Handbook of
Response to Intervention

Handbook of
Response to Intervention

The Science and Practice of Assessment
and Intervention

Edited by

Shane R. Jimerson
University of California
Santa Barbara, CA, USA

Matthew K. Burns
University of Minnesota
Minneapolis, MN, USA

Amanda M. VanDerHeyden
Education Research and Consulting
in Fairhope, Alabama

 Springer

Shane R. Jimerson
University of California, Santa Barbara
1332 Phelps Hall-Department of CCSP
Santa Barbara, CA 93106-9490
email: jimerson@education.ucsb.edu

Amanda M. VanDerHeyden
Education Research and Consulting,
Fairhope, Alabama
email: amandavande@gmail.com

Matthew K. Burns
University of Minnesota, Minneapolis
75 East River Road
346 Elliott Hall
Minneapolis, MN 55455-0208
email: burns258@umn.edu

Library of Congress Control Number: 2006939138

ISBN-10: 0-387-49052-3   e-ISBN-10: 0-387-49053-3
ISBN-13: 978-0-387-49052-6

Printed on acid-free paper.

9 8 7 6 5 4 3 2 1

springer.com

This handbook is dedicated to the professionals who work diligently to educate and enhance the success of students and to the scholars who inform our understanding of how to promote the social and cognitive competence of students. Through bringing the best of science to professional practice, and highlighting lessons learned from implementation efforts across the country, it is hoped that the information presented in this handbook serves as a catalyst that advances the science and practice of assessment and intervention at school, and ultimately promotes enhanced student outcomes for all students.

Acknowledgments

The Editors acknowledge the exceptional efforts of colleagues who contributed to this handbook as authors, and also to the individuals at Springer publications who were instrumental in bringing this handbook to print: Judy Jones, Angela Burke, Annè Meagher, Satvinder Kaur, and Peter Lewis. In addition, we are grateful for the extraordinary efforts of numerous individuals who provided reviews of chapters, which further enhanced the quality and contents; Michael Furlong, Cathi Christo, Chris Riley-Tillman, Aimee Higuita, Craig Albers, Mary Skokut, and the many chapter authors who also contributed their expertise by providing reviews of chapters. The collective efforts of all those involved have resulted in the timely publication of this extremely informative handbook.

Finally, it is important that we acknowledge the tremendous support, inspiration, and perspective that our families provided throughout the development of this handbook. The collective adventures, celebrations, and challenges we have shared has enriched each of us; our sincere appreciation to Kathryn O'Brien, Gavin O'Brien Jimerson, Mary Beth Burns, Kathleen Burns, Matthew Burns, Jr., Chad VanDerHeyden, and Benjamin VanDerHeyden.

Contents

III. Research-Based Prevention and Intervention

IV. Lessons Learned in Implementing Problem-Solving and Response-to-Intervention Strategies

Contents

Foreword

Response to Intervention (RTI) offers the best opportunity of the past three decades to ensure that every child, no matter how gifted or challenged, will be equally valued in an education system where the progress of every child is monitored, and individualized interventions with appropriate levels of intensity are provided to students as needed. Far too much attention has been focused on the different approaches to RTI by education leaders, researchers and implementers. It's time to look to what is common in our work and unite together so this opportunity is not wasted. The best science will prove itself over time, but while the field is waiting for the evidence base to grow, RTI must advance in a responsible manner. This handbook includes 31 chapters with essential reading for all stakeholders seeking to increase their knowledge base about RTI. It is an excellent and timely resource. I challenge everyone to read it, and then follow-up with actions to ensure that every child benefits from RTI.

Bill East, Executive Director
National Association of State Directors of Special Education (NASDSE)

Contributors

Randy Allison, EdS, NCSP, is Coordinator of System Supports for Educational Results, Heartland AEA 11, Johnston, IA. rallison@aea11.k12.ia.us

Stephanie Al Otaiba, PhD, is an Associate Professor in Special Education at Florida State University and the Florida Center for Reading Research. salotaiba@fcrr.org

Melissa Andersen, MA, is a graduate student in Educational (School) Psychology at the University of Nebraska Lincoln. melissandersen@gmail.com

David W. Barnett, PhD, is a Professor of School Psychology at the University of Cincinnati. david.barnett@uc.edu

George M. Batsche, EdD, is a Professor and Co-Director of the Institute for School Reform in the School Psychology Program at the University of South Florida in Tampa, Florida, and serves as the Co-Director of the Florida PSM/RTI Project. batsche@tempeset.coedu.usf.edu

Kerry A. Bollman, EdS, is an Academic Collaborative Planner with the St. Croix River Education District in Rush City, MN. kbollman@scred.k12.mn.us

Matthew K. Burns, PhD, is an Associate Professor of Educational Psychology and Coordinator of the School Psychology program at the University of Minnesota. burns258@umn.edu

Virginia Buysse, PhD, is a Senior Scientist at the Frank Porter Graham Child Development Institute at the University of North Carolina at Chapel Hill. Virginia_buvsse@unc.edu

Wayne A. Callender, EdS, is a Regional Coordinator and RTI Trainer/Consultant at the University of Oregon. waynec@uoregon.edu

José M. Castillo, MA, is a doctoral student and Presidential Fellow in the School Psychology Program at the University of South Florida. jcastillo@tampabay.rr.com

Theodore J. Christ, PhD, is an Assistant Professor of School Psychology at the University of Minnesota. tchrist@umn.edu

Sandra L. Christenson, PhD, is a Professor of Educational (School) Psychology at the University of Minnesota. chris002@umn.edu.

Melissa A. Clements, PhD, is a Research Scientist at the Wisconsin Center for Educational Research at the University of Wisconsin-Madison. maclements@wisc.edu

Melissa Coolong-Chaffin, EdS, is a graduate student in Educational (School) Psychology at the University of Minnesota. cool0044@umn.edu

Michael J. Curtis, PhD, is a Professor and Co-Director of the Institute for School Reform in the School Psychology Program at the University of South Florida and serves as the Co-Director of the Florida PSM/RTI Project. curtis@tempest.coedu.usf.edu

Edward J. Daly III, PhD, is an Associate Professor of Educational (School) Psychology at the University of Nebraska-Lincoln. edaly2@unl.edu

Stanley L. Deno, PhD, is a Professor of Educational Psychology with the Special Education program at the University of Minnesota. denox001@umn.edu

Clark Dorman, EdS, is the Project Leader for the Florida PSM/RTI Project and a former school psychologist in the Orange County (Orlando) School District. dorman@coedu.usf.edu

Ruth A. Ervin, PhD, is an Associate Professor of School Psychology and Special Education at University of British Columbia, Vancouver, Canada. ruth.ervin@ubc.ca

Dawn P. Flanagan, PhD, is a professor in the school psychology program at St. John's University in New York. flanagad@stjohns.edu

Kristin A. Gansle, PhD, is an Associate Professor in Special Education at Louisiana State University. kgansle@lsu.edu

Kimberly A. Gibbons, PhD, is the Special Education Director with St. Croix River Education District in Rush City, MN. KGibbons@scred.k12.mnn.us

Steven D. Goodman, is a Teacher Consultant at the Ottawa Area Intermediate School District, Holland, Michigan.

Janet L. Graden, PhD, is a Professor of School Psychology at the University of Cincinnati. janet.graden@uc.edu

Frank M. Gresham, PhD, is a Professor in the Department of Psychology at Louisiana State University. gresham@lsu.edu

Jeri K. Gustafson, MSEd, is a special education research practitioner on the Special Education Research Team at Heartland Area Education Agency 11, in Johnston, Iowa.

Terry B. Gutkin, PhD, is a Professor of Counseling, San Francisco State University. tgutkin@sfsu.edu

Kristi Hagans, PhD, is an Assistant Professor and School Psychology Program Coordinator, California State University, Long Beach. khagansm@csulb.edu

Renee O. Hawkins, PhD, is an Assistant Professor of School Psychology at the University of Cincinnati. renee.hawkins@uc.edu

John M. Hintze, PhD, is an Associate Professor of School Psychology at the University of Massachusetts at Amherst. hintze@educ.umass.edu

John L. Hosp, PhD, is an Assistant Professor in the Department of Childhood Education, Reading, and Disability Services at Florida State University and research faculty at the Florida Center for Reading Research. jhosp@fcrr.org

Martin J. Ikeda, PhD, is Coordinator of Special Projects at Heartland AEA 11, and an Assessment Consultant in Special Education for the Bureau of Children, Family, and Community Services of the Iowa Department of Education. marty.ikeda@iowa.gov

Shane R. Jimerson, PhD, is a Professor in the Department of Counseling, Clinical, and School Psychology at the University of California, Santa Barbara. jimerson@education.ucsb.edu

Kristen M. Kalymon, MS, is a graduate student in the School Psychology Program at the University of Wisconsin-Madison.

Kenneth A. Kavale, PhD, is a Distinguished Professor of Special Education at Regent University, Virginia Beach, VA. kkavale@cox.net

Christine Kerres Malecki, PhD, is an Associate Professor of Psychology at Northern Illinois University, DeKalb. cmalecki@niu.edu

Michelle Kilpatrick Demaray, PhD, is an Associate Professor of Psychology at Northern Illinois University, DeKalb. mkdemaray@niu.edu

Joseph F. Kovaleski, DEd, is a Professor of Educational and School Psychology at the Indiana University of Pennsylvania. jkov@iup.edu

Steven E. Knotek, PhD, is an Assistant Professor of School Psychology in the Human Development and Psychological Studies Department in the School of Education at the University of North Carolina, Chapel Hill. sknotek@email.unc.edu

Thomas R. Kratochwill, PhD, is a Sears–Bascom Professor in the School Psychology Program at the University of Wisconsin–Madison. tomkat@education.wisc.edu

Matthew Lau, PhD, is a school psychologist and program facilitator with Minneapolis Public Schools and Field Experience Coordinator with the University of Minnesota. lauxx008@tc.um.edu

Courtney LeClair, MA, is a graduate student in Educational (School) Psychology at the University of Nebraska–Lincoln. cleclai1@bigred.unl.edu

Sylvia Linan-Thompson, PhD, is an Associate Professor of Special Education at the University of Texas at Austin. sylvialt@mail.utexas.edu

Na'im Madyun, PhD, is an Assistant Professor in the College of Education and Human Development at the University of Minnesota. madyu002@umn.edu

Douglas Marston, PhD, is a special education administrator for research and evaluation in the Minneapolis Public Schools. doug.marston@mpls.k12.mn.us

Amy Matthews, PhD, is an Associate Professor of Psychology at Grand Valley State University, Allandale, Michigan. matthewa@gvsu.edu

Margaret T. McGlinchey, is an Educational Consultant at Kalamazoo Regional Educational Service Agency, Kalamazoo, Michigan. mmcglinc@kresanet.org

Scott McLeod, JD, PhD, is an Assistant Professor in Educational Policy and Administration with the University of Minnesota. mcleod@umn.edu

Kristen L. McMaster, PhD, is an Assistant Professor in Special Education at the University of Minnesota. mcmas004@umn.edu

Megan Miller, BA, is a graduate student of school psychology, California State University, Long Beach. mmiller8@csulb.edu

Christy S. Murray, MA, is a Senior Research Coordinator with the Vaughn Gross Center for Reading and Language Arts at the University of Texas at Austin. christymurray@austin.utexas.edu

Paul Muyskens, PhD, is a school psychologist and program facilitator with Minneapolis Public Schools. paul.muyskens@mpls.k12.mn.us

Jeanie E. Nam, is a School Psychology Graduate Student in the Graduate School of Education at the University of California-Riverside. jeanie.nam@email.ucr.edu

Melissa Nantais, PhD, is an Educational Consultant at the Southwest Ohio Special Education Regional Resource Center. nantais_m@swoserrc.org

Markeda Newell, MS, is a doctoral student in the School Psychology Program at the University of Wisconsin, Madison. mlnewell@wisc.edu

Bradley C. Niebling, PhD, is a School Psychologist/Curriculum Alignment Specialist at Heartland AEA 11, Johnston, IA. bniebling@aea11.k12.ia.us

George H. Noell, PhD, is a Professor of Psychology with the School Psychology program at Louisiana State University. gnoell@lsu.edu

Stephanie C. Olson, MA, is a graduate student in Educational (School) Psychology at the University of Nebraska–Lincoln. scolson@bigred.unl.edu

Wei Pan, PhD, is an Assistant Professor of Quantitative Educational Research at the University of Cincinnati. wei.pan@uc.edu

David W. Peterson, MS, is Co-Director of FED ED, an organization that represents the interests of suburban schools in Washington, peterson@nssed.org

Rita L. Poth, PhD, is Associate Director of the Southwestern Ohio Special Education Regional Resource Center, Cincinnati, OH. poth_r@swoserrc.org

Larry J. Porter, is a doctoral intern in the Pasco County School District in Land O' Lakes, Florida and a student in the School Psychology Program at the University of South Florida. ljporter@mail.usf.edu

Kristin Powers, PhD, is an Associate Professor of School Psychology, and Director of the Educational Psychology Clinic, California State University, Long Beach. kpowers@csulb.edu

David P. Prasse, PhD, is a Professor and Dean in the School of Education at the Loyola University Chicago. dprasse@luc.edu

Alecia Rahn-Blakeslee, PhD, is a Research & Evaluation Practitioner/School Psychologist at Heartland AEA 11, Johnston, IA. arahn@aea11.k12.ia.us

Amy L. Reschly, PhD, is an Assistant Professor of Educational Psychology & Instructional Technology at the University of Georgia. reschly@uga.edu

Donna M. Scanlon, PhD, is an Associate Professor in the Reading Department at the State University of New York at Albany. She is also the Associate Director of the University's Child Research and Study Center. dscanlon@uamail.albany.edu

Elizabeth Schaughency, PhD, is a Senior Lecturer in the Department of Psychology at University of Otago, Dunedin, New Zealand. schaughe@psy.otago.ac.nz

Mark R. Shinn, PhD, is a Professor of School Psychology at National Louis University, Evanston, IL. markshinn@mac.com

Benjamin Silberglitt, PhD, is Senior Consultant, Assessment and Implementation with Technology and Information Educational Services (TIES) in St. Paul. MN. Benjamin Silberglitt@ties.k12.mn.us

Robert O. Sornson, PhD, is the founder and President of The Early Learning Foundation, Brighton, Michigan. bobsornson@aol.com

Stephanie A. Stollar, PhD, is an Educational Consultant at the Southwestern Ohio Special Education Regional Resource Center, Cincinnati OH. stollar_s@swoserrc.org

James Stumme, EdD, is an Associate Administrator at Heartland AEA 11, Johnston, IA. jstumme@aea11.k12.ia.us

Mark E. Swerdlik, PhD, is a Professor of Psychology and Coordinator of Graduate Programs in School Psychology at Illinois State University, Normal. meswerd@ilstu.edu

Joseph Torgesen, PhD, is the W. Russell and Eugenia Morcom Chair of Psychology and Education at Florida State University and the Florida Center for Reading Research. torgesen@fcrr.org

James A. Tucker, PhD, is a Professor and McKee Chair of Excellence in Dyslexia and Related Learning Exceptionalities, University of Tennessee at Chattanooga. jatuck@mac.com

April Turner, MA, is a graduate student in Educational (School) Psychology at the University of Nebraska–Lincoln. april_d_turner@yahoo.com

Amanda M. VanDerHeyden, PhD, is a Private Researcher and Consultant living in Fairhope, Alabama. amandavande@gmail.com

Mike L. Vanderwood, PhD, is an Assistant Professor of School Psychology in the Graduate School of Education at the University of California–Riverside. mike.vanderwood@ucr.edu

Sharon Vaughn, PhD, is the H. E. Hartfelder/Southland Corp Regent Chair at the University of Texas at Austin. srvaughnum@aol.com

Frank R. Vellutino, PhD, is a Professor in the Department of Psychology and the Department of Educational and Counseling Psychology (joint appointment) at the State University of New York at Albany. He is also the director of the University's Child Research and Study Center. fvellutino@uamail.albany.edu

Dana Wagner, is a doctoral candidate in Special Education at the University of Minnesota. wagn0244@umn.edu

Jeanne Wanzek, PhD, is a Research Associate with the Vaughn Gross Center for Reading and Language Arts at the University of Texas at Austin. wanzek@mail.utexas.edu

Joseph C. Witt, PhD, is the Director of Research and Development iSTEEP Learning. joe@JoeWitt.org

James Ysseldyke, PhD, is a Birkmaier Professor in the School Psychology Program at the University of Minnesota. jim@umn.edu

Haiyan Zhang, MS, is a doctoral student in the Department of Educational and Counseling Psychology at the State University of New York at Albany. hz7494@albany.edu

Information About the Editors

Shane R. Jimerson, PhD, is a Professor in the Department of Counseling, Clinical, and School Psychology and Associate Dean for Research at the University of California, Santa Barbara. Among over 150 professional publications, he is a co-author of a five-book grief support group curriculum series *The Mourning Child Grief Support Group Curriculum* (2001, Taylor and Francis), co-author of *Identifying, Assessing, and Treating Autism at School* (2006, Springer), a co-editor of *Best Practices in School Crisis Prevention and Intervention* (2002, National Association of School Psychologists), the lead editor of *The Handbook of School Violence and School Safety* (2006, Lawrence Earlbaum, Inc.), and the lead editor of *The Handbook of International School Psychology* (2006, Sage). He serves as the Editor of *The California School Psychologist* journal, Associate Editor of *School Psychology Review*, and is on the editorial boards of the *Journal of School Psychology* and *School Psychology Quarterly*. Dr. Jimerson has chaired and served on numerous boards and advisory committees at the state, national, and international levels, including chair of the *Research Committee* of the *International School Psychology Association*. His scholarly publications and presentations have provided further insights regarding developmental pathways, the efficacy of early prevention and intervention programs, school psychology internationally, and school crisis prevention and intervention. The quality and contributions of his scholarship are reflected in the numerous awards and recognition that he has received. Dr. Jimerson received the *Best Research Article* of the year award from the *Society for the Study of School Psychology* in 1998, and then again in 2000. He also received the 2001 *Outstanding Article of the Year Award* from the National Association of School Psychologists' *School Psychology Review*. Dr. Jimerson's scholarly efforts were also recognized by the *American Educational Research Association* with the 2002 *Early Career Award in Human Development*. He and his UCSB research team received the 2003 *Outstanding Research Award* from the *California Association of School Psychologists*. Also during 2003, Dr. Jimerson received the *Lightner Witmer Early Career Contributions Award* from *Division 16 (School Psychology) of the American Psychological Association*. In 2005, he received an *Outstanding Service Award* from Division 16 of the American Psychological. In 2006, Dr. Jimerson received the *President's Award for Exemplary Contributions from the California Association of School Psychologists*. Also during 2006, Dr. Jimerson received the *President's Award of Excellence from the National Association of School Psychologists* (NASP) for his efforts in bringing science to practice. His scholarship continues to highlight the importance of early experiences on subsequent development and emphasizes the importance of research informing professional practice to promote the social and cognitive competence of children.

Matthew K. Burns, PhD, is an Associate Professor of Educational Psychology and coordinator of the School Psychology program at the University of Minnesota. He is a Co-Guest Editor of a special issue of *Assessment for Effective Intervention* addressing response to intervention and is a contributor to two other special series within different journals on the same topic. He has authored or co-authored over 60 professional publications and has conducted an equal number of local, state, national, and international presentations. The majority of Dr. Burns's scholarly work addresses matching instructional demands to student skill with curriculum-based assessment, and problem-solving team processes and outcomes. Dr. Burns is an Associate Editor for *Assessment for Effective Intervention* and is on the editorial board of *School Psychology Review Psychology in the Schools*, and *Remedial and Special Education*. Finally, Dr. Burns was a member of the task force and co-author of *School Psychology: A Blueprint for Training and Practice III*.

Amanda M. VanDerHeyden, PhD, is a private consultant and researcher living in Fairhope, Alabama. Dr. VanDerHeyden previously has held faculty positions at the Early Intervention Institute at Louisiana State University Health Sciences Center and in the School Psychology Program at University of California at Santa Barbara. She has also worked as a researcher and consultant in a number of school districts. In Vail Unified School District, Dr. VanDerHeyden led a district effort to implement the STEEP RTI model from 2002 to 2005. In this district, identification of children as having specific learning disabilities was reduced by half within 2 years, test scores increased, and the district was nationally recognized as a success story related to *No Child Left Behind* by the US Department of Education. Dr. VanDerHeyden has authored over 40 related articles and book chapters and has worked as a national trainer and consultant to assist districts to implement RTI models. In 2006, Dr. VanDerHeyden was named to an advisory panel for the National Center for Learning Disabilities to provide guidance related to RTI and the diagnosis of specific learning diability. She is associate editor of *Journal of Behavioral Education* and serves on the editorial boards for *School Psychology Review, School Psychology Quarterly*, and *Journal of Early Intervention*. Dr. VanDerHeyden recently co-edited special issues of Assessment for *Effective Intervention and School Psychology Review*, each focusing on RTI. In 2006, Dr. VanDerHeyden received the *Lightner Witmer Early Career Contributions Award* from *Division 16 (School Psychology) of the American Psychological Association* in recognition of her scholarship on early intervention, RTI, and models of data-based decision-making in schools.

I
Foundations of Problem-Solving and Response-to-Intervention Strategies

1
Response to Intervention at School: The Science and Practice of Assessment and Intervention

Shane R. Jimerson, Matthew K. Burns, and Amanda M. VanDerHeyden

Shane R. Jimerson, PhD is a Professor in the Department of Counseling, Clinical, and School Psychology at the University of California, Santa Barbara. Jimerson@education.ucsb.edu
Matthew K. Burns, PhD is an Associate Professor of Educational Psychology with the School Psychology program at the University of Minnesota. burns258@umn.edu
Amanda M. VanDerHeyden, PhD is a private Researcher and Consultant living in Fairhope, Alabama. amandavande@gmail.com

Promoting the success of students is the primary focus of educational professionals. Systematically identifying individual needs and subsequently providing appropriate interventions is central to the task of enhancing student outcomes. With the reauthorization of the federal *Individuals with Disabilities Education Act* (IDEA), referred to as the *Individuals with Disabilities Education Improvement Act* (IDEIA; signed into law in December 2004), the process of identifying students with learning disabilities (LDs) is at the forefront of education issues in the United States. Regulations accompanying the reauthorized IDEIA permit the use of data (*response*) obtained when scientifically based intervention is implemented with a student (*to intervention*) to make eligibility decisions under LDs. The regulatory provision reflects a fundamental paradigm shift that closes the gap between instruction and assessment.

Although response to intervention (RTI) was only recently defined in federal regulations, the concept is well established in other fields, such as medicine, which focus on response to treatment. Therefore, this chapter and handbook addresses research and application of RTI in K-12 schools by identifying the importance of RTI as related to IDEIA, discussing the functions of RTI, examining the historical basis for RTI, providing contemporary definitions of RTI, and, finally, emphasizing the essential role of research in advancing the science and practice of assessment and intervention (critical components of RTI).

1.1 Importance of Response to Intervention at School

The *Individuals with Disabilities Education Improvement Act* (IDEA, 2004) allows local education agencies to use a student's response to intervention (RTI) as part of the evaluation procedure for identifying students with specific learning disabilities [PL 108-446, Part B, Sec 614(b)(6)(b)]. The following excerpts from IDEIA highlight key changes regarding the assessment and identification of children with specific learning disabilities (portions in italic for emphasis).

SPECIFIC LEARNING DISABILITIES—(IDEIA; 614, b, 6, A, B)

(A) IN GENERAL—Notwithstanding section 607(b), when determining whether a child has a specific learning disability as defined in section 602, *a local educational agency shall not be required to take into consideration whether a child has a severe discrepancy between achievement and intellectual ability* in oral expression, listening comprehension, written expression, basic reading skill, reading comprehension, mathematical calculation, or mathematical reasoning.

(B) ADDITIONAL AUTHORITY—In determining whether a child has a specific learning disability, *a local educational agency may use a process that determines if the child responds to scientific, research-based intervention* as a part of the evaluation procedures described in paragraphs (2) and (3).

To further examine the role of RTI within special education, it is important to consider what exactly is special education? Federal special education mandates since P.L. 94-142 have all defined special education as "Individualized instruction, at no cost to the parents or guardians, to meet the unique needs of a child with a disability." Thus, assessing student needs and designing instructional modifications to meet those needs is at the very core of special education. Moreover, the definition of specific learning disability within special education law has always included the provision that prior to consideration for special education it must be demonstrated that "the child was provided appropriate instruction in regular education settings" (§§ 300.309, *Individuals with Disabilities Education Act* (IDEA), 2004). This latter mandate has often been overlooked in practice, until RTI entered the national vernacular that is.

1.2 Functions of Response to Intervention at School

Although RTI was included in the federal definition of specific learning disabilities, to view it as only a diagnostic tool is too limiting. We suggest that RTI be considered the systematic use of assessment data to most efficiently allocate resources in order to enhance student learning for all students and to effectively identify those who are eligible for special education services.

1.2.1 Brief Background

Gresham (2007) provides a brief summary of the historical antecedents of RTI, including: the National Research Council (NRC) report (see Heller, Holtzman, and Messick, 1982) in which the validity of the special education classification system was evaluated; the LD Initiative that was sponsored by the Office of Special Education Programs (U.S. Department of Education), which resulted in a national

conference held in Washington, DC, in 2001 (entitled the *LD Summit*); and the President's Commission on Excellence in Special Education (2002) that recognized RTI as an alternative to IQ-achievement discrepancy in the identification of SLD.

RTI is most often conceptualized as falling into two basic approaches to delivering interventions: (a) problem-solving approaches and (b) standard protocol approaches (Fuchs, Mock, Morgan, and Young, 2003). The problem-solving approach is conceptualized as a systematic analysis of instructional variables designed to isolate target skill/subskill deficits and shape targeted interventions (Barnett, Daly, Jones and Lentz, 2004). In the standard protocol approach, a standard set of empirically supported instructional approaches is implemented to remediate academic problems.

Although this dichotomous view of RTI is somewhat common, most RTI models described in literature combine the two approaches (Burns and Coolong-Chaffin, 2006; Reschly, 2003), which appears to indicate that this dichotomy is somewhat artificial (Christ, Burns, and Ysseldyke, 2005). Problem solving is a term with a more general meaning than that presented by Fuchs et al. (2003). Deno's (2002) seminal paper described problem solving as any set of activities that are designed to "eliminate the difference between 'what is' and 'what should be' with respect to student development" (p. 38). There is a fundamental difference between problem-solving and standard protocol approaches to RTI regarding the depth of problem analysis that occurs prior to the designing and implementing an intervention (Christ et al., 2005). However, both approaches are consistent with problem solving as described by Deno (2002), because both seek to reduce or eliminate the difference between what is and what should be. Thus, both approaches to RTI are actually problem solving and probably function optimally when integrated into one three-tiered service delivery system (O'Shaughnessy, Lane, Gresham, and Beebe-Frankenberger 2003).

What are commonly referred to as standard protocol interventions are actually standardized small-group interventions that can be implemented with 15% to 20% of the student population. This grouping and standardization allows for more intensive interventions that are provided in typical classroom instruction through a relatively cost efficient manner. Only when children fail to succeed in these standardized approaches is it necessary to isolate and manipulate individual environmental variables through a problem analysis approach, or what is commonly referred to as problem solving. An effective general education core curriculum and quality instructional methodology, and an effective small-group standardized intervention should result in only approximately 5% of the student population requiring such an intensive data collection and analysis procedure (VanDerHeyden, Witt, and Gilbertson, 2007; VanDerHeyden, Witt, and Naquin, 2003).

1.3 Essential Role of Research in Advancing Science and Practice

Rather than attempting to identify how RTI models differ, it is time to examine what they have in common, because language regarding RTI within federal special education regulations is quite limited and vague. Some of the core concepts of RTI as identified by the National Research Center on Learning Disabilities (2002) include (a) students receive high-quality instruction in their general education setting, (b) general education instruction is research based, (c) school staff conduct universal screenings and continuously monitor progress, (d) school staff implement specific, research-based interventions to address student difficulties and monitor progress to determine if they are effective, and (e) the fidelity or integrity with which instruction and interventions are implemented is systematically assessed.

Whereas information provided by National Research Center on Learning Disabilities is helpful, clearly the operationalization and implementation of RTI requires further research and clarification. The U.S. Department of Education, Institute of Education Sciences (Institute of Educational Sciences, 2006) emphasizes the importance of systematic and experimental application of RTI: (a) across the full range of school curricula and content areas at the preschool, primary, elementary and secondary schooling levels; (b) in which empirically established interventions are implemented with high fidelity in various combinations under a range of task and performance conditions within a three-tiered framework across the full range of grade levels or age groups; (c) across all levels of instructional intensity, frequency, and duration (e.g., high, moderate, or low levels of intensity, frequency, and duration in the presentation of stimuli and opportunities to respond within fixed or varied amounts of instructional time); and (d) across a range of measures designed for initial screening and progress monitoring (p. 29).

Additionally, further research is needed regarding the implementation of RTI at the district and/or school levels. Burns and Ysseldyke (2005) identified several questions regarding RTI implementation including: (a) are there validated intervention models; (b) are there adequately trained personnel; (c) what leadership is needed for success; (d) when should due process protection begin; (e) is RTI a defensible endpoint in the identification process; (f) what implementation procedures are needed at the secondary level; (g) what role should parents have in the process; and (h) how should implementation integrity be viewed and assessed? Previous studies have addressed some of the questions, but others remain unanswered.

Many equate implementation integrity with treatment fidelity, but the former term is more accurate to use in RTI because data are needed to assess the integrity with which interventions are developed *and* implemented (Noell and Gansle, 2006). For example, previous research has examined the predictive validity of RTI data and early reading measures in predicting future reading difficulties and disabilities (Jenkins, 2003; McMaster, Fuchs, Fuchs, and Compton, 2005; Ritchey and Foley, 2006). However, Institute of Educational Sciences (2006) recommends further studies examining how the accuracy of risk prediction is affected by: (a) the assessment approaches (i.e., static, dynamic, progress monitoring) or combination of assessment approaches implemented within a classroom or school; (b) the measures administered and skills assessed within a specified domain at particular grade levels and times of the school year; and (c) decision rules for defining cut-scores and statistical techniques for analyzing student performance data that determine inadequate response, predict future difficulties, and result in acceptable levels of *sensitivity* (e.g., indicates percentage of children who will be identified as having a specific learning disability out of all the children who actually have one), *specificity* (e.g., indicates percentage of children who will be identified as not having a specific learning disability out of all of the children who do not have one), *false positive rates* (e.g., indicates percentage of students who will be identified as having a specific learning disability out of all the children who actually do not have one), and *false negative rates* (e.g., indicates the percentage of children who will be identified as not having a specific learning disability out of all of the children who actually do have a specific learning disability) (p. 29).

Based on the extant empirical evidence, a number of key questions and principles are evident.

Key questions regarding the implementation of RTI models. There are many questions that remain to be addressed regarding wide-scale implementation, including:

1. What will the effects be on student and systemic outcomes? Although research has been conducted on the effects of RTI approaches on both student (e.g., increasing student reading, decreasing student difficulties) and systemic (e.g., reducing the number of referrals to and placements in special education) with positive effects (Burns, Appleton, and Stehouwer, 2005), these studies focused primarily on existing models with little experimental control. Thus, additional research is needed that examines the effects of RTI on systemic outcomes in tightly controlled studies. Moreover, very few studies used randomization or control groups.

2. What will the effects be on educational professionals? Reschly (2003) presented data regarding the effect that practicing in an RTI model had on the functions of school psychologists and Burns and Coolong-Chaffin (2006) discussed specific activities that school psychologists should engage in when using an RTI model. However, few data have been published regarding the roles and outcomes for other personnel. Moreover, how will RTI affect training programs? Do training programs graduate professionals with the skill set necessary to competently participate in RTI; and if not, how should the training change? Previous studies demonstrated that training preservice special education teachers in reading tutoring and curriculum-based measurement led to improved knowledge about reading instruction (Al Otaiba and Lake, 2006), but little is known about the frequency with which these skills are taught in training programs.

Principles regarding the implementation of RTI models. Successful wide-scale implementation will take considerable, time, resources, leadership, planning, preparation of professionals, and empirical evidence.

Time. Efforts to implement various RTI models (including Florida, Idaho, Iowa, Michigan, Ohio, Pennsylvania, and Minnesota) reveal that the process typically takes years, or even decades, and is better characterized as a dynamic ongoing process, rather than an event that is completed on a given date. Moreover, the more comprehensive the RTI model, the greater the duration to prepare, implement, and evaluate. School districts may benefit from implementing RTI procedures on a small scale with high quality while building local capacity for implementation on a wider scale.

Resources. States that appear to have made the most progress in implementing RTI models have also invested considerable resources. For example, Florida implemented a series of initiatives and invested millions of dollars during the past decade that have set the foundation for current efforts to implement RTI models state-wide, and the current funds invested in the implementation efforts involve millions of dollars each year. Other states have implemented smaller grant initiatives.

Leadership. Each of the states that have made significant efforts to implement RTI models (e.g., Florida, Michigan, and Ohio) includes strong leadership at the state level. This leadership is typically reflected at multiple levels of education in the state (e.g., State Department of Education, university faculty, and school administrators). Representation, buy-in, and contributions of multiple stakeholders are each important facets that may be facilitated by leaders. Moreover, successful state initiatives have been supported with considerable technical support from the State Department of Education, often in collaboration with a university.

Planning. Strategic plans for the preparation of professionals involved and implementation procedures are important for implementing RTI models. Research and focus are needed on pre-service professionals. In-service training was critical to previously successful RTI implementation, and this will continue to be critical to successful RTI implementation as professionals working in the field acquire the skills necessary to successfully implement RTI.

Preparation of professionals. Implementation requires training to provide essential knowledge and skills to educational professionals who will be responsible for implementing RTI models. Curricula of general education teachers, special education teachers, and school psychologists should address effective instruction in general and across multiple topical areas, data-based instructional decision making, involvement in effective problem-solving teams, individual differences for learners, school–home collaboration, and making instructional modifications to accommodate diversity within general education. Some of the specific skills associated with RTI (e.g., curriculum-based assessment and measurement, reading interventions) are perhaps best learned through case-based and service-learning activities (Al Otaiba, 2005). Thus, internships in teaching and school psychology training programs should include an RTI focus.

Empirical evidence. Quantifying the empirical base for RTI presents considerable challenges, as it is essential to identify the standards or criteria that will be used in determining evidence-based practices. One source of information is the extant literature base, but future RTI efforts must incorporate emerging empirical evidence regarding assessment and intervention strategies. There is a strong research base for many practices within the areas of reading instruction, reading assessment, and interventions for exceptional learners. However, more is needed regarding: small-group interventions for children at risk for reading failure; effective problem-solving practices; effective school-based screening and interventions for youth with social, emotional, and behavioral problems; and effective interventions for youth in secondary schools.

Evaluation. Systematic formative and summative evaluation of RTI implementation is essential to further understanding critical features of models. Establishing evaluation measures and processes to be shared throughout and across states would be especially valuable in advancing knowledge of processes and student outcomes associated with various RTI models.

The findings of the President's Commission on Excellence in Special Education (2001) emphasized that special education needs to focus on outcomes rather than processes. In addition, we believe process data are important when it comes to RTI. There is a growing consensus that implementation integrity will be the most significant obstacle to overcome when implementing RTI on a national level (Burns, Vanderwood, and Ruby, 2005; Burns and Ysseldyke, 2005; Noell and Gansle, 2006; Ysseldyke, 2005). Thus, assessing the fidelity with which RTI models are implemented will be critical to its success.

1.4 Conclusions

Educational practices are already being modified; however, there is a paucity of resources that synthesize essential knowledge regarding the conceptual and empirical underpinnings of RTI and actual implementation. In many ways, it appears that recent legislation and many RTI initiatives during the past decade serve as a catalyst for further efforts and future scholarship to advance understanding of the science and practice of assessment and intervention at school. *The Handbook of Response to Intervention* (Jimerson, Burns, and VanDerHeyden, 2007) provides a collection of chapters that address essential aspects of RTI.

RTI models have considerable promise for screening, intervention service delivery, and catalysts for system change. Research is needed to articulate purposes, operationalize procedures and judgments, and evaluate the decision-making utility of the models in practice. It is important to articulate how RTI can be judged (which behaviors to measure, how frequently, for how long, under what stimulus conditions, and compared with what reference group using what units of measurement) and demonstrate that this judgment is functionally meaningful (VanDerHeyden and Jimerson, 2005). Whereas the roots of RTI are discernible in a research base that stretches back over the last 30 years in the areas of behavior analysis, precision teaching, direct instruction, curriculum-based assessment, measurement, and evaluation, and effective teaching, RTI remains today an evolving science of decision-making. Over time, consensus may emerge about the purposes of RTI, the best ways to operationalize the independent variable or variables under RTI, and how technical adequacy of RTI implemented in schools can best be evaluated (VanDerHeyden, Witt, and Barnett,

2005). Today's schools operate within a challenging context that is best addressed by adherence to scientific principles and consistent implementation of the scientific method to examine system and individual variables (Ysseldyke et al., 2006). In other words, science should inform practice and practice should inform science. It is our intent that this handbook will do just that for RTI in order to advance both science and practice, and enhance the lives of the children we serve.

References

Al Otaiba, S. (2005). Response to early literacy instruction: Practical issues for early childhood personnel preparation. *Journal of Early Childhood Teacher Education, 25,* 201–209.

Al Otaiba, S. & Lake, V. E. (in press). Preparing special educators to teach reading and use curriculum-based assessments. *Reading and Writing Quarterly.*

Barnett, D. W., Daly, E. J., Jones, K. M., & Lentz, F. E. (2004). Response to intervention: Empirically based special service decisions from single-case designs of increasing and decreasing intensity. *The Journal of Special Education, 38,* 66–79.

Burns, M. K., Appleton, J. J., & Stehouwer, J. D. (2005). Meta-analytic review of response-to-intervention research: Examining field-based and research-implemented models. *Journal of Psychoeducational Assessment, 23,* 381–394.

Burns, M. K. & Coolong-Chaffin, M. (2006). Response-to-intervention: Role for and effect on school psychology. *School Psychology Forum, 1* (1), 3–15.

Burns, M. K., Vanderwood, M., & Ruby, S. (2005). Evaluating the readiness of prereferral intervention teams for use in a problem-solving model: Review of three levels of research. *School Psychology Quarterly, 20,* 89–105.

Burns, M. K. & Ysseldyke, J. E. (2005). Comparison of existing responsiveness-to-intervention models to identify and answer implementation questions. *The California School Psychologist, 10,* 9–20.

Christ, T. J., Burns, M. K., & Ysseldyke, J. E. (2005). Conceptual confusion within response-to-intervention vernacular: Clarifying meaningful differences. *Communiqué, 34(3).*

Deno, S. L. (2002). Problem solving as best practices. In A. Thomas & J. Grimes (Eds.), *Best practices in school psychology,* 4th ed. (pp. 37–56). Bethesda, MD: National Association of School Psychologists.

Fuchs, D., Mock, D., Morgan, P. L., & Young, C. L. (2003). Responsiveness-to-intervention: Definitions, evidence, and implications for the learning disabilities construct. *Learning Disabilities Research and Practice, 18,* 157–171.

Gresham, F. M. (2007). Evolution of the RTI concept: empirical foundations and recent developments. In Jimerson, S. R., Burns, M. K., and VanDerHeyden, A. M. (Eds.), *The Handbook of Response to Intervention: The Science and Practice of Assessment and Intervention.* New York: Springer.

Heller, K. A., Holtzman, W. H., & Messick, S. (1982). *Placing Children In Special Education: Theories and Recommendations.* Washington, DC: National Academy Press.

Institute of Educational Sciences (2006). Special Education Research Grants CFDA 84.324 (IES-NCSER-2007-01). Online at http://ies.ed.gov/ncser/funding/response/response.asp (downloaded 7.1.2006).

Jenkins, J. (2003). Candidate measures for screening at-risk students. Paper presented at the *National Research Center on Learning Disabilities Responsiveness-to-Intervention Symposium,* Kansas City, MO.

McMaster, K. L., Fuchs, D., Fuchs, L. S., & Compton, D. L. (2005). Responding to nonresponders: An experimental field trial of identification and intervention methods. *Exceptional Children, 71,* 445–463.

Noell, G. H. & Gansle, K. A. (2006). Assuring the form has substance: Treatment plan implementation as the foundation of assessing response to intervention. *Assessment for Effective Intervention, 32,* 32–39.

National Research Center on Learning Disabilities. (2002). *Core Concepts of RTI.* Online at http://www.nrcld.org/html/research/rti/concepts.html (downloaded 6.23.2006).

O'Shaughnessy, T. E., Lane, K. L., Greshman, F. M., & Beebe-Frankenberger, M. E. (2003). Children placed at risk for learning and behavioral difficulties: Implementing a school-wide system of early identification and intervention. *Remedial & Special Education, 24,* 27–35.

President's Commission on Excellence in Special Education (2001). *A New Era: Revitalizing Special Education for Children and their Families.* Washington, DC: US Department of Education.

Reschly, R. J. (2003). What if LD identification changed to reflect research findings? Paper presented at the *National Research Center on Learning Disabilities Responsiveness-to-Intervention Symposium,* Kansas City, MO.

Ritchey, K. D. & Foley, J. E. (2006). Responsiveness to instruction as a method of identifying at-risk kindergarten readers: a one-year follow-up. Paper presented at the *Council for Exceptional Children Annual Conference,* Salt Lake City, UT.

VanDerHeyden, A. M. & Jimerson, S. R. (2005). Using response to intervention to enhance outcomes for children. *The California School Psychologist, 10*, 21–32.

VanDerHeyden, A. M., Witt, J. C., & Barnett, D. A. (2005). The emergence and possible futures of response to intervention. *Journal of Psychoeducational Assessment, 23*, 339–361.

VanDerHeyden, A. M., Witt, J. C., & Gilbertson, D. A. (2007). A multi-year evaluation of the effects of a response to intervention (RTI) model on the identification of children for special education. *Journal of School Psychology, 45*, 225–256.

VanDerHeyden, A. M., Witt, J. C., & Naquin, G. (2003). Development and validation of a process for screening referrals to special education. *School Psychology Review*, 32, 204–227.

Ysseldyke, J. (2005). Assessment and decision making for students with learning disabilities: What is this is as good as it gets? *Learning Disabilities Quarterly, 28*, 125–128.

Ysseldyke, J., Burns, M., Dawson, P., Kelley, B., Morrison, D., Ortiz, S., et al. (2006). *School Psychology: A Blueprint for Training in Practice III*. Bethesda, MD: National Association of School Psychologists.

2
Evolution of the Response-to-Intervention Concept: Empirical Foundations and Recent Developments

Frank M. Gresham

Frank M. Gresham, PhD, is a Professor in the Department of Psychology at Louisiana State University.
gresham@lsu.edu

Traditionally, schools address students' academic and behavioral difficulties in terms of a predictable three-stage process that can be described as a "refer-test-place" approach. That is, students presenting academic and/or behavior problems are referred to a child study team that offers recommendations for an intervention to resolve the problem. Very often, however, these interventions are not evidence based and are often ineffective in solving the referral concern. These ineffective interventions then are followed by an official referral to a school psychologist or an assessment team to determine whether the student meets eligibility requirements for special education under a designated disability category (typically specific learning disabilities, emotional disturbance (ED), or mild mental retardation). Finally, if a team believes that the student is eligible for special education and related services, he or she is placed into special education and an individualized educational plan (IEP) is written (see Bocian, Beebe, MacMillan, and Gresham, 1999).

The aforementioned process has been the most common process in determining special education eligibility and placement since 1975, when the Education of All Handicapped Children Act was passed (Public Law 94-142). Despite over 30 years of experience with this approach, there are some major drawbacks and disadvantages inherent in this process. This approach often penalizes students by using arbitrary eligibility criteria that many times result in delaying services and often providing these students with ineffective and scientifically baseless interventions to remediate their academic

and behavioral difficulties (Denton, Vaughn and Fletcher, 2003; Gresham, 2002; Vaughn and Fuchs, 2003).

The purpose of this chapter is to present the evolution of the response to intervention (RTI) concept and discuss how that concept can be and is being used to provide more effective services to children and youth with both academic and social/behavioral difficulties. A definition of RTI is provided, along with a brief discussion of the historical antecedents of RTI in the literature. RTI is described as being presented in either a problem-solving or standard protocol approach; however, some applications of this process use a combination of both approaches. Recent empirical support for using RTI principles ais described, along with measurement challenges that present themselves when applying RTI to make intervention and eligibility determinations for both academic and behavioral difficulties.

2.1 Conceptual and Definitional Aspects of Response to Intervention

RTI is based on the notion of determining whether an adequate or inadequate change in academic or behavioral performance has been achieved because of an intervention (Gresham, 1991, 2002). In an RTI approach, decisions regarding changing or intensifying an intervention are made based on how well or how poorly a student responds to an evidence-based intervention that is implemented with integrity. RTI is used to select, change, or titrate interventions based on how the child responds to that intervention.

RTI assumes that if a child shows an inadequate response to the best interventions available and feasible in a given setting, then that child can and should be eligible for additional assistance, including more intense interventions, special assistance, and special education and related services. RTI is *not* used exclusively to make special education entitlement decisions, although it may be used for this purpose.

RTI is not a new concept in other fields. The field of medicine provides a particularly salient example of how physicians utilize RTI principles their everyday practice to treat physical diseases. Physicians assess weight, blood pressure, and heart rate every time they see a patient because these three factors are important indicators of general physical health and have scientifically well-established benchmarks for typical and atypical functioning. If weight and blood pressure exceed established benchmarks, then physicians may recommend that the patient diet, exercise, and quit smoking. The next time the patient sees the physician, these same indicators are measured; if the indicators show no change, then the physician may place the patient on a specific diet and exercise regimen and tell the patient to stop smoking. The next time the physician sees the patient these same indicators are taken; if they still show no change, then the physician may put the patient on medication, refer to a dietician, and send the patient to a smoking cessation clinic. Finally, the next time the physician sees the patient, the same indicator data are collected and if they are still in the atypical range, then, upon further assessments, the patient may require surgery to prevent mortality. Several important points should be noted in considering the above example. First, intervention *intensity* is increased only after data suggest that the patient shows an inadequate response to intervention. Second, treatment decisions are based on objective data that are collected continuously over a period of time (data-based decision-making). Third, the data that are collected are well-established indicators of general physical health. Finally, decisions about treatment intensity are based on the collection of more and more data as the patient moves through each stage of treatment intensification. RTI can and should be used in a parallel manner in schools to make important educational decisions for children and youth.

2.2 Historical Antecedents of Response to Intervention

The basis of the RTI approach, at least in special education, can be traced back to the National Research Council (NRC) report (see Heller, Holtzman, and Messick, 1982), in which the validity of the special education classification system was evaluated on the basis of three criteria: (a) the quality of the general education program, (b) the value of the special education program in producing important outcomes for students, and (c) the accuracy and meaningfulness of the assessment process in the identification of disability. Vaughn and Fuchs (2003) suggested that the first two criteria emphasized the quality of instruction (both general education and special education), whereas the third criterion involved judgments of the quality of instructional environments and the student's response to instruction delivered in those environments. The third criterion described in the NRC report is consistent with Messick's (1995) evidential and consequential bases for test *use* and *interpretation*. That is, there must be evidential and consequential bases for using and interpreting tests in a certain way. If these bases exist to a sufficient degree, then we may conclude that there is sufficient evidence for the validity of a given assessment procedure.

Speece (2002) described problems with IQ-achievement discrepancy in terms of unintended social consequences, such as the difficulty of young children qualifying under this criterion and the overrepresentation of males and minority children using this approach. Additionally, there are concerns that the discrepancy approach does not inform instructional decisions that might be used to improve student outcomes (Gresham, 2002). Heller et al. (1982) argued that a special education classification might be considered valid only when all three criteria are met.

2.2.1 Concept of Treatment Validity

Fuchs and Fuchs (1998) argued for a reconceptualization of the learning disabled (LD) identification process based on a treatment validity criterion. This approach does not classify as LD unless and until it has been demonstrated empirically that they are not benefiting from the general education curriculum. Treatment validity (sometimes called instructional utility) can be defined as the extent to which any assessment procedure contributes to beneficial outcomes for individuals (Cone, 1989; Hayes, Nelson, and Jarrett, 1987). A central feature of treatment validity is that there must be a clear and unambiguous relationship between the assessment data collected and the recommended intervention. Although the notion of treatment validity evolved from the behavioral assessment literature, it shares several common features and concepts with the traditional psychometric literature.

First, treatment validity is based, in part, upon the idea of incremental validity, in that it requires that an assessment procedure improve prediction beyond existing assessment procedures (Sechrest, 1963). As will be discussed later, a major advantage of an RTI approach is the collection of additional information over time that adds incremental validity to the assessment process. Second, treatment validity involves the concepts of utility and cost–benefit analysis that are common concepts in the personnel selection literature (Mischel, 1968; Wiggins, 1973). Third, treatment validity involves Messick's (1995) notion of the evidential and consequential bases of test use and interpretation as it relates to construct validity, relevance/utility, and social consequences of testing. It should be noted that an assessment procedure might have adequate evidence for construct validity, but have little, if any, relevance or utility for treatment planning (i.e., absence of treatment validity). As will be described later, *all* cognitive ability tests suffer from this fatal flaw of treatment invalidity (see Cronbach, 1975; Gresham and Witt, 1997; Reschly and Ysseldyke, 2002).

For any assessment procedure to have treatment validity, it must lead to identification-relevant areas of concern (academic or behavioral), inform treatment planning, and be useful in evaluating treatment outcomes. Traditionally, many assessment procedures in applied psychology have failed to demonstrate treatment validity because they do not inform instructional and behavioral intervention practices (Cronbach, 1975; Gresham, 2002). The concept of RTI depends largely upon the treatment validity of measures used to determine adequate or inadequate treatment response.

2.2.2 Operationalizing of the National Research Council Criteria

Fuchs and Fuchs (1997, 1998) operationalized the NRC criteria by using a curriculum-based measurement (CBM) approach that measures a student's responsiveness or unresponsiveness to intervention delivered in the general education classroom. In earlier work, Fuchs (1995) compared the RTI approach with the practice used in medicine, whereby a child's growth over time is compared with that of a same-age group. A child showing a large discrepancy between his or her height and that of a normative sample might be considered a candidate for certain types of medical intervention (e.g., growth hormone therapy). In education, a child showing a discrepancy between the current level of academic performance and that of same-age peers in the same classroom might be considered a candidate for special education. It should be noted that a low-performing child who shows a growth rate similar to that of peers in a low-performing classroom would not be considered a candidate for special education because the child is deriving similar educational benefits from that classroom (Fuchs, 1995). Thus, employing an IQ-achievement discrepancy criterion using national norms may identify this child as LD, whereas using an RTI approach using local norms would not.

Unlike traditional LD assessment, which measures students at one point in time using ability, achievement, and processing measures, the treatment validity approach repeatedly measures the student's progress in the general education curriculum using CBM. Special education is considered only if the child's performance shows a *dual discrepancy* (DD), in which performance is below the level of classroom peers and the student's learning rate (growth) is substantially below that of classroom peers.

The CBM-DD model for determining LD eligibility consists of three phases. Phase I involves the documentation of adequate classroom instruction and dual discrepancies. This phase meets the first criterion of the NRC report involving the adequacy of the general education curriculum (Heller et al., 1982). During this phase, overall classroom performance is compared with the performance relative to other classrooms or district norms. If classroom performance is adequate, then individual student data are evaluated to determine the presence of a DD based on: (a) a difference of one standard deviation between a student's CBM median score and that of classmates (level) and (b) a difference of one standard deviation between a student's CBM growth (slope) and that of classmates. Students meeting these criteria and who do not have accompanying exclusionary conditions (e.g., mental retardation, sensory disabilities, autism) move on to Phase II of the process.

Phase II of this process involves implementation of a prereferral intervention focusing on remediating the student's DD. CBM data are collected to judge the effectiveness of the intervention with the provision that the teacher implements a minimum of two interventions over a 6-week period. If a student does not show an adequate response to intervention in terms of level of slope, then the student enters Phase III of the process.

Phase III involves the design and implementation of an extended intervention plan. This phase represents a special education diagnostic trial period in which the student's responsiveness to a more intense intervention is measured. This phase often lasts 8 weeks, after which a team reconvenes and makes decisions about the student's most appropriate placement. The team could decide that the intervention was successful and an IEP would be developed and the plan continued. Alternatively, the team could decide that the intervention was unsuccessful in eliminating the DD and consider alternative decisions, such as changing the nature and intensity of the intervention, collecting additional assessment information, considering a more restrictive placement, or changing to a school having additional resources that better addresses the student's needs. In this CBM-DD model, a student qualifies for LD if he or she passes a three-pronged test: (a) a DD between the student's performance level and growth (one standard deviation for each), (b) the student's rate of learning with adaptations made in the general education classroom is inadequate, and (c) the provision of special education must result in improved growth. Speece and Case (2001) provided further validity evidence for the CBM-DD model in identifying students as LD. Children identified as being at risk for reading failure if their mean performance on CBM reading probes placed them in the lower quartile of their classes. A contrast group was identified that included five students from each classroom based on scores at the median (two students) and the 30th, 75th, and 90th percentiles (one student at each level). At-risk students were placed into one of three groups: CBM DD (CBM-DD), regression-based IQ-reading achievement discrepancy (IQ-DS), and low achievement (LA). Students in the CBM-DD group were given 10 CBM oral reading probes administered across the school year. Slopes based on ordinary least-squares regression for each child and classroom were computed and each student's performance level was based on the mean of the last two data points. Children were placed in the CBM-DD group ($n = 47$) if their slope across the year and level of performance at the end of the year was greater than one standard deviation below that of classmates. Students were placed in the IQ-DS group ($n = 17$) if their IQ-DS was 1.5 or more standard errors of prediction (approximately a 20-point discrepancy). Children were placed in the LA group ($n = 28$) if their total reading score was less than a standard score of 90.

Speece and Case (2001) showed that students in the CBM-DD group were more deficient on measures of phonological processing and were rated by teachers as having lower academic competence and social skills and more problem behaviors than students in the IQ-DS and LA groups. The CBM-DD and IQ-DS groups were not different on a standardized measure of reading achievement demonstrating the sensitivity of the CBM-DD model. These data offer further support for the CBM-DD model to identify students as LD, specifically those with phonological deficits. In later commenting on this study, Speece, Case, and Molloy (2003, p. 150) stated:

...by focusing on both level and growth in reading achievement as indexed by CBM, a valid group of children who experience reading problems was identified. Although much simpler identification methods would be preferred, other analyses indicated that single indicators of reading difficulty (letter sound fluency, oral reading fluency, phonological awareness) were not sensitive indicators of either DD or status as problem readers... The dual discrepancy method would require major challenges in the way children are identified; however, our initial evidence suggests that benefits may outweigh the costs of change.

2.2.3 The Learning Disabilities Summit

The RTI concept received further attention as a viable alternative to the IQ-achievement discrepancy approach from the LD Initiative that was sponsored by the Office of Special Education Programs (US Department of Education). The LD Initiative was a working group meeting held in Washington, DC, in May, 1999, and was attended by numerous researchers and leaders in the field over a 2-day period. Based on the LD Initiative, a national conference was held in Washington, DC, in August, 2001, entitled the *LD Summit*. Nine white papers were written and presented over a 2-day period to a group of LD professionals and stakeholders from all over the US. One paper (Gresham, 2002) specifically addressed the literature on *responsiveness to intervention* that was responded to by four professionals within the field of LD (Fuchs, 2002; Grimes, 2002; Vaughn, 2002; Vellutino, 2002). This paper argued that a student's inadequate response to an empirically validated intervention implemented with integrity can and should be used as evidence of the presence of LD and should be used to classify students as such. Gresham (2002) maintained that RTI was a viable alternative to defining LD, particularly in light of the myriad of difficulties with discrepancy-based models that were and are currently being used to identify this disability.

Subsequent to the LD Summit, the President's Commission on Excellence in Special Education (2002) emphasized RTI as a viable alternative to IQ-achievement discrepancy in the identification of LD. In December, 2004, President Bush signed into law the reauthorization of the Individuals With Disabilities Education Improvement Act (IDEIA, 2004). The law now reads with respect to specific learning disabilities:

Specific learning disabilities: (A) General: Notwithstanding section 607 of this Act, or any other provision of law, when determining whether a child has a specific learning disability as defined under this Act, the LEA shall *not be required* to take into consideration whether a child has a severe discrepancy between achievement and intellectual ability in oral expression, listening comprehension, reading recognition, . . . (B) Additional Authority: In determining whether a child has a specific learning disability, a LEA *may use* a process which determines if a child *responds to a scientific, research based intervention*. (Emphases added)

Clearly, the reauthorized version of IDEIA does not require nor does it eliminate IQ-achievement discrepancy as a basis of identifying children with LD. Moreover, it allows, but does not require, school districts (LEAs) to use an RTI approach to identifying LD.

2.3 Response-to-Intervention Models

There are two basic approaches to delivering interventions within an RTI model: (a) problem-solving approaches and (b) standard-protocol approaches (Fuchs, Mock, Morgan, and Young, 2003). These two approaches are described in the following section. Some RTI models combine the two approaches, particularly within a multi-tier model of service delivery, and may be particularly useful in school settings (Barnett, Daly, Jones, and Lentz, 2004; Duhon et al. 2004; Noell et al., 1998; Van DerHeyden, Witt, and Naquin, 2003). These models are best described as multi-tier RIT approaches to intervention.

2.3.1 Problem-Solving Approaches

Problem solving can be traced back to the behavioral consultation model first described by Bergan (1977) and later revised and updated by Bergan and Kratochwill (1990). Behavioral consultation takes place in a sequence of four phases: (a) problem identification, (b) problem analysis, (c) plan implementation, and (d) plan evaluation. The goal in behavioral consultation is to define the problem in clear, unambiguous, and operational terms, to identify environmental conditions related to the referral problem, to design and implement an intervention plan with integrity, and to evaluate the effectiveness of the intervention (Bergan and Kratochwill, 1990). More recently, the behavioral consultation model was described by Tilly (2002) in the form of four fundamental questions governing the identification and intervention of school-based academic and behavioral problems: (a) What is the problem? (b) Why is the problem happening? (c) What should be done about it? (d) Did it work? Each of these problem-solving steps is described briefly in the following section.

Problems are defined in a problem-solving approach as a discrepancy between current and desired levels of performance; as such, the larger the discrepancy, the larger the problem. For example, if the current rate of oral reading fluency is 50 words correct per minute and the desired rate is 100 words per minute, then there is a 50% discrepancy (or 50 words) between where the child is functioning and the child's desired level of performance. This same logic can be applied to any type of referral problem (academic or behavioral) as the first step in a problem-solving approach.

Another important aspect of problem solving is to determine why the problem is occurring. At this stage, the distinction between "Can't do" problems and "Won't do" problems becomes critical (Gresham, 1981; Elliott and Gresham, 1991). "Can't do" problems are considered to be *acquisition deficits*, meaning that the child does not have the skill or behavior in his or her repertoire. For instance, if a child does not engage in appropriate social interactions on the playground with peers, then it may be because the child lacks appropriate peer group entry strategies. In this case, the acquisition deficit must be remediated by directly teaching the child appropriate peer group entry strategies.

"Won't do" problems are considered to be *performance deficits*, meaning that the child knows how to perform the behavior or skill, but does not do so. Reasons for not performing the behavior or skill may be due to the lack of opportunities to perform the skill or the lack of or low rate of reinforcement for performing the behavior. In this case, remedial interventions would involve providing multiple opportunities or perform the behavior or skill and increase in the rate of reinforcement for the skill or behavior.

The final stage of a problem-solving model involves determining whether or not the intervention was effective in changing behavior. This process involves *data-based* decision making in which effectiveness is determined empirically by direct measurement of intervention outcomes. For example, outcomes of a reading intervention might be evaluated by direct measurement of oral reading fluency using standard CBM passages. If the child shows a significant increase in oral reading fluency (as indexed by either benchmarks or normative data), then the child would be considered as showing an adequate response to intervention.

2.3.2 Standard-Protocol Approaches

Another approach to RTI is the use of validated treatment protocols that can be implemented with students having either academic or behavioral difficulties. Many students classified as LD, for example, may fail to acquire basic reading skills not because of some underlying processing disorder, but because they have not be given adequate opportunities to learn (Clay, 1987). The use of IQ-achievement discrepancy and processing assessment in LD does not screen out those children whose reading difficulties might be due to either inadequate schooling or limited exposure to effective reading instruction (Clay, 1985; Foorman, Francis, Fletcher, Schatschneider, and Mehta, 1998; Vellutino et al., 1996). Vellutino et al. (1996) suggested that exposure to validated reading instruction for a period of time should be used as a "first cut diagnostic aid" in distinguishing between reading problems caused by cognitive deficits versus those caused by experiential deficits (e.g., poor reading instruction).

Other standard protocol approaches have shown similar positive outcomes in the area of reading instruction (Torgesen, Alexander, Wagner, Rashotte, Voeller, and Conway, 2001; Vaughn, Linan-Thompson, and Hickman, 2003). Standard-protocol approaches such as these have convincing empirical evidence that they can be used to effectively remediate reading difficulties in most, but not all, poor readers. The primary advantage of the standard-protocol approach compared with the problem-solving approach is that they may afford better quality control of instruction. Given that these protocols are scripted, they can be used to ensure the integrity of instruction. It should also be noted that the standard protocol approach has been used almost exclusively by researchers and not by school practitioners (Fuchs et al., 2003). This research-to-practice gap represents exciting avenues to RTI researchers and practitioners for the future.

2.3.3 Multi-Tiered Response to Intervention

Most proponents of the RTI approach adopt a multi-tiered model of intervention in which the intensity of services that are delivered is increased only after the child's skills or behavior have not shown an adequate response to intervention (Brown-Chidsey and

Steege, 2005; National Association of State Directors of Special Education, 2005; Reschly, Tilly, and Grimes, 1999). Thus, RTI involves both problem-solving and standard-protocol approaches depending on the intensity level required to remediate a student's academic and/or behavioral difficulties. Several advantages accrue from using a multi-tiered RTI approach; these are briefly discussed below.

2.3.3.1 Early Identification

First, this approach leads to early identification of learning and behavior problems that have a better chance of being effective than problems identified later in a child's school career. Perhaps the most compelling reason for adopting a RTI approach is that it provides the opportunity for providing assistance to struggling children immediately rather than waiting until these children have an entrenched pattern of academic and/or behavioral difficulties. The use of IQ-achievement discrepancy to identify children as LD, for example, has been termed a "wait-to-fail" approach because it requires that a child fail severely enough and long enough for the teacher to make a decision to refer and for a severe discrepancy to be psychometrically detected. For example, the developmental odds of being classified as LD in schools increases linearly by 450% between 1st and 4th grades (United States Department of Education, 2002). Discrepancy approaches penalize younger children because they are much less likely to show a discrepancy than older children (Fletcher et al., 1998).

In the area of children's emotional and behavioral difficulties, schools often wait until it is too late for interventions to be effective for these children's difficulties. Bullis and Walker (1994) suggested that it is ironic that teachers consistently rank children's severe behavioral difficulties as one of their highest service priorities, even though prevalence studies indicate that this school population continues to be underidentified and unidentified (Walker, Nishioka, Zeller, Severson, and Feil, 2000). Kauffman (1999) has argued that schools often "prevent prevention" of behavioral disorders of at-risk children through well-meaning efforts to "protect" them from such factors as labeling and stigmatization associated with the early identification process.

Research has indicated that children who do not learn to achieve their social goals other than through inappropriate and/or coercive behavior patterns by around 8 years of age (end of 3rd grade) will likely continue displaying some degree of antisocial behavior throughout their lives (Kazdin, 1987; Loeber and Farrington, 1998; Walker, Ramsey, and Gresham, 2004). Research also reveals that the longer such children go without access to effective intervention services, the more resistant their behavior problems will be to subsequent intervention efforts (Gresham, 1991). In the absence of early intervention, these problem behaviors will likely escalate and morph into more serious and debilitating behavior patterns. Early identification of problem behaviors and subsequent intervention efforts using a multi-tiered RTI approach is a promising practice in schools and may prevent more serious forms of behavior challenges from occurring.

2.3.3.2 Risk versus Deficit Approach

A second advantage of using an RTI approach is that it operates under a *risk model* that emphasizes early identification of learning and behavioral difficulties. Under this model, *all* students are screened for potential learning and behavioral difficulties early in their school careers (e.g., kindergarten–1st grade). Those students identified as being at risk are given supplemental instruction or behavioral support that has been shown to be an effective practice based on evidence-based research.

Historically, the field of LD has operated under a deficit model of practice in which underlying cognitive and processing deficits are identified and specifically designed instructional strategies are recommended to remediate those deficits (Mann, 1979; Ysseldyke, 2001). Current approaches to LD assessment rely heavily on aptitude by treatment interaction (ATI) logic, in which instructional treatments are matched to aptitude strengths presumably to produce better outcomes. After 20 years of disappointing research, Cronbach (1975) abandoned ATI for applied psychology and recommended a process akin to what is now called problem solving and short-run empiricism (see Reschly and Ysseldyke, 2002; Tilly et al., 1999).

The most important concept in any RTI model is the idea of matching the *intensity* of the intervention to the severity of the problem and the resistance of that problem to change. This approach characterizes interventions that differ in terms of their nature, comprehensiveness, and intensity, as well as in the degree of unresponsiveness of behavior to those interventions (Gresham, 2004). The RTI approach offers an opportunity to integrate services between general and special education (Vaughn and Fuchs, 2003).

2.3.3.3 Reduction of Identification Biases

Referral to special education in the public schools typically begins with a general education teacher's decision to refer a student for special education consideration. The decision to refer a child for special education consideration is usually based on academic and/or behavioral difficulties that are discrepant from the rest of that teacher's general education classroom. The principal guiding teacher referral is one of *relativity*; that is, what is the child's academic and/or behavioral performance relative to the modal performance.

Factors such as gender, socioeconomic status, and minority group membership often influence a teacher's decision to refer a child to special education (MacMillan and Siperstein, 2002; Reschly, 2002; VanDerHeyden and Witt, in press). Donovan and Cross (2002) argued that an RTI approach to the referral process has the potential of reducing and perhaps eliminating the disproportionate overrepresentation of certain minority groups in special education that result from biases in the teacher referral process. For example, it is well established that there is a bias in overidentifying boys and underidentifying girls as LD by the current teacher referral process (Donovan and Cross, 2002; Shaywitz, Shaywitz, Fletcher, and Escobar, 1990). The power of iterative problem-solving efforts implemented within an RTI model of identification to reduce disproportionate identification by race and sex, and its superiority to other methods of identification such as teacher referral, has been empirically demonstrated (see VanDerHeyden and Witt, in press).

2.3.3.4 Focus on Student Outcomes

RTI is based on the premise that measures and domains assessed should be determined by their relationships to child outcomes. Useful and appropriate measures and domains have a documented relationship to *positive child outcomes*, not just predictions of failure. Measures without such relationships do little for children and may cause harm because they deflect attention away from measures and domains that can be used to produce positive outcomes (Reschly and Tilly, 1999). RTI emphasizes *direct measurement* of achievement, behavior, and the instructional environment as the core foci of a comprehensive evaluation of learning and behavioral difficulties. RTI is concerned primarily with the assessment of measurable and changeable aspects of the instructional environment that are related to positive child outcomes. Assessment within an RTI approach concentrates on those factors that are related to achievement and positive behavior change.

In terms of academic achievement, RTI is based on the assumption that a significant proportion of children who might be identified as LD may be more accurately characterized as "instructional causalities" (Vaughn et al., 2003). Clay (1987) suggested that many children "learn to be learning disabled" because they are not exposed to early fundamental literacy skills in kindergarten and 1st grade (e.g., phoneme awareness, print concepts, letter–sound correspondence). Additionally, many of these children are exposed to marginally effective general education reading curricula and instruction that have either not been scientifically validated or that have been implemented with poor integrity (National Reading Panel, 2000).

RTI involves analyses or prior and current instructional opportunities and the application of evidence-based instructional strategies related to positive child outcomes. Instructional variables assessed include alterable factors such as time allocated for instruction, academic learning time, pacing of instruction, number of opportunities to respond, sequencing of examples and nonexamples of skills, and so forth (Carnine, Silbert, and Kame'enui, 1997; Denton et al., 2002; National Reading Panel, 2000; Witt, VanDerHeyden, and Gilbertson, 2004). An essential component of RTI involves the direct measurement of treatment integrity of instructional and behavioral intervention delivered in the general education classroom (Gresham, 1989, 1997).

2.4 Technical Challenges in Measuring Response to Intervention

The RTI approach to service delivery presents some unique measurement challenges that differ substantially from measurement issues involved in IQ-achievement discrepancy for LD or for determining an inadequate response to intervention for children at-risk for ED. The most fundamental issue in an RTI approach revolves around the notion of *adequate* versus *inadequate* responsiveness. That is: How does one define an adequate response to intervention and how does one measure it? In the area of academic performance, two basic approaches have been proposed for indexing response to intervention: (a) final status and (b) growth models (see Fuchs, 2003). For behavioral difficulties, several methods have been proposed to reflect response to intervention: (a) visual inspection of graphed data, (b) percentage change from baseline, (c) effect sizes estimates, and (d) social validation of behavior change. Owing to space constraints, only responses to intervention measurement issues for academic difficulties are presented. More detail on measuring response to intervention for social/behavioral difficulties can be found in other sources (Brown-Chidsey and Steege, 2005; Gresham, 2005, 2006).

2.4.1 Final Status

Perhaps the most straightforward way of determining adequate response to intervention is to evaluate where the student is at the end of an intervention. Students showing adequate functioning at posttest might be considered "treatment responders" and, therefore, not in need of additional intervention services. What constitutes adequate functioning? There is no right or wrong answer to this question; however, several guidelines might be suggested.

For example, one might consider a student to have adequately responded to intervention if he or she is now functioning in the normative range on a norm-referenced measure of academic achievement (e.g., >25th percentile). Another approach based on CBM might be whether or not the student meets or exceeds established benchmark criteria for a particular skill at a given grade level (e.g., reading 40 words correctly per minute in 1st grade). There are

well-established benchmark criteria for oral reading fluency, phoneme segmentation fluency, letter naming fluency, and nonsense word fluency using CBM strategies that can be used in decision-making in an RTI approach (Fuchs, 2000; Good, Gruba, and Kaminski, 2002; Shinn, 2002).

Torgesen et al. (2001) used final status in a sample of school-identified LD students to determine whether students responded adequately to intensive one-to-one reading instruction (67.5 h). These researchers showed that between one-half and two-thirds of students receiving the intensive reading intervention "normalized" their skills depending on the measure used. For example, students achieved scores in the normal range on the Word Attack ($M = 93.4$) and Passage Comprehension ($M = 92.4$) subtests of the Woodcock Reading Mastery Test-Revised (Woodcock, 1987). Additionally, students attained scores in the normative range on five of six phonological measures, including Phoneme Elision ($M = 99.5$), Digit Memory ($M = 90$), Nonword Repetition ($M = 102.0$), Rapid Automatized Naming Digits ($M = 90$), and Rapid Automatized Letters ($M = 94.5$). Interestingly, the reading interventions produced the most effective results on measures of reading comprehension, with 80 to 85% of students performing in the average range at the end of intervention.

The Torgesen et al. (2001) investigation provides useful information regarding how one might define adequate or inadequate responsiveness based on the RTI concept. About 25% of the school-identified LD students (a sample likely to have a greater number of inadequate responders relative to a general school population) in this study were *inadequate responders* to the intensive intervention with mean standard scores of about 70 on Word Attack, Word Identification, and Passage Comprehension. Approximately 40% of the students in the sample who the schools previously identified as LD were returned to general education and deemed no longer in need of special education and related services.

The problem with using final status as the criterion in an RTI approach is that it ignores the concept of growth that is a fundamental aspect of academic learning (Fuchs, 2003). For example, a student can make very good growth as measured by slope estimates, but may not meet normative or benchmark criteria as indexed by level estimates. Similarly, students can make relatively poor growth, but may have started the intervention relatively close to the criterion level standard. The concept of *growth* is an essential aspect of RTI and is considered in the following section.

2.4.2 Growth Models in Response to Intervention

The goal of all interventions is to produce an improvement between baseline and post-intervention levels of performance, and this logic forms the basis of any RTI approach (Gresham, 2002). Using final status as the criterion to evaluate intervention effectiveness (described above) uses this logic by comparing pretest with posttest levels of performance. The effects of intervention, at least in group design studies, are determined by some form of repeated measures logic to compute simple mean differences on dependent measures for groups. Although these types of analysis can tell us whether or not an intervention produced mean differences for *groups* (a significant group × time interaction), these are insufficient data to model *individual change* over time adequately.

Vellutino et al. (1996) used a growth curve analysis in a longitudinal study of 183 kindergarten children composed of poor readers ($n = 118$) and normal reader controls ($N = 65$). Poor readers were selected on the basis of scoring below the 15th percentile on measures of word identification or letter–sound correspondence using nonsense words. Children in the poor reader group were given 15 weeks of daily one-to-one tutoring (30 min per day) over 70–80 sessions. Using hierarchical linear modeling analyses, growth rates were calculated for each child from kindergarten to 2nd grade. Slopes from these analyses were rank-ordered and used to place children into one of four groups: Very Limited Growth, Limited Growth, Good Growth, and Very Good Growth. As such, approximately half the sample showed inadequate response to intervention (treatment resisters) and the other half showed adequate response to intervention (treatment responders).

Figure 2.1 depicts three hypothetical growth curve models that might be expected in an RTI approach. The solid line represents the average growth over time one might expect from the classmates who exhibit no reading difficulty. For those beginning the year exhibiting a reading disability, one might hypothesize that some number, when provided with an evidence-based reading implemented with integrity, will accelerate their progress and actually "catch up" (Hypothetical A) with those students showing no disability. These cases represent probable cases where instruction may have been inadequate and when taught well, they in fact do "catch up" to their normally achieving peers. Such cases might be considered *instructional causalities* and not "true" disabilities (Vaughn et al., 2003).

Another subgroup of children (Hypothetical B) begin the year well behind the nondisabled readers, but they progress at the same rate as nondisabled

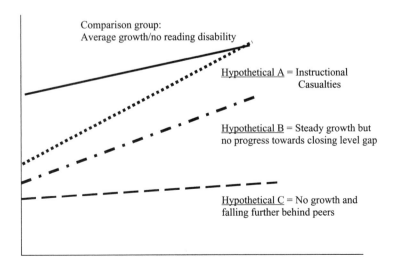

FIGURE 2.1. Hypothetical Responses to Reading Intervention by Students with Reading Problems

readers when provided with evidence-based reading instruction but fail to close the gap. That is, they show similar parallel slopes as the nondisabled readers (reflecting reading growth), but they never reach the desired grade-level of reading performance.

The third group (Hypothetical C) resembles the "nonresponders" or treatment resisters in a number of reading studies (e.g., Torgesen et al., 2001; Vaughn et al., 2003; Vellutino et al., 1996). They begin the year well behind the nondisabled readers but, despite exposure to evidence-based reading instruction delivered with integrity, they continue to fall further and further behind their nondisabled peers (i.e., they show both flat slopes and lower levels of reading performance). The research literature suggests that between 4 and 6% of a general school population (or 25% of a poor reading population) is expected to exhibit this pattern of inadequate response to instruction (Foorman et al., 1998; Torgesen et al., 2001; Vellutino et al., 1996, 2000).

2.5 Conclusions

Regarding learning to read, there is a convincing body of evidence to suggest that many children with reading difficulties can be effectively remediated by intensive exposure to evidence-based reading instruction. This evidence is based on research sponsored by the National Institute of Child Health and Human Development (NICHD) over the past 20 years that indicates reading difficulties are caused by weaknesses in the ability to process phonological aspects of language (Liberman, Shankweiler, and Liberman, 1989; Stanovich and Siegel, 1994; Vellutino, 1987; Vellutino and Scanlon, 2002). What the field does not have at this time is the availability of validated treatment protocols for other academic achievement areas, such as mathematics and written expression. This requires further research of the same quality as the aforementioned NICHD reading research.

Apart from the need for controlled outcome research in other academic areas, there is still the question of whether RTI is a legitimate basis for ruling in or ruling out the presence of a *disability*. Does the fact that a child responded adequately to an intervention rule out that he or she did not have a disability? Does this mean that the child's learning difficulties were caused exclusively by poor instruction? Does

the fact that the child did not respond adequately to an intervention mean that he or she has a "true" learning disability?

These questions may be of more interest to researchers than to treatment consumers such as parents or teachers. One could argue that the accuracy of a cancer diagnosis is not confirmed or disconfirmed by how a patient responds to treatment (e.g., radiation, chemotherapy, and/or surgery). In other words, the diagnosis of cancer is made independently of treatment considerations. Although this is true, professionals in education and psychology do not enjoy the same luxury when it comes to defining so-called "mild" or high-incidence disabilities (e.g., LD or ED). The field has always faced daunting conceptual and measurement difficulties in assessing processing, cognitive abilities, and EDs and relating this information to effective interventions (Reschly and Tilly, 1999; Reschly and Ysseldyke, 2002; Torgesen, 2002). A legitimate argument from an RTI perspective is that if a child's learning or behavioral difficulties have been remediated (i.e., "normalized"), then the issue of whether or not that child had a "true disability" in the first place is moot.

Another issue of concern relating to the adoption of an RTI approach is assessment considerations. What does a comprehensive assessment look like in an RTI approach? An in-depth presentation of this topic would constitute an entire chapter in its own right and, therefore, will not be comprehensively described herein. Briefly, RTI advocates argue that a comprehensive assessment must be related to child outcomes and must gather relevant functional information relating to those outcomes (Gresham et al., 2004; Witt, VanDerHeyden, and Gilbertson, 2004). Useful and appropriate measures and domains must have a documented relationship to positive child outcomes and not just predictions about failure. RTI uses *direct* measurement of achievement, behavior, and the instructional environment as the core foci of a comprehensive assessment. The emphasis of assessment in an RTI approach is on assessment of measurable and changeable aspects of behavior and the instructional environment that are related to child outcomes.

Comprehensive assessment in an RTI approach emphasizes teachable skills related to the curriculum that informs decision-makers about what to teach and how to teach it (Howell and Nolet, 1999). RTI assessment collects representative, direct, and low inference measures that concentrate on referral concerns and answer the assessment questions. Comprehensive assessment in an RTI approach also involves the direct measurement of treatment integrity of interventions delivered either in the general education classroom, small group, or individual instruction (Gresham, 1989). Child achievement and behavior outcomes in natural settings drive decisions at every step in the RTI comprehensive assessment process.

RTI uses a child's adequate or inadequate response to intervention as a decision-making tool to guide further actions, such as changing or intensifying interventions or changing a child's educational placement. Part of the appeal of an RTI approach is that it allows one to rule out inadequate instruction or poor classroom management practices as an explanation for insufficient academic achievement or behavioral difficulties. RTI protects against faulty decision-making, unsubstantiated causal inferences, and use of assessment tools that do not inform instruction (Gresham and Witt, 1997; Macmann and Barnett, 1999; Neisworth and Bagnato, 1992). Outcomes of interventions in RTI are judged based on whether or not these interventions produce acceptable levels of student performance.

The discussion of RTI is often contentious because it raises questions about very basic ideas in psychoeducational practice that the field has not resolved. Eligibility for specialized services lies at the vortex of many issues central to the field about how learning occurs and what limits there are to human potential for learning. Special education originated because of a need to sort and serve students of a wider range of experience and ability due to federal mandates (Hallahan and Mercer, 2002; MacMillan and Siperstein, 2002). One could argue that the field has developed under contingencies arranged primarily through litigation and promoted by advocacy-based arguments rather than by evidence-based arguments.

Current evidence suggests that RTI can be implemented responsibly while the evidence base continues to accumulate. To be sure, iterations and modifications of RTI are not only inevitable, but also desirable as the database evolves. The benefits of RTI far outweigh the potential costs to children and will only facilitate refinements toward a model supported by converging sources of evidence. The changes and challenges presented by an RTI approach necessarily will move the field from an exclusive reliance on eligibility determination into intervention-based practices in the schools for struggling learners.

References

Barnett, D., Daly, E., Jones, K., & Lentz, F. E. (2004). Response to intervention: Empirically-based special service decisions for increasing and decreasing intensity using single case designs. *The Journal of Special Education, 38*, 66–79.

Bergan, J. (1977). *Behavioral Consultation.* Columbus, OH: Merrill.

Bergan, J. & Kratochwill, T. R. (1990). *Behavioral Consultation and Therapy.* New York: Plenum Press.

Bocian, K., Beebe, M., MacMillan, D. L., & Gresham, F. M. (1999). Competing paradigms in learning disabilities classification by schools and variations in the meaning of discrepant achievement. *Learning Disabilities Research & Practice, 14*, 1–14.

Brown-Chidsey, R., & Steege, M. W. (2005). *Response to Intervention: Principles and Strategies for Effective Practice.* New York: Guilford Press.

Bullis, M. & Walker, H. M. (1994). *Comprehensive School-based Systems for Troubled Youth.* Eugene, OR: University of Oregon, Institute on Violence and Destructive Behavior.

Carnine, D., Silbert, J., & Kame'enui, E. (1997). *Direct Instruction in Reading* (3rd ed.). Upper Saddle, NJ: Prentice-Hall.

Clay, M. (1985). *The Early Detection of Reading Difficulties* (3rd ed.). Auckland, New Zealand: Heinemann.

Clay, M. (1987). Learning to be learning disabled. *New Zealand Journal of Educational Studies, 22*, 155–173.

Cone, J. D. (1989). Is there utility for treatment utility? *American Psychologist, 44*, 1241–1242.

Cronbach, L. J. (1975). Beyond two disciplines of scientific psychology. *American Psychologist, 30*, 116–127.

Denton, C. A., Vaughn, S., & Fletcher J. M. (2003). Bringing research-based practice in reading intervention to scale. *Learning Disabilities Research & Practice, 18*, 201–211.

Donovan, M. & Cross, C. (2002). *Minority Students in Special and Gifted Education.* Washington, DC: National Academy Press.

Duhon, G. J., Noell, G. H., Witt, J. C., Freeland, J. T., Dufrene, B. A., & Gilbertson, D. N. (2004). Identifying academic skill and performance deficits: the experimental analysis of brief assessments of academic skills. *School Psychology Review, 33*, 429–443.

Elliott, S. N. & Gresham, F. M. (1991). *Social Skills Intervention Guide.* Circle Pines, MN: AGS Publishing.

Fletcher, J., Francis, D., Shaywitz, S., Lyon, G. R., Foorman, B., Steubing, K., et al. (1998). Intelligent testing and the discrepancy model for children with learning disabilities. *Learning Disabilities Research & Practice, 13*, 186–203.

Foorman, B., Francis, D., Fletcher, J., Schatschneider, C., & Mehta, P. (1998). The role of instruction in learning to read: preventing reading failure in at-risk children. *Journal of Educational Psychology, 90*, 37–55.

Fuchs, L. (1995). Incorporating curriculum-based measurement into eligibility the decision-making process: a focus on treatment validity and student growth. Paper presented for the *National Academy of Sciences Workshop on Alternatives to IQ Testing*, Washington, DC.

Fuchs, L. (2002). Three conceptualizations of "treatment" in a responsiveness-to-treatment framework for LD identification. In R. Bradley, L. Danielson, & D. Hallahan (Eds.), *Learning Disabilities: Research to Practice* (pp. 521–529). Mahwah, NJ: Lawrence Erlbaum.

Fuchs, L. (2003). Assessing intervention responsiveness: conceptual and technical issues. *Learning Disabilities Research & Practice, 18*, 172–186.

Fuchs, L. & Fuchs, D. (1997). Use of curriculum-based measurement in identifying students with disabilities. *Focus on Exceptional Children, 30*, 1–16.

Fuchs, L. & Fuchs, D. (1998). Treatment validity: a unifying concept for reconceptualizing the identification of learning disabilities. *Learning Disabilities Research & Practice, 13*, 204–219.

Fuchs, D., Mock, D., Morgan, P., & Young, C. (2003). Responsiveness-to-intervention: definitions, evidence, and implications for the learning disabilities construct. *Learning Disabilities Research & Practice, 18*, 157–171.

Good, R., Gruba, J., & Kaminski, R. (2002). Best practices in using dynamic indicators of basic early literacy skills (DIBELS). In A. Thomas & J. Grimes (Eds.), *Best Practices in School Psychology* (4th ed., pp. 699–720). Bethesda, MD: National Association of School Psychologists.

Gresham, F. M. (1981). Social skills training with handicapped children: a review. *Review of Educational Research, 51*, 139–176.

Gresham, F. M. (1989). Assessment of treatment integrity in school consultation and prereferral intervention. *School Psychology Review, 18*, 37–50.

Gresham, F. M. (1991). Conceptualizing behavior disorders in terms of resistance to intervention. *School Psychology Review, 20*, 23–36.

Gresham, F. M. (1997). Treatment integrity in single-subject research. In R. Franklin, D. Allison, &

B. Gorman (Eds.), *Design and Analysis of Single-Case Research* (pp. 93–118). Mahwah, NJ: Lawrence Erlbaum.

Gresham, F. M. (2002). Responsiveness to intervention: an alternative approach to the identification of learning disabilities. In R. Bradley, L. Danielson, & D. Hallahan (Eds.), *Learning Disabilities: Research to Practice* (pp. 467–519). Mahwah, NJ: Lawrence Erlbaum.

Gresham, F. M. (2004). Current status and future directions of school-based behavioral interventions. *School Psychology Review, 33*, 326–343.

Gresham, F. M. (2005). Response to intervention: an alternative means of identifying students as emotionally disturbed. *Education and Treatment of Children, 28*, 328–344.

Gresham, F. M. (2006). Response to intervention. In G. Bear & K. Minke (Eds.), *Children's Needs – III*. Bethesda, MD: National Association of School Psychologists.

Gresham, F. M., Reschly, D. J., Tilly, W. D., Fletcher, J., Burns, M., Christ, T., et al. (2004). Comprehensive evaluation of learning disabilities: a response-to-intervention perspective. *Communique, 33*, 34–35.

Gresham, F. M. & Witt, J. C. (1997). Utility of intelligence tests for treatment planning, classification, and placement decisions: recent empirical findings and future directions. *School Psychology Quarterly, 12*, 249–267.

Grimes, J. (2002). Responsiveness to intervention: the next step in special education identification, service, and exiting decision making. In R. Bradley, L. Danielson, & D. Hallahan (Eds.), *Identification of Learning Disabilities: Research to Practice* (pp. 531–547). Bethesda, MD: National Association of School Psychologists.

Hallahan, D. & Mercer, C. (2002). Learning disabilities: historical perspectives. In R. Bradley, L. Danielson, & D. Hallahan (Eds.), *Identification of Learning Disabilities: Research to Practice* (pp. 1–67). Mahwah, NJ: Lawrence Erlbaum.

Hayes, S., Nelson, R., & Jarrett, R. (1987). The treatment utility of assessment: a functional approach to evaluating assessment quality. *American Psychologist, 42*, 963–974.

Heller, K. A., Holtzman, W. H., & Messick, S. (Eds.) (1982). *Placing Children in Special Education: A Strategy for Equity*. Washington, DC: National Academy Press.

Howell, K. & Nolet, V. (1999). *Curriculum-based Evaluation: Teaching and Decision Making*. Pacific Grove, CA: Brooks/Cole.

Individuals With Disabilities Education Improvement Act (2004). Public Law 108-446 (20 U.S.C. 1400 *et seq.*).

Kauffman, J. (1999). How we prevent emotional and behavioral disorders. *Exceptional Children, 65*, 448–468.

Kazdin, A. (1987). Treatment of antisocial behavior in childhood: Current status and future directions. *Psychological Bulletin, 102*, 187–203.

Liberman, I., Shankweiler, D., & Liberman, A. (1989). The alphabetic principle and learning to read. In D. Shankweiler & I. Liberman (Eds.), *Phonology and Reading Disability: Solving the Reading Puzzle* (pp. 1–33). Ann Arbor, MI: University of Michigan Press.

Loeber, R. & Farrington, D. (Eds.) (1998). *Serious and Violent Juvenile Offenders: Risk Factors and Successful Interventions.* Thousand Oaks, CA: Sage Publications.

Macmann, G. & Barnett, D. (1999). Diagnostic decision making in school psychology: understanding and coping with uncertainty. In C. Reynolds & T. Gutkin (Eds.), *Handbook of School Psychology* (3rd ed., pp. 519–548). New York: Wiley.

MacMillan, D. L. & Siperstein, G. (2002). Learning disabilities as operationally defined by schools. In R. Bradley, L. Danielson, & D. Hallahan (Eds.), *Identification of Learning Disabilities: Research to Practice* (pp. 287–333). Mahwah, NJ: Lawrence Erlbaum.

Mann, L. (1979). *On the Trail of Process.* New York: Grune & Stratton.

Messick, S. (1995). Validity of psychological assessment: validation of inferences from persons' responses and performances as scientific inquiry into score meaning. *American Psychologist, 50*, 741–749.

Mischel, W. (1968). *Personality and Assessment.* New York: Wiley.

National Association of State Directors of Special Education (2005). *Response to Intervention: Policy Considerations and Implementation.* Alexandria, VA: National Association of State Directors of Special Education.

National Reading Panel (2000). *Report of the National Reading Panel. Teaching Children to Read: An Evidence-based Assessment of the Scientific Literature on Reading and its Implications for Reading Instruction.* (NIH Publication No. 00-4769). Washington, DC: US Government Printing Office.

Neisworth, J. & Bagnato, S. (1992). The case against intelligence testing in early intervention. *Topics in Early Childhood Special Education, 12*, 1–20.

Noell, G. H., Gansle, K. A., Witt, J. C., Whitmarsh, E. L., Freeland, J. T., LaFoeur, L. H., et al. (1998). Effects of contingent reward on instruction in oral reading performance at differing levels of passage difficulty. *Journal of Applied Behavior Analysis, 31*, 659–663.

President's Commission on Excellence in Special Education (2002). *A New Era: Revitalizing Special Education for Children and their Families.* Washington, DC: United States Department of Education, President's Commission on Excellence in Special Education.

Reschly, D. J. (2002). Minority overrepresentation: the silent contributor to LD prevalence and diagnostic confusion. In R. Bradley, L. Danielson, & D. Hallahan (Eds.), *Identification of Learning Disabilities: Research to Practice* (pp. 361–368). Mahwah, NJ: Lawrence Erlbaum.

Reschly, D. J. & Tilly, W. D. (1999). Reform trends and system design alternatives. In D. Reschly, W. D. Tilly, & J. Grimes (Eds.), *Special Education in Transition: Functional Assessment and Noncategorical Programming* (pp. 19–48). Longmont, CO: Sopris West.

Reschly, D. J., Tilly, W. D., & Grimes, J. (Eds.) (1999). *Special Education in Transition: Functional Assessment and Noncategorical Programming.* Longmont, CO: Sopris West.

Reschly, D. J. & Ysseldyke, J. (2002). Paradigm shift: the past is not the future. In A. Thomas & J. Grimes (Eds.), *Best Practices in School Psychology – IV* (pp. 3–20). Bethesda, MD: National Association of School Psychologists.

Sechrest, L. (1963). Incremental validity: A recommendation. *Educational and Psychological Measurement, 23*, 153–158.

Shaywitz, S., Shaywitz, B., Fletcher, J., & Escobar, M. (1990). Prevalence of reading disability in boys and girls: results of the Connecticut longitudinal study. *Journal of the American Medical Association, 264*, 998–1002.

Shinn, M. (2002). Best practices in using curriculum-based measurement in a problem-solving model. In A. Thomas & J. Grimes (Eds.), *Best Practices in School Psychology* (4th ed., pp. 671–698). Bethesda, MD: National Association of School Psychologists.

Speece, D. L. (2002). Classification of learning disabilities: convergence, expansion, and caution. In R. Bradley, L. Danielson, & D. Hallahan (Eds.), *Learning Disabilities: Research to Practice* (pp. 279–285). Mahwah, NJ: Lawrence Erlbaum.

Speece, D. & Case, L. (2001). Classification in context: an alternative approach to identifying early reading disability. *Journal of Educational Psychology, 93*, 735–749.

Speece, D., Case, L., & Molloy, D. (2003). Responsiveness to general education instruction as the first gate to learning disabilities identification. *Learning Disabilities Research & Practice, 18*, 147–156.

Stanovich, K. & Siegel, L. (1994). Phenotypic performance profiles of children with reading disabilities: a regression-based test of the phonological-core-variable-difference model. *Journal of Educational Psychology, 86*, 24–53.

Tilly, W. D. (2002). Best practices in school psychology as a problem-solving enterprise. In A. Thomas & J. Grimes (Eds.), *Best Practices in School Psychology – IV* (pp. 21–36). Bethesda, MD: National Association of School Psychologists.

Tilly, W. D., Reschly, D. J., & Grimes, J. (1999). Disability determination in problem solving systems: Conceptual foundations and critical components. In D. Reschly, W. D. Tilly, & J. Grimes (Eds.), *Special Education in Transition: Functional Assessment and Noncategorical Programming* (pp. 285–321). Sopris West: Longmont, CO.

Torgesen, J. (2002). Empirical and theoretical support for direct diagnosis of learning disabilities by assessment of intrinsic processing weaknesses. In R. Bradley, L. Danielson, & D. Hallahan (Eds.), *Identification of Learning Disabilities: Research to Practice* (pp. 565–613). Mahwah, NJ: Lawrence Erlbaum.

Torgesen, J., Alexander, A. Wagner, R., Rashotte, C., Voeller, K., & Conway, T. (2001). Intensive remedial reading instruction for children with severe reading disabilities: immediate and long-term outcomes from two instructional approaches. *Journal of Learning Disabilities, 34,* 33–58.

United States Department of Education (2002). *Twenty-fourth Annual Report to Congress on Implementation of Individuals With Disabilities Education Act.* Washington, DC: United States Department of Education.

VanDerHeyden, A. M., Witt, J. C., & Naquin, G. (2003). The development and validation of a process for screening referrals to special education. *School Psychology Review, 32,* 204–227.

Vaughn, S. (2002). Using response to treatment for identifying students with learning disabilities. In R. Bradley, L. Danielson, & D. Hallahan (Eds.), *Identification of Learning Disabilities: Research to Practice* (pp. 549–554). Mahwah, NJ: Lawrence Erlbaum.

Vaughn, S. & Fuchs, L. (2003). Redefining learning disabilities as inadequate response to instruction: the promise and potential problems. *Learning Disabilities Research & Practice, 18,* 137–146.

Vaughn, S., Linan-Thompson, S., & Hickman, P. (2003). Response to instruction as a means of identifying students with reading/learning disabilities. *Exceptional Children, 69,* 391–409.

Vellutino, F. R. (1987). Dylexia. *Scientific American, 256,* 34–41.

Vellutino, F. R. (2002). On the role of intervention in identifying learning disabilities. In R. Bradley, L. Danielson, & D. Hallahan (Eds.), *Learning Disabilities: Research to Practice* (pp. 555–564). Mahwah, NJ: Lawrence Erlbaum.

Vellutino, F. & Scanlon, D. (2002). The interactive strategies approach to reading intervention. *Contemporary Educational Psychology, 27,* 573–635.

Vellutino, F. R., Scanlon, D., & Lyon, G.R. (2000). Differentiating difficult-to-remediate and readily remediated poor readers: More evidence against IQ-achievement discrepancy of reading disability. *Journal of Learning Disabilities, 33,* 223–238.

Vellutino, F. R., Scanlon, D., Sipay, E., Small, S., Pratt, A., Chen, R., et al. (1996). Cognitive profiles of difficult to remediate and readily remediated poor readers: early intervention as a vehicle for distinguishing between cognitive and experiential deficits as basic causes of reading disability. *Journal of Educational Psychology, 88,* 601–638.

Walker, H. M., Nishioka, V., Zeller, R., Severson, H., & Feil, E. (2000). Causal factors and potential solutions for the persistent under-identification of students having emotional or behavioral disorders in the context of schooling. *Assessment for Effective Intervention, 26,* 29–40.

Walker, H. M., Ramsey, E., & Gresham, F.M. (2004). *Antisocial Behavior in School: Evidence-based Practices* (2nd ed.). Belmont, CA: Wadsworth/Thomson Learning.

Wiggins, J. (1973). *Personality and Prediction: Principles of Personality Assessment.* Reading, MA: Addison-Wesley.

Woodcock, R. W. (1987). *Woodcock Reading Mastery Tests – Revised.* Circle Pines, MN: AGS Publishing.

Ysseldyke, J. (2001). Reflections on a research career: generalizations from 25 years of research on assessment and instructional decision-making. *Exceptional Children, 67,* 295–309.

3

Response to Intervention: Conceptual and Methodological Issues in Implementation

Thomas R. Kratochwill, Melissa A. Clements, and Kristen M. Kalymon

Thomas R. Kratochwill, PhD, is Sears–Bascom Professor, School Psychology Program, University of Wisconsin–Madison. tomkat@education.wisc.edu
Melissa A. Clements, PhD, is a Research Scientist at the Wisconsin Center for Educational Research, University of Wisconsin–Madison. maclements@wisc.edu
Kristen M. Kalymon, MS, is a graduate student in the School Psychology Program, University of Wisconsin–Madison. kmkalymon@wisc.edu

Response to intervention (RTI) has been referred to as the practice of using evidence-based instruction/intervention to address student needs while monitoring student progress over time in learning and/or behavioral domains (National Association of State Directors of Special Education (NASDSE), 2005). Although there are emerging variations in the definition of RTI, essentially the approach involves using outcome data *to make decisions* about the effectiveness of an intervention structured within a multi-tiered system that could include, among other options, eligibility determination for special education (Kratochwill, 2006).

There are two critical components in the RTI framework and a variety of models as to how each of these components is operationalized. Throughout this chapter the term "models" of RTI is used, as there is no one model of implementation. In fact, it is possible to construct many different models to address the many nuances of practice and contextual factors that exist in any educational setting. These two components can be conceptualized as dependent and independent variables that vary along a number of dimensions. Specifically, the "R" in RTI can involve selecting students at risk for a variety of academic and/or social-emotional concerns and usually is referred to as "screening" in the research literature (Glover and Albers, in press). The dependent variable in this case is the number of children identified in some "at-risk" status or base rate and/or the status of a particular child (ren) on the screening measures. In addition, implicit in the RTI model on the dependent variable side is the ongoing monitor-

ing of students exposed to an intervention and often called "progress monitoring." Sometimes the same measures are used for screening and progress monitoring. However, progress monitoring is typically an ongoing process with frequent measurement for the purpose of assessing intervention outcomes and making instructional/intervention decisions.

On the independent variable side, the "I" refers to one or more interventions that are scheduled for the student and implemented. Typically, the interventions are to be evidence based, which means they must have scientific research to support their implementation (see below for more detailed discussion). And in the current literature, there has been major emphasis on reading interventions, but other academic and social–emotional domains can be included in the RTI framework as well. Interventions are typically organized within the framework of a multi-tiered model of services (e.g., primary, secondary, and tertiary prevention; Caplan, 1964), which has its origins in the prevention science literature (see Simeonsson, 1994) but has been modified considerably to include a number of special features and characteristics that are unique to its application within educational settings (see Kratochwill, Albers, and Shernoff, 2004). In addition, interventions are typically developed through some type of problem-solving model, such as, for example, problem-solving consultation (Bergan and Kratochwill, 1990; see discussion below) and/or a format called the "standard treatment protocol" (see Fuchs and Fuchs, 2006). Within RTI models, it is further assumed that the intervention serves as a "test," inasmuch as the intervention is being implemented with the distinct purpose of assessing its efficacy in improving student performance to certain specified criteria (Fuchs and Fuchs, 2006). Intervention integrity/fidelity is an important component of the intervention implementation process and has been integrated into the discussions of RTI as well.

Within the evolving developments in RTI models, a central feature in the dialogue has been on using evidence-based intervention programs and procedures (often called scientifically supported or research-based programs and procedures) in the domain of curriculum, instructional procedures, social–emotional interventions, or combinations of these features. However, as will be argued later in this chapter, considerable ambiguity exists in the exact definitions of what is evidence based within the RTI model with a full range of opinions about how the intervention is developed, implemented, and evaluated (Kratochwill, 2006).

Implicit within the RTI framework is that a student's performance is monitored across time with decisions made based on learning rate and/or level of performance as established on various social validity criteria (i.e., decision criteria based on normative or subjective standards). The criteria might be specified a priori, as in using norm-referenced standardized achievement tests to establish a standard, through the use of certain benchmarks on curriculum-based measures in a particular school, and/or consensus judgments as applied to social–emotional behaviors. Technically, all of the criteria involve professional judgment either by individuals and/or a team of professionals who are interested in making certain psychoeducational decisions about the student. These decisions could be linked to screening to evaluate the need for services, further assessment to move to a more intense level of interventions services, the application of various instructional components related to curricula and teaching procedures and programs, eligibility for special education, and/or effectiveness of instruction or intervention. In the latter case, RTI has specifically been advanced as a framework for making eligibility decisions for special education, and in this context represents a new (and according to some professionals) a radical departure from traditional assessment and decision making processes.

This chapter provides an overview of some of the conceptual and foundation features of RTI.

The concept of RTI is an extension of public health service models and many of the practices of problem-solving consultation (and especially behavioral psychology) as applied to individual children. Yet, in adoption and extension of some of these early paradigms of problem solving there are some thorny issues that remain to be resolved and which are highlighted here. And, with the new features of RTI applied within a prevention framework, new challenges will emerge, especially as these models are applied in special education decision-making processes in practice. In many cases, the issues that emerge as primary considerations in implementation of RTI remain to be addressed in research.

3.1 Conceptual Foundations

The basic conceptual framework for RTI has existed in the psychological and educational literature for many years and some of its foundational characteristics can be traced to the prevention science literature, wherein Caplan (1964) featured multi-levels of prevention in work on mental health consultation. The Institute of Medicine (1994) featured a multi-tiered model of services for prevention; this framework has generally been adopted in most of the literature, although a number of conceptual issues remain (e.g., Durlak, 1997; Small and Memmo, 2004). The evidence-based and data-based decision-making aspects of RTI do not represent a radical departure from some of the scientist–practitioner approaches that have been used in psychology and education (Barlow, Hayes, and Nelson, 1984). The problem-solving features of RTI, in fact, can be traced to many of the early writings in the behavior analysis or behavior modification field, which represents many of the foundation elements of establishing a baseline, implementing an intervention, and continuing ongoing assessment to determine whether an intervention is effective; see Kratochwill and Bijou (1987) for a history of behavior modification.

Some writers refer to the origins of the current RTI problem-solving practices in terms of two particular models of research and practice; however, there is not consistency on this dimension, as Brown-Chidsey and Steege (2006) feature only data-based progress monitoring as foundational. NASDSE (2005) referenced the work of Deno

TABLE 3.1. The Bergan and Deno models.

Bergan model and modern problem-solving steps	Deno model and modern standard protocol reading interventions
Define the problem behaviorally.	Define problems in terms of performance level and skills deficits.
Measure performance in the national setting.	Assess reading skills through progress monitoring, curriculum-based measurement and criterion-referenced skills inventories.
Determine current status and performance gap compared with peers.	Determine current status and performance gap compared with peers.
State a goal based on peer performance expectations.	State goals in terms of benchmarks for reading performance and peer expectations.
Design intervention plan, applying scientific instructional and behavior change principles.	Apply scientifically based instruction emphasizing five components of reading.
Implement intervention over a reasonable period of time with good treatment integrity.	Implement intervention over a reasonable period of time with good treatment integrity.
Monitor progress frequently using a time-series analysis graph and make changes in the intervention as needed to improve effectiveness or raise goals, as indicated by data.	Monitor progress frequently using a time-series analysis graph and make changes in the intervention as needed to improve effectiveness or raise goals, as indicated by data.
Evaluate results compared with goals and peer performance.	Evaluate results based on attainment of reading benchmarks.
Make decisions based on data to continue, fade, discontinue or seek more intense interventions.	Make decisions about discontinuing or phasing out small group instruction if benchmarks are attained or after consideration of further, more intense interventions, including possible special education eligibility.

and co-workers in data-based program modification (e.g. Deno, 1985; Deno and Mirkin, 1977) and behavioral consultation, and specifically the work of Bergan and co-workers as a foundation for current RTI practices (see Bergan, 1977; Bergan and Kratochwill, 1990; Kratochwill and Bergan, 1990; Kratochwill, Elliott, and Stoiber, 2004; Sheridan, Kratochwill, and Bergan, 1996). Comparison of the two models is reproduced in Table 3.1 from NASDSE (2005).

The problem-solving approach used in RTI described in the behavioral consultation literature by Bergan (1977) and Bergan and Kratochwill (1990) can represent a comprehensive framework to RTI, as it is broad in focus of intervention targets (i.e., academic and social–emotional behavior) and specifies a multi-stage problem-solving process for services. However, early conceptualizations of behavioral and problem-solving consultation were not designed to be implemented within a multi-tiered system of services, although they were integrated into "prereferral" interventions as recommended decades ago. Moreover, behavioral consultation was not designed to establish a "disability" designation per se, as the model has its conceptual origins in problem solving outside the context of the social construction of disability status.

3.2 Recommendations from National Groups and Task Forces

The current development and interest in RTI also have their origins in concern about education and, specifically, the quality of education in the United States and children who have learning challenges and disabilities. In 1983, the quality of education in the United States was examined in the publication *A Nation at Risk*. Following this report, local and federal governments developed a focus on improving student performance. The standards for the identification of learning disabilities (LDs) were set in 1976 by requiring a discrepancy between IQ and achievement scores. It was not until 2004, with the reauthorization of the *Individuals with Disabilities Education Improvement Act* (IDEIA, 2004), that the discrepancy was no longer mandated.

Historically, there has been much concern over the identification of LDs. The current method of identification is the IQ-achievement discrepancy, which originated in 1976 with the passage of the *Education for All Handicapped Children Act* of 1975 (Public Law 94-142). This federal law affected the delivery of education services to students with disabilities by mandating a free and appropriate public education for students with disabilities; an education in the least restrictive environment; due process rights for parents; and access to adequate and nondiscriminatory evaluation procedures. To assure these services, a clause was included to find and identify all children suspected of having a disability. This legislation was renewed when the *Individuals with Disabilities Act* of 1991 (101-476, IDEA, 1991) was passed, and again reauthorized in 1997 (IDEA, 1997) and 2004 (IDEIA, 2004).

Public Law 94-142, defines specific learning disability (SLD) as: "... a disorder in one or more of the basic psychological processes involved in understanding or in using language, spoken or written, which may manifest itself in an imperfect ability to listen, think, speak, read, write, spell or to do mathematical calculations" [P.L. 94-142, 121a. 5b(9)]. As a result of the child find program, many students were qualifying for special education services as having an SLD. As more students entered special education programs, questions began to arise regarding the effectiveness of these services (Reschly, 2003; Ysseldyke and Marston, 1999).

When PL 94-142 was reauthorized as IDEA in 1997, the final regulations defined the criteria for LD eligibility as follows: (a) A team may determine that a child has a specific learning disability if

1. The child does not achieve commensurate with his or her age and ability levels in one or more of the areas listed in paragraph (a) (2) of this section, if provided with learning experiences appropriate for the child's age and ability levels
2. The team finds that a child has a severe discrepancy between achievement and intellectual ability in one or more of the following areas:
   (i) oral expression
   (ii) listening comprehension
   (iii) written expression
   (iv) basic reading skill
   (v) reading comprehension
   (vi) mathematics calculation
   (vii) mathematics reasoning.

(b) The team may not identify a child as having a specific disability if the severe discrepancy between ability and achievement is primarily the result of

1. a visual, hearing, or motor impairment;
2. mental retardation;
3. emotional disturbance; or

4. environmental, cultural or economic disadvantage.

These criteria allowed special education services to be received for students more broadly in varying forms. Changes in evaluation and assessment requirements from PL 94-142 to IDEA 97 provided districts with more flexibility to determine educational placements. The definition of LD as a discrepancy between intelligence and achievement, however, was operationalized by most state departments of education by having a significant discrepancy between ability and achievement serve as the identification criterion.

Unfortunately, the inconsistency in the definition has been the cause for the loss of faith in the past methods of identification (e.g., MacMillan, Gresham, and Bocian, 1998). The reliability of difference scores in ability and achievement is poor, various discrepancy formulas are used that do not always agree, and various test instruments measure constructs differently (Fuchs, Fuchs, and Compton, 2004). Other critics note that many deserving, but unidentified students are from low-income homes and have relatively low IQ scores which are not different enough from their achievement scores to qualify for special education services. Other complaints are that IQ tests are a poor predictor of achievement and that that the discrepancy model represents a "wait-to-fail" approach, as students may perform poorly for years before their achievement scores are significantly below their IQ scores (Fuchs, Mock, Morgan, and Young, 2003).

A major concern relates to the consistency of the LD definition. "Findings over the past 15 years have pointed out the lack of a consistent definition in policy or practice in the identification of LD students. Research findings indicate that substantial proportions of school-identified LD students—from 52 to 70 percent—fail to meet state or federal eligibility criteria" (Gresham, 2002, p. 1). This inconsistency in identification of LD results in significant differences in prevalence of LD across the nation (Ysseldyke, Algozzine, and Epps, 1983). For example, Reschly and Ysseldyke (2002) found prevalence rates to vary from 2.73% to 9.43% nationwide. These differences are thought to be the result of differences in identification and not from differences in school populations.

The reauthorization of IDEA (1997) occurred in November 2004 and was renamed the *Individuals with Disabilities Education Improvement Act* (IDEIA, 2004). Both the House version (H.R. 1350) and the Senate version (S. 1248) acknowledged the difficulties with the traditional IQ/achievement discrepancy. IDEIA (2004) states:

(A) In general—Notwithstanding section 607(b), when determining whether a child has a specific learning disability as defined in section 602, a local education agency shall not be required to take into consideration whether a child has a severe discrepancy between achievement and intellectual ability in oral expression, listening comprehension, written expression, basic reading skill, reading comprehension, mathematical comprehension, or mathematical reasoning.

(B) Additional Authority—In determining whether a child has a specific learning disability, a local education agency may use a process that determines if the child responds to scientific, research-based intervention as part of the evaluation procedures described in paragraphs (2) and (3).

The reauthorization makes clear that the current definition of SLD, as defined by PL 94-142, remains. In determining eligibility, however, the IQ achievement discrepancy is not disallowed, but is no longer required. The law also notes that scientific, research-based interventions should be used as part of the process of eligibility determination. Additionally, the use of any single measure for determining SLD is not permitted, as a variety of assessment tools is required.

Concerns over the number of children in the LD category of special education, and the disproportionate representation of minority children within the various special education categories set the stage for a number of national groups who issued various recommendations and/or statements regarding methods to address the concern. These groups have been reviewed briefly by NASDSE (2005) and will not be reviewed in detail here; rather, the following briefly describes some of these groups and their position that set the stage for the current emphasis on RTI. A summary of these groups and their contribution to the RTI movement is presented in Table 3.2.

The *National Institute for Child Health and Development* (NICHD) studies examined practices related to the IQ achievement discrepancy model of services and indicated that it has delayed services to students with disabilities (see the website at http:/www.Idonline.org/Id_indepth/general_info/future_children.html). The *National Reading Panel* (NRP, 2000) specifically identified various compo-

nents that are critical to reading instruction and disabilities, which represent one of the highest categories of disability in schools. They argued that early intervention for children with reading problems is critical, which, in part, sets the stage for embracing early intervention/prevention frameworks for RTI (see website at http:/www.nationalreadingpanel.org) clearly established with most discussions of RTI (Kratochwill, 2006).

The RTI approach was first proposed as a method of LD identification in the *National Research Council* report (see Heller, Holltzman, and Messick, 1982) although its applications have been extended to other disability categories. RTI models are designed to ensure that students who are at risk for failure receive an evidence-based intervention preventatively, before failure. To further extend the RTI model in eligibility determination for special education services, the focus is on the children who are not able to be successful despite early and intensive interventions (Wedl, 2005). As described by Fuchs et al. (2003), the process includes the following:

1. Students are provided with "generally effective" instruction by their classroom teacher;
2. Their progress is monitored;
3. Those who do not respond get something else, or something more, from their teacher or someone else;
4. Again, their progress is monitored; and
5. Those who still do not respond either qualify for special education or for special education evaluation.

The *National Research Council Panel on Minority Overrepresentation* (see Donovan and Cross, 2002; Heller et al., 1982) emphasized early intervention services and the importance of multi-tiered models of services that could serve as a basis for helping to reverse the failure trend of children identified with learning problems. The *National Summit on Learning Disabilities* (see Bradley, Danielson, and Hallahan, 2002) also noted that many of the traditional strategies used to identify students with learning problems do not have strong support. They embraced an RTI model(s) as well as problem-solving strategies within this framework to help deal with the large number of students experiencing learning problems. The *President's Commission on Excellence in Special Education* (PCESE) was critical of traditional services and emphasized prevention within the context of

TABLE 3.2. Major organizations and professional groups and their contribution to the RTI movement.

National groups and task forces	Major contribution	Key source or website
National Institute for Child Health and Development (NICHD)	The IQ-achievement discrepancy model for the identification of LD delays treatment to students. In RTI, early intervention is critical.	http://www.Ldonline.org/ld_indepth/general_info/ furture_children.html
National Reading Panel (NRP)	Prevention and early intervention, as is done in the RTI model, can prevent or lessen the risk of the overidentification of minority students in special education.	http://www.nationalreadingpanel.org
National Summit on Learning Disabilities	Traditional bases for the identification of SLD are not useful due to lack of research foundations. RTI is the most promising method of identification due to the strong research base.	Bradley, Danielson, and Hallahan (2002)
President's Commission on Excellence in Special Education (PCESE)	Special education services should be delivered in a model of prevention. The current system waits for the child to fail, rather than preventing and intervening prior to failure as is done in the RTI model.	http://www.ed.gov/inits/commissionsboards/ whspecialeducation.index.html
National Center for Learning Disabilities (NCLD)	There is little evidence that the IQ-achievement discrepancy is an accurate predictor of LD. RTI is based on evidence that informs the decision-making process and should be used to determine eligibility classification.	http://www.ncld.org
National Research Center on Learning Disabilities (NRCLD)	Increases in the number of students identified as having learning disabilities, reliance on IQ tests, exclusion of environmental factors, inconsistency in procedures and criteria, and reliance on the IQ-achievement discrepancy lead to support for RTI as a possible alternative for identifying students with LD.	http://www.nrcld.org.symposium2003
United States Department of Education (USDOE) Office of Special Education Programs	Current identification patterns for LD need to be changed. Connections between identification and treatment need to be made. Response to intervention has the promise of establishing the validity of the SLD diagnostic construct.	http://www.nrcld.org/research/states/index.shtml

general education, therefore, setting the stage for more intense services in the general education setting (http://www.ed.gov/inits/commissionsboards/ whspecialeducation/index.html).

There have been other compelling reasons for examining alternative models of services to children experiencing learning problems, again with the primary focus on students with academic learning problems (Vaughn and Fuchs, 2003). In particular, the cost of special education services to children labeled as LD has historically been indicated to be too high (Fuchs and Fuchs, 2006). As noted above, the effectiveness of special education as a service to children has been questioned (e.g., Kavale and Forness, 1999; Reschly, 2003). Given these concerns, it is no wonder that there is growing consensus that adopting models of prevention can help more children in our schools and reduce base rates of fail-

ure. The issue, of course, is whether the RTI framework and the various models that emanate from it will address the myriad of issues raised in the professional literature and by various professional groups.

3.3 Considerations in Implementation of the Response-to-Intervention Model: Some Unresolved Issues

As RTI has made its way into the professional literature and practice, a number of important methodological and conceptual issues have emerged that have a bearing on the evidence base and conceptual foundations of these models, as well as of their adoption in practice. In this section, we review some of the major considerations that have emerged to date (see Kratochwill, 2006). The following discussion identifies unresolved issues in three major domains, including those on the response side, the intervention side, and some general considerations that warrant future research and conceptual attention.

3.3.1 Unresolved Issues on the Response Side

The measurement of outcomes within RTI models essentially brings to the forefront a variety of assessment issues that have been of concern to psychology and education since measurement became a primary focus in research and practice (see Blanton and Jaccard, 2006). There are several unresolved issues on the response side that warrant future attention. A first issue is that an RTI model requires a decision on what is to be screened and, eventually, monitored. The decision is not straightforward. For example, much of the RTI literature is focused on academic skill assessment and usually a very focused and narrow skill is assessed (see below). Should assessment focus on both academic and social–emotional domains to obtain a more comprehensive picture of the child's functioning? Increasing evidence suggests that academic and social–emotional behaviors are interrelated (DiPerna and Elliott, 2000) and may even have a reciprocal influence in leading to more serious problems in both domains (Algozzine and Kay, 2002). Thus, basic questions remain in terms of the focus and content of screening and ongoing progress monitoring.

A second and related concern is the focus of assessment within the academic domain. The majority of progress monitoring measures focus on distinct aspects of academic skill content (e.g., reading fluency) and not on academic enablers or the behaviors of the student that promote skill acquisition. Academic enablers refer to ecological factors that promote academic skills and are usually under the control of the teacher during instruction (e.g., study skills, motivation). A strong case can be made for the assessment of academic enablers in addition to academic skill assessment in terms of understanding student learning and achievement and, most important, the focus of intervention (DiPerna and Elliott, 2000). Aside from this issue, a limited range of measures have actually been developed for

monitoring progress in the academic skills domain. Some advances have been made by the *National Center for Progress Monitoring* that has established criteria for effective progress monitoring measures (see Table 3.3). Yet, progress monitoring measures across domains other than reading have not been rapidly forthcoming. Although reading could be regarded as a primary "keystone" area for intervention that has the potential for pervasive positive influences on other academic areas of the curriculum, monitoring other areas of the curriculum depending on student's strengths and weaknesses would seem important (see Shapiro, 2004).

Third, when considering assessment that involves the initial identification of students through screening in academic and social–emotional domains, there are also a rather limited range of measures (see Albers, Kratochwill, and Glover, in press; Glover and Albers, in press). Although it is beyond the scope of this chapter to review each of these issues in detail (see the 2007 mini-series on screening in the *Journal of School Psychology* for further information), it is clear that the sheer number of instruments that serve in a screening capacity have not been well developed in the research literature. In addition, careful review of measures suggests that many are associated with some of the traditional assessments used for disability determination (e.g., IQ and achievement tests). Thus, a major research agenda in the future must focus on establishing reliability, validity, and utility data for a variety of screening measures to be used in RTI models.

Fourth, and related to this concern, there are also a limited number of standardized measures that have been developed for monitoring progress in social–emotional domains. Some of the recent efforts developed through positive behavior support (see Crone and Horner, 2003) show great promise for monitoring students at a system-wide level (e.g., the SWISS). Typically, measures for monitoring social–emotional progress need to be customized for students. This customization requires considerable time and effort for practitioners. A host of measures, as has been referenced in the writing on "target behaviors" in the behavioral assessment literature (e.g., Brown-Chidsey, 2005; Shapiro and Kratochwill, 2000) documents a long history within applied behavior analysis and will likely facilitate the selection and implementation of progress monitoring in this domain. Nevertheless, there is a lack

TABLE 3.3. Review of progress monitoring tools.

Area	Foundational psychometric standards		Progress monitoring standards				
	Reliability	Validity	Alternate forms	Sensitive to student improvement	AYP benchmarks	Improving student learning or teacher planning	Rates of improvement specified
AIMSWeb Tool							
Maze	●	●	●	●	●	●	●
Reading	●	●	●	●	●	●	●
* Test of early numeracy	●	●	●	O	●	O	●
Early literacy	●	●	●	●	●	●	●
Spelling	●	●	●	●	●	●	●
Dynamic Indicators of Basic Early Literacy Skills (DIBELS) Tool							
Initial sound fluency	●	●	●	●	●	O	●
Word use fluency	●	●	●	O	O	O	O
Retell fluency	●	●	●	O	O	O	O
* Oral reading fluency	●	●	●	●	●	●	●
Phonemic segmentation fluency	●	●	●	●	●	●	●
Nonsense word fluency	●	●	●	●	●	●	●
EdCheckup Tool							
Maze	●	●	O	●	●	●	●
Reading	●	●	●	●	●	●	●
Monitoring Basic Skills Progress (MBSP) Tool							
Reading	●	●	●	●	●	●	●
Math	●	●	●	●	●	●	●
Yearly Progress Pro Tool							
Early literacy	●	●	●	●	●	●	●
Reading	●	●	●	●	●	●	●
Math	●	●	●	●	●	●	●
STAR Tool							
Early literacy	●	●	●	●	O	●	O
Reading	●	●	●	●	O	O	●
*Math	●	●	●	●	●	●	●
Test of Word Reading Efficiency (TOWRE) Tool							
Sight word reading efficiency	●	●	●	O	O	O	O
Phonemic decoding efficiency	●	●	●	O	O	O	O
Test of Silent Word Reading Fluency (TOSWRF) Tool							
Reading	●	●	●	O	O	O	O

● The tool demonstrates sufficient evidence that meets the basic standard.
O The tool did not demonstrate sufficient evidence that meets the basic standard.
* New information from the 2005 review.
Note. From National Center for Progress Monitoring.

of standardization within this area of target behavior selection and monitoring that makes the process challenging from a measurement perspective (Cone, 2001; Kratochwill, 1985; Shapiro, 2004).

Fifth, the criteria established for determining responsiveness for reaching a particular intervention goal, for the purposes of moving to another level (more or less) of intervention in a multi-tiered framework and/or determining eligibility for special education, are not straightforward. The issues invoked in RTI raise a wide range of concerns that have been the subject of debate in the psychotherapy and intervention field for many decades (see Cone, 2001; Kazdin, 2006). Basically, the issue relates to the outcome's relation to general improvement in achievement and/or quality of life in social/emotional functioning. For example, it is not clear that the benchmarks established in DIBELS and other measures represent clear criteria for determining successful outcomes of an intervention, a stated purpose for using these measures in the first place. One option is to adopt social validation as a framework for decision-making (Kratochwill and Stoiber, 2002). When social validity criteria are invoked (Kazdin, 1977; Wolf, 1977), some conceptual assistance is offered to practitioners through a progress monitoring and intervention protocol such as *Outcomes: Planning, Monitoring, Evaluating* (Outcomes: PME; see Kratochwill and Stoiber, 2002). However, social validity criteria still mean relying heavily on local norms, or standardized tests, to establish a criterion for determining whether a student is making adequate progress. This issue, of course, raises the concern about the need for standardized assessment in this area.

3.3.2 Challenges on the Intervention Side

3.3.2.1 Challenges with Evidence-Based Interventions

In addition to the challenges likely to emerge on the response side of the RTI equation, there are a number of prominent issues that remain to be resolved with respect to the interventions used within RTI models. Federal guidelines in NCLB and reauthorization of IDEIA (2004) feature an emphasis on research-supported practices for implementation of prevention/intervention. Thus, proponents of RTI frameworks explicitly recommend that the interventions be based on strong research support or be evidence based (see NASDSE, 2005; Brown-Chidsey and Steege, 2006). The justification for these recommendations has its origin in recent initiatives within education and, to some extent, mental health (Kratochwill, Hoagwood, White, Levitt, Romanelli, and Saka, in press). With the creation of the Institute for Educational Sciences (IES) and the focus on randomized trials to establish the research base for educational practices, a premium has been placed on these models for use within RTI models. In addition, the creation of the *What Works Clearinghouse* (a US Department of Education, IES initiative) further reflects the emphasis on using evidence-based interventions within educational settings.

There is considerable consensus that successful implementation of RTI models requires that evidence-based interventions be selected and implemented for academic and/or social–emotional target domains. Yet, there are several challenges in the area of evidence-based interventions that merit attention and currently stand as potential hurdles in implementation of RTI models generally (Kratochwill, 2006; Kratochwill and Shernoff, 2004). To begin with, one of the common assumptions within application of an RTI model is that there are a wide range of science-based interventions available to implement. Actually the list of evidence-based interventions is quite small relative to the need, especially in the social/emotional domain (Kazdan, 2004; Kratochwill and Hoagwood, in press; Kratochwill and Shernoff, 2004). In the academic domain the major resource to help schools select interventions based on strong research, the *What Works Clearinghouse*, has been very limited to date in providing resources for schools. Thus, limited dissemination of interventions is likely to be a practical problem as individuals move forward in the application of RTI models in applied settings. In the absence of readily available evidence-based interventions the responsibility falls on local school professionals to document the effectiveness of services (Kratochwill, 2006). Models of evaluation that embrace single-case research design (Brown-Chidsey and Steege, 2006) are unlikely to meet the acceptability standards of most practitioners and even those who are well versed in their application (Kratochwill, 2006).

Another major limitation in the evidence-based intervention literature is the actual generalizability or transportability of the intervention to educational

TABLE 3.4. Select dimensions of studies and the degree of resemblance to the clinical situation.

	Resemblance to the clinical or nonresearch situation		
Dimension	Identity with or great resemblance	Moderate resemblance	Relatively low resemblance
Target problem	Problem seen in the clinic, intense or disabling.	Similar to that in clinic but less severe.	Nonproblem behavior or experimental task.
Population	Clients in outpatient treatment.	College students with no treatment interest.	Animals in laboratory studies; college students with no treatment interest.
Manner of recruitment	Clients who seek treatment.	Individuals recruited for available treatment.	Captive subjects who serve for course credit.
Therapists	Professional therapists.	Therapists in training.	Nontherapists or nonprofessionals.
Client set	Expect treatment and improvement.	Expect "experimental" treatment with unclear effects.	Expect treatment with nontreatment focus.
Selection of treatment	Client chooses therapist and specific treatment.	Client given choice over few alternative procedures in an experiment.	Client assigned to treatment with no choice for specific therapist or condition.
Specification of treatment	What to do is at the discretion of the therapist.	General guidelines, goals, and themes to direct focus of the session.	Treatment manual specifies procedures, foci, means, or ends treatment session including maybe, even many of the statements of the therapist.
Monitoring of treatment	Little or no monitoring of what is done with the client.	Case supervision or discussion to review what was done, how it was done, and client progress.	Careful assessment of how treatment was delivered (audio, videotape, direct observation, case supervision).
Setting of treatment	Professional treatment facility.	University facility that may not regularly offer treatment.	Laboratory setting.
Variation of treatment	Treatment as usually conducted.	Variation to standardize treatment for research.	Analogue of the treatment as in infrahuman equivalent of treatment.
Assessment methods	Direct unobtrusive measure of the problem that the client originally reported.	Assessment on psychological devices that sample behaviors of interest directly.	Questionnaire responses about the behaviors that are a problem.

Note. From Kazdin, (2004).

settings (see Kazdin, 2004). Interventions implemented within clinical trials research often vary considerably on a number of important dimensions from the setting in which practitioners implement these interventions in schools. The priority on research in the variety of studies that have been conducted to facilitate transportability of interventions documents this serious concern in the field (Kratochwill and Hoagwood, in press). Research can be framed on a continuum of multiple criteria that effect the generalization of results from research to applied and educational settings (Kazdin, 2004). Table 3.4 from Kazdin (2004) demonstrates several dimensions on which research is likely to vary from the educational setting in which the intervention is implemented.

Another concern with many interventions is the diverse criteria that have been established for determining whether an intervention is evidence based. The problem is pervasive in the traditional intervention literature and in prevention science (see Kratochwill and Shernoff, 2004; Kratochwill et al., in press). Many different organizations have invoked criteria to designate a program as evidence based. Table 3.5, developed by the Research-to-Practice Committee of the Task Force on Evidence-Based Interventions in School Psychology (see Kratochwill et al., in press), shows some of the major organizations that have been involved in the process of designating an intervention as evidence based, along with their designation criteria.

TABLE 3.5. Agency and practitioner rating categories and criteria for evidence based programs.

Key source and website	Rating category	Focus and criteria
American Youth Policy Forum		
Mendel, Richard A. (2001). *Less hype, more help: Reducing juvenile crime, what works—and what doesn't* Washington, DC: American Youth Policy Forum. www.aypf.org.	Effective	Programs dealing with reducing juvenile crime. Many programs are described based on a review of the scientific literature; however, no specific criteria for the inclusion of programs are provided.
Blueprints for Violence Prevention		
Elliott, D. S. (Editor) (1997). *Blueprints for Violence Prevention* (Vols. 1–11). Boulder, CO: Center for the Study and Prevention of Violence, Institute of Behavioral Science, University of Colorado. www.colorado.edu/cspv/blueprints	Model Promising	Main objective is that of violence prevention in children and adolescents from birth to age 19. Programs focus on violence, delinquency, aggression, and substance abuse. *Model and Promising programs*: evidence of deterrent effect with a *strong* research design (experimental or quasi-experimental) on one of the above outcomes. *Model programs*: must meet above criteria and include sustained effects for at least one year posttreatment and replication at more than one site with demonstrated effects.
Center for Mental Health Services, US Department of Health and Human Services		
Greenberg, Mark T., Domitrovich, Celene, and Bumbarger, Brian (1999). *Preventing mental disorders in school-aged children: A review of the effectiveness of prevention programs.* State College, PA: Prevention Research Center for the Promotion of Human Development, College of Health and Human Development, Pennsylvania State University. www.prevention.psu.edu/CMHS.html	Effective Promising	*Effective Programs* Differentintervention programs dealing with the reduction of risks or effects of psychopathology in school-aged children, from ages 5 to 18. Programs that met the review requirements had to be evaluated using an adequate comparison group with either randomized or quasi-experimental design with an adequate control group. Studies had to have pre- and post-test data and preferably follow-up data. They also had to have a written implementation manual. Universal, selective and indicated prevention programs were identified that produced improvements in specific psychological symptomology or factors directly associated with increased risk for child mental disorders. Programs showing reduction in psychiatric symptoms were also included in the review. *Promising Programs* Programs that seem promising but do not meet the above criteria (lack a controlled design, have a very small sample or the findings are only indirectly related to MH outcomes).
Center for Substance Abuse Prevention (CSAP), Dept. of Health & Human Services, National Registry of Effective Programs		
Substance Abuse and Mental Health Services Administration www.modelprograms.samhsa.gov	Model Promising Effective	Focus substance abuse prevention. Programs are scored 1 to 5, with 1 being the lowest and 5 being the highest score, relative to 15 criteria. *Model programs* are well implemented and evaluated according to rigorous standards of research, scoring at least 4.0 on the 5-point scale.

(Continued)

TABLE 3.5. (*Continued*)

Key source and website	Rating category	Focus and criteria
		Promising programs have been implemented and evaluated sufficiently and are considered to be scientifically defensible, but have not yet been shown to have sufficient rigor and/or consistently positive outcomes required for Model status.
		Promising programs must score at least 3.33 on the 5-point scale. *Effective programs* meet all the criteria as the Model programs, but for a variety of reasons these programs are not currently available to be widely disseminated to the general public.

Department of Education, Safe and Drug-free Schools

www.ed.gov (visit US Department of Education and search for OSDFS)	Exemplary Promising	Programs are related to making schools safe, disciplined, and drug-free: reducing substance use, violence, and other conduct problems.
		Positive changes in scientifically established risk and protective factors.
		Both Exemplary and Promising programs have: (1) evidence of efficacy/effectiveness based on a methodologically sound evaluation that adequately *controls for threats to internal validity*, including attrition; (2) the program's goals with respect to changing behavior and/or risk and protective factors are clear and appropriate for the intended population and setting; (3) the rationale underlying the program is clearly stated, and the program's content and processes are aligned with its goals; (4) the program's content takes into consideration the characteristics of the intended population and setting; (5) the program implementation process effectively engages the intended population; (6) the application describes how the program is integrated into schools' educational missions; and (7) the program provides necessary information and guidance for replication in other appropriate settings.

Communities That Care, Developmental Research and Programs

Posey, R., Wong, S., Catalano, R., Hawkins, D., Dusenbury, L., Chappell, P. (2000). *Communities That Care prevention strategies: A research guide to what works*. Seattle, WA: Developmental Research and Programs, Inc., Seattle, WA. www.preventionscience.com/ctc/CTC.html	Effective	Communities That Care focus on preventing adolescent substance abuse, delinquency, teen pregnancy, school dropout, and violence as well as promoting the positive development of youth and children. Programs focus on the family, school, and community. The criteria include programs that: (1) address research based risk factors for substance abuse, delinquency, teen pregnancy, school dropout and violence; (2) increase protective factors; (3) intervene at developmentally appropriate age; and (4) show significant effects on risk and protective factors in controlled studies or community trials.

TABLE 3.5. (*Continued*)

Key source and website	Rating category	Focus and criteria
		S. Mihalic and T. Aultman-Bettridge
Mihalic and Aultman-Bettridge (2004)	Exemplary Promising Favorable	Programs are all school-based.
		Model and Promising programs utilize Blueprints criteria and outcomes.
		Favorable programs broaden the outcomes to include factors relevant for school safety and success, such as school disciplinary problems, suspensions, truancy, dropout, and academic achievement. These programs may also have weaker research designs than the standard held for Blueprints; however, there is "reasonable" scientific evidence that behavioral effects are due to the intervention and not other factors. These programs all have experimental or matched control group designs.
		National Institute of Drug Abuse
National Clearing House for Alcohol and Drug Information, Preventing drug use among children and adolescents: A research-based guide, #734 at 1-800-729-6686).	Effective	The focus is on drug prevention and reduction.
		There are no specific criteria for program inclusion.
		Sherman et al. (1997)
Sherman et al. (1997). *What works, what doesn't, what's promising* College Park: University of Maryland Department of Criminology and Criminal Justice. NCJ 165366. www.ncjrs.org/works/wholedoc.htm or www.preventingcrime.org	Effective	The main focus is crime prevention.
		The methodological rigor of each program was rated on a scale of 1 to 5. In order to obtain a score of "3," programs had to employ some kind of control or comparison group. If the comparison was to more than a small number of matched or almost randomized cases, then the study was given a score of "4." If the comparison was to a large number of comparable units selected randomly, then the study was scored as a "5." Programs were assessed as "working" if they had two or more evaluations with 3 or higher and statistical significance tests showed the program effective. Programs were assessed as "promising" if they had at least one evaluation with a score of 3 or higher showing effectiveness. For this report, all "working" and "promising" programs were classified as "Effective."
		Strengthening America's Families
www.strengtheningfamilies.org	Exemplary I Exemplary II Model Promising	Focused on family therapy, family skills training, in-home family support, and parenting programs.
		Each program was rated on theory, fidelity, sampling strategy, implementation, attrition, measures, data collection, missing data, analysis, replications, dissemination capability, cultural and age appropriateness, integrity, and program utility and placed into the following categories:
		Exemplary I: Program has experimental design with randomized sample and replication by an independent investigator. Outcome data show clear evidence of program effectiveness.

(*Continued*)

TABLE 3.5. (*Continued*)

Key source and website	Rating category	Focus and criteria
		Exemplary II: Program has experimental design with randomized sample. Outcome data show clear evidence of program effectiveness.
		Model: Program has experimental or quasi-experimental design with few or no replications. Data may not be as strong in demonstrating program effectiveness.
		Promising: Program has limited research and/or employs nonexperimental designs. Data appear promising but require confirmation using scientific techniques.
Surgeon General's Report (2001)		
US Department of Health and Human Services (2001) *Youth violence. A report of the Surgeon General* Rockville, MD: US Department of Health and Human Services, Centers for Disease Control and Prevention, National Center or Injury Prevention and Control; Substance Abuse and Mental Health Services Administration, Center for Mental Health Services; and National Institutes of Health, National Institute of Mental Health. www.surgeongeneral.gov/library/youthviolence	Model Promising: Level 1— violence prevention Level 2—risk factor prevention	The focus is violence prevention and intervention. *Model programs* have rigorous experimental design (experimental or quasi-experimental), significant effects on violence or serious delinquency (Level 1) or any risk factor for violence with a large effect size of 0.30 or greater (Level 2), replication with demonstrated effects, and sustainability of effect. *Promising programs* meet the first two criteria (although effect sizes of 0.10 or greater are acceptable), but programs may have either replication or sustainability of effects (both not necessary).
Title V (OJJDP)		
Title V *Training and technical assistance programs for state and local governments: Effective & promising programs guide.* Washington, DC: Office of Juvenile Justice and Delinquency Prevention, Office of Justice Programs, US Dept. of Justice. www.dsgonline.com	Exemplary Effective Promising	The focus is on delinquency prevention strategies. *Exemplary*, the program-required evidence of statistical deterrent effect using randomized treatment and control groups. *Effective programs* had evidence obtained with a control or matched comparison group but without randomization. *Promising* programs had evidence of a correlation between the prevention program (generally pre/post) and a measure of crime.
Promising Practices Network		
http://www.promisingpractices.net/	Proven Promising	*Proven programs* affect relevant variables, with substantial effect size (at least one outcome changes by 20% or 0.25 standard deviation). Statistically significant at 0.05. Design: randomized-control trial (experimental design) or quasi-experimental design. Sample size exceeds 30 in each group. Program Evaluation Documentation is publicly available. *Promising programs* may impact an intermediary outcome for which there is evidence that it is associated with one of the PPN indicators. Change in outcome is more than 1%. Outcome change is significant at the 10% level.

TABLE 3.5. (*Continued*)

Key source and website	Rating category	Focus and criteria
		Study has a comparison group, but it may exhibit some weaknesses; e.g., the groups lack comparability on pre-existing variables or the analysis does not employ appropriate statistical controls. Sample size exceeds 10 in each group.
		Program Evaluation Documentation is publicly available.
The Hamilton Fish Institute		
http://www.hamfish.org/programs/	Demonstrated Promising	*Demonstrated programs* design: a control group (does not have to be randomized), no replication needed.
		Outcomes: the intervention group demonstrated a larger change in target variables over time than control group.
		Promising programs: Positive trends but not consistent significant outcomes. Designs were too weak to be sure that the programs caused the positive effect. Some programs were not evaluated but merely theoretically designed to achieve objectives outlined in the "comprehensive framework."
Center for Disease Control		
http://www.cdc.gov/hiv/pubs/hivcompendium/ hivcompendium.htm	Effective	Focus on AIDS prevention
		Random assignment to intervention and control groups, with at least post-intervention data, OR quasi-experimental designs with equivalence of groups or statistical adjustment, with pre- and post-data.
		Statistically significant positive results on target variables.
		Conducted in the US.
CASEL		
www.casel.org	Select	*Safe and Sound programs* (1) are school based, (2) have at least eight lessons in one of the years, (3) there are either lessons for at least two consecutive grades or grade spans, or a structure that promotes lessons reinforcement beyond the first program year, and (4) the program is nationally available.
		The select programs: have at least one well-designed evaluation study demonstrating their effectiveness; and
		Offer high-quality professional development.
Evidence-Based Program Database		
http://www.alted-mh.org/ebpd/index.htm	Model Promising	Evaluates evidence supporting program's claims of effectiveness, and makes recommendations for (or against) the use of the program in the government, academic, and non-profit sectors.
		Model Programs meet the satisfactory standards of their specific criteria as an effective program.
		Promising Programs shows characteristics of a model program without having proven itself through documented research and replication.

(*Continued*)

TABLE 3.5. (*Continued*)

Key source and website	Rating category	Focus and criteria
The International Campbell Collaboration		
http://www.campbellcollaboration.org/frontend. asp	Effective	Prepares, maintains and disseminates systematic reviews of studies of interventions through a registry of effective policies and programs.
		Randomization Classification: Clearly identify "verified randomized," "possibly randomized," and "nonrandomized" studies.
		Comprehensiveness: Include a fairly complete list of all randomized trials.
		Usefulness: Each record should have a reasonably informative uniform abstract which outlines the main features of the study.
Social Programs that Work		
http://www.evidencebasedprograms.org/	Effective Small/no effect Ineffective No effects/ adverse effects	Summarizes the effectiveness of studies in the fields of medicine, welfare policy, and education. Only reviews well-designed randomized controlled trials that are backed by rigorous evidence of effectiveness.
		Focus is on well-designed randomized controlled trials
What Works Clearinghouse		
http://www.whatworkshelpdesk.ed.gov/identify. asp	Meets evidence standards Meets evidence standards with reser- vations Does not meet evidence standards	*Meets Evidence Standards* are randomized controlled trials (RCTs) that do not have problems with randomization, attrition, or disruption, and regression discontinuity designs that do not have problems with attrition or disruption.
		Meets Evidence Standards with Reservations are strong quasi-experimental studies that have comparison groups and meet other WWC Evidence Standards, as well as randomized trials with randomization, attrition, or disruption problems and regression discontinuity designs with attrition or disruption problems.
		Does Not Meet Evidence Standards are studies that provide insufficient evidence of causal validity or are not relevant to the topic being reviewed.
		Includes a publicly available user-guide for identifying and implementing evidence-based educational practices.
National Reading Panel		
http://www.nichd.nih.gov/publications/nrp/ smallbook.htm	Evidence- based	Focus on reading
		Only reviewed studies published in a refereed journal focusing on children's reading development in the age/grade range from preschool to grade 12 and using an experimental or quasi-experimental design with a control group or a multiple-baseline method.
		Meets Evidence Based Standards have carefully described (age, demographic, cognitive, academic, and behavioral characteristics) study participants; study interventions are described in sufficient detail to allow for replicability, including how long the interventions lasted and how long

TABLE 3.5. (*Continued*)

Key source and website	Rating category	Focus and criteria
		the effects lasted; study methods must allow judgments about how instruction fidelity was insured; and studies must include a full description of outcome measures.
		Effect sizes were examined with regard to their difference from zero (i.e., does the treatment have an effect on reading?), strength (i.e., if the treatment has an effect, how large is that effect?), and consistency (i.e., did the effect of the treatment vary significantly from study to study?). The panel also compared the magnitude of a treatment's effect under different methodological conditions, program contexts, program features, outcome measures and for students with different characteristics.
Oregon Reading First Center		
http://reading.uoregon.edu/curricula/index.php	Overall representative rating	Focus on reading
		Provides a thorough and objective analysis of comprehensive programs in beginning reading.
		The review was conducted using *The Consumer's Guide to Evaluating a Core Reading Program*
		Grades K-3: A Critical Elements Analysis, which was designed to document and to quantify the design and delivery features of comprehensive reading programs.
		Reviewers rate each item according to a three point scale that is represented by a full circle (i.e., two points), a partial circle (one point), or an empty circle (zero points). A full circle indicates that the program consistently met or exceeded the criterion for that item. A partial circle indicates the program partially met the criterion for that item. An empty circle indicates that the program did not satisfy the criterion for that item.
Texas Reading First Initiative		
http://www.tea.state.tx.us/reading/readingfirst/ AppConfOtt.pdf	Endorsed	Focus on reading
		Endorses reading curriculum that rely on measurements or observational methods, provide valid data across evaluators and observers and across multiple measurements and observations, has been accepted by a peer-reviewed journal or approved by a panel of independent experts through a comparably rigorous, objective and scientific review.
		Endorsed programs: Have convergent research to support its effectiveness, address the five essential components of reading appropriately at each grade level, align with the NRP Report, align with the diagnostic tools teachers will be using to inform instruction, contain explicit and systematic instructional strategies, and Contain effective and efficient instructional activities.
Florida Center for Reading Research		
http://www.fcrr.org		

Source: Research-to-Practice Committee of the Task Force on Evidence-Based Interventions in School Psychology (2005).

As indicated (Kratochwill et al., in press), not only are the criteria quite variable across these groups, but also designation of a program as evidence based varies on a number of different dimensions beyond traditional methodological and statistical criteria in research. The major limitation in identifying evidence-based interventions relates to how one conceptualizes evidence (Kazdin, 2004). Does one compare an intervention with no intervention, or an intervention relative to another intervention? Traditional criteria for determining effectiveness relate not only to the statistical significance, but also to the clinical significance of the effects. The translation of these statistical and clinical criteria to effective outcomes for students remains a challenge; see Kazdin (2006) and the 2006 *American Psychologist* mini-series on this topic.

To address some of these concerns, Kazdin (2004, p. 931) recommended a continuum to evaluate the status of research progress for various prevention/treatment programs.

1. Not evaluated.
2. Evaluated but unclear effects, no effects, or possible negative effects at this time.
3. Promising (e.g., some evidence in its behalf).
4. Well established (e.g., criteria used by one of the systems cited for identifying evidence-based therapy (EBT)).
5. Better/best treatments (e.g., studies shown to be more effective than one or more other well-established techniques).

The argument is that an intervention can be represented best by determining where it would fall on a continuum *in relation to other interventions*. The criteria established by the Task Force in Evidence-Based Interventions in School Psychology allow this kind of determination. Specifically, the Task Force *Procedural and Coding Manual* allows determination of the effectiveness of an intervention along a variety of methodological, statistical, and conceptual criteria, allowing an examination of where a particular intervention study falls relative to others, although not all within-study research comparisons are based on tests relative to alternative treatments. This information can be very helpful as mental health and education move forward in selecting various intervention programs.

Another consideration is that many of the interventions that have been applied in school settings are, in fact, not based on a sample of individuals who represent the population of concern in the setting. In particular, the evidence base is limited on dimensions of cultural context, requiring researchers to invoke conceptual criteria to assist in the process of adapting and accommodating interventions for certain underrepresented groups (NCCRESt, 2005; Newell and Kratochwill, in press, see Chapter 5 of this book). The limitations in sampling for evidence-based interventions are widely recognized, but solutions are not easily at hand until researchers are forthcoming with investigations that address the wide spectrum of variables that have been raised in the literature.

3.3.2.2 Challenges with Multi-Tiered Interventions

Associated with RTI models is not just an emphasis on evidence-based interventions, a challenge in their own right, but interventions implemented within a multi-tiered framework. The multi-tiered framework is not new; as noted above, it has its origin in the prevention science literature. Over the years, several writers recommended that the multi-tiered approach be implemented within academic and social–emotional domains (Walker and Shinn, 1999). The focus typically is on universal, selected, and indicated (or primary, secondary, and tertiary, respectively) interventions that are structured so that a student can progress through *levels* of intervention with progress monitored throughout these tiers. It is the movement through the tiers that provides the decision-making framework of RTI approaches.

The dimensions of options within a multi-tiered framework challenge practitioners (and researchers) to consider numerous implementation variations. Interventions can be implemented with increasing intensity, frequency, and/or duration and by type as students receive interventions in the multi-tiered system. Table 3.6 provides an example of some of the ways that multi-tiered interventions might vary as a function of level and topography. Theoretically, the pattern of intervention provision is expected to follow an upward progression of intensity with students being exposed to primary intervention and, if progress monitoring reveals a need, they are then provided secondary or tertiary intervention. If more intense intervention is needed, then students may receive a higher dose of secondary or tertiary intervention or may receive a more intense level

TABLE 3.6. Response to intervention rubric: example of a type, level, and topography example application.

	Intervention domain type											
	Academic				Social–emotional				Academic + Social–emotional			
	Topography of intervention											
Prevention LEVEL	I	F	D	C	I	F	D	C	I	F	D	C
Primary												
Secondary	x		X	x								
Tertiary												
Other												
	Field notes											
	Open Court provided at primary level. Student provided Open Court Booster at secondary level. Intensity increased from 1 h to 2 h. Duration increased from 5 weeks to 10 weeks. Frequency remained one time per day. Context changed from whole group to small group instruction.				Positive behavior support provided at primary level.				No academic + social–emotional combination interventions provided.			

Note. I = Intensity; F = Frequency, D = Duration, C = Context. Topography categories denote changes in intervention provision based on response to intervention.

of intervention (e.g., tertiary intervention). If less intense intervention is needed, then students may move down a level to either secondary or primary intervention. Students receiving secondary/tertiary intervention generally continue to receive primary intervention for at least some portion of the school day, so that primary intervention is combined with secondary or tertiary intervention (e.g., primary + secondary and primary + tertiary). Note that students can receive more than one level of intervention at one time.

Figure 3.1 shows this theoretical pattern of intervention provision within the context of the multi-tiered system. In practice, however, intervention provision may follow a number of patterns depending on the practitioner's implementation design or philosophy. For example, students may only be provided tertiary intervention if they have already received a secondary intervention or they may only be eligible to receive secondary/tertiary intervention if they have been screened and the screening results provide the basis for this level of services. See Figures 3.2, 3.3 and 3.4 for some alternative patterns of intervention provision that might be implemented in practice. Note that the flexibility available when putting these models into practice does not preclude the use of progress monitoring and RTI ap-

proaches to decision-making regarding intervention provision. Multi-tiered models have been invoked to develop a framework for how RTI can be implemented ultimately, for eligibility determination, but also to reduce the base rates of problems such as LDs and other special education category disability designations. Moreover, the RTI approach can be used to evaluate the interventions implemented within a special education disability designation context (i.e., after the decision of disability designation has been made and the student is receiving special education services).

The interventions within the multiple tiers can be structured through a problem-solving approach (as outlined above, e.g., Bergan and Kratochwill, 1990) and/or more commonly in the reading domain, a "standard-protocol approach" (see Vaughn, Linan-Thompson, and Hickman, 2003). The problem-solving approach typically involves individual application of a professional and/or team customizing interventions for a child and can occur at any of the levels of intervention (see Tilly (in press) for an illustration of this model in applied settings), but may result in the selection of a standard-protocol approach for a student. The standard intervention protocol approach relies heavily on interventions that can be administered in a certain specified format,

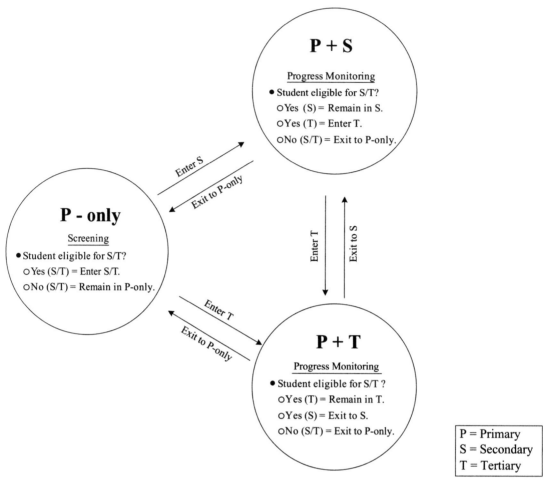

FIGURE 3.1. Theoretical patterns of intervention participation within a multi-tiered system.
Note. If eligible for S/T during initial screening, students may move from P-only to P + S or P-only to P + T. Based on progress monitoring scores, students may move between P + S and P + T (in either direction) or between P + S /T and P-only. Students who are not eligible for P + S/T receive P-only.

such as small group instruction for a predetermined or fixed period of time (e.g., 10 weeks). Although there is flexibility in how this approach is structured, children are typically assigned to some additional instructional protocol that is a priori structured with the intent of further reducing the base rates of concerns given responsiveness to the intervention being implemented.

A high priority in the field will be to establish the conceptual and theoretical links among multi-tiered interventions. The links are perhaps more clearly established in some areas than others. For example, reading interventions that build on a firm foundation of curriculum can be implemented with greater integrity and dosage levels to facilitate responsiveness to skill acquisition in core skill areas. However, in other areas, such as with social–emotional domains, the clear linkage among the three-tiered systems is not straightforward. For example, it is not clear how the components of intervention are organized and consistent as the student progresses through multiple tiers of an intervention. Conceptual and theoretical guidelines for how this linkage could be established would advance the field considerably (Kratochwill, 2006).

One template framework that has been adopted to assist practitioners in implementation of RTI is the review by Burns, Appleton, and Stehouwer (2005),

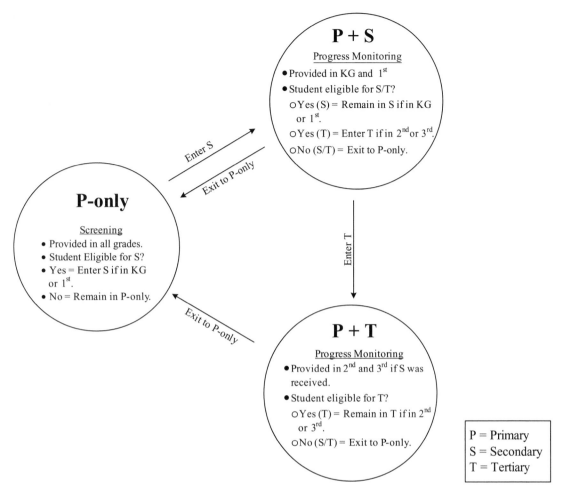

FIGURE 3.2. Alternative example of intervention provision: one-dose model with intervention provided according to grade level.

Note. If eligible for S during initial screening, kindergarten (KG) and first grade students may move from P-only to P + S. Based on progress monitoring scores, students may enter P + T when they get to second or third grades if they have already received a secondary intervention during KG or first grade. Students do not move from P + T to P + S but rather receive P + T until they are ready to exit to P-only.

in which "research-driven" and "practice-based" models of RTI were evaluated in a meta-analytic study. Burns et al. (2005) conducted a meta-analytic review of research on four existing large-scale models designated as RTI and various published single research studies that incorporated an RTI framework in the investigation (note that here we are referencing the conceptual features of this review; we have concerns about the methodological aspects of the research). The authors reported that RTI models in practice had stronger effect sizes than research-driven models, with both showing positive effects of the approach. The outcome for systemic

outcomes among field-based RTI models was nearly twice as large as for student outcomes. The authors used the conceptual framework work of Fuchs et al. (2003), who identified four basic models of problem solving that involve some applications of RTI. (The reader is referred to Fuchs et al. (2003) for a review of each of the models in greater detail.) The models identified by Fuchs et al. (2003) and incorporated in the Burns et al. (2005) review included the following: Heartland Area Education Agency model (Ikeda, Tilly, Stumme, Volver, and Alisson, 1996); Ohio's intervention-based assessment model (Telzrow and Hollinger, 2000); Pennsylvania's

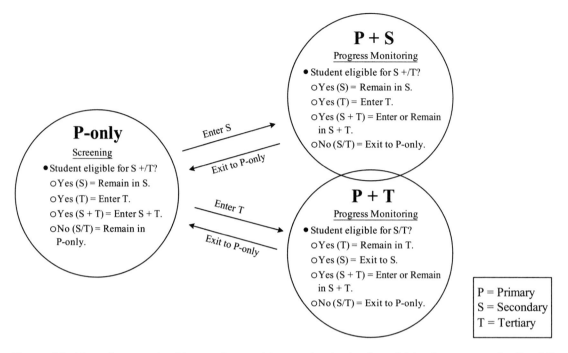

FIGURE 3.3. Alternative example of intervention provision: overlapping levels model (students may receive S and T simultaneously).

Note. If eligible for S and or T during initial screening, students may move from P-only to P + S/T or from P-only to P + S and P + T. Based on progress monitoring scores, students may move between P + S and P + T or may receive P + S and P + T simultaneously. Students who are not eligible for S/T receive P-only.

instructional support team model (Kovaleski, Tucker, and Duffy, 1995) and the Minneapolis Public Schools Problem Solving Model (Minneapolis Public Schools, 2001). It should be noted that these models are generic problem-solving models and can serve as a template for RTI. However, each of the models does not necessarily involve all the features of RTI discussed in this chapter and, therefore, may not represent a complete picture of how RTI might be implemented in practice.

Another template that can serve as a useful heuristic for RTI models is the K-3 Intervention Projects funded by the Office of Special Education Programs (OSEP) of the US Department of Education. Currently, there are six different centers, each with a somewhat different model of RTI (two behavior, two reading, and two reading-and-behavior combination centers). These research-based models are currently being evaluated, with outcomes expected to be reported in late 2007 or early 2008. Other information and descriptions on these models of RTI can be found at the Coordination, Consultation, and Evaluation Center website at the University of Wisconsin–Madison (www.wcer.wisc.edu/cce).

3.4 General Considerations

As if these considerations did not provide enough challenges to individuals in the field, there are other significant overarching issues that need to be addressed for RTI models to be implemented effectively in educational settings. In this section, four issues are identified that will need to be considered as the professionals move forward to embrace RTI (Kratochwill, 2006): (a) expanded models of prevention, (b) involvement of parents in the intervention process, (c) systemic intervention and change, and (d) professional development to adopt, implement, and sustain RTI and associated practices.

3.4.1 Models of Prevention

A first issue is that current conceptualizations of RTI (e.g., NASDSE, 2005; Gresham, 2006) are embedded in a certain approach to prevention of student concerns. Current conceptual models of prevention involve at least three prominent approaches to youth development and prevention: prevention based on risk and protective factors, resilience

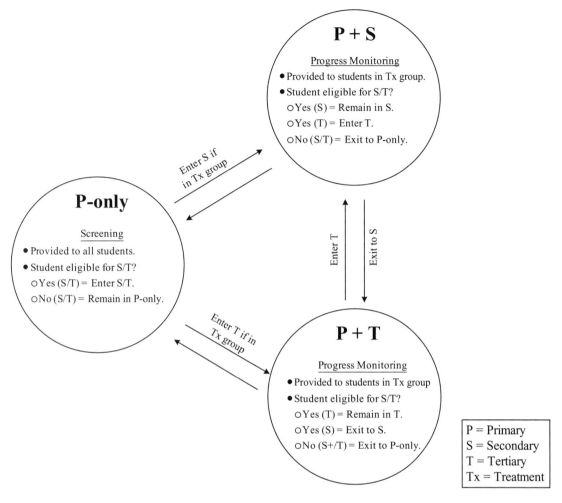

FIGURE 3.4. Alternative example of intervention provision: treatment group implementation model.
Note. If eligible for S/T during initial screening, and if assigned to a comparison group, students may move from P-only to P + S or P-only to P + T. Based on progress monitoring scores, students in the treatment group may move between P + S and P + T (in either direction) or between P + S/T and P-only. Students who are not eligible for S/T receive P-only.

approaches, and positive youth development approaches (Small and Memmo, 2004). RTI embraces the more traditional model which is designed to reduce risk factors and increase protective factors as well as enhance skills and competencies to help students cope better with future challenges and problems (see Durlak, 1997). There are at least three challenges with this framework of prevention relative to other approaches. First, it is a deficit approach that places a priority of deficits within the person (in this case, academic skill deficits and social/behavioral problems). In many respects the current conceptualizations of RTI embrace a medical model where the problems reside within the

child. As an example, consider the focus of academic progress monitoring assessment that is on deficits in the child as opposed to the instructional ecology of the learning environment as would be represented in the work of Ysseldyke and Christenson (1988). In contrast, resilience approaches focus on understanding factors that distinguish individuals who demonstrate good adaptation and skills from those that do not when confronted with challenging circumstances (e.g., poor instruction at school, child abuse and neglect). Positive youth development approaches place a premium on methods to promote development, and proponents of this model would suggest that preventing problems is not enough; see

Small and Memmo (2004) for more details of these three approaches and their advantages and limitations. Thus, from a prevention science perspective, greater attention should be given to expanding RTI to models that move beyond traditional prevention within multi-tier applications.

3.4.2 Parent Involvement in Multi-Tiered Interventions

Virtually all the literature on RTI features school-based interventions focused on traditional academics as delivered by teachers or other school-based professionals in the school. A compelling case can be made for involvement of parents in the intervention process at multiple levels of prevention and intervention (Kratochwill, 2006). Parent involvement can take many forms, with the empirical support variable across different dimensions of the involvement types (see Carlson and Christenson, 2005; Christenson and Sheridan, 2001; Ysseldyke and Christenson, 1988). As part of the problem-solving process affiliated with problem solving, more traditional models featured within RTI (e.g., traditional behavioral consultation; see Gresham, 2006) can be expanded to include conjoint models involving a collaborative relationship among teacher, parent, and support professional, such as the psychologist (and child where appropriate) (Sheridan and Kratochwill, in press). Thus, parent involvement can have a positive effect on the student and has demonstrated benefit for increasing motivation (see Gonzalez-DeHass, Willems, and Doan Halbein, 2005), an important academic enabler.

3.4.3 Systemic Intervention and Change

An important issue to be addressed pertains to the changes that may need to occur within systems for effective adoption, implementation, and sustainability of intervention practices in applied school settings. In particular, most of the RTI approaches that have been examined require systemic change for effective adoption of these programs (Osher, Dwyer, and Jackson, 2004). The Wisconsin Department of Public Instruction has adopted a model of systemic change called the Early Ongoing Collaborative Assistance (EOCA) project to help schools adopt prevention models and implement RTI. Ten EOCA framework components are designed to help schools

tackle system change for adoption, implementation, and sustainability of the intervention programs and practices. For example, in the EOCA model, adoption of prevention programs and procedures requires a commitment by administrators and general education professionals to consider these programs and their benefits. In many respects, the RTI framework is first and foremost a *system* of intervention within general education settings and practices. Traditional services of referring children for special education will have to be reconsidered and alternatives in the entire operation of the school and school teams reconsidered for such models to be sustainable over time. Thus, an intervention focused on system change will be critical to enact models of RTI.

3.4.4 Professional Development and Education

Related to the focus on system change, for RTI to be developed effectively considerable amount of professional development will need to be scheduled; individuals will need to learn new assessment technology and evidence-based intervention programs (Kratochwill et al., in press). The challenge of this task should not be underestimated and will involve consideration of evidence-base models of professional development for preservice and inservice education. The application of some of these programs and, in particular, application of multi-tier models in applied settings is challenging and will require considerable professional development extended beyond traditional formats with guided assistance and mentoring for effective implementation to occur. Some models of effective professional development are available, such as those through the K-3 intervention project's funded by the OSEP. However, in this case, the information has not been widely disseminated and will likely require years of effective dissemination practices to be of assistance with typical school systems.

3.5 Summary and Final Considerations

This chapter provides an overview of some of the features commonly presented in RTI approaches. Although there are some common elements of RTI models at the conceptual level (i.e., multi-tiered prevention, progress monitoring), nuances and variations in the actual application of these strategies in school settings will need to be considered. In considering these issues, important components of both the dependent and independent variable aspects of RTI were identified.

Application of RTI in applied settings also requires considerable conceptual and methodological engagement by researchers and practitioners in the professions that have a compelling interest in seeing these models work effectively to serve children, families, and schools. In particular, major developments must occur in measurement for advancements to be made in the application of these models. Traditional constructs of reliability and validity will be supplemented by treatment utility studies in a variety of construct validity requirements that have yet to emerge in the area of practice. Moreover, major challenges occur on the independent variable side of these educational innovations. A major issue pertains to the identification and implementation of evidence-based/science-based practices to facilitate using the intervention as a "test" in making decisions about students and determining the need for special education services.

There are also some general considerations that remain in application, adoption, and sustainability of these models, including reconsidering and expanding models of prevention, parent involvement, considerable professional development in the topical areas discussed in this chapter, as well as futures of systemic change that will be required for the model to be effective in its stated aims and purposes.

Perhaps the final challenge in this process is thinking about what RTI is designed to accomplish with respect to innovations and eligibility determination and effective outcomes for students. Once RTI is implemented, what kind of alignment will we have with potential of interventions within special education? Will the innovations and evidence-based strategies within the RTI framework be carried over into special education settings, itself a question of transportability? Will there be the trained personnel from our institutions of higher education and resources in schools to implement these approaches and make them sustainable so that students are cared for in the best possible way in our educational environments? These issues are of great interest nationally, and while RTI shows promise in being able to improve student outcomes, major issues remain to be resolved for this model to address the major concerns it has been designed to address.

Acknowledgments. The authors' appreciation is extended to Ms. Paula Volpiansky for her helpful comments on the chapter and to Ms. Cathlin Foy for her work on the manuscript.

References

Albers, C. A., Kratochwill, T. R., & Glover. T. A. (in press). Introduction to the special issue: How can universal screening enhance educational and mental health outcomes? *Journal of School Psychology.*

Albers, C. A., Kratochwill, T. R., & Glover. T. A. (in press). Where are we, and where do we go now? Universal screening for enhanced educational and mental health outcomes. *Journal of school Psychology.*

Algozzine, B. & Kay, P. (Eds.) (2002). *Preventing Problem Behaviors: A Handbook of Successful Prevention Strategies.* Thousand Oaks, CA: Corwin Press.

Barlow, D. H., Hayes, S. C., & Nelson, R. O. (1984). *The Scientist Practitioner: Research and Accountability in Clinical and Educational Settings.* New York, NY: Pergamon Press.

Bergan, J. R. (1977). *Behavioral Consultation.* Columbus, OH: Charles E. Merrill.

Bergan, J. R. & Kratochwill, T. R. (1990). *Behavioral Consultation and Therapy.* New York: Plenum Press.

Blanton, H. & Jaccard, J. (2006). Arbitrary metrics redux. *American Psychologist, 61,* 62–71.

Bradley, R., Danielson, L. C., & Hallahan, D. P. (2002). *Identification of learning Disabilities: Research to Practice.* Washington, DC: Lawrence Erlbaum Associates.

Brown-Chidsey, R. (2005). Response-to-intervention (RTI) training in school psychology programs: introduction to the RTI mini-series. *Trainer's Forum, 25,* 1–26.

Brown-Chidsey, R. & Steege, M. W. (2006). *Response to Intervention: Principles and Strategies for Effective Instruction.* New York: Guilford Press.

Burns, M. K., Appleton, J. J., & Stehouwer, J. D. (2005). Meta-analytic review of responsiveness-to-intervention research: examining field-based and research-implemented models. *Journal of Psychoeducational Assessment, 23,* 381–394.

Caplan, G. (1964). *The Principles of Preventive Psychiatry.* New York, NY: Basic Books.

Carlson, C. & Christenson, S. L. (2005). Evidence-based parent and family interventions in school psychology: overview and procedures. *School Psychology Quarterly, 20,* 345–351.

CASEL (n.d.). Retrieved July 5, 2006 from www.casel.org

Center for Disease Control (n.d.). Retrived July 5, 2006 from http://www.cdc.gov/hiv/pubs/hivcompendium/hivcompendium.htm.

Center for Substance Abuse Prevention (CSAP), Dept. of Health & Human Services, National Registry of Effective Programs. Substance Abuse and Mental Health Services Administration (n.d.). Retrieved July 5, 2006 from www.modelprograms.samhsa.gov.

Christenson. S. L. & Sheridan, S. M. (2001). *Schools and Families: Creating Essential Connections for Learning*. New York: The Gilford Press

Cone, J. D. (2001). *Evaluating Outcomes*. Washington, DC: American Psychological Association.

Crone, D. A. & Horner, R. H. (2003). *Building Positive Behavior Support Systems in Schools*. New York, NY: The Guilford Press.

Deno, S. (1985). Curriculum-based measurement: the emerging alternative. *Exceptional Children, 52*, 219–232.

Deno, S. & Mirkin, P. (1977). *Data-based Program Modification*. Minneapolis, MN: Leadership Training Institute for Special Education.

Department of Education, Safe and Drug-free Schools. Retrieved July 5, 2006 from www.ed.gov (Visit US. Department of Education and search for OSDFS)

DiPerna, J. C. & Elliott, S. N. (2000). *ACES Academic Competence Evaluation Scales Manual K-12*. The Psychological Corporation.

Donovan, M. S. & Cross, C. T. (2002). *Minority Students in Special and Gifted Education*. Washington, DC: National Academy Press.

Durlak, J. A. (1997). *Successful Prevention Programs for Children and Adolescents*. New York, NY: Plenum Press.

Elliott, D. S. (Editor) (1997). *Blueprints for Violence Prevention* (Vols. 1-11). Boulder, CO: Center for the Study and Prevention of Violence, Institute of Behavioral Science, University of Colorado. Retrieved July 5, 2006 from www.colorado.edu/cspv/blueprints.

Evidence-Based Program Database (n.d.). Retrieved July 5, 2006 from http://www.altedmh.org/ebpd/index.htm.

Florida Center for Reading Research (n.d.). Retrieved July 5, 2006 from http://www.ferr.org.

Fuchs, D. & Fuchs, L. S. (2006). Introduction to response to intervention: what, why, and how valid is it? *Reading Research Quarterly, 41*, 93–99.

Fuchs, D., & Fuchs, L. S., & Compton, D. L. (2004). Identifying reading disabilities by responsiveness-to-instruction: specifying measures and criteria. *Learning Disability Quarterly, 27*, 216–227.

Fuchs, D., Mock, D., Morgan, P. L., & Young, C. L. (2003). Responsiveness-to-intervention: definitions, evidence, and implications for the learning disabilities construct. *Learning Disabilities Research & Practice, 18*, 157–171.

Glover, T. A. & Albers, C. A. (in press). Considerations for evaluating universal screening assessments. *Journal of School Psychology*.

Gonzalez-DeHass, A. R., Willems, P. P., & Doan Halbein, M. F. (2005). Examining the relationship between parental involvement and student motivation. *Educational Psychology Review, 17*, 99–123.

Greenberg, Mark T., Domitrovich, Celene, & Bumbarger, Brian (1999). *Preventing Mental Disorders in School-aged Children: A review of the Effectiveness of Prevention Programs*. State College, PA: Prevention Research Center for the Promotion of Human Development, College of Health and Human Development, Pennsylvania State University. Retrieved July 5, 2006 from www.prevention.psu.edu/CMHS.html.

Gresham, F. M. (2002). Responsiveness to intervention: an alternative approach to the identification of learning disabilities. In R. Bradley, L. Danielson, & D. P. Hallahan (Eds.), *Identification of Learning Disabilities* (pp. 467–519). Mahway, NJ: Erlbaum.

Gresham, F. M. (2006). Response to intervention. In G. G. Bear & K. M. Minke (Eds.), *Children's Needs III: Development, Prevention, and Intervention* (pp. 525–540). Bethesda, MD: National Association of School Psychologists.

Heller, K. A., Holtzman, W. H., & Messick, S. (Eds.) (1982). *Placing Children in Special Education: A Strategy for Equity*. Washington, DC: National Academy Press.

Ikeda, M. J., Tilly, W. D., Stumme, J., Volmer, L., & Allison, R. (1996). Agency-wide implementation of problem solving consultation: foundations, current implementation, and future directions. *School Psychology Quarterly, 11*, 228–243.

IDEA (1991, 1997, 1999). *Individuals with Disabilities Education Act*. 20 U.S.C. §1400 et. seq., C.F.R. 300 (regulations), Regulations Implementing IDEA (1997), (Fed. Reg., 1999, March 12, 1999, vol. 64, no. 48).

IDEIA (2004). *Individuals with Disabilities Education Improvement Act*. Pub. L 108–446.

Institute of Medicine (1994). *Reducing Risks for Mental Health Disorders; Frontier for Preventive Intervention Research*. Washington, DC: National Academy Press.

Kavale, K. A. & Forness, S. R. (1999). Effectiveness of special education. In C.R. Reynolds & T. B Gutkin (Eds.), *The Handbook of School Psychology* (pp. 984–1024). New York: Wiley.

Kazdin, A. E. (1977). Assessing the clinical or applied importance of behavior change through social validation. *Behavior Modifications, 1*, 427–452.

Kazdin, A. E. (2004). Evidence-based treatments: challenges and priorities for practice and research. *Child and Adolescent Psychiatric Clinics of North America, 13*, 923–940.

Kazdin, A. E. (2006). Arbitrary metrics: implications for identifying evidence-based treatments. *American Psychologist, 61*, 42–49.

Kovaleski, J. F., Tucker, J. A., & Duffy, D. J. (1995). School reform through instructional support: the Pennsylvania Initiative (Part I). *Communiqué, 23*(8).

Kratochwill, T. R. (1985). Selection of target behaviors in behavioral consultation. *Behavioral Assessment, 7,* 49–61.

Kratochwill, T. R. (2006). Response to intervention: methodological and conceptual issues in research and practice. Invited address presented at the Annual Meeting of the American Psychological Association, New Orleans, LA, August.

Kratochwill, T. R., Albers, C. A., & Shernoff, E. S. (2004). School-based interventions. *Child and Adolescent Psychiatric Clinics of North America, 13,* 885–903.

Kratochwill, T. R. & Bergan, J. R. (1990). *Behavioral Consultation: An Individual Guide.* New York: Plenum Press.

Kratochwill, T. R. & Bijou, S. W. (1987). The impact of behaviorism on educational psychology. In J. A. Glover & R. R. Ronning (Eds.), *A History of Educational Psychology* (pp. 131–157). New York, NY: Pergamon.

Kratochwill, T. R., Elliott, S. N., & Stoiber, K. C. (2004). Problem solving consultation. In A. Thomas and J. Grimes (Eds.), *Best Practices.* Washington, DC: National Association of School Psychologists.

Kratochwill, T. R. & Hoagwood, K. E. (in press). Evidence-based interventions and system change: concepts, methods and challenges in implementing evidence-based practices in children's mental health.

Kratochwill, T. R., Hoagwood, K. E., White, J., Levitt, J. M., Romanelli, L. H., & Saka, N. (in press). Evidence-based interventions and practices in school psychology: Challenges and opportunities for the profession. In T. Gutkin & C. Reynolds (Eds.), *Handbook of School Psychology* (4 ed.). Hoboken, NJ: Wiley.

Kratochwill, T. R. & Shernoff, E. S. (2004). Evidence-based practice: promoting evidence-based interventions in school psychology. *School Psychology Review, 33,* 34–48.

Kratochwill, T. R. & Stoiber, K. C. (2002). Evidence-based intervention in school psychology: conceptual foundations of the Procedural and Coding Manual of Division 16 and the Society for the Study of School Psychology Task Force. *School Psychology Quarterly, 17,* 341–389.

MacMillan, D. L., Gresham, F. M., & Bocian, K. M. (1998). Discrepancy between definitions of learning disabilities and school practices: an empirical investigation. *Journal of Learning Disabilities, 31,* 314–326.

Mendel, Richard A. (2001). *Less Hype, more Help: Reducing Juvenile Crime, What Works and What Doesn't.* Washington D.C.: American Youth Policy Forum. Retrived July 5, 2006 from http://www.aypf.org/publications/mendel/MendelRep.pdf.

Mihalic, S. & Aultman-Bettridge, T. (2004). A guide to effective school-based prevention programs. In W. L. Tulk (Ed.), *Policing and School Crime.* Englewood Cliffs, NJ: Prentice Hall Publishers.

Minneapolis Public Schools (2001). *Problem-Solving Model: Introduction for all Staff.* Minneapolis, MN: Minneapolis Public Schools.

National Association of State Directors of Special Education (NASDSE) (2005). Response to intervention: policy considerations and implementation. Alexandria, VA: National Association of State Directors of Special Education.

National Clearing House for Alcohol and Drug Information, (n.d.). *Preventing Drug Use among Children and Adolescents: A Research-based Guide*, #734 Retrieved July 5, 2006 from http://ncadistore.samhsa.gov/catalog/ProductDetails.aspx?ProductID=16617. Also available at 1-800-729-6686.

National Reading Panel (n.d.). Retrieved July 5, 2006 from http://www.nichd.nih.gov/publications/nrp/smallbook.htm.

NCCRESt (2005). Cultural considerations and challenges in response-to-intervention models. Denver, CO: National Center for Culturally Responsive Educational Systems.

Newell, M. & Kratochwill, T. R. (in press). The integration of response to intervention and critical race theory-disability studies: a robust approach to reducing racial discrimination. In S. R. Jimmerson, M. K. Burns, & A. M. VanDerHeyden (Eds.), *The Handbook of Response to Intervention: The Science and Practice of Assessment and Intervention.* New York: Springer.

NRP (2000). *Teaching Children to Read: An Evidence Assessment of the Scientific Research Literature on Reading and its Implications for Reading Instruction.* Bethesda, MD: National Reading Panel.

Oregon Reading First Center (n.d.). Retrieved July 5, 2006 from http://reading.uoregon.edu/curricula/index.php.

Posey, Robin, Wong, Sherry, Catalano, Richard, Hawkins, David, Dusenbury, Linda, Chappel, Patricia (2000). *Communities That Care Prevention Strategies: A Research Guide to what Works.* Seattle, WA: Development Research and Programs, Inc., Seattle, WA. Retrieved July 5, 2006 from www.preventionscience.com/ctc/CTC.html.

Reschly, D. J. (2003). School psychology. In W. M. Reynolds & G. E. Miller (Eds.), *Handbook of Psychology* (Vol. 7, pp. 431–453). Hoboken, NJ: Wiley.

Office of Juvenile Justice and Delinquency Prevention (n.d.). *Title V Training and Technical Assistance Programs for State and Local Governments: Effective & Promising Programs Guide.* Washington D.C.: Office of Juvenile Justice and Delinquency Prevention, Office of Justice Programs, U.S. Dept. of Justice. Retrieved July 5, 2006 www.dsgonline.com.

Osher, D., Dwyer, K., & Jackson, S. (2004). *Safe, Supportive and Successful Schools: Step by Step*. Longmont, CO: Sopris West.

Promising Practices Network (n.d.). Retrieved July 5, 2006 http://www.promisingpractices.net/.

Reschly, D. J. & Ysseldyke, J. E. (2002). Paradigm shift: the past is not the future. In A. Thomas & J. Grimes (Eds.), *Best Practices in School Psychology* (4th ed., pp. 3–21). Bethesda, MD: National Association of School Psychologists.

Shapiro, E. S. (2004). *Academic Skills Problems: Direct Assessment and Intervention*. New York, NY: The Guilford Press.

Shapiro, E. S. & Kratochwill, T. R. (2000). *Behavior Assessment in Schools*. New York, NY: Guilford Press.

Sheridan, S. M., & Kratochwill, T. R. (in press). *Conjoint Behavioral Consultation:* Promoting Family-school Connections and Interventions. New York, NY: Springer.

Sherman et al. (1997). *What Works, What doesn't, What's Promising* College Park: University of Maryland, Department of Criminology and Criminal Justice. NCJ 165366. Retrieved July 5, 2006 from www.ncjrs.org/works/wholedoc.htm or www. preventingcrime.org.

Sheridan, S. M., Kratochwill, T. R., & Bergan, J. R. (1996). *Conjoint Behavioral Consultation: An Individual Guide*. New York: Plenum Press.

Simeonsson, R. J. (1994). *Risk, Resilience & Prevention: Promoting the Well-Being of all Children*. Baltimore: P.H. Brookes.

Small, S. & Memmo, M. (2004). Contemporary models of youth development and problem prevention: toward an integration of terms, concepts, and models. *Family Relations, 53*, 3–11.

Social Programs that work (n.d.). Retrieved July 5, 2006 from http://www.evidencebasedprograms.org/.

Strengthening America's Families (n.d.). Retrieved July 5, 2006 from www.strengtheningfamilies.org.

Telzrow, C. F., McNamara, K., & Hollinger, C. L. (2000). Fidelity of problem-solving implementation and relationship to student performance. *School Psychology Review, 29*, 443–461.

Texas Reading First Center (n.d.). Retrieved July 5, 2006 from http://www.tea.state.tx.us/readingfirst/AppConfOtt.pdf

The Hamilton Fish Institute (n.d.). Retrieved July 5, 2006 from http://www.hamfish.org/programs/.

The International Campbell Collaboration (n.d.). Retrieved July 5, 2006 from http://www. campbellcollaboration.org/frontend.asp.

Tilly III, D. W. (in press). The evolution of school psychology to science-based practice. In A. Thomas & J. Grimes, (Eds.), *Best Practices in School Psychol-*

ogy V. Bethesda, MD: National Association of School Psychologists.

U.S. Department of Health and Human Services (2001). *Youth Violence. A report of the Surgeon General* Rockville, MD: U.S. Department of Health and Human Services, Centers for Disease Control and Prevention, National Center of Injury Prevention and Control; Substance and Abuse and Mental Health Services Administration, Center for Mental Health Services; and National Institutes of Health, National Institute of Mental Health. Retrieved July 5, 2006 from www.surgeongeneral.gov/library/youthviolence.

Vaughn, S. & Fuchs, L. S. (2003). Redefining learning disabilities as inadequate response to instruction: The promise and potential problems. *Learning Disabilities Research & Practice, 18*, 137–146.

Vaughn, S., Linan-Thompson, S., & Hickman, P. (2003). Response to instruction as a means of identifying students with reading/learning disabilities. *Exceptional Children, 69*, 391–409.

Walker, H. M. & Shinn, M. R. (1999). Structuring school-based interventions to achieve integrated primary, secondary, and tertiary prevention goals for safe and effective schools. In M. R. Shinn, H. M. Walker, & G. Stoner (Eds.), *Interventions for Academic and Behavior Problems II: Preventive and Remedial Approaches* (pp. 1–25). Bethesda, MD: National Association of School Psychologists.

Wedl, R. J. (2005). *Response to Intervention: An Alternative to Traditional Eligibility Criteria for Students with Disabilities*. Saint Paul, MN: Education Evolving.

What Works Clearinghouse (n.d.). Retrieved July 5, 2006 from http://www.whatworkshelpdesk.edgov/identify.asp.

Wolf, M. M. (1977). Social validity: the case of subjective measurement or how applied behavior analysis is finding its heart. *Journal of Applied Behavior Analysis, 11*, 203–214.

Ysseldyke, J., Algozzine, B., & Epps, S. (1983). A logical and empirical-analysis of current practice in classifying students as handicapped. *Exceptional Children, 50*, 160–166.

Ysseldyke, J. & Christenson, S. L. (1988). Linking assessment to instruction. In J. Graden, J. E. Zins, & M. J. Curtis (Eds.), *Alternative Educational Delivery Systems: Enhancing Instructional Options for all Students* (pp. 91–107). Washington, DC: National Association for School Psychologists.

Ysseldyke, J. & Marston, D. (1999). Origins of categorical special education services in schools and a rationale for changing them. In D. J. Reschly, D. W. Tilly III, & J. P. Grimes (Eds.), *Special Education in Transition* (pp. 1–18). Longmong, CO: Sopris.

4
Consultation within Response to Intervention Models

Steven E. Knotek

Steven E. Knotek, PhD, is an Assistant Professor of School Psychology in the Human Development and Psychological Studies Department in the School of Education at the University of North Carolina, Chapel Hill
sknotek@email.unc.edu

The reauthorization of the Individuals with Disabilities Education Act (IDEA) opens the door for the general education system to revisit how it assesses and provides service for students who are experiencing academic and behavioral difficulties. As opposed to the current regular education practice of relying upon a refer-test-place approach to support students with special academic or behavioral needs, this alternative approach places an emphasis on both assessment and, importantly, intervention in regular education settings. Response to intervention (RTI) offers regular education teachers assessment options and intervention tools that encourages them to accept instructional responsibility for a broader range of students than the prior model.

The emphasis in RTI on curriculum-based assessment, multiple-level problem-solving, and intervention in regular education will require substantial changes in how teachers and psychologists individually and collectively conduct their professional duties (Hoagwood and Johnson, 2002). For example, how will teachers integrate their prior understandings of a student-focused etiology of learning disabilities into an ecologically oriented instructional model? How will teachers adopt "evidence-based interventions" that may work well under ideal conditions in a university learning laboratory, but are then implemented within the ecological complexity of their individual school sites? What mechanisms can be used to support teachers' professional development of skills such as the use of single-subject design to document intervention effectiveness? This chapter first outlines characteristics and components of the RTI process and highlights and discusses challenges to its successful implementation as an evidence-based intervention. Next, consultee-centered consultation is defined and a rationale presented for its use as a means to facilitate the development of skills that will be needed by consultees to implement and sustain the RTI model in individual school sites. Finally, the chapter ends with a discussion about the use of consultee-centered consultation to facilitate a consultee's acquisition of RTI-related skills within Showers and Joyce's (1996) four levels of professional development.

4.1 Conceptual Basis

Although several variants have been proposed, many RTI models share common conceptual frameworks and have overlapping content and process components (Gresham, 2002). An important component of a variety of RTI models is the use of a dual-discrepancy (DD) decision paradigm to assess and intervene with students who are exhibiting low-impact, higher incidence school problems. Additionally, as the name implies, RTI models universally use a process that is at some level based upon a student's response to evidence-based interventions (EBIs).

4.1.1 Dual Discrepancy

Like the IQ/Achievement model of learning disabilities the DD model uses the concept of establishing a discrepancy to identify students who are "learning disabled" (Reschly, 2003). However, in the DD model the discrepancy refers to students' pre- and post-levels of performance in response to an evidence-based intervention (Gresham, 2002). If a student is deficient in critical academic skills and exhibits a low rate of learning in response to effective instructional practices, then the student may be identified as having a learning disability (Kovaleski, 2003). This concept is a feature of many RTI models.

4.1.2 Response to Intervention

The RTI process has two defining characteristics: it is a multi-tiered problem-solving model and it requires the use of evidence-based interventions (Walker, 2004). Medical analogies are often used to explain the rationale. For example, when a person complains to a physician of shortness of breath a doctor does not immediately order a heart transplant or radiation therapy for the patient. Instead, a doctor undertakes a diagnostic approach in which information is gathered and then moves from lower intensity possibilities towards more severe possibilities. Ultimately, a course of scientifically validated medications or procedures is prescribed based upon the patient's response to treatment.

Schools also need to adopt the practice of "matching intensity of intervention to problem severity" (Gresham, 2004, p. 4) because, as the recent shifts in reading instruction between whole language and phonics have demonstrated, one size intervention does not fit all students. Within RTI, the intensity of an intervention is based upon the severity of a student's academic or behavioral issues. Consequently, depending upon their responsiveness, a student could potentially move through a tiered system of increasingly intensive interventions.

4.1.3 Tiered Levels of Problem Solving

The RTI process is typically described as occurring across three to four levels of increasingly intensive interventions that are administered to an increasingly smaller proportion of the student population (Kovaleski, 2003). For example, North Carolina is implementing a pilot RTI program that has four tiers: Level I, benchmark, all of general education; Levels II and III, strategic interventions, 15% of population; and Level IV, intensive interventions, 5% of population (Deni, 2004). Depending upon a student's responsiveness to an intervention, one may move from being in a skill-building small group to receiving individualized instructional modifications. Within each of these levels an intervention will be applied through a distinct problem-solving process: define the problem, develop the plan, implement the plan, and evaluate the student's response to the intervention. The general problem-solving process is facilitated at each level through either dyadic or team-based consultation.

4.1.4 New Skills

The implementation of RTI may require educational professionals, especially teachers and school psychologists, to acquire or bolster their skill sets. The Instructional Consultation (IC) team model (Rosenfield and Gravois, 1996), an RTI approach, has four core skill areas that team members need to develop: problem-solving strategies, communication skills, data collection, and curriculum-based analysis. Specific skills that are needed include: hypothesis formulation, defining concerns in observable terms, charting and graphing data, conducting a curriculum-based assessment in reading, and active/reflective listening. Most RTI models require knowledge of these core skill areas.

4.2 Description of the Issues

4.2.1 Sustaining Response to Intervention in a School

The scope of the RTI paradigm is broad and its implementation includes change in many school systems at the district, building, classroom, and individual levels. What challenges need to be met to transform the programmatic and professional infrastructure of schools from the current refer-test-place model to the RTI, assessment for intervention model? While the specific challenges are many and include fostering system buy-in, revamping schools' intervention practices, widening the scope of classroom instruction, and providing professional development, there is one overarching issue that subsumes many of these individual challenges: intervention implementation (Adelman and Taylor, 2003; Schoenwald and Hoagwood, 2001; Walker, 2004).

A core assumption of the RTI approach is that students will be better served when teachers and allied professionals use an empirically validated problem-solving process that results in the appropriate selection of EBIs to meet low-achieving students' academic and behavioral needs (Reschly, 2004). However, the seemingly straightforward process, first identifying a student's academic needs and then selecting and implementing an EBI, becomes complicated as it is applied in actual settings. Researchers have identified three key challenges to the problem of implementation: (a) efficacy, (b) transportability and effectiveness, and (c) transportability and dissemination (Hoagwood, 2001; Hoagwood and Johnson, 2002; Schoenwald and Hoagwood, 2001).

4.2.2 Efficacy

Traditionally, interventions focusing on behavioral and instructional problems have been developed in "ideal" settings (Burns and Hoagwood, 2002) in which the efficacy of an intervention is established. Initial studies of instructional interventions are often conducted in a setting that will allow for maximum effect and for control of variables. Accordingly, efficacy trials may exclude "low functioning" or "low IQ" students or be limited to teachers who self-select and volunteer for investigations that seem interesting to them. The experimental research process must normally begin with initial trials conducted in controlled settings to establish efficacy. School districts should not routinely adopt new interventions that have not had their effectiveness and efficacy empirically confirmed. However, once efficacy has been established for an intervention and it then moves from a laboratory or a highly staffed, research-funded school site, it will come face to face with complicated ecological realities inherent in ordinary schools. An intervention that has only been researched through initial efficacy may not be found to be effective or be evidence based in "natural settings." Thus, in many instances, additional implementation and efficacy research is needed.

4.2.3 Effectiveness and Transportability

Most veteran educators or school psychologists have had to devote time and energy to tackling the latest "intervention du jour." Every year, school districts across the country spend millions of professional development dollars and commit massive amounts of staff and student time to engaging in the newest educational "fix." Programs designed to ameliorate problems such as self-esteem, reading levels, citizenship, and motivation are introduced annually. Savvy educators have become skeptical of the promises of new programs and often adopt a "this too shall pass" attitude. What is at the root of this skepticism to innovation? Experienced educators will tell you that many of the programs do not work, were designed by people who have never been in a classroom, or are merely recycled ideas from "when I started as a teacher." These comments refer to the issue of the "research to practice gap," or transportability.

Schoenwald and Hoagwood (2001, p. 1192) describe transportability as "the movement of efficacious interventions to usual care settings." Modern schools are complex environments whose functioning is impinged upon by macrosystem issues (i.e., state of the economy, current legislative mandates), mesosystem issues (i.e., interactions between police and schools), and microsystem issues (i.e., current class size). Within this context, Schoenwald and Hoagwood (2001) describe six dimensions in which there may be contrasts between research and practice settings: (a) intervention characteristics, (b) practitioner characteristics, (c) client characteristics, (d) service delivery characteristics, (e) organizational characteristics, and (e) service system mandates. Intervention development has not traditionally focused on bridging the research to practice gap to ensure an intervention's transportability – implementation has often been left to chance.

4.2.3.1 Integrity

Once an intervention reaches a site and implementation has begun, the issue of integrity (Gresham, 1989; Walker, 2004) is very important. Is there consistency of delivery? Are central components ignored? Is consistency possible? For example, the curriculum-based assessment process requires that an intervention's effectiveness be evaluated, often through the use of a single-subject protocol. However, graphing intervention effectiveness requires a time-consuming, multiple-step process that necessitates fidelity to insure validity. Teachers and/or school psychologists used to the laxer implementation of many of the interventions undertaken in current pre-referral protocols may not understand or follow the more rigorous steps of data-based problem identification and charting needed for a valid evaluation of intervention effectiveness.

These questions address some of the salient issues related to integrity: Who has training in evaluation? Who should be responsible for carrying out the evaluation step? Can the intervention be adopted as originally designed (Hoagwood, 2003–2004; Schoenwald and Hoagwood, 2001)? The implementation of an RTI model may need to begin with the basic question of professional responsibility and contain some mechanism to support the transfer of knowledge and skill between professions.

4.2.4 Dissemination and Transportability

Dissemination refers to whether or not interventions are sustained beyond their original adoption within settings of normal practice (Burns and Hoagwood, 2002; Rones and Hoagwood, 2000). To realize dissemination an intervention must include a planned, directed path that addresses how sustainability will be achieved. How will an intervention's goals become a part of the school's goals? What processes will be used to facilitate training, buy-in, and organizational support? Who will conduct the intervention in question, under what circumstances and to what effect (Schoenwald and Hoagwood, 2001)? Factors known to be important to dissemination include: comprehensive training (Knoff and Batsch, 1995), participatory action and collaboration (Nastasi, 1998), and supervision and monitoring (McDougal, Clonan, and Martens, 2000).

In order for RTI models to successfully enter schools and then become a long-term presence they must address issues beyond efficacy and actively plan for transportability for effectiveness and dissemination. Programmatic content cannot simply be downloaded into schools via single-session workshops or through administrative mandate. Transportability of RTI models requires an embedded diffusion process that takes into account professional development needs, adaptation to the school's unique ecological context, a workable evaluation process, and a means to encourage system acceptance of the model (Glisson, 2002). The next section of this chapter discusses how consultation may be used to facilitate the implementation of RTI through the various phases of professional development of the personnel responsible for the process.

4.3 Application

RTI models are noteworthy for their ambitious reach across the entire population of general education students and for their multilayered range of interventions. The RTI initiative embraces a prevention perspective and reframes students' functioning from a point of view of deficit to one of potential; this conceptual shift, in turn, reframes how teachers and school psychologists should conduct their professional business. General education professionals are challenged to problem solve and use assessment in the service of effective intervention, and to use intervention within the context of regular education.

The process of implementing and sustaining an RTI model is daunting because of the requirement that educators effectively acquire new skills, effectively use data-based decision-making to inform intervention, and effectively master and adapt EBIs to their unique school setting. For example, some reading interventions require educators to administer a running record, take multiple "snap shots," and then chart the students' progress (Gickling and Rosenfield, 1995; Shapiro, 2004). How can these training challenges be met? One piece of the answer may be to focus on the process of professional development that is tied to RTI's implementation. The RTI model will not become embedded simply because of its conceptual merits, someone will have to be responsible for ensuring that skill acquisition, EBI implementation, and collaboration during problem solving really occurs. Consultation is an interpersonal problem-solving process that can be used to meet these challenges.

4.3.1 Consultation

Consultation is generally defined as an indirect service through which a consultee (i.e., a teacher) gains support for a client (i.e., a student) by engaging in a problem-solving process with a consultant (Bergan and Kratochwill, 1990; Caplan, 1970). For instance, in a school setting a teacher may initiate consultation with a school psychologist in order to problem solve about ways to provide classroom support for a child who is a frequent target of bullies. In this case the teacher has primary responsibility for the student, and the school psychologist has a primary responsibility to facilitate the teacher's acquisition of new perspectives and possible solutions to the work problem (classroom interventions to stop bullying). Within the field of consultation there is variation in the methods and goals associated with different types of consultation.

Behavioral consultation utilizes behavioral theory and is primarily defined by its emphasis on the use of behavioral technology and the systematic structure of consultation (Bergan, 1977). Mental health consultation utilizes psychodynamic theory and is defined by its use of an external consultant who works with the consultee to overcome issues such as theme interference (Caplan, 1970).

4.3.1.1 Consultee-Centered Consultation

This type of consultation evolved out of Caplan's (1970) original model and has developed to the point that it is in many ways distinct and incompatible with the form of consultation traditionally known as Caplanian Mental Health Consultation (Lambert, 2004). The contemporary definition of consultee-centered consultation was developed over three international seminars in the past 10 years and contains the following key elements (Knotek and Sandoval, 2003):

1. Consultee-centered consultation emphasizes a nonhierarchical helping role relationship between a resource (consultant) and a person or group (consultee) who seeks professional help with a work problem involving a third party (client).
2. This work problem is a topic of concern for the consultee who has a direct responsibility for the learning, development, or productivity of the client.
3. The primary task of the consultant is to help the consultee pinpoint critical information and then consider multiple views about well-being, development, intrapersonal, interpersonal and organizational effectiveness appropriate to the consultee's work setting. Ultimately, the consultee may reframe his/her prior conceptualization of the work problem.
4. The goal of the consultation process is the joint development of a new way of conceptualizing the work problem so that the repertoire of the consultee is expanded and the professional relationship between the consultee and the client is restored or improved. As the problem is jointly reconsidered, new ways of approaching the problem may lead to acquiring new means to address the work dilemma.

The term "consultee-centered" consultation itself reflects the core focus of the consultation relationship, which is predicated on facilitating change in the conceptual understandings of the consultee. While the expectation exists that clients will ultimately be better served through consultation, the prime goal of this type is to reframe consultees' knowledge and reconceptualize their understanding of the work problem. Consultee-centered consultation seeks to facilitate change through the interpersonal process of the relationship, and can be considered as open with respect to the content discussed during consultation. This type of consultation is well suited to support the implementation of the RTI model because (a) it is also prevention focused, (b) it is designed to foster the consultee's adaptation to novel work problems, such as deciding how to implement new interventions, and (c) it is content neutral and can be used to discuss implementation issues ranging from individual cases to system-wide sustainability.

4.3.2 A Need for Skill Acquisition and Integration

Acquisition of the skills, simple (i.e., filling out information forms) and complex (i.e., integrating intervention results into a coherent, data-based interpretation), that are needed to successfully impact the students for whom RTI is designed to benefit will not occur magically. Successful implementation of RTI will require that school personnel learn skills such as curriculum-based assessment, assessment for intervention, and intervention evaluation, and then conceptually integrate each of these discrete skills within a superordinate explanatory framework. Typically, professionals such as school psychologists learn these abilities, which are part and parcel of the problem-solving process, over several years of course work and internships. How, then, will these capabilities be acquired by other professionals, in the work environment? Classroom teachers, upon whom much of the RTI implementation process depends, are not usually trained in fine-grained academic and behavioral analysis, and intervention design. Rather, teachers' preservice training usually emphasizes grade-level curricular and instructional practices. Successful implementation of an RTI model will be more likely to occur when professional development occurs across four increasingly demanding levels of professional development (Showers and Joyce, 1996).

4.3.3 Qualities of Effective Professional Development

As school districts attempt to provide ongoing professional development, it has become apparent that some forms of training are more efficacious than others (Baldwin and Ford, 1988; Showers and Joyce, 1996). And while numerous training approaches have been attempted, from single-session presentations to year-long demonstrations, the bottom line for professional training programs is whether or not the programs ultimately contribute to the achievement and success of students in classrooms (Roy, 1998). Showers and Joyce (1996) suggest that four major levels of impact are needed to insure that education professionals can adequately implement a new intervention: awareness, conceptual understanding, skill acquisition, and application of skills. The levels are as follows:

Level 1. An awareness of the problem is heightened through didactic presentations that result in a person's ability to cite the general ideas and principles associated with the intervention. In RTI, the trainee would be able to cite important features of the model, such as research-based interventions and primary prevention.
Level 2. An individual's deepening conceptual understanding of an intervention is facilitated through modeling and demonstration. For example, within RTI an individual who had acquired conceptual understanding of the paradigm would be able to conceptually articulate the difference between assessment for referral and assessment for intervention.
Level 3. Skill acquisition occurs when a person engages in simulated practices that are observed and commented on by a facilitator. A person learning the RTI process would, for instance, be given the opportunity to simulate how to obtain district norms for curriculum-based measurement of third-graders' reading fluency.
Level 4. This level of professional development is reached when a person is able to demonstrate a successful application of the new intervention within the actual context of his or her school site. A teacher who is able to implement the RTI process with fidelity to meet the academic needs of students with a range of academic problems will have successfully attained this level of professional development.

When a person has achieved the tasks present in each of these four levels, they are able to conceptually understand the linkages between the goals and means of the training.

Training to implement RTI models will likely vary greatly and occur unevenly across schools, districts, and states. How many districts have the professional development funds to train the personnel who will implement RTI (referred to from hereon as implementers) beyond the usual didactic sessions? Further, how many districts will have a development structure in place that supports application of skills in the actual context of individual classrooms? While it would be preferable if districts had the funds to train RTI implementers through the level of application of their skills during actual implementation, in this era of restricted budgets this may be little more than wishful thinking. Consultee-centered consultation cannot replace a well-funded and staffed training program; however, it can be used within each of the four levels of impact to augment and support implementation of RTI models.

4.3.4 Consultee-Centered Consultation Applied Across Levels of Professional Development

4.3.4.1 Awareness

RTI is not yet a term automatically recognized by the education community at large. Disciplines such as school psychology and special education that have traditionally focused on serving students with special needs likely have a heightened awareness and professional investment in RTI. However, professionals whose roles are traditionally less defined by special education may not be as aware of the principles, motivations, methods, and goals involved in the process (see Table 4.1).

The implementation of RTI models generally requires the participation of professionals from a variety of disciplines, with a variety of experience, and with a variety of prior knowledge about RTI as an intervention. It would, therefore, be reasonable

TABLE 4.1. Uses of consultation to promote RTI.

Type of implementation	Description
Research to practice	
Level	
Effectiveness	Use consultation to match intervention, practitioner, client, service delivery, organizational, and service system mandate characteristics to adapt RTI to unique context of a school/district
Dissemination	Consultation to support embedded professional development to support diffusion and sustainability
Professional development	
Level	
Awareness	Provide educators with an initial exposure to RTI
Conceptual	Use of modeling and demonstration to support educator's conceptualization of core RTI principles and processes
Skill acquisition	Facilitate practice of simulated RTI methods
Application	Consult with educators as they apply RTI within their unique school

to expect that, as schools move on a large scale to adopt RTI, some educators in a district may not be as aware of the particulars of the model or even the overall reasons for its adoption. Teachers who are not aware of the problems that RTI is designed to impact may have a difficult time internalizing the conceptual foundations of the model. For example, assessment in RTI has purposes that may be new to a teacher. If the teacher is not aware of the assessment for intervention dynamic embedded in the model, then they will not be successful at implementing it with fidelity. Consultee-centered consultation can be used to facilitate change in the conceptual understandings of the consultee.

4.3.4.2 Conceptual Understanding

RTI represents a conceptual shift in the goals of the provision of academic and behavioral interventions in classroom settings (see Table 4.1). It presupposes that a careful assessment for intervention will allow many students to have their needs met through the targeted delivery of efficacious instruction. The concept of direct linkage of assessment and intervention in the service of primary prevention differs substantially from the more common practice of assessment for tertiary intervention. RTI supplants the more passive wait-to-fail approach that typifies how children currently receive support. Presently, many teachers understand assessment as associated with standardized assessments that will be used in what amounts to the first tertiary intervention. Ms. Turner, a second-grade teacher typified this perspective when she told her school psy-

chologist "I need this child assessed so that I can get him out of my class and into special ed so he can get some help. Those folks might be able to do something for him." How will teachers and other implementers reconcile their preexisting belief that the best support for many struggling students will be to give up responsibility for struggling students and remove them from their present instructional environment?

Some implementers will have little trouble reconceptualizing their beliefs about when and where to first begin to intervene with students experiencing academic and behavioral problems. However, for teachers such as Ms. Turner there may be an unresolved conceptual disconnect between their preexisting beliefs and those that under gird the RTI model. When Ms. Turner was told by the school psychologist that the new policy in her school was to first undertake an assessment that would lead to an actual intervention her response was "What do you mean I can't refer this student (immediately) to the CST (Child Study Team)? Don't you want to help this child?" Implementers who share Ms. Turner's beliefs may face a mismatch between their current belief and skill (refer unsuccessful students on to the experts) and the principles of RTI (primary prevention, shared responsibility).

Consultee-centered consultation offers a process to help the implementer address this work problem of conceptual mismatch. First, the consultant will work to understand the implementer's beliefs and conceptualization of the relevant issues (role of special education, role of assessment). Using questioning and other communication skills, the consultant might ask "How do you see the problem? How is your view of the problem different from the view embedded in the RTI/EBI? What are the similarities between the two views?" After the consultant and consultee have jointly explored alternate ways to see the problem, the consultant will then help the consultee consider alternative ways and means to address the problem.

4.3.4.3 Skill Acquisition

RTI will require many implementers to acquire new skills. Some districts may have the funds and training time available to offer the ongoing professional development that will allow implementers to move beyond conceptual understanding and simple awareness of the issues embedded in the RTI model. However, in districts that do not provide implementers with an opportunity to practice simulations or to get feedback from a supportive coach other, mechanisms may be needed to support an individual's acquisition of skill. Consultee-centered consultation can be used to problem solve with the consultee about possible ways and means to gain needed practice (see Table 4.1).

In a systems example, an intervention facilitator was having a difficult time arranging for her IC team to meet. During the meetings the team members would, among other things, role play and provide each other with scenarios in which to practice their own coaching skills. However, the principal would not allow the team to meet during school hours, instead suggesting that the team meet Friday nights for dinner at a local restaurant. The team's acquisition of skills was thought by the facilitator to be suffering as a result. The facilitator met with her project consultant and initially conceptualized the problem as being about the personal relationship between herself and the principal in which neither she nor principal were going to budge, on principle. The consultation task was to first understand the facilitator's view of the problem and to then jointly reconceptualize the problem as one of the institutionalization of the intervention. Upon further discussion it became evident that the team had managed to develop a very cohesive structure for its members to acquire and practice skills; the problem was actually in how to go about making it a part of the school's problem-solving culture.

4.3.4.4 Application of Skills

In the Showers and Joyce model, the final aspect of professional development needed to implement a new intervention occurs through the application of the skills the implementers have learned, "for real" in the school. Accordingly, the RTI model must be practiced during application with appropriate feedback and discussion. Consultee-centered consultation may be used to help the implementer reflect on best practice, mistakes, or unexpected road blocks (see Table 4.1). Consultees may bring problems both large and small to the consultation. "Based upon the screening, half of my students need help with fluency skills, our RTI model says I'm to only pick the lowest 10% to work with." Or, "We keep running out of evaluation forms and my copying allowance is all used up." In either case the consultant will endeavor to understand the consultee's conception of the problem and then discuss and formulate possible alternative explanations and interventions.

Consultation can be used at each level of professional development to increase an implementer's ability to carry out an RTI model with understanding and fidelity. One RTI model, IC (Rosenfield and Gravois, 1996), uses consultation along the dimensions of implementation and professional development to support an implementer's acquisition of skills and the transportability of the model.

4.3.5 Instructional Consultation Teams

IC (Rosenfield and Gravois, 1996) was originally conceived of as an ecologically grounded model of consultation that incorporated the consultee-centered approach described in Caplan's (1970) model of mental health consultation. It is a structured, systematic, and data-driven problem-solving consultation process focused upon improving the instructional ecology of schools. One of the central goals of IC is to change how consultees (teachers) frame students' school problems away from viewing them as internal, child-centered deficits and toward understanding student learning as a result of the interaction of instruction, task and student entry skills. This perspective provides an intervention framework in which a student's instructional difficulties can be described as an instructional mismatch between a student's current instructional level, and the curriculum and instruction presented to the student.

IC interventions are designed to bridge the gap between a student's instructional level and instructional delivery in his or her regular education classroom by using the consultation process to help the teacher or consultee acquire new means to address a student's academic/behavioral problems.

The IC/RTI protocol (Gravois, Knotek, and Babinski, 2002; Gravois and Rosenfield, 2002) consists of six problem-solving steps: (a) contracting; (b) problem identification and analysis; (c) strategy and intervention design; (d) strategy and intervention implementation; (e) evaluation of strategy and intervention; and (f) follow-up, redesign, and closure. Overall, this RTI problem-solving sequence looks similar to what is already required by many pre-referral teams. Yet, experience tells us that in many Student Success Teams this sequence is often not followed with a high degree of fidelity or effectiveness (Knotek, 2003a,b). The IC model is unique because it has procedures in place to ensure the implementation and dissemination of the intervention. Of particular interest is how the model makes use of consultee-centered consultation to support and sustain the transportability of the IC intervention to unique school sites.

4.3.6 Transportability of Effectiveness within Instructional Consultation

Teachers will not master the fine points of curriculum-based assessment, charting, and intervention evaluation through the force of mandate or a 1-day workshop: some process has to occur in which concepts and skills are introduced and then mastered within the context of the teacher's own classroom. In IC, the consultant assumes responsibility for fostering the teacher's new conceptualization of the work problem and for developing new skills, while the teacher assumes responsibility for figuring out how to carry out the RTI steps within the context of her classroom.

The IC/RTI process does not leave teachers to their own devices to conceptualize and undertake an ecologically valid problem-solving intervention. The consultant provides a problem-solving framework that allows the consultee to pinpoint critical information and operationalize an aspect of student's academic functioning. For example, a nebulous presenting problem of "can't read" would be narrowed down through the use of a jointly con-

ducted RTI protocol in which a curriculum-based assessment would be used to evaluate a student's language and prior knowledge, word recognition, word study, responding, reading fluency, comprehension, and metacognition.

4.3.6.1 Consultation in Instructional Consultation

Consultation also supports the integrity of the problem-solving intervention by fostering the consistency of the implementation of each discrete step (Gravois and Rosenfield, 2002; Knotek, Rosenfield, Gravois, and Babinski, 2003). Through the application of a reflective communication strategy the consultant helps the consultee monitor his or her fidelity of implementation of each segment. For instance, sometimes teachers are not familiar with the emphasis on data-driven decisions, and this is problematic because each successive step of the IC/RTI protocol relies upon outcome data from the previous one. Teachers who are new to the RTI process have occasionally struggled with allowing data to disconfirm their initial hypothesis. Consultation is used to increase the teacher's awareness of their inconsistent use of data and the result is to expand the teacher's problem-solving repertoire to include an increased fidelity to data-driven decision-making.

4.3.7 Transportability of Dissemination within Instructional Consultation

All too often, intervention programs that are introduced into schools, even effective programs, fail to become embedded in the culture of the site and are allowed to flounder because they fail to include a mechanism for transportability into the design of the intervention. The IC/RTI model includes the implementation of an embedded teaming structure that facilitates the institutionalization of the RTI process into the school's problem-solving culture. IC teams consist of a facilitator who undergoes extensive consultation training and case manager/consultants, drawn from both teaching and specialist staff members, who meet weekly throughout the school year. The meetings consist of professional development (i.e., practice with decision-making with curriculum-based assessments), case monitoring, documentation, and administrator participation. The development of a collaborative problem-solving team culture is fostered through the facilitator's consultative engagement with the IC members. For instance, the facilitator uses consultation skills, such as asking clarifying questions, perception checking or summarizing, to support the team's development of group norms, including decision-based problem-solving and a constructive communication process.

4.4 Relevant Research

While there is a strong intuitive appeal and theoretical rationale for the use of consultation in RTI, the efficacy and effectiveness of the use of the procedure has not been empirically established. However, there is evidence for the effectiveness of consultation in general. Meta-analyses (Medway and Updyke, 1984; Sheridan, Welch, and Orme, 1996) indicate that consultation overall has an impact on issues such as consumer satisfaction, process integrity, and generalization. Knotek, Kaniuka, and Ellings (2007) propose that future studies of the effectiveness of consultation in support of the implementation of the RTI process occur across the four levels suggested by Kratochwill and Shernoff (2004): (a) Type I efficacy studies, (b) Type II transportability studies, (c) Type III dissemination studies, and (d) Type IV system evaluation studies.

4.5 Additional Directions

4.5.1 Establishing an Evidence Base for Response to Intervention during Pre-Kindergarten

An important future direction with regard to RTI will be to extend these concepts downward to pre-kindergarten programs. A recognition-and-response system is being designed to help parents and teachers respond to learning difficulties in young children who may be at risk for learning disabilities as early as possible, beginning at age 3 or 4 years, before children experience school failure and before they are referred for formal assessment (for a full report, see Coleman, Buysse, and Neitzel (2006)). The recognition-and-response system is based on an assumption that is consistent with the rationale offered for RTI, namely that the earlier we intervene

with children who may be at risk for learning disabilities, the more likely we will be to support their subsequent development and learning and to prevent other learning difficulties from occurring later.

Several key trends in education and the early childhood field serve as a context and an impetus for implementing a recognition-and-response system. For example, the pre-kindergarten movement and recent policies that emphasize early literacy and children's academic preparation as key goals during pre-kindergarten appear to be changing the definition of school readiness. Another contextual factor is the provision within the reauthorized IDEA that allows a local education agency (LEA) to use Part B funds to develop early intervening services for students in kindergarten through grade 12 (with an emphasis on students in kindergarten through grade 3) who have not been identified as needing special education or related services, but who need additional academic and behavioral support to succeed in a general education environment (see section 613 (f)(1)].

The conceptual framework for the recognition-and-response system is being developed with grant support from the Emily Hall Tremaine Foundation (http://www.treaminefoundation.org) through a collaborative effort that involves the FPG Child Development Institute, The National Center for Learning Disabilities (NCLD), the National Association for the Education of Young Children (NAEYC), the Communication Consortium Media Center (CCMC), and several key state partners. Collectively, these organizations and partners bring expertise in learning disabilities and early childhood education, as well as diverse perspectives from research, policy, and practice in both fields.

4.6 Relative Advantages and Disadvantages

Implementation of an intervention is a daunting task that requires major thought, planning, training, and effort. The research-to-practice gap (Schoenwald and Hoagwood, 2001) that may be anticipated to occur with the implementation and sustainability of RTI will have to be accounted for in a systematic and programmatic fashion. RTI will not happen in schools, let alone within districts or across states, without a robust professional development mechanism in place. As was discussed in this chapter, consultation may be useful as a meta-intervention to support the implementation, transportability, and dissemination of RTI within schools. However, consultation in the service of professional development is effortful and requires commitment and the expenditure of resources, such as time and patience.

References

Adelman, H. & Taylor, L. (2003). On sustainability of project innovations as systemic change. *Journal of Educational and Psychological Consultation, 14*, 1–25.

Baldwin, T. T. & Ford, J. K. (1988). Transfer of training: A review and directions for Future research. *Personnel Psychology, 41*, 63–105.

Bergan, J. R. (1977). *Behavioral Consultation*. Columbus, OH: Charles E. Merrill.

Bergan, J. R. & Kratochwill, T. R. (1990). *Behavioral Consultation and Therapy*. New York: Plenum Press.

Burns, B. & Hoagwood, K. (2002). *Community Treatment for Youth: Evidence-based Interventions for Severe Emotional and Behavioral Disorders*. New York: Oxford University Press.

Caplan, G. (1970). *The Theory and Practice of Mental Health Consultation*. New York: Plenum.

Coleman, M.R., Buysse, V., & Neitzel, J. (2006). *Recognition and Response: An Early Intervening System for Young Children at-risk for Learning Disabilities*. Chapel Hill: The University of North Carolina, FPG Child Development Institute.

Deni, J. (2004). Response to intervention: a school-wide problem solving model. Paper presented at the North Carolina School Psychology Association Annual Meeting, Wilmington, NC.

Gickling, E. E. & Rosenfield, S. (1995). Best practices in curriculum-based assessment. In A. Thomas & J. Grimes (Eds.), *Best Practices in School Psychology III* (pp. 587–595). Washington, DC: National Association of School Psychologists.

Glisson, C. (2002). The organizational context of children's mental health services. *Clinical Child and Family Psychology Review, 5*(4), 233–253.

Gravios, T.A, Knotek, S. E., & Babinski, L.M. (2002). Educating practitioners as consultants: the instructional consultation team consortium. *Journal of Educational and Psychological Consultation, 13*, 113–132.

Gravois, T.A. & Rosenfield, S. (2002). A multidimensional framework for the evaluation of instructional consultation teams. *Journal of Applied School Psychology, 19*, 5–29.

Gresham, F. M. (1989). Assessment of treatment integrity in school consultation and prereferral intervention. *School Psychology Review, 17*, 211–226.

Gresham, F. M. (2002). Responsiveness-to-intervention: an alternative approach to the identification of learning disabilities. In R. Bradley, L. Danielson, & D. P. Hallahan (Eds.), *Identification of Learning Disabilities: Research to Practice* (pp. 467–519). Mahwah, NJ: Lawrence Erlbaum.

Gresham, F. M. (2004). Current status and future directions of school-based behavioral interventions. *School Psychology Review, 33*, 326–334.

Hoagwood, K. (2001). Evidence-based practice in children's mental health services: what do we know? Why aren't we putting it to use? *Emotional & Behavioral Disorders in Youth, 1*, 84–87.

Hoagwood, K. (2003–2004). Evidence-based practice in child and adolescent mental health: its meaning, application and limitations. *Emotional & Behavioral Disorders in Youth, 4*, 7–8.

Hoagwood, K. & Johnson, J. (2002). School psychology: a public health framework I. From evidence-based practices to evidence-based policies. *Journal of School Psychology, 41*, 3–21.

Knoff, H. M. & Batsch, G. M. (1995). Project achieve: analyzing a school reform process for at-risk and underachieving students. *School Psychology Review, 24*, 579–603.

Knotek, S. E. (2003a). Bias in problem solving and the social process of student study teams: A qualitative investigation of two SST's. *Journal of Special Education, 37*, 2–14.

Knotek, S. E. (2003b). Making sense of jargon during consultation: understanding consultees' social language to effect change in student study teams. *Journal of Educational and Psychological Consultation, 14*, 181–207.

Knotek, S. E., Kaniuka, M., & Ellings, K. (2007). Mental health consultation and consultee-centered approaches. In W. P. Erchul & S. M. Sheridan (Eds.), *Handbook of Research in School Consultation: Empirical Foundations for the Field*. Mahwah, NJ: Erlbaum.

Knotek, S. E., Rosenfield, S., Gravois, T., & Babinski, L. (2003). The process of orderly reflection and conceptual change during instructional consultation. *Journal of Educational and Psychological Consultation, 14*, 303–328.

Knotek, S. E. & Sandoval, J. (2003). Introduction to the special issue: consultee centered consultation as a constructivistic process. *Journal of Educational and Psychological Consultation, 14*, 243–250.

Kovaleski, J. F. (2003). The three tier model of identifying learning disabilities: Critical program features and system issues. Paper presented at the *National Research Center on Learning Disabilities Responsiveness-to-Intervention Symposium*, Kansas City, MO.

Kratochwill, T. R. & Shernoff, E. S. (2004). Evidence-based practice: promoting evidence-based practice in school psychology. *School Psychology Review, 33*, 34–48.

Lambert, N. M. (2004). Consultee-centered consultation: an international perspective on goals, process, and theory. In N. Lambert, I. Hylander, & J. Sandoval (Eds.), *Consultee-Centered Consultation: Improving the Quality of Professional Services in Schools and Community Organizations* (pp. 3–20). Mahwah, NJ: Erlbaum.

McDougal, J. L., Clonan, S. M., & Martens, B. K. (2000). Using organizational change procedures to promote the acceptability of prereferral interventions services: the school-based intervention team project. *School Psychology Quarterly, 15*, 149–171.

Medway, F. J. & Updyke, J. F. (1985). Meta-analysis of consultation outcome studies. *American Journal of Community Psychology, 13*, 489–505.

Nastasi, B. K. (1998). A model for mental health programming in schools and communities: introduction to the mini-series. *School Psychology Review, 27*, 165–174.

Reschly, D. J. (2003). What if LD identification changed to reflect research findings? Paper presented at the *National Research Center on Learning Disabilities Responsiveness-to-Intervention Symposium*, Kansas City, MO.

Reschly, D. J. (2004). Commentary: paradigm shift, outcomes criteria, and behavioral interventions: foundations for the future of school psychology. *School Psychology Review, 33*, 408–417.

Rones, M. & Hoagwood, K. (2000). School-based mental health services: a research review. *Clinical Child and Family Psychology Review, 3*, 223–241.

Rosenfield, S. A. & Gravois, T. A. (1996). *Instructional consultation teams: Collaborating for change*. New York: Guilford Press.

Roy, P. (1998). *Teacher Behaviours that Affect Discipline Referrals and Off-Task Behaviours*. Springfield, VA: Eric Clearinghouse.

Schoenwald, S. & Hoagwood, K. (2001). Effectiveness, transportability, and dissemination of interventions: what matters when? *Psychiatric Services, 52*, 1190–1197.

Shapiro, E. S. (1994). *Academic Skills Problems: Direct Assessment and Intervention* (3rd ed.). New York: Guilford Press.

Sheridan, S. M., Welch, M., & Orme, S. F. (1996). Is consultation effective? A review of outcome research. *Remedial and Special Education, 17*, 341–354.

Showers, B. & Joyce, B. (1996). The evolution of peer coaching. *Educational Leadership, 53*, 12-16.

Walker, H. M. (2004). Commentary: use of evidence-based interventions in schools: where we've been, where we are, and where we need to go. *School Psychology Review, 33*, 398–410.

5

The Integration of Response to Intervention and Critical Race Theory–Disability Studies: A Robust Approach to Reducing Racial Discrimination in Evaluation Decisions

Markeda Newell and Thomas R. Kratochwill

Markeda Newell, MS, is a doctoral student in the School Psychology Program at the University of Wisconsin, Madison. mlnewell@wisc.edu
Thomas R. Kratochwill, PhD, is a Professor in the School Psychology Program at the University of Wisconsin, Madison. tomkat@education.wisc.edu

The response-to-intervention (RTI) model is a treatment-based approach to determining special education eligibility based on the student's responsiveness to evidence-based interventions (Batsche et al., 2005; Fuchs, 2003; Kratochwill, Clements, and Kalymon, 2007). This model is increasingly becoming recommended as the preferred approach to assessment and intervention for addressing a wide range of problems and disabilities among students, including learning disabilities, mental retardation, and behavioral disorders (Batsche et al., 2005; Fuchs and Fuchs, 1998; Gresham, 2005; Individuals with Disabilities Education Act, 2004). The RTI framework has much appeal because it brings renewed focus on intervening early with students, identifying students' needs based on risk, potentially reducing bias in the identification process, and improving student outcomes (Gresham, Vanderheyden, and Witt, in press). Furthermore, the move away from an exclusive use of the IQ-achievement discrepancy model of identification to a problem-solving approach used in the RTI model gives it a distinct advantage over current approaches to serving students who are experiencing difficulties in school (Fuchs and Fuchs, 1998; Fuchs, Mock, Morgan and Young, 2003; Kratochwill et al., 2007).

It has been asserted that one of the most promising aspects of the RTI model is its potential not only to reduce the number of children identified with disabilities, but also to reduce the number of minority children being placed in special education, particularly in the categories of mental retardation and learning disabilities (Fuchs, Fuchs, and Speece, 2002; Heller, Holtzman, and Messick, 1982). The potential for reducing the number of racially/ethnically diverse students in special education by applying the RTI model is important, because the disproportionate representation of racially/ethnically diverse students in special education is one of the most prominent, controversial issues facing researchers, practitioners, and policymakers in education today (Coutinho and Oswald, 2000; Donovan and Cross, 2002; Losen and Orfield, 2002) and in fact, has been an issue in psychology and education for some time (see Kratochwill, Alper, and Cancelli, 1980). More important, although the disproportionate representation of racially/ethnically diverse students in special education has persisted over four decades, there has been little success in resolving it (Coutinho and Oswald, 2000: Donovan and Cross, 2002; Dunn, 1968; Heller et al., 1982). Addressing these issues will be especially important, as there is strong evidence for increasing behavioral variation in US classrooms due, in part, to the growing diversity of the student population (Baker, Kamphaus, Horne, and Winsor, 2006). Nevertheless, there is optimism in the RTI model because of the potential it has to eliminate discrimination in the special education evaluation process and bring about meaningful change in the disproportionate representation of racially/ethnically diverse students in special education (NCCREST, 2005). However, to bring the RTI model to its full potential of addressing minority representation in special education, factors that contribute to the over- and under-identification of racially/ethnically diverse children need to be explicitly addressed within the RTI approach. In particular, implementing the RTI model without specific examination of racial bias and discrimination will not necessarily eliminate racial discrimination in the assessment, intervention, and the eligibility determination processes.

Reducing bias in instruction, assessment, and special education evaluation, particularly among diverse populations, is an integral part of the RTI model, but it is currently limited in its approach to significantly reducing discrimination in special education placements. Specifically, it is unrealistic to believe that racial discrimination can be completely eliminated; rather, a more appropriate goal is to reduce it as much as possible. More important, the strategies used in RTI models to eliminate racial discrimination may not reflect the complexity of the dynamic interplay of race and disability as social constructions that are used to systematically marginalize and exclude racially diverse students in education settings (Delgado and Stefancic, 2001; Ferri and Connor, 2005; Watts and Erevelles, 2004). Therefore, the purpose of this chapter is to introduce the critical race theory (CRT)–disability studies theoretical framework and illustrate how it can be integrated into RTI models to provide a more complex analysis of racial discrimination in an effort to bolster the effectiveness of RTI in reducing racial discrimination in evaluation decisions. To this end, a detailed examination of an RTI model and the strategies used in it to eliminate discrimination in placement is warranted.

5.1 Eliminating Discrimination in Special Education Evaluations: The Development of Response to Intervention

In 1979, the National Research Council (hereafter called The Council) was commissioned to investigate the disproportionate representation of racially/ethnically diverse students and males in special education (Heller et al., 1982). This investigation was sparked by the results of national survey data collected by the Office of Civil Rights within the US Department of Education, which revealed years of persistent disproportionate representation of racially/ethnically diverse students and males in special education. The Council was faced with the dilemma of trying to identify factors that could explain the disproportionate representation of these groups in special education (Heller et al., 1982). They decided that, rather than identifying the myriad factors that caused disproportionality, they would focus on identifying the conditions under which placement in special education was inappropriate and discriminatory. The Council explained that discrimination occurs when the child has: (1) received poor instruction in the regular education environment or missed a significant amount of instruction due to absences or disciplinary actions; (2) undergone an invalid referral or assessment process; and/or (3) received inadequate instruction or programming in special education. The premise of this argument is that placement in special education is appropriate when these discriminatory practices are eliminated (Heller et al., 1982).

Fuchs and Fuchs (1998) proposed an RTI model based on The Council's conceptualization of discrimination in special education placement and incorporated the strategies that The Council recommended into the RTI model to eliminate discrimination. Hence, RTI was designed as a "nonbiased" approach to special education identification, evaluation, and placement. However, it is important to note that, although the focus is on eliminating discrimination, there is no guarantee that the overrepresentation of racially/ethnically diverse children in special education will be reduced by using this method (Fuchs and Fuchs, 1998; Heller et al., 1982). To understand how discrimination can be eliminated in this process, an explanation of the Fuchs and Fuchs (1998) RTI model and the components designed to prevent discrimination can illustrate the process.

5.1.1 Dual Discrepancy Response to Intervention Model

Fuchs and Fuchs (1998) proposed a four-phase dual discrepancy RTI model to reduce the number of students identified with learning disabilities, as well as to reduce the overrepresentation of racially/ethnically diverse students in special education by eliminating discrimination in the identification process. The adequacy of classroom instruction and presence of a discrepancy between performance level and rate of growth in learning are evaluated in Phase I and II of the model respectively. That is, poor classroom instruction must be ruled out before assessment of the student's performance is conducted. If classroom instruction is adequate and the target student exhibits a dual discrepancy that is significantly below that of classroom peers, then that student enters Phase III of the RTI process. During Phase III, the teacher implements at least two evidence-based interventions in the classroom targeted at the discrepancy, and if these interventions do not improve the discrepancy, then the student moves into Phase IV. In this phase, the student is provided an intensive intervention that is reflective of special education services, and if this intervention reduces the discrepancy, then the student is evaluated for special education placement (Fuchs and Fuchs, 1998; Fuchs, Fuchs, and Speece, 2002). When racially/ethnically diverse students go through this process of evaluation and there is continued disproportionate placement, then it should not be considered a problem because, ideally, discrimination did not influence the evaluation. In fact, researchers argue that placement under these conditions would not only be appropriate but also equitable, because bias and discrimination have been eliminated (Fuchs and Fuchs, 1998; Heller et al., 1982).

It is clear that use of an RTI model may address several key aspects of the referral to placement process where discrimination can taint the process and render placement inappropriate. To explain, evaluating the quality of instruction in the classroom, eliminating the IQ-achievement assessment, implementing evidence-based interventions, and identifying effective interventions that improve outcomes as part of the special education program are the essential elements of the RTI approach that address discrimination. Harry and Klingner (2006) suggest that schools that serve predominately African–American and/or Latino populations overwhelmingly have inadequately prepared teachers that provide low-quality instruction, subjective assessment practices, and ineffective special education programming; therefore, using the RTI

approach is an important and significant step in reducing discrimination in serving diverse populations (see also Donovan and Cross, 2002; Kozol, 1992, 2005). However, as stated earlier, RTI is limited in its approach to eliminating discrimination. For instance, racial discrimination is a pervasive and oftentimes hidden phenomenon, especially within educational contexts (Bell, 1987, 1992; Losen and Orfield, 2002). Therefore, it is important to understand the fundamental mechanisms that underlie and subsequently reflect racial discrimination, which is the use of stereotypical, deficit-based constructions of racially diverse students that result in biased, inequitable treatment and oftentimes placement in special education (Connor and Ferri 2005; Haney Lopez, 1995; Harry and Anderson, 1999; Watts and Erevelles, 2004). To identify racial discrimination, it is essential to understand the complexities of how racial discrimination may function, particularly in educational contexts.

5.2 Complexities in Identifying and Reducing Racial Discrimination

Before discussing fundamental elements of racial discrimination, it is important first to outline further the context within which RTI is attempting to reduce discrimination. According to the National Center for Culturally Responsive Educational Systems (Klingner et al., 2005), disproportionate representation refers to an under- as well as overrepresentation of a group in a special education category relative to that group's representation in the school population. However, the overrepresentation of racially/ethnically diverse students in special education, especially African-American children in categories such as emotional behavioral disorder, mental retardation, and to a lesser degrees, learning disabilities has garnered much of the attention (Artiles, 1998; Donovan and Cross, 2002; Klingner et al., 2005). Many scholars have argued that disproportionate representation is a problem because it reflects biased and discriminatory practices and policies against racially/ethnically, culturally, linguistically, and economically diverse populations in educational settings (Artiles, 1998; Harry and Anderson; 1999; Harry and Klingner, 2006; Losen and Orfield, 2002; Patton, 1998). However, there is not a consensus on whether discrimination is the reason these students are overrepresented in special education (Artiles, 1998; Donovan and Cross, 2002; Harry and Klingner, 2006; Losen and Orfield, 2002; MacMillan and Reschly, 1998; Oswald, Coutinho, Best, and Nguyen, 2001). Some researchers contend that poor schools with low-quality teachers and the biological effects of poverty, such as poor nutrition, low birth weight, and inadequate prenatal health care, provide a better reason why racially/ethnically diverse children, especially African–American children, are overrepresented in special education (see Donovan and Cross, 2002; MacMillan and Reschly, 1998). Nevertheless, most would agree that racial discrimination should not influence the placement of racially/ethnically diverse students in special education; thus, efforts to ensure that its influence in the process is as minimal as possible are critical in tempering the debate over this issue.

5.2.1 Racial Discrimination

There have been several definitions of racial discrimination put forth over the years; however, Mickelson (2003) provides a comprehensive description that resonates within many educational institutions. According to Mickelson (2003, p. 1052), "racial discrimination in education arises from actions of individuals as state actors or institutions, attitudes, and ideologies, or processes that systematically treat students from different racial/ethnic groups disparately and/or inequitably." In this description of racial discrimination, the importance of individuals, as well as the institution to which they belong, is integral to acts of discrimination. That is, individual acts of discrimination are ineffective unless the institution within which it is perpetrated supports it (see Chesler, 1976). The interaction of individuals and institutional practices in maintaining and normalizing discriminatory acts is what makes racial discrimination so elusive and difficult to identify (Losen and Orfield, 2002). Mickelson (2003, p. 1057) poignantly explained, "simple instances of discrimination by a racist teacher are more identifiable than identifying complex cases of discrimination because they result from the cumulative effects of institutions' and peoples' actions conditioned by structure and culture and framed by history." Therefore, in trying to disentangle discrimination from unbiased practices and procedures,

being able to identify how racial stereotypes are reified in decision-making is the key. Doob (1993, p. 6) explains, "institutional racism is the prime factor maintaining racism" and these biased institutional practices center on stereotypes. For instance, some scholars have stated that African–American students are often stereotyped as intellectually inferior, undisciplined, violent, and lazy (see Delgado and Stefancic, 2001; Graves, 2004; Reyna, 2000; Watts and Erevelles, 2004) and these stereotypical views influence school professionals' views of a child and cause an increase in referrals to special education based on bias and prejudice (Harry and Klingner, 2006). Consequently, these beliefs can become inherent within the practices of the school and the schools can become reinforcers of racism.

Racial discrimination reflects a dynamic interaction between individual and collective acts of bias and inequitable treatment. In examining how racial discrimination explains the disproportionate representation of racially/ethnically diverse students in special education, researchers point to several examples of systematic inequities in education. For example, researchers have argued that unequal treatment of diverse populations, particularly in educational institutions (Artiles, 1998; Delgado and Stefancic, 2001; Graves, 2004; Southern Regional Council and 20 Robert F. Kennedy Memorial Foundation, 1974), is a fundamental reason why racial bias and discrimination, at least in part, explains the disproportionate representation of racially/ethnically diverse students in special education (Artiles, 1998; Connor and Ferri, 2005; Watts and Erevelles, 2004). This unequal treatment is largely manifested in the structural inequities, such as unequal funding in schools, inferior school structures, and resources at predominately racially/ethnically diverse schools. Moreover, poor-quality teachers and instruction are considered prominent forms of institutional bias that adversely affect students' opportunities to learn (Harry and Klingner, 2006; Klingner et al., 2005; Kozol, 2005). Moreover, the overrepresentation of students of color in the more subjective special education categories (i.e., mental retardation, learning disabilities, and emotional behavioral disorder) has provided evidence that the special education identification process is oftentimes biased and discriminatory. That is, deficit-based, negative constructions of racially/ethnically diverse students have contributed greatly to these disparities because these students are seen as less capable, inferior, deficient, and, thereby, disabled (Ferri and Connor, 2005; Gould, 1996; Harry and Anderson, 1999).

This conflation of race and ability at the individual and institutional levels forms the foundation of racial discrimination, which makes the placement of racially/ethnically diverse students in special education a complex issue. Harry and Klingner (2006, p. 6) remind us that "there may be bias in an institution not one individual who professes or explicitly displays bias, yet all members [of the institution] may be, by virtue of uncritical participation in the system, purveyors of biased practices." Hence, the focus of RTI on regular education instruction, assessment, and effectiveness of special education may not be sufficient strategies to significantly reduce racial discrimination in the placement of racially/ethnically diverse students in special education. Therefore, we advance the CRT–disability studies framework as a theoretical approach that can be integrated with RTI models to better identify potential racial discrimination when meeting the needs of racially diverse students.

5.3 Critical Race Theory–Disability Studies Framework

Integrating the CRT–disability studies framework with the RTI model can provide a comprehensive examination of individual as well as institutional bias and discrimination in the evaluation of racially/ethnically diverse students for special education. CRT–disability studies is an analytical framework that is the integration of CRT and disability studies, which are two theoretical approaches for understanding the problematic underpinnings of the social constructions of race and disability, respectively (Watts and Erevelles, 2004). By combining these two theoretical frameworks, not only are the distinctive features of each construction (i.e., race and disability) evident, but also the interaction between the two is made clear. It is the focus on the distinctive and concomitant effects of race and disability that facilitates a better understanding and recognition of racial discrimination. Historically, disability studies scholars have focused on ability, whereas critical race theorists have focused on race; however, there is growing recognition of how these two areas

of study inform and affect each other, particularly in schools (see Artiles and Trent, 1994; Ferri and Connor, 2005; Watts and Erevelles, 2004).

CRT is a theoretical approach to exposing how racism functions in America to oppress racially/ethnically diverse students, particularly African–Americans, to diminish its effects and achieve equality (Crenshaw, Gotanda, Peller, and Thomas, 1995; Delgado, 1995). On the other hand, disability studies is an area of study that is concerned with how disabilities are constructed and used to marginalize people who have differences in normative expectations of ability and behavior (Davis, 1997; Watts and Erevelles, 2004). The intersection of these two theories brings forth three major issues in the disproportionate representation of racially/ethnically diverse students in special education: (1) discrimination of racially/ethnically diverse students, (2) difference as disability, and (3) marginalization of racially/ethnically diverse students (Connor and Ferri, 2005; Erevelles, 2000; Ferri and Connor, 2005; Haney Lopez, 1995). Understanding these issues is integral to using the CRT–disability studies framework to reduce racial discrimination in the evaluation of racially/ethnically diverse students for special education.

The discrimination of racially/ethnically diverse students and difference as disability are predicated on the social construction of race and disability, which is a fundamental tenet of CRT and disability studies. Haney Lopez (1995) explains that race is a social construction because racial categories overlap, are fluid, and make sense only in relation to other racial categories and have no meaningful independent existence. On the other hand, the social construction of disability lies in how difference is received in the environment (Davis, 1997). That is, if the environment does not fit/accommodate individual differences or areas of impairment, then that person becomes disabled in that environment, such as general education classrooms or society (Davis, 1997; Erevelles, 2000; Foufeyrollas and Beauregard, 2001). These social constructions are problematic because they are based on the physical, intellectual, and behavioral norms of Whites, who are constructed as superior (Graves, 2004; Haney Lopez, 1995; Watts and Erevelles, 2004; West, 1993). Graves (2004) explained that Europeans, when they came to colonize America, brought with them their beliefs in a racial hierarchy. Consequently, to create social order in America, they used "physical differences . . . to determine an individual's worth" (p. x). As Graves (2004, p. x) explained, this use of physical differences "justified racism, [which is] the belief that groups were different in their very natures, and that these differences should be used to stratify society." In the creation of this racial hierarchy, Whites were defined as superior to other racial/ethnic groups (Haney Lopez, 1995); therefore, Whites were in the position to define acceptable norms, beliefs, and behaviors by which all other racial/groups were judged. Hence, deviations from those White norms were constructed or defined as problematic and indicative of inferiority to Whites (Watts and Erevelles, 2004). Therefore, racially/ethnically diverse students and those who have differences that do not reflect those normative expectations are constructed as inferior, deviant, and deficient (Artiles, 1998; Haney Lopez, 1995; Harry and Anderson, 1999; Watts and Erevelles, 2004). For this reason, it is important to realize that races and ability are not constructed in isolation, that is ". . . [as] races are constructed, ideas about race form part of a wider social fabric into which other relations, not least gender, class, and [ability], are also woven" (Haney Lopez, 1995, p. 170). Therefore, as races are socially constructed, gender, class, and ability are also tied into those racial constructions, resulting in specific views of gender, class, and ability within certain groups. For example, constructing African–Americans as intellectually inferior (see Gould, 1996) creates the belief that all African–Americans are less capable of academic endeavors, which can adversely influence school professionals' views, attitudes, and treatment of these students in educational settings (Harry and Klingner, 2006).

In explaining the issues of racial discrimination and difference as disability, CRT–disability studies shows us how the construction of racial groups has negatively influenced society's views of racially/ethnically diverse students, which precipitates discriminatory behavior. Moreover, it reveals how differences from White norms are seen as problematic. More important, when these two views intersect, racially/ethnically diverse groups are seen as different, thereby being conceptualized as a physical, academic, and behavioral problem in US society and its institutions. Herein lies how deficit-

based, stereotypical views of racially/ethnically diverse students are used to marginalize (i.e., expel/suspend or place in special education) them from educational environments.

The RTI model does not bring attention to the use of deficit-based constructions to discriminate and systematically marginalize students of color (see also NCCREST, 2005). Therefore, integrating it with the CRT–disability studies framework is a promising step towards reducing the multiple permutations of racial discrimination in education instead of isolating specific acts (e.g., poor instruction). Specifically, CRT–disability studies can be integrated in the RTI model to analyze how schools as institutions are biased against racially/ethnically diverse students, when school professionals interact with and make decisions about racially/ethnically diverse students based on deficit notions, and when disability is being used as a means to marginalize racially/ethnically diverse students in educational settings.

5.4 Integration of Response to Intervention with Critical Race Theory–Disability Studies

The multi-tier model of service delivery (e.g., three or four tiers) has been described as an efficient system to support the implementation of RTI in school-based settings (e.g., Batsche et al., 2005). For example, within a three-tier model of service delivery, students' needs are grouped into three tiers as a means to identify the level of intervention required to improve the performance of the students within that tier of service. Tier I represents the largest level of service delivery because it involves the provision of a high-quality curriculum and instruction and intervention to all students. Students are screened at this level to determine which students are not performing at a level comparable to their peers, and those students who lag behind receive Tier II services. In Tier II, students who are exhibiting academic or behavioral difficulties are provided interventions to remediate their challenges while maintaining their place in the regular educational environment. However, those students whose do not make sufficient progress receive Tier III services, where individual assessment and intervention

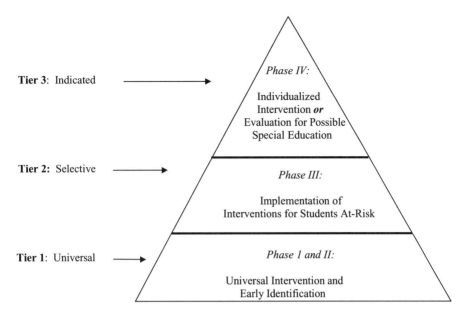

Tier 3: Indicated

Tier 2: Selective

Tier 1: Universal

Phase IV:

Individualized
Intervention *or*
Evaluation for Possible
Special Education

Phase III:

Implementation of
Interventions for Students At-Risk

Phase 1 and II:

Universal Intervention and
Early Identification

FIGURE 5.1. Dual discrepancy RTI approach in a three-tier model.

take place. At this level, students may be evaluated for intensive services such as special education. This three-tier model of service delivery is a useful framework to organize the provision of services within the RTI approach. Figure 5.1 depicts the dual discrepancy RTI approach within a multi-tier model of service delivery.

As can be seen in Figure 5.1, universal evidence-based interventions are implemented and early identification based on students' responses to those interventions occurs within the first tier of service delivery. As Fuchs and Fuchs (1998) explained in the dual discrepancy model, students who are experiencing difficulties can be identified early based on their response to a high-quality curriculum via screening measures (e.g., curriculum-based approaches). Once students with difficulties are identified, they enter Phase III of the RTI model or Tier II of service delivery. At this level, interventions are implemented to address specific area(s) of concern. Students who do not respond adequately at this level enter Phase IV of the RTI process or Tier III of services, which provides individualized evaluation for intensive services. Although this approach to service delivery allows for an efficient, treatment-based approach to identification of students for special education, the mechanisms to reduce the overrepresentation of racially/ethnically

diverse students in special education are unclear.

Thus, the dual discrepancy RTI model is designed to prevent specific acts of discrimination (i.e., poor instruction, invalid assessment, and ineffective special education programming) in the evaluation of students for special education (Fuchs and Fuchs, 1998; Heller et al., 1982). These critical steps in the RTI evaluation process provide practical, concrete areas to analyze how the social constructions of race and disability are inappropriately influencing the evaluation procedures, which would constitute racial discrimination. To analyze whether racial discrimination is occurring, school professionals need to be equipped with the analytical tools to recognize racial discrimination no matter what form it manifests. Thus, the dual discrepancy RTI approach within a three-tier model needs to be reconceptualized to include steps that help school professionals prevent and/or rectify racial discrimination during this process. The CRT–disability studies framework is an analytical tool that can be integrated into the process to meet this goal. In Figure 5.2, the CRT–disability studies framework (represented by the solid line) has been infused with the RTI approach (represented by the dashed line). The CRT–disability studies RTI approach occurs within a multi-tier model of service delivery.

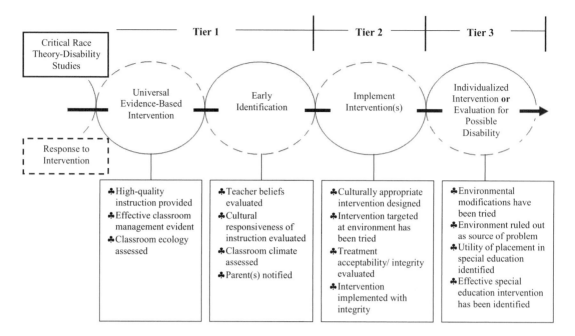

FIGURE 5.2. Dual discrepancy RTI model integrated with CRT–disability studies framework.

It is important to understand that, by implementing RTI using CRT–disability studies framework within a three-tier model, the goal of RTI expands from eligibility determination to the broader purpose of serving all students regardless of the level of services needed. This is an important distinction, because under this reconceptualized model the school professionals approach service delivery with the goal of providing interventions that improve the performance of the child and not identifying a disability for placement in special education. One of the primary goals of CRT–disability studies is to move professionals away from identifying within-person disabilities to identifying how the environment disables people and changing it so that the environment is accepting of and accommodating to individual differences (Davis, 1997; Foufeyrollas and Beauregard, 2001).

This environmental or "outside-the-individual" focus pervades every tier of service delivery within the CRT–disability studies RTI process. Nevertheless, the goal of this approach is not to focus solely on the environment; however, it is the starting point when identifying the source(s) of a problem because school psychologists traditionally have relied heavily on a within-child medical model of service delivery (Sheridan and Gutkin, 2000). This is under-

standable given that the three-tier model of service was developed in the medical field (see Kratochwill, 2006); therefore, the onus is on researchers and practitioners in school psychology to broaden this model to reflect the social context of education and the environmental factors that can contribute to and/or cause student difficulties. Figure 5.2 is described further below to illustrate how infusing the CRT–disability studies framework with RTI brings an ecological orientation to service delivery that can reduce racial discrimination and improve education for all students.

5.4.1 Early Identification

At Tier I, students who are not performing at expected levels, either academically and/or behaviorally, are identified. It is important to note, within this approach, that early identification can occur at the school-wide level (e.g., kindergarten screening) or classroom-level. Nonetheless, the process of identifying these students is critical, because it sets the educational trajectory for those students. That is, students who are appropriately identified can get the services they need and potentially thrive in the general education environment; however, those students who are not identified or inappropriately identified can have significant difficulties throughout their schooling. For this reason, accurate screening is essential in the early identification of students who experience educational difficulties.

In the process of screening ethnic minority students, under the CRT–disability studies RTI approach, school professionals should ask, "How are this child's difficulties different from that of other students and why do those differences warrant a more intensive level of service?" The rationale for asking this question is to determine whether the difficulties of racially/ethnically diverse children are perceived as more deviant/pathological than students who are not racially/ethnically diverse students. In this stage of service delivery, it is also important to evaluate whether the identification of difficulties among racially/ethnically diverse children is based on socially constructed, deficit-based views of the racial group of which that child is a member. To make this evaluation, the problem identification step has been emphasized in this reconceptualized model. The nature of the problem dictates future assessment and intervention decisions; therefore, when determining the problem, particularly when serving racially/ethnically diverse children, understanding whether and how racialized, deficit-based thinking is influencing school professionals is essential.

5.4.2 Problem Identification

During this stage of the process, students are in Tier I of service delivery and Phase II of the RTI process. More attention is given to problem identification in this model because, within the original dual discrepancy model, the area of difficulty is identified (e.g., reading below grade level) and the teacher implements a reading intervention (Fuchs et al., 2003). However, what if the problem lies outside of the technical aspects of reading? RTI models may fall short in thoroughly analyzing the problem and examining many potential causes or contributing factors to the problem. Therefore, within this model, problem identification becomes a more robust, ecological assessment-based approach to identifying why a child may be lagging behind his/her peers. Thus, during problem identification, it is important to determine the degree to which the teacher's attitude, expectations, and beliefs are adversely affecting the student's learning of the material. That

is, the curriculum may be effective; however, the effectiveness of the teacher in teaching racially diverse children may be the problem. CRT–disability studies work informs us that students of color are often seen as intellectually inferior and lazy (see Delgado and Stefancic, 2001; Watts and Erevelles, 2004); these beliefs can influence a teacher's attitude towards and effort in teaching that student (Doob, 1993; Reyna, 2000). Therefore, it is important during this phase to inquire about the strategies the teacher has used to help the student, the teacher's beliefs as to whether the child can learn the material, and the reason why the teacher thinks the student is not learning. The rationale for asking these questions is to determine whether the teacher and other professionals believe the student is the problem (e.g., lazy, uninterested in education, or incapable of learning) instead of the strategies being used to provide instruction. Secondly, the influence of the classroom climate should be evaluated to determine its affect on the delivery and reception of the instruction. This issue is important for all students, but in relation to racially diverse children the influence of race becomes central. Ferri and Connor (2005) argued that disability status is increasingly being used to marginalize students of color; therefore, professionals should consider whether the students are having trouble because the student feels excluded from the class.

Moreover, school professionals should directly observe the ecology of the classroom, evaluate the cultural responsiveness of the instruction, and rule out situational stressors that could be contributing to the development of the discrepancy. Under the CRT–disability studies framework, taking these steps moves the sole focus of the problem from within the child to the environment. Given the pervasive manner in which students of color are constructed as inherently inferior and pathological (Gould, 1996), explicit steps are needed to help school professionals evaluate external factors and directly analyze potential links to the problem. In addition, evaluating whether the instruction is culturally responsive may explain if the student is not performing well as the result of inadequate or inappropriate instruction. Ladson-Billings (1994) reveals that students of color perform better when the pedagogy is culturally relevant to the students, because it intellectually and socially empowers them in educational settings, which is integral to academic success. Finally, interviewing the student and/or family can shed light on situational stressors that may not be evident to the school professionals.

A prominent aspect of CRT–disability studies is that students of color experience a significant amount of stress due to their daily experiences as members of certain groups (Delgado and Stefancic, 2001; Ferri and Connor, 2005). For this reason, understanding how their experiences and life stressors are influencing their academic performance is essential in identifying the cause of the problem instead of moving forward with the belief that the child has an academic problem instead of a socio-emotional response to life events. It is important to realize that there is evidence of a problem if a student has made it to this phase. Therefore, whether there is a significant dual discrepancy or not, these steps should be taken to address the problem to prevent a significant discrepancy from developing later.

After these steps have been taken to accurately identify a child and the problem, the parents of the child should be notified. Excluding parents from participating in their child's education, particularly when concerns are raised, may reflect institutional marginalization of racially/ethnically diverse parents and reifies stereotypes that these parents do not value education or they do not care about their child's education (Harry, 1992). Therefore, if students are identified during this stage then parents should be notified and included in deciding how to proceed with the student. To decide whether the child should move to the next level of services (i.e., Tier II of service delivery or Phase III of RTI), school professionals along with parents and the child (if possible) should be able to answer the following questions: (1) Is the identification of the problem based on socially constructed, deficit-based views of the child? (2) How is the child's classroom/instructional ecology influencing the problem? (3) Does the problem primarily lie in the classroom ecology and not within the child? If the answer to the first question is yes then school professional(s) need to evaluate their own beliefs and determine how it influences their actions to certain racial groups of students so that it can be changed. Answering questions two and three can help professionals identify where the problem is situated so that they can intervene on the problem and not only target the student. Once these questions are answered, intervention(s) can begin.

5.4.3 Intervention

At the intervention phase, it is important to address how bias can be reduced during the selection, implementation, and evaluation of the intervention. When selecting an evidence-based intervention, within the CRT–disability studies framework, environmental variables (e.g., instructional format, classroom management procedures, and style) should be considered intervention targets first. Examining the environment or classroom ecology is a fundamental aspect of this approach to service delivery because the environment can be disabling the student. For example, the classroom may lack structure that exacerbates student behavior, peer relationships may be problematic, as well as teacher–student–family relationships, and differences in teacher tolerance for various types of behavior may pose problems for students. Therefore, examining the interaction between the child and the ecology of the classroom is necessary to select interventions that address the appropriate intervention target, which might not be the student.

Conversely, if the intervention is focused on the child then school professionals should attempt to better understand the student in a number ways. Oftentimes, if the problem manifests as academic failure there is a tendency to focus only on the academic needs of the child; however, other factors could be contributing to an academic problem. Hence, there needs to be a more comprehensive understanding of the student and their experience of the educational environment. To that end, school professionals can read literature from fields such as ethnic studies, anthropology, curriculum and instruction, sociology, and other fields of psychology related to the racial/ethnic, cultural, and linguistic characteristics of the child to better understand their experiences as members of this group within the United States educational system. Some comprehensive works on explaining issues related to racially/ethnically diverse students in the United States include Gibbs (2003), Ladson-Billings (1994), and Sue and Sue (2003). In addition, meeting with the child and the parents can provide invaluable insight into the strengths of the student, as well as what elements in the classroom environment may be adversely influencing performance. Furthermore, having professionals who are of similar racial/ethnic, cultural, linguistic, or economic background of the student can be useful in providing additional perspectives on the behavior that can lead to different explanations, interpretations, and, ultimately, interventions for the behavior.

In better understanding the student, professionals can design interventions that are more accurately designed to meet the needs of the child in a way that does not diminish or conflict with cultural attributes of the child. For this reason, culturally relevant interventions are important. There is a resurgence of focus on maximizing the cultural strengths of racially/ethnically diverse students to improve their educational experience and outcomes (APA, 2002; Ladson-Billings, 1995; NASP, 2006). Culture is important in education, because oftentimes miscommunication and misunderstanding between European–American educators and racially and culturally different children and families arise within educational contexts due to cultural differences in behaviors and beliefs (Hosp and Hosp, 2001; Ladson-Billings, 1995; Townsend, 2002). Tharp (1991) hypothesized those interventions that are more culturally compatible with the student the increased likelihood of the success of the intervention. Therefore, embracing a culture-centered approach to the education of diverse populations becomes integral to academic and social success of diverse students (Banks, 1998).

Culture-centered approaches have been integrated into educational settings in several ways. Most prominent of these approaches is multicultural competence of service providers (APA, 2002; Sue and Sue, 1999), multicultural education (Banks, 1998; Ladson-Billings, 1994), and culturally specific/relevant interventions (Gibbs, 2003; Hudley, 2001; Nastasi, Moore, and Varjas, 2004). Each of these approaches is distinctly important in educating diverse students; however, Banks (1993) asserted that multicultural education issues are equally important to the education of European–American students. However, it is important to understand that multicultural education has unique implications for diverse students. For example, Ladson-Billings (1994, p. 17–18) explained that "culturally relevant teaching is a pedagogy that empowers students intellectually, socially, emotionally, and politically by using cultural referents to impart knowledge, skills, and attitudes." As a result, students feel connected to the curriculum, instruction, and educational environment. Professionals may attempt to find specific interventions that are described as culturally relevant for the target student (e.g., see Banks, Hogue, Timberlake, and Liddle, 1996; Coard, Wallace, Stevenson, and Brotman, 2004; Hudley, 2001; Nagayama Hall, 2001). On the other hand, a more promising approach to designing culturally relevant interventions is the work of Nastasi et al. (2004). They developed a participatory model that assists professionals in developing interventions for diverse populations of students. The appealing aspect of this model is that professionals can design an intervention based on the needs and individual characteristics of the child, particularly if there is not an evidence-based intervention available. This model is useful in the RTI model because it does not set a specific type of intervention for specific types of student. Rather, the goal is to facilitate the design of interventions that are individualized to the unique needs and contexts of the student.

When implementing the intervention, it is also important to monitor treatment acceptability. It is important because the voices and perspectives of racially/ethnically diverse students have been, in some ways, silenced or devalued (Delgado and Stefancic, 2001). Therefore, in monitoring the progress of the intervention it is also important to monitor how the student and parents feel about the intervention and ideas they have to improve it or maintain it. Finally, in evaluating the intervention, if the outcomes are less than desirable then it is important to consider whether the intervention is effective with this population of students instead of attributed low outcomes to the student. CRT–disability studies informs us that institutional practices may not be representative of diverse populations and may in fact be inherently biased against diverse populations (Banks, 1998; Harry and Klingner, 1996). The intervention should be implemented with integrity; not all school professionals may believe the intervention will work, which may result in lower treatment integrity. At the end of this stage, school professionals and parents should answer the following question: "Have ecological interventions that are not focused on the child been implemented and evaluated?"

5.4.4 Evaluation for Special Education Services

During this phase, professionals are determining whether intensive services that are reflective of more traditional special education services will improve the discrepancy. During this phase, CRT–disability studies forces us to challenge the definition of disability. Specifically, professionals should ask themselves to what degree is the environment disabling students of color (Ferri and Connor, 2005). If there are clear patterns of how the educational environment is not serving large numbers of students of color, then how much of the problem is disability and how much of the problem reflects an unwillingness of professionals to effectively serve these students in the general education environment. Moreover, this situation begs the question of the utility of identification and classification. Is the goal marginalization? Is the goal to identify the other or rather those who are different? These important questions need to be raised and addressed in deciding whether the student should be placed in special education.

5.5 Concluding Perspectives

Implementing the CRT–disability studies RTI process within a multi-tier model of service delivery marks a shift in focus from eligibility determination to the provision of services to all children regardless of need. Therefore, when students at risk of school failure are identified early, the goal is to improve outcomes instead of identifying a disability. This is a significant paradigm shift in school psychology, because the decisions made in this field are often based on arbitrary metrics, which means the measures used to assess and evaluate students do not reveal all about that individual's stance on that construct (Blanton and Jaccard, 2006). Therefore, school psychology researchers and practitioners have to constantly challenge (and be critical) of the information gleaned from a score on a measure, particularly those that attempt to quantify abstract constructs such as intelligence, self-esteem, and prejudice. Kazdin (2006, p. 43) explained, "what we *call* measures or how we label individuals with a particular standing on a measure can be misleading in relation to the characteristic or construct of interest to us." Hence, identifying a disability may be of interest to school professionals, but the measures used to make those determinations may be flawed, which can result in inaccurate and inappropriate decisions. For this reason, CRT–disability studies is needed to create a critical approach to identi-

fying and intervening with students, particularly racially diverse students, so that negative, socially constructed realities are not reinforced by arbitrary metrics.

In this chapter, we explained how the CRT–disability studies theoretical framework could be integrated into the RTI model to provide a richer, more complex analysis of racial discrimination in an effort to bolster the effectiveness of RTI in reducing racial discrimination in evaluation decisions. It is important to recognize the significant strides that the RTI model has made in refining our thinking about identifying students with disabilities; and it has provided a foundation on which more refined, nuanced approaches can be built to continually improve the identification process. The racial discrimination of racially diverse children in education is an amorphous and oftentimes obscure phenomenon, and the conceptualization of discrimination within the RTI model has made it possible to meaningfully redress this problem in education. By layering the CRT–disability studies framework over the RTI process, school professionals can begin to ask questions that facilitate their ability to recognize when racial discrimination is interfering with an appropriate and valid evaluation of racially diverse students for special education. The integrated model advanced in this chapter is not exhaustive of all the questions and strategies that can be used to help reduce discrimination; however, it is a starting point that can be used to spur richer discussions and more in-depth analyses of biased decision-making. As discriminatory acts are revealed in these analyses, significant steps can be taken to create a more fair and equitable educational experience.

Acknowledgments. We would like to extend a special thanks to Jennifer Moy West, Kathy Short, and Paul Volpiansky for their valuable comments on this chapter.

References

APA (2002). *Guidelines on Multicultural Education, Training, Research, Practice, and Organizational Change for Psychologists*. Washington, DC: American Psychological Association.

Artiles, A. J. (1998). The dilemma of difference: enriching the disproportionality discourse with theory and context. *Journal of Special Education, 32*, 32–36.

Artiles, A. J. & Trent, S. C. (1994). Overrepresentation of minority students in special education: a continuing debate. *Journal of Special Education, 27*, 410.

Baker, J. A., Kamphaus, R. W., Horne, A. M., & Winsor, A. P. (2006). Evidence for population-based perspectives on children's behavioral adjustment and needs for service delivery in schools. *School Psyhology Review, 35*, 31–46.

Banks, J. A. (1998). Multicultural education. *Phi Delta Kappan, 75*, 21.

Banks, J. A. (1999). *An Introduction to Multicultural Education*. Boston: Allyn and Bacon.

Banks, R., Hogue, A., Timberlak, T., & Liddle, H. (1996). An Afrocentric approach to group social skills training with inner-city African American adolescents. *The Journal of Negro Education, 65*, 414–423.

Batsche, G., Elliott, J., Graden, J. L., Grimes, J., Kovaleski, J. F., Prassee, D., et al. (2005). *Response to Intervention: Policy Considerations and Implementation*. Alexandria, VA: National Association of State Directors of Special Education, Inc.

Bell, D. A. (1987). *And We Are Not Saved: The Elusive Quest for Racial Justice*. New York: Basic Books.

Bell, D. A. (1992). *Faces at the Bottom of the Well: The Permanence of Racism*. New York, NY: BasicBooks.

Blanton, H. & Jaccard, J. (2006). Arbitrary metrics in psychology. *American Psychologist, 61*, 27–41.

Chesler, M. A. (1976). Contemporary sociological theories of racism. In P. A. Katz (Ed.), *Towards the Elimination of Racism* (p. 21–72). New York: Pergamon.

Coard, S. I., Wallace, S. A., Stevenson, H. C., & Brotman, L. M. (2004). Towards culturally relevant preventative interventions: the consideration of racial socialization in parent training with African American families. *Journal of Child and Family Studies, 13*, 277–293.

Connor, D. J. & Ferri, B. A. (2005). Integration and inclusion – a troubling nexus: race, disability, and special education. *Journal of African American History, 90*, 107–127.

Coutinho, M. J. & Oswald, D. P. (2000). Disproportionate representation in special education: a synthesis and recommendations. *Journal of Child and Family Studies, 9*, 135–156.

Crenshaw, K, Gotanda, N., Peller, G., & Thomas, K. (Eds.) (1995). *Critical Race Theory: The Key Writings that Formed the Movement*. New York: New Press.

Davis, L. J. (1997). *The Disability Studies Reader*. New York: Routledge.

Delgado, R. (1995). *Critical Race Theory: The Cutting Edge*. Philadelphia: Temple University Press.

Delgado, R. and Stefancic, J. (2001). *Critical Race Theory: An Introduction*. New York: New York University Press.

Donovan, M. S. & Cross, C. T. (2002). *Minority students in special and gifted education. National Research Council. Committee on Minority Representation in Special Education*. Washington, DC: National Academy Press.

Doob, C. B. (1993). *Racism: An American Cauldron*. New York, NY: HarperCollins College.

Dunn, L. M. (1968). Special education for the mildly retarded: is much of it justifiable? *Exceptional Children, 23*, 5–21.

Erevelles, N. (2000). Educating unruly bodies: critical pedagogy, disability studies, and the politics of schooling. *Educational Theory, 50*, 25.

Ferri, B. A. & Connor, D. J. (2005). Tools of exclusion: race, disability, and (re)segregated education. *Teachers College Record, 107*, 453–474.

Foufeyrollas, P. & Beauregard, L. (2001). An interactive person–environment social creation. In G. L. Albrecht, K. D. Seelman, & M. Bury (Eds.), *Handbook of Disability Studies* (pp. 171–194). Thousand Oaks, CA: Sage Publications.

Fuchs, D., Mock, D., Morgan, P. L., & Young, C. L. (2003). Responsiveness-to-intervention: definitions, evidence, and implications for the learning disabilities construct. *Learning Disabilities Research & Practice, 18*, 157–171.

Fuchs, L. S. (2003). Assessing intervention responsiveness: conceptual and technical issues. *Learning Disabilities Research & Practice, 18*, 172–186.

Fuchs, L. S. & Fuchs, D. (1998). Treatment validity: a unifying concept for reconceptualizing the identification of learning disabilities. *Learning Disabilities Research & Practice, 13*, 204–219.

Fuchs, L. S., Fuchs, D., & Speece, D. L. (2002). Treatment validity as a unifying construct for identifying learning disabilities. *Learning Disability Quarterly, 25*, 33–45.

Gibbs, J. T. (2003). Children of color: Psychological interventions with culturally diverse youth. San Francisco: Jossey-Bass.

Gould, S. J. (1996). *The Mismeasure of Man* (revised and expand ed.). New York: Norton.

Graves, J. L. (2004). *The Race Myth: Why we Pretend Race Exists in America*. New York: Dutton.

Gresham, F. M. (2005). Response to intervention: an alternative means of identifying students as emotionally disturbed. *Education & Treatment of Children, 28*, 328–344.

Gresham, F., VanDerHeyden, A., & Witt, J. (In press). Response to intervention in the identification of learning disabilities: empirical support and future challenges. *School Psychology Review*.

Haney Lopez, I. F. (1995). The social construction of race. In R. Delgado (Ed.), *Critical Race Theory: The Cutting*

Edge (pp. 163–175). Philadelphia: Temple University Press.

Harry, B. (1992). *Cultural Diversity, Families, And The Special Education System: Communication and Empowerment*. New York: Teachers College Press.

Harry, B. & Anderson, M. G. (1999). The social construction of high-incidence disabilities: the effect on African American males. In V. C. Polite & J. E. Davis (Eds.), *African American Males in School and Society: Practices and Policies for Effective Education* (pp. 34–50). New York: Teachers College Press.

Harry, B. & Klingner, J. (2006). *Why are so Many Minority Students in Special Education? Understanding Race and Disability in Schools*. New York: Teachers College Press.

Heller, K.A., Holtzman, W.H., & Messick, S. (Eds.) (1982). *Placing Children in Special Education: A strategy for Equity. National Research Council. Panel on Selection and Placement of Students in Programs for the Mentally Retarded*. Washington, DC: National Academy Press.

Hosp, J. L. & Hosp, M. K. (2001). Behavior differences between African American and Caucasian students: issues for assessment and intervention. *Education and Treatment of Children, 24*, 336–350.

Hudley, C. (2001). The role of culture in prevention research. *Prevention & Treatment, 4*(1).

Individuals with Disabilities Education Act (1997, 2004). 20 U.S.C. §§1400–1487.

Kazdin, A. E. (2006). Arbitrary metrics. *American Psychologist, 61*, 42–49.

Klingner, J. K., Artiles, A. J., Kozleski, E., Harry, B., Zion, S., Tate, W., et al. (2005). Addressing the disproportionate representation of culturally and linguistically diverse students in special education through culturally responsive educational systems. *Education Policy Analysis Archives, 13*(38). Retrieved January 2005 from http://epaa.asu.edu/epaa/v13n38/.

Kratochwill, T. R. (2006). Response to intervention: conceptual dimensions, methodological limitations, and practice guidelines. Paper presented at the *Annual Meeting of the American Psychological Association*, New Orleans, August.

Kratochwill, T. R., Alper, S., & Cancelli, A. A. (1980). Nondiscriminatory assessment: perspectives in psychology and education. In L. Mann and D.A. Sabatino (Eds.), *The Fourth Review of Special Education* (pp. 229–286). New York: Grune & Stratton.

Kratochwill, T. R., Clements, M. A., & Kalymon, K. M. (2007). Response to intervention: conceptual and methodological issues in implementation. In S. R. Jimerson, M. K. Burns, & A. M. VanDerHeyden (Eds), *The Handbook of Response to Intervention: The Sci-*

ence and Practice of Assessment and Intervention (chapter 3). New York: Springer.

Kozol, J. (1992). *Savage Inequalities: Children in America's Schools* (1st Harper Perennial ed.). New York: HarperPerennial.

Kozol, J. (2005). *The Shame of the Nation: The Restoration of Apartheid Schooling in America* (1st ed.). New York: Crown Publishers.

Ladson-Billings, G. (1994). *The Dreamkeepers: Successful Teachers of African American Children* (1st ed.). San Francisco: Jossey-Bass Publishers.

Ladson-Billings, G. (1995). Toward a theory of culturally relevant pedagogy. *American Educational Research Journal, 32* (3), 465–491.

Losen, D. J. & Orfield, G. (2002). *Racial Inequity in Special Education*. Cambridge, MA: Harvard Education Press.

MacMillan, D. L. & Reschly, D. J. (1998). Overrepresentation of minority students: the case for greater specificity or reconsideration of the variables examined. *Journal of Special Education, 32*, 15–24.

Mickelson, R. A. (2003). When are racial disparities in education the result of racial discrimination? A social science perspective. *Teachers College Record, 105*, 1052–1086.

Nagayama Hall, G. C. (2001). Psychotherapy research with ethnic minorities: empirical, ethical, and conceptual issues. *Journal of Consulting and Clinical Psychology, 69*, 502–510.

NASP (2006). *The Provision of Culturally Competent Services in the School Setting*. Bethesda, MD: National Association of School Psychologists.

Nastasi, B. K., Moore, R. B., & Varjas, K. M. (2004). *School-based Mental Health Services: Creating Comprehensive and Culturally Specific Programs*. Washington, DC: American Psychological Association.

NCCREST (2005). *Cultural Considerations and Challenges in Response to Intervention Models*. Denver, CO: National Center for Culturally Responsive Educational Systems.

Oswald, D. P., Coutinho, M. J., Best, A. M., & Nguyen, N. (2001). Impact of sociodemographic characteristics on the identification rates of minority students as having mental retardation. *Mental Retardation, 39*, 351–367.

Patton, J. M. (1998). The disproportionate representation of African Americans in special education: looking behind the curtain for understanding and solutions. *Journal of Special Education, 32*, 25–31.

Reyna, C. (2000). Lazy, dumb, or industrious: when stereotypes convey attribution information in the classroom. *Educational Psychology Review, 12*, 85–110.

Sheridan, S. & Gutkin. T. B. (2002). The ecology of school psychology: examining and changing our paradigm for the 21st century. *School Psychology Review, 29*(4), 485–502.

Southern Regional Council & 20 Robert F. Kennedy Memorial Foundation (1974). *The Student Pushout: Victim of Continued Resistance to Desegregation.* Washington, DC; Atlanta, GA: Robert F. Kennedy Memorial/Southern Regional Council.

Sue, D. & Sue, D. (1999). *Counseling the Culturally Different (3rd edition).* New York, NY: John Wiley & Sons, Inc.

Sue, D. W. & Sue, D. (2003). *Counseling the Culturally Different: Theory and Practice.* New York: Wiley.

Tharp, R. G. (1991). Cultural diversity and treatment of children. *Journal of Consulting and Clinical Psychology, 59,* 799–812.

Townsend, B. L. (2002). "Testing while Black": standards-based school reform and African American learners. *Remedial and Special Education, 23,* 222–230.

Watts, I. E., & Erevelles, N. (2004). These deadly times: reconceptualizing school violence by using critical race theory and disability studies. *American Educational Research Journal, 41,* 271–299.

West. C. (1993). Race matters. Boston: Beacon Press.

6
Potential Pitfalls of Response to Intervention

Joseph F. Kovaleski

Joseph F. Kovaleski, DEd, is a Professor of Educational and School Psychology at the Indiana University of Pennsylvania. jkov@iup.edu

The inclusion in the Individuals with Disabilities Educational Improvement Act (IDEIA, 2004) of the option for local education agencies (LEAs) to use an assessment of a student's response to intervention (RTI) as an alternative to the evaluation of a student's ability–achievement discrepancy in determining whether the student can be classified as having a learning disability (LD) has spawned much controversy and much hope. Because RTI is embedded in the nation's special education law, and is particularly connected with procedures for determining LD, much of the public discussion about RTI has focused on whether the assessment of RTI is psychometrically defendable and sufficiently comprehensive to verify the existence of LD (Batsche, Kavale, and Kovaleski, 2006). In addressing potential pitfalls of RTI, then, there is a temptation to conceptualize elements of this controversy as the critical issues facing the field in implementing RTI and the multi-tier model that has been inextricably tied to RTI (Batsche et al., 2005).

However, from a larger perspective, this controversy is rather isolated and probably time-limited. The more important issues relate to the potential of RTI, and the multi-tier model in particular, to provide a seamless system of evidence-based, proactive curricula and instruction, along with support structures that will allow school districts to bring all students to acceptable levels of proficiency in basic skills. The assessment of RTI assumes that students have been provided with explicit, evidence-based instruction of sufficient intensity and duration so that their responses to it can be genuinely determined. Such interventions are not conceptualized merely as short-term, analogue experiments to appraise how

students would respond to individualized instructional packages, but presuppose that an entire system of effective curricula and instruction is in place and that teachers use these practices pervasively and with high fidelity. Kovaleski (2005) has noted that the determination of RTI depends on the building of a sufficient infrastructure of evidence-based curricula and instruction and effective support services in every school so that the integrity of the interventions implied in RTI can be ensured.

When considering the future of RTI, then, it is important to reflect on how this concept and the multi-tier model impact on larger issues of school improvement as LEAs strive to meet the requirements of the No Child Left Behind Act (NCLB, 2002). It is clear that Congress created NCLB and IDEIA as mutually referential laws, in the expectation that schools would make adequate yearly progress (AYP) in bringing all students, including those in disaggregated groups (e.g., children with disabilities), to proficiency, with the goal of 100% proficiency by 2013–2014 (NCLB, 2002, §1111(b)(2)(F)). Consequently, in this analysis of potential pitfalls of RTI, it is necessary to emphasize the challenges that school districts will face in building the infrastructure that not only provides for the comprehensive and reliable implementation of RTI, but also creates the necessary environment so that all students will learn.

In this chapter, what school districts will have to do to establish a multi-tier model will be reviewed. Reflections will be presented on how school districts: (1) choose and implement evidence-based foundational curricula, (2) establish the system-wide use of effective teaching strategies, (3) use universal assessment and monitoring of students' basic skills to inform the instructional process for all students and to make programmatic decisions about individual students, (4) design and implement supplementary programs that impact students who display insufficient responding to the core curriculum, and (5) restructure and manage these activities with existing staff. Following this discussion, issues surrounding the use of RTI data that emerge from the implementation of the multi-tier will be addressed, leading to further thoughts about the future of special education and the construct of LD.

6.1 The Multi-Tier Model

As previously indicated, the assessment of RTI has been universally conceptualized as occurring within a multi-tier model (Batsche et al., 2005; Berninger, Stage, Smith, and Hildebrand, 2001). The number of tiers involved (typically three or four) has been formulated differently by various authors and organizations, and seems largely an issue of semantics at this point. To avoid this potential confusion, in this chapter the tiers will be identified as the benchmark phase, the targeted phase, and the ongoing support phase, and are described below.

6.1.1 Benchmark Phase

This phase corresponds to tier 1 in most depictions, and refers to provision of evidence-based practices to all students in general education classroom settings. It includes the selection and provision of scientifically validated core curricula; universal screening of all students on measures that are tied to local, state, or national standards of performance; and structures in which teachers work collaboratively to use the results of the universal screening to design instructional practices for all students.

6.1.2 Targeted Phase

In this phase, students who do not respond at an acceptable level to benchmark instruction are provided with individualized supports. This phase corresponds to "the middle tiers" of most multi-tier models and includes the provision of supplemental materials by support personnel both in the general education classroom ("push-in" services) and potentially outside of it ("pull-out" services). In this phase, the use of standard-protocol approaches, as described by Vaughn and Fuchs (2003), are emphasized. It is also at this stage that problem-solving teams such as instructional consultation teams (Rosenfield and Gravois, 1996), instructional support teams (Kovaleski and Glew, 2006), and problem-solving teams (Heartland Area Education Agency, 2001) are typically used to customize interventions. It should be noted that, although Fuchs, Mock, Morgan, and Young (2003) have conceptualized standard-protocol approaches and problem-solving approaches as alternative and different ways of delivering supports in this phase, it appears that this distinction is historical at this point, and that many LEAs will incorporate aspects of both approaches in the actual implementation of multi-tier models.

6.1.3 Ongoing Support Phase

This final phase addresses supports and services for students who display RTI profiles that indicate that it will take extensive amounts of time and intensity to approach desired levels of proficiency. This phase includes special education and its requisite comprehensive evaluation, as well as other long-term services for students who have extensive needs, but who are not eligible for special education.

6.2 Challenges in Establishing a Multi-Tier Model

6.2.1 Challenges at the Benchmark Phase

It has been suggested that the first tier of the multi-tier model is most critical, in that the provision of a robust core instructional program is the essential foundation on which the other tiers are based (Kovaleski and Glew, 2006). Batsche et al. (2005) have suggested that this phase should be capable of bringing at least 80% of students in general education to proficiency. For schools to realize these attainments, the following challenges will have to be met.

6.2.1.1 Provision of Scientifically Validated Core Curricula

The publication of the report of the National Reading Panel (2000) was a watershed moment for

American education. It can be argued that with this event American educators came to embrace scientific research as the basis for steering educational policy (in spite of some nay-sayers to the contrary). Sweet (2004) noted that NCLB used the term "scientifically based instruction" over 100 times in stating the expectation that research should serve as the basis for curriculum, instruction, and assessment, particularly in reading. The challenge for LEAs, then, is to construct core curricula that are based on scientific research and can be expected to facilitate the development of proficiency in students' basic skills when implemented with appropriate fidelity. Although curriculum publishers have been quick to change their advertising to claim that their products are research based, LEAs have rightly begun to take a *caveat emptor* approach to expensive curriculum purchases. In the reading area, a number of independent organizations, such as the University of Oregon (www.uoregon.edu) and the Florida Center for Research in Reading (www.fcrr.org), have developed internet websites in which guidelines for reviewing commercially available curricular products are presented. There are also reviews of various curricular products, in which the extent to which they provide coverage of the essential components of reading instruction (National Reading Panel, 2000) are rated. In the face of some cynicism regarding "what is scientifically based?", these services can help LEAs avoid the pitfall of setting teachers and students up for failure by not providing a sufficiently robust core program. Unfortunately, there seems to be less of a consensus on the evidence base of other curricular domains at this point in time (e.g., mathematics, science, social studies). There is also a lack of clear evidence-based practices in working with some population subgroups, notably English-language learners.

6.2.1.2 Provision of Effective Instructional Strategies

It has long been understood that there is a set of teaching strategies that are differentially effective in facilitating student learning (Stevens and Rosenshine, 1981). Nonetheless, there have been ongoing indications that teachers do not routinely use these practices (Kavale, 1990). For schools to attain high rates of proficiency in their general education programs, it is necessary for teachers not only to have

evidence-based curricula, but also to use effective teaching strategies in delivering them. The failure of LEAs to promote the widespread use of these practices is likely a result of a number of factors; however, one in particular is worthy of note in this context. Until very recently, school districts have not used research findings to guide selection and adoption of effective teaching strategies that are expected of all teachers. Rather, as noted by Ellis (2005, p. 12), "... we move from fad to fad ... ready ... to grasp at anything as long as it is *new.*" One need inspect any issue of *Educational Leadership*, the flagship publication of the influential Association of Supervision and Curriculum Development, to realize that American educators have too many ideas and not enough focus on the few that have been shown to work. What is needed at the local school district level is a full understanding of educational research, as well as methods of using research to identify effective instructional strategies, and single-minded adoption of a limited number of these strategies for widespread use in the school district. Once these strategies have been identified, it is critical for districts to ensure that all teachers are provided with comprehensive training and guided practice in their use. This training needs to include not only typical in-service vehicles (e.g., presentations by experts), but, more importantly, peer coaching (Joyce and Showers, 1988) and other tactics that facilitate actual use in classroom settings.

6.2.1.3 Universal Screening

In the last few years, many LEAs have realized the value of and have begun to implement periodic screening of all students on measures that are linked to established standards of proficiency. Widespread use of the *Dynamic Indicators of Basic Early Literacy Skills* (Good and Kaminski, 2005) and *AIMSweb* (Shinn and Garman, 2006) are two notable examples. Many districts have implemented these assessments in the benchmark phase as a way to predict students' eventual performance on high-stakes statewide and national proficiency exams, and evidence is emerging that these measures are useful for that purpose (Shapiro, Keller, Lutz, Santoro, and Hintze, 2006). However, it is also common to hear the report that districts do not share these data with teachers or provide little guidance as to how to use the data to guide daily instructional practice. To address this situation, Kovaleski and Glew (2006) have proposed that schools create "data analysis teams" in which the problem-solving process is used in the benchmark phase to review the data on all students, set goals for attainment for the entire group, and select strategies that will be used to reach the set goals by the next review. Based on procedures developed by Schmoker (2002), these teams are composed of all teachers in each grade level, the school principal, and other specialists as needed. Because an important feature of these teams is the reliable collection and analysis of the assessment data, school psychologists and other specialists have been frequently utilized as consultants in this process. Teams at each grade level meet approximately three times per year, soon after the collection of the periodic universal screening data. While many of the efforts toward periodic universal screening have focused on early literacy, the advent of assessment tools geared for upper grades, such as the *4Sight Benchmark Assessments* (Slavin and Madden, 2006), allow the data-analysis team process to occur at all levels. Based on some preliminary results (Lillenstein and Pedersen, 2006), it appears that this process supports teachers in using evidence-based core curricula and strategies of effective teaching, with commensurate gains in overall proficiency levels.

6.2.2 Challenges at the Targeted Phase

In the benchmark phase, school personnel work at the level of the whole group in general education, with the goal of improving overall instruction and realizing proficient performance for 80–90% of the school population (Batsche et al., 2005). In the targeted phase, students who lag behind their peers on universal screening measures are provided with additional supports. As in the benchmark phase, a number of challenges for implementing these procedures are apparent.

6.2.2.1 Identification of Evidence-Based Supplemental Materials

In spite of staggering financial expenditures, remedial education programs (e.g., Title I) have been frequently criticized for having minimal impact on the improvement of student attainments (Allington and Walmsley, 1995). Even intensive programs that provide one-to-one tutoring, such as Reading

Recovery, have displayed only moderate gains and have been criticized for not incorporating explicit instructional techniques (Hiebert, 1994). Recently, however, a number of researchers have reported impressive results with intensive instructional packages based on the essential elements of reading instruction (Rashotte, MacPhee, and Torgesen, 2001; Vaughn, Linan-Thompson, and Hickman, 2003). These "standard protocol" approaches feature the use of tightly structured teaching using commercially available instructional packages. These programs supplement the core curriculum and can be used by general education teachers, specialists, or trained instructional assistants to differentiate instruction in the general education classroom on an ongoing basis, or can be used in small homogeneous groups (three to six students) over approximately 10-week periods of intensive services (e.g., 30 min per day, 3 days per week). Similar to the reviews of core curriculum products, the aforementioned organizations (University of Oregon and Florida Center for Reading Research) provide internet-based analyses of the research on a number of these programs, which allows school districts to make prudent choices of these supplemental instructional materials. Once acquired, school districts will also need to ensure that support personnel use these materials at appropriate levels of fidelity. Although it is likely that many of these specialists will embrace the explicit approach to teaching basic skills that is embedded in these supplemental programs, for others these changes will require shifts in both philosophy and practice. It should be noted that, at this time, the availability of evidence-based supplemental materials in other areas (e.g., mathematics, science) is limited, and helpful product-review sources have not yet been developed.

6.2.2.2 Deployment of Resources

A historic problem with the provision of supplemental services is the failure to coordinate them into workable organizational structures. Reynolds, Wang, and Walberg (1987, p. 391) described the following scenario:

The principal reports that growing numbers of children with problems are being referred to her office, possibly because the existing specialized programs have been organized into a set of little "boxes" that leave many children "falling through the cracks."

Nearly 20 years later, this situation could aptly describe today's educational milieu. The problem often appears to be not a paucity of resources but the lack of the planful and strategic orchestration of them. What is called for is the systematic deployment of existing personnel targeted to students' needs as indicated by assessed data. Clearly, the school principal can be seen as the central coordinator of this function; however, a building-level team composed of key service providers to consult with the principal on how staff are assigned to various remedial activities can be readily imagined. Key to the creation of a more seamless system of supports is a regular review of the assessed progress of students (through the tiers) and the flexible assignment and reassignment of staff based on these needs.

For such a flexible, seamless system to emerge, some critical issues must be addressed. First, the proliferation of specialists who see themselves as performing only very narrow functions needs to end and must be replaced by a cadre of generic service providers (e.g., literacy coaches), who can flexibly be deployed to various groups of students across grade levels using an array of evidence-based supplemental materials. Second, rather than having different personnel who are trained in one type of intervention (e.g., Reading Recovery), these specialists must be cross-trained in a core set of the evidence-based practices that can be targeted to students with identified instructional needs. The challenge of revising job descriptions and blurring the lines between disciplines that have historically fostered unique professional identities (e.g., reading specialists, speech and language clinicians, etc.) will be substantial.

6.2.2.3 Progress Monitoring

It has long been understood that teachers who use ongoing progress monitoring to guide instruction evidence superior attainments with their students (Fuchs, 1986). Nonetheless, procedures such as curriculum-based measurement (CBM) have been only sporadically implemented on a large scale in special education, and are virtually nonexistent among remedial educators. To monitor the effectiveness of the intensive interventions called for in the targeted phase, the critical features of CBM must be embraced and implemented by the staff that are providing these interventions. Specifically,

in this phase, direct assessment of students' progress should occur, ranging from twice a month to twice a week (depending on the extent of the student's deficiency), and the data should be graphed for inspection and reflection by the intervention specialists. Typical CBM conventions (e.g., aim lines, data-utilization rules) should be incorporated. The use of this assessment technology by nonspecial educators will require extensive training and, in many cases, paradigm shifts regarding the nature, purpose, and specific procedures of assessment. These changes of assessment practices will require informed leadership at the local, state, and national levels, so that expectations are set (e.g., changes in Title I plan requirements) and appropriate training provided.

6.2.2.4 Problem-Solving Teams

As indicated above, Fuchs et al. (2003) articulated the standard-protocol and problem-solving approaches to RTI in somewhat dichotomous terms. However, because both of these approaches have extensive empirical support, it appears there is no reason that practitioners need to choose between the two. Instead, these approaches can be seen as complementary in designing a comprehensive array of services in the targeted phase. In general, what seems reasonable is for standard protocol techniques to be used as the initial default interventions for typically observed performance deficiencies (e.g., poor performance on measures of phonemic awareness). When a student fails to respond satisfactorily to these approaches, the use of a problem-solving team to customize an intervention that matches the student's unique performance profile would be necessary. Kovaleski (2002) suggested a number of critical program features of problem-solving teams that are often overlooked in their implementation. These include so-called "system" factors, including strong principal support, collaborative teaming procedures, and the assignment of specific team tasks (i.e., student assessment, progress monitoring) to individual team members, as well as "process" factors, including the use of curriculum-based assessment, assigning team members to establish the intervention in the classroom and to plan for long-term instructional changes, and meaningfully involving parents in the process. Given Flugum and Reschly's (1994) seminal critique of the lack of fidelity of interventions designed by these teams, close adherence to these hallmarks of team functioning is indicated.

6.2.3 Challenges at the Ongoing Support Phase

Ongoing support in a multi-tier model is best conceptualized as including options provided by both general and special education. How this support is operationalized in both service areas will be addressed in this section. Because the multi-tier process has unique implications for special education, those challenges will be presented first.

6.2.3.1 Determining Eligibility for Special Education

As indicated earlier, the controversy surrounding RTI (Batsche, Kavale, and Kovaleski, 2006) has been limited to the question of whether RTI procedures alone are sufficient to identify students with LD. There seems to be only a few published concerns (Allington, 2006) about other ramifications of RTI and the multi-tier model. Even among critics of RTI, there is acknowledgement that the multi-tier model should be used at the "pre-referral" level (Kavale, Kaufman, Naglieri, and Hale, 2005). On the other hand, proponents of RTI acknowledge that procedures beyond the assessment of RTI are needed to screen other domains to rule out other disabling conditions (e.g., mental retardation, emotional disturbance) (Gresham et al., 2005). It is also widely understood that what comprises the full and individual comprehensive evaluation required by IDEIA for determination of eligibility will always be a prerogative of individual multidisciplinary teams.

Under an RTI model, the determination of LD would be made if the student displays a dual discrepancy (Vaughn and Fuchs, 2003)—academic skills that are significantly below benchmarks for the grade and a subnormal slope of progress in response to research-based interventions (along with the demonstrated need for special education that is required for eligibility under IDEIA). That these measures can be used to identify students with LD has been well established (Deno, Fuchs, Marston, and Shin, 2001). However, a number of questions remain that will need to be addressed as multi-tier models are brought to scale in individual LEAs or in

larger areas (i.e., regions, states). Yet to be addressed through empirical research are these issues:

- What percentage of students reaches proficiency solely by the provision of evidence-based core curricula in the benchmark phase?
- Is the percentage of students reaching proficiency in the benchmark phase improved by the systematic use of data-analysis teaming?
- What percentage of students needs intervention at the targeted phase?
- What percentage of students in the targeted phase succeeds and returns to the benchmark phase?
- What percentage of students in the targeted phase fails to display adequate progress and requires referral for evaluation for special education eligibility?
- How long do students spend in the targeted phase before they are returned to the benchmark phase or are referred for evaluation for special education eligibility?
- What are the profiles (extent of deficiency and slope of progress) of students identified as LD versus those not identified?

It is not proposed that these issues need to be ascertained before multi-tier models are implemented by LEAs. There is enough evidence from school districts and regions that have implemented dual discrepancy procedures (Marston, Muyskens, Lau, and Canter, 2003) that indicate that appropriate numbers of qualified students are identified as LD. Rather, these data will be useful in guiding new implementers of multi-tier models.

6.2.3.2 What is Special Education?

A question typically heard in discussions of RTI is: "If the interventions provided in the targeted phase are so intensive, what would be different in special education?" Indeed, descriptions of the interventions in the targeted phase often appear to be more intensive than what many students currently receive in special education. For example, McMaster, Fuchs, Fuchs, and Compton (2003) described these interventions as "special-education-like." What these musings reveal is how "watered down" special education has become in many areas since the passage of Public Law 94-142 in 1975. There is no evidence that the types of research-based intervention described above are routinely used in special education. Many special education programs still do not use CBM or other systematic methods of monitoring students' progress. In many special education programs, especially at upper grades, the teaching of basic skills has been abandoned and replaced by instruction in compensating skills or by tutoring in content subjects. It is little wonder that the outcomes for special education have been so dismal for so many years (Kavale, 1990; Reschly and Ysseldyke, 2002).

In a multi-tier system, in which intensive interventions in basic skill areas are provided both proactively in the general curriculum and reactively for students who display inadequate RTI, special education would look very different than what is seen in many programs today. Simply stated, special education in these systems would include pervasive and consistent use of research-based strategies for extended durations per day and over extended time periods. Barnett, Daly, Jones, and Lentz (2004) clearly illustrated the gradations of intensity needed at various phases of the multi-tier model in a number of relevant aspects of the educational program, including intervention management and planning, instructional routines, amount and type of assistance provided to students, increased individualized instruction, unique intervention episodes, specialized curricular materials, and specially trained personnel. One hope of the multi-tier model is that, if the number of students who are successful in the benchmark and targeted phases increases, fewer students will need special education, which would allow for the reduced teacher/student ratio that would be required for these changes to occur.

6.2.3.3 Ongoing Support in General Education

It would be overly optimistic to believe that the programs and supports provided in a multi-tier model will succeed immediately in bringing all students to acceptable levels of proficiency. Indeed, the goals set for this model at various tiers (Batsche et al., 2005) are ambitious, but genuine. Nonetheless, for a number of years it is likely that there will be substantial numbers of students who will be below basic levels of proficiency, but who will not qualify for special education. These students fall in one or both of the following categories: students who have not been exposed to evidence-based teaching, espe-

cially during the primary and intermediate grades, and students who have experienced frequent disruptions of schooling due to transience. These students would not qualify for special education because of the prohibition in IDEIA of identifying students as disabled if their deficiencies are a result of a lack of instruction. In addition, it is likely that many of these students, if provided with intensive instruction in the basic skills, would display deficiencies in level, but not in slope of improvement. Consequently, what is likely to emerge (or actually be acknowledged by school personnel) is a group of students in the middle to upper grades who are not in special education, are far behind benchmarks in basic skills, do not qualify for special education, yet need special-education-like programming to reach proficiency. The obvious answer to this challenging situation is that schools need to create general-education options that will provide the requisite level of explicit teaching in the basic skills using evidence-based instructional packages. At present, most secondary schools appear to be in denial about this obvious problem and its straightforward solution. A hopeful aspect of this situation is that the numbers of students in these situations should decrease over time if high percentages of students leaving elementary school reach proficient levels.

6.3 A Final Challenge: What is Learning Disability?

A particularly salient aspect of the controversy surrounding RTI is the significant disagreement about the nature and definition of the core construct in the debate (i.e., LD). This paradigmatic difference was graphically portrayed in the article by Batsche et al. (2006), in which differing viewpoints were presented in a debate format. Interestingly, both the pro-RTI respondent (Batsche) and the anti-RTI respondent (Kavale) agreed that deficiency from grade-level benchmarks is a *sine qua non* for LD. This perspective would eliminate from consideration for LD those students with high IQs who display average (or benchmark) performance in basic skills. That some students with this profile are currently identified as LD seems to reflect an erroneous belief among some assessment specialists that an ability–achievement discrepancy is the signal marker for

LD, regardless of the student's actual level of classroom performance. That is, bright students may be considered to have LD even if they are meeting benchmarks of proficiency. One ramification is that, in an RTI model, these students would not even be referred for evaluation for special education eligibility because they would be deemed as successful in the benchmark phase. This issue may have particular resonance for various advocacy groups and special education attorneys, who have often supported the notion that LD may include not only students who are significantly discrepant from grade- or age-level benchmarks, but also students who are proficient, but not working to "potential." This belief about the nature of LD is frequently different from that held by many practitioners, and considerable rancor between parents and LEAs (often in the form of due-process hearings) has resulted. State departments of education will have to provide training for administrative hearing officers, attorneys, and advocacy groups on the implications of the local adoption of RTI procedures for dispute-resolution procedures.

Both respondents also agreed that students with average ability who displayed persistent underachievement could qualify as LD, although the methods by which they would qualify were different. Batsche supported RTI procedures in making this determination, while Kavale argued that tests of psychological processing should be used to identify those students who display profiles indicative of LD.

The most significant difference between the two viewpoints, however, was whether students with subnormal IQs (although above the level of mental retardation) can be considered LD. Kavale's view was that the basic definition of LD includes only those students who have average IQs, and for whom underachievement is "unexpected." Batsche, on the other hand, took the position that IQ is not a marker for students' ability to learn basic skills (Fletcher et al., 2002) and that students previously viewed as slow learners, and historically excluded from special education, could qualify as LD if they displayed poor RTI. Kavale correctly pointed out that what is at stake here is the very definition of LD. Many authors who have challenged RTI desire to preserve the historic interpretation that students with LD must display IQs in the average range and prevent "diagnostic chaos" (Kavale et al., 2005, p. 24). The opposing view is that the construct of LD needs to change. As indicated by Fletcher et al. (2002), because there is no empirical connection between IQ and a student's ability to respond to effective instruction, all students (in ranges above mental retardation) should be expected to learn basic skills and, therefore, display "unexpected underachievement" (i.e., LD) when they fail to respond. As indicated by Stanovich (1999, p. 353):

[I]t is rare for advocates of discrepancy-based definitions to articulate the theory of social justice that dictates that society has a special obligation to bring up the achievement of individuals whose achievements fall short of their IQs, rather than simply to bring up the skill of those with low skills, period.

This issue is not merely a scholarly debate, however. School psychologists, special educators, parents, advocacy groups, lawmakers, and other critical stakeholders are likely to be challenged by the conceptual change regarding LD that logically follows from an RTI perspective. It can be predicted that many disagreements over eligibility for special education and individualized education plans will be based, not on procedural conflicts, but on these very different beliefs about what LD is or should be. As indicated previously, one group that will particularly need to grapple with this issue is hearing officers and administrative law judges who oversee due-process hearings. A full understanding of not only RTI procedures, but also who is legitimately diagnosable as LD through these procedures will be needed. Failure to adequately train these arbiters will create substantial hesitation among LEAs in adopting RTI procedures.

6.4 Summary

In reflecting on potential pitfalls in implementing a multi-tier model and RTI as its central operating procedure, a number of challenges were raised. Some of these challenges relate to the paradigms under which school personnel function: Can all children be expected to learn? What is LD? Others are about the hard work of putting into practice what is known to work in research settings. It is hoped that, in meeting these challenges, educators have reached consensus that their efforts should be judged by the impact they have on student outcomes.

References

Allington, R. L. (2006). Research and the three-tier model. *Reading Today, 23*, 20.

Allington, R. L. & Walmsley, S. A. (Eds.) (1995). *No Quick Fix: Rethinking Literacy Problems in America's Elementary Schools.* Newark, DE: International Reading Association.

Barnett, D. W., Daly, E. J., Jones, K. M., & Lentz, F. E. (2004). Response to intervention: Empirically based special service decisions from single-case designs of increasing and decreasing intensity. *Journal of Special Education, 38*, 66–79.

Batsche, G., Elliott, J., Graden, J., Grimes, J., Kovaleski, J. F., Prasse, D., et al. (2005). *IDEA 2004 and Response to Intervention: Policy Considerations and Implementation.* Alexandria, VA: National Association of State Directors of Special Education.

Batsche, G., Kavale, K. A., & Kovaleski, J. F. (2006). Competing views: a dialogue on response to intervention. *Assessment for Effective Intervention, 32*, 6–19.

Berninger, V. W., Stage, S. A., Smith, D. R., & Hildebrand, D. (2001). Assessment for reading and writing intervention: a 3-tier model for prevention and remediation. In J. W. Andrews, D. H. Saklofske, & H. L. Janzen. (Eds.), *Handbook of Psychoeducational Assessment: Ability, Achievement, and Behavior in Children.* San Diego, CA: Academic Press.

Deno, S. L., Fuchs, L. S., Marston, D., & Shin, J. (2001). Using curriculum-based measurement to establish growth standards for students with learning disabilities. *School Psychology Review, 30*, 507–524.

Ellis, A. (2005). *Research on Educational Innovations* (4th ed.). Larchmont, NY: Eye on Education.

Fletcher, J. M., Lyon, G. R., Barnes, M., Stuebing, K. K., Francis, D. J., Olson, R. K., et al. (2002). Classification of learning disabilities: an evidence-based evaluation. In L. D. R. Bradley & D. P. Hallahan (Eds.), *Identification of Learning Disabilities: Research to Practice.* Mahwah, NJ: Lawrence Erlbaum.

Flugum, K. R. & Reschly, D. J. (1994). Prereferral interventions: quality indices and outcomes. *Journal of School Psychology, 32*, 1–14.

Fuchs, L. S. (1986). Monitoring progress among mildly handicapped pupils: review of current practice and research. *Remedial and Special Education, 7*, 5–12.

Fuchs, D., Mock, D., Morgan, P. L., & Young, C. L. (2003). Responsiveness-to-intervention: definitions, evidence, and implications for the learning disabilities construct. *Learning Disabilities Research and Practice, 18*, 157–171.

Good, R. H. & Kaminski, R. A. (2005). *Dynamic Indicators of Basic Early Literacy Skills* (6th ed.). Longmont, CO: Sopris West Educational Services.

Gresham, F. M., Reschly, D. J., Tilly, W. D., Fletcher, J., Burns, M., Christ, T., Prasse, D., Vanderwood, M., & Shinn, M. (2005). Comprehensive evaluation of learning disabilities: a response to intervention perspective. *The School Psychologist, 59*, 26–30.

Heartland Area Education Agency (2001). *Procedures Manual for Special Education.* Johnston, IA: Heartland Area Education Agency.

Hiebert, E. (1994). Reading recovery in the United States: what difference does it make to an age cohort? *Educational Researcher, 23*, 15–25.

IDEIA (2004). *Individuals with Disabilities Education Improvement Act.* H. R. 1350, 108 Cong., 2nd Sess. (2004). Available online at http://frwebgate.access.gpo.gov/cgi-bin/getdoc.cgi?dbname=108_cong_public_laws&docid=f:publ446.108 on June 14, 2006.

Joyce, B. & Showers, B. (1988). *Student Achievement Through Staff Development.* White Plains, NY: Longman.

Kavale, K. A. (1990). Effectiveness of special education. In T. B. Gutkin & C. R. Reynolds (Eds.), *The Handbook of School Psychology* (pp. 868–898). New York: John Wiley.

Kavale, K. A., Kaufman, A. S., Naglieri, J. A., & Hale, J. B. (2005). Changing procedures for identifying learning disabilities. *The School Psychologist, 59*, 16–25.

Kovaleski, J. F. (2002). Best practices in operating prereferral intervention teams. In J. Grimes & A. Thomas (Eds.), *Best Practices in School Psychology IV* (pp. 645–655). Washington, DC: National Association of School Psychologists.

Kovaleski, J. F. (2005). IDEA reauthorization includes RTI: now what? *Communique, 34*, 26.

Kovaleski, J. F., & Glew, M. C. (2006). Bringing instructional support teams to scale: Implications of the Pennsylvania experience. *Remedial and Special Education, 27*, 16–25.

Lillenstein, J. & Pedersen, J. (2006). Data analysis teams: results from Cornwall–Lebanon School District. Unpublished manuscript, Lebanon, PA.

Marston, D., Muyskens, P., Lau, M., & Canter, A. (2003). Problem-solving model for decision making with high-incidence disabilities: the Minneapolis experience. *Learning Disabilities Research and Practice, 18*, 187–200.

McMaster, K. L., Fuchs, D., Fuchs, L. S., & Compton, D. L. (2003). Responding to nonresponders: An experimental field trial of identification and intervention methods. Paper presented at the *Responsiveness to Intervention Symposium*, Kansas City, MO.

National Reading Panel (2000). *Report of the National Reading Panel: Teaching Students to Read: An Evidence-Based Assessment of the Scientific Research Literature on Reading and its Implications for Reading*

Instructions. Washington, DC: National Institute of Child Health and Human Development, National Institutes of Health, US Government Printing Office.

NCLB (2001). *No Child Left Behind Act*. P.L. No. 107-110, 115 Stat. 1425 (2002). Retrieved online at http://www.ed.gov/policy/elsec/leg/esea02/index.html, June 14, 2006.

Rashotte, C. A., MacPhee, K., & Torgesen, J. K. (2001). The effectiveness of a group reading instruction program with poor readers in multiple grades. *Learning Disabilities Quarterly, 24*, 119–134.

Reschly, D. J. & Ysseldyke, J. E. (2002). Paradigm shift: the past is not the future. In J. Grimes & A. Thomas (Eds.), *Best Practices in School Psychology IV I* (pp. 3–20). Bethesda, MD: National Association of School Psychologists.

Reynolds, M. C., Wang, M. C., & Walberg, H. J. (1987). The necessary restructuring of special and regular education. *Exceptional Children, 53*, 391–398.

Rosenfield, S. & Gravois, T. (1996). *Instructional Consultation Teams: Collaborating for Change*. New York: Guilford.

Schmoker, M. (2002). *Results: The key to Continuous School Improvement* (2nd ed.). Alexandria, VA: Association for Supervision and Curriculum Development.

Shapiro, E. S., Keller, M. A., Lutz, J. G., Santoro, L. E., & Hintze, J. M. (2006). Curriculum based measures and performance on state assessment and standardized tests: reading and math performance in Pennsylvania. *Journal of Psychoeducational Assessment, 24*, 19–35.

Shinn, M. R. & Garman, G. (2006). *AIMSweb*. Eden Prairie, MN: Edformation, Inc.

Slavin, R. & Madden, N. A. (2006). *4Sight Benchmark Assessments*. Baltimore, MD: Success for All Foundation.

Stanovich, K. E. (1999). The sociopsychometrics of learning disabilities. *Journal of Learning Disabilities, 32*, 350–361.

Stevens, R. & Rosenshine, B. (1981). Advances in research on teaching. *Exceptional Education Quarterly, 2*, 1–9.

Sweet, R. W. (2004). The big picture: where we are nationally on the reading front and how we got here. In P. McCardle & V. Chhabra (Eds.), *The Voice of Evidence in Reading Research* (pp. 13–44). Baltimore, MD: Paul H. Brookes.

Vaughn, S. & Fuchs, L. S. (2003). Redefining learning disabilities as inadequate response to instruction: the promise and potential pitfalls. *Learning Disabilities Research & Practice, 18*, 137–146.

Vaughn, S., Linan-Thompson, S., & Hickman, P. (2003). Response to instruction as a means of identifying students with reading/learning disabilities. *Exceptional Children, 69*, 391–409.

II
Assessment and Measurement

7

Psychometric Considerations when Evaluating Response to Intervention

Theodore J. Christ and John M. Hintze

Theodore J. Christ, PhD, is an Assistant Professor of School Psychology at the University of Minnesota.
tchrist@umn.edu
John M. Hintze, PhD, is an Associate Professor of School Psychology at the University of Massachusetts at
Amherst. hintze@educ.umass.edu

As a part of eligibility determination, response-to-intervention (RTI) models use both the level and rate of skill acquisition to evaluate student response to both core instructional and supplemental interventions (Case, Speece, and Molloy, 2003; Fuchs, 2003; Fuchs and Fuchs, 1998; Fuchs, Mock, Morgan, and Young, 2003). As such, the level of student performance in targeted domains is compared with benchmark expectations and local peer performances (i.e., local norms). A substantial discrepancy in level is often an indication that an instructional change or intervention is necessary. The rate of student performance is also to standard expectations and local peer performances. Persistent and ongoing discrepancies in both level and rate are indicators that more intensive services are necessary, which might include those associated with special education (NASDE, 2005).

This chapter provides an integrative approach to measurement as it is likely to be applied to assessment and evaluation within an RTI framework. The approach is integrative in the sense that assessment and evaluation within RTI should rely on the best traditions of direct observation, time-series ideographic analysis, and an ecological orientation. However, RTI should also benefit from the psychometric literature. This chapter will provide an overview of psychometric theory and psychometrically oriented research to be considered when developing, selecting, or implementing measurement strategies within an RTI model. For those who evaluate RTI, this chapter will provide insight into the psychometric foundation for the most common methods of RTI.

7.1 The Relevance of a Psychometric Perspective

Assessment refers to the procedures and outcomes that are used to compile information that describe phenomena. Procedures and outcomes encompass the multiple methods (e.g., qualitative and quantitative) that might be used to gather information that is descriptive of the target phenomena. Within the realm of school psychology and special education, these methods are likely to include reviews of educational records, interviews, observations, and testing. Such multi-method procedures help to develop an understanding of the target phenomena and relevant influences. Such influences might include instruction, curriculum, environment, and learner characteristics (Heartland AEA 11, 2000; Howell, Kurns, and Antil, 2002).

Measurement refers to the procedures and outcomes that are used to quantify a phenomenon. Well-established measurement procedures and metrics have the potential to communicate information with precision and efficiency. It is useful to integrate common measurements into decision-making systems. For example, schools systems that adopt the procedures and metrics that correspond with curriculum-based measurement (CBM) of oral reading fluency (R-CBM) are likely to benefit from the commonalities associated with standardized approach to assessment. Members of the system can communicate information about the child's early reading development in terms of words read correctly per minute (WC/min). Rather than describing students as good decoders or poor decoders, educators can define the absolute level of student performance, such as 25 WC/min, or relative level of student performance, such as the 10th percentile. Throughout this chapter we will discuss important implications for how measurement procedures are developed and how measurement outcomes are used to guide educational decisions.

Within education and psychology, *psychometrics* is the study of measurement procedures and outcomes. In brief, psychometrics is the science that guides the development, selection, and compilation of procedures and instrumentation to quantify assessment targets. Such procedures and instrumentation include each of the following components: (a) tasks and/or stimuli that cue responses for measurement; (b) procedures that translate responses into numerical quantities (frequency, proportion, rate, duration, and latency); (c) transformation and contextualization of those quantities onto common scales and distributions; (d) the establishment of procedures to facilitate interpretation; and (e) evidence of outcomes to justify each proposed interpretation and use. Whereas issues of both reliability and validity are relevant to this discussion, the primary focus will be on the accuracy and reliability of measurement.

Finally, *evaluation* is the process of consuming data along with the results of interpretation that guide educational decisions. The implications of psychometric theory for RTI evaluations relate to both measurement (i.e., quantification of phenomena) and evaluation (i.e., interpretation and use) components.

7.2 Relevance of Multiple Measurement Perspectives

Psychometric support for specific assessment procedures should be developed and presented for each intended interpretation of a measurement outcome (AERA, APA, and NCME, 1999). There are unique expectations for assessments within the context of RTI. Data must be collected to facilitate the evaluation of both the level and trend of student performance. This expectation has been well established within the dual discrepancy model of RTI evaluations (Fuchs, 1995; Fuchs and Fuchs, 1998). Within an RTI dual discrepancy model, the validity of el-

igibility decisions hinges on the reliability of measurement and sound evaluation practices.

Relative (or *vaganotic*) measurement yields values that are dependent on some standard set of references (Johnston and Pennypacker, 1993). The meaning of any relative measurement outcome is interpreted in reference to a normative distribution (e.g., national or local norms) or criterion of reference (e.g., benchmark). Student performance on traditional achievement tests are typically interpreted *relative* to the performance of their peers. Within the context of an RTI approach, relative measurements are used to compare an individual's academic or social performance with that of their peer group or criterion value. Local data might be collected in the fall, winter, and spring of the academic year to establish distributions that define typical performance. These distributions are then summarized by statistics such as the mean and standard deviation, which then establish *what is typical* at each of three points in the academic year. Subsequently, the performance of each child is interpreted relative to the performance of their same-age and/or same-grade peers. With relative measures, it is common to use percentile ranks, stanines, quartiles, *t*-scores, *z*-scores, standard scores, or cut scores to facilitate interpretation. Such standard scales are common, and indicative of, measurements that are inherently relative. This is true of many measurements within the social sciences. *Their meaning is tied to the context, content, and normative sample* that was used to devise the psychometric characteristics of the instrument. The properties of measurement for most tests in education and psychology are substantially dependent on the calibration of the instrument for particular samples.

Absolute (or *idemnotic*) measurements yield values that have meaning independent of the measurement context (Johnston and Pennypacker, 1993). Such values are distinct from relative measurements, which were defined above. Absolute measurements (and interpretations) are more common in the natural sciences where scales of measurement are established in space and time. For example, liters, gallons, inches, and centimeters all have absolute values that may be interpreted independent of a comparison group. A person is 66 inches tall regardless of which ruler is used for measurement. The measurement value retains its absolute meaning regardless of the height among those in the cohort group. That raw score in inches has an absolute quality inherent to the outcome, which is distinct from a raw score on an achievement test. The raw score on an achievement test is dependent on the composition of the achievement test, item weights, and the references for interpretation (e.g., normative sample or criterion reference). Therein are the functional distinctions between relative and absolute measurements. The practical distinction is that absolute measurements are interpretable in and of themselves, whereas relative measurements are only interpretable in reference to an external criterion. A raw score of 50% on an achievement test is meaningless unless we have peer/age norms, criteria for expected performance, or additional measures of the individual's response (to establish growth or intraperson strengths and weaknesses).

Measurement outcomes have the property of either relative or absolute values. However, the interpretation and use of measurements can also be classified as either relative or absolute. That is, although a person's height can be measured in inches, which we have defined as an absolute measurement, the actual interpretation of that measurement outcome may depend, in part, on the age and gender of the individual. The mean height plus/minus standard deviation (SD) of an adult male is 70 (± 2.5) inches and the mean height ($\pm SD$) for an adult female is 64 (± 2.5) inches. Sixty-six inches is within the average range for a typical adult female, but below the average range for a typical adult male. The 66-inch tall adult female approximates the 79th percentile, whereas the 66-inch adult male approximates the 5th percentile. The intervention decision (e.g., to provide growth hormones) depends not simply on the absolute value of the measurement outcomes, but on expectations such as norms, as used above, or criterion values. In this way, absolute values are often interpreted within a relative context. This analogy extends to measurement and interpretation within RTI.

RTI combines the core features of both absolute and relative measurements (Hintze, 2006). Currently, CBM is the most likely procedure to be used for RTI evaluations of academic performance. CBM yields a direct measure of academic achievement in the basic skill areas of reading (R-CBM), mathematics (M-CBM), spelling (S-CBM), and written expression (Deno, 1985; Deno, Mirkin, and Chiang, 1982; Shinn, 1989). Each of these direct measurement procedures yields an absolute measurement outcome. In the case of R-CBM, the measurement yields a measurement outcome in WC/min. WC/min quantifies behavior in terms of time and space (i.e., oral reading), which establishes it as an absolute measure. A student who read 20 WC/min read half as many words as the student who read 40 WC/min. There is an absolute quality to R-CBM outcomes, so that a student who progresses from 20 WC/min to 35 WC/min over 3 weeks has indeed improved his/her oral reading fluency by 15 WC/min (i.e., 5 WC/min per week gain).

The metric of WC/min has an absolute measurement quality. The relative measurement quality is contributed by the context of observation. That is, assessors and evaluators must know the context in which the student read 20 or 40 WC/min. Some content is more difficult to read and other content is less difficult to read. Passage difficulty is likely to vary both within and across grade-level curricula (Fuchs and Deno, 1992; Hintze and Christ, 2004; Hintze, Daly, and Shapiro, 1998; Hintze, Owen, Shapiro, and Daly, 2000; Shinn, Gleason, and Tindal, 1989). If individual R-CBM outcomes are used as indicators of general performance in the curriculum (Fuchs, 2003; Fuchs and Deno, 1991) then there is an implicit assumption that one set of observations corresponds with a larger number of observations. That is, we assume our measurements are reliable across measurement occasions despite variability of stimuli (e.g., sentence complexity, vocabulary) across measurement instruments (e.g., reading probes). In this sense, it is insufficient to establish measurement accuracy and it is necessary to establish psychometric reliability and dependability.

7.2.1 Accuracy or Reliability

The accuracy and reliability of measurement are two related but distinct concepts. An evaluation of either accuracy or reliability is an evaluation of the correctness or trustworthiness of measurement outcomes. However, the two terms reference distinct properties of measurement. Cone (1981) defined *accuracy* as "how faithfully a measure represents objective topographic features of a behavior of interest (p. 59)." That is, an evaluation of measurement accuracy is an appraisal of the extent that quantified objective descriptions represent a confirmed/confirmable description of what occurred at some point in time.

Accuracy is frequently emphasized within the applied behavior analytic literature, where the correctness or trustworthiness of measurement is evaluated by comparing the consistency of outcomes across observers on a specific occasion (Hintze, 2006). There is no presumption that measurement outcomes should be consistent across measurement occasions. On the contrary, the assumptions of direct measurement and situational specific environmental influences are fundamental to applied behavior analysis. These assumptions support the use of accuracy as the most relevant criterion to determine correctness or trustworthiness or measurement. For example, when the rate of disruptive verbalizations is measured during a specified class period, the causal attributions relate to situational factors (e.g., environmental or biological events) that are free to vary across measurement occasions. The influential/causal factors are free to vary so that the rate of disruptive verbalizations is likely to fluctuate along with those factors. As a result of these commonly held assumptions within the field of applied behavior analysis, accuracy is typically used to evaluate correctness or trustworthiness instead of reliability.

In contrast to measurement accuracy, Cone (1981) defined *reliability* as "the consistency with which repeated observations of the same phenomena yield equivalent information (p. 59)." That is, an evaluation of measurement reliability is an appraisal of the extent that quantified descriptions represent a repeated/repeatable indication of some stable trait (across time, forms, situations, and occasions). It is assumed within the psychometric paradigm that measurement outcomes are substantially determined by stable internal characteristics that persist across measurement occasions. Therefore, variability across measurement occasions is attributed to measurement error. In contrast with the above example, where applied behavior analysts might measure the rate of classroom disruption, the psychometrically oriented psychologist is more likely to assess stable internal traits such as impulsivity or hyperactivity (which may be *inferred* from behavioral observations). The true state of an internal construct is generally thought to be a stable overriding influence on behavior. This point will become more explicit when the classical test theory (CTT; i.e., true score model) is presented below. The use of either accuracy or reliability criteria to

evaluate measurement outcomes corresponds with behavior analytic or psychometric orientations. Is the purpose of measurement to describe the relationship and corresponding environmental or biological contingencies? Or, do we assess to describe a persistent internal trait that guides the behavior of individuals? These two orientations correspond with the distinctions between accuracy (i.e., correct measurement representation) and reliability (i.e., consistent measurement representation) respectively. Accuracy is a necessary feature of measurement. This necessity is recognized within the psychometric framework, although it is substantially subsumed by inter-rater reliability (different term, but a concept substantially similar to accuracy). In that sense, accuracy is necessary but not sufficient within a psychometric framework. It is likely that accuracy is also necessary but not sufficient for RTI evaluations.

There are at least two general forms of reliability. The first is the reliability of measurement and the second is the reliability of effect. Both relate to consistency and replication. The *reliability of measurement* is the consistency of measurement outcomes within a specified set of conditions. It is established through intra-individual measurement across time, setting, and/or forms (Crocker and Algina, 1986; Sattler, 2001; Ysseldyke, Algozzine, and Thurlow, 2000). The *reliability of effect* is the consistency of behavior change across experimental conditions (Baer, Wolf, and Risley, 1968). It is established through repeated measurements across conditions/phases. Within an RTI framework, both the reliability of measurement and the reliability of effect are important to consider. However, the primary focus of this chapter is on the reliability of measurement rather than the reliability of effect. That is, it is necessary to infer that a set of measurement outcomes is indicative of typical performance. When R-CBMs are administered to assess oral reading fluency, the construct of interest is typically the child's oral reading within grade-level material, and it is not their oral reading performance on any specific passage. Psychometric reliability (especially alternate form and test–retest) is relevant because it depicts the likelihood that a single set of measurements corresponds with an alternate set of measurements that is derived from theoretically similar (testing) situations. That is, the psychometric framework facilitates the development of theoretical estimates of stability and confidence intervals. It is dangerous to guide decisions with measurements that vary substantially as a function of which alternate form(s) are used. It is generally assumed that students will perform at similar levels across alternate test forms and on alternate measurement occasions. Such assumptions should be tested using psychometric methods.

In the case of R-CBM, the measurement procedures are accurate to the extent that a single administration and observation reflects the occurrence of the target behavior (i.e., WC/min). A single observation could be recorded, measured/coded repeatedly, and agreement could be calculated (cf., Hintze, 2006). In a technical sense, that single measurement can have the property of accuracy, but it might not have the property of reliability. Accuracy can be derived from a single measurement; however, reliability cannot be derived from a single measurement. That single measurement is neither consistent nor inconsistent. The notion of reliability and consistency necessitate real, or theoretical, instances of repeated measurement. This is true from both behavior analytic and psychometric interpretations of reliability. Reliability of effect requires replication across conditions (e.g., demonstration of prediction, verification, and replication of effect within single-subject experimental designs, such as the reversal or multiple baseline design) to demonstrate the consistency of effect. Reliability of measurement requires either repeated observations of the same individual or the use of a theoretical foundation to infer consistency. What follows is a brief description of test theory that provides just such a foundation.

7.3 A Theoretical Perspective: Test Theory

The most substantial threats to RTI relate to the reliability and dependability of measurement. Both researchers and practitioners must develop an improved understanding of these issues. The following discussion attempts to clarify the theoretical foundation of two psychometric theories that are used to estimate the reliability and dependability of measurement. These are CTT and generalizability theory (GT) respectively.

7.3.1 Classical Test Theory and Reliability

CTT has been the foundation and predominant model for most psychometric work that has occurred over the past 100 years. The tenets of CTT were established by Spearman (1904, 1907, 1913), who proposed that the outcomes from educational and psychological measurements are test and sample dependent. That means measurement outcomes depend on both the context of measurement (e.g., difficulty of task demands) and th relative preparedness/ability of the individuals who are assessed. Those are foundational tenets of CTT that have been retained as it continued to develop through the 1950s, when its assumptions and applications were substantially developed (Crocker and Algina, 1986). The purpose of this section is to briefly describe the foundational ideas and implications of CTT as they relate to reliability.

7.3.1.1 True Score Model

The first assumption of CTT is that the observed test score is the sum of two theoretical components: the true score and the error score. Within the literature, the observed test score is denoted as X, true score is denoted as T, and error score is denoted as E. Using that notation, the *true score model is denoted as $X = T + E$*. Neither the true score nor error score can be observed directly. Instead, the true score and error score are both theoretical values that are used to explain and analyze the inconsistencies (i.e., variance) in test scores across repeated measurements.

The true score is a latent, or within-person, trait. As analyzed within CTT, the purpose of assessment is to estimate the true score value of a latent trait, such as oral reading fluency. However, the true score cannot be observed directly, so its value is estimated from the observed score. This estimation is done by first positing a set of assumptions. Although these assumptions can be set out in much greater detail, they can be summarized in three general statements: (a) the true scores and error scores are uncorrelated $[\rho(TX) = 0]$; (b) the error scores across parallel tests are uncorrelated $[\rho(EE') = 0]$; and (c) the mean of error scores is zero whenever there are a sufficient number of responses $[M(E) = 0]$ (Hambleton and Jones, 1993). When the true score model is combined with these assumptions, it can be shown that *the observed score is an unbiased estimate of the true score* for a particular test with a particular group. The clause "for a particular test with a particular group" implies that the *psychometric values are both test and sample dependent*. Stated another way, the observed scores and estimates of true score are substantially dependent on the measurement process. True scores across measurement instruments and alternate forms are not necessarily equivalent.

7.3.1.2 Sample-Dependent Behavior

A test is developed to estimate the true score value for a particular characteristic. For example, R-CBM is often described as an *indicator of early reading development*. Each person has an underlying ability (or skill set) to rapidly decode words in connected text. That characteristic is demonstrated and assessed within the specific conditions of an R-CBM test. It is erroneous to expect that an individual is likely to perform the same WC/min across test forms unless they are parallel. *Parallel test forms* are defined by two or more tests where a group of examinees have the same true score and error variance across forms. The practical method to evaluate test forms is to assess the same content and demonstrate substantially similar distributions of observed scores. In practice, parallel forms are difficult, and often impossible, to achieve. The solution is to depart from the parallel test assumption, to transform the observed test scores onto a common scale (e.g., z-scores), or to use one of the common methods to equate alternate forms. In practice, raw scores are rarely used in educational and psychological assessment. Scaled scores, such as standard scores ($M = 100, SD = 15$), t-scores (50, 10), and z-scores (0, 1), are much more common. In practice, the properties of both measurement and interpretation are relative in psychology and education. As discussed, the exceptions are those measurements derived from direct observation procedures.

Estimates of true score depend on the sample of items that comprise a test. That is, the reading performance among those in a group will depend, in part, on the items that comprise an R-CBM test. The sample group will perform at a lower level if the test is more difficult and at a higher level if the test is easier. In terms of R-CBM, the WC/min will

be lower when passages are more difficult ($M = 55$, $SD = 15$ WC/min) and higher when passages are less difficult ($M = 74$, $SD = 15$ WC/min). Typically, items are selected and tests are constructed to approximate average difficulty so that the distributions of test scores are approximately normal and equivalent across alternate test forms. In the case of R-CBM, researchers have used various indirect measures, such as readability, to estimate and control passage difficulty (Hintze and Christ, 2004; Hintze et al., 1998, 2000; Hintze and Pelle Petitte, 2001). However, recent research has begun to establish that direct measures of passage difficulty are superior (Ardoin, Suldo, Witt, Aldrich, and McDonald, 2005; Poncy, Skinner, and Axtell, 2005).

Estimates of item and test characteristics depend on the sample of examinees. Item characteristics, such as item difficulty and proportion correct, depend on the performance of the sample group. Test characteristics, such as the mean, variance, and reliability, are also sample dependent. Moreover, CTT has a limited flexibility to evaluate items independently of a fixed test. The majority of analysis and procedures have been developed to evaluate test outcomes, not particular items.

7.3.2 Generalizability Theory

GT is an extension of CTT that defines each behavior sample (i.e., student response or behavior) as a potential estimate of the universe score. The universe score is distinct from the notion of true score because it incorporates alternate nonparallel measures (discussed below). The language and conception of an observed score is also replaced with reference to *observations* or samples of behavior. These are minor shifts in language that represent more substantial shifts in test theory. GT is developed around a more flexible approach to assessment and less around a rigid approach to fixed tests and parallel test assumptions. The conditions of assessment are not strictly fixed prior to field testing and norming. Instead, the potential dimension for behavior samples and assessment is defined by measurement facets, which can be tinkered with after field testing to establish the most efficient assessment procedure for particular types of decision or purpose. These *facets* define the relationship between particular observations and the universe of generalization.

7.3.2.1 Universe and Universe Score

The universe score is similar but distinct from the true score within CTT. The *universe score* is the average level of performance for every admissible observation. Those observations are not necessarily restricted to a specific test or set of parallel tests. The definition for "every admissible observation" may be defined broadly or narrowly depending on the intended use of assessment data. For example, R-CBM procedures might be used to estimate the universe score on third-grade probes as administered by a school psychologist in a quiet test room. In contrast, R-CBM procedures might be used to estimate the universe score on second- through fourth-grade curriculum samples that are administered by either a school psychologist or paraprofessional in the setting of either a classroom or test room. GT can be used to analyze either the former more restrictive scenario or the latter more general set of scenarios. The latter case includes more facets, which are domains of generalization, such as probe difficulty, rater, and setting, and the levels of which (i.e., probe difficulty) might influence the outcomes of assessment.

GT is more flexible than CTT. GT provides a framework to analyze the *accuracy of generalizations from a particular set of observations to a larger universe of potential observations*. GT contextualizes the interaction between the individual and conditions of assessment, whereas CTT establishes a single assessment context (i.e., one test or parallel tests). There are a large number of possible R-CBM contexts, or facets, which might characterize observations and the corresponding universe of generalization. Of course, the total number of possible observations is too large to observe them all. GT provides a framework to analyze the accuracy of generalizing one or more observations to the estimate the universe score. Moreover, analysis can be conducted to examine the relative influence of multiple facets of measurement and for multiple interpretations of assessment outcomes.

7.3.2.2 Generalizability Study

A generalizability study (G-study) is used to estimate the proportion of measurement variance associated with the objects of measurement, which are usually person(s), facets of measurement, rele-vant interactions, and error. Assuming that R-CBM scores will be generalized across alternate forms and raters, then the model to examine variance will include persons (p), alternate forms (f), and raters (r), along with any relevant interactions and error. In this example, persons are the object of measurement. Both alternate forms and raters are the facets. A G-study is conducted to estimate the magnitude and proportion of total variance associated with each main effect and any interactions between persons, forms, and raters. Those outcomes are then used in the second (decision) study.

7.3.2.3 Decision Study

A decision study (D-study) is run to establish the accuracy of generalization from one observed score to the universe score of an individual (Brennan, 2003). D-studies are used to estimate the accuracy and sufficiency of a test score to estimate the universe score. The universe of generalization can be specified to include any or all of the facets from a G-study. In the example above, students were the object of measurement, and both alternate forms and raters were defined as facets. D-studies might be designed to evaluate the accuracy and dependability of scores to predict outcomes across various combinations of alternate forms and raters. Various D-study designs can be used if, for example, it was observed that generalization across alternate forms accounted for a relatively large proportion of the variance in the G-study. Such an outcome would suggest that R-CBM observations are substantially inconsistent across alternate forms. D-studies might be conducted to examine the consistency of measurement when a single form is used or combinations of multiple forms. The same could be done for raters (i.e., one rater versus multiple raters).

As discussed, estimates of reliability and the standard error of measurement (SEM) within CTT depend on a parallel test assumption. In GT there are two coefficients that are reliability-like (Brennan, 2003). The generalizability coefficient ($E\rho^2$) is an estimate of consistency that is substantially similar to reliability coefficients within CTT. Interpretation requires a parallel test assumption. However, within GT a dependability coefficient (Φ) can also be generated which *does not require a parallel test assumption*. The dependability coefficient can inform interpretation and generalization of absolute scores across facets that are not strictly parallel. For this reason, dependability coefficients and their corresponding estimates for standard error have the potential to contribute unique and useful information to the RTI literature, which often relies on absolute score interpretations.

7.4 Implications

This chapter was written to address one of the more substantial threats to RTI evaluations: the reliability and dependability of measurement. The validity of measurement methods within RTI is founded first on the consistency of measurement and second on the construct and criterion relevance. That is, unreliability prevents validity. Measures that yield inconsistent depictions of academic achievement have limited generalizability, or external validity. The distinction between reliability and accuracy was previously established. Accuracy is the extent to which a quantified objective description faithfully represents what occurred at some point in time. Accurate measurement does not necessarily yield consistent outcomes across time (only across raters at one point in time). In contrast, reliability is the extent that quantified descriptions yield a consistent indication of some stable trait. Reliable measurement(s) do yield consistent outcomes across time, forms, situations, and occasions. Measurement accuracy is sufficient only when measurement outcomes are not generalized beyond the specific circumstances of measurement. However, reliability (and/or dependability) is necessary if measurement outcomes are generalized beyond the specifics of measurement circumstances. Both accuracy and reliability are important features of measurement procedures that are used for RTI evaluations. Reliability is particularly important when the level and trend of academic achievement is examined.

7.4.1 Development of Instrumentation

Most of the instruments and procedures that are used for RTI evaluations were developed across both behavior analytic and psychometric frameworks. As discussed, the underlying assumptions of behavioral and psychometric paradigms might conflict or establish inconsistent assumptions (e.g., difference between relative and absolute measurements). For example, behavioral traditions are consistent with low-inference analyses of behavior through direct observation. Psychometric traditions are consistent with higher inference analyses of behavior to examine latent traits through indirect observation. In the case of R-CBM, the behavior analyst is likely to describe the target phenomenon as oral reading, whereas the psychometrician is likely to describe the target phenomenon as early reading development (and cite validity evidence to support the inference). The psychometric interpretation is both higher inference and more generalized than that of the behavior analytic interpretation.

The advent and development of G-theory has ameliorated some inconsistencies between behavioral conceptions of accuracy and reliability (Cone, 1986, 1987; Cronbach, Nanda, and Rajaratnam, 1972; Hintze, 2006; Hintze and Pelle Petitte, 2001). This is because G-theory can be used to analyze measurement variance disaggregated across sources/facets of measurement. Within G-theory, measurement outcomes can be used to estimate variance due to alternate test forms, items, raters, and observations. G-theory can also be used to examine relative and absolute score interpretations. Future research should continue to employ G-theory to examine measurements that are used within RTI.

7.4.2 Precision of Estimates: Standard Error

A dual discrepancy model for RTI evaluation requires the assessment and evaluation of both level and slope. An assessment of level is used to evaluate the student performance using either criterion or normative references. Students who are substantially discrepant from expected levels of performance are likely to be assessed further and/or receive additional services. Once students are provided additional services, the students' responses are assessed in terms of their slopes of performance. The rate of student growth may be evaluated against criterion, normative, or self-references. As assessment outcomes are used to estimate the level and trend of student achievement, the consumers of those data must be aware that some proportion of the variance associated with measurement outcomes is due to error. Such error is often associated with the conditions of assessment, including the particular raters, instruments, items, and environmental conditions operating during each measurement occasion. Despite the accuracy and sensitivity to student performance, the reliability of measurements is an important consideration when interpreting assessment outcomes. The evaluator must determine if a result would replicate given additional assessments.

The outcomes of recent research on CBM and related procedures guide the use of assessment and evaluation procedures within RTI. The majority of research has been optimistic in the potential applications of CBM and presented relatively few cautions. However, research by Hintze, Christ, and Keller (2002) has provided cause for caution. CBM and other direct observation rate-based procedures are highly sensitive to variations in student performance across measurement occasions (Christ, 2006; Christ and Schanding, 2007; Christ and Silberglitt, in press). Although such rate-based procedures are highly sensitive to instructional effects, they are also highly sensitive to variations in measurement conditions. That is, they are often highly accurate, but less reliable. This observation should encourage caution when using CBM or other highly sensitive rate-based procedures to infer the presence of an underlying stable construct.

The relevance of CBM within RTI evaluation has been well established (Deno, Fuchs, Marston, and Shin, 2001; Fuchs and Fuchs, 1998; Fuchs, Fuchs, Hosp, and Jenkins, 2001; Hintze and Pelle Petitte, 2001; Hintze and Silberglitt, 2005; Stage and Jacobsen, 2001). The previously cited research has established the need to improve reliability and dependability. For example, researchers must develop alternate forms of academic assessment that yield equitable estimates of performance across forms and measurement occasions. Until evidence is presented to support both relative and absolute interpretations of CBM outcomes, then assessors and evaluators might consider scaling and/or equating performance across CBM forms. In addition, assessment outcomes should be reported along with estimates of measurement error.

7.4.3 Scaling and Equating Tests

Optimal measurement conditions will employ parallel measurement forms across occasions. In lieu of those optimal conditions, test scores can be scaled and equated to enhance comparisons of measurement outcomes across alternate forms. In the previous sections of this chapter, we discussed relative and absolute values as they relate to both measurement and interpretation. We defined that the measurement metric for CBM (e.g., WC/min) is a measurement with an absolute value. Subsequently, we explained that the absolute value of WC/min might be subject to either an absolute or relative interpretation. The standard practice in school psychology and special education has been to maintain the absolute scale values of WC/min. However, an alternative is to transform those values on standard scaled scores (e.g., z-scores, t-scores, standard scores) or a unique set of scaled scores. Such values may be derived from local, regional, or national standards with aggregated and disaggregated normative groups. The actual comparison sample is determined by its relevance to an instructional decision. It seems the most relevant comparison sample would typically be that of the local schools and classrooms.

The majority of psychometric evidence that is cited in the literature to support the use of CBM (e.g., Marston, 1989) provides insufficient information to inform absolute interpretations of measurement outcomes. The majority of reliability evidence in the literature is based on CTT, which might overestimate the consistency of absolute values across assessment sessions. This means that, although there is evidence to support "alternate form reliability," those reliability coefficients are reported in the absence of the mean and SDs across forms. CTT reliability typically depends on Pearson correlation coefficients, which are based on deviation scores (i.e., relative interpretations). That level of analysis does not inform the interpretation of absolute values, especially if there are substantial inconsistencies in the means and variances across alternate forms. For example, two R-CBM passages of divergent difficulty could rank-order students with perfect consistency, which would yield a reliability coefficient of 1.00. Nevertheless, performance across passages could correspond with means of 50 WC/min and 75 WC/min. The first passage is more difficult and the second passage is easier (as indicated by student performance). Despite identical rank ordering across passages, any absolute interpretation of test scores would be confusing and might have an adverse effect on educational decisions. The average difference in performances across those two passages would approximate 25 WC/min. Thus, any one student could perform 60 WC/min on passage one (deviation score $= 50 - 60 = 10$ WC/min) and 85 WC/min on passage two (deviation score $= 75 - 85 = 10$ WC/min). The relative performance (and deviation scores) across passages might be identical (i.e., percentile rank of 60), whereas the absolute values of the measurement outcomes diverge substantially. If the data were graphed for self-referenced (within-subject) analysis, then interpretation would be error prone because of this discrepancy in the performances demonstrated to be associated with task difficulty.

Interpretation might be improved by scaling the mean level of performance across alternate forms. This is the most basic form of horizontal equating, which is only appropriate if the SDs across alternate forms are substantially similar given the target population (Crocker and Algina, 1986). That is, the mean level of performance across multiple passages (i.e., easy and difficult) could be placed at a fixed central mid-point to equate performance across tests. Data could be collected in the winter (e.g., mid-year) of an academic year. Group-level performance could then be analyzed across multiple passages within grades. If all students were administered all passages and equivocal standard deviations across forms, which typically range between 30 and 40 WC/min (Christ and Silberglitt, in press), the mean performance for each passage can be adjusted to a consistent grade-specific number. Given the available research on typical performance across grades, the R-CBM mean might be scaled to 30 WC/min for all first-grade probes, 70 WC/min for all second-grade probes, 100 WC/min for all third-grade probes, 120 WC/min for all fourth-grade probes, and so on. This practice would reduce the measurement error associated with variable passage difficulty, especially during progress monitoring. The procedure simply removes the absolute difference between mean performances across passages. For example, all second-grade passages would be scaled to have an absolute mean level of performance equal to 70 WC/min in the winter. If passage "A" had a mean performance level of 60 WC/min, then 10 points would be added to each student's score. If passage "B" has a mean performance level of 80 WC/min, then 10 points would be subtracted from each student's score. The effect is that the absolute level of performance on passages "A" and "B"

becomes comparable. Equated/scaled passages are more comparable than the raw scores of passages with inconsistent difficulties.

The mean equating method might be too simplistic for some applications. For example, this practice would be problematic if the SD across passages diverged substantially. In the case that the SDs were inconsistent across passages, evaluators might consider a full linear transformation onto an appropriate scale. The procedure is straightforward: (a) transform the WC/min to z-scores, (b) multiply each z-score by a predetermined value to fix the SDs, and (c) add the grade-specific value to each z-score value to adjust the mean. A simple Excel spreadsheet can be set up to transform all scores onto a common scale. Unfortunately, these transformed scores should be interpreted as relative and not absolute values, because the equal-interval scale is not maintained. The transformation removes the equal-interval property that previously existed in the absolute measurement values for WC/min. For that reason, a full linear transformation should be distinct from the distribution of likely WC/min values (e.g., second grade, $M = 75$ WC/min and $SD = 30$ WC/min). The new scale might be entitled the reading fluency scale (RF-scale) with a fixed SD of 20 and grade-specific means for first through fifth of 150, 250, 350, 450, and 550. This is not an optimal solution, but it is one solution to equate alternate forms with highly variable outcomes.

The use of a fixed scale and/or constant SD across passages will facilitate the use of common error estimates. The discussion in the next section encourages the use of error estimates whenever measurement outcomes are reported or interpreted. Because standard errors are derived from SDs and reliability coefficients, common scales or equated passages are likely to have fixed standard errors, which will facilitate their use.

7.4.4 Standard Error

The results of recent research provide impetus to integrate standard error when interpreting direct observation of social skills (Chafouleas, Christ, Riley-Tillman, Briesch, and Chanese, in press; Hintze, 2006) or academic behaviors (Christ, 2006; Hintze and Christ, 2004; Poncy et al., 2005). In relation to R-CBM, the results of recent research suggest that the SEM, as derived within CTT, is likely to approximate 5 to 15 WC/min (Christ and Silberglitt, in press). The actual magnitude of the SEM is likely to vary as a function of the assessment conditions, which include variables related to the administrator, distractions in the environment, and passage characteristics. The most typical generic estimates for SEM are likely to range from 8 to10 WC/min. In reference to the previous section on scaling, the estimate of SEMs in the range 8–10 WC/min does not account for inconsistencies in the absolute level of WC/min across alternate forms. Estimates of SEM can, and should (AERA et al., 1999), be used to construct confidence intervals around estimates of levels of performance. A 64% confidence interval may be constructed by multiplying 1 (z-score unit) by the SEM, and a 95% confidence interval may be constructed by multiplying 1.96 (z-score units) by the SEM.

A similar procedure can be used to evaluate slope. Recent estimates for the standard error of the slope (SEb) have been shockingly large, especially when growth is evaluated over relatively brief progress monitoring durations. For example, when R-CBM data are collected twice per week for 2 weeks the SEb is likely to approximate 2–17 WC/min per week (Christ, 2006). The actual magnitude of SEb will substantially depend on the conditions of assessment (e.g., consistency and control over administration conditions). Those estimates of SEb are very large relative to the likely magnitude of R-CBM weekly growth, which typically range from 0.5 to 2.5 WC/min (Deno et al., 2001; Fuchs, Fuchs, Hamlett, Walz, and Germann, 1993). The outcomes of such research suggest that high-stakes RTI-type decisions should not rely on R-CBM data that are collected over relatively brief periods. The magnitude of SEb after 10 weeks of data collection is likely to be within the range of 0.2 to 1.4 WC/min per week, and the magnitude after 15 weeks is likely to be within the range of 0.1 to 0.8 WC/min per week. Estimates of stability and confidence should be considered and evaluated whenever such data are used to guide educational and diagnostic decisions.

7.5 Concluding Comments

The graphic depictions of measurement data may be analyzed to glean the level, trend, and variability of assessment data. Multiple measurements are col-

lected and plotted to evaluate behavior within and across phases or conditions. RTI evaluations are not distinct from such practices that are fundamental to an inductive hypothesis testing framework. RTI evaluations are consistent with the analysis of effect; however, causal inferences are likely to be attributed without establishing experimental control. Experimental control is typically established by analyzing response across intervention phase reversals (ABA, ABAB, and multi-element designs), intervention phase delays (multiple-baseline and/or extended baseline conditions) or changing criterion designs. These designs that instill high internal validity and experimental control are not likely to be employed in practice. Instead, it is most likely that quasi-experimental designs will be used to evaluate RTI (e.g., AB or even B designs where treatment is evaluated without adequate baseline data). *In the absence of designs to establish experimental control, the reliability of effects cannot be established, which places much greater reliance on the reliability of measurement.* That is, the change in level or trend between phases is likely to be construed as causally related to an intervention. A nonexperimental design is much more susceptible to erroneous conclusions, especially when reliability and measurement error are ignored. Future research and implementation of RTI evaluations should examine psychometric issues of reliability more closely, especially as they relate to absolute and relative interpretations of measurement outcomes.

References

AERA, APA, & NCME. (1999). *Standards for Educational and Psychological Testing.* Washington, DC: American Educational and Psychological Research Association.

Ardoin, S. P., & Christ, T. J. (in press). Evaluating curriculum based measurement slope estimate using data from tri-annual universal screenings. *School Psychology Review.*

Ardoin, S. P., Suldo, S. M., Witt, J. C., Aldrich, S., & McDonald, E. (2005). Accuracy of readability estimates predictions of CBM performance. *School Psychology Quarterly, 20,* 1–22.

Baer, D. M., Wolf, M. M., & Risley, T. R. (1968). Some current dimensions of applied behavior analysis. *Journal of Applied Behavior Analysis, 1,* 91–97.

Brennan, R. L. (2003). Generalizability theory. *Journal of Educational Measurement, 40,* 105–107.

Case, L. P., Speece, D. L., & Molloy, D. E. (2003). The validity of a response-to-instruction paradigm to identify reading disabilities: a longitudinal analysis of individual differences and contextual factors. *School Psychology Review, 32*, 557–582.

Chafouleas, S. M., Christ, T. J., Riley-Tillman, T. C., Briesch, A. M., & Chanese, J. A. M. (in press). Generalizability and dependability of daily behavior report cards to measure social behavior of preschoolers.*School Psychology Review*.

Christ, T. J. (2006). Short term estimates of growth using curriculum-based measurement of oral reading fluency: Estimates of standard error of the slope to construct confidence intervals. *School Psychology Review, 35*, 128–133.

Christ, T. J. & Schanding, T. (2007). Practice effects on curriculum based measures of computational skills: Influences on skill versus performance analysis. *School Psychology Review*, 147–158.

Christ, T. J. & Silberglitt, B. (in press). Curriculum-based measurement of oral reading fluency: the standard error of measurement. *School Psychology Review.*

Christ, T. J. & Vining, O. (2006). Curriculum based measurement procedures to develop multiple-skill mathematics computation probes: Evaluation of random and stratified stimulus-set arrangements. *School Psychology Review, 35*, 387–400.

Cone, J. D. (1981). Psychometric considerations. In M. Hersen & J. Bellack (Eds.), *Behavioral Assessment: A Practical Handbook* (2nd ed., pp. 38–68). New York: Pergamon Press.

Cone, J. D. (1986). Ideographic, nomothetic, and related perspectives in behavioral assessment. In R. O. Nelson & S. C. Hayes (Eds.), *Conceptual Foundations of Behavioral Assessment* (pp. 111–128). New York: Guilford Press.

Cone, J. D. (1987). Psychometric considerations and multiple models of behavioral assessment. In M. Hersen & J. Bellack (Eds.), *Behavioral Assessment: A Practical Handbook* (2nd ed., pp. 42–66). New York: Pergamon Press.

Crocker, L. & Algina, J. (1986). *Introduction to Classical and Modern Test Theory*. Orlando, FL: Harcourt Brace.

Cronbach, L. J., Nanda, H., & Rajaratnam, N. (1972). *The Dependability of Behavioral Measures*. New York: Wiley.

Deno, S. L., Fuchs, L. S., Marston, D., & Shin, J. (2001). Using curriculum-based measurement to establish growth standards for students with learning disabilities. *School Psychology Review, 30*, 507–524.

Fuchs, L. S. (1995). Incorporating curriculum-based measurement into the eligibility decision-making process: a focus on treatment validity and student growth. Paper presented at the *National Academy of Sciences Workshop on Alternatives to IQ Testing*, Washington, DC.

Fuchs, L. S. (2003). Assessing intervention responsiveness: Conceptual and technical issues. *Learning Disabilities Research & Practice, 18*, 172–186.

Fuchs, L. S. & Deno, S. L. (1991). Paradigmatic distinctions between instructionally relevant measurement models. *Exceptional Children, 57*, 488–500.

Fuchs, L. S. & Deno, S. L. (1992). Effects of curriculum within curriculum-based measurement. *Exceptional Children, 58*, 232–242.

Fuchs, L. S. & Deno, S. L. (1994). Must instructionally useful performance assessment be based in the curriculum? *Exceptional Children, 61*, 15–24.

Fuchs, L. S. & Fuchs, D. (1998). Treatment validity: a unifying concept for reconceptualizing the identification of learning disabilities. *Learning Disabilities Research & Practice, 13*, 204–219.

Fuchs, L. S., Fuchs, D., Hamlett, C. L., Walz, L., & Germann, G. (1993). Formative evaluation of academic progress: how much growth can we expect. *School Psychology Review, 22*, 27–48.

Fuchs, L. S., Fuchs, D., Hosp, M. K., & Jenkins, J. R. (2001). Oral reading fluency as an indicator of reading competence: a theoretical, empirical, and historical analysis. *Scientific Studies of Reading, 5*, 239–256.

Fuchs, D., Mock, D., Morgan, P. L., & Young, C. L. (2003). Responsiveness-to-intervention: definitions, evidence, and implications for the learning disabilities construct. *Learning Disabilities Research & Practice, 18*, 157–171.

Hambleton, R. K. & Jones, R. W. (1993). Comparison of classical test theory and item response theory and their applications to test development. *National Council on Measurement in Education: Instructional Topics in Educational Measurement (ITEMS)*. Retrieved September, 2004, from http://ncme.org/pubs/items.cfm.

Heartland AEA 11. (2000). *Program Manual for Special Education*. Johnston, IA: Heartland AEA.

Hintze, J. M. (2006). Psychometrics of direct observation. *School Psychology Review, 34*, 507–519.

Hintze, J. M. & Christ, T. J. (2004). An examination of variability as a function of passage variance in CBM progress monitoring. *School Psychology Review, 33*, 204–217.

Hintze, J. M., Daly III, E. J., & Shapiro, E. S. (1998). An investigation of the effects of passage difficulty level on outcomes of oral reading fluency progress monitoring. *School Psychology Review, 27*, 433.

Hintze, J. M., Owen, S. V., Shapiro, E. S., & Daly, E. J. (2000). Generalizability of oral reading fluency measures: application of G theory to curriculum-based measurement. *School Psychology Quarterly, 15*, 52–68.

Hintze, J. M. & Pelle Petitte, H. A. (2001). The generalizability of CBM oral reading fluency measures across general and special education. *Journal of Psychoeducational Assessment, 19*, 158–170.

Hintze, J. M. & Silberglitt, B. (2005). A longitudinal examination of the diagnostic accuracy and predictive validity of R-CBM and high-stakes testing. *School Psychology Review, 34*, 372–386.

Howell, K. W., Kurns, S., & Antil, L. (2002). Best practices in curriculum-based evaluation. In A. Thomas & J. Grimes (Eds.), *Best Practices in School Psychology.* (pp. 753–772). Bethesda, MD: National Association of School Psychologists.

Johnston, J. M. & Pennypacker, H. S. (1993). *Strategies and Tactics of Behavioral Research* (2nd ed.). Hillsdale, NJ: Lawrence Erlbaum Associates.

Marston, D. B. (1989). A curriculum-based measurement approach to assessing academic performance: What it is and why do it. In M. R. Shinn (Ed.), *Curriculum-Based Measurement: Assessing Special Children* (pp. 18–78). New York: Guildford Press

NASDE. (2005). *Response to Intervention: Policy Considerations and Implementation.* Alexandria, VA: Author.

Poncy, B. C., Skinner, C. H., & Axtell, P. K. (2005). An investigation of the reliability and standard error of measurement of words read correctly per minute. *Journal of Psychoeducational Assessment, 23*, 326–338.

Sattler, J. M. (2001). *Assessment of Children: Cognitive Applications* (4th ed.). San Diego, CA: Sattler.

Shinn, M. R. (Ed.). (1989). *Curriculum-Based Measurement: Assessing Special Children.* New York: Guildford Press.

Shinn, M. R., Gleason, M. M., & Tindal, G. (1989). Varying the difficulty of testing materials: implications for curriculum-based measurement. *Journal of Special Education, 23*, 223–233.

Spearman, C. (1904). The proof and measurement of associations between two things. *American Journal of Psychology, 15*, 72–101.

Spearman, C. (1907). Demonstration of formulae for true measurement of correlation. *American Journal of Psychology, 18*, 161–169.

Spearman, C. (1913). Correlations of sums and differences. *British Journal of Psychology, 5*, 417–426.

Stage, S. A. & Jacobsen, M. D. (2001). Predicting student success on a state-mandated performance-based assessment using oral reading fluency. *School Psychology Review, 30*, 407–419.

Ysseldyke, J. E., Algozzine, B., & Thurlow, M. L. (2000). *Critical Issues in Special Education: Issues in assessment* (3rd ed.). Boston: Houghton Mifflin Company.

8
Decision-Making Validity in Response to Intervention

David W. Barnett, Renee Hawkins, David Prasse, Janet Graden, Melissa Nantais, and Wei Pan

David W. Barnett, PhD, is Professor of School Psychology at the University of Cincinnati. david.barnett@uc.edu
Renee O. Hawkins, PhD, is Assistant Professor of School Psychology at the University of Cincinnati.
renee.hawkins@uc.edu
David P. Prasse, PhD, is Professor and Dean, School of Education, Loyola University Chicago. dprasse@luc.edu
Janet L. Graden, PhD, is Professor of School Psychology at the University of Cincinnati. janet.graden@uc.edu
Melissa Nantais, PhD, is Educational Consultant at the Southwest Ohio Special Education Regional Resource
Center. nantais_m@swoserrc.org
Wei Pan, PhD, is Assistant Professor of Quantitative Educational Research at the University of Cincinnati.
wei.pan@uc.edu

Validity can be defined as the "approximate truth of an inference" (Shadish, Cook, and Campbell, 2002, p. 33). *Decision-making validity* can be viewed as the process of marshaling and weighing evidence to support actions (Messick, 1995). At first glance, these definitions alone do not sound too bad as criteria for professional decisions, but in considering response to intervention (RTI) we would need to include the validity of prevention efforts, measures and approaches to student selection, interventions in appropriate intensity sequences, and outcomes, among other variables, since we make inferences (i.e., conclusions) about all of these. Perhaps not surprisingly, there is a vast amount of literature that applies to the discussion of *decision-making* and *validity* that communicates both the strengths and weaknesses of human choice, the challenges of intervention evaluation, and, therefore, the many possible vulnerabilities of professional roles.

Professionals are valued when they assist with the highly challenging decisions needed to promote positive outcomes for individuals. To prepare for this role of decision-making consultant, professionals do the best they can by reviewing intervention research, applying problem-solving steps, and teaming. Consumers expect that professionals have mastered decision skills as well as validity ideals and apply them in a way that approximates perfection when offering advice, making instructional decisions, and

intervening with children. Decision-making validity addresses this tension in RTI practice through examining prior and ongoing evidence of effectiveness.

This chapter provides both a general discussion of issues relevant to decision-making validity and more specific recommendations for strengthening validity arguments when implementing an RTI model. The first part of the chapter provides an overall context for decision-making validity in RTI, highlights the importance of establishing validity as a way to improve confidence in decisions, and examines the types and sources of validity evidence. The second part of the chapter offers suggestions for ways to build validity arguments.

8.1 Overview of Decision-Making Validity Issues

8.1.1 Context for Validity of Decision-Making within Response to Intervention

Decisions made within an RTI model operate from a different set of assumptions, practices, and areas of focus relative to traditional decisions made in a test-based model, so it is important to first recognize some of these critical differences. Foremost is the emphasis in RTI on demonstrated student need based on outcomes using time-series data. This on-going consideration and use of data differs from the traditional approach that focuses on eligibility determination based on child disability conditions at a single point in time. Consistent with recommendations from the President's Commission on Special Education (2002) and the National Association of State Board of Directors of Special Education (Batsche et al., 2005), and as described in other chapters in this book, we rely on a tiered model for RTI implementation. Decision-making validity is central in this model, with emphasis on determining child service needs using scientifically based and empirically demonstrated instruction and intervention, making decisions based on time-series data across tiers of varying intensity of services, and using important, or socially valid, child outcome data to judge success or need for instructional or intervention changes. In some well-developed RTI models (see other chapters), decisions are solely based on need for services, with no categorical differentiation, which is most consistent with the emphasis of RTI. Specific issues for decision-making validity within this approach will be highlighted throughout this chapter.

8.1.2 A Primer on Intervention Decision-Making

Many human information variables have been studied in decision-making that impact professional behaviors (Hastie and Dawes, 2001; Kahneman, 2003). Among them include time pressures, the types and amount of information available, qualities of information displays, and the order in which information becomes available (Barnett, 1988). Even simply recasting the descriptions of children's behavior may significantly influence judgments (i.e., "a child is aggressive towards peers" versus a replacement behavior such as "we need to increase successful play bouts") (e.g., Hall, Ashley, Bramlett, Dielmann, and Murphy, 2004). A complicated array of data can increase feelings of confidence in decisions ("looks like we have everything well covered") while potentially increasing actual error (i.e., a critical variable is more likely to be obfuscated by a clutter of data).

Examples of judgment errors include (1) diagnosing and intervening based on ideas that come easily

to mind (*availability*), (2) limiting goals that may be set for children due to preconceived ideas about what they may be able to learn (*anchoring*), and (3) maintaining these initial biases, even despite data to the contrary, in favor of the preconceived ideas (insufficient *adjustment*) (Kahneman, 2003). In fact, individuals may not handle ambiguity and uncertainty all that well but these are pervasive characteristics of problem situations (Kahneman, 2003). Professionals may find themselves offering interventions that have been reinforcing to them because of past successes.

Errors of inference may be ubiquitous in decision-making and thus are not necessarily stamped out by RTI and problem solving or by another method. Answering questions addressed by validity is a major way to achieve confidence in decisions. However, new validity territory is introduced by RTI by shifting the focus to child outcomes and, therefore, raising questions of how to sequence interventions. A poorly planned sequence will consume unnecessary resources (if too intense), or unnecessarily keep a child in a prolonged failure experience (not sufficiently intense), or lead to erroneous conclusions (eligible as a child with a disability versus poor intervention sequence). Strategies to help reduce errors of intervention judgment include (1) applying a keystone target variable selection strategy functionally linked to success in typical environments and base rate information (Kame'enui, Good, and Harn, 2005; VanDerHeyden and Witt, 2005), (2) creating a range of plausible interventions based on prior research linked to the targeted variables, child characteristics, and supported by contextual or setting variables (Lentz, Allen and Ehrhardt, 1996), (3) communicating uncertainty, in that interventions result in likely *patterns* of outcomes and not specific outcomes, and (4) graphing student response data and applying valid decision rules to interpret data.

8.1.3 Confidence in Decision-Making

Practical validity questions for RTI have a dual role. First, practitioners will need to monitor progress at the system level to know that the overall RTI model is healthy and is doing its job in the best way possible. Outcomes supporting RTI validity indicating system health include reduced risk for children (e.g., improved reading outcomes, improved behavioral outcomes), as well as satisfaction from consumers and participants, and indicators of sustainability. For example, system (school or district) data would indicate increased reading performance in third and fourth grade as a result of K-1 early literacy skill screening and interventions (Tier I). Since RTI will continue evolving with regard to research on instructional and social interventions, interpreting and implementing research are significant examples of decision-making validity. Validity checks will lead to ongoing RTI design modifications with new research.

Second, RTI requires monitoring decisions made for selected groups of children and individual children. Decision-making validity includes questions about the psychometric adequacy and utility of measures and criteria (benchmarks) selected for RTI use. Measures need to be correctly selected and accurate, and, when interpreted by teams, they need to link children to the most promising instructional or intervention alternatives. Decision-making through development of rules for selecting students for interventions and determining adequate progress for students receiving interventions, and problem solving, are used to satisfy the objectives pertaining to group and individual outcome determination. In summary, validity evidence for measures, selection procedures, and intervention sequences stand at the center of the RTI decision process.

8.1.4 Validity Evidence

8.1.4.1 Reliability Jumpstarts Validity

Many measures may be used throughout RTI in order to create data for decision-making. Reliability, typically defined as the consistency of measurement, has a direct relationship to RTI validity evidence as it connotes the allowable confidence in scores or observations used for decisions (Nunnally and Bernstein, 1994). Reliability facets would include internal consistency and accuracy of administration and scoring (before starting), as well as consistency in measuring a set of skills, behavior, or performance during intervention (ongoing). Decision confidence increases with the number of observations, items, or scores, but not justifiably if measures are not reliable, valid, or well sampled. Error rates for combined facets of reliability (e.g., scoring, internal consistency, and retest) that mirror natural decision-making, in that error sources are simultaneously

active, are likely to be much higher than typically represented in test manuals (Macmann and Barnett, 1999).

Beyond instrument reliability, *procedural reliability* and the subset of intervention measurements known as fidelity, integrity, or adherence also underlie what can be said with confidence about intervention outcomes. Measures include not only student skill, performance, or behavior, but also include RTI model adherence and, ostensibly, instructional quality indicators from a verifiable model of instruction (e.g., Barnett, Ihlo, Nichols and Wolsing, 2006; McCardle and Chhabra, 2004; Twyman, Layng, Stikeleather, and Hobbins, 2005). In intervention research, low procedural reliability creates greater variability in outcomes that cannot be directly attributed to the intervention. By doing so, low procedural reliability creates lower effect sizes in research (Cohen, 1988) and questionable ethics in practice if decisions are made *as if* the intervention were carried out as planned (Gresham, 2004).

8.1.4.2 Construct Validity Connects the Dots

Construct use is pervasive in RTI, in that socially derived constructs are found in many areas of prevention, risk, and disability status, even though RTI constructs may not be recognized as such. Construct validity includes bigger ideas, such as academic achievement, social/behavioral risk, learning disability (chiefly because of its use as a federal category, although implementation varies by state – Iowa, for example, bases decision on need, not category), and RTI itself (e.g., Fuchs, Fuchs, and Speece, 2002). Construct validity also includes narrower domains or associated variables, such as reading (e.g., Fletcher and Francis, 2004; Kame'enui et al., 2005), academic or social engagement (e.g., Greenwood, Delquadri, and Hall, 1984), and intervention intensity (e.g., Barnett, Daly, Jones, and Lentz, 2004; Daly, Witt, Martens, and Dool, 1997; Gresham, 1991). From these examples, constructs are supported by networks of measurement as evidence. In RTI, child outcomes, the instructional environment, and interventions are measured. Construct validity gives this process of aligning measurement of construct-guided variables (i.e., risk), selection of children, and intervention the possibility of coherent analyses for cause-and-effect relationships. Construct validity addresses the unifying links and evidence, including sampling adequacy, what is measured, how the data are interpreted (decision rules), how interventions are designed and evaluated, and how the next decisions are made. In other words, in intervention outcome research, construct validity provides the conceptual basis and foundation for understanding change based on measurement *and* intervention (Kazdin, 1998; Shaddish et al., 2002).

For example, a new instructional intervention may not only (a) provide creative and engaging lessons, but also (b) add considerable opportunities to practice the skill, (c) teach self-graphing to children for progress monitoring, and (d) provide additional rewards for improvements (i.e., reinforcement for increasing rates of fluency). In addition, the selection of certain children for the intervention is a critical part of analysis. Inadequate attention to selection may minimize or possibly exaggerate results (make outcomes difficult or relatively easy to achieve). Also, what is measured and how measurement samples are obtained allow different views of intervention outcome. Ideally, the intervention construct would include all key intervention facets (with corresponding measurement) as possible active ingredients in change. *Internal validity* provides arguments for attributing change to the intervention (cause and effect). *Statistical conclusion validity* addresses the analyses of any differences that might be found, but the processes or variables that *explain* change are questions of construct validity and would require ongoing measurement of relevant variables (Shaddish et al., 2002). In this example, significant independent variables, if measured, could include the engagement value of lessons (i.e., stimulus or conditions sampling), practice opportunities, scheduling and type of performance monitoring, self-graphing (i.e., accuracy of procedures, etc.), and reinforcement procedures (i.e., functional), plus undoubtedly other variables as well. Dependent variables could include different aspects of reading behavior if the focus is on students (e.g., Kame'enui et al., 2005) and instructional variables (i.e., changes in the qualities of practice) as the focus shifts to teachers or curriculum.

In summary, construct validity is used to help design and interpret studies through the selection and measurement of dependent and independent variables, and samples of students and teachers. The interventions are expected to move the children's performance measures consistent with measures used to select children and assign them to the appropriate

intervention, and to help select criteria to judge outcomes. Interventions are construct linked, in that the children, measures, and interventions selected fit some conception of prevention, risk, or disability that could be used to explain change.

8.1.4.3 It Looks Like a Great Intervention, But Will it Work in My School?

Questions addressed by construct validity also help answer the questions of *external validity* or the degree that causal relationships are upheld over different settings, students, and other implementation variables (Shaddish et al., 2002). Selection of children for research may create samples that are quite different than child populations that professionals may face in schools. The best that we can do in most practice situations is "logical generalization" based on similarities between the research and our practice objectives, settings, and participants (e.g., Edgington, 1966; Hayes, Barlow, and Nelson-Gray, 1999).

8.1.4.4 Efficacy and Effectiveness Research

What validity evidence would support intervention practices? There have been a number of influential position papers addressing this question (Chambliss and Hollon, 1998; Kratochwill and Stoiber, 2002). *Efficacy* research shows the potential intervention outcomes under carefully controlled conditions. These conditions include screening and selecting participants, randomly assigning participants to groups (control and experimental, often not feasible in educational practice), and ensuring adherence to research protocols. Rather than comparing a new intervention with no intervention, comparisons with the best available rival intervention make efficacy studies critically important (Chambliss and Hollon, 1998). *Effectiveness* research looks at how well the intervention of proven efficacy can work in actual or more natural conditions. Questions include generalization, feasibility, and cost effectiveness, setting the bar quite high for researchers (Chorpita, 2003).

8.1.4.5 Single-Case Designs and Validity Evidence

Single-case designs provide a flexible and valid methodology for empirically evaluating interventions (Horner, Carr, McGee, Odom, and Wolery,

2005) and allow educators to assess the effectiveness of interventions for individual students, classes, and school systems in natural settings (Skinner, 2004). Both internal and external validity can be established through the use of single-case designs. Withdrawal, multiple-baseline, and changing-criterion designs allow for the repeated demonstration that an intervention systematically changes a given target variable (Barlow and Hersen, 1984). As a functional relation between intervention and behavior change is demonstrated and replicated, internal validity is established and the intervention becomes a plausible cause of behavior change. In practice, the internal validity of single-case designs can be strengthened by using control conditions and interventions with an empirical evidence base (Barnett et al., 2004). Designs such as alternating treatments also enable the rapid comparisons of alternative interventions to evaluate the most promising for a child (discussed later).

Of great potential importance for practice is the usefulness of single-case designs to address the actual application from the external validity evidence of interventions. Single-case designs provide a method for determining the generalizability of findings from controlled experimental studies to specific populations and individuals under applied conditions (Gresham, 2004). As procedures from efficacy research are replicated in natural settings, intervention effects in less-controlled environments can be evaluated.

8.1.4.6 Social Validity

Social validity evolved from single-case research (Wolf, 1978) to help evaluate intervention research through an expanded evaluation (i.e., participants, consumers, potential consumers) of satisfaction, appropriateness, and effectiveness of intervention goals, procedures, and outcomes. Methods for social validation include use of rating scales by teachers/parents to judge social validity, comparisons with various norms (i.e., peer comparisons), and evidence of sustainability (Kennedy, 2005). Social validity addresses many aspects of RTI, including the viability of the goals and methods of an intervention program prospectively and the viability of the goals, methods, and outcomes once the process is underway (Schwartz and Baer, 1991).

8.2 Response to Intervention Decision-Making Validity

RTI involves ongoing decision-making regarding instruction and intervention. Each decision affects the next as the process unfolds. Permanent product documentation, including graphs of universal screening results, group as well as individualized intervention outcomes (demonstrated through single-case design graphs), and decision rule use, is critical for decision confidence based on a comprehensive and cumulative record of the process.

8.2.1 Examining Validity Evidence

8.2.1.1 Target Variable Selection

Before selecting and implementing intervention procedures, a target variable is selected. There should be documented evidence that the variable targeted for intervention is appropriate. Data collected on the target variable must be evaluated by members of the problem-solving team to ensure that it is a direct measure of the problem, can be reliably measured over time, and will be sensitive enough to detect change resulting from the intervention (Macmann et al., 1996). Indirect measures (e.g., interviews, questionnaires) have generally not been shown to meet these criteria (i.e., reliable measurement over time, sensitive to growth), but may be used to generate a broader picture of the problem situation.

8.2.1.2 Instruction and Interventions, Vetting Criteria, and Sources

Once the target variable for change is clear, appropriate instruction and interventions need to be identified. There are numerous web resources available describing instruction and interventions for school-based problems (Table 8.1), but it is still necessary to be cautious with regard to evaluating effectiveness research and generalizing research to one's school and students. The challenges lie in determining which intervention will be most effective, most positive and natural, least costly, and least time consuming at a given point of time. Potential instructional approaches and interventions should be evaluated to determine (1) if they are appropriate and acceptable for universal (Tier 1), selected (Tier 2) or

TABLE 8.1. Examples of vetting sources.

University of Oregon	http://reading.uoregon.edu/curricula/index.php
Florida Center For Reading Research	http://www.fcrr.org/FCRRReports/index.htm
National Registry of Effective Practices	http://www.modelprograms.samhsa.gov/
What Works Clearinghouse	http://www.whatworks.ed.gov/
Intervention Central	http://www.interventioncentral.org
Edformation	www.edformation.com
Institute for the Development of Educational Achievement (IDEA)	www.idea.uoregon.edu
Positive Behavioral Interventions and Supports	http://www.PBIS.org

intensive (Tier 3) implementation (Gresham, 2004), (2) if they are designed to improve selected target variable performance, (3) if they are appropriate for the age and skill level of the students, and (4) if the school system has the resources to support proper implementation. If a chosen instructional approach or intervention is poorly matched on these criteria, then it is unlikely to have the desired effects on student performance and may lead to invalid decisions about the need for additional services. Also, although an intervention is empirically supported by efficacy research, the effectiveness of the intervention may still need to be determined in a natural setting, and these studies are rare (Chorpita, 2003). Interventions may need to be adjusted to meet the needs of a student or the resources of the system without losing effectiveness. Single-case methods may be used to provide answers about the feasibility of an intervention in a real-life situation and empirically "fine-tune" interventions to fit ecologies and children's needs.

8.2.1.3 Criteria for Judging Research Outcomes

Consumers of research need to judge the adequacy of the research design and procedures, statistical significance (the degree the results might be chance related?), size of effect (amount of change?), and social or clinical significance of the outcomes (Cohen, 1988; Foster and Mash, 1999; Kazdin, 1999; Wolf, 1978). Effect sizes estimate the amount of change measured in standard deviation units. An effect size of "1" means that data points represented in the intervention condition improved by one standard deviation over the control condition. Social validity includes broad methods relating change back to societal functioning.

8.2.1.4 Replicated Studies

Replications of efficacy and effectiveness strengthen intervention validity evidence and, thus, the validity of decisions to implement those procedures. Even when an intervention has been investigated through the primary methodology of efficacy research (i.e., randomized experiments), replicated studies of intervention effectiveness are especially important (Chambliss and Hollon, 1998; Horner et al., 2005; Stoiber and Kratochwill, 2000) to estimate and to purposefully influence external validity.

An intervention should not be overlooked as a potential solution to problem behavior for the sole reason that it has not been investigated through a randomized experiment. Single-case design researchers consider within- and between-series replication (i.e., ABAB, multiple baseline across participants, behavior, settings), not random assignment, to be the *sine qua non* of valid design, with replication across different participants and researchers building justifiable confidence in conclusions even further. Horner et al. (2005, pp. 175–176) suggest that an intervention may be considered *evidence based* by using single-case designs when:

(a) a minimum of five . . . studies that meet minimally acceptable methodological criteria and document experimental control have been published in peer-reviewed journals, (b) the studies are conducted by at least three different researchers across at least three different geographical locations, and (c) . . . a total of at least 20 participants [are included across studies].

Practitioners in the field are continuously developing new and effective interventions to address student problems but are unable to establish cause–effect relationships for a variety of reasons (i.e., limited resources, teacher/parent preference not to return to baseline) (Skinner, 2004). However, by sharing data on interventions developed and applied in the field, practitioners can begin the process to more extensively replicate procedures in order to establish the relationship and boundaries between the intervention and behavior change. From the parents' view, permissions and informed consent for services at Tier 3 would be based on estimates of established empirical confidence in the intervention, or an agreement to try newer procedures based on full knowledge of intervention alternatives.

8.2.1.5 Researched Principles of Learning

Familiarity with basic principles of learning also can help with the process of sorting through research to find the most appropriate intervention. Although there are numerous empirically supported interventions for school-related academic and behavior problems in research, many of these interventions share key components. Recognizing these important principles of learning can help when modifications of interventions are deemed necessary or when judging newer interventions. Common features of effective academic or social interventions include clarifying objectives, practice, feedback, and reinforcement principles (e.g., Shapiro, 2004; Sugai et al., 2000).

8.2.1.6 Decision Rules

Problem-solving teams should have data to support pre-established (nonarbitrary) decision rules that will be used to determine when adjustments to intervention protocols are needed. Empirically set decision rules are based on generalizations from past research with specific interventions (e.g., significant characteristics of sessions usually needed to produce effects; how long to keep a child in an intervention without making changes). As part of the permanent product record of the RTI process, these data provide evidence of the validity of decision rules for new student groups or individuals. Graphs of established benchmarks or local norms can provide a point of comparison as student response to intervention is monitored. Decision rules should also take into account base rate data (VanDerHeyden and Witt, 2005). Recognizing the prevalence of reading or social problems within a school or school system can inform decisions about what level of intervention support is needed (e.g., school-wide versus small

group). In summary, by pre-establishing decision rules, decision-making validity can be examined.

8.2.2 Ongoing Assessment of Validity Evidence

8.2.2.1 Intervention is Implemented as Intended

The validity of decisions made through the RTI process can be significantly threatened if interventions are not implemented accurately (Gresham, 1989). "Accuracy" should include adherence to procedures and appropriate schedules of contact between student and the intervention (i.e., "dose" of intervention). The use of intervention scripts helps address this issue by providing a detailed outline of how intervention plans are to be implemented (Ehrhardt, Barnett, Lentz, Stollar, and Reifin, 1996). Scripts provide the individuals responsible for intervention implementation with a step-by-step contextual and natural guide, increasing the likelihood that the intervention will be implemented as intended. The scripts can also be used to document intervention adherence by providing a checklist of the implementation steps completed and occasions of use. Thus, scripts can be completed by the individual responsible for the intervention as a guide and used by an individual observing the intervention being implemented. Adherence data provide evidence that an intervention was implemented accurately and that change in behavior was likely due to effects of the intervention. These data are particularly important when a student is not making desired progress. Without evidence that the intervention was implemented accurately and as scheduled, it will be unclear as to whether a student's failure to make desired levels of progress is an indicator that they need additional intervention supports or an artifact of a poorly implemented intervention protocol. This evidence would need to be included in some format (e.g., co-plotted or referenced on a progress-monitoring graph; scripts with completed items checked off) as a permanent product in the intervention file (Ehrhardt et al., 1996). It is worth noting that some curricula (e.g., direct instruction approaches) have built-in methods to determine and provide a record of implementation. In general, evidence suggests that teachers may need considerable support for implementation (e.g., Noell et al., 2000).

8.2.2.2 Is the Intervention Having the Desired Effect?

As intervention procedures are implemented, the effects must be continuously monitored and documented. Graphs of student progress over time that include goal lines, aim lines, and conditions, can be used to provide evidence of intervention effectiveness or ineffectiveness. Pre-established decision rules from past research provide guidelines for data interpretation and when adjustments to interventions should be made. The frequent collection of progress-monitoring data will be needed to inform the ongoing evaluation process.

8.2.2.3 Intervention Components and Sequences

Comprehensive, multifaceted intervention packages have proven to effectively address the needs of students at high risk of school failure due to poor academic performance and/or highly disruptive behavior. However, all components of an intervention package may not be necessary for individual students to demonstrate progress and may unnecessarily and inefficiently use system resources. In addition, the more time consuming and difficult that intervention procedures are to implement, the less likely they will be implemented as designed (Gresham, 1989). If an intervention package includes components unnecessary for student progress and unlikely to be implemented accurately,

then the validity of the decision to continue providing such services is significantly threatened.

Intervention sequence data can help problem-solving teams determine the level of support necessary for student success by examining the effects of increasing and decreasing the intensity of intervention designs (Barnett et al., 2004). Increasing-intensity designs start with the least intensive instructional intervention and add additional intervention components as necessary based on progress-monitoring data. Alternatively, decreasing-intensity designs start with more comprehensive interventions and elements of the intervention are systematically withdrawn. With both increasing- and decreasing-intensity designs, the goal is to ensure that intervention procedures are at the minimum level necessary to achieve desired levels of student performance. The data collected on the effects of systematically adding or withdrawing intervention components provides empirical evidence to validate decisions about necessary services for students.

8.2.2.4 Which Intervention is Best?

Using well-established methods, the validity of alternative interventions or reinforcers for individual students can also be established by behavioral assessments and single-case designs (e.g., Steege, Wacker, Berg, Cigrand, and Cooper, 1989). Referred to as *brief experimental analysis* (or *brief trial* designs in Table 8.2), exposures to alternative interventions that are pre-planned with regard to prior

TABLE 8.2. How to address decision-making validity in RTI.

Unit of analysis	Prior validity evidence	Ongoing validity evidence
RTI model	Validity evidence for model or at least components in reducing risk, etc.; social validity	Progress monitoring for key service delivery "events"; outcomes show reduced risk; social validity
Universal screening	Reliability and validity of measures, cut scores, or benchmarks	Progress-monitoring data leads to accurate decisions about risk
Universal prevention and intervention	Efficacy and effectiveness research on construct (academic or social risk prevention)	Progress-monitoring data leads to accurate conclusions about risk reduction
Target variable selection	Research in academic achievement and social behavior and its measurement	Progress-monitoring data allows evaluation of intervention effectiveness
Targeted interventions	Efficacy and effectiveness research; replicated single-case designs; replicated principles of learning	Single-case research, "brief trial" or accountability designs
Individualized intervention	Replicated single-case designs; replicated principles of learning	Single-case research or accountability designs; functional assessment and analysis
Eligibility for special services	Validity of specialized services	Validity of intervention "intensity" variables

efficacy for specific targeted behaviors may rapidly yield validity evidence. Applied to academic skills problems, brief experimental analysis has been used to test various empirically supported individualized interventions to improve reading performance (e.g., Daly and Martens, 1994; Daly, Martens, Dool, and Hintze, 1998). Students are exposed to different hierarchically arranged intervention conditions for a few sessions. Brief withdrawals and replications are then used to validate the most effective interventions (Daly et al., 1997). The alternating treatment design can show the relative effectiveness of two candidate interventions (Steege et al., 1989).

8.2.2.5 Functional Analysis

Rather than trying out likely interventions even briefly, functional analysis allows an understanding of a behavior by first examining hypothesized functional relationships, or patterns of behavior, that vary systematically by antecedents (or predictors) and/or consequences of behavior. First, teams hypothesize and establish the function, and then design the intervention based on function. *Brief functional analysis* procedures include brief exposure to manipulated conditions with replication of results (Steege and Northup, 1998). Crone and Horner (2003) provide decision rules to guide the levels of functional assessment and analysis based on risk appraisals for highly concerning behaviors. The primary objective is increasing the validity of an intervention design by establishing its function and, through the design, making the problem behavior irrelevant, inefficient, or ineffective. A primary example is functional communication training (Carr and Durand, 1985; Horner et al., 2005).

8.3 Conclusions

RTI is construct-linked with regard to theories of prevention (achievement and social risk), interventions ordered by intensity for struggling children, and decisions for special services eligibility for challenging-to-serve children. Many types of research are needed to support RTI, not only large-scale and single-case intervention research, but also research addressing measurement, selection, progress monitoring, and outcome evaluation. All of these involve complex decision processes and, thus,

vulnerabilities to inaccurate decision-making. A strong model, procedures, and validity evidence for procedures are ways to improve decision-making. We have stressed validity evidence for interventions. While not meant to be inclusive, Table 8.2 is organized by the roles of examining existing and ongoing sources for validity evidence for RTI for practice.

On the surface, validity discussions look like they are for professionals and researchers. However, if one considers the consequences of decisions made, then RTI validity evidence is relevant to parents and any stakeholders who are invested in attaining positive outcomes for individual and groups of children. Such evidence will permit stakeholders to make informed choices about available services as much as it will help researchers and practitioners to evaluate potential RTI models and formatively enhance existing ones.

Acknowledgments. This work was partially funded by an Ohio Board of Regents grant.

References

Barlow, D. H. & Hersen, M. (1984). *Single Case Experimental Designs: Strategies for Studying Behavior Change* (2nd ed.). New York: Pergamon.

Barnett, D. W. (1988). Professional judgment: a critical appraisal. *School Psychology Review, 17*, 656–670.

Barnett, D. W., Daly III, E. J., Jones, K. M., & Lentz Jr., F. E. (2004). Response to intervention: empirically based special service decisions from single-case designs of increasing and decreasing intensity. *The Journal of Special Education, 38*, 66–79.

Barnett, D. W., Ihlo, T, Nichols, A., & Wolsing, L. (2006). Preschool teacher support through class-wide intervention: a description of field initiated training and evaluation. *Journal of Applied School Psychology, 23*, 77–96.

Batsche, G., Elliott, J., Graden, J. L., Grimes, J., Kovaleski, J. F., Prasse, D., et al. (2005). *Response to Intervention: Policy Considerations and Implementation.* Alexandria, VA: National Association of State Board of Directors of Special Education.

Carr, E. G. & Durand, V. M. (1985). Reducing problem behaviors through functional communication training. *Journal of Applied Behavior Analysis, 18*, 111–126.

Chambliss, D. L. & Hollon, S. D. (1998). Defining empirically supported therapies. *Journal of Consulting and Clinical Psychology, 66*, 7–18.

Chorpita, B. F. (2003). The frontier of evidence-based practice. In A. E. Kazdin & J. R. Weisz (Eds.),

Evidenced-based Psychotherapies for Children and Adolescents (pp. 42–59). New York: Guilford.

Cohen, J. (1988). *Statistical Power Analysis for the Behavioral Sciences* (2nd ed.). Hillsdale, NJ: Erlbaum.

Crone, D. A. & Horner, R. H. (2003). *Building Positive Behavior Support Systems in Schools: Functional Behavioral Assessment.* New York: Guilford.

Daly III, E. J. & Martens, B. K. (1994). A comparison of three interventions for increasing oral reading performance: application of the instructional hierarchy. *Journal of Applied Behavior Analysis, 27*, 459–469.

Daly III, E. J., Martens, B. K., Dool, E. J., & Hintze, J. M. (1998). Using brief functional analysis to select interventions for oral reading. *Journal of Behavioral Education, 8*, 203–218.

Daly III, E. J., Witt, J. C., Martens, B. K., & Dool, E.J. (1997). A model for conducting a functional analysis of academic performance problems. *School Psychology Review, 26*, 554–574.

Edgington, E. S. (1966). Statistical inference and nonrandom samples. *Psychological Bulletin, 66*, 485–487.

Ehrhardt, K. E., Barnett, D. W., Lentz, F. E., Jr., Stollar, S. A., & Reifin, L. H. (1996). Innovative methodology in ecological consultation: use of scripts to promote treatment acceptability and integrity. *School Psychology Quarterly, 11*, 149–168.

Fletcher, J. M. & Francis, D. J. (2004). Scientifically based educational research. In P. McCardle & V. Chhabra (Eds.), *The Voice of Evidence in Reading Research* (pp. 59–80). Baltimore: Brookes.

Foster, S. L. & Mash, E. J. (1999). Assessing social validity in clinical treatment research: Issues and procedures. *Journal of Consulting and Clinical Psychology, 67*, 308–319.

Fuchs, L. S., Fuchs, D., & Speece, D. L. (2002). Treatment validity as a unifying construct for identifying learning disabilities. *Learning Disabilities Quarterly, 25*, 33–44.

Greenwood, C. R., Delquadri, J. C., & Hall, V. R. (1984). Opportunities to respond and student academic performance. In W. L. Heward, T. E. Heron, D. S. Hill, & J. Trap-Porter (Eds.), *Focus on Behavior Analysis in Education* (pp. 58–88). Columbus, OH: Merrill.

Gresham, F. (1989). Assessment of treatment integrity in school consultation and prereferral intervention. *School Psychology Review, 18*, 37–50.

Gresham, F. (2004). Current status and future directions of school-based behavioral interventions. *School Psychology Review, 33*, 326–343.

Gresham, F. M. (1991). Conceptualizing behavior disorders in terms of resistance to intervention. *School Psychology Review, 20*, 23–36.

Hall, J. D., Ashley, D. M., Bramlett, R. K., Dielmann, K. B., & Murphy, J. J. (2004). ADHD assessment: a comparison of negative versus positive symptom formats. *Journal of Applied School Psychology, 21*, 163–173.

Hastie, R. & Dawes, R. M. (2001). *Rational Choice in an Uncertain World: The Psychology of Judgment and Decision Making.* Thousand Oaks, CA: Sage.

Hayes, S. C., Barlow, D. H., & Nelson-Gray, R. O. (1999). *The Scientist Practitioner: Research and Accountability in the Age of Managed Care.* Boston: Allyn & Bacon.

Horner, R. G., Carr, E. G., McGee, G., Odom, S., & Wolery, M. (2005). The use of single subject research to identify evidence-based practice in special education. *Exceptional Children, 71*, 165–179.

Kahneman, D. (2003). A perspective on judgment and choice. *American Psychologist, 58*, 697–720.

Kame'enui, E. J., Good III, R. G., & Harn, B. A. (2005). Beginning reading failure and the quantification of risk: reading behavior as the supreme index. In W. L. Heward, T. E. Heron, N. E. Neef, S. M. Peterson, D. M. Sainato, G. Cartledge, et al. (Eds.), *Focus on Behavioral Analysis in Education: Achievements, Challenges, and Opportunities* (pp. 68–88). Upper Saddle River, NJ: Pearson.

Kazdin, A. E. (1998). *Research Design in Clinical Psychology* (3rd ed.). New York: Harper & Row.

Kazdin, A. E. (1999). The meanings and measurement of clinical significance. *Journal of Consulting and Clinical Psychology, 67*, 332–339.

Kennedy, C. H. (2005). *Single-Case Designs for Educational Research.* Boston Allyn & Bacon.

Kratochwill, T. R. & Stoiber, K. C. (2002). Evidence-based interventions in school psychology: conceptual foundations of the Procedural and Coding Manual of Division 16 and the Society for the Study of School Psychology Task Force. *School Psychology Quarterly, 17*, 1–55.

Lentz Jr., F. E., Allen, S. J., & Ehrhardt, K. E. (1996). The conceptual elements of strong interventions in school settings. *School Psychology Quarterly, 11*, 118–136.

Macmann, G. & Barnett, D. (1999). Diagnostic decision making in school psychology: understanding and coping with uncertainty. In C. R. Reynolds & T. B. Gutkin (Eds.), *Handbook of School Psychology* (3rd ed., pp. 519–548). New York: Wiley.

Macmann, G. M., Barnett, D. W., Allen, S. J., Bramlett, R. K., Hall, J. D., & Ehrhardt, K. E. (1996). Problem solving and intervention design: guidelines for the evaluation of technical adequacy. *School Psychology Quarterly, 11*, 137–148.

McCardle, P. & Chhabra, V. (Eds.) (2004). *The Voice of Evidence in Reading Research.* Baltimore: Brookes.

Messick, S. (1995). Validity of psychological assessment: validation of inferences from persons' responses and performances as scientific inquiry into score meaning. *American Psychologist, 50*, 741–749.

Noell, G. H., Witt, J. C., LaFleur, L. H., Mortenson, B. P., Ranier, D. D., & LeVelle, J. (2000). Increasing intervention implementation in general education following consultation: a comparison of two follow-up strategies. *Journal of Applied Behavior Analysis, 33*, 271–283.

Nunnally, J. C. & Bernstein, I. H. (1994). *Psychometric Theory* (3rd ed.). New York: McGraw-Hill.

President's Commission on Excellence in Special Education. (2002). A new era: revitalizing special education for children and their families. Retrieved August 2, 2002 from http://www.ed.gov/inits/ commissionsboards/whspecialeducation/reports.html

Schwartz, I. S. & Baer, D. M. (1991). Social validity assessment: is current practice state of the art? *Journal of Applied Behavior Analysis, 24*, 189–204.

Shaddish, W. R., Cook, T. D., & Campbell, D. T. (2002). *Experimental and Quasi-Experimental Designs for Generalized Causal Inference*. Boston: Houghton Mifflin.

Shapiro, E. S. (2004). *Academic Skills Problems* (3rd ed.). New York: Guilford.

Skinner, C. H. (2004). *Single-Subject Designs for School Psychologists*. Binghamton, NY: Haworth.

Steege, M. W. & Northup, J. (1998). Brief functional analysis of problem behavior: A practical approach for school psychologists. *Proven Practice: Prevention and Remediation Solutions for Schools, 1*, 4–11, 37–38.

Steege, M. W., Wacker, D. P., Berg, W. K., Cigrand, K. K., & Cooper, L. J. (1989). The use of behavioral assessment to prescribe and evaluate treatments for severely handicapped children. *Journal of Applied Behavior Analysis, 22*, 23–33.

Stoiber, K. C. & Kratochwill, T. R. (2000). Empirically supported interventions and school psychology: Rationale and methodological issues. Part I. *School Psychology Quarterly, 15*, 75–105.

Sugai, G., Horner, R. H., Dunlap, G., Hieneman, M., Lewis, T. J., Nelson, C. M., et al. (2000). Applying positive behavioral support and functional behavioral assessment in schools. *Journal of Positive Behavioral Interventions, 2*, 131–143.

Twyman, J. S., Layng, T. V. J., Stikeleather, G., & Hobbins, K. A. (2005). A nonlinear approach to curriculum design: the role of behavior analysis in building an effective reading program. In W. L. Heward, T. E. Heron, N. E. Neef, S. M. Peterson, D. M. Sainato, G. Cartledge, et al. (Eds.), *Focus on Behavioral Analysis in Education: Achievements, Challenges, and Opportunities* (pp. 55–68). Upper Saddle River, NJ: Pearson.

VanDerHeyden, A. M. & Witt, J. C. (2005). Quantifying context in assessment: Capturing the effect of base rates on teacher referral and a problem solving model of identification. *School Psychology Review, 43*, 161–183.

Wolf, M. M. (1978). Social validity: the case for subjective measurement or how applied behavior analysis is finding its heart. *Journal of Applied Behavior Analysis, 11*, 203–214.

9

Assessing Student Response to Intervention

Stephanie C. Olson, Edward J. Daly III, Melissa Andersen, April Turner, and Courtney LeClair

Stephanie C. Olson, MA, is a graduate student in Educational (School) Psychology at the University of Nebraska-Lincoln. scolson@bigred.unl.edu

Edward J. Daly III, PhD, is Associate Professor of Educational (School) Psychology at the University of Nebraska-Lincoln. edaly2@unl.edu

Melissa Andersen, MA, is a graduate student in Educational (School) Psychology at the University of Nebraska-Lincoln. melissandersen@gmail.com

April Turner, MA, is a graduate student in Educational (School) Psychology at the University of Nebraska-Lincoln. april_d_turner@yahoo.com

Courtney LeClair, MA, is a graduate student in Educational (School) Psychology at the University of Nebraska-Lincoln. cleclai1@bigred.unl.edu

Seen by many as a significant educational innovation with far-ranging implications for how school districts respond to the needs of their students, the notion of "Response to Intervention" (RTI, upper case) has taken on immense proportions; justifiably so, in our view. RTI will directly affect the educational experience of millions of students nationwide. School districts are revamping their processes for classifying students with learning disabilities. Educators are now investing significant time, effort, and resources in screening processes to identify students' risk status. School personnel are combing the intervention literature to find strategies that can be implemented locally. Administrators are stuttering like David Bowie when considering the "*ch-ch-ch-changes*" that need to take place in their schools to live up to this new mandate.

The importance of these events for the overall integrity of RTI as a broad innovation cannot be overstated. Yet, if we lose sight of the elegant simplicity of the fundamental rationale, logic, and methods associated with RTI, there is a risk of drifting off course and forgetting the purpose of these changes. The pattern is clear and has been established through many cycles of educational reform: innovations have a tendency to eventually become simply a series of procedural steps that represent nothing more than an "add on" to existing, ineffec-

tive educational practices (Fullan, 2001). Someone somewhere will make up a checklist that fulfills RTI requirements and haggard-looking former visionaries will resign themselves to routinely complying so as to dig themselves out from under the overwhelming case loads that snuffed out their spark.

At the risk of oversimplifying the many complex dimensions of RTI, this chapter will unfold the basic concept of response to intervention (lowercase) as an organizing rubric for the activity of assessment. Our goal is to bring clarity to how practitioners conceptualize and carry out their assessment role in the RTI process as it relates first of all to student learning. After all, the primary purpose of assessment should always be improving student learning. However, the data generated through these assessments will likely provide a database for categorical decisions, like eligibility for special education, as schools move toward full-scale implementation of RTI. Therefore, we hope that the principles and practices described in this chapter will also help to improve the quality of the databases that will be used for high-stakes decisions like eligibility for special education when administrative action is in order. The purpose of this chapter is to provide a conceptual map for assessment activities to guide the questions that are asked and how one goes about answering those questions within RTI.

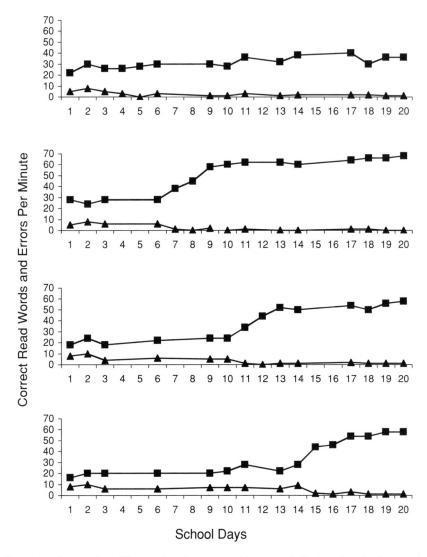

FIGURE 9.1. Hypothetical examples of fluency data (corrects and incorrects) displayed in single-case, A–B designs.

9.1 Use of an Evaluation Design in Response to Intervention

Psychologists get themselves into trouble when they fail to use predetermined evaluation criteria for important decisions about human problems (Dawes, 1994). Having a strong evaluation design reduces the likelihood of cognitive heuristics, post-hoc explanations, and other judgment errors (Barnett, 1988). The standard that has developed for data-based problem solving is the use of single-case accountability designs, like the A–B design (Barnett, Daly, Jones, and Lentz, 2004). Hypothetical exam-

ples of intervention outcomes arranged as a series of A–B designs appear in Figure 9.1. In the RTI process, the evaluation design involves repeated measures across different phases of instruction, each of which includes an assortment of instructional and/or motivational variables that reflect elements of the natural environment. In Figure 9.1, each graph has a baseline which serves as the point of comparison for an intervention that is applied repeatedly over time. Each graph in the example also has an intervention phase in which some planned modification of the environment is carried out. The result is that projections are made about the trajectory of student learning under various instructional conditions.

Decisions about intervention effectiveness are based on visual analysis of level, trend, and variability in the data across and within phases (Kazdin, 1982; Parsonson and Baer, 1992). Structured criteria for visual inspection which determine statistical significance and which do a good job of controlling decision errors have been recently developed and could be used as well (Fisher, Kelly, and Lomas, 2003). Problems with academic skills are most frequently behavioral deficits. Interventions, therefore, are expected to lead to increases in performance over time (i.e., changes in level and trend). An unsuccessful intervention phase would lead to results that do not differ from the baseline phase.

Comparisons between conditions are planned to test hypotheses about when a student is more or less likely to respond to some kind of environmental arrangement. When these comparisons are done within an adequate evaluation design with variables that reflect elements of the natural setting, generalizations (i.e., inferred meaning) are stronger because competing explanations have been ruled out and the results have direct implications for students' instructional needs. Although it is the student's responding that is being measured, it is the *instruction* that is being scrutinized (Englemann, Granzin, and Severson, 1979). Therefore, assessment is essentially a process of testing instruction through *response-guided experimentation* (Barlow and Hersen, 1984). Changes in student responding (or a lack thereof) within and across phases of instruction serve as feedback about the effectiveness and appropriateness of the instruction. The evaluation design and the data in the graphs are used as a basis for determining what should be done next. Within this model of assessment, an accurate description of the relationship of student responding to instruction is vital to guiding how instruction should be changed over the course of time. If student responding does not improve as expected following instruction, then subsequent instruction should increase in intensity and/or be differentiated in some way from previous instruction. The process is iterative until a solution is achieved. If student learning does not improve before the process is terminated, then *we* are the nonresponders (and not the students). The discussion will return to the examples in Figure 9.1 several times as assessment questions and practices are addressed. The graphs within the figure will be labeled in different ways throughout the chapter for purposes of illustration across examples. In addition, data from an actual case will be

presented to round out illustration of many of the points.

9.2 Using Skills Assessment to Describe Problems with Student Responding

"Assessing student response to intervention" is a fitting description of the underlying purpose of assessment. Assessments are designed to detect responses which are presumed to have significance that transcends their measured occurrence. A student's response is the focal point of inference about the "meaning" of assessment results. The meaning directs the evaluator's decisions and future actions regarding the student. For example, student responses are used daily by evaluators across the country to deduce disabilities and risk status. However, the response is loaded with implications that may escape the attention of the evaluator if they fail to take note of the events that precede a measured response. The evaluator can avoid speculation about the meaning of student responses and instead make those responses all the more significant when he or she purposefully arranges or manipulates the events that precede student responding during assessment. By intentionally investigating how student responding changes as a function of instructional materials and demands, the evaluator enhances the meaning of assessment (Barnett et al., 2004).

The most natural starting point for assessing student learning in a classroom or curriculum is to note whether student responses to instructional tasks are correct or incorrect. Obviously, over time, correct responses should increase and incorrect responses should decrease as a function of instruction. More specifically, the nature of academic responding is such that correct responses should increase in frequency, rapidity, and consistency across instructional tasks. An observer will note that a response that was not initially in the student's repertoire may begin to increase in frequency (as errors decrease) when the student is presented with an instructional item. In other words, the learner's responses become *accurate* when presented with the instructional task. As accuracy improves, responses become more rapid and *fluency* develops. *Consistency* in responding emerges when the student answers correctly when presented with similar instructional items and/or instructional items that require the same or a similar response. For instance, a second grader who has "mastered" double-digit addition with regrouping can presumably calculate any combination of numbers, even combinations not directly taught by the teacher. Consistency also is a factor when the skill is used to accomplish a larger task that requires a broader repertoire of skills; the skill is used in conjunction with other skills to achieve an overarching outcome. For example, this same student should also eventually be able to use their computation skills to accomplish other tasks, like completing a science experiment. In this case, the double-digit addition with regrouping skill is one *component* of a *composite* skill that requires multiple component skills (e.g., reading the science text, following directions in order).

Student response to intervention, therefore, is the degree to which responding changes in terms of accuracy, fluency, and consistency within and across a variety of tasks, with improvements in *all* of these areas being critical to successful student performance. A deficiency in any of these areas signals that there is a problem and a need for further investigation. At the risk of overstating the obvious, it is worth noting that students are referred to evaluators because they exhibit fewer correct responses than desired or expected and a more systematic evaluation of student responding is necessary. Fortunately, there are highly developed, standardized procedures for directly assessing accuracy and fluency of basic skills. Curriculum-based measurement (CBM; Shinn, 1989) provides information regarding rate of responding, which reflects a combination of both accuracy and fluency of responding. CBM is widely popular and has become a standard practice in graduate training programs in school psychology (Shapiro, Angello, and Eckert, 2004). Given that fluency is an indicator of both accuracy and speed of responding and that it is a better measure of response strength than accuracy alone (Binder, 1996), assessments of basic skills should measure fluency.

Having a fluency score is only a part of knowing what the score means, however. An analysis of student responding will be incomplete if it does not account for the type of academic material given to the student as a part of the assessment. The material used for assessment will reflect the type of consistency and generality of responding being investigated. For instance, repeatedly assessing responding in materials instructed by the teacher yields information regarding consistency over time, referred to as *response maintenance*. Graphs B, C, and D in Figure 9.1 might reflect outcomes of instruction or a planned intervention across three different passages used by the teacher. Results are staggered because the teacher instructs the stories sequentially. If the teacher stopped instruction in earlier stories when moving on to subsequent stories, the latter data points in each graph would reflect maintenance once instruction was withdrawn.

An actual example of maintenance data from a reading intervention done with a ninth-grade student appears in Figure 9.2. Intervention was carried out over several days and the results were measured across three conditions: reward, instruction/taught materials, and instruction/untaught materials (these conditions will be described in more detail below). In order to measure response maintenance, the student was assessed two more times in each condition the week following withdrawal of the intervention. For the instruction/taught materials condition (the top data series in Figure 9.2), the data reveal that the student improved significantly throughout the intervention phase, and the performance leveled off following withdrawal of the intervention. It can be concluded that the student maintained his improvements because the performance during the maintenance phase was close in level to the performance during intervention. In the instruction/untaught materials condition (the middle data series), minor improvements in performance occurred during intervention. During the maintenance phase, there was a drop in performance. Finally, in the reward condition (the bottom data series), which served as a type of control condition, no performance increases were witnessed. These maintenance data reveal that the student's performance in the instructional conditions led to performance improvements that persisted when instruction was terminated.

A complete assessment should go beyond merely measuring what has been taught. The curriculum material taught by the teacher really only represents a subset of material in which the student should show improvement (Alessi, 1987). In an earlier example of consistency of responding, we pointed out that it is highly unlikely that the teacher would directly teach the student every possible number combination for double-digit addition with

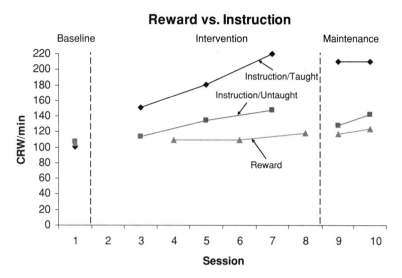

FIGURE 9.2. Example of correct read works per minute (CRW/min) in reward versus instruction conditions and in taught versus untaught passages.

regrouping problems. Curriculum material can be divided into *directly taught* tasks, or instructional materials, and *untaught* (but presumably equal difficulty level) tasks, or instructional materials. Assessing skill proficiency in untaught tasks provides information about the degree to which student responding is generalizing to similar instructional items. For example, an evaluator who assesses a second-grade student's reading fluency in a second-grade reading series that differs from the one used by the teacher in the classroom is assessing generalization of reading fluency across second-grade passages. The evaluator might choose to sample student performance over time using classroom instructional materials, which could be represented by the results in graph A, and separately sample student performance over time using an independent reading series, which could be represented by the results in graph B. Graph A provides information about changes in student responding in directly taught materials. Graph B provides information about how well the student is generalizing to untaught but equivalent difficulty level material. This information is probably even more important than the information in graph A, because it reveals how broad the effects of instruction are.

Figure 9.2 also displays an example of generalization to untaught materials. The ninth-grade student participated in a fluency intervention, in which he worked one-on-one with an experimenter,

repeatedly reading a particular passage and receiving corrective feedback on his performance. Following practice, assessment data were collected by having the student read two different passages: the instructional passage, which was practiced as part of the intervention (instruction/taught materials); and another passage, which had not been practiced during the intervention (instruction/untaught materials). One would expect to see large increases in the instruction/taught materials condition, since the student practiced with those exact materials. In addition, one would hope to see increases in the instruction/untaught materials condition, since that would suggest overall improvements across grade-level materials (generalization). However, it would be expected that such improvements would be modest and gradual. Figure 9.2 reveals that these expectations were, indeed, met: the student demonstrated significant improvements in the taught materials and modest improvements in the untaught materials, suggesting some degree of generalization.

If a student improved in taught materials but did not improve in untaught materials, then the teacher's job is not done. The student is likely to struggle if he is moved up in the curriculum before consistency in responding across grade-level instructional tasks is achieved. For these reasons, priority should be given to measuring responding to untaught material over time as a basis for judging whether the effects of instruction have generalized sufficiently for the student to be ready to move on in the curriculum.

Consistency of responding is also vital to skill use when the skill is a necessary part of a larger repertoire of skills which are coordinated into a composite skill. For example, a student may be able to pronounce phonemes (sounds) when presented with letters on flashcards (e.g., pronouncing "b") and even be able to blend those phonemes to form words that the student was previously unable to read (e.g., "tab" and "cab"). However, the student still needs to be able to read those words in connected text and even blend untaught phonemes when he encounters an unfamiliar word in text. An assessment that evaluates skill proficiency in the context of critical composite skills produces valuable information about the student's ability to generalize the skill (and hence about its consistency in the presence of new and more complex problems or tasks). In this case, the results of graph A might reflect outcomes of phoneme blending assessments (in which fluency with phoneme tasks is repeatedly assessed with words) and the results of graph B might reflect oral reading fluency outcomes in phonetically regular passages that contain phonemes instructed in isolation by the teacher. As in the prior example, graph A indicates progress in the taught skill and graph B indicates progress in use of the skill when applied to a composite skill that appears as a later objective in the curriculum.

Similarly, reading comprehension could be viewed as a composite skill requiring the component skill of reading fluency (e.g., Pinnell et al., 1995). Thus, improvements in reading fluency may contribute to improved comprehension outcomes. For example, the ninth-grade student was asked to practice reading high-school-level passages. The student repeatedly practiced the first third of the passage. Fluency was then assessed in the second third of the passage, and comprehension was assessed through a cloze procedure in the final third of the passage. In the cloze procedure, every sixth word was replaced with a blank, and the student was instructed to provide words to replace the blanks. Figure 9.3 displays the results for two separate passages. The data indicate that improvements in reading comprehension correspond to improvements in generalized reading fluency. Indeed, the comprehension data show similar trends and changes in level as the fluency data.

9.3 Arranging Assessment Conditions to Figure Out What to Do About the Problem

Evaluating accuracy, fluency, and consistency/generalization may not be very satisfactory if assessment information is not related in some way to what can be done about the problem. Fortunately, the evaluation of these various dimensions of responding can also guide assessors in determining what to do about the problem. If one treats the assessment process as an opportunity to ask a series of questions, then assessments of skill fluency can be designed as mini-experiments that shed light on potentially effective and ineffective interventions that can be examined over time (Daly, Witt, Martens, and Dool, 1997). A series of questions is proposed that can be readily answered through planned instructional trials and ongoing fluency assessments. Our recommendation is to examine simple solutions first and progress to more complex interventions only as necessary.

A relatively simple initial question about how to change student performance is whether it can improve with rewards (Daly et al., 1997). If responding improves with rewards contingent on prespecified goals, then additional instructional support may be unnecessary to promote accurate, fluent, and consistent responding (Duhon et al., 2004; Eckert, Ardoin, Daisey, and Scarola, 2000; Eckert, Ardoin, Daly, and Martens, 2002; Noell et al., 1998). The advantage is that demands on those responsible for the intervention are minimized. For example, Duhon et al. (2004) developed a simple strategy for examining whether rewards or additional instruction were necessary to improve the performance of four students who had been referred for writing or math difficulties. A 2-min math calculation probe and a 3-min writing probe were administered to an entire class that included the four referred students. Brief, individual assessments were then conducted with each of the four students. During these assessments, performance goals were communicated to the students and rewards were offered for meeting the performance goals. Two of the students significantly improved their scores with rewards only. The other two students did not respond to rewards and required additional instructional assistance. Extended analyses of results confirmed the

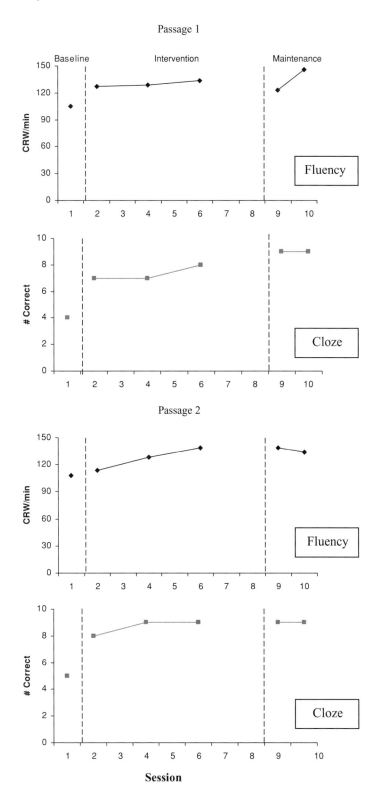

FIGURE 9.3. Relationship between fluency and comprehension.

conclusions of the initial assessment. In this study, Duhon et al. (2004) expanded standard CBM procedures by adding procedures to determine whether students would respond to a motivational strategy or an instructional strategy.

If a student does not improve responding following rewards, then instructional strategies should be investigated as a next step. For example, use of rewards might lead to limited outcomes like those presented in graph A. Instructional strategies might then be applied to other instructional materials, leading to results like those depicted in graphs C and D. Strategies that improve accuracy and fluency include modeling, practice, error correction, and performance feedback (Daly, Lentz, and Boyer, 1996a; Eckert et al., 2002).

Instructional strategies can be directly compared with a reward condition. As alluded to previously when discussing Figure 9.2, the study involved comparison of the student's performance in instruction and reward conditions. The instructional package included practice, error correction, and performance feedback, and fluency effects were assessed in taught and untaught materials. In addition, another passage was used to assess fluency improvements when the student did not receive instruction and was instead offered a reward for improving upon his previous score. The data which appear in Figure 9.2 indicate that the student hardly improved in the reward condition but did better in the instructional condition in both taught and untaught passages. Therefore, an effective intervention for that student would clearly require the use of instructional strategies.

Teachers, parents, and students themselves have been taught to use reading fluency interventions, such as listening passage preview (modeling fluent reading for the student), repeated readings (having the student repeatedly practice a passage), phrase drill error correction (having the student repeatedly practice phrases with error words), and performance feedback (telling the student how accurately and fluently they read the passage) (Bonfiglio, Daly, Persampieri, and Andersen, 2006; Daly, Persampieri, McCurdy, and Gortmaker, 2005; Gortmaker, Daly, McCurdy, Persampieri, and Hergenrader, in press; Persampieri, Gortmaker, Daly, Sheridan, and McCurdy, 2006). These strategies can be examined individually (Daly, Martens, Dool, and Hintze, 1998; Jones and Wickstrom, 2002) or in combination with one another. For example, Daly, Martens, Hamler, Dool, and Eckert

(1999) systematically evaluated combinations of intervention strategies by sequentially adding treatment components. The results suggested that some students required simpler interventions and some required more complex intervention packages. For example, if the strategy used for intervention in graph C was procedurally simpler than the strategy used for intervention in graph D, then the former strategy is preferred for that student. Each of these strategies is directly applicable to any reading text and easily tested out in a single or a small number of sessions (Daly, Chafouleas, and Skinner, 2005).

Figure 9.4 also illustrates this point. In this case, the ninth-grade student with deficits in reading fluency was exposed to two different intensities of intervention; both involved repeated readings, phrase drill error correction, and performance feedback, but one was very brief, lasting about 5 min (low-intensity condition), while the other was more time consuming, lasting about 25 min (high-intensity condition). Assessment data were collected immediately following intervention in the same passage in which intervention occurred. The data indicate that the high-intensity intervention led to greater improvements than the low-intensity intervention. This could especially be seen in the maintenance data. Although the high-intensity intervention was more effective, strong effects were also seen with the low-intensity intervention, suggesting that it could be an appropriate replacement if significant time constraints were present.

In some cases, generalization to untaught material might not be observed. Therefore, as a next step, rewards should be combined with instructional strategies. Daly, Bonfiglio, Mattson, Persampieri, and Yates (2005) improved generalized reading fluency when instructional strategies like listening passage preview, repeated readings, and error correction were carried out prior to offering a reward for meeting performance goals. The instructional strategies were applied to different passages from those in which rewards were promised. What both types of passage shared in common were many of the same words (written in a different order). Therefore, combining instructional and reinforcement strategies may produce generalized word reading in some cases, especially when generalized improvements are reinforced.

If student responding still does not improve, then two strategies should be tried. First, consider reducing the difficulty level of instructional material

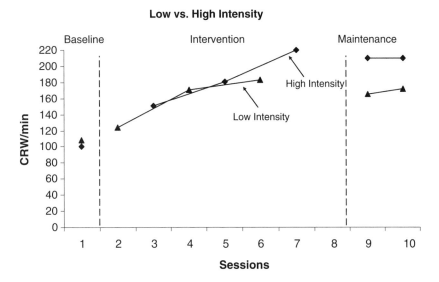

FIGURE 9.4. Example of correct read works per minute (CRW/min) in low-intensity versus high-intensity instructional conditions.

by moving down in the curriculum. Daly, Martens, Kilmer, and Massie (1996b) found greater generalization of reading fluency when difficulty level was better matched to students' instructional level (i.e., the materials were not too hard). Similar results were found by VanAuken, Chafouleas, Bradley, and Martens (2002). A second strategy is to teach responding in isolation first (e.g., by using flashcard exercises for word reading or math problems) before having the student practice in context (Daly et al., 1996b). For example, the teacher may have the student practice difficult words from texts on flashcards before having the student practice reading the story that contains those words.

9.4 Instructional Validity: Directly Assessing Instruction

We have emphasized how assessment of student responding repeatedly over time is the measure of instructional effectiveness. Unfortunately, however, intervention plans are seldom followed consistently in the absence of some type of direct observation and follow-up on the part of a consultant (Noell et al., 2005). Therefore, a critical step in the process of assessing a student's response to intervention is documenting the validity of instruction. Even the most carefully and systematically chosen and tested intervention is limited by the extent to which it is

delivered frequently and reliably and reflects sound principles of instruction.

Direct observation of instruction can be facilitated (and structured) by the use of the Instructional Validity Checklist that appears in Appendix A. Academic engagement improves student learning (Greenwood, 1994) and can serve as a valid indicator of student response to instruction (Barnett et al., 1999). Part I of the Instructional Validity Checklist allows for the collection of momentary time sampling data. Results can be summarized to indicate the percentage of time the student is actively engaged during instruction.

The assessment team should directly observe the instructional methods and behavior management strategies used by the teacher. Part II of the Instructional Validity Checklist contains principles of effective teaching that have been shown to be related to student outcomes (Witt, Daly, and Noell, 2000). These behaviors are listed on the second form of the Instructional Validity Checklist in a rating-scale format to guide your observation. Strong instruction is responsive to the student's responding and each of the strategies on the checklist should be used by the teacher *as necessary* to facilitate student engagement with the instructional task. The items on the checklist can serve as a point of departure for analyzing the quality of instruction or intervention episodes. It is important for teachers to be clear and direct when explaining and giving directions for a task. Eliminating ambiguity increases the amount of time a student can spend correctly engaging in the task rather than figuring out what they are to do or practicing incorrectly. Teachers can bolster clear and direct explanation through modeling the task and prompting the correct answer, two critical strategies for increasing response accuracy and fluency. Praising and rewarding student effort, good behavior, and even the smallest of successes are an important part of instruction because they increase student motivation and effort and help decrease behavior problems. Watching student practice increases both teacher awareness of the student's progress and the opportunities to provide positive and corrective feedback for the student's errors, which in turn facilitates accurate practice to increase correct responding. Note also items related to student proficiency, difficulty level and relevance of instruction to the student's problem, all of which address the appropriateness of instructional match. Finally, it is worth observing whether misbehavior is a problem that needs to be addressed directly during instructional sessions. If misbehavior seems to be a problem, then the reader is referred to Witt, VanDerHeyden, and Gilbertson (2004) for guidelines about what to do.

9.5 Implications for Practice

Table 9.1 includes a summary of implications for practice for each of the topics discussed in this chapter. The evaluation design should be chosen before anyone engages in assessment. It establishes the rules for determining the effectiveness of instruction in advance and acts as a deterrent to the temptation to make post-hoc judgments about effectiveness. Post-hoc judgments are notoriously biased and inconsistent (Dawes, 1994), which will have an adverse effect on student outcomes. Use of single-case designs for evaluation and accountability purposes is strongly advised.

With respect to assessments to be conducted, an evaluator may spend almost as much time planning what will be assessed as actually conducting the assessments. Assessments should reflect important dimensions of student learning. Simple fluency assessment procedures for basic skills are readily available to educators, with CBM being the most prominent version. What requires careful deliberation is the selection of assessment tasks that produce

TABLE 9.1. Implications for Practice

1. Choose an evaluation design *prior* to student evaluation.
2. Plan repeated fluency assessments that examine consistency and generality of student responding.
3. Implement a planned intervention.
   a. Try rewards. If that doesn't work:
   b. Try instructional methods like modeling, practice, error correction, and performance feedback. If that doesn't work:
   c. Try combining rewards and instruction. If that doesn't work:
   d. Try reducing difficulty level of the material and/or teaching component skills in isolation.
4. Evaluate the instructional validity of intervention sessions by examining both student engagement and the teacher's instructional behaviors.
5. Use outcome data to validate or sequentially modify instruction until student responding reaches desired level of performance.

information about the consistency and generality of students' skill proficiency. At a minimum, evaluators should routinely sample untaught but equal-difficulty-level tasks over time to check for generalization of responding. Failure to assess generalization provides an incomplete account of learning and may have a negative effect on the student if they are moved on prematurely in the curriculum. If instruction is targeted toward component skills (e.g., letter reading, phoneme blending) that should contribute to composite skills (e.g., reading words in text), then serious consideration should be given to monitoring the composite skill to determine whether instruction is impacting a student's ability to generalize use of the skill.

A wide variety of interventions appear in the literature and it is beyond the scope of this chapter to go into much detail on this topic. However, we have tried to provide guidelines in principles of instruction that are derived from our understanding of how accuracy, fluency, and consistency develop and which are broadly generalizable across skill types. For example, modeling of reading and modeling of math calculations look different in many ways. Functionally, though, they reflect the same principle of learning. The other guiding principle that we recommend is to begin with simpler interventions and increase in complexity only as necessary. It is important to keep in mind that the task may be a new one for the person who is responsible for implementing the intervention and also that they probably have other demands going on at the same time. A simpler intervention is more likely to be carried out (Lentz, Allen, and Ehrhardt, 1996).

If a student's data do not improve during an intervention phase, then it may be that the intervention was not carried out as planned. We provided an observation format that will allow documentation of instructional validity across a broad range of interventions. The best thing to do is to organize intervention steps into a step-by-step protocol (Witt et al., 2000). However, there will be many cases in which it might not be possible to do this. Evaluating student engagement and the teacher's instructional and management behaviors will provide some information about the quality of the intervention. Documenting intervention episodes over time may provide information about the frequency of intervention use, which is also likely to be an important factor in intervention effectiveness.

The real strength of this model is how data help educators be responsive to students' instructional needs. Outcome data will always indicate one of two things: (a) validation of intervention effectiveness (the desired outcome), or (b) the need for modification of the intervention plan. Fortunately, even when modification is necessary, previous intervention phases can be very "instructive" to educators, who often see ways that the intervention can be changed to promote better engagement and learning. In principle, the process repeats itself until student performance reaches an acceptable level. If we accept anything short of this, then we may be depriving a student of his or her right to a free and appropriate public education. Furthermore, this kind of direct, professional engagement with student outcomes is more likely to fan the spark of visionaries into a burning flame.

Appendix A

A.1 Instruction Validity Checklist Part I: Student Behavior

Student: Date: Instructor/Tutor: Time of Day: Length of Lesson:

Lesson Topic(s): (Check all that apply)	Phonemic awareness	Phonics/word study	Reading fluency	Comprehension	Spelling/writing

Active Student Engagement: Record student behavior at 10 second intervals using momentary time sampling; includes reading aloud, answering an academic question, asking an academic question, writing in response to teacher request, and silent reading (eye movements indicate student is scanning text).

Total for Row:

10	20	30	40	50	1 min	10	20	30	40	50	2 min	10	20	30	40	50	3 min	↓
10	20	30	40	50	4 min	10	20	30	40	50	5 min	10	20	30	40	50	6 min	
10	20	30	40	50	7 min	10	20	30	40	50	8 min	10	20	30	40	50	9 min	
10	20	30	40	50	10 min	10	20	30	40	50	11 min	10	20	30	40	50	12 min	
10	20	30	40	50	13 min	10	20	30	40	50	14 min	10	20	30	40	50	15 min	
10	20	30	40	50	16 min	10	20	30	40	50	17 min	10	20	30	40	50	18 min	
10	20	30	40	50	19 min	10	20	30	40	50	12 min	10	20	30	40	50	21 min	
10	20	30	40	50	22 min	10	20	30	40	50	23 min	10	20	30	40	50	24 min	
10	20	30	40	50	25 min	10	20	30	40	50	26 min	10	20	30	40	50	27 min	
10	20	30	40	50	28 min	10	20	30	40	50	29 min	10	20	30	40	50	30 min	

Minutes of Observation ×6 = _____ Observation Intervals   Sum of Last Column = _____

Sum of Last Column/Observation intervals = _____% Active Student Engagement for the observation.

A.2 Instruction Validity Checklist Part II

Student: Date: Instructor/Tutor:

To be filled out during or immediately after observation of student engagement during instruction.

__Instruction__: Record the degree to which each of the teaching behaviors was observed to occur.

Explaining task/Giving directions	☐ Not done at all	☐ Done some of the time	☐ Done consistently, as necessary
Modeling/Demonstrating	☐ Not done at all	☐ Done some of the time	☐ Done consistently, as necessary
Prompting correct answer	☐ Not done at all	☐ Done some of the time	☐ Done consistently, as necessary
Praising and/or rewarding	☐ Not done at all	☐ Done some of the time	☐ Done consistently, as necessary
Watched student practice	☐ Not done at all	☐ Done some of the time	☐ Done consistently, as necessary
Corrected student errors	☐ Not done at all	☐ Done some of the time	☐ Done consistently, as necessary

How **proficient** was the student with assigned work during instruction?	Student answers were often incorrect (inaccurate)	Student answers were often accurate but slow (accurate but not fluent)	Student had difficulty giving correct answers across instructional tasks (generalization problem)

Was the task at an appropriate **difficulty level** for the student?   YES   NO

Was instruction stopped more than once to correct **misbehavior**?   YES   NO

Was **instruction relevant** to the student's skill problems?   YES   NO

Notes and Observations: _____

_____

_____

_____

References

Alessi, G. (1987). Generative strategies and teaching for generalization. *The Analysis of Verbal Behavior, 5*, 15–27.

Barlow, D. H. & Hersen, M. (1984). *Single Case Experimental Designs: Strategies for Studying Behavior Change* (2nd ed.). Boston: Allyn & Bacon

Barnett, D. W. (1988). Professional judgment: a critical appraisal. *School Psychology Review, 17*, 658–672.

Barnett, D. W., Bell, S. H., Gilkey, C. M., Lentz Jr., F. E., Graden, J. L., Stone, C. M., et al. (1999). The promise of meaningful eligibility determination: functional intervention-based multifactored preschool evaluation. *The Journal of Special Education, 33*, 112–124.

Barnett, D. W., Daly III, E. J., Jones, K. M., & Lentz Jr., F. E. (2004). Empirically-based special service decisions from increasing and decreasing intensity single case designs. *Journal of Special Education, 38*, 66–79.

Binder, C. (1996). Behavioral fluency: evolution of a new paradigm. *The Behavior Analyst, 19*, 163–197.

Bonfiglio, C. M., Daly III, E. J., Persampieri, M., & Andersen, M. N. (2006). An experimental analysis of the effects of reading interventions in a small group reading instruction context. *Journal of Behavioral Education, 15*, 92–108.

Daly III, E. J., Bonfiglio, C. M., Hauger, T., Persampieri, M., & Yates, K. (2005). Refining the experimental analysis of academic skill deficits, part I: an investigation of variables affecting generalized oral reading performance. *Journal of Applied Behavior Analysis, 38*, 485–498.

Daly III, E. J., Chafouleas, S. M., & Skinner, C. H. (2005). *Interventions for Reading Problems: Designing and Evaluating Effective Strategies.* New York, NY: Guilford Press.

Daly III, E. J., Lentz, F. E., & Boyer, J. (1996a). The instructional hierarchy: a conceptual model for understanding the effective components of reading interventions. *School Psychology Quarterly, 11*, 369–386.

Daly III, E. J., Martens, B. K., Dool, E. J., & Hintze, J. M. (1998). Using brief functional analysis to select interventions for oral reading. *Journal of Behavioral Education, 8*, 203–218.

Daly III, E. J., Martens, B. K., Hamler, K., R., Dool, E. J., & Eckert, T. L. (1999). A brief experimental analysis for identifying instructional components needed to improve oral reading fluency. *Journal of Applied Behavior Analysis, 32*, 83–94.

Daly III, E. J., Martens, B. K., Kilmer, A., & Massie, D. (1996b). The effects of instructional match and content overlap on generalized reading performance. *Journal of Applied Behavior Analysis, 29*, 507–518.

Daly III, E. J., Persampieri, M., McCurdy, M., & Gortmaker, V. (2005) Generating reading interventions through experimental analysis of academic skills: demonstration and empirical evaluation. *School Psychology Review, 34*, 395–414.

Daly III, E. J., Witt, J. C., Martens, B. K., & Dool, E. J. (1997). A model for conducting a functional analysis of academic performance problems. *School Psychology Review, 26*, 554–574.

Dawes, R. M. (1994). *House of Cards: Psychology and Psychotherapy Built on Myth.* New York: The Free Press.

Duhon, G. J., Noell, G. H., Witt, J. C. Freeland, J. T., Dufrene, B. A., & Gilbertson, D. N. (2004). Identifying academic skills and performance deficits: the experimental analysis of brief assessments of academic skills. *School Psychology Review, 33*, 429–443.

Eckert, T. L., Ardoin, S. P., Daisey, D. M., & Scarola, M. D. (2000). Empirically evaluating the effectiveness of reading interventions: the use of brief experimental analysis and single-case designs. *Psychology in the Schools, 37*, 463–474.

Eckert, T. L., Ardoin, S. P., Daly III, E. J., & Martens, B. K. (2002). Improving oral reading fluency: an examination of the efficacy of combining skill-based and performance-based interventions. *Journal of Applied Behavior Analysis, 35*, 271–281.

Englemann, S., Granzin, A., & Severson, H. (1979). Diagnosing instruction. *The Journal of Special Education, 13*, 355–363.

Fisher, W. W., Kelley, M. E., & Lomas, J. E. (2003). Visual aids and structured criteria for improving visual inspection and interpretation of single-case designs. *Journal of Applied Behavior Analysis, 36*, 387–406.

Fullan, M. G. (2001). *The New Meaning of Educational Change* (3rd ed.). New York, NY: Teachers College Press.

Gortmaker, V. J., Daly III, E. J., McCurdy, M., Persampieri, M. J., & Hergenrader, M. (in press). Improving reading outcomes for children with learning disabilities: Using brief experimental analysis to develop parent tutoring interventions. *Journal of Applied Behavior Analysis.*

Greenwood, C. R. (1994). Confirming a performance-based instructional model. *School Psychology Review, 23*, 652–668.

Jones, K. M. & Wickstrom, K. F. (2002). Done in sixty seconds: Further analysis of the brief assessment model for academic problems. *School Psychology Review, 31*, 554–568.

Kazdin, A. E. (1982). *Single-Case Research Designs: Methods for Clinical and Applied Settings.* New York: Oxford.

Lentz, F. E., Allen, S. J., & Ehrhardt, K. E. (1996). The conceptual elements of strong interventions in school settings. *School Psychology Quarterly, 11*, 118–136.

Noell, G. H., Gansle, K. A., Witt, J. D., Whitmarsh, E. L., Freeland, J. T., LaFleur, L. H., et al. (1998). Effects of contingent reward and instruction on oral reading performance at differing levels of passage difficulty. *Journal of Applied Behavior Analysis, 31*, 659–664.

Noell, G. H., Witt, J. C., Slider, N. J., Connell, J. E., Gatti, S. L., Williams, K. L., et al. (2005). Treatment implementation following behavioral consultation in schools: A comparison of three follow-up strategies. *School Psychology Review, 34*, 87–106.

Parsonson, B. S. & Baer, D. M. (1992).The visual analysis of data, and current research into the stimuli controlling it. In T. R. Kratochwill & J. R. Levin (Eds.), *Single-Case Research Design and Analysis* (pp. 15–40). Hillsdale, NJ: Lawrence Erlbaum Associates.

Persampieri, M., Gortmaker, V., Daly III, E.J., Sheridan, S. M., & McCurdy, M. (2006). Promoting parent use of empirically supported reading interventions: Two experimental investigations of child outcomes. *Behavioral Interventions, 21*, 31–57.

Pinnell, G. S., Pikulski, J. J., Wixson, K. K., Campbell, J. R., Gough, P. B., & Beatty, A. S. (1995). *Listening to Children Read Aloud.* Washington, DC: Office of Educational Research and Improvement, US Department of Education.

Shapiro, E. S., Angello, L. M., & Eckert, T. L. (2004). Has curriculum-based assessment become a staple of school psychology practice? An update and extension of knowledge, use, and attitudes from 1990 to 2000. *School Psychology Review, 33*, 249–257.

Shinn, M. R. (1989). *Curriculum-based Measurement: Assessing Special Children.* New York: Guilford Press.

VanAuken, T., Chafouleas, S. M., Bradley, T. A., & Martens, B. K. (2002). Using brief experimental analysis to select oral reading interventions: an investigation of treatment utility. *Journal of Behavioral Education, 11*, 163–181.

Witt, J. C., Daly III, E. J., & Noell, G. H. (2000). *Functional Assessments: A Step-by-Step Guide to Solving Academic and Behavior Problems.* Longmont, CO: Sopris West.

Witt, J. C., VanDerHeyden, A. M., & Gilbertson, D. (2004). Troubleshooting behavioral interventions: a systematic process for finding and eliminating problems. *School Psychology Review, 33*, 363–381.

10

Ability–Achievement Discrepancy, Response to Intervention, and Assessment of Cognitive Abilities/Processes in Specific Learning Disability Identification: Toward a Contemporary Operational Definition

Kenneth A. Kavale and Dawn P. Flanagan

Kenneth A. Kavale is Distinguished Professor of Special Education at Regent University, Virginia Beach, VA.
kkavale@cox.net
Dawn P. Flanagan, PhD, is professor in the school psychology program at St. John's University in New York.
flanagad@stjohns.edu

The category of specific learning disability (SLD) remains the largest and most contentious area of special education. A primary problem is overidentification of students with SLD as evidenced by the SLD category representing approximately 5% of the school population and 50% of the special education population. Partially responsible for this problem is the overreliance on the ability–achievement discrepancy criterion as the sole indicator of SLD, a practice that remains widespread. Recently, new ways to conceptualize and define SLD have been proposed in an attempt to remedy the overidentification problem (e.g., Fletcher, Coulter, Reschly, and Vaughn, 2004). Most popular is a model that conceptualizes SLD in terms of a failure to respond to intervention (RTI) (Berninger and Abbott, 1994).

The purpose of this chapter is to briefly review these two methods of SLD identification, the ability–achievement discrepancy criterion and RTI. It is our belief that neither of these methods, when used as the sole indicator of SLD, can identify this condition reliably and validly. This is because SLD may be present in students with *and without* a significant ability–achievement discrepancy (see Aaron (1997) for a comprehensive review) and in students who fail to respond *and who do respond favorably to* scientifically based interventions. We believe the missing component in both of these SLD methods is information on the student's functioning across a broad range of cognitive abilities and processes, particularly those that explain significant variance in academic achievement. Indeed, the federal definition of SLD is "a disorder in one or more of the basic psychological processes..." (Individuals with Disabilities Education Act [IDEA] 2004). Therefore, this chapter discusses evaluation of cognitive abilities/processes as defined by contemporary Cattell–Horn–Carroll (CHC) theory and its research base. Inherent in this discussion is a summary of the research on the relations between cognitive abilities/processes and academic achievement, information we believe is necessary to (a) determine whether a processing deficit(s) is the probable cause of a student's academic difficulties and (b) restructure and redirect interventions for nonresponders in an RTI model.

Keogh (2005) discussed criteria for determining the adequacy and utility of a diagnostic system, such as the ability–achievement discrepancy and RTI models. The criteria include *homogeneity* (Do category members resemble one another?), *reliability* (Is there agreement about who should be included in the category?), and *validity* (Does category membership provide consistent information?). Keogh (2005, p. 101) suggested that, SLD "is real and that it describes problems that are distinct from other conditions subsumed under the broad category of problems in learning and achievement." The question is how to best capture the distinctiveness of SLD. Having a significant ability–achievement discrepancy or being nonresponsive to treatment does not appear sufficient. Therefore, we offer an operational definition of SLD that (a) begins with an RTI method, (b) focuses on documentation of cognitive ability/processing deficits and integrities for nonresponders, (c) identifies a link between below-average processes and academic skills, and (d) does not require the identification of a significant ability–achievement discrepancy. As such, our operational definition is consistent with IDEA 2004 and its attendant regulations (34 CFR Part 300). It is our hope that this operational definition will meet Keogh's criteria for an adequate diagnostic system.

10.1 The Ability–Achievement Discrepancy Criterion

The discrepancy criterion has been the primary operational definition of SLD since 1977 when it was codified in federal law (US Office of Education, 1977). The origins of discrepancy and SLD identification are found in Bateman's (1965) definition and the discrepancy criterion is the primary means of identifying SLD to date (Reschly and Hosp, 2004). Nevertheless, over time, the discrepancy model has come under increasing criticism (e.g., Aaron, 1997; Gresham, 2002; Sternberg and Grigorenko, 2002), leading to recommendations that this method be eliminated (e.g., Lyon et al., 2001). Despite these recommendations, the reauthorization of IDEA does not eliminate the historically important discrepancy criterion but instead states that agencies shall *not be required* to use discrepancy in SLD identification procedures.

Whereas many of the arguments against the ability–achievement discrepancy method can be challenged on several bases (as discussed below; see also Kavale, Kaufman, Naglieri, and Hale, 2005, for a review), some of the arguments against ability–achievement discrepancy have merit. One of the major problems with the discrepancy model has been the failure to implement it in a steadfast manner (MacMillan, Gresham, and Bocian, 1998; MacMillan and Siperstein, 2002). Consequently, sometimes

up to 50% of SLD populations have been found not to meet the required discrepancy criterion (Kavale and Reese, 1992). When the single stipulated identification criterion is not met, the basis for SLD status is not attained and the validity of the classification must be called into question. The implementation problem is not remedied by discrepancy models such as the one described by Peterson and Shinn (2002). For example, the *absolute achievement discrepancy* model represents SLD simply as the low end of the achievement distribution. The *relative achievement discrepancy* model compares individual student performance with other students in a particular school. These models fail because they make the context of evaluation (i.e., individual school setting) the primary influence on SLD determination. For example, in a school where the average student scores 90 on a norm-referenced assessment with a mean of 100 and a standard deviation of 15, a student with an IQ of 110 and achievement score of 85 would not appear to possess an academic problem, but a student with an IQ of 80 and achievement score of 75 might appear to be SLD in that context.

A related problem is the failure to recognize that discrepancy is actually the operational definition of *underachievement* (Thorndike, 1963); discrepancy is not the operational definition of SLD. It is, consequently, incorrect to assume that meeting the discrepancy criterion completes an SLD diagnosis (Kavale and Forness, 2000b). As originally conceptualized, the SLD construct was predicated on the presence of underachievement, not simply low achievement (LA) (Chalfant and King, 1976).

Complicating the notion of discrepancy as the operational definition of underachievement is the fact that all total intelligence test scores are not created equal. Therefore, whether or not a student displays a discrepancy is partly a function of the intelligence test used in an evaluation of suspected SLD. Suppose a student has reading difficulties because of slow processing speed (with other abilities within the average range). If the total test score from the Cognitive Assessment System (CAS; Das and Naglieri, 1997) were used in a discrepancy formula, then the student would be less likely to display a discrepancy than if the Kaufman Assessment Battery for Children–Second Edition (KABC-II; Kaufman and Kaufman, 2004) were used. This is because approximately half of the subtests that contribute to the CAS total test score are speeded (e.g., Keith,

Kranzler, and Flanagan, 2001), whereas none of the subtests that contribute to the total test scores of the KABC-II are speeded.[1] A non-significant discrepancy may be found simply because the cognitive abilities/processes that are responsible for low achievement have attenuated the total test score, such as in the CAS example. If those specific abilities/processes could be removed from the total test score and in so doing a significant discrepancy emerged, then this finding would suggest underachievement. In short, while the finding of a non-significant discrepancy may rule out underachievement in some cases, it does not rule out underachievement in all cases.

Furthermore, while a significant discrepancy between ability and achievement represents underachievement in some cases, it does not represent underachievement in all cases. For example, an average reader (with standard scores of about 100 on reading tests) may have a full-scale IQ in the very superior range (e.g., > 130) because of specific cognitive strengths in some, but not all, abilities that encompass the full-scale score. Practitioners who interpret this type of significant discrepancy (30 points or two standard deviations in this example) as underachievement have mistakenly assumed that a student who has superior ability in one area ought to have superior ability in all areas. This assumption is simply wrong. Significant variability in an individual's cognitive ability profile is common and, therefore, is to be expected (see McGrew and Knopik, 1996; Oakley, 2006). In summary, good readers may have IQs that are significantly above their standardized reading test scores simply because they have significant strengths in specific cognitive abilities/processes that make up IQ. It is important to recognize that these strengths are unusual, and indeed valuable, deviations from the norm. A student with significant strengths in some areas should not be diagnosed with SLD simply because they have average abilities in other areas. Average ability is not a disability. Nevertheless, average readers with superior IQs are mistakenly diagnosed as SLD routinely.

Critiques of the discrepancy model are often linked to calls for eliminating IQ tests in the SLD

identification process (e.g., Siegel, 1989). These calls are part of the continuing vilification of IQ testing that, in reality, possesses little justification (see Carroll and Horn, 1981; Flanagan, Ortiz, Alfonso, and Dynda, 2006; Flanagan, Ortiz, Alfonso, and Mascolo, 2006; Gottfredson, 1997a, 1997b). Nevertheless, the wrongheaded view of IQ testing continues in the SLD field with the patently false view that intelligence tests are either not useful, irrelevant, or discriminatory in the identification process (Fletcher et al., 1998; Siegel, 1999). The IQ score is assumed irrelevant because it is confounded by achievement, but such a perception fails to consider how an IQ score can be a "good" predictor of academic skills if IQ and achievement are unrelated. The correlations between IQ and reading achievement range from $r = 0.30$ to $r = 0.80$ depending upon age, IQ test, and achievement assessment. These correlations are hardly irrelevant and support the predictive validity of intelligence tests. By accounting for about 50% of the variance in global achievement, an IQ score does not impose limits on academic performance as suggested by Siegel (1999). Additionally, the large proportion of unexplained variance makes it difficult to accept the assumption that low IQ *causes* SLD (Stanovich, 1999). In fact, most of the variability in specific academic skills is due to factors other than global IQ (e.g., *specific* cognitive abilities and processes, motivation, appropriateness of instruction, etc.), but IQ remains the best single predictor of global achievement as measured by standardized achievement tests (e.g., a total score from a standardized comprehensive achievement battery) (see Glutting, Yongstrom, Ward, Ward and Hale, 1997).

Because, the discrepancy model has historically sought to document underachievement at a global level (IQ–achievement difference), it is not surprising that IQ was found not to differentiate between reading disabled groups (i.e., IQ-discrepant versus IQ-nondiscrepant). Unfortunately, current research and critiques of SLD definitions continue to treat IQ under the outdated assumption that intelligence is solely "g" or general intelligence (Buckhalt, 2000). Although g is important for dealing with the complexity of everyday life (Gottfredson, 1997b), its sole value for SLD identification is in providing an expected achievement level (along with other variables such as motivation) necessary for determining the presence of under- or over-achievement and only

---

[1] The KABC-II has no timed subtests for children aged 3–7 years. A non-timed condition may be used for older children.

when the IQ is not attenuated by deficits in specific cognitive abilities/processes.[2]

Over time, cognitive ability tests have moved away from "g" (i.e., providing a single IQ score) and now, besides providing a total test score, assess multiple and complex theoretically validated cognitive abilities/processes (Flanagan and Kaufman, 2004; Flanagan and Ortiz, 2001; Kaufman and Kaufman, 2001). Consequently, new intelligence tests (e.g., WJ III, KABC-II) possess significant value for identifying individual differences in cognitive functioning *and* insight into the nature of underlying cognitive deficits and integrities. Would the body of research showing no differences between RD groups have differed using current intelligence tests that contain measures of valid cognitive constructs with known relations to reading achievement (e.g., phonological processing, working memory, processing speed, fluid reasoning)? We believe the answer to this question is "yes." There is much research available to support this conclusion (e.g., Evans, Carlson and McGrew, 1993; Flanagan, 2000; McGrew, Flanagan, Keith, and Vanderwood, 1997; Vanderwood, McGrew, Keith, and Flanagan, 2002). The interested reader is referred to Flanagan et al.'s (2006b) comprehensive summary of the relations between specific cognitive abilities/processes and reading, math, and written language achievement.

SLD also has been associated with "average" IQ levels, but there have been long-standing suggestions that SLD occurs at all IQ levels (e.g., Ames, 1968; Cruickshank, 1977). This seems ill-advised, because IQ levels in the below-average range (e.g., <85) introduce the "slow learner" problem and eliminate unexpected school failure from the SLD construct. Conversely, IQ levels in the above average to superior ranges are also problematic for SLD identification as mentioned above. To illustrate, Siegel (2003) criticized the discrepancy model for not identifying a student with an IQ of 130 and achievement score of 110. This criticism was unfounded be-

cause it is inappropriate to use the SLD designation for "relatively well-functioning students" (Flanagan, Keiser, Bernier, and Ortiz, 2003; Flanagan et al., 2006a; Gordon, Lewandowski, and Keiser, 1999). As a disability classification, SLD should only be associated with *significantly below-average achievement levels*. Special services may be beneficial for all students experiencing academic difficulties (including those who have average achievement levels), but the need for some type of educational intervention provides an inadequate reason for SLD identification. That is, the SLD category should not be made the convenient entry to special education for any and all students who might otherwise not receive special services.

In sum, the ability–achievement discrepancy criterion does not meet Keogh's (2005) criteria for determining the adequacy and utility of a diagnostic system. There is ample evidence to show that the discrepancy criterion does not capture the distinctiveness of SLD. At best, the discrepancy criterion may serve as a means of identifying underachievement when the ability measure is not attenuated by ability/processing deficiencies.

10.2 Response to Intervention

The RTI process is based on the concept of treatment validity whose goal is "to simultaneously inform, foster, and document the necessity for and effectiveness of special treatment" (Fuchs and Fuchs, 1998, pp. 204–205). The viability of an RTI model has been tested (e.g., Fletcher et al., 2002; McMaster, Fuchs, Fuchs, and Compton, 2005; Vaughn, Linan-Thompson, and Hickman, 2003), but the RTI model is far from complete (Mellard, Deshler, and Barth, 2004). To enhance the RTI process, a National Research Center on Learning Disabilities was established to conduct research on SLD identification and classification (Fuchs, Deshler, and Reschly, 2004).

In the context of special education, the RTI model is best viewed as a process aimed at prevention of significant reading difficulties (Kavale, Holdnack, and Mostert, 2005). However, as presently constituted, RTI appears to erroneously equate reading disability/difficulty (RD) and SLD. Almost all studies questioning the validity of discrepancy-based classifications have studied students with reading disability/difficulty, not other types of SLD (e.g.,

---

[2] For example, if one or more abilities/processes that make up the total test score on an intelligence battery is deficient (e.g., <85), then the total test score would be higher if those scores were removed from its calculation. The assumption is that the abilities/processes in which the student is deficient are responsible for the low achievement; see Flanagan et al. (2006b) for a comprehensive discussion.

Stanovich, 1991; Stuebing et al., 2001; Vellutino, Scanlon, and Lyon, 2000). Consequently, these investigations may influence decisions about "specific reading retardation" (Rutter and Yule, 1975), but they do not necessarily generalize to other types of SLD. The rationale that RD is the most common form of SLD (see Stanovich, 2005) fails to acknowledge that other types of SLD, such as mathematics disorder, can stand alone as a construct independent of RD (Kavale and Forness, 1995). Nevertheless, in the RTI model, students experiencing early reading difficulties are provided with increasingly frequent and intensive interventions; and if they continue to be "treatment resisters" (Torgeson, 2000), then they are deemed eligible for special education under the SLD designation. To date, the RTI process only confirms the presence of significant reading difficulties. The question of whether the student is RD or has another type of SLD remains.

Although one may have some justification for inferring RD from the RTI process, the SLD designation in the RTI model seems to be conferred by decree. As suggested by Kavale et al. (2005a, p. 12), "What is the basis for the SLD designation? In reality, there is none, unless there is some legerdemain whereby all [reading difficulties] magically transform... into SLD." With its lack of diagnostic validity, the RTI model is best viewed as a prereferral process (Pugach and Johnson, 1989). The prereferral process has, however, been marked by inconsistent implementation with problems in terminology, professional ownership, and practical matters (e.g., size of team, nature of problems addressed, extent of team involvement in intervention) (e.g., Buck, Polloway, Smith-Thomas, and Cook, 2003; Truscott, Cohen, Sams, Sanborn, and Frank, 2005). Notwithstanding, the real value of RTI lies in the prospect of providing a systematic and rigorous prereferral process (e.g., Fuchs, Fuchs, and Compton, 2004; Mellard, Byrd, Johnson, Tollefson, and Boesche, 2004).

When the RTI model deems a student eligible for special education services (even though SLD status remains unknown), it is because scientifically validated interventions did not result in an expected positive response. Such a finding suggests the presence of unique and idiosyncratic learning needs. However, the RTI model does not suggest the type of individualized instruction that should be provided next, precisely because the model does not contain

a mechanism for identifying the presumptive cause of the student's learning needs. A student who does not demonstrate a positive response to scientifically validated interventions should not be placed in special education without essential diagnostic and instructional planning information. It is our contention that this information is best obtained from a comprehensive evaluation of cognitive abilities/processes, academic achievement, and psychosocial functioning (Flanagan et al., 2006b; Kavale et al., 2005). In the absence of such information, students who fail to respond to intervention will be educated no differently in special education classrooms than the hundreds of thousands of students who have been placed there based *solely* on a discrepancy between ability and achievement. This is because each model fails to provide a crucial element that is necessary for constructing *individualized* educational plans, information about students' specific cognitive ability/processing integrities and deficiencies and their relationship to academic skills. Whereas some operational definitions of SLD use an ability–achievement discrepancy as a foundation for SLD, or as a necessary but not sufficient condition for an SLD diagnosis (Kavale and Forness, 2000a, 2000b), the RTI process offers no direction for further diagnostic activities even with the tedious operationalization of unexpected underachievement in "hybrid models" combining low achievement and RTI (see Fletcher, Denton, and Francis, 2005).

By clustering all low-achieving (LA) students into a single group, the RTI model offers no means for differentiating among members to determine who can be designated SLD. Besides the presence or absence of underachievement, exclusionary criteria are often considered, but there is no justification for assuming those remaining are SLD. For example, IDEA guidelines exclude students with mental retardation (MR) from SLD classification. Without information from an intelligence test, how is it possible to determine if overall ability is below the requisite level of 70 (or perhaps 75) for MR classification? Although MR is specifically excluded from SLD consideration, the student with an IQ of 70 (or 75) to 85 (or 90) represents the "slow learner" for who there is increasing desire to provide special education services even though never a recognized special education category. The problem is that the slow learner is not an underachiever; achievement is at a level consonant with cognitive ability (Keogh,

1994). When underachievement is not documented, an RTI process that selects students solely on the basis of LA will likely include those whose academic problems are expected ("slow learners").

The RTI model seems predicated on the assumption that those who fail to respond possess the same cognitive deficits regardless of IQ level. Although RTI is presently based on a limited conceptualization of reading (i.e., word decoding), it, nevertheless, remains important to identify cognitive strengths to facilitate better understanding of SLD and the best ways to develop intervention plans. In essence, the RTI model does not provide an answer to the question, "which cognitive abilities/processes are deficient and which ones remain intact?"

The SLD construct has long been associated with intra-individual differences. To understand an individual student's array of strengths and weaknesses, a comprehensive cognitive assessment is the most efficient means to reveal cognitive integrities, as well as deficiencies. With the neurological bases for SLD supported (e.g., Galaburda, 2005; Kibby and Hynd, 2001), it becomes important to determine how specific cognitive deficits may be causally linked to specific academic deficits. Such an analysis describes the nature of SLD, which is not captured by simply describing achievement deficits that are not amenable to remedial efforts.

In sum, although a variety of RTI models are available (see Fuchs, Mock, Morgan, and Young, 2003), like the ability–achievement discrepancy models, none of the RTI models appears to meet all of Keogh's criteria (homogeneity, reliability, validity) for determining the adequacy and utility of a diagnostic system. If the question is how to best capture the distinctiveness of SLD, then simply being nonresponsive to treatment does not appear sufficient. Although it is our contention that the RTI model cannot legitimately identify SLD, the process does serve to create a pool of at-risk students who may or may not have SLD.

10.3 Cognitive Ability/Processing Assessment

As stated above, cognitive ability/processing deficits define SLD: "The term 'specific learning disability' means a disorder in one or more of the basic psychological processes...." Yet, cognitive ability/processing deficits have not been a primary identification criterion and have not been included in many states' operational definitions of the federal definition. Consequently, there has been a long-standing disconnect between elements stipulated in the formal definition and the elements selected for inclusion in operational definitions which undermines valid scientific principles (Kavale and Forness, 2000a, 2000b). Cognitive ability/processing deficits represent the *essence* of SLD and, in a sense, make SLD what it is (Flanagan, 2003; Flanagan, Ortiz, Alfonso, and Mascolo, 2002, 2006b; Kavale and Forness, 1995). In other words, it is our belief that an SLD diagnosis cannot be made in the absence of well-documented processing deficits (along with other variables).

Early conceptualizations of SLD emphasized the role of perceptual-motor processes, but these were shown to lack sufficient reliability and validity (Coles, 1978; Mann, 1971). The subsequent downgrading of perceptual-motor processes was clearly seen in the decision to ensconce discrepancy as the primary operational indicator of SLD. Nevertheless, when asked the question "What shall we do with psychological processes?", Torgesen (1979, p. 520) responded, "we should keep the concept of psychological processes alive. The notion of deficiencies in the processing activities required for learning is essential to the maintenance of concern with learning disabled children as a special subgroup within the general population of underachievers." Torgesen's response is consistent with that of many current researchers (e.g., Flanagan, 2003; Flanagan and Kaufman, 2004; Flanagan et al., 2006a, 2006b; Gregg, Coleman, and Knight, 2003; Kaufman, Lichtenberger, Fletcher-Janzen, and Kaufman, 2004; Kavale et al., 2005; Mather and Schrank, 2003; Naglieri, 2005). In fact, all current intelligence tests are far more differentiated than their predecessors. Each test includes multiple theoretically validated measures of broad and specific cognitive ability/processing constructs, thereby reflecting the importance of evaluating processing strengths and integrities, particularly for evaluation of SLD (Kaufman, Kaufman, Kaufman, and Kaufman, 2005; Kavale et al., 2005; Naglieri, 2005; Roid and Pomplun, 2005; Schrank, 2006).

In examining the relationship between auditory and visual perception and reading ability, Kavale and Forness (2000a) found a correlation of $r = 0.597$ between the ITPA-Sound Blending subtest and reading, indicating a 60% increase in accurately predicting reading ability. Presently, sound blending would be viewed in terms of a phonological processing deficit affecting reading ability (Stanovich, 1985). This hypothesis has been validated by findings showing that phonological processing deficits are a primary characteristic of students who fail to respond in the RTI model (Al-Otaiba and Fuchs, 2002).

Whereas phonological processing deficits may differentiate "dyslexic" and "garden-variety poor readers" (Stanovich, 1988), they represent a deficit associated with reading difficulties; the SLD status of the individual student still needs to be determined. Just like the studies that questioned the validity of discrepancy classifications of students with reading disability/difficulty, the focus on phonological processing and early reading suggests that conclusions may be valid for "specific reading disability/difficulty" but not SLD (Rutter and Yule, 1975). The continuing failure to differentiate reading disability/difficulty from other types of SLD leads to erroneous and misguided suggestions, like defining SLD solely in terms of phonological and orthographic processing deficits because they differentiate types of reading disability/difficulty that the discrepancy model presumably cannot (see Spear-Swerling and Sternberg, 1996). Similarly, Dean and Burns (2002) suggested that a processing component in SLD definitions does not differentiate students with SLD from low achievers but provides research support focusing almost exclusively on students with reading disability/difficulty. The confound between SLD and reading disability/difficulty must be eliminated if efforts to improve SLD identification are to be successful.

The emphasis on phonological processing in the RTI model may be misleading. First, Swanson, Trainin, Necoechea, and Hammill (2003), after examining the correlational evidence, concluded that the importance of phonological awareness and rapid naming in accounting for reading may be overstated (see also Vukovic and Siegel, 2006). Second, Nelson, Benner, and Gonzalez (2003) found nonresponsiveness to be associated with a number of other learner characteristics in addition to phonological processing. Third, beyond RD, Kavale and Nye (1991) demonstrated how a variety of processing deficits may contribute to SLD. Processes related to attention, memory, perception, metacognition, and motivation, among others, have been similarly associated with SLD and essentially define SLD status. Consequently, the presence of processing deficits needs to be confirmed by a comprehensive evaluation. We agree with Francis et al. (2005) that IQ and achievement scores are not sufficient for SLD identification. As such, it seems clear that information about specific cognitive abilities/processes is necessary to insure reliable and valid SLD identification and to provide insight regarding individual functioning.

In moving away from a strict "g" interpretation, a number of theories about the structure of cognitive abilities have been developed (see Flanagan, Genshaft, and Harrison, 1997; Flanagan and Harrison, 2005). Among the most comprehensive and empirically validated is the CHC theory of cognitive abilities, which is used for selecting, organizing, and interpreting tests of intelligence and cognitive abilities (Flanagan and Ortiz, 2001; Flanagan, Ortiz, and Alfonso, 2007) and was recently expanded to include tests of academic achievement (Flanagan et al., 2002, 2006b). The CHC model includes 10 broad cognitive abilities that subsume over 70 narrow abilities. For example, the Broad Stratum II ability of long-term storage and retrieval (*Glr*) is composed of 13 Narrow Stratum I abilities (e.g., meaningful memory, word fluency, originality/creativity). Other Broad Stratum II abilities include crystallized intelligence (*Gc*), fluid reasoning (*Gf*), short-term memory (*Gsm*), visual processing (*Gv*), auditory processing (*Ga*), processing speed (*Gs*), and decision speed/reaction time (*Gt*). These cognitive abilities represent "processes" and, as suggested by Carroll (1993, p. 10), "A cognitive task is one in which suitable processing of mental information is the major determinant of whether the task is successfully performed." Assessment of these broad and narrow CHC abilities/processes is thus useful for identifying specific cognitive processing deficits and providing insight into the nature of unique learning needs.

The CHC model also includes two "achievement" Broad Stratum II abilities: reading and writing (*Grw*) and quantitative knowledge (*Gq*). The *Grw* domain includes eight narrow Stratum I abilities (reading decoding, reading comprehension, verbal language comprehension, cloze ability, spelling ability, writing ability, english usage knowledge, reading speed) and the quantitative knowledge domain includes two (math knowledge and math achievement). These achievement domains are included in CHC theory because there is virtually no distinction made between *cognitive* ability and *academic* ability in the cognitive psychology literature. The difference between cognitive and academic abilities is partially related to the different types of learning (formal and experiential) involved in their development. Carroll (1993, p. 510) suggested that cognitive and academic abilities are on a continuum extending from "the most general abilities to the most specialized types of knowledges," with the latter developing as a function of more formal and direct instructional and educational experiences. Simply put, "Cognitive abilities are measures of achievements, and measures of achievements are just as surely measures of cognitive abilities" (Horn, 1988, p. 655).

In reviews of the relations between cognitive abilities/processes and reading, math, and written language achievement, Flanagan et al. (2002, 2006b) demonstrated the importance of specific or narrow CHC abilities in explaining and predicting academic achievement. That is, many broad and narrow CHC abilities/processes are directly linked to achievement. The CHC theoretical framework provides a common terminology and set of definitions that reduces the possibility of misinterpretation of findings. Additionally, the CHC model permits assessments to be individually matched to student needs which can then provide data more closely linked to intervention: "Evaluation of individuals with learning difficulties that are *theory focused* and grounded in current research are more psychometrically respectable and have more accountability than those that are *test-kit focused* or devoid of a firm grounding in contemporary theory and research" (Flanagan et al., 2002, p. 62, italics in original).

The evaluation of the specific abilities/processes that are most closely associated with referral concerns (e.g., reading difficulties, math difficulties) is often based on "cross-battery assessment (XBA)" (Flanagan and Ortiz, 2001; Flanagan et al., 2007) where testing proceeds by "crossing" batteries (i.e., the careful selection of tests needed to supplement standard battery information). Based on an operational definition provided by Kavale and Forness (2000a, 2000b), Flanagan et al. (2002, 2006b)

defined SLD in terms of CHC theory and its research base. This definition is described below.

10.4 An Operational Definition of Learning Disability

Kavale and Forness (2000a, 2000b) published one of the first general operational definitions of SLD. Their model included several levels, each of which was a "necessary but not sufficient" condition for SLD. When all conditions were met, however, sufficient data existed to make the SLD diagnosis. This model was an important development because it provided the specificity necessary to allow SLD to be operationalized more reliably. A modified version of this definition was presented by Flanagan et al. (2002, 2006b). These researchers incorporated CHC theory into the definition, thereby allowing both theory and research to guide the SLD identification process. They also restructured the component levels of Kavale and Forness's operational definition to provide a better correspondence with the assessment and evaluation process (Flanagan et al., 2006a). Whereas their operational definition introduced the concept of *consistency between cognitive and academic deficits*, it still allowed for use of a discrepancy approach, but only after the consistency was documented. Like Kavale and Forness's definition, the definition provided by Flanagan and colleagues consists of different levels (see Figure 10.1). As will become evident, it is only when the criteria at each of the four levels are met that SLD can be diagnosed under this model.

Consistent with IDEA 2004 and its attendant regulations (34 CFR Parts 300, 301, and 304) we see the use of norm-referenced ability testing as only one method among many that may be used in the evaluation of SLD. We wish to emphasize that, prior to engaging in the use of norm-referenced ability testing, other important and significant data sources should have already been collected, preferably within the context of RTI and other prereferral activities, including results from informal testing, direct observation of behaviors, work samples, reports from people familiar with the student's difficulties, such as teachers or parents, information provided by the student, and so forth. The operational definition is used when RTI methods meet with little to no success.

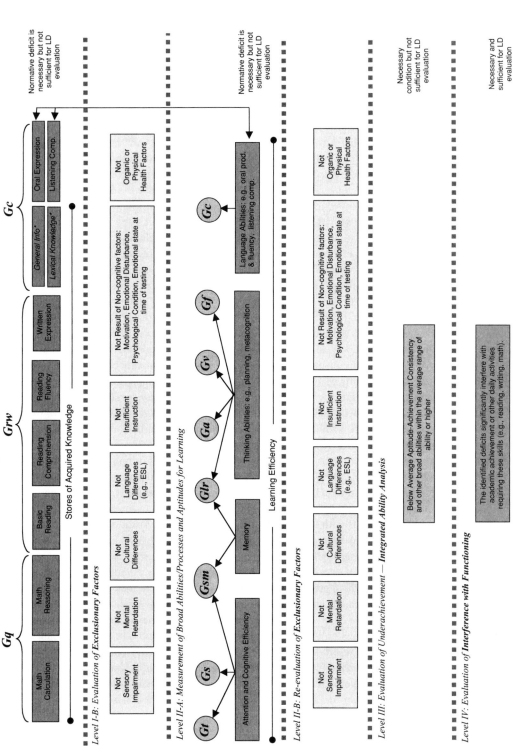

FIGURE 10.1. A definition of SLD incorporating CHC theory and research.

Note. This figure was developed by Flanagan, Ortiz, Alfonso, and Mascolo (2002) and was adapted with permission from John Wiley & Sons. All rights reserved.

10.4.1 Level I-A: Measurement of Specific Academic Skills and Acquired Knowledge

Level I represents perhaps the most basic concept involved in SLD, that academic learning is somehow disrupted from its normal course on the basis of some type of internal dysfunction. Although the specific mechanism that inhibits learning is not directly observable, we can proceed on the assumption that it does manifest itself in observable phenomena, particularly in areas of academic achievement. Thus, the most logical and initial component of an operational definition of SLD should be establishing the fact that some type of *learning* dysfunction exists apart from reported low achievement (e.g., teacher reports). If no academic deficit or documented failure to respond to appropriate instruction can be found, whether through the use of standardized tests, RTI, or any other viable method, then the issue of SLD becomes moot because such dysfunction is a necessary component of the definition.

Assessment activities at Level I-A usually involve comprehensive assessment of the major areas of academic achievement (e.g., reading, writing, and math abilities). For convenience, as well as practical reasons, the academic abilities depicted in Figure 10.1 at this level in the hierarchy are organized according to the eight areas of achievement specified in IDEA 2004 (i.e., the regulation), math calculation, math problem solving, basic reading, reading comprehension, reading fluency, written expression, oral expression, and listening comprehension. The definitions of these academic domains are neither provided in IDEA 2004 nor based on any particular theoretical formulation. As such, they remain vague and nonspecific. Therefore, for theoretical and psychometric reasons, the academic abilities depicted at this level have also been organized according to the broad CHC abilities that encompass these achievement domains (i.e., *Gq*, *Grw*, and *Gc*). Generally speaking, Level I abilities tend to represent an individual's *stores of acquired knowledge*. These specific knowledge bases (i.e., *Gq*, *Grw*, and *Gc*) develop almost exclusively as a function of formal instruction, schooling, and educationally related experiences.

At Level I-A, the performance of the student is compared with the test's norm sample. The evaluator must answer the following question: Is performance relative to individuals of the same age in the general population within normal limits or higher? If yes, SLD is ruled out; if no, then further assessment is needed to rule out SLD. Note that the comparison is not based on performance within the individual, but rather performance of the individual contrasted with other individuals. Thus, person-relative discrepancies, no matter how large, are generally not useful as indicators of dysfunction unless one of the student's scores falls below the normative range (e.g., standard score of less than 85). Unless test data indicate a normative deficit in one or more areas of academic functioning, advancement to Level I-B analysis is unwarranted. If the criterion of a normative deficit in academic achievement is not met, then the evaluator should either reassess the sufficiency of the academic evaluation or reexamine the referral questions and concerns. For example, it is entirely possible that the test selected for initial evaluation simply failed to adequately assess the specific area of presumed dysfunction.

10.4.2 Level I-B: Evaluation of Exclusionary Factors

Level I-B involves evaluating whether the documented academic skill or knowledge deficit found through Level I-A analysis is *primarily* the result of factors other than an intrinsic cognitive dysfunction. Because the potential reasons for low performance are many and do not always reflect an actual manifestation of SLD, clinicians must be careful not to ascribe causal links to SLD prematurely and should develop reasonable hypotheses related to other potential causes. For example, cultural or language differences are factors that can adversely affect test performance and result in data that appear to suggest SLD. In addition, factors such as insufficient instruction, lack of motivation, emotional disturbance, performance anxiety, psychiatric disorders, sensory impairments, and medical conditions (e.g., hearing or vision problems), need to be ruled out as potential explanatory correlates to any deficiencies identified at Level I-A.

Noteworthy is the fact that the use of RTI methods prior to evaluation of specific abilities via norm-referenced ability testing can be used to assist in evaluating the data collected to this point. If RTI methods were employed prior to referral for testing, it is very likely that many of the plausible external reasons for the academic deficiency have already been ruled out (e.g., lack of sufficient instruction, lack of motivation, cultural and linguistic differences). Alternatively, some relevant and important exclusionary factors may not be uncovered until later in the assessment process. This is because it may not be possible to rule out certain conditions at this level, such as MR, which may necessitate Level II-A assessment (i.e., assessment of cognitive abilities/processes). When the conditions listed at Level I-B have been assessed, at least those that can be reliably evaluated and determined not to be the primary reason for the observed academic deficits, assessment may advance to Level II-A.

10.4.3 Level II-A: Measurement of Abilities/Processes and Aptitudes for Learning

Level II-A evaluation is similar to Level I-A evaluation, except that it focuses on cognitive ability/processes rather than on academic skills. In general, the process of assessment at Level II-A proceeds with the expectation that an individual will perform within normal limits (i.e., standard scores of 85 to 115, inclusive) in all or nearly all of the areas listed in this level in Figure 10.1. The questions that must be answered at this level are as follows: (1) Is performance on tests of cognitive ability or processing within normal limits relative to people of the same age in the general population? (2) If a deficit in cognitive ability/processing is found, is it empirically or logically related to the academic skill deficit? Of the more salient aspects involved in creating an operational definition of SLD, none is more central than the need to establish the potential presence of a *normative deficit* in a particular cognitive ability/process that is related to and is the presumptive cause of the observed academic deficit(s). This is because SLD is defined as a *disorder* in one or more psychological processes. Although the term "disorder" may be defined in numerous ways, it seems clear that this term is not synonymous with *average* ability. A disorder implies "dysfunction," "deficit," or "disability." Therefore, documenting a disorder should be based on population-relative comparisons.

The cognitive abilities depicted at this level in the evaluation hierarchy in Figure 10.1 are organized according to the broad abilities specified by CHC theory (i.e., Gs, Gsm, Glr, Ga, Gv, Gf, and Gc). These CHC abilities are organized further according to the processes they represent primarily from an information processing perspective, including attention and cognitive efficiency, memory, "thinking abilities," and language abilities (e.g., Dean and Woodcock, 1999; Woodcock, 1993). The latter category represents the collection of Gc narrow abilities that more accurately reflect processing skills as opposed to the abilities that represent stores of acquired knowledge that were included at Level I-A. Generally speaking, the abilities depicted at Level II-A provide valuable information about an individual's *learning efficiency*. Development of most of the cognitive abilities/processes represented at this level tend to be less dependent on formal classroom instruction and schooling as compared to the abilities presented at Level I-A (Carroll, 1993, 1997). Furthermore, specific or narrow abilities within many of the CHC areas listed in Level II-A may be combined to yield specific aptitudes for learning in different areas (e.g., reading, math, writing). These aptitudes are expected to be related to and consistent with academic outcomes. For example, deficiency in phonetic coding (a narrow Ga ability), naming facility (a narrow Glr ability), or working memory (a Gsm ability), or some combination thereof, may be used to explain a deficit in basic reading skill (when other factors have been ruled out; see Table 10.1). This is because these abilities/processes have been found to explain significant variance in basic reading skill (e.g., Fletcher et al., 2002). Moreover, deficiency in one or more of these cognitive abilities/processes is consistent with the "disorder in one or more of the basic psychological processes" terminology used in the federal definition of SLD.

Data generated at Level II-A, like the data generated at Level I-A, provide input for Level III analyses, should the process advance to the third level. The evaluator may progress to Level III when the following two criteria are met: (1) identification of a normative deficit in at least one area of cognitive ability/processing; and (2) identification of an empirical or logical link between low functioning in any identified area of cognitive ability or processing and a corresponding weakness in academic

TABLE 10.1. Summary of findings on relations between CHC abilities/processes and academic achievement.

CHC ability	Reading achievement	Math achievement	Writing achievement
Gf	Inductive (I) and general sequential reasoning (RG) abilities play a moderate role in reading comprehension.	**Inductive (I) and general sequential (RG) reasoning abilities are consistently very important at all ages.**	Inductive (I) and general sequential reasoning abilities are related to basic writing skills primarily during the elementary school years (e.g., 6 to 13) and consistently related to written expression at all ages.
Gc	**Language development (LD), lexical knowledge (VL), and listening ability (LS) are important at all ages. These abilities become increasingly more important with age.**	**Language development (LD), lexical knowledge (VL), and listening abilities (LS) are important at all ages. These abilities become increasingly more important with age.**	**Language development (LD), lexical knowledge (VL), and general information (K0) are important primarily after age 7. These abilities become increasingly more important with age.**
Gsm	Memory span (MS) is important especially when evaluated **within the context of working memory.**	Memory span (MS) is important especially when evaluated **within the context of working memory.**	**Memory span (MS) is important to writing, especially spelling skills, whereas working memory has shown relations with advanced writing skills (e.g., written expression).**
Gv	Orthographic processing	May be important primarily for higher level or advanced mathematics (e.g., geometry, calculus).	
Ga	**Phonetic coding (PC) or "phonological awareness/processing" is very important during the elementary school years.**		Phonetic coding (PC) or "phonological awareness/processing" is very important during the elementary school years for both basic writing skills and written expression (primarily before age 11).
Glr	**Naming facility (NA) or "rapid automatic naming" is very important during the elementary school years.** Associative memory (MA) may be somewhat important at select ages (e.g., age 6).		Naming facility (NA) or "rapid automatic naming" has demonstrated relations with written expression, primarily the fluency aspect of writing.
Gs	**Perceptual speed (P) is important during all school years, particularly the elementary school years.**	**Perceptual speed (P) is important during all school years, particularly the elementary school years.**	**Perceptual speed (P) is important during all school years for basic writing and related to all ages for written expression.**

Note: The absence of comments for a particular CHC ability and achievement area (e.g., *Ga* and mathematics) indicates that the research reviewed either did not report any significant relations between the respective CHC ability and the achievement area, or if significant findings were reported, they were weak and were for only a limited number of studies. Comments in bold represent the CHC abilities that showed the strongest and most consistent relations with the respective achievement domain. Information in this table was reproduced from McGrew and Flanagan (1998) and Flanagan, McGrew, and Ortiz (2000) with permission from Allyn and Bacon. All rights reserved.

performance (as identified in Level I-A analysis). The first criterion is necessary in order to establish the presence of a disorder in a psychological process. Low achievement performance, in the absence of cognitive deficiencies, does not meet criteria presented here as well as in other current conceptualiza-

tions of SLD, although it does meet criteria under RTI models. In addition, the cognitive deficiency must be normatively based, not person based. The so-called weaknesses derived from ipsative analysis (also called intra-individual analysis) are irrelevant, regardless of statistical significance, unless the "weakness" also falls within the normative weakness range (generally about one standard deviation or more below the mean of 100). The second criterion is necessary in order to establish a valid basis for linking the cognitive deficit with the academic deficit.

10.4.4 Level II-B: Reevaluation of Exclusionary Factors

Although the presence of a cognitive ability/processing deficit that is related to the academic deficit is fundamental to the operational definition of SLD described herein, these deficits must not be primarily the result of exclusionary factors. Hypotheses regarding reasonable explanations (particularly situation-specific factors, such as motivation and fatigue) for the observed cognitive deficit(s) must be rejected in order to conclude that the data represent an accurate and valid reflection of true ability. When all appropriate exclusionary factors have been evaluated and excluded as the primary reason for the observed cognitive deficits, the process may advance to Level III.

10.4.5 Level III: Evaluation of Underachievement

Advancement to Level III automatically implies that three necessary conditions for determination of SLD have been met: (1) one or more academic ability deficits have been identified; (2) one or more cognitive ability/processing deficits have been identified; and (3) the identified academic and cognitive deficits are related and have been determined not to be the primary result of exclusionary factors. What has not yet been determined, however, is whether the pattern of results supports the notion of underachievement in the manner that might be expected in cases of suspected SLD or whether the pattern of results may be better explained via alternative causes such as mild MR or other factors known to have an adverse effect on both academic and cognitive performance (e.g., sensory-motor handicaps, lack of English language proficiency). Thus, Level III involves evaluation of all data to verify (1) that the student possesses specific and related academic and cognitive deficits (e.g., an aptitude-achievement *consistency*) and (2) that these deficits

exist within an otherwise *normal ability/processing* profile.

Given the historical predominance of the discrepancy model, evaluation of consistency may appear unusual at first. An aptitude score is comprised specifically of tests that are most directly relevant to the development and acquisition of specific academic skills, and, thus, is the best predictor of the corresponding achievement area. For example, an individual with low reading ability and isolated cognitive deficits in one or more areas (or aptitudes) related to reading achievement (e.g., phonological awareness, processing speed, short-term memory) will most likely demonstrate consistency between scores of reading aptitude and reading achievement. Likewise, a high reading aptitude score would predict high reading achievement (i.e., the two scores are more likely to be *consistent* with each other than to be discrepant).

Because consistency in scores that are within normal limits or even above would have already failed to demonstrate normative-based deficits, SLD determination at this level is concerned with scores that fall below the average range. A low aptitude score coupled with a low academic achievement score is insufficient, however, to meet our criterion for SLD unless it occurs within the context of an otherwise average or better pattern of functioning. Meeting these requirements involves evaluation of consistency between low aptitude and low achievement scores, as well as a pattern of results that demonstrates average or better functioning in other cognitive abilities/processes. Low aptitude scores across the board (i.e., all or nearly all cognitive abilities/processes in the deficient range) may be more suggestive of mild MR, a condition that would preclude determination of SLD under this definition (and most others). In the case of an individual with reading difficulties, it would be necessary to determine the level of performance or functioning in all cognitive areas, including those that are largely unrelated to reading. If the majority of these abilities are within normal limits relative to same-aged peers in the general population, then the practitioner can be reasonably confident that the consistency between reading aptitude deficits (e.g., below-average performance on cognitive abilities/processes related to reading, such as phonological processing and working memory) and academic deficits in reading represents underachievement.

10.4.6 Level IV: Evaluation of Interference with Functioning

When SLD determination reaches this point, criteria at the previous three levels have been met, thus supporting the presence of SLD. Further evaluation may seem unnecessary, but an operational definition of SLD based only on the previous criteria would be incomplete. One of the basic eligibility requirements contained in both the legal and clinical definitions for establishing SLD refers to whether the suspected learning disorder actually results in significant or substantial academic failure or other restrictions/limitations in daily life functioning. This final criterion reflects the need to take a broad survey of all collected data and the real-world manifestations of any presumed disability. In general, if the principles specified in Levels I through III have been followed and the criteria adhered to, then it is very likely that Level IV analysis serves only to support conclusions that have already been drawn up to this point. However, in cases where data may be equivocal, Level IV analysis becomes an important safety valve, ensuring that any representations of SLD suggested by the data are indeed manifest in observable impairments in one or more areas of functioning in real-life settings.

The advantage of the Flanagan et al. (2006b) operational definition lies in its integration of established notions about the nature of SLD with theories about the structure of cognitive abilities into "an inherently practical method for LD assessment that clearly specifies relationships between and among both cognitive and academic abilities, definitions of aptitude and global ability scores, and a recursive process that accommodates essential elements necessary for high-quality evaluation of learning difficulties" (p. 360).

10.5 Summary and Conclusion

It is well known that the ability–achievement discrepancy criterion is unreliable and invalid when used as the sole criterion for SLD identification and that its use has led to overidentification of this disability category in the special education population. Fortunately, there is a movement away from this method toward potentially more viable methods, with RTI being the most prominent.

The RTI model is part of an effort to (a) develop defensible methods of SLD identification, (b) develop and implement scientifically valid interventions, and (c) ensure that students with SLD benefit from school improvement and accountability efforts (Danielson, Doolittle, and Bradley, 2005). To date, the RTI model does not appear to meet all of Keogh's (2005) criteria (homogeneity, reliability, validity) for determining the adequacy and utility of a diagnostic system. At best, the RTI model identifies students who are at risk for reading failure, but the narrowly focused reading achievement problem, the single processing deficit, and the limited intervention options suggest that what is being identified is a far cry from SLD in any significant sense (Kavale, 2005). RTI has offered little for SLD identification except for the unwarranted presupposition that nonresponsiveness equates to SLD status. Although the RTI model cannot legitimately identify SLD at this time, the process does serve to create a pool of at-risk students who may or may not have SLD.

In its present form, the RTI model lacks reliability and validity as a diagnostic system for SLD. There can be little confidence in the SLD status of students identified through RTI because SLD determination is essentially by fiat: nonresponsive *ipso facto* SLD. If RTI is properly viewed as a systematic and rigorous prereferral activity that identifies *potential* SLD, then final determination of SLD status needs to be based on a comprehensive psychometric evaluation. When that evaluation is structured within a defensible operational definition of SLD supported by a validated theory of cognitive functioning, such as the one presented herein, decisions about who is and who is not SLD will be significantly enhanced. This is because a defensible operational definition of SLD includes all facets of the condition, including criteria for documenting a disorder in one or more basic psychological processes. By organizing a set of criteria that is consistent with IDEA 2004 and its attendant regulations, the probability of identifying SLD in a reliable and valid manner increases.

In conclusion, we believe that RTI and evaluation of cognitive abilities/processes are complementary (not competing) approaches, and the integration of the two may provide the most viable means of SLD identification to date. The operational definition presented here describes current attempts to integrate RTI methods and their scientific rigor with modern theory on the structure of cognitive and academic abilities/processes in a manner that may lead to better consistency in accepted notions of SLD. Future directions in SLD identification should focus on evaluating the SLD diagnostic system described in this chapter (i.e., the operational definition) following Keogh's criteria.

References

Aaron, P. G. (1997). The impending demise of the discrepancy formula. *Review of Educational Research, 67*, 461–502.

Al-Otaiba, S., & Fuchs, D. (2002). Characteristics of children who are unresponsive to early literacy intervention: a review of the literature. *Remedial and Special Education, 23*, 300–315.

Ames, L. B. (1968). A low intelligence quotient often not recognized as the chief cause of many learning difficulties. *Journal of Learning Disabilities, 1*, 735–739.

Bateman, B. D. (1965). An educator's view of a diagnostic approach to learning disabilities. In J. Hellmuth (Ed.), *Learning Disorders* (Vol. 1, pp. 217–239). Seattle: Special Child Publications.

Berninger, V. W. & Abbott, R. D. (1994). Redefining learning disabilities: moving beyond aptitude–achievement discrepancies to failure to respond to validated treatment protocols. In G. R. Lyon (Ed.), *Frames of Reference for the Assessment of Learning Disabilities* (pp. 163–183). Baltimore: Paul H. Brookes.

Buck, G. H., Polloway, E. A., Smith-Thomas, A., & Cook, K. W. (2003). Prereferral intervention processes: a survey of state practices. *Exceptional Children, 69*, 349–360.

Buckhalt, J. A. (2002). A short history of j: psychometrics' most enduring and controversial construct. *Learning and Individual Differences, 13*, 101–114.

Carroll, J. B. (1993). *Human Cognitive Abilities: A Survey of Factor-Analytic Studies.* Cambridge, UK: Cambridge University Press.

Carroll, J. B. (1997). The three-stratum theory of cognitive abilities. In D. P. Flanagan, J. L. Genshaft, & P. L. Harrison (Eds.), *Contemporary intellectual assessment: Theories, tests, and issues* (pp. 122–130). New York: Guilford.

Carroll, J. B. & Horn, J. L. (1981). On the scientific basis of ability testing. *American Psychologist, 36*, 1012–1020.

Chalfant, J. D. & King, F. S. (1976). An approach to operationalizing the definition of learning disabilities. *Journal of Learning Disabilities, 9*, 228–243.

Coles, G. S. (1978). The learning-disability test battery: empirical and social issues. *Harvard Educational Review, 48*, 313–340.

Cruickshank, W. M. (1977). Myths and realities in learning disabilities. *Journal of Learning Disabilities, 10*, 51–58.

Danielson, L., Doolittle, J., & Bradley, R. (2005). Past accomplishments and future challenges. *Learning Disability Quarterly, 28*, 137–139.

Das, J. P. & Naglieri, J. A. (1997). *Das-Naglieri Cognitive Assessment System.* Itasca, IL: Riverside Publishing.

Dean, Y. J. & Burns, M. K. (2002). Inclusion of intrinsic processing difficulties in LD diagnostic models: a critical review. *Learning Disability Quarterly, 25*, 170–176.

Dean, R. & Woodcock, R. W. (1999). *The WJ-R and Bateria-R in Neuropsychological Assessment.* (Woodcock Psychological and Educational Assessment Research Report no. 3.) Itasca, IL: Riverside.

Evans, J. H., Carlsen, R. N., & McGrew, K. S. (1993). Classification of exceptional students with the Woodcock-Johnson Psycho-Educational Battery-Revised. *Journal of Psychoeducational Assessment* [Monograph Series: WJ-R Monograph], 6–19.

Flanagan, D. P. (2000). Wechsler-based CHC cross-battery assessment and reading achievement: Strengthening the validity of interpretations drawn from Wechsler test scores. *School Psychology Quarterly, 15*, 295–229.

Flanagan, D. P. (2003). Use of the WJ III within the context of a modern operational definition of LD. In F. Schrank & D. P. Flanagan (Eds.), *Clinical Use and Interpretation of the WJ III.* Burlington, MA: Elsevier, Academic Press.

Flanagan, D. P., Genshaft, J. L., & Harrison, P. L. (Eds.) (1997). *Contemporary Intellectual Assessment: Theories, Tests, and Issues.* New York: Guilford.

Flanagan, D. P. & Harrison, P. L. (Eds.). (2005). *Contemporary Intellectual assessment (2nd ed.) Theories, Tests, and Issues.* New York: Guilford.

Flanagan, D. P. & Kaufman, A. S. (2004). *Essentials of WISC-IV assEssment.* Hoboken, NJ: Wiley.

Flanagan, D. P., Keiser, S. Berneir, J., & Ortiz, S. O. (2003). *Diagnosing Learning Disability in Adulthood.* Boston: Allyn & Bacon.

Flanagan, D. P. & Ortiz, S. O. (2001). *Essentials of Cross-Battery Assessment.* New York: Wiley.

Flanagan, D. P., Ortiz, S. O., Alfonso, V. C., & Dynda, A. M. (2006a). Integration of response-to-intervention and norm-referenced tests in learning disability identification: Learning from the tower of Babel. *Psychology in the Schools, 43(7)*, 807–825.

Flanagan, D. P., Ortiz, S. O., Alfonso, V. C ., & Mascolo, J. T. (2002). *The Achievement Test Desk Reference (ATDR): Comprehensive Assessment and Learning Disabilities.* Boston: Allyn & Bacon.

Flanagan, D. P., Ortiz, S. O., Alfonso, V. C., & Mascolo, J. T. (2006b). *The Achievement Test Desk Reference – Second Edition (ATDR-II): A Guide to Learning Disability Identification.* New York: Wiley.

Flanagan, D. P., Ortiz, S. O., & Alfonso, V. C. (2007). *Essentials of Cross-Battery Assessment with C/D ROM* (2nd ed.). New York: Wiley.

Fletcher, J. M., Coulter, W. A., Reschly, D. J., & Vaughn, S. (2004). Alternative approaches to the definition and identification of learning disabilities: some questions and answers. *Annals of Dyslexia, 54,* 304–331.

Fletcher, J. M., Denton, C., & Francis, D. J. (2005). Validity of alternative approaches for the identification of learning disabilities: operationalizing unexpected underachievement. *Journal of Learning Disabilities, 38,* 545–552.

Fletcher, J. M., Foorman, B. R., Boudousquie, A., Schatschneider, C., & Francis, D. J. (2002). Assessment of reading and learning disabilities: a research-based intervention-oriented approach. *Journal of School Psychology, 40,* 27–63.

Fletcher, J. M., Francis, D. J., Shaywitz, S. E., Lyon, G. R., Foorman, B. R., Stuebing. K. K., et al. (1998). Intelligent testing and the discrepancy model for children with learning disabilities. *Learning Disabilities Research and Practice, 13,* 186–203.

Francis, D. J., Fletcher, J. M., Stuebing, K. K., Lyon, G. R., Shaywitz, B. A., & Shaywitz, S. A. (2005). Psychometric approaches to the identification of LD: IQ and achievement scores are not sufficient. *Journal of Learning Disabilities, 38,* 98–108.

Fuchs, D., Deshler, D. D., & Reschly, D. J. (2004). National Research Center on Learning Disabilities: multimethod studies of identification and classification issues. *Learning Disability Quarterly, 27,* 189–195.

Fuchs, L. S., & Fuchs, D. (1998). Treatment validity: a unifying concept for reconceptualizing identification of learning disabilities. *Learning Disabilities Research and Practice, 13,* 204–219.

Fuchs, D., Fuchs, L. S., & Compton, D. L., (2004). Identifying reading disabilities by responsiveness-to-instruction: specifying measures and criteria. *Learning Disability Quarterly, 27,* 216–227.

Fuchs, D., Mock, D., Morgan, P. L., & Young, C. L. (2003). Responsiveness-to-intervention: definitions, evidence, and implications for the learning disabilities construct. *Learning Disabilities Research and Practice, 18,* 157–171.

Galaburda, A. M. (2005). Neurology of learning disabilities: what will the future bring? The answer comes from the successes of the recent past. *Learning Disability Quarterly, 28,* 107–109.

Glutting, J. J., Youngstrom, E. A., Ward, T., Ward. S., & Hale, R. L. (1997). Incremental efficiency of WISC-III factor scores in predicting achievement: What do they tell us? *Psychological Assessment, 9,* 295–301.

Gordon, M., Lewandowski, L., & Keiser, S. (1999). The LD label for relatively well-functioning students: a critical analysis. *Journal of Learning Disabilities, 32,* 485–490.

Gottfredson, L. S. (1997a). Mainstream science on intelligence: an editorial with 52 signatories, history, and bibliography. *Intelligence, 24,* 13–24.

Gottfredson, L. S. (1997b). Why g matters: The complexity of everyday life. *Intelligence, 24,* 79–134.

Gregg, N. Coleman. C. & Knight, D. (2003). Use of the Woodcock-Johnson III in the diagnosis of learning disabilities. In Schrank, F. A. and Flanagan, D. P. (Eds.), *WJ III Clinical Use and Interpretation: Scientist-Practitioner Perspectives* (pp. 176–199). New York: Academic Press.

Gresham, F. M. (2002). Responsiveness to intervention: an alternative approach to the identification of learning disabilities. In R. Bradley, L. Danielson, & D. Hallahan (Eds.), *Identification of Learning Disabilities: Research to Practice* (pp. 467–519). Mahwah, NJ: Lawrence Erlbaum.

Horn, J. L. (1988). Thinking about human abilities. In J. Nesselroade & R. Cattell (Eds.), *Handbook of Multivariate Psychology* (rev. ed., pp. 645–683). New York: Academic Press.

Johns, B. H. (2003). NCLB and IDEA: never the twain should meet. *Learning Disabilities: A Multidisciplinary Journal, 12,* 89–91.

Kaufman, A. S. & Kaufman, N. L. (2001). Assessment of specific learning disabilities in the new millennium: Issues, conflicts, and controversies. In A. Kaufman & N. Kaufman (Eds.), *Specific Learning Disabilities and Difficulties in Children and Adolescents: Psychological Assessment and Evaluation* (pp. 433–461). Cambridge, UK: Cambridge University Press.

Kaufman, A. S. & Kaufman, N. L. (2004). *Kaufman Assessment Battery for Children—Second Edition.* Circle Pines, MN: American Guidance Service.

Kaufman, J. C., Kaufman, A. S., Kaufman-Singer, J., & Kaufman, N. L. (2005). The Kaufman Assessment Battery for Children-Second Edition and the Kaufman Adolescent and Adult Intelligence Test. In D. P. Flanagan and P. L. Harrison (Eds.), *Contemporary intellectual assessment: Theories, Tests, and Issues* (2nd ed.) (pp. 344–370). New York: Guilford.

Kaufman, A. S., Lichtenberger, E. O., Fletcher-Janzen, E., & Kaufman, N. L. (2004). *Essentials of KABC-II Assessment.* New York: Wiley.

Kavale, K. A. (2002). Discrepancy models in the identification of learning disability. In R. Bradley, L. Danielson, & D. Hallahan (Eds.), *Identification of Learning Disabilities: Research to Practice* (pp. 287–333). Mahwah, NJ: Lawrence Erlbaum.

Kavale, K. A. (2005). Identifying specific learning disability: is responsiveness to intervention the answer? *Journal of Learning Disabilities, 38,* 553–562.

Kavale, K. A. & Forness, S. R. (1995). *The Nature of Learning Disabilities: Critical Elements of Diagnosis and Classification.* Mahwah, NJ: Lawrence Erlbaum.

Kavale, K. A. & Forness, S. R. (2000a). Auditory and visual perception processes and reading ability: a quantitative reanalysis and historical reinterpretation. *Learning Disability Quarterly, 23*, 253–270.

Kavale, K. A. & Forness, S. R. (2000b). What definitions of learning disability say and don't say: a critical analysis. *Journal of Learning Disabilities, 33*, 239–256.

Kavale, K. A., Holdnack, J. A., & Mostert, M. P. (2005). Responsiveness to intervention and the identification of specific learning disability: a critique and alternative proposal. *Learning Disability Quarterly, 28*, 2–16.

Kavale, K. A. & Nye, C. (1991). The structure of learning disabilities. *Exceptionality, 2*, 141–156.

Kavale, K. A. & Reese, J. H. (1992). The character of learning disabilities: an Iowa profile. *Learning Disability Quarterly, 15*, 74–94.

Kavale, K. A., Kaufman, A. S., Naglieri, J. A., & Hale, J. B. (2005). Changing procedures for identifying learning disabilities: the danger of poorly supported ideas. *The School Psychologist, 59*, 16–25.

Keogh, B. K. (1987). Learning disabilities: in defense of a construct. *Learning Disabilities Research, 3*, 4–9.

Keogh, B. K. (1994). A matrix of decision points in the measurement of learning disabilities. In G. R. Lyon (Ed.), *Frames of Reference for the Assessment of Learning Disabilities: New Views on Assessment Issues* (pp. 15–26). Baltimore: Paul H. Brookes.

Keogh, B. K. (2005). Revisiting classification and identification. *Learning Disability Quarterly, 28*, 100–102.

Kibby, M. Y. & Hynd, G. W. (2001). Neurobiological basis of learning disabilities. In D. Hallahan & B. Keogh (Eds.), *Research and Global Perspectives in Learning Disabilities: Essays in Honor of William M. Cruickshank* (pp. 25–42). Mahwah, NJ: Lawrence Erlbaum.

Lyon, G. R., Fletcher, J. M., Shaywitz, S. E., Shaywitz, B. A., Torgensen, J. K., Wood, F. B., et al. (2001). Rethinking learning disabilities. In C. Finn, R. Rotherham, & C. Hokanson (Eds.), *Rethinking Special Education for a New Century* (pp. 259–287). Washington, DC: Thomas B. Fordham Foundation.

MacMillan, D. L. & Siperstein, G. N. (2002). Learning disabilities as operationally defined by schools. In R. Bradley, L. Danielson, & D. Hallahan (Eds.), *Identification of Learning Disabilities: Research to Practice* (pp. 287–333). Mahwah, NJ: Lawrence Erlbaum.

MacMillan, D. L., Gresham, F. M., & Bocian, K. M. (1998). Discrepancy between definitions of learning disabilities and school practices: an empirical investigation. *Journal of Learning Disabilities, 31*, 314–326.

Mann, L. (1971). Psychometric phrenology and the new faculty psychology: the case against ability assessment and training. *Journal of Special Education, 5*, 3–14.

Mather, N. & Schrank, F. A. (2003). Using the Woodcock-Johnson III discrepancy procedures for diagnosing learning disabilities. In F. A. Schrank and D. P. Flanagan (Eds.), *WJ III Clinical Use and Interpretation: Scientist-Practitioner Perspectives* (pp. 176–199). New York: Academic Press.

McGrew, K. S. & Flanagan, D. P. (1998). *The Intelligence Test Desk Reference (ITDR): Gf–Gc Cross-Battery Assessment.* Boston: Allyn & Bacon.

McGrew, K. S., Flanagan, D. P., Keith, T. Z., & Vanderwood, M. (1997). Beyond g: The impact of Gf-Gc specific cognitive abilities research on the future use and interpretation of intelligence tests in the schools. *School Psychology Review, 26*, 177–189.

McGrew, K. S., & Knopik, S. N. (1996). The relationship between intra-cognitive scatter on the Woodcock-Johnson Psycho-Educational Battery–Revised and school achievement. *Journal of School Psychology, 34*, 351–364.

McMaster, K. L., Fuchs, D., Fuchs, L. S., & Compton, D. L (2005). Responding to nonresponsiveness: an experimental field trip of identification and intervention methods. *Exceptional Children, 71*, 445–463.

Mellard, D. F., Deshler, D. D., & Barth, A. (2004). LD identification: it's not simply a matter of building a better mousetrap. *Learning Disability Quarterly, 27*, 229–243.

Mellard, D. F., Byrd, S. E., Johnson, E., Tollefson, J. M., & Boesche, L. (2004). Foundations and research on identifying model responsiveness-to-intervention sites. *Learning Disability Quarterly, 27*, 243–256.

Naglieri, J. A. (2005). The Cognitive Assessment System. In D. P. Flanagan and P. L. Harrison (Eds.), *Contemporary Intellectual Assessment: Theories, Tests, and Issues* (2nd ed.) (pp. 441–460). New York: Guilford.

Nelson, J. R., Benner, G. J., & Gonzalez, J. (2003). Learner characteristics that influence the treatment effectiveness of early literacy interventions: a meta-analytic review. *Learning Disabilities Research and Practice, 18*, 255–267.

Oakley, D. (2006). *The Relationship between Intra-Cognitive Scatter on the WJ III and School Achievement.* Unpublished doctoral dissertation. St. John's University, New York.

Peterson, K. M. H. & Shinn, M. R. (2002). Severe discrepancy models: which best explains school identification practices for learning disabilities? *School Psychology Review, 31*, 459–746.

Pugach, M. & Johnson, L. J. (1989). Prereferral interventions: progress, problems, and challenges. *Exceptional Children, 56*, 217–226.

Reschly, D. J. & Hosp, J. L. (2004). State SLD identification policies and practices. *Learning Disability Quarterly, 27*, 197–213.

Roid, G. H. & Pomplun, M. (2005). Interpreting the Stanford-Binet Intelligence Scales, Fifth Edition. In D. P. Flanagan and P. L. Harrison (Eds.), *Contemporary Intellectual Assessment: Theories, Tests, and Issues* (2nd ed.) (pp. 325–343). New York: Guilford.

Rutter, M. & Yule, W. (1975). The concept of specific reading retardation. *Journal of Child Psychology and Psychiatry, 16*, 181–197.

Schrank, F. A. (2006). *Assessment Service Bulletin 7: Specification of the Cognitive Processes Involved in Performance on the Woodcock-Johnson III NU.* Itasca, IL: Riverside.

Scruggs, T. E. & Mastropieri, M. A. (2002). On babies and bathwater: addressing the problems of identification of learning disabilities. *Learning Disability Quarterly, 25*, 155–168.

Shepard, L. A. & Smith, M. L. (1983). An evaluation of the identification of learning disabled students in Colorado. *Learning Disability Quarterly, 6*, 115–127.

Siegal, L. S. (1989). IQ is irrelevant to the definition of learning disabilities. *Journal of Learning Disabilities, 489*, 469–478.

Siegel, L. S. (1999). Issues in the definition and diagnosis of learning disabilities: a perspective on Guckenberger v. Boston University. *Journal of Learning Disabilities, 32*, 304–319.

Siegel, L. S. (2003). IQ-discrepancy definitions and the diagnosis of LD: introduction to the special issue. *Journal of Learning Disabilities, 36*, 2–3.

Spear-Swerling, L. & Sternberg, R. J. (1996). *Off Track: When Poor Readers Become "Learning Disabled."* Boulder, CO: Westview Press.

Stanovich, K. E. (1985). Explaining the variance in reading ability in terms of psychological processes: what have we learned? *Annals of Dyslexia, 35*, 67–96.

Stanovich, K. E. (1988). Explaining the differences between the dyslexic and the garden-variety poor reader: the phonological–core-variable–difference model. *Journal of Learning Disabilities, 21*, 141–156.

Stanovich, K. E. (1991). Discrepancy definitions of reading disability: has intelligence led us astray? *Reading Research Quarterly, 26*, 7–29.

Stanvich, K. E. (1999). The sociopsychometrics of learning disabilities. *Journal of Learning Disabilities, 32*, 350–361.

Stanovich, K. E. (2005). The future of a mistake: will discrepancy measurement continue to make the learning disabilities field a pseudoscience? *Learning Disability Quarterly, 28*, 103–106.

Sternberg, R. J. & Grigorenko, E. L. (2002). Difference scores in the identification of children with learning disabilities: it's time to use a different method. *Journal of School Psychology, 40*, 65–83.

Stuebing, K. K., Fletcher, J. M., LeDoux, J. M., Lyon, G. R., Shaywitz, S. E., & Shaywitz, B. A. (2002). Validity of IQ-discrepancy classifications of reading disabilities: a meta-analysis. *American Educational Research Journal, 39*, 469–518.

Swanson, H. L., Trainin, G., Necoechea, D. M., & Hammill, D. D. (2003). Rapid naming, phonological awareness, and reading: a meta-analysis of the correlation evidence. *Review of Educational Research, 73*, 407–440.

Thorndike, R. L. (1963). *The Concepts of Over- and Under-Achievement.* New York: Teachers College Press.

Torgensen, J. K. (1979). What shall we do with psychological processes? *Journal of Learning Disabilities, 12*, 514–521.

Torgensen, J. K. (2000). Individual differences in response to early interventions in reading: the lingering problem of treatment resisters. *Learning Disabilities Research and Practice, 15*, 55–64.

Truscott, S. D., Cohen, C. E., Sams, D. P., Sanborn, K. J., & Frank, A. J. (2005). The current state(s) of prereferral intervention teams: a report from two national surveys. *Remedial and Special Education, 26*, 130–140.

US Office of Education (1977). Assistance to states for education of handicapped children: Procedures for evaluating specific learning disabilities. *Federal Register, 42*, (250), 65082–65085. Washington, DC: US Government Printing Office.

Vanderwood, M. L., McGrew, K. S., Flanagan, D. P., & Kieth, T. Z. (2002). The contribution of general and specific cognitive abilities to reading achievement. *Learning and Individual Differences, 13*, 159–188.

Vaughn, S., Linan-Thompson, S., & Hickman, P. (2003). Response to instruction as a means of identifying students with reading/learning disabilities. *Exceptional Children, 69*, 391–410.

Vellutino, F. R., Scanlon, D. M., & Lyon, G. R. (2000). Differentiating between difficult-to-remediate and readily remediated poor readers: more evidence against the IQ–achievement discrepancy definition for reading disability. *Journal of Learning Disabilities, 33*, 223–238.

Vukovic, R. K. & Siegel, L. S. (2006). The double-deficit hypothesis: a comprehensive analysis of the evidence. *Journal of Learning Disabilities, 39*(1), 25–47.

Wagner, R. K. & Torgensen, J. K. (1987). The nature of phonological processing and its causal role in the acquisition of reading skills. *Psychological Bulletin, 101*, 192–212.

Woodcock, R. W. (1993). An information processing view of *Gf-Gc* theory. *Journal of Psychoeducational Assessment, 8*, 231–258.

Ysseldyke, J. (2005). Assessment and decision making for student with learning disabilities: what if this is as good as it gets? *Learning Disability Quarterly, 28*, 125–128.

11
Contextual Influences and Response to Intervention: Critical Issues and Strategies

Amy L. Reschly, Melissa Coolong-Chaffin, Sandra L. Christenson, and Terry Gutkin

Amy L. Reschly, PhD, is an Assistant Professor of Educational Psychology and Instructional Technology at the University of Georgia. reschly@uga.edu

Melissa Coolong-Chaffin, EdS, is a doctoral student in Educational (School) Psychology at the University of Minnesota. cool0044@umn.edu

Sandra L. Christenson, PhD, is Professor of Educational (School) Psychology at the University of Minnesota. chris002@umn.edu

Terry B. Gutkin, PhD, is Professor of Counseling, San Francisco State University. tgutkin@sfsu.edu

The psychological and educational literature is replete with lists of the shortcomings of traditional educational assessment and intervention practices and concomitant calls for reform (e.g., Reschly, 1988, Sheridan and Gutkin, 2000; Ysseldyke and Christenson, 1987), and yet *change has been slow*. Much of current practice may still be characterized by said shortcomings, such as: predominately within-child conceptualizations of educational difficulties; too little time allotted for prevention and early intervention; more rhetoric than action in creating significant opportunities for parent engagement; assessment conducted for the purpose of eligibility determination, rather than intervention; and the reliance on placement as a means of addressing students' difficulties. An emerging alternative, response to intervention (RTI), addresses many of these limitations. However, to meet the spirit of those calls for reform, an RTI approach requires consideration of the complex interaction among environmental influences in multiple contexts, those in which children learn and develop. Conceptualized in this way, RTI is an opportunity to fully realize the assessment to intervention link.

11.1 Systems Ecological Theory

Students develop, learn, and behave within a context. This idea is not new or controversial. Indeed, there are few individuals within the field of education who lack at least a passing familiarity with the seminal work of Bronfenbrenner (1977), and the notion that there is "something about context" that might be important has permeated the consciousness of those who study and work with children. However, with few exceptions, a meaningful integration of systems ecological theory with research or practice has yet to occur. A true application of this theory has significant implications for how we conceptualize students' successes and difficulties, collect data, conceive of interventions, and define not only who stakeholders are, but how to work with them.

In the classic model proposed by Bronfenbrenner (1977, 1992), children are viewed as developing within a series of nested contexts, or structures (see Figure 11.1). These structures range from immediate settings the child is part of, such as home, school, or community, to broad cultural norms. In addition, these structures interact, or have reciprocal influence, over time. Development, then, is understood as a process of ongoing adaptation between the individual and the environments in which the individual is embedded. Further, development is affected by the interactions between these contexts, those that are immediate and more distal from the individual, formal and informal, across the lifespan (Bronfenbrenner, 1977). The influential variables from the four levels must be recognized to understand child functioning in schools. Applied to the mesosytem of home and school, Christenson and Sherdian (2001) have argued that parent and teacher input are essential to understand children's learning difficulties

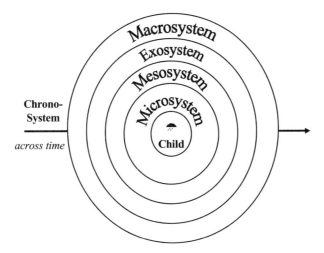

FIGURE 11.1. Graphic representation of Bronfenbrenner's ecological model.

in academic, social, emotional, and behavioral domains; the total picture of child functioning must be "co-constructed." Also, as children grow and develop, they interact directly with more systems; therefore, complexity is increased in understanding adolescent behavior.

There are several organizational principles of systems ecological theory that not only enrich our understanding of children's development over time, but also are particularly influential for intervention planning and implementation. These principles include multifinality, equifinality, nonsummativity, and circular causality (Christenson, Abery, and Weinberg, 1986; Christenson and Anderson, 2002). *Multifinality* refers to the idea that similar initial conditions, or antecedents, may result in different outcomes. For example, a standard, uniform prescription for parental assistance with homework may achieve the desired goal for some children and families but not work with others. The principle of *equifinality* suggests that different initial conditions may lead to similar end states. For instance, families whose interactional styles are diverse (authoritarian, permissive, authoritative) may have children who experience similar degrees of school success. *Nonsummativity* suggests that the system is greater than the sum of its parts. The interactions among the parts contained within the system create something greater than each of the parts taken in isolation (i.e., synergy). Finally, the principle of *circular causality* refers to the notion that every action within a system, which is comprised of a number of

individuals, is also a reaction. Changes are nonlinear. For example, changes in a child's home environment may affect their behavior and achievement at school and perhaps, interactions with peers. The notion that change in any one system in which a student interacts creates ripple effects (i.e., changes) in other systems and among systems is a classic theoretical underpinning of systems ecological theory.

Pianta and colleagues (Pianta and Walsh, 1996; Rimm-Kaufman and Pianta, 2000) have made significant contributions to our understanding of systems theory and educational processes. One important consideration for understanding systems and development is the relationship that exists among socializing agents, or contexts, such as home and school or family and peers. These relationships are affected by history and the quality, nature, and quantity of contact. The *pattern of relationships* among socializing agents may either enhance or thwart students' learning in our schools. By drawing attention to relationships and interactions among contexts, it is understood that risk, and by extension, competence, cannot be located within any one level – child, family, school, or community – but rather, resides in the interactions and relationships among these agents. Of particular relevance is that any discontinuity between home and school is a risk factor with respect to expectations, value placed on learning, and communication patterns (Pianta and Walsh, 1996) that is alterable with changes in assessment and intervention practices.

Instructional Support	Home Support	Home-School Support
Instructional Match	Home Expectations and Attributions	Shared Standards and Expectations
Instructional Expectations	Discipline Orientation	Consistent Structure
Classroom Environment	Home-affective Environment	Cross-setting Opportunity to Learn
Instructional Presentation	Parent Participation	Mutual Support
Cognitive Emphasis	Structure for Learning	Positive, Trusting Relationships
Motivational Strategies		Modeling
Relevant Practice		
Informed Feedback		
Academic Engaged Time		
Adaptive Instruction		
Progress Evaluation		
Student Understanding		

FIGURE 11.2. Ysseldyke and Christenson's support for learning components.

The work of other theorists, such as Vygotsky (1962), Carroll (1963), Bandura (1978), Sameroff (1983), and Ysseldyke and Christenson (2002), has helped those interested in schooling conceptualize students' behavior and learning from an ecological systems theoretical framework and describe variables of interest in the learning environment. The work of Vygotsky (1962) and Carroll (1963) indicated the importance of individualized support from the learning context. Vygotsky's (1962) "zone of proximal development" opined a match between an appropriate, or ideal, level of difficulty and the provision of instructional supports, or scaffolding, from teachers, allowing students to benefit optimally from instruction; in contrast, in Carroll's (1963) model of student learning, how much a student learns is a function of the amount of time spent learning and the amount of time needed to learn (comprised of aptitude, ability to learn, and quality of instruction). The concept of *reciprocal determinism* (Bandura, 1978) portends that behavior is a function of the context in which it occurs, resulting from a continuous interaction between cognition, affect, and the environment.

After reviewing the literature, Ysseldyke and Christenson (2002) proposed a model of student learning based on systems ecological theory. In this model, the learning environment is broadly con-

ceived to include the critical contexts in which children learn (school, classrooms, home) and the interface between these contexts. Student learning, or academic behavior, is understood as a function of instructional, home, and home–school supports for learning. Further, they delineated important alterable variables for assessment and intervention planning within each of these contexts (see Figure 11.2).

11.2 Implications for Assessment and Intervention

Several implications of systems ecological theory for assessment and intervention practices exist. For example, if individuals are understood as developing, learning, and behaving within multiple contexts, then assessment and intervention practices must attend to these settings and contexts. Assessments that focus primarily on within-student characteristics are not consistent with a systems ecological framework. In the words of Sheridan and Gutkin (2000, p. 489), "We cannot serve children effectively by decontextualizing their problems as internal pathologies . . . ." Furthermore, individuals and systems change with time. Assessment, then, must also be an ongoing, dynamic process – one that is not complete until interventions have altered student responses in a positive direction. In addition, important outcomes, such as achievement or dropout, are complex with multiple determinants. These outcomes cannot be accounted for by examining single variables in isolation. Rather, students and their environments must be viewed systemically.

In the next section, three assessment tools that may be used to assess critical contextual influences within an RTI model are described. Those included in this chapter are not all inclusive, nor does using one or more of these ensure an ecologically valid assessment. Rather, an important principle of systems ecological theoretical framework is that of *integrating information from multiple sources*. A relevant distinction may be made between a systems approach and general systems theory for understanding children's development (Sameroff, 1983) and, by extension, assessment practices. A systems approach refers to examining aspects of context in relative isolation (e.g., parenting *or* teaching practices related to student achievement), whereas systems theory may be used as the structure for organizing information from the contexts, settings, and interactions related to development. A meaningful integration of systems theory and assessment requires the latter perspective.

11.3 Tools for Conducting an Ecological Assessment

The challenge for educators is to conduct assessments that take into account the multiple contexts in which the child is learning. The goal of assessment in an RTI model is not simply to determine whether or not a student qualifies for special education services; rather, the assessment process helps practitioners pinpoint what variables/characteristics of/alterations in the environment bring out the best response from the targeted student. Assessment is not a finite step on the road to eligibility; rather, it is an ongoing process through which the most appropriate intervention for the student's specific problem is identified, implemented, and its effectiveness evaluated – the core elements of problem-solving methodology.

Three specific tools for conducting an ecological assessment are described, including brief experimental analysis (Daly, Witt, Martens and Dool,

1997), the Ecobehavioral Assessment Systems Software (EBASS; Greenwood, Carta, Kamps, Terry, and Delquadri, 1994), and the Functional Assessment of Academic Behavior (FAAB; Ysseldyke and Christenson, 2002).

11.3.1 Functional Analysis of Academic Behavior

From a behavioral perspective, RTI involves a functional rather than a structural explanation for performance deficits (Christ, Burns and Ysseldyke, 2005). In contrast to focusing on within-child deficits as an explanation for learning problems (i.e. the structural approach), the functional approach focuses on external, alterable variables affecting the child's performance, such as time allotted for instruction, level of difficulty of material, and teacher feedback (Daly et al., 1997). Since the explanatory variables for performance deficits are alterable, they can be manipulated to test various hypotheses about why the problem is occurring. Once a plausible functional explanation is determined, appropriate interventions can be selected based on that function.

Daly et al. (1997) pioneered the use of brief experimental analysis for choosing and evaluating academic interventions. Each intervention is designed to test one of the following hypotheses:

1. The child does not want to do the task.
2. The child has not had enough practice to do the task.
3. The child has not had enough help to do the task.
4. The child has not had to do it that way before.
5. The task is too difficult.

By manipulating each independent variable successively (i.e. incentive, practice, modeling, rehearsal and feedback, and task difficulty, respectively), while measuring the same dependent variable (e.g. oral reading fluency), and then replicating the results, the most successful intervention can be chosen for each student. The hypotheses are arranged in ascending order from least intrusive to most intrusive, and when tested in that succession they allow the interventionist to determine the most simple, effective intervention for the student.

Using a brief experimental analysis technique within an RTI framework allows practitioners to determine not only whether a student has "responded to intervention" for special education placement decisions (i.e., where to teach), but also answers the more practical questions of how to teach and what to teach (i.e., produces data with instructional utility). An added benefit of this approach is that the five hypotheses are very understandable to parents and, in addition, build on the consistent finding that parents want practical strategies to know how to assist their children's learning (Christenson and Sheridan, 2001). The relevance of this approach is that realistic, and yet optimistic communication about children's learning progress can occur between home and school.

11.3.2 Ecobehavioral Assessment Systems Software

EBASS enables observers to record behaviors in a classroom setting using a laptop computer. The Code for Instructional Structure and Student Academic Response (CISSAR) is one component of the EBASS system designed for use with students in general education settings. The CISSAR focuses on three main areas: student behaviors, teacher behaviors, and the ecology of the classroom.

Student behaviors include *academic responses*, in which the student is actively engaged in the appropriate task (e.g., answering a question, reading aloud); *task management responses*, in which the student is preparing to make an academic response (e.g., raising hand, looking for a pencil, paying attention to lecture); and *competing responses*, or behaviors that are considered inappropriate in the classroom (e.g., talking out of turn, hitting a classmate). Teacher behaviors include what the teacher is doing (e.g., asking an academic question, disciplining a student) and the position of the teacher in the room. Classroom ecological variables include activity (e.g., reading, math, transition), task (e.g. worksheet, reader, pencil-and-paper task), and instructional grouping (e.g. whole class or small group).

Once observations are completed, it is possible to compute the percentage of time during the observations that the various student, teacher, and ecological events were occurring. An ecobehavioral analysis can then be conducted to determine which setting events are most associated with positive and negative behaviors from the student. Thus, EBASS allows assessors to analyze the instructional environment of the classroom in order to identify multiple points for intervention within that classroom en-

vironment. Information gathered with EBASS has ecological validity; identification of student and teacher variables can be used to create home support for learning interventions.

11.3.3 Functional Assessment of Academic Behavior

The brief experimental analysis procedures previously described focus on manipulating factors in the student's immediate instructional environment that affect academic performance (i.e. antecedents and consequences of specific academic behaviors), while EBASS allows observers to identify events and behaviors in the classroom environment that contribute to or inhibit student learning. Ysseldyke and Christenson's *FAAB* takes an even broader ecological approach. As an assessment tool, the focus of FAAB is on designing interventions to enhance the student's performance through identifying and coordinating instructional, home, and home–school support for learning (Ysseldyke and Christenson, 2002).

Ysseldyke and Christenson (2002) draw on the work of Bronfenbrenner, defining the instructional environment as the school, classrooms, and home contexts in which students learn, as well as the interface of these contexts. Beyond classroom variables, FAAB gathers information across home and school in order to develop comprehensive interventions across socializing agents. Twenty-three alterable variables related to academic performance are subsumed under three categories: instructional support for learning, home support for learning, and home–school support for learning (see Figure 11.2). Nine steps in the assessment and intervention process similar to other models of problem solving and consultation are described, including identifying and clarifying the reason for referral, gathering parent and teacher perspectives on the student's instructional needs, collecting data on the student's total learning environment, selecting interventions based on priorities and needs, identifying complementary home supports for learning, implementing the intervention, evaluating the intervention's effectiveness, revising the plan, and documenting and reporting results.

FAAB provides the philosophical framework as well as specific assessment tools for gathering information, including reproducible parent, teacher, and student interview and classroom observation forms. Once information is gathered, interventions to address the fit, or lack thereof, between student characteristics and the total instructional environment can be developed. FAAB takes into account the important influence of home support for learning, whereas many other assessment tools do not.

11.4 Promise for Practice

The shift from traditional models that search for within-child variables to explain learning difficulties, to an RTI approach that focuses on finding the best instructional match for students, holds much promise for practitioners seeking to move beyond asking *where* a student should be taught to asking *how* and *what* to teach. However, for the promise of RTI to be fully realized, practitioners must take an ecological systems approach, addressing the complex interactions between the child and the multiple environmental systems in which they live and learn. Sheridan and Gutkin (2000, p. 486) eloquently explain the need for ecological assessment:

When children experience difficulty learning to read, for example, this "dysfunction" is best understood as the product of multilayered, proximal, distal, and interactive systems. Among these systems are the individual children themselves, educational contexts, prevailing social environments, societal influences, and the interactions among and across all of these systems.

Consideration of students' learning within the broad educational environment in an RTI model represents a significant change in practice for educational personnel, with implications for assessment and intervention in terms of what is assessed (e.g., home and school support for learning, opportunity to learn, antecedents), roles for parents, and the timing and ongoing nature of assessment and intervention. No longer focusing on testing the student using standardized measures in a contrived setting (Dean, Burns, Grialou, and Varro, 2006), school professionals will potentially have more time to partner with parents (should they choose to use it), to discover the child's unique instructional needs (e.g., motivational support, increased opportunities for practice, appropriate instructional level, specific skill remediation, homework completion strategies, etc.) and develop effective interventions across home and school environments. Parents are necessary, not optional, in a well-conceived application of RTI. Family–school interventions have demonstrated positive effects on

students' school performance and behavior (Carlson and Christenson, 2005). A recent review of the literature on parent and family interventions implemented at or in conjunction with school settings found that the most effective elements of programs were those that emphasized dialogue about programming and shared communication/monitoring of student performance, had specific intervention targets, strategies that emphasized the role of parents as teachers, and consultation with parents about child-specific concerns (Carlson and Christenson, 2005).

The changes in practice inherent with an RTI model, such as the focus on screening, early intervention, and progress monitoring, provide an opportunity for active parent engagement and partnering between family and school personnel much earlier in the development and identification of a student's academic or behavioral difficulty (i.e., before problems are severe and often intractable) than is typically the case in traditional practice, thereby pairing the promise of early intervention with partnership between primary socializing agents – home and school. In addition, teachers are integral to the success of school–family partnerships (Dauber and Epstein, 1993; Westat & Policy Studies Associates, 2001). For example, the more that parents perceived teachers as valuing their contributions, keeping them informed of their child's strengths and weaknesses, and providing them with suggestions, the higher was the parental engagement in children's learning in urban settings (Patrikakou and Weissberg, 2000). From a preventive point of view, early teacher–parent consultation in the assessment to intervention process is invaluable. Parents and teachers can share their perspectives with respect to the school- or parent-based concern, generate ideas for intervention, and begin to understand the questions each has with respect to assisting the students' adaptation to the demands of the school environment. Maintaining a partnership focus rests on school personnel *inviting* parents to partner, *informing* parents of child progress relative to classmates and school demands and *being informed by* parental input, and *including* parents in the development of instructional programming.

In addition, a fully realized RTI approach has the potential to change how the various adults (i.e. teachers, parents) in a child's life interact to improve outcomes. The shift from questions of *where* to *what*, *how*, and *did it work* necessitate changes in the roles of teachers, psychologists, administrators, and parents. Assessment and intervention are far too often viewed as separate, albeit interrelated, functions of the school psychologist. Seldom do assessment teams address and integrate how parents might be involved as active participants in the assessment plan. The work of Harry (1992), a special education researcher, is beneficial for creating the assessment to intervention link within the RTI model. She suggested that the parent–professional discourse must change to provide official channels for reciprocal rather than one-way discourse, and that this can be achieved best by having parents assume active roles – specifically, parents as assessors, presenters of reports, policymakers and advocates, and peer supports. School psychologists and other

school personnel can facilitate parent participation in these roles (e.g., discussing data collection ideas and sharing strategies and forms; ensuring there is opportunity and time for parents to give input, view data, and be involved in intervention planning; connecting parents to each other to share experiences and information). When educators actively engage parents in these roles, they begin the process of developing collaborative practice or create conditions whereby parents and educators understand the "bigger" picture about children's development and educational needs. Examples excerpted from Christenson and Sheridan (2001) are provided in Table 11.1.

Public Law 108-446, the Individuals with Disabilities Education Improvement Act (IDEA; 2004), mandates that parents are part of the special

TABLE 11.1. Potential parental roles in assessment and intervention.*

Assessors and presenters

- Parents sharpen the referral by providing questions for the assessment to address.
- Observation techniques are demonstrated to parents (e.g., ABC analysis) and then used to gather data to answer specific questions.
- Parents monitor and record ways in which students spend their time.
- Parents are given time to ask questions of educators.
- Parents are included as part of the assessment team on intervention planning and other required forms.
- Parents describe the kinds of messages given to their child about schoolwork and effort for learning.
- Parents provide teachers and teams with information regarding what motivates the child, what reinforcements have worked, successes in previous years, etc.
- Parents provide the home input and educators the school input on the same, specifically defined behavior. Discussion and interpretation of the findings occurs together.
- Parents collect data for and evaluate interventions.
- Parents offer recommendations for implementation of interventions.
- Parents present observational data from home/school/community.
- Parents explain cultural context for child behavior to educators.
- Parents report on community events (gang activity, stressors) to give an ecological dimension to understanding child behavior.
- Parents report on child strengths in general and child strengths relative to a specific mutually identified concern. Gather same information from school personnel.
- Parents use half of the conference time to report about their child (send home sample questions for their consideration).
- Parents present intervention strategies that have worked well in the past.
- Parents present information regarding child's personal or medical history/background.

Policymakers

- Parents co-conduct forums to educate parents re: policy issues.
- Parents suggest agenda items, issues for consideration for advisory meetings.
- Parents serve on policy-making committees and have voting power.
- Forums/discussion groups are created to allow parents to meet independently from teachers/administrators.

Advocates and supporters of other parents

- Parents with experience with intervention planning and/or special education process, rules, and policies serve as advocates and encourage other parents to be active participants.
- Provide opportunities to parents for advocacy training and make it a routine part of service delivery to include parent advocates/partners.
- Provide parents with opportunities to have contact with other families who share similar backgrounds and/or experiences.
- Parents serve as advocates for each other (e.g., bring another parent to IEP meeting for support).

*Excerpted from Christenson and Sheridan (2001).

education process, including: providing informed consent to conduct initial evaluations and begin special education services upon finding the child eligible; contributing information to the evaluation; and participating in the development of the individual education plan, detailing students' special education needs, goals, and services. Information from existing RTI models indicates that parents are only included explicitly as part of the process in two of the four widely disseminated RTI models (i.e., the Heartland model in Iowa and the intervention-based assessment (IBA) model in Ohio) (Burns and Ysseldyke, 2005; Fuchs, Mock, Morgan and Young, 2003). However, the positive effect of the family environment and school–family partnerships for enhancing children's learning outcomes is undisputed (Carlson and Christenson, in press; Christenson and Sheridan, 2001). It is our contention that opportunities for partnering should not begin with, or be limited to, special education eligibility. As RTI moves to scale across the USA, we must be careful not to repeat the mistakes of the past. RTI is an opportunity to partner with and engage parents throughout the problem-solving process.

McNamara, Telzrow, and DeLamatre (1999) conducted a study that looked at how parents of children referred to an Ohio IBA team for problem solving reacted to the IBA process, and how those reactions related to student goal attainment. The results indicated that parents generally wanted to be involved in the process, felt that adequate opportunities existed for them to participate, and did in fact participate. In addition, parents who reported greater involvement in developing the intervention plan for their child also reported that they felt the plan adequately addressed their child's unique needs, were more satisfied with their child's progress in school, and reported higher ratings of their child's feelings of success in school. Finally, students were more likely to meet their goals when parents supported the intervention plan at home.

Christenson, Rounds and Gorney (1992, p. 192) identified several family factors correlated with positive academic outcomes for students in their classic literature review. These factors are:

... high, realistic parent expectations for school performance, parents' use of effort attributions for school performance, parents' structure and support for learning in the home, positive emotional interaction between parents and children ... parents' use of an authoritative parenting style, and parent involvement in education at home and school.

Two of these factors (i.e., high, realistic expectations and parents' use of effort attributions) may be directly affected by the shift away from a within-child, medical model of learning disabilities. Traditionally, the message parents presumably received throughout their interaction with the special education evaluation and service process was that something is "wrong" with their child and this "disability" is causing that child's learning problems. Contrast this with the message parents may receive in an RTI model, where the focus is on alterable, environmental variables, as the reason for learning difficulties. The message may be *we as educators need to work with you to determine how to best help your child learn*. No longer are educators seeking to diagnose a problem within the child; rather, they are trying to identify what factors in the environment occasion the best learning outcomes for the child. This is a fundamentally different message for parents and students to receive, a message that reinforces the definition of school–family partnerships as shared goals plus shared contribution plus shared accountability (Fantuzzo, Tighe, and Childs, 2000).

11.5 Benefits of Active Parental Engagement

The benefits of increasing active parental engagement in the RTI model are many and varied. Active parental engagement in RTI offers the chance to focus parent participation in children's learning on reinforcing and meeting students instructional needs, something Edwards (2004) has referred to as making "strategic connections" with the curriculum. These strategic connections would be apparent in collaborative home–school interventions, maximizing students' out-of-school learning time, and joint monitoring of a student's learning progress. Other expectations and benefits of RTI for key stakeholders are presented in Table 11.2.

A recent example of the integration of RTI and parent engagement in assessment and intervention may be found in Figure 11.3. Dunsmuir et al. (2005), at the training program for educational psychologists at London College University, have

TABLE 11.2. Expectations and benefits of RTI for key stakeholders.

Students

- Greater opportunities for
  - screening and early intervention for academic or behavioral concerns;
  - congruence in messages between home and school;
  - participation in their own interventions, including data collection, goal setting, preferences, self-reported conditions surrounding academic and behavioral difficulties.

Parents

- Opportunity to be involved at the first indication of a problem or concern.
- Critical source of information about the student.
- Necessary partner in the assessment and intervention process.
- Shared responsibility for student outcomes.

School professionals

- Less time in traditional assessment practices; more time spent in consultation, screening, direct intervention, and program evaluation.
- Consideration of the broad learning environment.
- Shared responsibility for student outcomes.

systematically created connections between parents and teachers throughout six phases representing the assessment to intervention link. In this figure, parent and teacher perspectives are gathered primarily to address two questions: What can be manipulated in the broad learning environment to bring about better student performance? And what resources do parents and teachers need to be actively involved in supporting student learning?

11.6 Potential Contributions to Public Health and Prevention

As has been documented in both the general mental health and school psychology literature, it is becoming increasingly clear that public health and prevention models must be implemented if there is to be any realistic hope of providing effective and systemic solutions to the "tidal wave" of educational and psychological problems facing our nation in the 21st century. The statistics are indeed grim, particularly for children and youth (Garbarino, 1995). Recently, Gutkin and Mills (2005) characterized our current state of affairs as nothing short of a "pandemic." A few dramatic examples suffice to make the point.

Nearly half of the US population will experience at least one diagnosable DSM-IV mental illness during the course of their lifetime, with half of these cases starting as early as age 14 (Kessler, Berglund, Demler, Jin, and Walters, 2005). Approximately one-third of fourth graders read at or above basic levels in reading proficiency and another one-third are behind a year or more in school (Sheridan and Gutkin, 2000). Problems of this breadth and scope will not respond to "business as usual." They call for significant alternative approaches to educational and psychological service delivery. Public health and prevention methodologies with school-aged populations hold the key to success (Gutkin and Mills, 2005; Strein, Hoagwood and Cohn, 2003).

RTI, if properly conceptualized, can play an important role in these public health and preventive approaches. Although born out of IDEA and special education legislation, it would be an enormous mistake to limit its application to this restricted population. RTI can and should be applied universally to enhance educational achievement for all children and youth. Looking back in our history, we can see similar pedagogical systems being advocated in the early 1970s in the form of diagnostic teaching (e.g., Cartwright, Cartwright, and Ysseldyke, 1973; Sabatino, 1971), but these were mistakenly framed within the limited context of serving special education and handicapped students and thus never achieved their full potential. Scanning the discussion of RTI to date, it would appear that school psychologists and educators are vulnerable yet again to falling into this trap. We want to suggest in the strongest of terms that this would be a serious mistake and that it would dramatically limit the potential systemic benefits of RTI approaches.

The rationale and logic behind RTI, which is essentially the logic of data-based decision-making, applies just as much to students in general education as it does to those being considered for special education. Limiting the application of RTI to special education diagnostic determinations is to miss the point and possibilities of this methodology. As argued convincingly by Stoner and Green (1992), all school-based and educational practice can be best approached in much the same manner as a research project. Hypotheses should be developed and then tested by gathering data. Successful educational methods should be retained and implemented over time with students. Unsuccessful

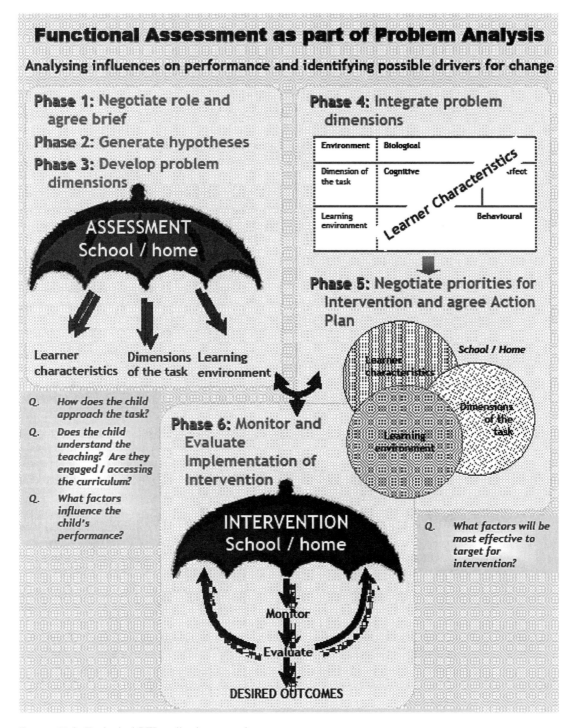

FIGURE 11.3. Ecological-RTI application example.

methods should be revised and replaced by alternative hypotheses that are tested subsequently via ongoing data gathering and analysis. While the terminology differs, Stoner and Green are essentially describing the core elements of RTI.

Our central point is that RTI should be understood as an approach and process with the potential to provide meaningful, scientifically driven, data-based decision-making services to all students. While it can most certainly be used as a diagnostic tool in relationship to special education, restricting its application in this manner would nullify its enormous potential as a tool in the service of public health and prevention. RTI can play a significant role in addressing the educational and mental health pandemic described earlier if it is thought of as a tool with universal rather than restricted application. To do otherwise would be to squander our latest opportunity to serve America's school-aged populations.

11.7 Concluding Remarks

Much attention and recent debate regarding RTI has focused on definitional and eligibility issues; however, RTI represents a much broader reform initiative for assessment and intervention practices. Indeed, it is perhaps best conceptualized as a product of years of calls for reform. However, to meet the spirit of those calls for reform, RTI applications must also include consideration of the multiple contexts in which children learn and develop. RTI will require a significant change in practice, with new or sharpened skills needed not only in program evaluation, evidence-based practices, and direct intervention, but also in consultation, collaboration, multi-systemic assessment and intervention, and the integration of this information across time. These changes are long overdue. Paired with a systems-ecological framework, RTI is an incredible opportunity to bring about positive changes in assessment, intervention, collaborative partnerships, and student outcomes.

The centrality of the learning context for improving student outcomes can no longer be ignored (Christenson and Anderson, 2002). Fortunately, the remarkable opportunity through implementing an RTI model may serve as the essential stimulus needed for school psychologists to make a substantial contribution to learning outcomes for students.

These contributions would be reflected in improved treatment and ecological validity, the use of more evidence-based interventions, improved parent and teacher knowledge about how the child learns best (i.e., how and what we can do together to help child meet the demands of the school environment), and altering the learning environment to increase student opportunity and supports for learning. The focus on functional behaviors in RTI (both academic and behavioral comparisons to norms, grade-level expectations, or same-grade peers for measurable outcomes, like words read correct, rate per hour, and problems completed) serves as an entrée for building constructive relationships with parents.

Despite these contributions to children's learning, we must acknowledge that RTI, especially conceptualized from systems ecological theory, is in its inception. Systems change is difficult and, admittedly, the prospect of organizing and measuring the confluence of contextual variables involved in students' academic and behavioral performance is daunting. RTI with parents and teachers as change agents is more complex than the current, albeit deeply flawed, system of diagnoses and labels. Nevertheless, there are tools and problem-solving structures for beginning to address the complexity. We need to recognize that these are implemented as a science and as an iterative process with hypotheses and data-based decision-making. Because RTI provides a very important, fundamental message that we will work together to identify "what," "how," and "did it work" for the target student, school psychologists can fill in the gaps with respect to how different students learn best.

Sound research and scholarship are needed to advance the understanding and implementation of RTI. More specifically, however, research from a systems ecological perspective has lagged considerably behind theoretical work. Most studies fail to account for the interactional nature of social contexts, settings, and child development and are fairly narrow in scope (Boyce et al., 1998). Similar comments could be made regarding the state of RTI. Although there is a theoretical basis (i.e., hypothesis testing, problem solving) and initial models and studies that support RTI, it, too, requires additional scholarship in terms of implementation and student outcomes. Ellis (2005) suggests that evidence at three levels is needed to determine whether an educational innovation is not simply another fad, but has enough research support to merit widespread use. First, the educational innovation must have a strong theoretical basis, derived from basic research in learning or behavior, or both. Second, it must have empirical support in real-world settings; and third, its effectiveness must be demonstrated in widespread implementation. As discussed throughout this chapter, implementing RTI using a systems ecological approach has strong theoretical support (Ysseldyke and Christenson, 2002). In addition, the implementation of RTI has been described in the literature (e.g., Iowa; Minneapolis Public Schools; Ohio; Horry County, SC). However, more research is needed to implement an RTI model that fully integrates the systems ecological perspective.

References

Bandura, A. (1978). The self system in reciprocal determination. *American Psychologist, 33,* 344–358.

Boyce, W. T., Frank, E., Jensen, P. S., Kessler, R. C., Nelson, C. A., Steinberg, L., et al. (1998). Social context in developmental psychopathology: recommendations for future research from the MacArthur Network on Psycholopathology and Development. *Development and Psychopathology, 18,* 143–164.

Bronfenbrenner, U. (1977). Toward an experimental ecology of human development. *American Psychologist, 32,* 513–531.

Bronfenbrenner, U. (1992). Ecological systems theory. In R. Vasta (Ed.), *Annals of Child Development. Six Theories of Child Development: Revised Formulations and Current Issues* (pp. 187–249). London: Jessica Kingsley.

Burns, M. K. & Ysseldyke, J. E. (2005). Questions about responsiveness to intervention: seeking answers from existing models. *The California School Psychologist, 10,* 9–20.

Carlson, C. & Christenson, S. L. (Eds.). (2005). Evidence-based parent and family interventions in school psychology [Special issue]. *School Psychology Quarterly, 20*(4).

Carroll, J. B. (1963). A model for school learning. *Teachers College Record, 64,* 723–733.

Christ, T. J., Burns, M. K., & Ysseldyke, J. E. (2005). Conceptual confusion within response-to-intervention vernacular: clarifying meaningful differences. *Communique, 3,* 1, 6–7.

Christenson, S., Abery, B., & Weinberg, R. A. (1986). An alternative model for the delivery of psychology in the school community. In S. N. Elliott & J. C. Witt (Eds.), *The delivery of psychological services in schools: Con-*

cepts, processes, and issues (pp. 349–391). Hillsdale, NJ: Lawrence Erlbaum.

Christenson, S. L., & Anderson, A. R. (2002). Commentary: the centrality of the learning context for students' academic enabler skills. *School Psychology Review, 31,* 378–393.

Christenson, S. L. & Carlson, C. (2005). Evidence-based parent and family intervention in school psychology: state of scientifically-based practice. *School Psychology Quarterly, 20*(4), 525–528.

Christenson, S. L., Rounds, T., & Gorney, D. (1992). Family factors and student achievement: an avenue to increase students' success. *School Psychology Quarterly, 7,* 178–206.

Christenson, S. L. & Sheridan, S. M. (2001). *School and Families: Creating Essential Connections for Learning.* New York: Guilford Press.

Cartwright, G. P., Cartwright, C. A., & Ysseldyke, J. E. (1973). Two decision models: identification and diagnostic teaching in handicapped children in regular classrooms. *Psychology in the Schools, 10,* 4–11.

Daly, E. J, Witt, J. C., Martens, B. K., & Dool, E. J. (1997). A model for conducting a functional analysis of academic performance problems. *School Psychology Review, 26,* 554–575.

Dauber, S. L. & Epstein, J. L. (1993). Parents' attitudes and practices of involvement in inner city elementary and middle schools. In N. F. Chavkin (Ed.), *Families and Schools in a Pluralistic Society* (pp. 53–72). Albany: State University of New York Press.

Dean, V. J., Burns, M. K., Grialou, T., & Varro, P. (2006). Comparison of ecological validity of learning disabilities diagnostic models. *Psychology in the Schools, 43,* 157–168.

Dunsmuir, S.,[1] Cameron, R. J., Cline, T., Frederickson, N., Graham, B., Hudson, J., et al. (2005). Functional assessment as part of problem analysis. Unpublished poster guidance for Educational Psychologists in Training. London: University College London.

Edwards, P. A. (2004). *Children's Literacy Development: Making it Happen Through School, Family, and Community Involvement.* Boston: Pearson Education.

Ellis, A. K. (2005). *Research on Educational Innovations* (4th ed.). Larchmont, NY: Eye on Education.

Fantuzzo, J., Tighe, E., & Childs, S. (2000). Family involvement questionnaire: a multivariate assessment of family participation in early childhood education. *Journal of Educational Psychology, 92,* 367–376.

Fuchs, D., Mock, D., Morgan, P., & Young, C. (2003). Responsiveness to intervention: definitions, evidence, and implications for the learning disabilities construct.

---

[1] Email: s.dunsmuir@ucl.ac.uk

Learning Disabilities Research and Practice, 18, 157–171.

Garbarino, J. (1995). *Raising Children in a Socially Toxic Environment*. San Francisco: Jossey-Bass.

Greenwood, C. R., Carta, J. J., Kamps, D., Terry, B., & Delquadri, J. (1994). Development and validation of standard classroom observation systems for school practitioners: Ecobehavioral Assessment Systems Software (EBASS). *Exceptional Children, 61*, 197–210.

Gutkin, T. B. & Mills, R. C. (2005). Public health services: Conceptual rationale and sample evidence-based contributions. Presented at the *Annual Convention of the American Psychological Association*. Washington, DC.

Kessler, R. C., Berglund, P., Demler, O., Jin, R., & Walters, E. E. (2005). Lifetime prevalence and age-of-onset distributions of DSM-IV disorders in the national comorbidity survey replication. *Archives of General Psychiatry, 62*, 593–602.

Harry, B. (1992). *Cultural Diversity, Families, and the Special Education System: Communication and Empowerment*. New York: Teachers College Press.

McNamara K., Telzrow, C., & DeLamatre, J. (1999). Parent reactions to implementation of intervention-based assessment. *Journal of Educational and Psychological Consultation, 10*, 343–362.

Patrikakou, E. N. & Weissberg, R. P. (2000). Parents' percetions of teacher outreach and parent involvement in children's education. *Journal of Prevention and Intervention in the Community, 20*, 103–119.

Pianta, R. & Walsh, D. B. (1996). *High-Risk Children in Schools: Constructing Sustaining Relationships*. New York: Routledge.

Reschly, D. J. (1988). Special education reform: school psychology revolution. *School Psychology Review, 17*, 459–475.

Rimm-Kaufman, S. E. & Pianta, R. C. (2000). An ecological perspective on the transition to kindergarten: a theoretical framework to guide empirical research. *Journal of Applied Developmental Psychology, 21*, 491–511.

Sabatino, D. A. (1971). A scientific approach toward a discipline of special education. *Journal of Special Education, 5*, 15–22.

Sameroff, A. J. (1983). Developmental systems: contexts and evolution. In P. H. Mussen (Ed.), *Handbook of Child Psychology* (4th ed., pp. 237–293). New York: Wiley.

Sheridan, S. & Gutkin, T. (2000). The ecology of school psychology: examining and changing our paradigm in the 21st century. *School Psychology Review, 29*, 485–502.

Stoner, G. & Green, S. K. (1992). Reconsidering the scientist–practitioner model for school psychology practice. *School Psychology Review, 21*, 155–166.

Strein, W., Hoagwood, K., & Cohn, A. (2003). School psychology: a public health perspective I. Prevention, populations, and, systems change. *Journal of School Psychology, 41*, 23–38.

Vygotsky, L. (1962). *Thought and Language,* E. Hanfmann & G. Vakar (Eds. & Trans.). Cambridge, MA: MIT Press.

Westat and Policy Studies Associates (2001). *The Longitudinal Evaluation of School Change and Performance in Title 1 Schools: Volume I: Executive Summary*. Washington, DC: US Department of Education, Office of the Deputy Secretary, Planning and Evaluation Service. http://www.ed.gov/offices/OUS/PES/esed/lescp_highlights.html.

Ysseldyke, J. E. & Christenson, S. L. (1987). Evaluating students' instructional environments. *Remedial and Special Education, 8*, 17–24.

Ysseldyke, J. E. & Christenson, S. L. (2002). *FAAB: Functional Assessment of Academic Behavior: Creating Successful Learning Environments*. Longmont, CO: Sopris West.

12
Social Behavior Assessment and Response to Intervention

Christine Kerres Malecki and Michelle Kilpatrick Demaray

Christine Kerres Malecki, PhD, is an Associate Professor of Psychology at Northern Illinois University, DeKalb.
cmalecki@niu.edu
Michelle Kilpatrick Demaray, PhD, is an Associate Professor of Psychology at Northern Illinois University,
DeKalb. mkdemaray@niu.edu

This chapter presents information on assessment strategies for social behaviors in schools that may be used in a problem-solving approach that incorporates response to intervention (RTI). As a point of communication, although many associate RTI solely as a method for identifying and qualifying students for special education services, this chapter discusses RTI within the context of a problem-solving approach. The "interventions" in RTI can be thought of as general education curriculum and instruction, interventions for students at risk of academic or behavior problems, or interventions that are intense enough to warrant special education funding. Thus, this chapter does not focus solely on RTI as an eligibility tool. The importance of the assessment of social behaviors in a problem-solving or RTI approach will be presented along with a detailed description of specific measures and example applications. The use of RTI with social behaviors will also be critiqued, along with suggestions for future directions for the field.

12.1 Importance

Educators are continually struggling with the increasing number of students that have academic or behavioral difficulties, or both, in the classroom. For example, there are an increasing number of children being served in special education programs for children with emotional disturbance (US Department of Education, National Center for Education Statistics, 2003). Researchers have reported a high prevalence of bullying behavior in US schools, with 15 to 20% of students reporting being regular victims of bullying behavior (Batsche and Knoff, 1994). Social behavior problems in schools, unfortunately, also include serious crimes and offenses. For example, according to the US Department of Education, National Center for Education Statistics (2004), in 1999–2000, 20% of public schools reported at least one violent crime (e.g., rape, assault), 71% reported violent incidents, and 46% reported thefts. Not only are externalizing behaviors of concern, but students may also experience high rates of internalizing disorders, such as depression and anxiety. Prevalence rates of depression in children and adolescents range from 20 to 55% (Diekstra and Garnefski, 1995). As the number of students with emotional or behavioral difficulties continues to rise, this creates challenges for educators in dealing with these behaviors. Schools are forced to address these increasing social behavior challenges in order to educate children. Too often, the approaches within schools to address behavior problems are reactive and do not emphasize a proactive or preventative component. Ideally, schools would utilize a more preventative approach based on evidence-based interventions (Deno, 2005). Using a problem-solving model in schools to prevent problem behavior and academic difficulties is crucial. If schools only focus on intervening when problems are severe, then they will be doing a great disservice to the students they are serving (Shinn, 2005).

School psychologists are well positioned in the schools to advocate, and in some contexts provide leadership for, a proactive and preventative approach to social behavior problems in schools. They have the knowledge and skills that allow them to design, implement, and evaluate interventions aimed at prevention and behavior change (Gresham, 2004). Future directions for school-based intervention models will be based on evidence-based intervention practices and response to intervention in a problem-solving model (Gresham, 2004). Thus, it is important for educators and school psychologists to have the knowledge and skills to prevent or intervene with social behavior problems. This requires educators to utilize knowledge from the literature on evidence-based intervention, RTI, and problem-solving.

12.2 Historical Need/Use

Many components or aspects of RTI have been utilized in schools in the past; however, they have not been conceptualized as part of a larger model or system (Brown-Chidsey and Steege, 2005). Prior models of identifying students in need of services in schools have had many problems, such as lacking prevention efforts, relying on one-time assessments, and assuming that deficits are within the student (Barnett, Daly, Jones, and Lentz, 2004; Brown-Chidsey and Steege, 2005; Gresham, 2004). Brown-Chidsey (2005) describes the two main components of RTI that distinguish it from other practices are that it is systematic and data based. Thus, a large part of the RTI process involves *assessments* that are both systematic and data based. This chapter details these assessments for social behavior problems in schools. The RTI model has more of a preventative focus as opposed to traditional models, where educators wait for referrals of children or adolescents who are failing or severely struggling in school. Within the RTI model, educational professionals proactively monitor and screen for various academic and social behaviors. Based on those assessment data, interventions are provided that match the students' needs. Much more has been written about proactively screening and monitoring important academic outcomes, such as reading. However, there is clearly also a need to screen and provide interventions for important social behaviors in the schools (Crone and Horner, 2003).

12.3 Three-Tiered Model of Intervention

Researchers have discussed the importance of identifying and intervening with students based on the level of symptom severity and need. Given the context of social behaviors in schools, first one must identify children that are typically developing and not at risk for various social behavior problems. Ideally, at least 80 to 85% of students would be functioning in a typical (nonproblematic) range of behavior at this level (Walker and Shinn, 2002). Next, one must identify those children and adolescents that are at risk for developing social behavior problems and those that are currently exhibiting social behavior problems. Given the large domain of social behavior, this task may seem overwhelming to some educational professionals. It may be difficult for school personnel to know what specific social behaviors to focus on for prevention/intervention. The list of social behavior problems that may be affecting children in schools today is large. This could include bullying, drug and alcohol use, poor social skills, depression, skipping school, and anxiety. See Table 12.1 for a list of some of the many social

TABLE 12.1. List of possible social behaviors for schools to target for prevention/intervention.

Affective problems
  Depression
  Anxiety
  Self-esteem/self-concept
Externalizing problems
  Aggression
  Bullying
  School violence
  Conduct problems
  Hyperactivity
  Truancy
Social/relationship behaviors
  Peer relationships
  Social Skills
  Prosocial behaviors
Risky behaviors
  Alcohol and drug use
  Smoking
  Sexual behaviors
  Health behaviors
School factors/positive behaviors
  School climate
  Social support
  Resiliency (risk and protective factors)

Model/Framework

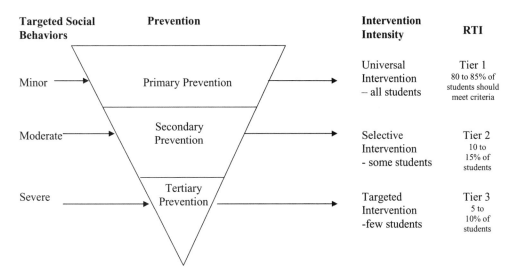

FIGURE 12.1. Relationships among severity of targeted social behavior, prevention framework, intervention intensity framework, and RTI.

behaviors that schools may potentially focus on as target behaviors in an RTI model.

Figure 12.1 depicts the three levels of severity for social problems that children and adolescents may be exhibiting. Granted, children and adolescents who are already exhibiting social behavior problems are going to have more negative outcomes associated with their difficulties than children at risk or not exhibiting a specific social behavior problem. Children exhibiting different levels of behavior problems require different levels of intervention (e.g., intensity, complexity, expense) due to the severity of their problems or their responsiveness to prevention/intervention strategies (Gresham, 2004; Walker and Shinn, 2002). These levels of intervention are primary, secondary, and tertiary prevention. Primary prevention programs (i.e., universal interventions) focus on the entire school and may be focused on building protective factors, increasing resilience, or preventing social behavior problems from starting in the first place. Basically, at the primary prevention level one is trying to *prevent* social behavior problems from beginning and to achieve or maintain the 80 to 85% benchmark for the behavior of interest. Secondary prevention programs (i.e., selective interventions) focus on providing interventions to students that are *at risk* for social behavior

problems. These interventions are typically used to target at-risk students and are often carried out in small groups. Interventions at the third level, tertiary (i.e., targeted intervention), are used to address the needs of children already displaying social behavior problems and are much more intensive and typically individual in focus (Walker and Shinn, 2002).

It is assumed that, within the three-tiered approach to service delivery, all of the requisite problem-solving steps would be used. Although the steps are often numbered differently or labeled differently, the basic tenets include problem identification, problem analysis, intervention development, intervention implementation, and intervention evaluation (Tilly, 2002). In this chapter, it should be assumed that the assessment techniques being discussed would be tailored to the purpose called for within each of these five steps. For example, for intervention evaluation (progress monitoring) purposes, the assessment technique would need to be able to be given repeatedly and reliably over time and would need to be sensitive to change. If a team is determining whether or not a child is eligible for and needs interventions that are intensive enough to warrant special education funding, then the data collected and or reviewed would need to be appropriate for making that eligibility determination. Although the steps of the problem-solving process may not be referred to specifically throughout the chapter, this "fit the assessment to its appropriate purpose" philosophy should be assumed.

12.4 Assessment Approaches Within the Three Tiers

One assumption of the authors is that all assessment methodology within a problem-solving model would take a functional behavior assessment (FBA) approach. In order to conserve space, the remainder of the chapter will focus on the general assessment techniques that might fit within a three-tier assessment/intervention approach, but it should be assumed that, especially at the higher tiers, school personnel would be using FBA as their orientation in approaching behavioral assessment.

Just as the intensity of interventions increases as student needs increase from Tier 1 to Tier 3, the "intensity" of assessment also increases. As stated by Grimes and Kurns (2003, p. 14), "Assessment data are gathered at all levels of the problem solving process, but the breadth and depth of these data increase as the needs become more intensive." One framework that is helpful for educators to guide assessment practices is the review, interview, observe, test (RIOT) approach (Heartland Area Education Agency, 2003). Descriptions and examples of each of the RIOT domains are described below.

If RIOT is followed in assessment approaches, the breadth of assessment data would refer to multiple methods and multiple sources, with data first being gathered via review, interview, and observations. If more information is needed (more breadth and depth needed), then one may move to the most "intrusive" method of assessment by gathering new data via "testing." The idea is to test (typically involving time one-on-one with the student) only if necessary. Testing in the RIOT approach does not just refer to tests per se, but refers to methodologies that gather new data in a way that involves the student or gathering data systematically from others (e.g., experimental intervention piloting, gathering rating-scale data from the student, teacher, or parent). The following sections describe how data on social behaviors can be collected via the RIOT approach in a three-tiered model of service delivery (Table 12.2).

12.4.1 Review for Tier 1

School staff can identify first whether they can simply gather existing data via "review." Are the data available in students' cumulative records, teachers' gradebooks, or behavioral referral databases? If so, this data would be the first to collect, organize, and analyze. Several types of important behavioral data may be found in students' cumulative files (National Center for Education Statistics, 1997). Attendance rates could be aggregated by grade level or other meaningful demographics (e.g., special education status, if students are receiving after-school programming). School staff can use these data to determine what the local norms are regarding attendance and use those data in conjunction with staff expectations for students' attendance. Is there a mismatch between local norms and teacher expectations? Are 85% of students attending school at an acceptable rate?

Collecting behavioral referral data can also be very informative (Crone and Horner, 2003; National Center for Education Statistics, 1997). How many students are being referred to the office for behavioral issues each week, each semester, or each year? Are the levels of behavioral referrals acceptable? Staff could also organize the data by behavioral offense if that information is available. For example, perhaps most of the students are referred due to dress code violations. These initial data may lead to hypotheses for changes at Tier 1, such as a revised dress code, better communication about the dress code, or a reward system for students consistently following the dress code. The methods of analyzing the last year or two of office referral data and using those data to make decisions (an ideal Tier 1 review assessment) are described in the work of the researchers behind Positive Behavioral Interventions and Supports (PBIS) (e.g., Sugai, Sprague, Horner, and Walker, 2000; Crone and Horner, 2003).

12.4.2 Review for Tiers 2 and 3

Reviewing for Tiers 2 and 3 would involve examining data for individual students more closely. Rather than reviewing existing products to develop normative data or to screen for problems, the review would take place to facilitate problem analysis and hypothesis development (Tilly, 2002). For example, personnel could examine a middle-school student's assignment completion rates across all of their class

TABLE 12.2. Summary table to guide implementation of assessment for social behaviors with RTI.

Question to answer	Assessments to use	Considerations	Purpose of assessment
What is the target behavior?	Choose appropriate target social behavior(s)	The target behavior must be clearly and operationally defined	To choose an appropriate target behavior for prevention/intervention based on school need or goals
What are the current levels of this behavior? Are 80 to 90% of students succeeding in this area at Tier 1?	Conduct Tier 1 assessment with review, interview, observe, and/or test	Tier 1 assessments should be easy to collect on entire school population	To understand the current levels of the target social behavior in the school, to create normative data or benchmark criteria

Implement Tier 1 universal interventions school-wide and continue data collection.

Assess at-risk students for potential Tier 2 interventions.

Do *some* children need more intensive intervention (Tier 2)?	Conduct Tier 2 assessment with review, interview, observe, and/or test	Tier 2 assessments should provide information to aid problem analysis and intervention development	To determine how to develop interventions for children that are not responding to Tier 1 interventions
Are the interventions being implemented effective (at Tier 2)?	Conduct Tier 2 assessment with primarily observe & test	Data collected to monitor Tier 2 interventions should be able to be gathered repeatedly and reliably	To determine students' response to intervention at Tier 2
Are the Tier 1 interventions being implemented effective?	Conduct Tier 1 screening assessment with review, interview, observe, and/or test	Tier 1 assessments should be easy to collect on entire school population	To monitor the levels of the target social behavior in the school and compare against previously identified benchmark criteria

Continue Tier 1 universal interventions school-wide with necessary changes and continue data collection.
Implement and progress monitor Tier 2 interventions.
Identify and develop interventions for Tier 3

Do a *few* children need more intensive intervention?	Conduct Tier 3 assessment with review, interview, observe, and/or test	Tier 3 assessments should provide information to aid problem analysis and intervention development	To determine children that did not respond to Tier 2 interventions and are in need of more intensive interventions
Are the interventions being implemented effective (at Tier 3)?	Conduct Tier 3 assessment with primarily observe & test	Data collected to monitor Tier 3 interventions should be able to be gathered repeatedly and reliably	To determine students' response to intervention at Tier 2

periods. Is the problem occurring in some classes more than others? Is there a pattern of not turning work in on certain days (e.g., Mondays, or on days when work was taken home as opposed to completed in class?). As mentioned above, the purposes of Tier 2 and 3 assessments are to be more diagnostic; that is, to identify the conditions under which the student is successful and not successful. This information can then be used for developing interventions for groups of students or individuals, for evaluating the effectiveness of those interventions, and potentially to determine eligibility for special education services (Gresham, 2005). Reviewing

data is appropriate at every level of the service delivery model.

12.4.3 Interviewing and Observing for Tier 1

Interviewing and observing every child in a school for Tier 1 purposes would be inefficient, if not impossible. However, gathering staff interviews can be helpful for anecdotal information about a target concern. Select parent and student interviews may also help provide a direction if more information is needed before doing more Tier 1 assessment; for example, to narrow down the scope of a target behavior. Similarly, conducting school-wide observations to gather universal data is impractical. However, choosing a random classroom at each grade level and conducting observations during a common time (e.g., observing reading instruction) may provide useful data. For example, many teachers refer students for poor peer relations. However, teachers and school staff may not have local peer comparison data for that social behavior. Observing random recess times and gathering systematic data on the number of peer interactions typically occurring on the playground would provide useful data that may be used for comparison or goal setting (particularly in Tiers 2 and 3). Additionally, these data could be used to determine whether more students than expected have poor peer relationships, thus leading to a Tier 1 intervention.

12.4.4 Interviewing and Observing for Tiers 2 and 3

As part of the problem analysis and intervention development steps of problem solving, gathering data via interviews (e.g., student, parent, and teachers) and via observations of the target behavior in context can be crucial. Most interviews conducted within a problem-solving framework are more behavioral in nature and are critical in conducting a functional assessment of behavior (Busse and Beaver, 2000). Furthermore, doing structured, formal observations of the student in context provide more data to develop hypotheses that will lead to intervention development.

There are several types of interview (e.g., traditional techniques, behavioral interviews, and structured or semi-structured interviews) and several types of observation (e.g., naturalistic observation, analogue observation, self-monitoring), all of which are documented in detail in many resources (e.g., Merrell, 2003; Sattler and Hoge, 2006). More important for the context of the current chapter is to discuss how interviews and observations generally fit into the RTI approach.

First, interviews and observations should be focused on the target behavior rather than being general and comprehensive. Furthermore, these methods should be used to help develop or confirm hypotheses generated as part of problem analyses. Finally, data from observations should be collected

systematically, as those data may be used as baseline data in the intervention evaluation step of the problem-solving process (Tilly, 2002).

Ecological data may also be gathered via interviews and observations. Important questions include: Is there a mismatch in the curriculum being used and the student's instructional level? Is the classroom environment conducive to that student's learning? Is instructional pace appropriate for the target student? These questions can be answered via review (e.g., of the curriculum), interview (e.g., teacher, student, parent), and observation (e.g., classroom instruction, environment).

Another methodology that fits within interview and observation is teacher referral. To screen at Tier 1 for various social behavior concerns, all teachers could be requested to identify children in their classrooms that they are concerned about regarding a particular social behavior (e.g., peer relationship problems, inattention, poor classroom behavior, depression). The accuracy of teachers' judgments surrounding academic behaviors has been documented by research (Demaray and Elliott, 2001; Gresham, MacMillan, and Bocian, 1997; Hoge and Coladarci, 1989); however, several cautions have also been discussed (Feil, Severson, and Walker, 2002). Although much more research needs to be conducted on the validity of teacher identification of social behavior problems, relying on teacher identification of children in need of intervention at Tier 1 may be a very realistic methodology for schools with limited resources.

12.4.5 Testing at All Tiers

As part of the RIOT process, school psychologists may need to employ various "tests" or tools in order to collect additional data to inform decisions at each of the three tiers. These may be for screening, diagnostic, progress-monitoring, or eligibility purposes. These various tools will be briefly reviewed below.

12.4.5.1 Rating Scales

While there are numerous methods to collect new data (e.g., sociometric analyses, goal attainment scaling), the use of rating-scale screening methodology is probably the most efficient "testing" method for social behaviors. The rating scales used on a school-wide basis (Tier 1) need to be relatively brief, easy to score, and cost effective. Ratings scales can be used to assess students' social behavior in a number of domains, including bullying, depression, alcohol and drug use, gang involvement, social skills, anxiety, externalizing behavior, attention problems, and social support. At Tiers 2 and 3, more comprehensive rating scales may be used. For example, the child behavior checklist (Achenbach and Rescorla, 2001) and the behavioral assessment system for children (Reynolds and Kamphaus, 2004) are commonly used broad-band measures for the assessment of a wide variety of social and emotional problems in children and are often used in the determination of eligibility for services. These comprehensive ratings scales have their limitations for use at Tiers 2 and 3. For example, they are not designed to be used frequently and repeatedly to track the effect of interventions; they frequently focus on negative behaviors, are time intensive, and are based on the reporters' perceptions.

There are also narrow-band rating scales that can assess a particular targeted behavior. For example, screening for problems at a school-wide level (Tier 1) could be done using brief narrow-band measures such as the Reynolds child depression scale (Reynolds, 1989) for depression, the child and adolescent social support scale (Malecki, Demaray, and Elliott, 2000) for social support, and the social skills rating system (Gresham and Elliott, 1990). The ADHD-IV rating scale (DuPaul, Power, Anastopoulos, and Reid, 1998) and the BASC ADHD monitor (Kamphaus and Reynolds, 1998) are both brief measures that can be used to assess and monitor intervention effectiveness for symptoms of ADHD. These measures average around 10 to 15 min to administer (some can be collected from multiple informants) and can be scored quickly. They have been found to be valid and reliable measures of their stated constructs. There are a wide variety of other behavior rating scales available across various domains of behavior (Merrell, 2003). It is important to note that, although they are relatively brief, schools may not have the resources to purchase, administer, and score these measures. In addition, some of these measures may not be ideal for progress monitoring behavior change.

12.4.5.2 Self-Monitoring

In a self-monitoring assessment a child or adolescent records specific target behaviors and may include monitoring circumstances surrounding that behavior (Sattler, 2002). An advantage of self-monitoring is that it may also serve as an intervention to change the targeted social behavior (Reid, 1996). Another advantage is that children can monitor internal thoughts and feelings as well as overt behaviors (Merrell, 2003). Some concerns around self-monitoring include training children and adolescents to properly conduct self-monitoring, the accuracy of self-monitoring, and limited reliability and validity. An excellent review of the literature and a guide to using self-monitoring is provided in Shapiro, Durnan, Post, and Levinson (2002). Self-monitoring could be used both as part of an intervention and to monitor intervention effectiveness at Tiers 2 and 3. Given the cautions around the accuracy of self-monitoring (Shapiro et al., 2002), self-monitoring data would need to be used along with several types of convergent data if part of an eligibility decision.

12.4.5.3 Goal Attainment Scaling and Daily Behavior Report Cards

Two similar methods of rating behavior can be used as progress monitoring tools in a problem-solving approach: goal attainment scaling (GAS; Roach and Elliott, 2005) and daily behavior report cards (DBRCs; Chafouleas, McDougal, Riley-Tillman, Panahon, and Hilt, 2005). GAS ratings involve (a) identifying the target behavior, (b) operationalizing the behavior in objective, measurable terms, and (c) creating three to five operational descriptions of the behavior ranging from the criterion (e.g., 100% immediate compliance to teacher requests) to the least favorable outcome (e.g., 0 to 10% immediate compliance to teacher requests). The numeric indicators for each of the descriptions typically range from "+2," representing the most favorable description, to "−2," representing the least desirable description, and "0," representing the description of the baseline level of the behavior (Albers, Elliott, Kettler, and Roach, 2005).

DBRCs are very similar to GAS. They are developed very similarly by identifying a target behavior, creating operational descriptions of various levels of that behavior ranging from least to most desirable, and assigning numeric values to each descriptor (Chafouleas et al., 2005). Chafouleas et al. compared DBRC data with direct observations and found that there is a moderate association between DBRC ratings and direct observations of behavior. Future research is warranted on the use of GAS and DBRC data collection methods, as they may be very useful tools to monitor progress associated with interventions at Tier 2 and Tier 3. One caution is that the GAS and DBRC operational descriptors need to be developed very carefully by a school psychologist or other professional trained to create behavioral, observable, and measurable behavioral descriptors.

12.4.5.4 Direct Observation

Using direct observation techniques would also add to the convergent data necessary when making decisions within a problem-solving or RTI model. Frequency recording, duration recording, latency recording, interval recording, antecedent, behavior, and consequence (ABC) recordings, (Albers et al., 2005) can all be used at Tiers 2 and 3 to monitor progress and to help determine peer comparison data to help in making eligibility decisions. The direct observation data can be crucial in helping confirm or provide convergent evidence of the GAS or DBRC ratings described above.

12.4.5.5 Treatment Acceptability and Treatment Integrity

An important consideration in gathering new assessment data within the three-tier model of service delivery is to monitor the acceptability and integrity of the interventions being implemented at all three levels of intervention. If progress monitoring is planned and conducted perfectly, then the data will still be meaningless if the intervention is not carried out as planned. At least two factors may influence this: treatment acceptability and treatment integrity (Elliott, Witt, Kratochwill, and Stoiber, 2002). For example, knowing a teacher's perceptions of an intervention in terms of the time it will take, how intrusive it is, and how positive (versus punitive) the intervention is can all affect treatment acceptability (Albers et al., 2005). An intervention will be more likely to be implemented with integrity when it is time efficient, simple, requires minimal resources and staff, if staff are highly motivated, and if it is perceived as effective (Albers et al., 2005). Thus, collecting acceptability and integrity data should al-ways be considered as part of intervention development and evaluation in a problem-solving approach.

12.5 An Example: Bullying

Perhaps a school administrator noticed that they had experienced increased complaints about bullying in their school but they were not sure of the significance of the issue in their building. As a Tier 1 assessment approach, the administrator might elicit teacher feedback via informal interviews and teacher referrals. Additionally, a school may use one of several rating scales that were developed to measure bullying behavior that may be appropriate for school-wide screening. The Reynolds Bully Victimization Scale (Reynolds, 2003) is a 46-item rating scale (23 assess being bullied and 23 assess being the aggressor) that assesses the frequency of experiencing various aggressive behaviors at school. The Olweus Bully/Victim Questionnaire (Olweus, 2004) provides a lengthy definition of bullying and asks students to answer questions about their experiences of bullying behavior. The Bully Survey (Swearer, 2001) provides a very brief definition of bullying to students and then asks questions about the frequency of bullying, and reasons why students think they are bullied. Furlong and Greif (2006) provide a contemporary review of bullying measures that may provide further direction in choosing measures of bullying. These rating scales would be appropriate for Tier 1 screening, as it is feasible for all students in the school to complete them to provide data on levels of bullying in the school. Again, schools with limited resources may not have the means to collect and analyze this data. It may require a staff person in charge of data collection and analysis or collaboration with a local university.

If a problem was identified, then a committee could be developed to gather more information about the nature of the problems and develop a universal intervention plan. In the meantime, groups of students could be identified for more selective intervention. This could involve working with small groups of children that were identified through the screening as being frequently targeted for bullying. Further interviews could be done with those students as a Tier 2 assessment approach to do problem analysis and intervention development. Perhaps it is identified that, for many of the students who have been victimized, they need help in learning how to effectively respond to bullying when it happens to them. Educational professionals often target bullies for intervention and prevention by creating no-tolerance rules, trying to create a culture that does not accept bullying behavior; however, educators may fall short when it comes to providing victims of bullying with appropriate levels of intervention. Thus, along with anti-bullying interventions, interventions could also focus on the victims. This could consist of a series of small group informational skill-building interventions. These students would be followed via progress monitoring using an appropriate rating scale, a GAS or a self-monitoring procedure (how often were they bullied, and if they were, did they respond using the skills they were being taught, what help do they need). Additionally, of course, problem solving is a cyclical process. The universal intervention in place would need to be monitored, new students targeted for Tier 2 interventions, those students monitored, and, finally, potentially identified for more intensive Tier 3 interventions if necessary.

12.6 Limitations and Concerns

The idea of screening and implementing prevention and intervention strategies in schools for social behavior problems in an RTI model also creates some concerns and roadblocks. First, many schools are so busy "putting out fires" and dealing with day-to-day issues that it is often difficult to communicate the wisdom of prevention. As stated by Walker and Shinn (2002, p. 4), "it is not just a question of knowing what to do but, rather, of whether we are aware of what we need to do, and whether we are willing to do it." There are evidence-based interventions and prevention programs that have been shown to be effective for addressing various social and behavioral problems. It is just a matter of developing systems to be certain they get implemented in a comprehensive, systematic, and appropriate manner. Part of the difficulty for schools in implementing the screening and intervention/prevention efforts is a lack of available resources. The task of screening the entire school for benchmark data and to identify children who need higher levels of intervention may be overwhelming. First, the schools have to

have the necessary resources for screening, staff to implement, score, systematically analyze, and interpret. An additional problem for many schools is what to do with the children they identify as needing more intensive intervention, especially in high-risk schools where they many identify numerous social and behavioral problems among their student population. Schools will need resources to implement prevention and intervention programs. Particularly for prevention programs, money can be difficult to secure to solve "problems that do not yet exist." However, given the emphasis on evidence-based interventions, the growing number of endorsed programs, and the reauthorization of IDEA (2004), including resource provision to prevention and intervention in general education, there may be support to be found. Additionally, strong leadership within a school or district and staff commitment to implement would be crucial.

12.7 Future Directions and Conclusions

In academic domains, the three-tier model has a great deal of research and support, particularly in the area of reading (Grimes and Kurns, 2003; National Institute of Child Health and Human Development, 2000). National benchmarks have been identified using early literacy skills and oral reading fluency that inform educational professionals regarding whether young children are on track to be successful readers. However, such benchmarks do not currently exist in the vast area of social behavior. One future direction will be to identify "benchmarks" for certain social behaviors that schools can use as they conduct Tier 1 screening. These data may be there, but a comprehensive meta-analysis of the existing empirical literature may help in the area of social behavior as it has for reading (National Institute of Child Health and Human Development, 2000).

Although educators may find the task of implementing a three-tiered approach to addressing social behavior needs daunting, it is a worthy pursuit. The amount of time and school resources used to assess, intervene, and progress monitor social behaviors increases along with the level of intensity of the target behavior. Therefore, if schools take a preventative approach, beginning with Tier 1 assessment and intervention procedures, then it is anticipated that there would be a savings of both time and resources by catching problems early or before they even begin and grow in intensity and need. Additionally, research has shown repeatedly that positive behavior is related to positive academic achievement (e.g., Malecki and Elliott, 2002; Wentzel, 1993). Thus, spending resources in creating a preventative framework for behavior may also have positive results for academics. Hopefully, a continuing empirical research base will help provide more specific guidelines in implementing a three-tiered model of service delivery for social behaviors in the schools.

References

Achenbach, T. M. & Rescorla, L. A. (2001). *Manual for the ASEBA School-Age Forms & Profiles.* Burlington, VT: University of Vermont, Research Center for Children, Youth, & Families.

Albers, C. A., Elliott, S. N., Kettler, R. J., & Roach, A. T. (2005). Evaluating intervention outcomes. In R. Brown-Chidsey (Ed.), *Assessment for Intervention: A Problem-Solving Approach* (pp. 329–351). New York: Guilford Press.

Barnett, D. W., Daly, E. J., Jones, K. M., & Lentz Jr., F. E., (2004). Empirically based special service decisions from single-case designs of increasing and decreasing intensity. *The Journal of Special Education, 38,* 66–79.

Batsche, G. M. & Knoff, H. M. (1994). Bullies and their victims: understanding a pervasive problem in the schools. *School Psychology Review, 23,* 165–174.

Brown-Chidsey, R. (Ed.). (2005). *Assessment for Intervention: A Problem-Solving Approach.* New York: The Guilford Press.

Brown-Chidsey, R. & Steege, M. W. (2005). *Response to Intervention: Principles and Strategies for Effective Practice.* New York: The Guilford Press.

Busse, R. T. & Beaver, B. R. (2000). Informant reports: parent and teacher interviews. In E. S. Shapiro & T. R. Kratochwill (Eds.), *Conducting School-Based Assessment of Child and Adolescent Behavior.* (pp. 235–273). New York: Guilford Press.

Chafouleas, S. M., McDougal, J. L., Riley-Tillman, T. C., Panahon, C. J., & Hilt, A. M. (2005). What do daily behavior report cards (DBRCs) measure? An initial comparison of DBRCs with direct observation for off-task behavior. *Psychology in the Schools, 42,* 669–676.

Crone, D. A. & Horner, R. H. (2003). *Building Positive Behavior Support Systems in Schools.* New York: The Guilford Press.

Demaray, M. K. & Elliott, S. N. (2001). Teachers' judgments of students' academic functioning: a comparison of actual and predicted performances. *School Psychology Quarterly, 13,* 8–24.

Deno, S. L. (2005). Problem-solving assessment. In R. Brown-Chidsey (Ed.), *Assessment for Intervention: A Problem-Solving Approach* (pp. 10–30). New York: Guilford Press.

Diekstra, R. F. & Garnefski, N. (1995). On the nature, magnitude and causality of suicidal behaviors: an international perspective. *Suicide and Life-Threatening Behavior, 25,* 36–57.

DuPaul, G.J., Power, T. J., Anastspoulos, A.D., & Reid, R. (1998). *ADHD-IV Rating Scale IV.* New York: Guilford Press.

Elliott, S. N., Witt, J. C., Kratochwill, T. R., & Stoiber, K. C. (2002). Selecting and evaluating classroom interventions. In M. R. Shinn, H. M. Walker, & G. Stoner (Eds.), *Interventions for Academic and Behavior Problems II: Preventative and Remedial Approaches* (pp. 243–294). Bethesda, MD: The National Association of School Psychologists Publications.

Feil, E. G., Severson, H. H., & Walker, H. M. (2002). Early screening and intervention to prevent the development of aggressive, destructive behavior patterns among at-risk children. In M. R. Shinn, H. M. Walker, & G. Stoner (Eds.), *Interventions for Academic and Behavior Problems II: Preventative and Remedial Approaches* (pp. 143–166). Bethesda, MD: The National Association of School Psychologists Publications.

Greif, J. L. & Furlong, M. J. (2006). The assessment of school bullying: using theory to inform practice. *Journal of School Violence, 5,* 33–50.

Gresham, F. M. (2004). Current status and future directions of school-based behavioral interventions, *School Psychology Review, 33,* 326–343.

Gresham, F. M. & Elliott, S. N. (1990). *Social Skills Rating System.* Circle Pines: AGS.

Gresham, F. M., MacMillan, D. L., Bocian, K. M. (1997). Teachers as "Tests": Differential validity of teacher judgments in identifying students at-risk for learning difficulties. *School Psychology Review, 26,* 47–60.

Gresham, F. M. (2005). Response to intervention (RTI): an alternative means of identifying students as emotionally disturbed. *Education and Treatment of Children, 28,* 328–344.

Grimes, J. & Kurns, S. (2003). An intervention-based system for addressing NCLB and IDEA expectations: a multiple tiered model to ensure every child learns.

Paper presented at the *National Research Center on Learning Disabilities Responsiveness-to-Intervention Symposium*, Kansas City, MO.

Heartland Area Education Agency (2003). *Program Manual for Special Education*. Johnston, IA: Heartland Area Education Agency.

Hoge, R. D. & Coladarci, T. (1989). Teacher-based judgments of academic achievement: a review of the literature. *Review of Educational Research, 59*, 297–313.

Kamphaus, R. W. & Reynolds, C. R., (1998). *Behavior Assessment System for Children (BASC) ADHD Monitor*. Circle Pines, MN: American Guidance Service.

Malecki, C. K., Demaray, M. K., & Elliott, S. N. (2000). *The Child and Adolescent Social Support Scale*. DeKalb, IL: Northern Illinois University.

Malecki, C. K. & Elliott, S. N. (2002). Children's social behaviors as predictors of academic achievement: a longitudinal analysis. *School Psychology Quarterly, 17*, 1–17.

Merrell, K. W. (2003). *Behavioral, Social, and Emotional Assessment of Children and Adolescents*. Mahway, NJ: Lawrence Erlbaum Associates.

National Center for Education Statistics (1997). *Basic Data Elements for Elementary and Secondary Education Information Systems*. Washington, DC: US Department of Education.

National Institute of Child Health and Human Development (2000). *Report of the National Reading Panel. Teaching Children to Read: An Evidence-based Assessment of the Scientific Research Literature on Reading and its Implications for Reading Instruction* (NIH Publication No. 00-4769). Washington, DC: US Government Printing Office.

Olweus, D. (2004). *The Olweus Bully/Victim Questionnaire*. Bergen, Norway: Olweus.

Reid, R. (1996). Research in self-monitoring with students with learning disabilities: the present, the prospects, the pitfalls. *Journal of Learning Disabilities, 29*, 317–322.

Reynolds, C. R. & Kamphaus, R. W. (2004). *Behavior Assessment System for Children* (2nd ed.). Circle Pines, MN: American Guidance Service.

Reynolds, W. (2003). *Reynolds Bully Victimization Scales*. San Antonio, TX: The Psychological Corporation, Harcourt Assessment.

Reynolds, W. M. (1989). *Reynolds Child Depression Scale*. Odessa, FL: Psychological Assessment Resources.

Roach, A.T. & Elliott, S.N. (2005). Goal attainment scaling: An efficient and effective approach to monitoring student progress. *Teaching Exceptional Children, 37* (4), 8–17.

Sattler, J. M. (2002). *Assessment of Children. Behavioral and Clinical Applications* (4th ed.). San Diego, CA: Jerome M. Sattler.

Sattler, J. M. & Hoge, R. D. (2006). *Assessment of Children: Behavioral, Social, and Clinical Foundations* (5th ed.). San Diego, CA: Jerome M. Sattler.

Shapiro, E. S., Duman, S. L., Post, E. E., & Levinson, T. S. (2002). Self-Monitoring procedures for children and adolescents. In M. R. Shinn, H. M. Walker, & G. Stoner (Eds.), *Interventions for Academic and Behavior Problems II: Preventative and Remedial Approaches* (pp. 433–454). Bethesda, MD: The National Association of School Psychologists Publications.

Shinn, M. R. (2005). Identifying and validating academic problems in a problem-solving model. In R. Brown-Chidsey (Ed.), *Assessment for Intervention: A Problem-Solving Approach* (pp. 219–246). New York: Guilford Press.

Sugai, G., Sprague, J. R., Horner, R. H., & Walker, H. M. (2000). Preventing school violence. The use of office discipline referrals to assess and monitor school-wide discipline interventions. *Journal of Emotional and Behavioral Disorders, 8*, 94–101.

Swearer, S. M. (2001). *The Bully Survey*. Unpublished manuscript, The University of Nebraska–Lincoln.

Tilly, W. D. (2002). Best practices in school psychology as a problem solving enterprise. In A. Thomas & J. Grimes (Eds.), *Best Practices in School Psychology IV* (pp. 21–36). Bethesda, MD: The National Association of School Psychologists Publications.

US Department of Education, National Center for Education Statistics (2003). *Digest of Education Statistics, 2003* (NCES 2005-025), Chapter 2.

US Department of Education, National Center for Education Statistics (2004). *Indicators of School Crime and Safety, 2004* (NCES 2005–002), Table 3.1.

Walker, H. M. & Shinn, M. R. (2002). Structuring school-based interventions to achieve integrated primary, secondary, and tertiary prevention goals for safe and effective schools. In M. R. Shinn, H. M. Walker, & G. Stoner (Eds.), *Interventions for Academic and Behavior Problems II: Preventative and Remedial Approaches* (pp. 1–25). Bethesda, MD: The National Association of School Psychologists Publications.

Wentzel, K. R. (1993). Does being good make the grade? Social behavior and academic competence in middle school. *Journal of Educational Psychology, 85*, 357–364.

13
Addressing Disproportionality with Response to Intervention

John L. Hosp and Na'im H. Madyun

John Hosp, PhD, is an Assistant Professor of Special Education at the University of Utah. john.hosp@ed.utah.edu
Na'im Madyun, PhD, is an Assistant Professor in the College of Education and Human Development at the
University of Minnesota. madyu002@umn.edu

Fifty years ago, the United States' educational system began a transformation to accommodate the large increase in background diversity resulting from the Brown v. Board of Education (1954) decision. Large-scale studies, like the Moynihan (1965) and Coleman (1966) reports, were conducted to better assess and evaluate the health of this transformation both inside and outside school systems, and programs such as Head Start and Upward Bound were created to increase the probability of success for people of color. Efforts were noble, but results were found to be less than ideal because poor students, ethnic minorities, and/or non-native speakers of English were found to be more likely to be placed in special education programs than their white peers (Dunn, 1968). This trend of disproportionate representation of minorities in special education has continued for the next 40 years (Chinn and Hughes, 1987; Heller, Holtzman, and Messick, 1982; Hosp and Reschly, 2004; MacMillan and Reschly, 1998; Skiba, Poloni-Staudinger, Simmons, Feggins-Assiz, and Chung, 2006).

Disproportionality in special education is concerning because of the effects of labeling, segregation, and low exit rates from special education services. Consistent with the classic research on the power of labels (Rosenthal and Jacobsen, 1968), students identified as having behavior problems are perceived and addressed in a more negative manner by teachers regardless of whether or not there is a difference in behavior compared with their peers (Mehan, Hertweck, and Miehls, 1986). They may suffer from a diminished self-concept (Campbell-Whatley and Comer, 2000), and poor postsecondary outcomes (Malmgren, Edgar, and Neel, 1998). De-

spite the least restrictive environment provisions of the Individuals with Disabilities Education Act (IDEA, 2004, 2006), students of color receiving special education services are more likely to be taught in segregated environments than Caucasian students (Donovan and Cross, 2002; Hosp and Reschly, 2002). These realities have pushed educators to examine the disproportionate representation of minorities in special education more closely.

Research examining disproportionality has generally been conducted at the district level, or occasionally the state level (i.e., comparing identification rates among districts or states). Although this is important work to establish the presence or severity of a problem, it has not been fruitful at identifying *solutions* to the problem (Chinn and Hughes, 1987). One reason for this could be that this research has focused on placement rates rather than reasons for identification for special education services or the outcomes from their provision. Some scholars have examined methods of predicting disproportionality (cf., Finn, 1982; Oswald, Coutinho, Best, and Singh, 1999), but these have not yielded educationally relevant solutions perhaps because most of the identified predictors are inalterable variables (Hosp and Reschly, 2004). While this research is important from a civil rights perspective, it has failed to yield solutions to inequitable education outcomes among different groups of students.

In recent years, some have called for studies that extend the literature to the individual level (i.e., looking at what variables specific to individual students might predict disproportionality) so that more sensitive analyses can be conducted regarding the reasons for identification of special education eligibility and to compare educational outcomes for minority groups. These foci align well with the purposes and procedures of response to intervention (RTI; Gresham, 2002), as defined in recent federal special education regulations. The remainder of this chapter will present some principles and methods of monitoring disproportionality of minority students in remedial and special education. Because RTI aims to improve educational outcomes for all students, it is important to be able to identify those outcomes for all students, as well as to compare them for traditionally marginalized groups of students.

13.1 Examining Disproportionate Representation at the Individual Level

Monitoring disproportionality at the individual level within a school or district should focus on three general principles:

1. Reliable, valid data are collected and used to make educationally relevant decisions.
2. The focus of instruction and assessment is on socially valid or important outcomes.
3. Effectiveness of intervention is demonstrated through improved performance on important outcomes.

When these three principles are met it can be inferred that each individual's needs are being met, no matter what race, ethnicity, socioeconomic status, gender, native language, or any other factor that can be used to "differentiate" a student from their peers.

Even in schools or districts that have histories of disproportionate identification rates, if focusing on each student's education decisions and outcomes shows that every individual's needs are being met, then it can generally be assumed that those needs are also being sufficiently addressed at the group level. In addition to this general principle, there are several specifics to keep in mind that can help ensure that each student's educational needs are being met, and, therefore, disproportionality is more a result of need than a lack of fairness in provision of services.

13.1.1 Do Not Assume That Culture Equals Race/Ethnicity (or Any Other Student Characteristic)

The expression of culture varies across communities, families, and individuals. It is no secret that variability is higher within groups than between. What may be true of one family's approach to education may not be true of another's, even within the same cultural community. It is important to note that many ethnic minorities struggle to resolve as many disconnects as possible between their home life/culture and the demands/expectations of schooling (Boykin, 1994; Ogbu, 2004; Phelan, 1998). Their academic success is dependent upon their ability to navigate efficiently between the contexts of home and school. Given differences in personality, family histories, and resources, we can imagine an endless list of approaches and strategies to education among the "typical" African American, Asian, Latino and/or American Indian communities, not including the countless variations in applying the approaches within each family of the respective communities.

Unsure about their own ability to contribute effectively, many ethnic families may see the school system as a necessary extension of their own family and place their trust entirely in the schools (Chavkin and Gonzalez, 1995; Walker, Wilkins, and Dallaire, 2005). This perspective grants teachers license to demand more of the student personally, but also puts them in the position to address psychosocial concerns of identity and relationship development. Other ethnic families may see the school system as entirely separate from the home. The families may view schooling as a nine-to-five job, figuratively clocking in and out and bringing the "office" home as little as possible. The home provides the morals and the discipline, the school provides the knowledge (Chavkin and Gonzalez, 1995). Many ethnic minorities view the school system as the key to success, but vary in the degree to which they trust the school system to ensure or assist in reaching their career aspirations (Graham, Taylor, and Hudley, 1998; Jackson, Kacanski, Rust, and Beck, 2006; Viadero, 2004). Obviously, there are variants and hybrids of each of the previous perspectives, so where does one begin in order to properly understand and apply contextual factors that may explain disproportionality?

13.1.2 Find Out the Individual's Wants, Needs, and Preferences

One of the most important steps to ensure meeting a student's needs is, of course, to identify what those needs are. As far as educational needs (i.e., which skills have not yet been mastered that the student is expected to master), these should be identified through assessment, evaluation, and the problem-solving process. Student wants and preferences are not always as easy to determine. Preferences can often be determined by watching what a student selects when given the choice, e.g.: Does the student prefer small-group work, whole-class work, or individual assignments? Does the student prefer reading about animals, cars, or a different topic? (Cooper, 2001; Morgan, 2006). If the student is able to state his preferences, asking about them is also an easy and direct method. A student's wants are often the most difficult to determine, since they can often vary among settings or occasions (i.e., Does the student want more take-home projects? Does the student want someone at home to talk to about school?) (Cooper, 2001; Livingston and Nahimana, 2006).

13.1.3 Include Parents in Decision-Making

Parent involvement historically has been low among racial/ethnic minorities. It is imperative that this historical precedent does not reduce efforts to include all stakeholders in the process. Parent involvement to some degree is an indicator of the climate and mirrors the outreach of the school. Often, low parent involvement is not a result of a lack of interest or caring, but rather is impeded by economic factors (e.g., the need for a parent to work multiple jobs), social factors (e.g., the parent not speaking English and/or no one in the school speaking the parent's native language well enough to communicate effectively), or knowledge factors (e.g., the parent may not be familiar with educational jargon or expectations, school personnel may not be familiar with the parents' expectations; Casas, Furlong, Solberg, and Carranza, 1990).

While working to include the parents in decision-making, it is also important to include the student. Students know their wants, needs, and preferences better than anyone. Considering possible problems with trust, motivation, and an academic attitude, a participative process that increases the probability of student buy-in by default improves the capacity of any potential intervention.

In addition to including the parents and student in the process of decision-making, it is useful to have someone else involved who is familiar with the student and their family, especially if the student and their parents are not able to participate. If the student is having difficulty with schooling, then there is a possibility that one of the parents may have had similar school problems. What this creates is a potential dynamic in which both the parent and the student are uncomfortable, anxious, and possibly intimidated by the school system. A significant step toward reducing this discomfort and ensuring cooperation and follow-through occurs when the family has an ally within the school system (Trotman, 2001). This person should not be a neighbor or relative, but rather a school staff or faculty member who has taken the time to get to know the family and student and that the student and family can trust (Salas et al., 2005; Trotman, 2001). This would function to increase parental involvement for two reasons: (1) the parent will feel more connected to the school and (2) teacher–parent discourse can occur without concerns of negative stereotypes and low expectation (Chavkin and Gonzalez, 1995; Trotman, 2001). Some schools have community liaisons whose role it is to do exactly this. If a school does not have such a position, then often the school psychologist, counselor, social worker, or classroom teacher will perform this function.

The school-based family ally can function merely as an interpreter of spoken word or of tradition and cultural expectations. This would ensure that someone on the team is familiar with language and cultural issues that may affect the student and their family. Regardless, the presence of an ally facilitates communication and may allow for a better fit between student and the instructional intervention.

13.1.4 Enhance Cultural Sensitivity in Instruction

Researchers have argued that minority students are sometimes placed into special education to make it easier for teachers to deal with culturally diverse populations (Gravois and Rosenfield, 2006). In these instances, the teachers do not have to adjust as much to the culturally diverse students who do not fit their pedagogical philosophy or delivery. Artiles and McClafferty (1998) argued that a resistance to the training necessary to pedagogically evolve to diverse populations is a key factor in referral and placement rates. This resistance should not necessarily be seen as a manifestation of some inherent bias or discomfort with culturally diverse students when the opposite may very well be the case. Many teachers believe that adjusting to students of diverse backgrounds will be acknowledging differences and not adopting a color-blind approach which opens the door to prejudices and discrimination by others (Keyes, Burns, and Kusimo, 2006). Their natural response in being fair to all students is to treat everyone the same. A problem with this approach is that, for various reasons outside of a teacher's control, students are not the same.

There should be little debate that not all students are equally proficient in English. If a student is communicating in their second (or third, or fourth) language, then it is possible that critical ideas will get lost in translation. This will make it more difficult to follow directions or understand and perform tasks in the classroom—things that are crucial to learning the material being presented. While bilingual programs can offer this in several different ways to meet students' language needs, it can also be accomplished along with content instruction in English. If at least part of the instruction or directions are presented in the student's native language (or one she is more familiar with than English), then when the student begins to convert her ideas it increases the odds that no idea would get left behind and, therefore, that she would have a better chance of learning the material. Moreover, students may also bring different background knowledge and experiences to school. One way to address this is to again explore the student's preferences and interests. Of course, this is the kind of thing that is important to do with *every* child, since it is likely to enhance their interest and motivation and it helps them to make important connections among their knowledge bases.

13.1.5 Enhance Cultural Sensitivity in Assessment

Previous chapters in this volume go into greater detail on issues of assessment within RTI (Barnett et al., Chapter 8; Christ and Hintze, Chapter 7;

Kavale and Flanagan, Chapter 10; Olson, Daly, Andersen, Turner, and LeClair, Chapter 9); however, in relation to disproportionality, there are a few key principles to remember. First, it is important to ensure that the assessment method is aligned with the purpose for which data are collected. This means that the data being collected should be the most relevant to the decision being made. Related to this is having a clear understanding of the decision and why that decision is needed. It also means ensuring that the student understands the assessment task and its parameters (e.g., that it is timed and she only has 3 minutes to do as much work as possible).

When using norm-referenced tests (NRTs), it is important to make sure there is adequate representation of students similar to the one you are working with in the norm group. For example, if the student is American Indian, it is important to check the technical manual that there were enough American Indians to make a reliable comparison or that studies were conducted to demonstrate similar predictive power and discriminant (i.e., discriminating mastery/nonmastery of a skill) ability for American Indian students compared with other racial/ethnic groups. If the norm group only included 80 American Indians of ages ranging from 5 to 75 and only one of those was in the same grade as the student you are working with, then the test may not be appropriate for making decisions about that student's performance.

Just as with NRTs, there are issues to be aware of with criterion-referenced tests (CRTs). First, make sure that the tasks performed for the assessment are similar to those expected of or taught to the students. If a student is taught to summarize paragraphs as a demonstration of her reading comprehension, but then is asked to answer factual questions for the assessment of her reading comprehension, she is not likely to accurately demonstrate her reading comprehension skills (Dochy, Moerkerke, and Martens, 1996; Snyder, Caccamise, and Wise, 2006). Thus, her poor performance may be an indication of the testing conditions rather than skill performance, and the decision made about this performance could be inaccurate. One instance when it might be appropriate to use a different task for assessment than instruction is when trying to determine how well a student can generalize a skill to a different task; then, it is important to select a different task.

Tasks used in the CRTs should also be predictive of future success on important outcomes. Many times performance on a CRT *is* the actual outcome that is being used (the same is true for NRTs). However, even outcome measures should be compared with others that purport to measure the same content and should be compared with other outcomes that are important (e.g., Does earning a mastery score on this test predict high-school graduation?).

13.2 Examining Disproportionate Representation at the School/District Level

Disproportionality of identification for special education services for an entire school or district is generally identified through statistical methods. This can happen because groups of students are being compared; however, when there are only a few students of any one group in the school or district, statistical analyses become unreliable and perhaps unusable. The most common method of statistical analysis of disproportionate representation is to compare proportionality between or among groups.

13.2.1 Comparing Proportionality

Two indices and two ratios are the most common methods used to compare disproportionality. These are the composition index, the risk index, the odds ratio, and relative risk. Each has pros and cons. For a more thorough discussion of each, as well as a comparison, see MacMillan and Reschly (1998) and Hosp and Reschly (2003).

13.2.1.1 Composition Index

The composition index is calculated by finding the percentage of students in a certain special education category that are from a specific group. For example, if there are 50 students identified as having a learning disability (LD) in a district (the category) and 20 of these students are African American, then the composition index for African American students in that district is 40%. If African American students make up 20% of the population of that district, then it looks like there is overrepresentation of African

American students in the category of LD. However, a problem with the composition index is that this kind of comparison is not reliable and has a tendency to overstate the issue (MacMillan and Rechly, 1998). Thus, composition index is rarely used in isolation.

13.2.1.2 Risk Index

The risk index is calculated by finding the percentage of a group placed into a certain category. For example, if in our example district 20 of the 1000 African American students are identified as having LD, then the risk index for African American students is 2% (i.e., 20/1000). Use of the risk index provides an easier comparison of proportionality, since a risk index can be calculated for each racial/ethnic group and this can be compared; however, solely using the risk index does not make this comparison explicit (i.e., it is not turned into a single statistic).

13.2.1.3 Odds Ratio

The odds ratio was the first statistic used that incorporated the comparison of groups into it. An odds ratio compares the odds of placement of one group to the odds of placement of all others. The odds of placement for a group equal the number of students identified for a category divided by the number of students not identified for that category. For example, the odds of African American students identified as LD would be 20 divided by 980, or 0.020. As is probably apparent, the "odds" is not an easy statistic to interpret by itself. Where the ratio comes in is when African American students (odds = 0.020) is divided by all other students (e.g., odds = 0.015). Using this ratio, the odds ratio for African American students in the category of LD is 1.33, meaning African American students are 1.33 times more likely to be identified as having an LD than their non-African American peers.

13.2.1.4 Relative Risk

Because of the difficulty interpreting the odds (and its accompanying ratio), and the benefit of comparing the risk index of two groups, some researchers have advocated using a ratio of rates called relative risk. Relative risk divides the risk index of one group by the risk index of another. Since the risk index is the rate of identification for a group, it is easy to interpret; therefore, the accompanying ratio (the relative risk) is also easier to interpret. It does not come without some controversy though.

13.2.1.5 Difference of Denominators

Some researchers have tried to overcome the problems of the odds ratio by changing denominators. Interestingly, this is also the difficulty some people have had with relative risk. Two different approaches are to compare the group of interest with (1) another group or (2) all other students.

When comparing with another group, white students are often used as the standard. The reasoning for this is that white students are the majority nationally and are generally the standard that others are compared with. This may not be true in a specific school or district, and it also assumes that the representation rate of the white students is "correct" or ideal. Again, this may not be true.

The alternative is to compare the group of interest with all other students (as the odds ratio does). While this could eliminate the need for a correct or ideal comparison group, it raises the problem of when there are two or more groups with disproportionate representation. For example, a school might have a population that is 1/3 African American, 1/3 Latino, and 1/3 White. The risk index for each group is 3% for African American and Latino, but 1% for White. If the white students are used as the denominator (i.e., the comparison group), then the relative risk for each other group is 3.0, or a rate that is three times that for white students. If all other students are used as the denominator, then the relative risk becomes 1.5 for each group—half what it would be using a different denominator. This is said to mask disproportionality, because a very different decision could be made about a relative risk of 1.5 than 3.0.

13.2.1.6 Multiple Gating Procedures

To offset the limitations of different disproportionality indices, some have used a multiple gating procedure (e.g., Reschly, Hosp, and Fox, 2003). Multiple gating procedures use one statistic first, followed by use of another (and sometimes a third) in order to find out whether a school or district has a "true" disproportionate representation. The rationale for this approach is that if representation looks dispropor-

tionate despite the statistic being used, it is probably the most severe and a "true" disproportionality.

Many of these issues are not just statistical arguments though. There are pedagogical issues that arise, such as the value of special education and the appropriate provision of services. Coutinho and Oswald (2000) argue that the primary problem is not necessarily which index is used, but the failure to properly reference the chosen index and outline its impact on subsequent interpretations.

13.2.2 Comparing Group Outcomes

Another comparison that could be made between or among groups is to compare the outcomes between them. This is occasionally known as the achievement gap, since these comparisons often yield a gap between groups. The first step in comparing outcomes is to select the outcomes that are important to measure and determine how they will be measured. Because group performance on state CRTs is now used across all states and districts for Adequate Yearly Progress (AYP) reporting for No Child Left Behind (NCLB; 2002), this is an outcome that is likely to be important to administrators at the school, district, and state level. Generally, it can be used in multiple grades and multiple content areas (but not all grades or content areas). Any other measure can be used as long as the scores can be converted to a metric that is useful for comparison.

Once outcomes and measurement thereof are identified, how to compare them needs to be determined. The benefit of CRTs is that they can be divided into performance categories, or even a proficient/nonproficient decision. This allows easy calculation of the percentage of each group achieving proficiency. This is simple to calculate, simple to display, simple to interpret, and can be used to show changes over time. It also lends itself to statistical analysis, such as using the chi square statistic, because it is easily placed into a 2×2 grid. Chi square is a reasonable statistic to use because it does not require large groups and can be calculated readily using common spreadsheet software. One problem with the chi square statistic is that it is affected by the size of the total population being compared. Large populations are more likely to show statistical difference than small ones. Conversely, in small populations each individual is given a greater "weight." This means that the change of one student from proficient to nonproficient in a small population might change the chi square decision (i.e., is the difference significant or not), whereas with a large population it might take a change of 5, 10, or even 50 individuals. This is a somewhat paradoxical effect, but illustrates why it is important to look at disproportionate representation in various ways.

13.3 Developing a System for Monitoring Disproportionality

In any school or district, it is important to have a clear plan for monitoring disproportionality. Consistent with most RTI approaches, this requires a system-wide plan that covers individuals, classrooms, schools, and possibly an entire district. The more that the same data can be used for multiple purposes, or to make decisions at multiple levels, the more efficient the system will be.

When making decisions at the school or district level, it is important to examine the patterns over time rather than at a single point in time. Significant fluctuation in representation or performance rates can occur from year to year. If only looking at a single point in time, then a very different conclusion could be reached than if multiple years' worth of data are used. Consistent patterns of disproportionality are stronger evidence of systematic unfairness than a single year's worth.

While also comparing data across years, it is important to look across comparisons. Monitoring proportionality in representation rates is an important component, but it should not be considered in isolation. Adding a comparison of outcomes provides a sort of cross-check that representation is not due to unfairness, but rather a differential need for services. For example, finding that African American students in a specific district are identified as having LD at three times the rate of their peers for several years in a row is a shocking finding. By looking at these data only, a reasonable conclusion is that there is an overrepresentation of African American students in the category of LD and that it might be caused by some systematic unfairness. However, if we couple those data with the fact that African American students in this district also are half as likely to reach proficiency on the state CRTs, then we might not be as alarmed, because there *appears* to be a greater educational need of the African American students. What this also gives is an indication for solutions (i.e., the need to focus academic interventions to improving the performance of the African American students).

Although there may appear to be a greater need for African American students, we are not in a position to infer causality between disproportionality and achievement. Lower achievement might "cause" overrepresentation just as much as overrepresentation might cause low achievement. More likely is the explanation that there are other factors involved and they require more detailed analyses. While disproportionality (in placement or outcomes) at school/district level can *suggest* a problem, this decision must be confirmed/disconfirmed by using individual level data. School- or district-level data cannot identify what the decision-making process looks like for each individual and, therefore, how "accurate" those decisions turned out to be. Decisions about disproportionality are subject to following the convergence of evidence as much as instructional decisions made for individual students.

A promising approach to accomplishing this at a systemic and individual level is the tiered system of instructional delivery coupled with a problem-solving approach that is generally associated with RTI (Ikeda et al., Chapter 19). With effective instruction provided to all students, the proportion of students needing additional help (which could include special education) is reduced and the related problems of disproportionality are also reduced. Below is the description of a district that used this approach to address disproportionality while being monitored by the Office of Civil Rights.

13.4 An Example of Response to Intervention Being Used to Address Disproportionate Representation

The disproportionate representation of minorities in special education was addressed in one Mid-Western school district with a problem-solving model. As described by Marston, Muyskens, Lau, and Canter (2003), decisions were made based on a continuous teach–test–teach–test model.

There were four steps included in the model:

1. Specifically describe the student's problem.
2. Generate and implement strategies for instructional intervention.
3. Monitor student progress and evaluate effectiveness of instruction.
4. Continue the cycle as necessary.

First, students were screened to determine current academic levels and inform necessary instructional changes. Those identified as not meeting expectations from the screening were targeted for classroom interventions. The interventions and modifications were implemented and the progress of the student was monitored. In addition, background and cultural data were gathered. If the classroom teacher felt as though interventions were not necessary, then a multidisciplinary team was assembled to review the data and develop stronger, more specific interventions and to continue monitoring progress. Because a team was developing the general education interventions, setting the goals, and monitoring the progress, it reduced the probability of individual bias significantly influencing the referral process. If there was inadequate progress made toward the goals, the team could decide to refer the student for a comprehensive evaluation to determine eligibility for special education services. It is important to note that the instructional interventions created by the multidisciplinary team were still modified and monitored during eligibility determination. This model places greater emphasis on general education teachers to provide classroom interventions to help guide instruction rather than relying solely on the grade-level curriculum.

The Office of Civil Rights concluded that the problem-solving model reduced bias in the referral, evaluation, and eligibility process for students of color. The number of referrals increased from 657 students to 1303. However, the number of students placed in special education increased only slightly, from 327 students to 364. Even though more students were screened using this model, it did not lead to overidentification, similar to the results of a meta-analysis by Hosp and Reschly (2003). For example, the African American population went from a 25% overrepresentation in referrals to special education down to 10% overrepresentation for placement.

13.5 Conclusions

Disproportionate representation of minorities in special education has been a constant and contentious topic for nearly 40 years. RTI provides a promising foundation for addressing disproportionality through its reliance on collecting and using data to make decisions and its focus on outcomes. Through a closer focus on disproportionality data and a careful examination of educational outcomes for all students, we can finally begin to realize the promise of the Brown v. Board of Education decision.

References

Artiles, A. & McClafferty, K. (1998). Learning to teach culturally diverse learners: Charting change in preservice teachers' thinking about effective teaching. *Elementary School Journal, 98*, 189–200.

Boykin, A. W. (1994). Harvesting talent and culture: African American children and educational reform. In R. J. Rossi (Ed.), *Schools and Students at Risk: Context and Framework for Positive Change* (pp. 116–138). New York: Teachers College Press.

Brown v. Board of Education (1954). 347 U. S. 483, 486 n. 1, 493, 495.

Campbell-Whatley, G. D. & Comer, J. P. (2000). Self-concept and African–American student achievement: related issues of ethics, power and privilege. *Teacher Education and Special Education, 23*, 19–31.

Casas, J. M., Furlong, M., Solberg, V. S., & Carranza, O. (1990). An examination of individual factors associated with the academic success and failure of Mexican–Americans and Anglo students. In A. Barona & E. E. Garcia (Eds.), *Children at Risk: Poverty, Minority Status, and Other Issues in Educational Equity* (pp. 103–118). Washington, DC: National Association of School Psychologists.

Chavkin, N. F. & Gonzalez, D. L. (1995). *Forging Partnerships between Mexican American Parents and the Schools*. Charleston, WV: ERIC Clearinghouse on Rural Education and Small Schools. ED388489.

Chinn, P. C. & Hughes, S. (1987). Representation of minority students in special education classes. *Remedial and Special Education, 8*, 41–46.

Coleman. J. (1966). *Equality of Educational Opportunity*. Washington, DC: Department of Health, Education, and Welfare.

Cooper, H. M. (2001). Homework for all—in moderation. *Educational Leadership, 58*, 34–38.

Coutinho, M. J. & Oswald, D. C. (2000). Disproportionate representation in special education: A synthesis and recommendations. *Journal of Child and Family Studies, 2*, 135–156.

Dochy, F. J. R. C., Moerkerke, G., & Martens, R. L. (1996). Integrating assessment, learning, and instruction. Assessment of domain-specific and domain-transcending prior knowledge and progress. *Studies in Educational Evaluation, 22*, 309–339.

Donovan, M. S. & Cross, C. T. (Eds.) (2002). *Minority Students in Special and Gifted Education*. Washington, DC: National Academy Press.

Dunn, L. M. (1968). Special education for the mildly mentally retarded: is much of it justifiable? *Exceptional Children, 23*, 5–21.

Finn, J. D. (1982). Patterns in special education placement as revealed by the OCR survey. In K. A. Heller, W. Holtzman, & S. Messick (Eds.), *Placing Children in Special Education: A Strategy for Equity* (pp. 322–381). Washington, DC: National Academy Press.

Graham, S., Taylor, A. Z., & Hudley, C. R. (1998). Exploring achievement values among ethnic minority early adolescents. *Journal of Educational Psychology, 90*, 606–620.

Gravois, T. & Rosenfield, S. (2006). Impact of instructional consultation teams on the disproportionate referral and placement of minority students in special education. *Journal of Remedial and Special Education, 27*, 42–52.

Gresham, F. M. (2002). Responsiveness to intervention: An alternative approach to the identification of learning disabilities. In R. Bradley, L. Danielson, & D. P. Hallahan (Eds.), *Identification of Learning Disabilities: Research to Practice* (pp. 467–519). Mahweh, NJ: Lawrence Erlbaum Associates.

Heller, K. A., Holtzman, W., & Messick, S. (Eds.) (1982). *Placing Children in Special Education: A Strategy for Equity*. Washington, DC: National Academy Press.

Hosp, J. L. & Reschly, D. J. (2002). Predictors of restrictiveness of placement for African–American and Caucasian students with learning disabilities. *Exceptional Children, 68*, 225–238.

Hosp, J. L. & Reschly, D. J. (2003). Referral rates for intervention or assessment: A meta-analysis of racial differences. *The Journal of Special Education, 37*, 67–80.

Hosp, J. L. & Reschly, D. J. (2004). Disproportionate representation of minority students in special education: Academic, economic, and demographic predictors. *Exceptional Children, 70*, 185–200.

IDEA (2004, 2006). *Individuals with Disabilities Education Act*, 20 U. S. C. 1400 et Seq (Statute). 34 C.F.R. 300 (Regulations).

Jackson, M. A., Kacanski, J. M., Rust, J. P., & Beck, S. E. (2006). Constructively challenging diverse inner-city youth's beliefs about educational and career barriers and supports. *Journal of Career Development, 32*, 203–218.

Keyes, M., Burns, R., & Kusimo, P. (2006). *It Takes a School: Closing Achievement Gaps Through Culturally Responsive Schools*. Charleston, WV: Edvantia.

Livingston, J. N. & Nahimana, C. (2006). Problem child or problem context: An ecological approach to young black males. *Reclaiming Children & Youth, 14*, 209–214.

MacMillan, D. L. & Reschly, D. J. (1998). Overrepresentation of minority students: The case for greater specificity of the variables examined. *The Journal of Special Education, 32*, 15–24.

Malmgren, K. Edgar, E. B., & Neel, R. S. (1998). Postschool status of youths with behavioral disorders. *Behavioral Disorders, 24*, 257–263.

Marston, D., Muyskens, P., Lau, M., & Canter, A. (2003). Problem-solving model for decision making with high-incidence disabilities: The Minneapolis experience. *Learning Disabilities: Research & Practice, 18*, 187–200.

Mehan, H., Hertweck, A., & Miehls, J. L. (1986). *Handicapping the Handicapped*. Stanford, CA: Stanford University Press.

Morgan, P. L. (2006). Increasing task engagement using preference or choice-making: Some behavioral and methodological factors affecting their efficacy as classroom interventions. *Remedial and Special Education, 27*, 176–187.

Moynihan. D. P. (1965). *The Negro Family: The Case for National Action*. Washington, DC: United States Department of Labor.

Ogbu, J. (2004). Collective identity and the burden of "acting white" in black history, community, and education. *The Urban Review, 36*, 1–35.

Oswald, D. P., Coutinho, M. J., Best, A. M., & Singh, N. N. (1999). Ethnic representation in special education: The influence of school-related economic and demographic factors. *The Journal of Special Education, 32*, 194–206.

Phelan, P. (1998). *Adolescents' Worlds: Negotiating Family, Peers, and School*. New York: Teachers College Press.

Reschly, D., Hosp, J., & Fox, R. (2004). *Special Education Disproportionality Evaluator* (SEDE) [Computer software]. Albany, NY: New York State Education Department.

Rosenthal, R. & Jacobsen, L. (1968). *Pygmalion in the Classroom, Teacher Expectations & Pupils' Intellectual Development*. New York: Rhinehart & Winston.

Salas, L., Lopez, E. J., Chinn, K., & Menchaca-Lopez, E. (2006). Can special education teachers create parent partnerships with Mexican-American families? Si se pueda! *Multicultural Education, 13*(2), 52–55.

Skiba, R. J., Poloni-Staudinger, L., Simmons, A. B., Feggins-Assiz, L. R., & Chung, C. G. (2006). Unproven links: Can poverty explain ethnic disproportionality in special education? *The Journal of Special Education, 39*, 130–144.

Snyder, L., Caccamise, D., & Wise, B. (2006). The assessment of reading comprehension: Considerations and cautions. *Topics in Language Disorders, 25*, 33–50.

Trotman, M. F. (2001). Involving the African American parent: Recommendations to increase the level of parent involvement within African American families. *The Journal of Negro Education, 70*, 275–285.

Viadero, D. (2004). Panel outlines strategy for raising minority achievement. *Education Week, 24* (6), p. 10.

Walker, J. M., Wilkins, A. S., & Dallaire, J. R. (2005) Parental involvement: Model revision through scale development. *The Elementary School Journal, 106*, 85–104.

III
Research-Based Prevention and Intervention

14

Identifying Reading Disability Based on Response to Intervention: Evidence from Early Intervention Research

Frank R. Vellutino, Donna M. Scanlon, and Haiyan Zhang

Frank R. Vellutino, PhD, is a Professor in the Department of Psychology and the Department of Educational and Counseling Psychology (joint appointment) at the State University of New York at Albany. He is also the director of the University's Child Research and Study Center. fvellutino@uamail.albany.edu

Donna M. Scanlon, PhD, is an Associate Professor in the Reading Department at the State University of New York at Albany. She is also the Associate Director of the University's Child Research and Study Center. dscanlon@uamail.albany.edu

Haiyan Zhang, MS, is a doctoral student in the Department of Educational and Counseling Psychology at the State University of New York at Albany. hz7494@albany.edu

For well over four decades the dominant approach to identifying specific learning disabilities has been what has come to be called the psychometric/exclusionary approach (Gresham, 2002; Vellutino et al., 1996). This approach typically entails assessment of achievement, intelligence, and cognitive abilities believed to underlie acquisition of a given academic skill, along with assessment of exclusionary criteria, such as uncorrected sensory deficits, emotional disorder, general learning problems, socioeconomic disadvantage, and like factors. The psychometric/exclusionary approach can be traced back to Kirk and Bateman (1962–1963), who initially defined learning disabilities as a collection of neurodevelopmental disorders having a deleterious effect on academic learning in children who do not have serious intellectual limitations, and whose learning difficulties are not caused by extraneous factors such as those just mentioned. The essential components of Kirk and Bateman's exclusionary definition of learning disability were later codified as part of Public Law 94–142 (US Office of Education, 1977), but the most notable effect of this legislation was the status it gave to the IQ–achievement discrepancy as the central criterion for defining specific learning disabilities (Frankenberger and Fronzaglio, 1991). Indeed, the IQ–achievement discrepancy was soon after adopted as a basic prerequisite for diagnosing learning disabilities in schools

and other institutions, and it also became widely adopted as the central criterion for defining learning disabilities in empirical research (Vellutino, Scanlon, and Lyon, 2000).

In discussing issues concerned with the identification of specific reading disability (RD), the most common form of learning disability, Vellutino, Scanlon, and Tanzman (1998) identified several problems with the psychometric/exclusionary approach that are worth a brief mention here. One problem with this approach is that it does not adequately distinguish between children whose learning difficulties are caused primarily by experiential and instructional deficits and children whose learning difficulties are caused primarily by biologically based cognitive deficits. This is because those who adopt this approach typically do not control for or assess the child's preschool and educational history (Clay, 1987). A second problem is that it often makes use of assessment instruments that have little or no diagnostic validity in terms of the cognitive underpinnings of the academic skill of concern; for example, tests evaluating visual sequencing ability, perceptual speed, or visual–motor functions to determine the cause of specific RD. A third is that it gives undue weight to the IQ–achievement discrepancy in classifying children as disabled readers. This third problem is particularly disconcerting, because the validity of the discrepancy definition of RD has been seriously undermined in recent research (Fletcher et al., 1994; Gresham, 2002; Siegel, 1989; Stanovich and Siegel, 1994; Vellutino et al., 2000). A fourth problem with the psychometric/exclusionary approach is that it tends to inflate estimates of the number of children classified as disabled learners, most estimates ranging from 10% to 20% of the population of school children (Lyon, Fletcher, and Barnes, 2002). A fifth is that it tends to create low expectations for children so classified, which, of course, says nothing about the low expectations for children who are not classified as disabled learners because of the failure to meet the IQ–achievement discrepancy criterion. Finally, the psychometric/exclusionary approach to identifying learning disability provides no direction for either classroom or remedial instruction (Clay, 1987).

These concerns motivated our research team to initiate a program of intervention research to begin to develop the means for distinguishing between basic cognitive deficits as opposed to experiential and instructional deficits as primary causes of early and long-term reading difficulties. Of particular importance was the need to evaluate the utility of using the child's initial response to remedial intervention rather than psychometric assessment as a "first-cut" approach to identifying specific RD. A secondary objective was to generate criteria and procedures for identifying children at risk for early reading difficulties, in the interest of developing a preventative approach to such difficulties. The final and most important objective was to develop assessment and instructional procedures that would facilitate literacy development in all children. The remainder of this paper discusses selected findings from two consecutive intervention studies designed to pursue these objectives. Because results from the first of these studies have been extensively discussed elsewhere (e.g. Vellutino et al., 1996; Vellutino and Scanlon, 2002; Vellutino, Scanlon, and Jaccard, 2003), the focus in the ensuing sections is on the second of the two studies, with the results from the first study being briefly summarized.

14.1 First-Grade Intervention Study

In the first of the two intervention studies just mentioned (Vellutino et al., 1996, 2003; Vellutino

and Scanlon, 2002), literacy development in struggling and normal readers was tracked for a period extending from the beginning of kindergarten (before reader group membership was determined) through the end of fourth grade. Participants in both groups were sampled from a larger population of middle to upper middle class children ($n = 1407$) who were initially assessed on entry into kindergarten. Reader group membership was determined in mid-first grade, and the struggling readers were provided with daily one-to-one tutoring for up to two school terms (mid-first grade to mid-second grade), depending on the child's progress. In order to compare the cognitive profiles of children who were found to be difficult to remediate with those of children who were found to be less difficult to remediate, all of the tutored children were divided into four roughly equal groups based on a rank ordering of regression slopes obtained by regressing time in months on the WRMT-R Basic Skills Cluster administered at several different time periods before and after one school semester of tutoring. To further evaluate the relationship between intelligence and reading achievement, the normal readers were divided into two groups, one that included only children with average intelligence and another that included only children with above-average intelligence. To evaluate the influence of home and preschool literacy experiences on early reading achievement, emergent literacy skills, such as print concepts, print awareness, alphabet knowledge, and phonological awareness, were assessed when the children entered kindergarten or shortly before kindergarten entry. Cognitive abilities believed to underlie reading ability were also assessed in kindergarten and again in first and third grades. All three assessments included measures evaluating language-based abilities, such as phoneme analysis, name retrieval, verbal memory, and verbal learning, as well as visual abilities, such as visual analysis and visual memory. Verbal and nonverbal intelligence were also assessed in first and third grades. To evaluate the possibility that early reading difficulties in some struggling readers may be due, in part, to deficiencies in kindergarten literacy instruction, systematic observations of the kindergarten language arts program were carried out at all schools participating in the study (Scanlon and Vellutino, 1996).

There were several important findings that emerged from this study. First, whereas almost 10%

of the children sampled from the first-grade population ($n = 1284$ after attrition) would have been classified as "disabled readers" (i.e., $\leq$15th percentile on the WRMT-R Basic Skills Cluster), prior to implementation of the intervention program, only 1.5% of this population would have been so classified after one semester of remediation. And, although several of the tutored children had difficulty maintaining the gains they achieved in acquiring basic reading skills, especially during the summer hiatus (often called "backsliding"), this pattern was observed primarily among children who showed the least amount of initial growth in response to remediation (Vellutino and Scanlon, 2002; Vellutino et al., 2003). A second important finding is that children who proved to be difficult to remediate generally performed below both children who proved to be readily remediated and normal readers on tests evaluating phonological skills, such as phonological awareness, verbal memory, and fluency in name retrieval, as well as on tests evaluating literacy skills. In contrast, the children who were readily remediated often performed at levels close to those of the normal readers on the same measures. A third notable finding is that all children identified as struggling readers in mid-first grade were found to be deficient in emergent literacy skills, such as letter identification and phonological awareness at the beginning of kindergarten. A fourth is that kindergarten children were less likely to demonstrate reading problems in first grade if they had received a comprehensive and balanced language arts program while in kindergarten, one that included both word-level and text-processing components in the instructional program (Scanlon and Vellutino, 1996).

Finally, pairwise comparisons on measures of verbal and nonverbal intelligence produced no statistically significant differences, either between any of the tutored groups compared or between each respective tutored group and a group of normal readers of average intelligence. In addition, there were no substantial differences between normal readers of average intelligence and normal readers of above average intelligence on tests of basic word-level skills (i.e., word identification and phonological decoding). At the same time, IQ–achievement discrepancy scores were not significantly correlated with growth in reading ability, indicating that intelligence test scores did not predict initial response to intervention (RTI; Vellutino et al., 2000).

Results from this study led to the conclusion that early reading difficulties in most struggling readers can be successfully remediated and that experiential and instructional factors are more likely to be the primary causes of such difficulties in children who are readily remediated than are basic cognitive deficits of biological origin. It was also concluded that assessing a child's ability to profit from remedial intervention may be a more valid means of distinguishing between cognitive versus experiential/instructional causes of reading difficulties than is the psychometric/exclusionary approach. At the same time, results from the kindergarten assessment and classroom observation components of the study led to the conclusion that childrens' pre-first-grade literacy experiences, especially the instruction to which they were exposed, may be critically important determinants of early reading achievement. Thus, it seemed that the logical sequel to the first-grade intervention study just described would be a study that evaluated the utility of identifying children "at risk" for early reading difficulties at the beginning of kindergarten and implementing intervention during kindergarten, both to prevent long-term reading difficulties in these children and to develop benchmarks for identifying those who will no longer require remedial services at the beginning of first grade and those who will continue to require such services, some of whom may well have biologically based reading difficulties. In addition, there was great interest in further evaluating an RTI approach to diagnosing RD. The ensuing sections discuss selected findings from a study that was designed to accomplish these objectives.

14.2 Kindergarten and First-Grade Prevention/Intervention Study

The RTI model evaluated in the study to be described adopted a gated approach to intervention, in that children identified as being "at risk " for early reading difficulties were given small-group instruction in kindergarten in order to prevent the emergence of significant reading difficulties and those who continued to be at risk at the beginning of first grade were given daily one-to-one tutoring throughout first grade in order to help them overcome their difficulties (Vellutino, Scanlon, Small, and Fanuele,

2006). To evaluate RTI, literacy development in both groups was assessed from the beginning of kindergarten through the end of third grade. Thus, the model, in essence, is a preventative model that can be described as a variant of the different "tiered" approaches to remedial intervention, the most common one being the three-tiered model described by Denton and Mathes (2003) and Fuchs and Fuchs (1997). In brief, the three-tiered model is defined by three sequentially ordered intervention strategies. The first strategy (Tier 1) involves analysis and possible modification of the classroom language arts program to insure that all children in the classroom receive balanced, comprehensive, and evidence-based literacy instruction, including the children found to be experiencing literacy difficulties. The second strategy (Tier 2) involves supplementary small-group intervention for children whose difficulties are not ameliorated by modifications in the classroom program. The third (Tier 3) involves more intensive and more individualized instruction (e.g., one-to-one tutoring) for children who continue to experience significant reading difficulties, despite Tier 2 intervention. Thus, the model implemented in the present study deviated somewhat from the three-tiered model, in that intervention was initiated on behalf of at-risk kindergartners before they had any extensive exposure to their classroom language arts programs and no attempt was made to modify these programs.

14.2.1 Kindergarten Screening

The study was initiated in late summer of 1997 and was terminated in late spring of 2002. Participants in the study were kindergarten children from lower middle, to middle class home environments being educated in rural and suburban schools in upstate New York. The initial sample consisted of two cohorts of kindergartners ($n = 1373$ total) assessed at the beginning of the school year. There were approximately equal percentages of boys and girls in the sample (54% boys in cohort 1 and 50% boys in cohort 2). In addition, approximately 98% of the sample consisted of Caucasian children, and the remaining percentage was divided among African–American (0.67%), Hispanic (0.59%) and Asian children (0.39%). Finally, 0.33% of the children in the total sample were English-language learners and 8.4% of the sample was eligible for free or reduced-price lunch.

Because knowledge of the alphabet has been found to be a good predictor of early reading achievement (Adams, 1990) and because virtually all of the struggling readers in the Vellutino et al. (1996) intervention study were found to be deficient in letter name knowledge at the beginning of kindergarten, children in the present intervention study were initially judged to be at risk for early reading difficulties on the basis of a test evaluating letter identification accuracy (Woodcock, 1987) administered at the beginning of kindergarten (fall 1997, 1998). A cut-off at the 30th percentile was the criterion used to determine risk status. The decision to use only letter identification to identify at-risk children and to set the criterion at the 30th percentile was based on analyses of classification accuracy using data from the first-grade intervention study (Scanlon and Vellutino, 1996), which revealed that classification accuracy was not improved by adding additional child indices and that both false negative and false positive rates would be optimized using this criterion. However, to provide baseline data in other skill areas, all children in the entire sample were also administered experimental tests evaluating phonological awareness (sensitivity to rhyme and alliteration), rapid naming of objects, number identification, and the ability to count by 1's. Table 14.1 presents results on all of these measures for children in the two cohorts (combined) who qualified for either the at-risk or the not-at-risk groups (respectively). It is apparent that the children who qualified for the at-risk group performed well below the children who did not qualify for the at-risk group on all measures, in accord with results obtained in the previous intervention study (Vellutino et al., 1996; Scanlon and Vellutino, 1997). Thus, it seems reasonable to suggest that assessing a child's knowledge of letter names may be a relatively economical way of identifying at-risk children who may be deficient in a variety of emergent literacy skills, and who may, therefore, need additional support in the early phases of learning to read.

14.2.2 Kindergarten Intervention

The kindergarten intervention component of the study was initiated in mid to late October (approximately 6 weeks after the beginning of school). Approximately half of the children in the at-risk group were randomly assigned to a project treatment

TABLE 14.1. Performance levels for the at risk and not at risk groups on the kindergarten screening battery.

| Measures | Reader groups | |
	At risk[1]	Not at risk[2]
WRMT-R letter identification raw score (51)[3]		
M	5.75	25.26
SD	4.21	5.82
(n)	(475)	(898)
WRMT-R letter identification standard score		
M	84.05	105.75
SD	6.05	8.74
(n)	(475)	(898)
Rhyme detection raw score (12)[3]		
M	6.71	8.93
SD	2.76	2.86
(n)	(474)	(676)
Alliteration detection raw score (12)[3]		
M	4.16	6.02
SD	1.46	2.70
(n)	(475)	(677)
Rapid automatized naming time (seconds)		
M	83.36	73.00
SD	21.29	17.48
(n)	(470)	(668)
Counting by 1's (highest number) (40)[3]		
M	23.49	32.94
SD	9.58	8.48
(n)	(475)	(895)
Number identification raw score (12)[3]		
M	4.97	8.67
SD	2.80	1.69
(n)	(475)	(895)

[1] n = 475.
[2] n = 898.
[3] Number in parentheses indicates maximum possible score on the measure.

TABLE 14.2. Performance levels for the Project Treatment and School-Based Comparison groups on the kindergarten screening battery.

| Measures | Reader groups | |
	Project Treatment[1]	School-Based Comparison[2]
WRMT-R letter identification raw score (51)[3]		
M	5.33	6.29
SD	4.01	4.40
WRMT-R letter identification standard score		
M	83.53	84.71
SD	5.98	6.13
Rhyme detection raw score (12)[3]		
M	6.65	6.72
SD	2.87	2.67
Alliteration detection raw score (12)[3]		
M	4.09	4.23
SD	1.45	1.43
Rapid automatized naming time (seconds)		
M	83.62	82.24
SD	21.81	20.15
Counting by 1's (highest number) (40)[3]		
M	22.81	24.09
SD	10.10	9.02
Number identification raw score (12)[3]		
M	4.70	5.31
SD	2.86	2.71

[1] n = 232.
[2] n = 230.
[3] Number in parentheses indicates maximum possible score on the measure.

condition (Project Treatment), and the other half were assigned to a school-based comparison condition (School-Based Comparison). The children in the School-Based Comparison condition were not expected to receive any form of supplementary instruction at the outset of the study. Table 14.2 presents results for these two groups on the kindergarten screening battery. It can be seen that the groups were not appreciably different on any of the screening measures.

Children assigned to the Project Treatment condition received small-group supplementary instruction throughout kindergarten implemented by certified teachers who were trained by project staff.

There were no more than two to three children in a group. The children in each group met with their teachers twice a week for 30 min each session in a room outside their regular classroom. These children received between 50 and 60 intervention sessions during their kindergarten year for a total of 25 to 30 hours of supplementary instruction. The instructional program was similar to that implemented in the Vellutino et al. (1996) study and was designed to promote motivation for reading and writing and to facilitate development of foundational reading skills, particularly phonological awareness, letter identification, letter-sound knowledge, functional use of the alphabetic principle, knowledge of print concepts, and the ability to identify high-frequency sight words. Although many of these skills were initially introduced in an isolated context, every instructional session included the opportunity for the children to (learn to) apply them in authentic reading and writing contexts. Heavy emphasis was placed on helping the children become strategic in their reading and writing. Moreover, lessons were tailored to meet the individual needs of the children in given groups and were designed to support them in their individual classroom programs as well (see Scanlon, Vellutino, Small, Fanuele, and Sweeney (2005a) for a more detailed description of this program).

In order to evaluate the short-term effects of the intervention, the letter identification and phonological awareness tests from the initial screening battery were readministered to children in both the Project Treatment and School-Based Comparison conditions in December, March, and June of the children's kindergarten year. In addition, experimental tests evaluating print concepts, word identification (Primary Word Identification), knowledge of letter sounds, letter-sound decoding (Primary Decoding), spelling, and two additional phonological awareness skills (phoneme segmentation and phoneme blending) were also administered. These tests were constructed and normed by the authors in order to avoid the floor effects typically observed with kindergarten and first-grade children on most commercially available tests.

For the sake of economy, results are presented only for the June assessment. These results are presented in Table 14.3. It can be seen that the children in the Project Treatment condition, on average, performed better than the children in the School-Based Comparison condition on most measures. However, effect sizes of 0.50 or better (a widely accepted standard) were obtained only on the (primary) word identification, letter-sound (primary) decoding, and phoneme segmentation tests. This was likely due to the fact that many of the children assigned to the School-Based Comparison condition came from schools that decided to implement their own intervention (contrary to our expectations), which served to weaken the effects of the Project Treatment intervention.

However, since several schools did not provide their at-risk kindergarten children with any form of intervention, it was possible to conduct a more valid treatment/control comparison. Table 14.4 presents results for comparisons of the children in these schools and children in the same schools who received the small-group intervention provided by project teachers. As is evident, the magnitudes of group differences are greater and more consistent in these comparisons than in comparisons involving the larger Project Treatment and School-Based Comparison samples. Effect sizes of 0.50 or

TABLE 14.3. Performance levels for the Project Treatment and School-Based Comparison groups on the kindergarten June follow-up battery.

| Measures | Reader groups | | Effect size |
	Project Treatment[1]	School Based Comparison[2]	
WRMT-R letter identification raw score (51)[3]			
M	28.91	27.07	0.29
SD	5.13	6.33	
Letter sounds raw score (35)[3]			
M	24.49	20.80	0.41
SD	7.80	9.05	
Primary word ID raw score (25)[3]			
M	6.68	4.32	
SD	5.18	4.14	0.57
WRMT-R word identification raw score (106)[3]			
M	3.24	2.11	0.35
SD	3.84	3.19	
WRMT-R word attack raw score (45)[3]			
M	0.91	0.28	0.47
SD	2.33	1.32	
Primary decoding (30)[3]			
M	6.51	4.15	0.52
SD	6.50	4.56	
Print concepts raw score (12)[3]			
M	10.88	10.43	0.27
SD	1.31	1.68	
Rhyme detection raw score (12)[3]			
M	8.43	8.03	0.14
SD	2.99	2.90	
Alliteration detection raw score (12)[3]			
M	8.38	7.53	0.28
SD	3.12	3.03	
Phoneme blending raw score (20)[3]			
M	14.80	12.97	0.47
SD	3.59	3.89	
Phoneme segmentation raw score (22)[3]			
M	6.22	2.76	0.65
SD	7.45	5.27	
Spelling (30)[3]			
M	13.00	10.62	0.40
SD	6.36	6.00	

[1] $n = 214$.
[2] $n = 214$.
[3] Number in parentheses indicates maximum possible score on the measure.

TABLE 14.4. Performance levels for Project Treatment and School-Based Comparison groups in schools that did not offer school-based intervention on the kindergarten June follow-up battery.

| Measures | Reader groups | | Effect size |
	Project Treatment[1]	School-Based Comparison[2]	
WRMT-R letter identification raw score (51)[3]			
M	28.52	24.37	0.51
SD	3.86	8.14	
Letter sounds raw score (35)[3]			
M	24.69	15.23	0.99
SD	7.17	9.54	
Primary word ID raw score (25)			
M	4.38	2.06	1.07
SD	3.30	2.16	
WRMT-R word identification raw score (106)[3]			
M	2.29	1.02	0.44
SD	3.07	2.86	
WRMT-R word attack raw score (45)[3]			
M	0.92	0.01	_[4]
SD	2.37	0.12	
Primary decoding (30)			
M	6.81	2.36	1.30
SD	7.51	3.42	
Print concepts raw score (12)			
M	10.96	10.48	0.25
SD	1.13	1.92	
Rhyme detection raw score (12)			
M	8.13	7.88	
SD	2.78	2.93	0.09
Alliteration detection raw score (12)			
M	7.75	6.65	0.36
SD	3.36	3.04	
Phoneme blending raw score (20)			
M	14.29	12.44	0.47
SD	3.49	3.91	
Phoneme segmentation raw score (22)			
M	6.25	1.05	1.66
SD	7.50	3.13	
Spelling (30)			
M	11.35	7.60	0.69
SD	5.99	5.41	

[1] $n = 48$.
[2] $n = 65$.
[3] Number in parentheses indicates maximum possible score on the measure.
[4] Effect size not reported because of floor effects.

greater were obtained on tests evaluating knowledge of letter names, knowledge of letter sounds, primary word identification, letter-sound (primary) decoding, phoneme segmentation, and spelling. In contrast, effect sizes were below traditional standards on tests evaluating detection of rhyme and alliteration, print concepts, and phoneme blending. Thus, given that group differences were relatively large on most of the emergent literacy measures, it can be concluded, with some degree of confidence, that early intervention to institute basic literacy skills in children judged to be at risk for early reading difficulties at the beginning of kindergarten can significantly improve such skills and, thereby, assist in preparing them for first-grade literacy instruction. It can also be concluded that many children who are judged to be at risk for early reading difficulties when they enter kindergarten will continue to be at risk if they are not provided with supplementary instruction in kindergarten.

14.2.3 First-Grade Screening

As already noted, a major objective of the model evaluated in the present study was to distinguish between at-risk children who responded positively to the remedial assistance they received in kindergarten and were no longer at risk in first grade and beyond, and at-risk children who continued to need remedial assistance in first grade, despite having received such assistance in kindergarten. Accordingly, all children from the full sample of at-risk kindergartners who had been assigned to either the Project Treatment or School-Based Comparison groups in kindergarten, and who were not lost through attrition, were re-evaluated at the beginning of first grade, using the measures periodically administered in kindergarten to evaluate growth in emergent literacy skills. These included the experimental measures evaluating knowledge of letter sounds, letter-sound (primary) decoding, and (primary) word identification, in addition to the Letter Identification, Word Identification, and Word Attack subtests from the Woodcock Reading Mastery Test-Revised (Woodcock, 1987). Raw scores for each measure were transformed into z scores (using either national norms or local norms for the instruments developed locally) and a composite based on summed z scores was computed for each child. Because a major objective of the first-grade intervention component of the study was to compare two different approaches to remedial intervention (i.e., text emphasis versus code emphasis) and because it was important to insure that there would be an adequate number of continued-risk children in each of the treatment groups, a relatively lenient cut-off score was adopted for constituting the continued-risk and no-longer-at-risk (NLAR) groups. Accordingly, the z scores of the at-risk children who had been in the Project Treatment group in kindergarten were rank ordered and children whose summed z scores were at or below the midpoint (median) of this distribution were defined as "poor readers" (PR). All other children were defined as NLAR readers. Thus, by definition, 50% of the at-risk kindergartners who had been in the Project Treatment group qualified as poor readers in first grade (this resulted in the lowest 15% of the original kindergarten sample being identified as poor readers). However, using the same cut-off score, 60% of the children from the kindergarten School-Based Comparison sample qualified as poor readers when the entire group was included in the count and 80% qualified when only children from schools that did not offer their own kindergarten intervention were included in the count. Thus, it can be inferred that the kindergarten intervention program implemented by project teachers was reasonably successful in reducing the number of children who may have qualified as "disabled readers" in first grade.

However, to further evaluate the utility of the preventative approach to early and long-term reading difficulties implemented in this study, the progress of the NLAR children was followed until the end of third grade, when the project ended. The intent was to evaluate the extent to which these children would be able to consolidate the gains they made in kindergarten and become independent readers with no further remedial assistance. The progress of the children identified as poor readers at the beginning of first grade was also followed. Some of these children were given daily one-to-one tutoring by project-trained teachers throughout first grade, and the remainder received whatever remedial services were available at their home schools. However, for purposes of evaluating the effects of the prevention/intervention model evaluated in the present study, the focus here is only on the poor readers who received both kindergarten and first-grade intervention provided by project teachers and the NLAR readers who received only kindergarten intervention provided by project teachers. In order to provide a normative standard, two groups of normally achieving readers were identified at the beginning of first

grade and their progress was also followed through the end of third grade. Both groups consisted of children who had summed z scores on the first-grade screening battery that were at or above zero and who were not identified as being at risk for early reading difficulties in kindergarten. Following a procedure used in the first intervention study discussed earlier (Vellutino et al., 1996), one group included children who had average intelligence (AvIQNorm) and the other group included children who had above average intelligence (AbAvIQNorm). These groups were constituted on the basis of the mean of the distribution generated by the entire sample of normal readers on the WISC III Full Scale IQ (Wechsler, 1991), which was administered to all target children in third grade. The intent here was to cross-validate previous findings as to the relationship between intelligence and reading ability.

Table 14.5 presents results for the PR, the NLAR, and the two groups of normal readers on the first-grade screening battery. It can be seen that the results approximate a linear trend on most measures, with the PR group, on average, performing at the lowest levels, the AvIQNorm, and the AbAvIQNorm groups performing at the highest levels and the NLAR group performing at levels intermediate to children in the poor and normal reader groups. The finding that the NLAR group performed at levels close to those of the normal readers on most of the screening measures is of special importance. It provides additional support for the preventative model evaluated in the present study, insofar as it suggests that identifying at-risk children at the beginning of kindergarten and providing them with supplemental (Tier 2) small-group instruction to institute foundational literacy skills may be a useful way to distinguish between at-risk children who may only need a modest degree of support to allow them to profit from first-grade literacy instruction and become independent readers and more basically impaired at-risk children who may require more individualized and more intensive (Tier 3) remedial instruction in first grade, or even beyond first grade, to become independent readers. Results on reading achievement measures administered at the end of first, second, and third grade provide additional support for this suggestion. These results are discussed below. However, the focus, in the next section, is on results from analyses evaluating different RTI models using incremental growth in kindergarten literacy

TABLE 14.5. Performance levels for the poor, no longer at risk, and two average reader groups on the first grade screening battery.

Measures	Reader group			
	PR ($n = 95$)	NLAR ($n = 94$)	AvIQNorm control ($n = 27$)	AbAvIQNorm control ($n = 27$)
WRMT-R letter identification (51)[1]				
M	25.32	32.04	33.12	34.74
SD	5.50	3.09	2.28	3.08
Letter sounds (35)[1]				
M	16.63	28.54	28.08	29.63
SD	6.89	3.10	4.17	4.46
Primary word identification (25)[1]				
M	3.41	10.02	13.70	16.56
SD	2.38	5.41	7.46	6.43
WRMT-R word identification (106)[1]				
M	1.19	6.57	13.68	19.78
SD	1.71	4.96	9.87	13.43
WRMT-R word attack (45)[1]				
M	0.12	2.83	4.19	6.96
SD	0.35	3.45	4.80	5.29
Primary decoding (30)[1]				
M	2.43	10.21	10.24	14.89
SD	2.07	6.09	5.38	8.26
Rhyme detection (12)[1]				
M	7.13	9.33	9.96	10.37
SD	3.09	2.32	2.46	1.52
Alliteration detection (12)[1]				
M	6.91	10.68	10.26	10.89
SD	2.79	1.72	1.89	1.74
Phoneme blending (20)[1]				
M	12.34	14.01	16.26	16.89
SD	2.51	1.20	3.29	3.26
Phoneme segmentation (22)[1]				
M	2.76	12.14	9.00	11.33
SD	5.32	6.65	7.29	7.45

[1] Number in parentheses indicates maximum possible score on the measure.

skills to classify Project Treatment children who received small-group intervention in kindergarten into the PR and NLAR groups identified at the beginning of first grade.

14.2.4 Modeling Response to Kindergarten Intervention

A series of logistic regression analyses were carried out to assess the accuracy with which measures of response to kindergarten intervention would predict PR and NLAR group membership, relative to static measures of emergent literacy skills and related abilities. Four different models were compared. The predictors for the first model were measures from the screening battery used to identify at-risk children at the beginning of kindergarten. This was the psychometric classification model. The predictors for the second and third models were measures of incremental growth in emergent literacy skills along with baseline measures of these skills. The predictors for the fourth model included all of the emergent literacy measures used as predictors in the third model along with measures of performance differences that emerged from the end of kindergarten to the beginning of first grade (i.e., during the summer hiatus, henceforth called the "summer drop off"). Selection of these predictors was the end result of a two-stage process. First, hierarchical linear modeling (HLM) procedures (Bryk and Raudenbush, 1992) were used to identify kindergarten that predicted growth in both primary word identification and primary word (letter-sound) decoding from kindergarten through the beginning of first grade, as well as level of performance on these measures at the beginning of first grade. Several of these predictors were simple difference scores representing change in a given literacy skill (e.g. letter-sound knowledge) from one assessment period to the next (e.g. first to second versus first to third). Next, multiple variable HLM procedures were used to identify unique combinations of predictors that accounted for the largest percentage of variance on the same word identification and word decoding measures. The primary intent of these preliminary analyses was to identify measures of kindergarten literacy development that, together, would be the strongest predictors of individual differences in RTI, as assessed, initially, by variability on measures of growth and level of performance in basic word-level skills (for the sake of economy, results from the HLM analyses are not reported in this chapter). Note also that because certain of these predictors were composites created by averaging standard scores derived from each predictor, all of the measures used as predictors were standardized for consistency.

Before discussing results from each of the regression models, it should be noted that logistic regression was used for classifying Project Treatment children into the PR and NLAR groups because it is an appropriate procedure for binary classification and it entails fewer assumptions than other classi-fication procedures, such as discriminant function analysis (e.g., linearity, homogeneity of variance, multivariate normality). Moreover, the output for lo-gistic regression not only provides percentages for accuracy in classification, but it also provides re-gression coefficients that reflect the importance of given predictors in classifying children into given groups. However, it is noteworthy that parallel anal-yses were conducted using the discriminant func-tion procedure in comparing classification models and the results were essentially the same as those obtained with the logistic regression procedure.

To evaluate the various classification models, metrics associated with receiver operating charac-teristic (ROC) curves were used to classify poor readers (true positives) versus NLAR readers (true negatives): "sensitivity," defined by the ratio of true positives to the sum of true positives and false nega-tives; "specificity," defined by the ratio of true nega-tives to the sum of true negatives and false positives; and the "area under the ROC curve" (AUC), which is a measure of accuracy in classification (Swets, 1992; Swets, Dawes, and Monahan, 2000). A ROC curve is a plot of the relationship between the true positive rate (sensitivity) and the false positive rate (1.00 minus specificity) in classifying individuals from two populations using prespecified criteria for classification (e.g. an arbitrary cut-off on a crite-rion measure). If, in any given sampling from the two populations (the PR and NLAR readers in the present instance) there are about as many false pos-itives as true positives, then the relationship be-tween the two quantities would be represented by a linear function and the ROC curve would resem-ble a straight line, thereby indicating classification that is no better than chance. If, however, the true positive rate greatly exceeds the false positive rate, then the ROC curve would be a steeply acceler-ating ogive that begins to asymptote at a point at which true positives can no longer be distinguished from false positives. The AUC represents the per-centage of randomly drawn pairs of individuals that have been accurately classified in the two popula-tions of interest and ranges from 0.50 (i.e. chance classification) to 1.00. An AUC of greater than 0.90 is considered excellent; 0.80 to 0.90 is considered good; 0.70 to 0.80 is considered fair; and below 0.70 is considered poor. To compare classification accu-racy across models, we computed critical ratios for

differences between pairs of AUC values generated by given models, corrected for correlations between the AUCs of the models being compared. Follow-ing Hanley and McNeil (1983), z scores for AUC differences were calculated using

$$z = \frac{AUC_1 - AUC_2}{\sqrt{SE_1^2 + SE_2^2 - 2r\,SE_1\,SE_2}}$$

where AUC_1 and SE_1 refer to the area under the curve and standard error for one model, AUC_2 and SE_2 refer to the area under the curve and standard error for a second model, and r represents the es-timated correlation between AUC_1 and AUC_2. The SPSS 13 software program was used to obtain all of these statistics.

Table 14.6 presents results from the classifica-tion analyses. Columns 2–5 (respectively) present regression coefficients for given predictors, along with standard errors, Wald significance tests, and probability values for those coefficients. The re-maining columns (respectively) present percentages for overall classification accuracy rate, the classifi-cation accuracy rate for poor readers (ROC sensitiv-ity), the classification accuracy rate for NLAR read-ers (ROC specificity), AUC estimates, and standard errors for these estimates. Model 1 consists of all of the measures included in the initial screening bat-tery administered at the beginning of kindergarten, save for the "counting-by-1's measure," which was not a significant predictor in preliminary analyses. It can be seen that the classification rates are less than optimal while the AUC is only "fair" (PR = 68.4%; NLAR = 72.3%; AUC = 0.79). Yet, all of these indices are better than chance, which in-dicates that the initial screening battery was able to accurately classify the majority of children into the PR and NLAR groups. Nevertheless, the false negative (FN) and false positive (FP) rates are both unacceptable (FN = 32.6%; FP = 27.7%), sug-gesting that entry-level tests of emergent literacy and related skills may not, by themselves, be ad-equate for predicting response to kindergarten in-tervention. Note, also, that the only measures that accounted for significant unique variance in the clas-sification equation were the tests of number identi-fication and rhyme detection. This is not surprising, given that both tasks are proxy measures of cogni-tive abilities that are important for learning to read (e.g., name encoding and retrieval, visual–verbal

TABLE 14.6. Classification indices for PR versus NLAR readers produced by four logistic regression models.

| Measure[1] | B | SE | Wald | p | Classification accuracy rate | | | ROC | |
					Overall	PR	NLAR	AUC	SE
Model 1					70.4	68.4	72.3	0.790	0.033
Letter ID S	0.020	0.013	2.113	0.146					
Number ID S	0.057	0.014	17.169	0.000					
Alliteration S	− 0.005	0.011	0.209	0.648					
Rhyme detection S	0.036	0.012	9.202	0.002					
Rapid object naming S	0.006	0.012	0.277	0.599					
Model 2					82.0	81.1	83.0	0.917	0.020
Letter ID S	0.017	0.017	1.025	0.311					
Letter-sound D	0.071	0.018	15.233	0.000					
Word ID and decoding D	0.038	0.022	2.939	0.086					
Letter ID M-D	0.003	0.016	0.042	0.838					
Letter sound M-D	0.069	0.016	18.227	0.000					
Word ID and decoding M-D	0.098	0.032	9.594	0.002					
Model 3					88.4	89.5	87.2	0.961	0.012
Letter ID S	0.037	0.030	1.466	0.226					
Letter sound D	0.139	0.036	14.529	0.000					
Word ID and decoding D	0.067	0.031	4.561	0.033					
Letter ID J-D	0.049	0.032	2.387	0.122					
Letter sound J-D	0.114	0.039	8.624	0.003					
Word ID and decoding J-D	0.136	0.037	13.464	0.000					
Model 4					95.2	94.7	95.7	0.994	0.003
Letter ID S	0.052	0.073	0.520	0.471					
Letter sound D	0.288	0.100	8.250	0.004					
Word ID and decoding D	0.119	0.056	4.507	0.034					
Letter ID J-D	0.097	0.080	1.475	0.225					
Letter sound J-D	0.309	0.105	8.734	0.003					
Word ID and decoding J-D	0.392	0.100	15.243	0.000					
Letter ID S-J	0.034	0.040	0.695	0.405					
Letter sound S-J	0.197	0.072	7.427	0.006					
Word ID and decoding S-J	0.143	0.061	5.579	0.018					

[1] S: kindergarten September assessment; D: kindergarten December assessment; M-D: kindergarten difference score from December to March assessment; J-D: kindergarten difference score from December to June assessment; S-J: difference score from June in kindergarten to September in first-grade assessment

learning, phonological awareness). Moreover, both share variance with emergent literacy skills, such as letter identification and knowledge of print concepts, and, like these latter skills, are likely influenced by home environment (Vellutino et al., 1996). That the test of letter identification did not account for unique variance in the classification equation is also not surprising, given that this measure was used for initial screening of all of the children in the at-risk group and was likely affected by range restriction.

Models 2, 3 and 4 provide more direct tests of RTI than does Model 1, in that each employs, as predictors, measures of growth in early literacy skills over periods in which remedial intervention was provided for the at-risk children. Predictors for Model 2 include difference scores representing growth in basic word-level skills from the December to the March assessments of the kindergarten year, along with baseline measures of these skills. The specific skills assessed include letter identification (the initial screening measure), letter-sound knowledge, primary word identification, and primary (letter-sound) decoding. (Note that the measures of phonological sensitivity were not included in the prediction equations because the composite measure of this skill did not contribute unique variance in the preliminary HLM analyses beyond that contributed by the letter-sound measures and the word identification/word decoding composite measures. However, the phonological sensitivity composite did significantly predict both level of performance and growth in both word identification and word decoding in the single variable analyses conducted.) The baseline measures were obtained in December, which, for all but the test of letter identification, was the first measuring period. The baseline measure of letter identification was obtained in September. The baseline and growth indices for primary word identification and primary word decoding were composites of both of these measures.

As is evident (Table 14.6), classification rates for Model 2 are substantially better than classification rates for Model 1 (PR = 81.1%; NLAR = 83%; AUC = 0.92), However, the AUC comparison indicates that this improvement in classification accuracy was not statistically significant ($z = 1.17$, $p > 0.05$). Similarly, the false negative and false positive rates are also substantially reduced, compared with Model 1 (FN = 18.9%; FP = 17%). Yet, by some standards, both percentages would still be considered unacceptable, especially the false negative rate. For example, Jenkins (2003) suggests that, in order for RTI to be an effective approach for determining degree of risk for long-term reading difficulties, the false negative rate for any given classification model should be no more than 10% (0.90 sensitivity).

The only significant predictors for Model 2 were the letter-sound baseline (December) measure, along with the letter-sound and the word identification/word decoding (December/March) difference scores. The letter identification baseline measure and the measure of growth in letter identification did not contribute significantly to the classification equation. Neither did the word identification/word decoding baseline measure. Thus, it appears that measures of growth in word level skills, especially early alphabetic skills, were the strongest predictors in the classification equation in Model 2, which essentially measured progress in acquiring emergent literacy skills during the better part of the children's kindergarten year. Here, it should be noted that to refer to assessments of literacy skills obtained initially in December as "baseline" measures of these skills is somewhat of a misnomer, because the children had already been in school for several months and had received approximately 6 weeks (a total of 6 hrs.) of the kindergarten intervention program before this assessment was conducted. However, since these children began the school year with very limited knowledge of letter names, it was anticipated

that assessment of decoding and word identification skills would have resulted in uniformly low scores and would have potentially frustrated the children. Thus, although a true baseline measure of those skills was not obtained, it seemed likely that there would have been little or no variability in performance had the assessments been administered at an earlier point.

Model 3 employed the same predictors as Model 2, except that the difference scores used as measures of growth in word-level skills were based on progress from December to June rather than progress from December to March. In other words, the growth indices used as predictors for Model 3 reflect incremental change in the skills assessed after an additional 3 months of remedial intervention compared with the growth indices used as predictors in Model 2. Not surprisingly, classification rates for Model 3 are even better than classification rates for Model 2 (PR = 90%; NLAR = 87.2%). In addition, the false negative rate (10%) is acceptable and the false positive rate (12.8%) is tolerable. At the same time, the AUC index (0.96) for Model 3 is excellent, and it is significantly different from the AUC index for Model 2 ($z = 2.27$, $p < 0.05$). Significant predictors for Model 3 were the same as those for Model 2, except that the coefficient for the baseline measure of the word identification/word decoding composite was now statistically significant. Evidently, the December/June difference scores used as predictors in Model 3 freed up some shared variance that was not available in Model 2, thereby allowing the word identification/word decoding composite to contribute significantly to the classification equation.

Model 4 was the final model evaluated. This model employed all of the predictors employed in Model 3, along with the difference scores reflecting the "summer drop off." It was intuited that these measures would substantially improve classification because they take account of individual and group differences in consolidating gains achieved through the intervention program during a period when no intervention was provided. This was found to be the case. As shown in Table 14.6, Model 4 produced the highest classification rates of all of the models (PR = 95%; NLAR = 96%) and the lowest false negative and false positive rates (FN = 5%; FP = 4%). It also produced the highest AUC index (0.99). In fact, the difference between the AUC index for

Model 4 and that for Model 3 was statistically significant ($z = 2.95$, $p < 0.05$). In addition, both the letter-sound and the word identification/word decoding summer drop-off measures contributed significant variance to the classification equation. Moreover, all of the baseline and growth measures that contributed significant and unique variance to the Model 3 classification equation also did so in Model 4.

Three important conclusions can be reasonably drawn from the results generated by the four classification models assessed. One is that dynamic measures of response to kindergarten supplementary intervention, such as the incremental growth measures employed in Models 2, 3, and 4, are more powerful predictors of continued risk status (and possible "RD" classification) than are static psychometric measures of early literacy skills and related cognitive abilities, such as those administered at the beginning of kindergarten, before any intervention was implemented. The second is that such incremental growth measures must be based on an amount (and quality) of remediation that generates enough variability in RTI to produce acceptable classification estimates. The third is that measures of success in maintaining gains accrued through remedial intervention, after such intervention has been discontinued, add significant variance to the classification equation and may be critically important components of any RTI classification model.

Finally, parallel analyses were conducted for each of the classification models evaluated using one standard deviation below the mean of the first-grade composite to constitute the PR and NLAR groups rather than a median split to do so. The pattern of results obtained in these analyses was essentially the same as those obtained when the median split was used to dichotomize the two groups, in terms of the relative contributions of given predictors. However, there were two important differences in the outcomes produced by these two classification criteria. First, the classification rates for the PR group ($n = 78$) were not acceptable for any of the models, except for Model 4, which included the summer drop off as a predictor (Model 1 = 66.7%; Model 2 = 78.2%; Model 3 = 82.1%; Model 4 = 92.3%). In contrast, classification rates for the NLAR group ($n = 111$) were acceptable for all models, except for Model 1 (Model 1 = 80.2%; Model 2 = 89.2%;

Model 3 = 96%; Model 4 = 95%). Second, all of the summer drop-off measures contributed significant variance to the Model 4 classification equation, including the letter identification difference score. The disparity in the classification rates generated by the two different cut-points is likely due to the fact that many of the children who fell one standard deviation below the mean on the first-grade screening battery were borderline candidates for the poor reader group at the middle and end of kindergarten (i.e., prior to the summer hiatus), no doubt because they had made enough progress in acquiring the emergent literacy skills used as predictors in the classification equations to be misidentified as NLAR readers, prior to inclusion of the summer drop-off measures as predictors. And, given that letter name knowledge was not a significant predictor in any of the classification analyses that used the median of the first-grade composite to dichotomize the reader groups, the finding that letter name difference score was found to be a significant predictor when the summer drop off was included in the classification equation suggests that the more severely impaired readers are likely to have difficulty consolidating their knowledge of even very basic literacy skills, such as letter name knowledge, despite extended periods of supplementary remedial assistance. Thus, the results provide additional support for our suggestion that measures of the child's ability to maintain the gains they acquired through remedial intervention is an important component of any RTI classification model that will likely increase the probability of identifying children most in need of continued remedial assistance and, in some cases, long-term and more intensive (Tier 3) remedial assistance. Still more support for this suggestion is provided by the first-grade intervention component of this study, which is discussed in the following section.

14.2.5 First-Grade Intervention

As noted in a previous section, literacy development in (available) children in the PR, the NLAR reader, and the two normal reader groups (AvIQNorm and AbAvIQNorm) was tracked from the beginning of first grade through the end of third grade. Some of the children in the poor reader group received daily one-to-one tutoring in first grade implemented by project teachers and the remainder received the remedial services provided by their home schools.

However, as already indicated, the focus herein is on the poor readers who received both the kindergarten small-group intervention and the first-grade one-to-one intervention provided by project trained teachers. To assess response to the more individualized and more intensive (Tier 3) intervention given these children throughout first grade, the PR groups were divided into two groups: one consisting of children who proved to be "difficult to remediate" (DR) and a second consisting of children who proved to be "less difficult to remediate" (LDR). Children in the DR group all received standard scores below 90 on the basic skills cluster (BSC) of the WRMT-R at the end of third grade. Children in the LDR group all received standard scores at or above 90 on the BSC at the end of third grade. Children in the LDR group are referred to as "less difficult to remediate" because, although they responded more positively to first-grade intervention than did the difficult-to-remediate children, in terms of their ability to maintain at least average level performance on measures of reading skill after the first-grade intervention program was discontinued (see discussion below), they were not as responsive to the small-group kindergarten intervention they received as the children in the NLAR group. Thus, they were more difficult to remediate than children in the latter group.

The first-grade intervention component of the project involved random assignment of all of the children identified as poor readers at the beginning of first grade to one of three treatment conditions, two that entailed one-to-one daily tutoring implemented by project-trained teachers, and a school-based comparison condition in which children received the intervention normally provided by their home schools (we do not discuss results produced by the latter condition in this chapter). The two project treatment conditions differed with respect to the amount of time spent on given remedial activities. In one of these conditions, the majority of time in each lesson was allotted to activities designed to facilitate development of phonological skills (e.g., phonological awareness, letter-sound decoding, etc.). In the other condition, the majority of time was allotted to activities designed to facilitate development of text processing skills (e.g., conjoint use of code-based and meaning-based strategies for word identification, comprehension monitoring, etc.). However, each treatment condition included both types

of activity, as well as equivalent amounts of time allotted to sight word learning and writing activities; see Scanlon et al. (2005a) for more detail. It should also be pointed out that, because the two conditions produced statistically equivalent results on measures of basic word-level skills, the DR and LDR reader groups just defined were dichotomized on the basis of sores on the WRMT-R BSC collapsed across these conditions. (Note that although the phonological skills emphasis and text emphasis conditions did not produce significant differences on measures of word level skills at the end of third grade, they did produce a significant difference on a measure of reading comprehension at the end of third grade; see Scanlon et al. (2005a) for more detail).

Table 14.7 presents results, in standard score units, for the reading outcome measures obtained from follow-up assessments at the end of first, second, and third grade. For purposes of comparison, a graph presents the raw scores on these measures (see Figure 14.1). Once again, there is a linear trend similar to that observed on the first-grade screening measures (Table 14.5), in that the DR children performed at the lowest levels on all measures, the AvIQNorm and AbAvIQNorm children performed at the highest levels, and the LDR and NLAR children performed at levels intermediate to the children in the DR and normal reader groups. Note also that the children in the LDR and NLAR groups were solidly in the average range on all of the reading measures across grade levels. Moreover, the performance levels in both the LDR and NLAR groups approach those of the normal readers on the word-level measures. Thus, of the total sample of at-risk children who were available at the end of third grade, and who either received only kindergarten intervention or both kindergarten and first-grade intervention provided by project-trained teachers ($n = 117$), 84% (98/117) achieved at least average levels of performance on all of the reading measures by the end of third grade (i.e., children in the LDR and NLAR groups) and 73 % of the latter subsample (72/98) received only kindergarten intervention (i.e., children in the NLAR group).

Results from the kindergarten and first-grade intervention components of this project are encouraging and important. Taken together, they provide strong support for the type of preventative approach to early intervention evaluated in the present study,

TABLE 14.7. Performance levels for the poor, NLAR, and normal reader groups on the first-, second-, and third-grade achievement measures.

| | | Poor reader | | NLAR ($n = 72$) | AvIQNorm controls ($n = 27$) | AbAvIQNorm controls ($n = 27$) |
		DR ($n = 19$)	LDR ($n = 26$)			
Word identification[1]						
Grade 1	M	94.63	105.73	109.24	118.89	127.33
	SD	8.50	5.72	11.71	13.05	14.69
Grade 2	M	83.94	102.73	107.47	117.67	125.78
	SD	11.46	8.37	12.19	14.68	12.21
Grade 3	M	79.16	99.50	103.44	109.74	114.81
	SD	11.58	6.63	9.70	11.37	8.13
Word attack[1]						
Grade 1	M	93.32	102.23	102.15	109.19	114.52
	SD	7.87	8.80	9.70	10.66	13.08
Grade 2	M	84.68	101.54	102.26	110.11	114.96
	SD	10.49	7.61	12.81	11.98	13.34
Grade 3	M	79.95	101.62	101.38	107.74	109.56
	SD	6.69	9.61	11.37	10.54	11.39
Reading comprehension[2]						
Grade 1	M	86.63	96.27	100.61	107.85	117.15
	SD	5.92	7.16	8.95	11.64	12.68
Grade 2	M	86.37	99.65	102.85	108.44	114.81
	SD	9.36	7.81	10.14	10.74	11.64
Grade 3	M	88.47	98.23	105.99	109.30	120.11
	SD	7.24	7.00	9.86	9.75	12.73

[1] Woodcock Reading Mastery Test-R standard scores.
[2] Wechsler Individual Achievement Test standard scores.

insofar as they suggest that early and long-term reading difficulties can be prevented in most children found to be at risk for such difficulties if they are identified at the beginning of kindergarten (if not sooner) and are provided with appropriate remedial intervention to institute foundational literacy skills throughout kindergarten. The data also suggest that many at-risk kindergartners will require less intensive (small-group) intervention to prepare them for first-grade literacy instruction and allow them to become independent readers beyond first grade, while other at-risk kindergartners will require more intensive and extensive instruction to attain the same outcome levels. Children of the latter description will continue to need additional remedial (Tier 3) support in first grade, and in some instances beyond first grade, to prevent them from experiencing long-term reading difficulties. Thus, of the 45 children who qualified for first-grade intervention, 42% (19/45) performed well below average on the word-level measures at the end of third grade and only in the low average range on the reading comprehension measure. These were the 19 children in the DR group. At the same time, one can be sanguine about the fact that 58% (26/45) of the kindergarten Project Treatment children who needed and received more intensive remedial services in first grade had solidly average levels of performance on all of the outcome measures of reading achievement at the end of first, second, and third grade. These were the 26 children in the LDR group.

Finally, it is of some significance that although the children in the DR group performed at below-average levels on all of the reading outcome measures at the end of second and third grade, they generally performed within the average range on measures of basic word-level skills at the end of first grade, suggesting that they were able to profit from the more individualized and more intensive remediation they received in first grade. The data also suggest, however, that these children had not yet consolidated their gains when the remedial program was discontinued and, once again, underscore the need to assess the child's ability to do so before making a determination as to the basic origin of their reading difficulties.

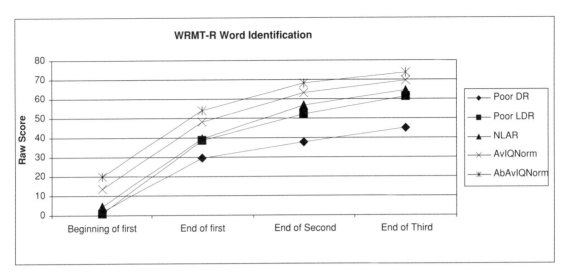

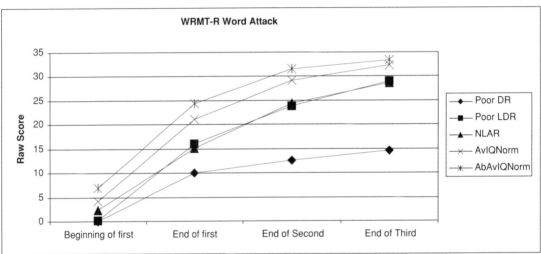

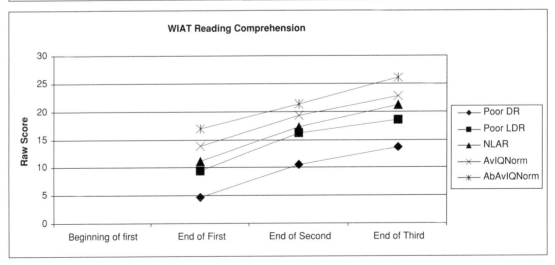

FIGURE 14.1. Performance levels across grades for poor, NLAR, and normal reader groups on the reading measures.

14.2.6 Cognitive Profiles of Reader Groups

As pointed out in a previous section, reading difficulties in some struggling readers may be caused primarily by biologically based cognitive deficits, whereas reading difficulties in others may be caused primarily by experiential and instructional deficits. Thus, it might be expected that the cognitive profiles of struggling readers would be appreciably different than the cognitive profiles of normal readers on measures of reading-related cognitive abilities. It might also be expected that the cognitive profiles of struggling readers who are difficult to remediate would be appreciably different than the cognitive profiles of struggling readers who are readily remediated. Initial evidence for both possibilities was provided by results from the first intervention study, as discussed earlier (Vellutino et al., 1996, 2003). Recall that, in this study, poor readers generally performed below normal readers on tests of phonological abilities, such as phonological awareness, letter-sound decoding, rapid naming, and verbal memory, administered in kindergarten, first, and third grades. It was also found that the poor readers who were difficult to remediate often performed below the poor readers who were readily remediated on many of the same measures. At the same time, the cognitive profiles of the readily remediated children were more like the cognitive profiles of the average IQ normal readers than like the cognitive profiles of the difficult to remediate children. Essentially the same pattern of results emerged in the present study.

Table 14.8 presents results for each of the five reader groups (DR, LDR, NLAR, AvIQNorm, AbAvIQNorm) on selected cognitive measures administered in first and/or third grade. The measures selected for these comparisons include tests evaluating rapid automatized naming, phonological memory (memory for nonsense words), digit span, receptive vocabulary, listening comprehension, and verbal and nonverbal intelligence. In accord with the pattern of results observed on both the first-grade screening measures and the reading achievement measures, we see a linear trend across groups with the DR and LDR groups performing at the lowest levels, the AvIQNorm and the AbAvIQNorm groups performing at the highest levels and the NLAR group performing at levels intermediate to the former and the latter groups. And, aside from substan-

tial gains in performance levels on measures administered in both first and third grade, the trend across groups is rather stable in both grades. Note, however, that the LDR children generally performed at levels closer to those of the DR children on the cognitive measures, despite the fact that they performed at levels closer to the NLAR children on the reading achievement measures (Table 14.7). At the same time, performance levels of children in the NLAR group approximated performance levels of children in the AvIQNorm group on the cognitive measures. One exception to this pattern of results, however, was observed on the test of nonverbal intelligence. On this test, the DR group mean was not substantially different from that of either the LDR or the AvIQNorm group means, and all three were lower than the NLAR group mean. These results suggest that it is not so much general cognitive abilities that distinguish between skilled and less-skilled readers, but language-based cognitive abilities that do so. Finally, except for tests evaluating rapid naming skills, the AbAvIQNorm group generally performed above the AvIQNorm group on the cognitive measures, which is not surprising.

These findings are consistent with results obtained in the first intervention study discussed above (Vellutino et al., 1996, 2003), as well as with results obtained in similar intervention studies (e.g., Foorman, 2003; Torgesen, 2000; Torgesen, Rose, Lindamood, Conway, and Garvan, 1999). In each of these studies, language-based abilities, especially phonological abilities, were found to distinguish between poor and normally developing readers more strongly and more reliably than did nonverbal abilities. Thus, the present findings provide additional support for the preeminence of language-based abilities as determinants of the ability to learn to read and the combined results speak for the importance of assessing such abilities to aid in distinguishing between biological and experiential/instructional causes of reading difficulties.

One other point might be usefully made about results from the cognitive measures. In discussing linear trends with poor and normal reader groups on such measures, similar to those obtained in the present study, Vellutino et al. (1996) suggested that reading ability along with the cognitive endowments underlying reading ability may both be placed on a continuum, relative to the types of literacy experience and instruction to which developing readers are

TABLE 14.8. Performance levels for the poor, NLAR, and normal reader groups on the first and third grade cognitive measures.

	Poor reader		NLAR ($n = 72$)	AvIQNorm controls ($n = 27$)	AbAvIQNorm controls ($n = 27$)
	DR ($n = 19$)	LDR ($n = 26$)			
Rapid naming letters (time in seconds)					
Grade 1					
M	45.74	40.58	38.71	33.26	32.74
SD	8.28	9.55	9.45	10.47	8.12
Grade 3					
M	33.89	30.35	28.42	25.67	26.65
SD	6.86	8.39	5.82	5.31	5.25
Rapid Naming objects (time in seconds)					
Grade 1					
M	63.84	57.69	57.88	51.89	49.89
SD	13.41	12.73	11.90	14.62	12.58
Grade 3					
M	52.42	51.15[2]	47.65	42.81	42.27
SD	12.61	17.31	9.43	8.14	8.04
Boston Naming spontaneously correct (60)[1]					
Grade 3					
M	32.68	34.50	37.22	38.89	42.81
SD	5.51	4.54	4.43	3.41	4.80
Phonological memory raw score (48)[1]					
Grade 1					
M	15.79	14.96	17.42	18.04	20.67
SD	4.52	4.56	5.62	3.97	6.82
Grade 3					
M	18.89	20.62	24.19	25.07	28.04
SD	3.89	4.77	5.34	4.87	5.83
WISC-III Digit Span scaled score					
Grade 3					
M	8.58	8.15	10.46	11.19	13.15
SD	2.17	2.43	3.05	3.03	2.57
Peabody Picture Vocabulary Test standard score					
Grade 3					
M	97.95	99.73	103.53	102.70	115.33
SD	9.49	9.22	11.19	9.71	10.37
WIAT Listening Comprehension standard score					
Grade 3					
M	98.00	98.85	105.75	106.00	115.59
SD	10.97	9.33	10.33	10.02	12.11
WISC-III Verbal IQ score					
Grade 3					
M	93.89	97.15	105.51	107.19	120.56
SD	8.84	11.84	9.02	8.17	7.75
WISC-III Performance IQ score					
Grade 3					
M	98.68	96.04	105.89	99.93	120.67
SD	10.66	11.49	11.78	8.46	7.42
WISC-III Full IQ score					
Grade 3					
M	95.63	95.92	106.03	103.81	122.59
SD	6.06	10.31	9.41	7.62	5.10

Key. WISC-III: Wechsler Intelligence Scale for Children III; WIAT: Wechsler Individual Achievement Test.

[1] Number in parentheses indicates maximum possible score on the measure.

[2] Note that one LDR child's naming speed on the Object Naming task was atypical (107 s). When this child's score was removed from the distribution the mean LDR score for object naming was 48.92 and the standard deviation was 13.30.

exposed. Thus, children who are endowed with an optimum or near-optimum mix of reading-related cognitive abilities may acquire strong and perhaps even superior literacy skills with little or no difficulty, despite even less than optimum experience and instruction. Conversely, children who are endowed with a less than optimum mix of reading-related cognitive abilities may find it difficult to acquire even the most basic literacy skills (e.g. letter identification), and will require supplemental instruction to acquire functional literacy skills. By logical extension, children who are at the low end of the continuum of reading-related cognitive abilities, especially language-based abilities such as phonological awareness, name retrieval, and verbal memory, may have difficulty learning to read even when provided with optimal or near-optimal literacy instruction. Such children will, in most cases, require more intensive and more individualized instruction to become functionally literate. In keeping with this analysis, some scholars have suggested that there is a "gradation of risk" for becoming "reading disabled" that is uniquely determined by the dynamic interaction of the developing reader's natural endowment and the amount and quality of the types of experience and instruction that facilitate reading acquisition (Snowling, Gallagher, and Frith, 2003; Vellutino et al., 2003). The data from the intervention studies discussed in this paper are consistent with this suggestion.

14.3 Implications of the Present Findings

14.3.1 Diagnosing Reading Disability

The present findings extend results from the first intervention study discussed above (Vellutino et al., 1996) and have several important implications regarding the role of early identification and early intervention in diagnosing RD. First, the results provide support for the gated approach to RTI classification evaluated in the present study, insofar as they document that children at risk for early and long-term reading difficulties can be efficiently and economically identified at the beginning of kindergarten and that such difficulties can be prevented in many of these children with small-group (Tier 2) supplementary intervention implemented

during kindergarten. Conversely, the data imply that many at-risk children who do not receive supplementary instruction in kindergarten will continue to be at risk when they enter first grade. Yet, the data also imply that most children who may continue to need remedial assistance in first grade can be successfully remediated with more intensive and more individualized (Tier 3) instruction implemented in first grade. Thus, in line with a similar conclusion drawn in the previous intervention study (Vellutino et al., 1996), some of the children in the latter group may be classified as "reading disabled" (for whatever official reason such classification is necessary), especially those who do not demonstrate accelerated growth in literacy skills when provided with more intensive and more individualized intervention.

However, the present study provides more definitive support for the RTI approach to diagnosing RD than that provided by the Vellutino et al. (1996) intervention study, in that measures of growth in early literacy skills, used as indices of response to kindergarten intervention, were found to be excellent predictors in classification models designed to distinguish between children who continued to be at risk for long-term reading difficulties at the beginning of first grade, and, thereby, required additional remedial assistance, and children who were no longer at risk for such difficulties and became independent readers without such assistance. Indeed, the finding that the NLAR group continued to perform at average levels in first through third grades provides especially strong support for the approach to RD classification evaluated in the present study. Moreover, the models that used measures of literacy growth as predictors in the classification equations were much more successful in distinguishing between these two groups, in terms of classification accuracy rates, than was the psychometric screening model (Model 1) that used only reading-related cognitive measures as predictors; see Compton, Fuchs, Fuchs, and Bryant (in press) for similar findings. In fact, results from both the growth curve and classification analyses quite clearly indicated that children who received small-group (Tier 2) intervention in kindergarten, and, yet, continued to show marginal growth in acquiring early literacy knowledge and skills (i.e., knowledge of print concepts, phonological awareness, knowledge of letter names, knowledge of letter sounds, letter-sound decoding, and primary word identification) were the most likely candidates for Tier 3 intervention in first grade. Thus, it seems reasonable to conclude, in accord with results obtained in the Vellutino et al. (1996) study, that an RTI approach to classification is a more effective means of identifying children who will require more intensive Tier 3 remediation (and may qualify for RD status), than a purely psychometric approach to classification.

The findings reported above also have important implications for the widespread use of intelligence tests for diagnosing RD. First, as noted in a previous section, these measures did not reliably distinguish between children in the DR group and children in the LDR group. Second, none of the intelligence tests distinguished between children in the NLAR group and children in the AvIQNorm group. At the same time, the nonverbal test of intelligence did not distinguish between children in the DR, LDR, and NLAR groups, on the one hand, and children in the AvIQNorm group, on the other hand. And, whereas the DR and LDR children did perform below children in the NLAR and AvIQNorm groups on the verbal intelligence test, this finding could be a consequence of the less accomplished reading ability of children in the DR and LDR groups, rather than a basic cause of reading difficulties in these children (Stanovich, 1986). This seems a likely possibility, given that intelligence was not assessed in any of the target groups until third grade (see Vellutino et al. (2003) for similar findings). Yet, in view of the finding that children in the DR and LDR groups generally performed below children in the NLAR and normal reader groups on the language-based measures administered in the cognitive battery, we cannot rule out the possibility that the lower verbal IQs of children in the DR and LDR groups are due, in some measure, to limited verbal ability, relative to children in the NLAR and normal reader groups. These two hypotheses are not mutually exclusive.

Thus, in sum, results from group contrasts on the intelligence tests make it clear that measures of intelligence do not reliably correlate with response to Tier 3-type intervention in at-risk children, in accord with results obtained in the Vellutino et al. (1996) intervention study. Neither do they distinguish between at-risk children who respond positively to Tier 2-type intervention and normally developing readers. When coupled with similar results

obtained elsewhere (Fletcher et al., 1994; Siegel, 1989; Stanovich and Siegel, 1994; Vellutino et al., 2000), along with results from the classification analyses reported above, the data further undermine the use of psychometric exclusionary approaches to RD classification, especially those that have the IQ–achievement discrepancy as their central defining criterion.

The present findings also provide additional support for the contention that reading difficulties in most beginning readers are caused primarily by experiential and instructional inadequacies rather than biologically-based cognitive deficits (Clay, 1987; Vellutino et al., 1996). Support for this contention is provided by the finding that deficiencies in foundational literacy skills were remediated in many of the at-risk children by the end of kindergarten. Moreover, performance levels in these children, on follow-up measures of reading achievement, were solidly in the average range from the beginning of first grade (after the summer hiatus) through the end of third grade, when the project ended. Yet, these results are also consistent with the possibility that reading difficulties in some beginning readers may be caused primarily by biologically based cognitive deficits. Support for this possibility is provided by the finding that the cognitive profiles of the children who continued to need remedial assistance in first grade were generally weaker than the cognitive profiles of the NLAR children and those of the normal readers.

Taken together, the results discussed thus far imply that an at-risk child's response to supplementary intervention in kindergarten can be a reasonably good barometer of whether that child will become a functionally independent reader without any additional remedial assistance, or continue to have difficulty acquiring functional literacy skills, as manifested in performance levels that necessitate continued and more intensive remedial assistance. And, in accord with a view expressed in the previous intervention study (Vellutino et al., 1996), the present results also imply that the nature of the child's RTI can act as a "first-cut diagnostic" that aids in determining whether impediments to acquiring functional literacy skills are caused primarily by experiential and instructional inadequacies or by cognitive deficits of biological origin. Thus, by this analysis, the at-risk children in the present study, who no longer needed remedial assistance after having received small-group supplemental intervention in kindergarten (NLAR children), in most cases, would be least defensibly classified as "reading disabled," whereas the at-risk children in the study who continued to need remedial assistance in first grade and beyond first grade, despite having received both kindergarten and first-grade intervention (i.e., the DR children), would be most defensibly classified as "reading disabled."

Of course, using RTI as the primary means of distinguishing between those children who are reading disabled and those who are not reading disabled does not necessarily rule out the use of psychometric tests with well-established measurement properties to evaluate cognitive abilities that have been found to reliably distinguish between children who do and do not respond positively to intervention (e.g., tests evaluating phonological awareness, verbal memory, name encoding and retrieval), as suggested elsewhere (Vellutino et al., 1996, 2002, 2003). However, the finding, in the present study, that children in the DR and LDR groups were not appreciably different on such measures, coupled with the finding that classification based only on psychometric tests was not nearly as good as RTI-based classification, together suggest that RTI would be a more accurate and more useful means of distinguishing between reading-disabled and non-reading-disabled children than would the sole use of psychometric tests for this purpose, in instances where psychometric tests are yet required.

The practical implications of the present findings should be apparent. That is, it should be possible for experienced educators to develop predictive RTI benchmarks based on growth in foundational literacy skills in kindergarten, relative to appropriate criterion-referenced standards (e.g., curriculum-based standards), to distinguish between those children who will continue to need supplementary assistance in first grade and those who will no longer need such assistance. However, results from the classification analyses make it clear that accuracy in identifying such children will be greater if such growth indices reflect change over the entire kindergarten year and will be even greater if a measure of the child's ability to maintain their gains during the summer hiatus is one of the benchmarks used to distinguish between these two groups. Yet, these analyses also indicate that well over 75% of the children in both the continued risk (PR) and NLAR groups

can be accurately classified using mid-kindergarten growth indices as predictors (Model 2). So, it should be possible, for purposes of remedial planning, to accurately classify at least those children in the extreme ranges of the distributions generated by measures of literacy growth as likely candidates for each respective group during this period of time. Such data could also be used as a signal to intensify preventative services offered in kindergarten in hopes of further reducing the number of children who would require support in first grade.

Finally, one other finding concerned with the diagnosis of RD merits some discussion. It will be recalled that classification analyses based on dichotomizing the first-grade PR and NLAR groups using one standard deviation below the mean of the composite measure used to define these groups, rather than the median score on this measure to do so, produced unacceptable classification rates for children in the PR group in all but the model that included the summer drop off in the classification equation (Model 4) and acceptable classification rates for children in the NLAR group in all but the psychometric screening model (Model 1). Given that, in many schools, remedial planning for children who may be at continued risk for reading difficulties in first grade is undertaken at the end of kindergarten, this finding cautions that adopting a stringent criterion (e.g., one standard deviation cutoff) for predicting continued risk status at the beginning of first grade may greatly inflate the false negative rate, if classification is based only on end of kindergarten RTI indices, whereas adopting a less stringent criterion (e.g., median split) may serve to minimize the false negative rate at the end of kindergarten and produce an acceptable false positive rate at this point in time.

14.3.2 Questions Raised by the K-1 Preventative Model

The preventative approach to early reading difficulties described in this paper raises several related questions that might be usefully addressed. First, one can legitimately question the efficacy of using a measure of letter identification to identify children at risk for early reading difficulties and doing so at the beginning of kindergarten before these children are exposed to classroom literacy instruction. The concern here would be that this procedure would produce an intolerably high number of false positives by placing children in the at-risk category prematurely and providing them with remediation they may not need. Identification of at-risk children at the beginning of kindergarten was justified on the basis of results obtained in the Vellutino et al. (1996) intervention study, in which it was found that almost all of the children identified as poor readers in first grade were lacking in foundational literacy skills (e.g., phonological awareness, knowledge of the alphabet) on entry into kindergarten. A measure of letter identification was used to determine at-risk status, because research has shown that this measure was the single best predictor of early and long-term reading achievement (e.g. Adams, 1990; Scanlon and Vellutino, 1997; Vellutino et al., 2003). Moreover, in accord with results obtained in the present study, kindergarten children who were found to be deficient on a test of letter identification at the beginning of kindergarten were also found to be deficient on a wide range of tests evaluating reading-related cognitive abilities.

Nevertheless, it is acknowledged that identifying at-risk children at the beginning of kindergarten risks inflating the false positive rate. This, of course, raises the valid question of what the false positive rate was in the case of identified at-risk children who did not receive supplementary intervention in kindergarten. Because the majority of the at-risk children in the present study received either project-based or school-based remedial assistance in kindergarten, it was not possible to assess the false positive rate on the full sample of these children. However, as indicated in a previous section, there were a number of at-risk children who did not receive supplemental intervention in kindergarten and who were still available for testing at the beginning of first grade, when the first-grade screening battery was administered ($n = 55$). Of these children, 78% received standard scores below 90 on the WRMT-R word identification subtest; 96% received standard scores below 90 on the WRMT-R word attack subtest; and 98%, 93%, and 89% received scores below the means of the NLAR and AvIQNorm groups on the experimental tests evaluating primary word identification, primary (letter-sound) decoding, and phoneme segmentation (respectively). If these percentages are averaged and if these averages are considered to be reasonable estimates of the true positive and false positive rates (respectively), then the

"true positive" rate for this group would be 91% and the "false positive" rate would be 9%. And, considering the fact that the children in this group had scores on the kindergarten screening battery that were not appreciably different from the total sample of at-risk children (data not shown), it seems reasonable to suggest that the false positive rate associated with the use of letter identification to identify at-risk children at the beginning of kindergarten would generally be more tolerable than a false negative rate of similar proportion.

A second question that may be profitably raised about the preventative approach assessed in the present study concerns the efficacy of using response to supplemental kindergarten intervention as the primary basis for providing more individualized and more intense (Tier 3) intervention in first grade, before making any attempt to evaluate and modify the at-risk children's classroom literacy program in kindergarten (Fuchs, 2002). Essentially the same question can be raised about the Tier 3 intervention provided for the poor readers identified at the beginning of first grade. It will suffice to point out that this procedure was motivated by two related findings obtained in the previous intervention study (Vellutino et al., 1996). First, in the kindergarten observation component of the latter study, it was found that, in the typical kindergarten classroom, relatively little time was spent on activities designed to institute foundational literacy skills (Scanlon and Vellutino, 1996). Therefore, it was intuited that, because of this circumstance, far too many kindergartners were entering first grade with limited ability to profit from the language arts curriculum, even if they had not been lacking in foundational literacy skills when they entered kindergarten. Second, it was also found that, in kindergarten classrooms that devoted more time to the development of foundational literacy skills, the probability of identifying children as poor readers in first grade was less than in the kindergarten classrooms where comparatively less time was devoted to foundational literacy skills. Thus, in view of these findings, and because it is widely recognized that attempts to change classroom literacy practices often meet with only limited success, it seemed important to evaluate the efficacy of an approach that incorporated supplementary instruction to prevent early reading difficulties in first grade. The present results would appear to justify the decision to evaluate this approach. Indeed, the finding that a very large majority of the (available) at-risk children who had not received any supplementary instruction in kindergarten were found to be seriously lacking in basic literacy skills at the beginning of first grade speaks for the validity of the concerns.

There is, of course little doubt that it is critically important to evaluate the classroom literacy programs of at-risk children and to take steps to modify such programs when necessary. In fact, it is entirely possible that the (at-risk) children in the present study, who profited from Tier 3 intervention in first grade, but were unable to consolidate their gains after the intervention was discontinued (DR children), were subsequently exposed to classroom instruction that made it difficult for them to do so. This same question was raised in discussing similar findings in the previous intervention study (Vellutino et al., 2003). Thus, addressing possible problems in the classroom literacy program would be a potentially vital component of any preventative intervention model. However, it is suggested that the most efficient and most effective preventative model would identify children as being at risk for early reading difficulties at the beginning of their kindergarten year (if not sooner) and implement both enhanced classroom instruction and appropriate (Tier 2) supplemental instruction on behalf of these children simultaneously rather than in tandem, as would be dictated by a strict rendering of the traditional three-tier model. A similar model is suggested in addressing the needs of those children who qualify for Tier 3 type intervention at the beginning of first grade. Of course, the decision to adopt such models would necessitate appropriate professional development for classroom teachers as well as for teachers implementing both Tier 2 and Tier 3 remedial assistance in order to insure compatibility of classroom and supplementary instruction. Our research team is currently conducting yet another intervention study to evaluate such a model, and initial results suggest that professional development for both classroom teachers and remedial intervention specialists is a necessary component of any effective preventative intervention model (Gelzheiser, Scanlon, Schatschneider, and Vellutino, 2006; Scanlon, Vellutino, Gelzheiser, Dunsmore, and Schatschneider, 2005b). In fact, the results indicate that providing kindergarten classroom teachers with professional development based on the kindergarten intervention model was as effective as direct intervention for children in reducing the proportion of kindergartners who qualified as at-risk for reading difficulties from the beginning to the end of the school year (Gelzheiser et al., 2006).

14.3.3 What Accounts for Limited Progress Among Difficult to Remediate Children?

Because children in the DR group were unable to consolidate and build upon the substantial gains they achieved by the end of first grade, despite having received both kindergarten and first-grade intervention, the question of what accounts for their limited progress naturally arises. One possible answer to this question is that the classroom and/or remedial instruction the DR children received when our intervention project ended did not sufficiently address their individual needs, as was already suggested. Although the design of the project did not involve collecting data to evaluate the types and amounts of classroom and remedial instruction these children received in second and third grade, school-level outcomes were examined for the schools ($n = 9$) that participated in the project and it was found that whereas 80% to 100% of the children who received project-based intervention in first grade obtained a standard score of 90 or greater on the BSC at the end of first grade, less than 60% of the project children in four of the schools achieved this level of performance on the BSC at the end of third grade. Percentages in the other five schools were about the same at the end of third grade as they were at the end of first grade. Thus, the data provide suggestive evidence that the quality of second- and third-grade instruction may at least partially explain the limited progress made by the DR children in these grades.

A second and related explanation for the "backsliding" observed among children in the DR group during second and third grade is that the gains these children made by the end of first grade were not stable enough to allow them to consolidate these gains without remedial assistance tailored to their individual needs. The fact that the DR children scored substantially below the LDR children on all of the reading measures makes this a likely possibility. It also points to a third possible explanation for the limited progress made by the DR children, relative to that made by the LDR children, specifically that the LDR children were cognitively better equipped than the DR children to profit from the intensive instruction they received in first grade. The fact that the LDR children performed only slightly better than the DR children on the cognitive measures included in the third-grade battery makes this the weakest of the three explanations. It is also possible that the LDR children received more effective classroom instruction in first grade than did the DR children and that this allowed them to better consolidate and maintain their gains in second and third grade. These explanations are not mutually exclusive, and additional research is necessary to address the question.

14.4 Summary

A major purpose of the present study was to further evaluate RTI as the primary vehicle for diagnosing specific RD. The RTI approach to RD classification was initially evaluated in a first-grade intervention study conducted by Vellutino et al. (1996, 2002, 2003). However, the RTI approach implemented in the kindergarten/first-grade intervention study that was the primary focus of the present paper (Vellutino et al., 2006) differs from that implemented in the Vellutino et al. (1996) study in several important respects. First, it is a preventative approach to intervention and classification that identified children who were judged to be at risk for early and long-term reading difficulties at the beginning of kindergarten using a test of an emergent literacy skill (letter identification) as the identifying measure, rather than at mid-first grade using a test of reading skill as the identifying measure. Second, the children who qualified for at-risk status were provided with small-group supplemental instruction initiated early in kindergarten, before they had received a substantial amount of literacy instruction, rather than intensive one-to-one instruction initiated at mid-first grade, after they had received a substantial amount of literacy instruction. Third, the approach to intervention used in the kindergarten/first-grade intervention study was a gated one, in that children received intensive one-to-one instruction throughout first grade, if they did not demonstrate accelerated learning (close the gap) when provided with a rather limited amount of remedial support in kindergarten, whereas in the Vellutino et al. (1996)

study the children received intensive one-to-one instruction initiated at mid-first grade (and extended through mid-second grade, depending on progress), on the basis of their response to first-grade classroom instruction. Fourth, reading achievement measures reflecting response to kindergarten supplementary intervention were used to determine eligibility for intensive intervention, which essentially ensured that the children who were served in the intensive first-grade program, as a group, were those who needed more intensive and more individualized instruction in order to make accelerated gains in reading skills. In contrast, in the Vellutino et al. (1996) study, no attempt was made to intervene with the at-risk children before intensive intervention was initiated in mid-first grade. As a result, there was a greater probability that many children served in that project were false positives in terms of their RD status. Fifth, in the kindergarten/first-grade intervention study discussed in this chapter, a comprehensive battery of tests evaluating reading-related cognitive abilities and intelligence was administered in third grade, whereas in the Vellutino et al. (1996) study such a battery was administered in kindergarten, first, and third grade. Finally, the classification analyses undertaken in the present study were not undertaken in the previous study because the number of children in the DR and readily remediated groups was not large enough to justify such analyses.

The major findings from the kindergarten/first-grade intervention study discussed in this chapter are quite in keeping with those from the Vellutino et al. study (Vellutino et al., 1996, 2002, 2003). However, they appreciably extend those findings. The present findings provide strong support for the preventative model evaluated in the study, insofar as they suggest that small-group supplemental intervention provided in kindergarten can significantly reduce the number of children who may be at risk for reading difficulties in first grade. It is also clear, from the results, that more intensive and more individualized intervention provided in first grade can facilitate the acquisition of functional and independent reading skills in most of the children who continue to be at risk for reading difficulties at the beginning of first grade, despite having received remedial assistance in kindergarten. Moreover, results from classification analyses suggest that measures of growth in basic literacy skills can identify all but a small percentage of the kindergarten children who will continue to be at risk for reading difficulties in first grade and all but a small percentage of those who will no longer be at risk for such difficulties in that grade by no later than the end of kindergarten. However, analogous to results obtained by Vellutino et al. (1996), the data also suggest that a small percentage of at-risk children will likely have difficulty consolidating and maintaining any gains they achieve through supplementary intervention and will require additional assistance to become functionally literate, even after they have received the extensive remedial instruction of the types provided in the present study. And, although there is reason to believe that inadequate classroom instruction may contribute significantly to the difficulty such children have in becoming independent readers, results from the cognitive battery suggest that at least some of them may be impaired by biologically based cognitive deficits that would make it difficult for them to learn to read, even under the most optimal experiential and instructional circumstances. It is children of this description that may be reasonably classified as "disabled readers." Yet, the results of this study make it clear that this classification would only be justified in cases where children have received intensive (Tier 3) remedial instruction tailored to their individual needs.

Finally, the analyses of the intervention data presented herein further undermine the use of psychometric/exclusionary approaches to the diagnosis of specific RD, especially those having the IQ–achievement discrepancy as their central defining criterion. In accord with results obtained in the Vellutino et al. study (Vellutino et al., 1996, 2000, 2003), the nonverbal measure of intelligence did not distinguish between the different at-risk groups. Neither did it distinguish between these groups and the normal readers of average intelligence. And, although the test of verbal intelligence did distinguish between some of these groups, this is likely a consequence of prolonged reading difficulty rather than a cause of reading difficulty (Stanovich, 1986). Moreover, the classification model that used only psychometric measures in the prediction equation was not as effective in distinguishing between continued risk and NLAR children as the classification models using measures of literacy growth in the prediction equation. Thus, this chapter reaffirms the major conclusion drawn by Vellutino et al. (1996) that RTI ap-

proaches to diagnosing RD are more effective than approaches that rely solely on psychometric measures to make this diagnosis.

Acknowledgments. Virtually all of the work discussed in this paper was supported by grants from the National Institute of Child Health and Human Development to Vellutino and Scanlon. The data for the prevention/intervention study that is the primary focus of the present chapter were collected under the auspices of NICHD grant R01HD34598. The data for the intervention study reported in Vellutino et al. (1996) were collected as part of a project conducted under the auspices of a special Center grant (P50HD25806) awarded to the Kennedy Krieger Institute by NICHD. The data for the Scanlon et al. (2005b) intervention study briefly mentioned in this paper were collected under the auspices of a grant (R01HD04235005) funded by the National Institute of Child Health and Human Development and sponsored by the Interagency Educational Research Initiative. The authors are grateful to Dr. Donald Compton (personal communication) for his assistance in obtaining estimated correlations for the AUCs generated by the models being compared. The authors express their sincere gratitude to the teachers, students, and secretarial and administrative staff in participating schools. We are also grateful to the intervention teachers and data-collection personnel who participated in these projects. Finally, special thanks and gratitude are extended to our colleagues Sheila Small, Diane Fanuele, and Joan Sweeney, who assisted immensely in the implementation of all three of the intervention studies discussed in this paper.

References

Adams, M. J. (1990). *Beginning to Read: Thinking and Learning about Print*. Cambridge, MA: MIT Press.

Bryk, A. S. & Raudenbush, S. W. (1992). *Hierarchical Linear Models: Applications and Data Analysis Methods*. Newbury Park, CA: Sage Publications.

Clay, M. M. (1987). Learning to be learning disabled. *New Zealand Journal of Educational Studies, 22*, 155–173.

Compton, D. L., Fuchs, D., Fuchs, L. S., & Bryant, J. D. (2006). Selecting at-risk readers in first grade for early intervention: A two-year longitudinal study of decision rules and procedures. *Journal of Educational Psychology, 98*, 394–409.

Denton, C. A. & Mathes, P. G. (2003). Intervention for struggling readers: possibilities for change. In B. R. Foorman (Ed.), *Preventing and Remediating Reading Difficulties: Bringing Science to Scale* (pp. 229–251). Baltimore, MD: York Press.

Fletcher J. M., Shaywitz, S. E., Shankweiler, D. P., Katz, L., Liberman, I. Y., Stuebing, K. K., et al. (1994). Cognitive profiles of reading disability: comparisons of discrepancy and low achievement definitions. *Journal of Educational Psychology, 86*, 6–23.

Foorman, B. R. (Ed.) (2003). *Preventing and Remediating Reading Difficulties: Bringing Science to Scale* (pp. 73–120). Baltimore, MD: York Press.

Frankenberger, W. & Fronzaglio, K. (1991). States' definitions and procedures for identifying children with mental retardation: comparison over nine years. *Mental Retardation, 29*, 315–321.

Fuchs, L. (2002). Three conceptualizations of "treatment" in a responsiveness to treatment framework for LD identification. In R. Bradley, L. Danielson, & D. Hallahan (Eds.), *Identification of Learning Disabilities: Research to Practice* (pp. 521–529). Mahwah, NJ: Erlbaum.

Fuchs, L. & Fuchs, D. (1997). Use of curriculum-based measurement in identifying students with learning disabilities. *Focus on Exceptional Children, 30*, 1–16.

Gelzheiser, L. M., Scanlon, D. M., Schatschneider, C., & Vellutino, F. R. (2006). Measuring the effects of professional development in effective literacy instruction. Paper presented at the *Annual Meeting of the Pacific Coast Research Conference*, Coronado, CA.

Gresham, F. K. (2002). Responsiveness to intervention: an alterative approach to the identification of Learning disabilities. In R. Bradley, L. Danielson, & D. Hallahan (Eds.), *Identification of Learning Disabilities: Research to Practice* (pp. 467–419). Mahwah, NJ: Erlbaum.

Hanley, J. A., & McNeil, B. J. (1983). A method of comparing the areas under receiver operating curves derived from the same cases. *Radiology, 148*, 839–843.

Jenkins, J. R. (2003). Candidate measures for screening at-risk students. Paper presented at the *Conference on Response to Intervention as Learning Disabilities Identification*, Kansas City, MO.

Kirk, S. A. & Bateman, B. (1962–1963). Diagnosis and remediation of learning disabilities. *Exceptional Children, 29*, 73–78.

Lyon, G. R., Fletcher, J. M., & Barnes, M. C. (2002). Learning disabilities. In E. J. Mash & R. A. Barkley (Eds.), *Child Psychopathology* (2nd ed., pp. 520–586). New York: Guilford Press.

Scanlon, D. M. & Vellutino, F. R. (1996). Prerequisite skills, early instruction, and success in first grade reading: Selected results from a longitudinal study. *Mental Retardation and Developmental Disabilities Research Reviews, 2*, 54–63.

Scanlon, D. M. & Vellutino, F. R. (1997). A comparison of the instructional backgrounds and cognitive profiles of poor, average, and good readers who were initially identified as at risk for reading failure. *Scientific Studies of Reading, 1*, 191–215.

Scanlon, D., Vellutino, F. R., Gelzheiser, L. M., Dunsmore, K., & Schatschneider, C. (2005b). Instructional and teaching characteristics of kindergarten teachers whose at-risk students make the greatest and least gains. Paper presented at the *Annual Meeting of the Pacific Coast Research Conference*, Coronado, CA.

Scanlon, D. M., Vellutino, F. R., Small, S. G., Fanuele, D. P., & Sweeney, J. (2005a). Severe reading difficulties: can they be prevented? A comparison of prevention and intervention approaches. *Exceptionality, 13*, 209–227.

Siegel, L. S. (1989). IQ is irrelevant to the definition of learning disabilities. *Journal of Learning Disabilities, 22*, 469–478.

Snowling, M. J., Gallagher, A., & Frith, U. (2003). Family risk of dyslexia is continuous: individual differences in the precursors of reading skill. *Child Development, 74*, 358–373.

Stanovich, K. E. (1986). Matthew effects in reading: some consequences of individual differences in the acquisition of literacy. *Reading Research Quarterly, 21*, 360–407.

Stanovich, K. E. & Siegel, L. S. (1994). Phenotypic performance profile of children with reading disabilities: a regression-based test of the phonological–core variable–difference model. *Journal of Educational Psychology, 86*, 24–53.

Swets, J. A. (1992). The science of choosing the right decision threshold in high-stakes diagnostics. *American Psychologist, 47*, 522–532.

Swets, J. A., Dawes, R. M., & Monahan, J. (2000). Psychological science can improve diagnostic decisions. *Psychological Science in the Public Interest, 1*, 1–26.

Torgesen, J. K. (2000). Individual differences in response to early interventions in reading: the lingering problem of treatment resisters. *Learning Disabilities Research and Practice, 15*, 55–64.

Torgesen, J. K., Rose, E., Lindamood, P., Conway, T., & Garvan, C. (1999). Preventing reading failure in young children with phonological processing disabilities: group and individual responses to instruction. *Journal of Educational Psychology, 91*, 579–594.

US Office of Education (1977). Assistance to states education of handicapped children: procedures for evaluating specific learning disabilities. *Federal Register, 42*, 665082–665085.

Vellutino, F. R. & Scanlon, D. M. (2002). The interactive strategies approach to reading intervention. *Contemporary Educational Psychology, 27*, 573–635.

Vellutino, F. R., Scanlon, D. M., & Jaccard, J. (2003). Toward distinguishing between cognitive and experiential deficits as primary sources of difficulty in learning to read: a two year follow-up of difficult to remediate and readily remediated poor readers. In B. R. Foorman (Ed.). *Preventing and Remediating Reading Difficulties: Bringing Science to Scale* (pp. 73–120). Baltimore, MD: York Press.

Vellutino, F. R., Scanlon, D. M., & Lyon, G. R. (2000). Differentiating between difficult-to-remediate and readily remediated poor readers: more evidence against the IQ–achievement discrepancy definition of reading disability. *Journal of Learning Disabilities, 33*, 223–238.

Vellutino, F. R., Scanlon, D. M., Sipay, E. R., Small, S. G., Pratt, A., Chen, R. S., et al. (1996). Cognitive profiles of difficult to remediate and readily remediated poor readers: early intervention as a vehicle for distinguishing between cognitive and experiential deficits as basic causes of specific reading disability. *Journal of Educational Psychology, 88*, 601–638.

Vellutino, F. R., Scanlon, D. M., Small, S., & Fanuele, D. P. (2006). Response to intervention as a vehicle for distinguishing between reading disabled and non-reading disabled children: evidence for the role of kindergarten and first grade intervention. *Journal of Learning Disabilities. 38*, 157–169.

Vellutino F. R., Scanlon D. M., & Tanzman M. S. (1998). The case for early intervention in diagnosing specific reading disability. *Journal of School Psychology, 36*, 367–397.

Wechsler, D. (1991). Wechsler Intelligence Scale for Children—Third Edition. New York: Psychological Corporation.

Woodcock, R. W. (1987). *Woodcock Reading Mastery Tests–Revised*. Circle Pines, MN: American Guidance Services.

15

Effects from Intensive Standardized Kindergarten and First-Grade Interventions for the Prevention of Reading Difficulties

Stephanie Al Otaiba and Joseph Torgesen

Stephanie Al Otaiba, PhD, is an Associate Professor in Special Education at Florida State University and the Florida Center for Reading Research. salotaiba@fcrr.org

Joseph Torgesen, PhD, is the W. Russell and Eugenia Morcom Chair of Psychology and Education at Florida State University and the Florida Center for Reading Research. torgesen@fcrr.org

The purpose of this chapter is to describe reading interventions that might be used within a response-to-intervention (RTI) framework when students do not show adequate progress in learning to read from their current instruction. We will provide information about the nature of these interventions, the settings in which they have been studied, and the strength of their impact on early reading growth. There is a critical need for effective early interventions in reading, since current data (NAEP, 2005) indicate that 36% of students in the United States cannot meet basic standards of reading competence by the end of fourth grade. The situation is even more troublesome for poor and minority students, in that the latest national assessment indicates that 56% of poor, 61% of African American, and 57% of Hispanic students currently fail to meet basic reading standards in fourth grade. The need for strengthening early reading instruction is underlined when we consider that the incidence of students identified as learning disabled during elementary school has grown exponentially since the establishment of the category in 1977 (over 200%), and most LD students are identified because of difficulties in learning to read.

The importance of work to develop effective early identification and interventions for students who struggle in reading is also supported by the fact that it becomes much more difficult to remediate reading difficulties after students have struggled in learning to read for several years. For example, Torgesen (2005) has recently reported data showing that, once students fall seriously behind in reading fluency,

even the most powerful remedial interventions are not able to help them "close the gap" in fluency with students who are learning to read normally. Other data point out a variety of negative consequences for early difficulties in reading that include relatively weak vocabulary growth (Cunningham and Stanovich, 1998), changes in attitude and motivation for reading (Wigfield and Guthrie, 1997), and loss of opportunities for development of increasingly sophisticated reading strategies (Brown, Palinscar, and Purcell, 1986). Finally, there is the sobering fact obtained in several longitudinal studies that children who are poor readers at the end of first grade almost never acquire average-level reading skills by the end of elementary school (Francis, Shaywitz, Stuebing, Shaywitz, and Fletcher, 1996; Juel, 1988; Torgesen and Burgess, 1998).

15.1 Conceptual Framework

The first part of our conceptual framework for discussing interventions to prevent reading difficulties involves the *content*, or focus of intervention, and it comes from the rich knowledge base about early reading development that has been the product of at least three decades of intensive research (Adams, 1990; National Reading Panel, 2000). In the first chapter of the report of the National Research Council (Snow, Burns, and Griffen, 1998), the authors identify three basic problems that constitute early stumbling blocks on the road to becoming a good reader. These difficulties involve: (1) problems in understanding and using the alphabetic principle to acquire fluent and accurate word reading skills; (2) failure to acquire the verbal knowledge and strategies that are specifically needed for comprehension of written material; and (3) absence or loss of initial motivation to read, or failure to develop a mature appreciation of the rewards of reading. Children can struggle in learning to read for any of these reasons, and many students struggle in all three areas.

It is important that children be prevented from lagging behind in the development of both word reading ability and vocabulary/thinking skills, because each of these areas is critical for proficient reading comprehension (Snow, 2002). Students who can recognize the words in text accurately and fluently are able to focus better on the meaning of the text than those who must stop to laboriously "decode" or guess at words they are unfamiliar with (Fuchs, Fuchs, Hosp, and Jenkins, 2001). Even more obviously, perhaps, students who do not understand the meaning of many of the words in a passage, or do not have basic knowledge assumed by the author, or who cannot make appropriate inferences, will also struggle to comprehend the meaning of the text (Nation, 2005).

Given that children must acquire knowledge and skills in the two broad areas outlined above if they are to be proficient readers, and given the large diversity in students' abilities to acquire these skills and knowledge (Share and Stanovich, 1995; Whitehurst and Lonigan, 1998), we can directly infer that RTI models applied within early elementary schools are likely to identify students that need interventions in either one or both of these areas. In fact, the science of reading disabilities has produced compelling evidence that there is a large group of students who enter school with limitations in phonological processing ability that interfere with their ability to acquire alphabetic reading skills (Raynor, Foorman, Perfetti, Pesetsky, and Seidenberg, 2001). These children must receive very specific kinds of instructional support if they are to succeed in learning to read. Another large group of students, primarily those from poor and minority homes, enter school with significant deficits in vocabulary and background knowledge that make it difficult for them to comprehend text that places heavy demands in these areas (Beck, McKeown, and Kucan, 2002; Hart and Risley, 1995). These children also frequently struggle with acquisition of early word

reading skills because limited experience with letters, print, and language in their preschool environment does not prepare them well to profit from early reading instruction (Whitehurst and Lonigan, 1998).

In order to prevent serious reading difficulties, early interventions must be available that can powerfully accelerate development in early word reading skills (phonemic awareness, phonics, fluency), and they must also be available to support the development of vocabulary, conceptual knowledge, reading comprehension, and thinking skills. Of course, instruction in these areas must also address motivational or learning behavior management issues, since this is frequently an area of challenge for students who struggle in learning to read.

The second aspect of the conceptual framework of this chapter involves the most important dimensions of instructional *methods* that are characteristic of successful early interventions in reading. The successful interventions we will describe in this chapter invariably increase both the intensity and the explicitness of instruction. Intensity typically is increased in one of two ways. Either extra time is added for instruction, or instructional group size is reduced. A number of research syntheses, for example, have demonstrated the value of grouping practices that increase instructional intensity (Elbaum, Vaughn, Hughes, and Moody, 1999; Lou et al., 1996; Swanson, Hoskyn, and Lee, 1999). Interventions that provide instruction in small groups are generally more successful than those that provide instruction in larger, classroom-sized groups.

Students who struggle in learning to read within one environment may profit from interventions that increase both the explicitness of instruction and the systematic way that instruction and practice/review are integrated (Foorman and Torgesen, 2001). Considering this dimension of instruction, replacing a less explicit and systematic classroom curriculum with one that is more explicit and systematic is, in a very real sense, an "intervention" given to all students. If most of the students in a class are "at risk" for reading difficulties, adopting an explicit whole-classroom approach to instruction has been shown to produce positive effects when compared with a less explicit curriculum (Foorman, Francis, Fletcher, Schatschneider, and Mehta, 1998). By the same token, the combination of explicit and systematic classroom instruction coupled with even more explicit and intensive interventions is likely to produce higher overall outcomes than if interventions are the only explicit instruction a child receives. As we consider studies in the next section, at least part of the variability in overall outcomes can be attributed to differences in the classroom instruction that is also being provided to the students, and not solely to differences in power of the interventions.

15.2 Relevant Research and Evidence of Effectiveness of Interventions

In this section of the chapter, we describe the nature and results of early interventions to provide an understanding of the instructional conditions that need to be in place to prevent reading problems for most students. Owing to space limitations, we focus on a small number of *standardized* interventions that have been evaluated using common standardized measures and that have been demonstrated to powerfully accelerate development in beginning reading skills.

The focal studies we will review are organized in order of increasing intensity, beginning with relatively less intensive standard class-wide interventions, continuing with intensive explicit interventions that supplement implicit classroom instruction, and ending with intensive interventions provided in addition to enhanced explicit classroom instruction. For each study, we describe the children who received intervention, the overall school context, and the nature and effectiveness of the intervention. For the purposes of the chapter, in lieu of a widely accepted performance standard, we consider reading scores above the 30th percentile on a standardized measure a benchmark of success; performance below this benchmark is then an indicator of poor readers who will likely need additional/ongoing intervention services. When available, characteristics of these children are described. Table 15.1 provides a summary of implications for practice that is intended to demonstrate the resources that schools need to carry out the interventions and the proportion of students who are likely to need additional support after the intervention.

15.2.1 Lower Intensity Class-Wide Interventions

To understand how well a low-intensity class-wide peer-mediated intervention can reduce the incidence of reading problems, we examine three recent and related studies (Al Otaiba and Fuchs, 2006; Fuchs, Fuchs, Thompson et al., 2001; McMaster, Fuchs, Fuchs, and Compton, 2005). In each study, Peer Assisted Learning Strategies, or PALS, was an explicit supplement to an implicit core reading program that did not systematically provide instruction that explicitly taught phonemic awareness and phonics. During PALS, teachers provide brief teacher-led reading and reading readiness lessons, and then they pair higher and lower performing readers to practice the lessons together. Converging findings from over a decade of research have shown that teachers and students can conduct PALS with a high degree of fidelity and that PALS has significantly improved reading achievement for beginning readers, including many poor and minority students (Fuchs, Fuchs, Thompson et al., 2001; Mathes, Torgesen, and Allor, 2001; Mathes, Fuchs, Fuchs, Henley, and Sanders, 1994). Denton and Mathes (2003) examined findings related to PALS's success for children estimated to be in the 30% most at risk for reading difficulties based on their performance on pretreatment measures. The percentage of students who remained poor readers in these three studies after receiving the PALS treatment ranged from 18% to 31%. These findings allowed the authors to estimate that, if PALS were available in a broad range of similar classrooms, all but about 5 to 6% of students could be brought to achieve word-level reading scores above the 30th percentile

Fuchs, Fuchs, Thompson et al. (2001) randomly assigned 33 kindergarten teachers in eight urban schools to one of two treatment or control conditions; all students participated (70% attended Title 1 schools; 66% were minorities, roughly 15% of received special education services, and 6% had English as a second language). The 20 week intervention took one of two forms: teachers either provided three 15 minute phonological (first sound identification, rhyming, blending, and segmenting) and print awareness activities selected from *Ladders to Literacy* (or "Ladders"; O'Connor, Notari-Syverson, and Vadasy, 1998) (totaling 15 hours) or a combination of these teacher-directed activities

TABLE 15.1. Summary table of implications for practice.

Study	Interventionist and training	Duration in years; grades	Hours of instruction; sessions per week	Grouping ratio	Diversity of participants; school setting	Reading percentile of participants	Percent reading below 30th percentile	Percent of total population estimated to read below 30th percentile
Low-intensity intervention/implicit classroom instruction								
Al Otaiba and Fuchs, 2006; Fuchs et al., 2001	Classroom teacher; 1 day	2 years; KG-1st grade	35 hrs per year; 3–30 min	Peer tutoring	Diverse participants; Title I and non-Title I schools	nr	nr	Est. 4% Word Attack Est. 2% Word ID
McMaster et al., 2004	Classroom teacher; 1 day	1 year; 1st grade	35 hrs; 3–35 min	Peer tutoring or adult 1:1	Diverse participants; Title I and non-Title I schools	nr	nr	Est. 2% Word ID or Word Attack
High-intensity intervention/implicit classroom instruction								
Vellutino et al., 1996	Teachers; 30 hrs	1 year; 1st grade	35–65 hrs; 5–30 min	1:1	Middle and upper middle SES schools	15	33	5% Basic Skills
Torgesen et al., 1999	Teachers and instructional aides; well-trained	2.5 years; KG-2nd grade	88 hrs; 4–20 min	1:1	Diverse participants; Mixed SES	12	23	4% Word Attack 5% Word ID
Torgesen et al., 2001	Teachers well-trained and computer-assisted	1 year; 1st grade	92 hrs; 4–50 min	1:3	Diverse participants; Mixed SES	18	8	2% Word Attack 2% Word ID
High-intensity intervention/explicit classroom instruction								
Torgesen et al., 2004	Teacher or instructional aide; well-trained	1 year; 1st grade	80 hrs; 5–45 min	1:3 or 1:5	Diverse participants; mixed SES	20	5	1.0% Word Attack 1.5% Word ID 3.2% Comprehension
Mathes et al. 2005	Teachers; 42 hrs	1 year; 1st grade	100 hrs; 5–40 min	1:3	Diverse; non-Title I	20	1–3	<1% Basic Skills

and kindergarten Peer Assisted Learning Strategies (K-PALS; Fuchs, Fuchs, Thompson et al., 2001) (totaling 35 hours). K-PALS activities included phonological awareness, letter-sound and decoding, and sight word training and occurred three times a week for 20 minutes. Ladders and Ladders plus PALS students outperformed controls on phonological measures and Ladders plus PALS children performed best on reading and spelling measures.

The following year, all first-grade teachers in the same eight schools were randomly assigned to first-grade PALS or control conditions. PALS teachers led three 20-minutes sessions a week for 20 weeks. The peer-mediated practice provided phonological awareness, decoding, and sight word training, as well as reading in connected text. PALS students outperformed controls across most measures of reading achievement, with large effects favoring children identified as low achieving at the start of the study.

At the end of first grade, we determined the percentage of students who had received an intervention in either kindergarten or first grade, but still scored below the 30th percentile on a standardized reading measure. Only 2% had low word attack skills and 4% had low word identification skills. Al Otaiba and Fuchs (2006) reported the characteristics that reliably distinguished children who did not benefit from PALS: they scored 1.5 standard deviations (SDs) lower on measures of vocabulary, rapid naming, and problem behavior and 1.0 SD lower on a measure of verbal memory. Thus, a well-implemented peer tutoring program can play an important role in reducing the incidence of reading difficulties for many low-achieving beginning readers in Title 1 schools, but may not be intensive enough to prevent reading problems for children with very low vocabulary, phonological processing deficits, and/or attention and behavior issues. When children's school records were examined at the end of third grade, all but one of these nonresponsive students received special education services in reading (Al Otaiba and Fuchs, 2006).

In the next study (McMaster et al., 2005), first graders who did not benefit (defined as 0.50 SD below average on level of performance and rate of growth) from an initial 7 weeks of intervention (October–December) were randomly assigned to an additional 13 weeks of (a) typical first-grade PALS, (b) modified PALS, or (c) tutoring by an adult. All

three approaches lasted 35 minutes, 3 days per week. The modified PALS condition was somewhat more individualized than typical PALS: letters and sounds were modeled and introduced more slowly. In the tutoring condition, children received one-to-one instruction from a research assistant and the pacing of instruction was tailored to student mastery of skills; as motivation, students graphed their own progress toward instructional goals.

No statistically significant differences favored any of the treatments; however, effect sizes favored tutoring by the adults. McMaster et al. (2005) reported at the end of first grade approximately 2% of PALS, modified PALS, or adult-tutored students performed below the 30th percentile on either word identification or word attack. As McMaster et al. suggested, these students may have needed a longer duration of more intensive instruction than was provided.

15.2.2 More Intensive Interventions as Supplements to Implicit Primary Instruction

To understand the short- and long-term effect of more intensive preventive intervention studies in kindergarten and/or first grade, we examine findings from two teams of researchers led by Vellutino and Torgesen. In an ongoing series of investigations, Vellutino and colleagues have examined the effects of intensive supplemental interventions across time. At the beginning of first grade, Vellutino et al. (1996) selected 118 students from an initial pool of 1284 students in 17 schools. In contrast to the remaining studies in this chapter, students attended schools only in middle to upper socio-economic status (SES) neighborhoods. Students met the following criteria: (a) their teachers nominated them as poor readers, (b) they scored in the lowest 15th percentile on either the word attack or word identification subtests of the *Woodcock Reading Mastery Test–Revised* (WRMT-R; Woodcock, 1998), and (c) they performed above a standard score of 90 on an individually administered intelligence test. Teachers also identified two normal readers from their classrooms and, among these, 65 were selected randomly to participate in a normal reader control group.

Poor readers were tutored daily for 30 minutes over one or two semesters by experienced research staff that were certified teachers and who received 30 hours of training. Treatment sessions were tailored to each student's individual needs, incorporating phonemic awareness, decoding, sight-word practice, comprehension strategies, and reading connected text. The total duration of intervention ranged from 35 to 65 hours. Most of the tutored children (67%) responded well to tutoring after one to two semesters of intervention and were reading on grade level. However, 25 children (approximately 33% of poor readers) were more difficult to remediate and they remained in the lowest 30th percentile on the word attack and word Identification subtests of the WRMT-R.

Vellutino et al. (1996) noted some potentially important pretreatment (kindergarten) characteristics that differentiated the children who were difficult to remediate from children who benefited from tutoring. These children had significantly lower pretreatment scores on phonological tasks (such as segmentation and retrieval) and on syntactic awareness, visual–verbal learning, counting, and number identification and letter naming measures. Because each of these tasks requires encoding in phonological memory, Vellutino et al. (1996) suggested the pattern of their results provides some cautionary evidence that children with severe phonological coding deficits may require more intensive or sustained interventions.

Vellutino and colleagues have followed students in the 1996 study through the end of fourth grade (Vellutino, Scanlon and Jaccard, 2003; Vellutino, Scanlon and Lyon, 2000). The protective effects of tutoring on word reading skills faded somewhat, with the percentage of students achieving within the average range on the basic skill cluster of the WRMT-R falling from 73% to 54%. This decline was steeper for the difficult-to-remediate children.

More encouragingly, in terms of comprehension, the percentage of students scoring on grade level grew between first and fourth grade from 23% to 62%, which suggests that most tutored children had acquired rudimentary comprehension skills. Considering that all children were from upper- and middle-class backgrounds, it is unclear whether this finding would be replicable in schools serving higher proportions of students living in poverty who have more limited vocabulary and conceptual background knowledge.

To learn whether providing earlier (and longer) intervention could further reduce the percentage of

difficult-to-remediate children, we examine findings from Torgesen et al. (1999). This study compared the effects of three intensive one-to-one interventions on the decoding and comprehension skills of beginning readers with very weak phonological skills. Students were identified by December of their kindergarten year who lagged behind in the development of phonemic awareness and letter knowledge. All children in the sample obtained verbal IQ scores above 75, with an average score of 92. The children came from a wide range of socio-economic backgrounds, and were 53% minorities (primarily African American).

The children were randomly assigned to one of four instructional conditions: (1) phonological awareness plus synthetic phonics (PASP), which involved explicit instruction in phonological awareness using articulatory cues plus extensive practice in decontextualized phonetic decoding; (2) embedded phonics, which also provided explicit instruction in phonics but placed more emphasis on applications to reading and writing connected text, along with acquisition of a functional sight vocabulary; (3) a regular classroom support group that received direct tutorial support for the reading instruction provided in the regular classroom; and, (4) a no treatment control group. Children in each of the instructional conditions received one-to-one tutoring in 20 minutes sessions, four days a week for 2.5 years beginning in the second semester of kindergarten. Half the sessions were led by well-trained teachers, and half were led by less well-trained instructional aides; over the entire period of instruction the children received an average of 47 hours of instruction from teachers and 41 hours from aides.

Classroom instruction was "primarily literature based and guided by a whole-language philosophy, with phonics being taught on an as-needed basis rather than systematically" (Torgesen et al., 1999, p. 583). Two of the interventions were both more intensive and more explicit than the classroom instruction; but, since the students received the intervention during their regular reading period, the total time for reading instruction was not different from students who did not receive the interventions. Only the most phonologically explicit method (PASP) produced significantly greater growth in word-level reading skills than students who received no intervention. Although the most explicit instructional method also produced the largest gains in reading comprehension at the end of second grade, these differences among the intervention methods in reading comprehension were not statistically reliable.

Because the interventions in this study were focused specifically on the development of phonemic decoding skills and early reading accuracy (neither vocabulary nor comprehension strategies were explicitly or systematically taught), Torgesen et al. (1999) evaluated the extent to which this level of intervention was sufficient to prevent students from falling seriously behind in these areas. For the most effective intervention, they found that the percentage of the group scoring below the 30th percentile on measures of phonemic decoding and reading accuracy was 30% and 39% respectively. Given that the children in this study were selected to be the 12% most at-risk for reading failure, they estimated that, if the strongest condition from this study were applied more broadly, approximately 4% of children would remain weak in phonemic decoding ability and 5% would perform below the 30th percentile in reading accuracy at the end of second grade, assuming that classroom reading instruction was similar to that received by students in this study.

One study that focused primarily on word-level reading skills in young students at risk for reading disabilities utilized computer software to provide intensive interventions to small groups of first-graders selected to be the 18% most at risk for reading (Torgesen, Wagner, Rashotte, and Herron, 2001). At the beginning of first grade, children were screened using measures of letter knowledge, phonemic awareness, and rapid automatic naming for digits. Participants were selected from the 18% of children obtaining the lowest scores on an index of risk status derived from the screening measures, who also obtained a verbal intelligence score above 80. The sample represented a wide range of SES and contained 35% minorities (primarily African American) with an average verbal intelligence score of 95.5.

Children were randomly assigned to two instructional conditions, and to a no treatment control group. One of the programs was *Auditory Discrimination in Depth* (ADD; Lindamood and Lindamood, 1984), which provided the core instructional methods for the PASP condition in the study just described. In this program, children spend a large amount of time practicing word reading skills out of context, but they also read phonetically controlled text in order to learn how to apply their word reading skills to passages that convey meaning. The other program was *Read, Write, and Type* (RWT; Herron, 1995), which provides explicit instruction and practice in phonological awareness, letter sound correspondences, and phonemic decoding, but does so primarily in the context of encouraging children to express themselves in written language. In this program, children spend a greater proportion of their time processing meaningful written material, and they are encouraged to acquire "phonics" knowledge to enable written communication. The classroom instruction provided to all students in the study was similar to that in the Torgesen et al. (1999) study.

Instruction in both conditions was provided in 50 minutes sessions, 4 days a week from October through May of the first-grade year. Children were taught in groups of three. The first 25 minutes of each session involved teacher-led activities and instruction to prepare children for work on the computer, and the last half of the session involved individual work on the computer using software specifically designed to support the program of instruction. Because the intervention instruction was provided, for the most part, during times other than the regularly scheduled reading block, these interventions represented not only an increase in explicitness and intensity, but also an increase in total amount of time for reading instruction.

Both instructional conditions significantly accelerated growth in reading compared with students from the same classes that did not receive the interventions. Whereas students in the ADD and RWT conditions had begun the year with standard scores (Mean = 100, SD = 15) on a measure of phonemic decoding skill of 74.2 and 74.7 respectively, their scores at the end of the year were 109.7 and 106.3. Corresponding end-of-year standard scores for the reading accuracy measure were 107.1 and 105.1. Within the ADD condition, the percentage of children obtaining scores below the 30th percentile on these measures was 12% (phonemic decoding) and 10% (reading accuracy), while for the RWT group the figures were 20% and 16%. Taking into consideration that the children in this study were the 18% most at risk for reading difficulties, the estimated proportion of the general population from which these children were selected who would remain weak in word reading skills if the ADD intervention were applied more broadly is 2% for both phonemic decoding and reading accuracy, again assuming that classroom instruction was relatively implicit in relationship to word-level reading skills.

15.2.3 Explicit Intervention Delivered as Supplements to Explicit Instruction

Two final studies provide some extremely promising findings about the combined successfulness of explicit instruction and supplemental interventions. The first study (Torgesen et al., 2004) provided a more broadly based intervention (strong focus on word reading accuracy and fluency, but also explicit instruction in vocabulary and comprehension strategies) to first-grade students who were also receiving relatively explicit and systematic instruction during their regular classroom reading block. The study took place in six elementary schools and 23 classrooms, and involved 230 first-grade children who were selected as the 20% most at risk for reading difficulties at the beginning of first grade based on their letter knowledge and phonemic awareness. An additional criterion for admission to the study was estimated verbal IQ above 70 (the final average for students receiving intervention was 93.1). Approximately 40% of the students were African American, and 42% qualified for free and/or reduced price lunch.

Children were randomly assigned to one of four instructional groups or to a "no treatment" group. Children in the treatment groups received instruction in 45 minutes sessions, 5 days a week in groups of either three or five children with either a highly trained, experienced teacher, or a well-trained paraprofessional teacher. The children in the treatment groups were all taught using a highly scripted curriculum based on direct instruction principles, and designed to be consistent with the children's classroom reading curriculum. The intervention included phonemic awareness, decoding, and spelling instruction, and provided cumulative review, practice, and feedback to ensure mastery. Children re-read decodable text to develop fluency and comprehension.

The combination of high-quality classroom instruction and intensive interventions provided in this study was very effective. All of the intervention groups made remarkable progress in reading during the intervention year. Whereas all groups began with word reading ability more than one SD below

average, by the end of the year all the groups were performing above average on this skill. Although the children's estimated level of general verbal ability fell at about the 32nd percentile, their average score on a group test of reading comprehension at the end of first grade was slightly above the 50th percentile. Assuming that these students were the 20% most at risk for reading difficulties in their classes, the authors estimated that, if interventions similar to those used in this study were provided to all students who needed them within similarly strong classroom contexts, only 1% of students would still score below the 30th percentile in phonemic decoding skills at the end of first grade. Similar estimates for students continuing to struggle with reading accuracy and reading comprehension at the end of first grade were 1.5% and 3.2%.

In a second study that provided powerful supplemental interventions in addition to enhanced classroom instruction, the effects of two intensive first-grade supplemental interventions were compared with an enhanced classroom instruction control condition (Mathes et al., 2005). Thirty first-grade teachers and nearly 400 students participated. At the start of first grade, children were screened to identify students at risk who scored in the lowest 20th percentile on the *Texas Primary Reading Inventory* (Texas Education Agency, 1998) and then were randomly assigned to condition. Teachers used core reading programs that were consistent with evidence-based practices, received professional development on using data to differentiate instruction provided by Mathes and staff, and were provided classroom consultation upon request.

Children in both supplemental intervention conditions received daily sessions lasting 40 minutes per day in groups of three students. Both interventions were delivered by trained teachers, and each was conducted with high rates of fidelity. One of the interventions (Proactive) was similar to the intervention described in the study by Torgesen et al. (2004), and the other (Responsive) was equally explicit, but was structured so that instruction was guided by student need rather than a preplanned sequence. The results indicated that children in both of the supplemental intervention conditions made significantly more growth than students in the classroom condition on measures of phonological awareness, word reading, and passage fluency, and effect sizes were moderate to large. Although the children in both intervention groups performed comparably on most posttreatment outcome measures, there were some minor differences in performance for students related to differences in the two supplemental interventions. Students in the Proactive program received more code-focused instruction; at the end of the year, their effect sizes (compared with controls) on phonological awareness, untimed word reading, nonword reading fluency, and word attack skills were higher than students in the Responsive condition. By contrast, students in the Responsive intervention focused more on practicing reading skills in connected text and achieved higher effect sizes at the end of the year on oral reading fluency. Mathes et al. (2005) reported that, at the end of the study, 16% of students in the classroom condition, 7% of the Responsive students, and only 1% of the Proactive students were still below the 30th percentile on basic skills. Thus, given that the sample was drawn from the lowest 20th percentile, the number of poor readers was reduced to about 3% in the enhanced classroom instruction and less than 1% in responsive or proactive intervention conditions.

15.3 Lessons Learned and Some Important Limitations

The studies we have considered suggest that schools, if they applied powerful interventions combined with explicit core reading programs within an RTI framework, could reduce the percentage of children who remain poor readers (word-level reading skills below the 30th percentile) to about 1% by the end of first or second grade. Because the samples in these studies came from a broad cross-section of students with regard to demographic characteristics, these findings are startlingly different from current data indicating that more than half of poor and minority students are not reading even at basic levels by the end of fourth grade.

An important finding replicated across several of the studies is that initial response to interventions may serve as an important "first cut diagnostic" (Vellutino et al., 1996, p. 114), in that children who respond well to even brief or less-intensive interventions frequently maintain a trajectory of stronger reading growth than children who were more difficult to remediate. In several studies, there appeared

to be a strong association between initial status, especially on phonological awareness, letter naming, vocabulary knowledge, and problem behavior, on reading development (Al Otaiba and Fuchs, 2006; Mathes et al., 2005; Vellutino et al., 1996, 2003).

The intensity of standardized interventions provided in the studies present a challenge for school personnel to deploy the necessary resources to prevent reading problems in all students. Clearly, just enhancing classroom instruction is not enough for children who begin school with the lowest skills; yet ,encouragingly, a variety of interventions that provide common components (phonemic awareness, phonics, and fluency) powerfully accelerated development in early word reading skills. However, to date, most of the intensive interventions have been conducted by well-trained project staff rather than school personnel and even researchers who did train classroom teachers to implement intervention provided considerable support. Furthermore, very few of these early prevention studies have followed children to third and fourth grade or attempted to examine "success" in terms of passing rates on statewide group-administered comprehension tests. Given that these latter tests require a much broader range of knowledge and skill than the word-level tests used to estimate success rates in this review, it is likely that poor and minority students, in particular, will not achieve the same success rates on them as for the simpler tests that assess only word reading accuracy.

Another limitation of the current research is that we still know little about how best to support the development of vocabulary, conceptual knowledge, reading comprehension, and thinking skills or how to address motivational or behavior management issues. Although Vellutino et al. (2003) found that tutored children continued to improve their comprehension skills from the first to fourth grade, these children were from upper and middle SES backgrounds. We found no demonstrations that students at high risk of reading problems because of low vocabulary were "normalized" in vocabulary or comprehension by grade three. In conclusion, the results of the studies we have summarized in this chapter demonstrate that we have learned many lessons about the conditions that need to be in place to substantially reduce word-level reading problems. What we know less about are the instructional conditions that need to be in place to insure that all students are prepared to meet the requirements for comprehending the more complex texts that they begin to experience in late elementary school, middle, and high school.

References

Adams, M. J. (1990). *Beginning to Read: Thinking and Learning About Print*. Cambridge, MA: MIT Press.

Al Otaiba, S. & Fuchs, D. (2006). Who are the young children for whom best practices in reading are ineffective? An experimental and longitudinal study. *Journal of Learning Disabilities, 39*, 414–431

Beck, I. L., McKeown, M. G. & Kucan, L. (2002). *Bringing Words to Life: Robust Vocabulary Instruction*. New York: The Guilford Press.

Brown, A. L., Palincsar, A. S., & Purcell, L. (1986). *Poor Readers: Teach, Don't Label. The School Achievement of Minority Children: New Perspectives* (pp. 105–143). Hillsdale, NJ: Lawrence Erlbaum Associates.

Cunningham, A. E. & Stanovich, K. E. (1998). What reading does for the mind. *American Educator, 22*(Spring/Summer), 8–15.

Denton, C. A. & Mathes, P. G. (2003). Intervention for struggling readers: possibilities and challenges. In B. R. Foorman (Ed.). *Preventing and Remediating Reading Difficulties: Bringing Science to Scale* (229–252). Baltimore, MD: York.

Elbaum, B., Vaughn, S., Hughes, M. T. & Moody, S. W. (2000). How effective are one-to-one tutoring programs in reading for elementary students at risk for reading failure? A meta-analysis of the intervention research. *Journal of Educational Psychology, 92*, 605–619.

Foorman, B. R., Francis, D. J., Fletcher, J. M., Schatschneider, C., & Mehta, P. (1998). The role of instruction in learning to read: preventing reading failure in at-risk children. *Journal of Educational Psychology, 90*, 37–55.

Foorman, B. R. & Torgesen, J. (2001). Critical elements of classroom and small-group instruction promote reading success in all children. *Learning Disabilities Research & Practice, 16*, 203–212.

Francis, D. J., Shaywitz, S. E., Stuebing, K. K., Shaywitz, B. A., & Fletcher, J. M. (1996). Developmental lag versus deficit model of reading disability: a longitudinal, individual growth curve analysis. *Journal of Educational Psychology, 88*, 3–17.

Fuchs, L. S., Fuchs, D., Hosp, M., & Jenkins, J. R. (2001). Oral reading fluency as an indicator of reading competence: a theoretical, empirical, and historical analysis. *Scientific Studies of Reading, 5*, 239–256.

Fuchs, D., Fuchs, L. S., Thompson, A., Al Otaiba, S., Yen, L., Yang, N., et al. (2001). Is reading important in reading-readiness programs? A randomized field trial with teachers as program implementers. *Journal of Educational Psychology, 93*, 251–267.

Hart, B. & Risley, T. R. (1995). *Meaningful Differences in the Everyday Experiences of Young American Children*. Baltimore: Brookes.

Herron, J. (1995). *Read, Write, & Type!* Freemont, CA: The Learning Company.

Juel, C. (1988). Learning to read and write: a longitudinal study of 54 children from first through fourth grades. *Journal of Educational Psychology, 80*, 437–447.

Lou, Y., Abrami, P. C., Spence, J. C., Poulsen, C., Chambers, B. & d'Apollonia, S. (1996). Within-class grouping: a meta-analysis. *Review of Educational Research, 66*, 423–458.

Mathes, P. G., Denton, C. A., Fletcher, J. M., Anthony, J. L., Francis, D. J., & Schatschneider, C. (2005). An evaluation of two reading interventions derived from diverse models. *Reading Research Quarterly, 39*, 450–480.

Mathes, P. G., Fuchs, D., Fuchs, L. S., Henley, A. M. & Sanders, A. (1994). Increasing strategic reading practice with Peabody classwide peer tutoring. *Learning Disabilities Research and Practice, 9*, 44–48.

Mathes, P. G., Torgesen, J. K., & Allor, J. H. (2001). The effects of peer-assisted literacy strategies for first-grade readers with and without additional computer assisted instruction in phonological awareness. *American Educational Research Journal, 38*, 371–410.

McMaster, K. L., Fuchs, D., Fuchs, L. S., & Compton, D. L. (2005). Responding to nonresponders: an experimental field trial of identification and intervention methods. *Exceptional Children, 71*, 445–463.

NAEP (2005). Retrieved January 19, 2006, from http://nces.ed.gov/nationsreportcard/.

Nation, K. (2005). Picture naming and developmental reading disorders. *Journal of Research in Reading, 28*, 28–38.

National Reading Panel (2000). Report of the National Reading Panel. Washington, DC: National Institute of Child Health and Development (www. natonalreadingpanel.org).

O'Connor, R. E., Notari-Syverson, A., & Vadasy, P. F. (1998). *Ladders to Literacy: A Kindergarten Activity Book*. Baltimore, MD: Paul Brookes.

Raynor, K., Foorman, B. R., Perfetti, C. A., Pesetsky, D., & Seidenberg, M. S. (2001). How psychological science informs the teaching of reading. *Psychological Science in the Public Interest, 2*, 31–73.

Share, D. L. & Stanovich, K. E. (1995). Cognitive process in early reading development: a model of acquisition and individual differences. *Issues in Education: Contributions from Educational Psychology, 1*, 1–57.

Snow, C. E. (2002). *Reading for Understanding: Toward an R & D Program for Comprehension.* Santa Monica, CA: RAND.

Snow, C. E., Burns, M. S., & Griffin, P. (Eds.) (1998). *Preventing Reading Difficulties in Young Children.* Washington, DC: National Academy Press.

Swanson, H. L., Hoskyn, M., & Lee, C. (1999). *Interventions for Students with Learning Disabilities: A Meta-Analysis of Treatment Outcomes.* Guilford: New York.

Texas Education Agency (1998). *Texas Primary Reading Inventory.* Austin, TX: Texas Education Agency.

Torgesen, J. K. (2005). Remedial interventions for students with dyslexia: national goals and current accomplishments. In S. Richardson & J. Gilger (Eds.), *Research-Based Education and Intervention: What We Need to Know* (pp. 103–124). Boston: International Dyslexia Association.

Torgesen, J. K., Alexander, A. W., Wagner, R. K., Rashotte, C. A., Voeller, K., Conway, T. et al. (2001). Intensive remedial instruction for children with severe reading disabilities: immediate and long-term outcomes from two instructional approaches. *Journal of Learning Disabilities, 34,* 33–58.

Torgesen, J. K. & Burgess, S. R. (1998). Consistency of reading-related phonological processes throughout early childhood: evidence from longitudinal-correlational and instructional studies. In J. Metsala & L. Ehri (Eds.), *Word Recognition in Beginning Reading* (pp. 161–188). Hillsdale, NJ: Lawrence Erlbaum.

Torgesen, J. K., Mathes, P. G., Rashotte, C. A., Menchetti, J. C., Grek, M. L., Robinson, C. S., et al. (2004). Effects of teacher training and group size on reading outcomes for first grade children at-risk for reading difficulties. Florida State University and Florida Center for Reading Research, Tallahassee, FL.

Torgesen, J. K., Rashotte, C. A., Wagner, R. K., Herron, J. & Lindamood, P. (2003). A comparison of two computer assisted approaches to the prevention of reading disabilities in young children. Unpublished manuscript, Florida State University, Tallahassee.

Torgesen, J. K., Wagner, R. K., Rashotte, C. A., Lindamood, P., Rose, E., Conway, T., et al. (1999). Preventing reading failure in young children with phonological processing disabilities: group and individual responses to instruction. *Journal of Educational Psychology, 91,* 579–593.

Vellutino, F. R., Scanlon, D. M., & Jaccard, J. (2003). Toward distinguishing between cognitive and experiential deficits as primary sources of difficulty in learning to read: a two-year follow-up of difficult to remediate and readily remediated poor readers. In B. R. Foorman (Ed.), *Preventing and Remediating Reading Difficulties. Bringing Science to Scale* (pp. 73–120). Baltimore: York Press.

Vellutino, F. R., Scanlon, D. M., & Lyon, G. R. (2000). Differentiating between difficult-to-remediate and readily remediated poor readers. *Journal of Learning Disabilities, 33,* 223–238.

Vellutino, F. R., Scanlon, D. M., Sipay, E. R., Small, S., Chen, R., Pratt, A., et al. (1996). Cognitive profiles of difficult-to-remediate and readily remediated poor readers: early intervention as a vehicle for distinguishing between cognitive and experiential deficits as basic causes of specific reading disability. *Journal of Educational Psychology, 88,* 601–638.

Whitehurst, G. J. & Lonigan, C. J. (1998). Child development and emergent literacy. *Child Development, 69,* 335–357.

Wigfield, A. & Guthrie, J. T. (1997). Relations of children's motivation for reading to the amount and breadth of their reading. *Journal of Educational Psychology, 89,* 420–432.

Woodcock, R. W. (1998). *Woodcock Reading Mastery Tests—Revised: Normative Update.* Bloomington, MN: Pearson Assessments.

16
Monitoring Response to General Education Instruction

Kristen L. McMaster and Dana Wagner

Kristen L. McMaster, PhD, is an Assistant Professor in Special Education at the University of Minnesota.
mcmas004@umn.edu
Dana Wagner is a doctoral candidate in Special Education at the University of Minnesota. wagn0244@umn.edu

The purpose of this chapter is to describe a critical component of the response-to-intervention (RTI) process: monitoring student response to general education instruction. First, we discuss the importance of the role of general educators in monitoring students' response to intervention. Second, we provide the conceptual framework for an RTI model within which general educators play a critical role in identifying students at risk and monitoring their progress during classroom-based instruction. Third, we describe specific approaches for each of the steps included in this model. We then illustrate this process using a case example from research. We end with a summary of recommendations for general educators, and emphasize the need for further research if RTI is to be adopted as part of the special education identification process.

16.1 Importance of Monitoring Student Response to General Education Instruction

Current educational reforms place increasing emphasis on the role of general educators in ensuring that *all* students progress toward high academic standards. Provisions of the *No Child Left Behind Act* (NCLB, 2002) stress that schools must work to close achievement gaps, placing heavy emphasis on evidence-based instruction, early intervention, and accountability. Under NCLB, schools must show that all students are making "adequate yearly progress" as determined by state-defined measures

of academic achievement. Schools that do not meet accountability standards may face tough sanctions.

The recent reauthorization of the *Individuals with Disabilities Education Act* (IDEA, 2004) aligns closely with these standards-based reforms. IDEA also emphasizes early, preventative intervention and accountability. Further, IDEA allows local education agencies to use RTI in place of traditional discrepancy models for identifying students with learning disabilities. This approach involves early identification of students at risk, progress monitoring, and implementation of increasingly intensive levels of intervention when best practices in the general education classroom do not appear beneficial. Only those students who do not make adequate progress despite intervention continue on to special education referral.

If schools and districts are to adopt RTI as a way to address student learning difficulties, then general educators must be prepared to play a pivotal role in this process. They will likely work with a team responsible for administering and using screening data to identify students at risk of academic failure, implementing instruction to maximize those students' likelihood of making progress in the general classroom, and monitoring students' progress to evaluate the effectiveness of instruction and decide when a student may be in need of more intensive intervention. All of this will require general educators to make data-based decisions using sound assessment practices, implement effective classroom instructional practices with integrity, and differentiate instruction for students at risk of failure.

16.2 Conceptual Framework

A major assumption of RTI is that it is necessary to establish that academic difficulties experienced by the child cannot be attributed to lack of effective instruction (Fuchs and Fuchs, 1998; Heller, Holtzman, and Messick, 1982; Vellutino et al., 1996). Therefore, it is critical that the child has the opportunity to profit from generally effective instruction. If many students in the general education classroom are not making progress under existing instructional conditions, then a necessary first step is to put into place instructional practices that are beneficial to most students. However, if most students in the classroom are thriving academically, then one can infer that the instruction is generally effective and that the child who is not making sufficient progress requires more intensive or individualized instruction to address specific academic difficulties. Continued difficulties despite more intensive, individualized instruction targeting critical skill areas may indicate that a child requires special education services (Fuchs, 2003; Fuchs and Fuchs, 1998; Vellutino et al., 1996).

Two general models of RTI have emerged from this assumption (see Fuchs, 2003). One model conceptualizes RTI as response to intensive, preventative intervention. In this model, students identified as at risk are immediately placed in a specialized intervention program provided in small groups by a specialist (e.g., Torgesen et al, 2001; Vellutino et al., 1996). Those who continue to perform at low levels or make very little growth despite intervention are deemed unresponsive to intervention and are candidates for special education.

The second RTI model is rooted in general education (Fuchs, 2003; Fuchs and Fuchs, 1998; Speece, Case, and Molloy, 2003), in that high-quality general classroom instruction is provided to students at risk before the decision is made to implement more intensive intervention. This model relies on three critical assumptions. The first assumption is that academic outcomes vary across learners, such that some students will make more progress and achieve at higher levels than others. Hence, low-performing students may not necessarily be unresponsive to instruction: they may just fall at the lower end of the continuum of academic ability. This leads to the second assump-

tion: If lower performing students are making good progress within general education instruction, then they are probably benefiting from that instruction. In such a case, no alternative interventions would seem necessary because it is unlikely that different instruction would yield better growth. On the other hand, in an environment in which most children are progressing, a low-performing student who is making little or no progress can be assumed to be unresponsive to general education instruction, and alternative instructional methods may be warranted.

The third assumption is that, if low performers are demonstrating little or no growth and a majority of their classmates are also demonstrating little or no growth, the adequacy of the general instruction should be questioned and steps to improve the overall quality of this instruction should be taken. Only when most students are making progress can decisions about individual responsiveness be made. In this chapter, we focus on monitoring student response to instruction as conceptualized by this second model, because it emphasizes effective instruction for all, reserving resources for more intensive instruction for students who are not benefiting from general instruction.

In the RTI model described in this chapter, progress monitoring occurs within increasingly intensive "tiers" of intervention, which should help establish whether a student's academic difficulties can be attributed to an underlying disability (Fuchs and Fuchs, 2006). Tier 1 consists of general classroom instruction that at least reflects sound teaching practices, and at best consists of evidence-based instructional programs implemented with integrity and supported by strong professional development (Fuchs and Fuchs, 2005a). Tier 2 is provided to students for whom Tier 1 is not beneficial, as evidenced by inadequate growth within a set period (e.g., 8 to 10 weeks). Tier 2 is more intensive, in that it is provided in small groups, is conducted more frequently or for longer periods, includes explicit instruction targeting specific skill areas, and/or is delivered by a specialist (Fuchs and Fuchs, 2005a). Subsequent tiers are implemented with students for whom Tier 2 does not effect sufficient progress, are even more intensive, and may lead to special education referral or are provided *within* special education.

16.3 Approaches to Monitoring Response to General Education Instruction

Specific steps in the RTI process include (1) screening students to identify those at risk of failing to meet important academic standards, (2) monitoring those students' response to general education (Tier 1) instruction and (3) identifying students in need of more individualized or intensive (Tier 2) intervention. After identifying children in need of more intensive services, specific interventions within Tier 2 are selected and implemented, and response to the interventions is monitored. Within each of these steps, general educators play an important role that should be supported by special educators, school psychologists, and administrators. Below, we describe specific components of each step.

16.3.1 Step 1: Screening

In the proposed RTI framework, general educators are responsible for screening students to identify those at risk of failing to meet grade-level expectations (Fuchs and Fuchs, 2005a). Screening allows schools to quickly identify problems and intervene early, which increases the likelihood that academic difficulties will be successfully remediated (Juel, 1988; Francis, Shaywitz, Stuebing, Shaywitz, and Fletcher, 1996). Screening approaches vary, and may include the use of high-stakes assessments, standardized achievement tests, or other assessment tools, such as general outcome measures shown to predict achievement in important academic areas. Below, we briefly discuss each approach and the criteria for determining risk status.

16.3.1.1 High-Stakes Assessments

One screening option is for schools to use results obtained from high-stakes state or district assessments. High-stakes assessment data may be useful for at least two reasons. First, many of these tests have reasonable technical adequacy (e.g., Minnesota Department of Education, 2003). Second, the data are already available, as they are typically collected at the end of the school year. End-of-year data might be used the following fall by the next grade-level team. For example, fourth-grade teachers may use

end-of-year third-grade test results to screen their incoming students.

Potential downfalls to using end-of-year high-stakes assessment data include the possibility that not all students will have taken the test in the spring. New students to a district may enter with results from different tests with different normative groups. Moreover, student skill levels may change over the summer in different ways (Cooper, Nye, Carlton, Lindsay, and Greathouse, 1996). For example, the effects of one student's summer experiences, such as hours of daily academic tutoring, could be positive academic growth, whereas the effects of another student's summer experiences, such as hours of daily video gaming, could be negative academic growth, or regression. For these reasons, screening data collected at the beginning of the school year may be a better choice. An alternate form of an end-of-year high-stakes test could be given to all students at the beginning of the school year; however, development of technically adequate alternate forms is resource intensive.

16.3.1.2 Standardized Achievement Tests

Alternatively, some norm-referenced standardized achievement tests, such as the *Woodcock–Johnson Achievement Battery–III* (Woodcock and Johnson, 1989) and the *Wechsler Individual Achievement Test–II* (Psychological Corporation, 2001), are reasonable choices for their technical adequacy and direct assessment of multiple skills within an academic domain (Fletcher, Francis, Morris and Lyon, 2005). However, a potential drawback to using standardized tests is that they are expensive, are often individually administered, and can require a substantial amount of training and time.

16.3.1.3 General Outcome Measures

Another screening alternative is the use of general outcome measures that sample a broad range of skills related to a given academic domain (Deno, Fuchs, Marston, and Shin, 2001) providing a global index of student proficiency (Deno, 1992). One of the most well-known, well-researched general outcome measurement approaches is curriculum-based measurement (CBM; Deno, 1985). CBM employs standardized administration and scoring methods that yield accurate, meaningful information about student performance (Fuchs and Deno, 1991). Researchers have demonstrated criterion validity of CBM with widely used standardized assessments and state standards tests (e.g., Crawford, Tindal, and Stieber, 2001; Hosp and Fuchs, 2005; Marston, 1989; Stage and Jacobsen, 2001), as well as test–retest, alternate-form, and interrater reliability (e.g., Marston, 1989). Because CBM can produce a broad dispersion of scores across students of the same age, with rank orderings that correspond to important external criteria, it is a good candidate for use as a screening tool.

Another benefit of using CBM for screening is that it can be administered with relative ease and efficiency. For example, in reading, a 1-min timed oral reading task has been demonstrated to be a reliable and valid indicator of overall reading proficiency (Marston, 1989). CBM is also designed to be administered repeatedly, using alternate forms of equivalent difficulty (see Deno et al., 2001). Thus, CBM can be administered multiple times during the school year. A benefit to collecting screening data multiple times during the year is that schools may "catch" students who were not initially identified as at risk but who, as the year progresses, fail to make adequate growth and thus require more intensive intervention.

16.3.1.4 Criteria for Risk Status

In addition to selecting screening tools, criteria for risk status must be established. Currently, there is not a consensus regarding what these criteria should be. One approach involves using normative data to establish a percentile below which risk status is determined. For example, all students scoring below the 25th percentile may be considered at risk (Fletcher et al., 2005; Fuchs and Fuchs, 2005a). A potential problem with this method is that, by definition, there will always be students who fall in the lowest percentile, and will thus always appear at risk, regardless of their performance level (Torgesen, 2000).

Alternatively, absolute performance levels, or benchmarks, may be used to determine risk status (e.g., Good, Simmons, and Kame'enui, 2001). For example, third-graders who score below the reading benchmark of 70 words read correctly per minute at the beginning of the school year may be considered at risk. Benchmarks may be based on na-

tional or local data, and can be determined by using inferential statistics to calculate scores that predict later success, such as meeting end-of-year academic standards or passing high-stakes tests (Hintze and Silberglitt, 2005; Good et al., 2001).

16.3.2 Step 2: Monitoring Progress to Tier 1 Instruction

16.3.2.1 Implementing Tier 1 Instruction

Within an RTI model rooted in general education, it is the responsibility of general educators to ensure that generally effective instruction is in place before a student may qualify for special education services (Fuchs, 2003; Fuchs and Fuchs, 1998). In other words, the student must have received high-quality, evidence-based classroom instruction, referred to as Tier 1 instruction. We suggest the use of an evidence-based core curriculum, supplemented as needed with additional evidence-based strategies or programs.

A core curriculum is comprehensive, covering all necessary grade-level skills in an academic area. It contains lessons that meet short-term objectives that align with overall curricular goals, and thus meets the grade-level needs of the majority of students. Schools or individual teachers may also choose to implement supplemental instructional programs to emphasize critical skills addressed in the core curriculum. Supplemental programs should align with core curriculum objectives, provide students with practice or application of critical skills, and be supported by scientific evidence of their effectiveness.

"Evidence-based" refers to a practice for which scientific evidence obtained through research has shown positive effects on student outcomes. A school should consider adopting core curricula and supplemental programs that have undergone rigorous research and shown positive results. Peer-reviewed journals are a good source for identifying such practices. Within peer-reviewed journals, some studies more appropriately test instructional practices than others. Studies that use a group design with random assignment to intervention and comparison groups are currently considered the gold standard (e.g., Gersten et al., 2005). In determining whether to adopt a particular instructional program, schools should also be especially attentive to the population of students on whom the program was evaluated, as well as the context in which it was implemented successfully (Klingner and Edwards, 2006). Just because a program is empirically supported does not ensure that it will be equally effective across different schools, classrooms, and students. Thus, attending to information about participants and settings included in the research should be central to decisions about which programs to implement.

Examples of instructional programs that do have substantial empirical support include direct instruction programs that emphasize student acquisition of basic academic skills, such as reading and math (Carnine, Silbert and Kame'enui, 1990; Stein, Silbert and Carnine, 1997). In addition, there is substantial support for peer-mediated instructional programs such as classwide peer tutoring (Delquadri, Greenwood, Whorton, Carta, and Hall, 1986) and peer-assisted learning strategies (PALS; Fuchs, Fuchs, Mathes, and Simmons, 1997) that are designed to enhance critical skills and concepts taught in reading, mathematics, spelling, and content areas. Comprehensive reviews such as the report of the National Reading Panel (2000) and databases such as the What Works Clearinghouse (US Department of Education, 2002) provide summaries of other such programs that schools may consider using. Finally, schools can learn about core curricula and supplemental instruction from other schools with good academic outcomes. Morningside Academy is one example of a school where research-based instructional practices are applied system-wide and student achievement levels and growth rates are high (Johnson and Street, 2004).

16.3.2.2 Fidelity of Tier 1 Instruction

Once evidence-based, Tier 1 instruction is in place, the integrity with which it is implemented, or fidelity, must be monitored (Fletcher et al., 2005). If Tier 1 instruction is implemented poorly and several students in the classroom fail to progress toward grade-level expectations, then the assumption that generally effective instruction is in place is compromised. To assess fidelity, an outside observer directly observes specific, operationally defined teacher and student behaviors based on a task analysis of the instructional program. This task analysis might take the form of a checklist of all components that should be included in the lesson. Operational definitions minimize subjectivity, such that multiple observers can independently observe instruction and agree on the behaviors that occurred. Lead teachers, administrators, and school psychologists are all good candidates for conducting fidelity observations. Fidelity observations would ideally include immediate feedback and follow-up coaching or mentoring activities for teachers (Fletcher et al., 2005; O'Shaughnessy, Lane, Gresham, and Beebe-Frankenberger, 2003).

It is important to note that initiating and maintaining change in the beliefs and practices of educators is complex, and it may take several years to fully implement and observe the benefits of evidence-based practices (Fuchs and Fuchs, 1998; Stanovich and Stanovich, 1997). To increase the likelihood of good implementation fidelity and sustainability of such practices, schools should ensure that appropriate professional development and support, such as adequate training and follow-up, team planning, and mentoring, are in place (Gersten, Chard and Baker, 2000; O'Shaughnessy et al., 2003). When fidelity is low, it is important to examine why this low fidelity is occurring and to determine the best ways to support teachers in improving their implementation (Klingner and Edwards, 2006).

16.3.2.3 Progress Monitoring

Implementation of Tier 1 instruction is not only a means of providing all students in the general education classroom, including those at risk, with presumably effective instruction, but is also an important assessment component within an RTI framework (Fuchs and Fuchs, 2006). Once Tier 1 instruction is in place, students identified as at risk should be monitored regularly to determine responsiveness to general education. Students who do not make sufficient progress in Tier 1 move on to Tier 2. The current recommended time-period for monitoring response to general education instruction is 8–10 weeks (Fuchs and Fuchs, 2005a; Vaughn, Linan-Thompson, and Hickman, 2003).

Different approaches have been used to monitor student response to instruction. Some have used standardized testing. For example, Vellutino et al. (1996) used pre- and post-intervention performance on the Woodcock reading mastery test–revised (Woodcock, 1987) to estimate at-risk student responsiveness. Students who made the least progress were identified as needing more intensive intervention. A drawback of using standardized tests is that most are not sensitive to growth made in very brief periods, and indeed were not designed for this purpose.

Others have used measures designed specifically for progress monitoring, such as CBM, to monitor student progress on a frequent basis (e.g., McMaster, Fuchs, Fuchs, and Compton, 2005; Speece et al., 2003; Vaughn et al., 2003). As described earlier, researchers have established CBM's technical adequacy as a general indicator of students' overall proficiency in core academic domains. CBM is also useful for documenting progress over brief periods (Deno et al., 2001). Multiple CBM probes of equivalent difficulty can be administered repeatedly (e.g., once per week), yielding a reliable estimate of growth (e.g., Fuchs, Fuchs, Hamlett, Walz, and Germann, 1993). Currently, CBM is viewed as one of the more promising and viable approaches to monitoring students' response to instruction (Fuchs, 2003; Speece and Case, 2001) because of its capacity to model academic growth and inform evaluation of instructional effectiveness (Fuchs and Fuchs, 1998; Vaughn and Fuchs, 2003).

Whereas CBM has a well-established empirical basis for monitoring student progress, it is important to note that it is not necessarily "RTI ready." Historically, special education teachers have used CBM to set long-term goals, monitor student progress toward those goals, assess the effectiveness of instruction for individual students, and make instructional changes when needed. This use of CBM data has been demonstrated to result in improvements in student achievement (e.g., Fuchs, Fuchs, Hamlett, and Stecker, 1991). However, RTI requires that progress monitoring data be used to make high-stakes decisions that can determine the course of a child's entire school career. For this reason it is critical that CBM, or other progress-monitoring tools, are technically adequate for making such decisions in relatively brief timeframes. Thus, whether CBM is appropriate for making high-stakes decisions in a relatively brief time period, as RTI would require, remains an important question.

One major concern that has been raised is the amount of measurement error associated with estimating growth across brief intervals (e.g., Hintze, Shapiro, and Daly, 1998; Jenkins, Zumeta, Dupree, and Johnson, 2005). For example, Jenkins et al. questioned the assumption that oral reading passages drawn from a pool of grade-level passages are truly "equivalent" and suggested that measurement error introduced by varying passage difficulties could compromise estimates of student growth across short time intervals. There is some evidence that exerting tight control of passage readability (Hintze and Christ; 2004) or even using identical passages (Jenkins et al., 2005) can reduce this measurement error; however, whether this reduction in error is sufficient for accurately estimating response to instruction requires further investigation. Moreover, error associated with other variables, such as within-student variability, may also compromise accuracy in estimating response to instruction (Jenkins et al., 2005). Thus, while CBM is promising in many ways, we recommend caution in its use for RTI decisions.

16.3.3 Step 3: Identifying Students in Need of Tier 2 Instruction

Researchers have operationalized response to instruction in various ways. Fuchs (2003) identified three general approaches: the final status approach, the growth approach, and the dual discrepancy approach. Researchers who have used the final status approach defined inadequate response as performance below a given percentile (e.g., the 16th percentile) on a given measure (e.g., Torgesen et al., 2001; Vellutino et al., 1996). Researchers who have used the growth approach defined inadequate response as no growth (e.g., Berninger et al., 1999) or limited growth (e.g., Vellutino et al., 1996).

There are some conceptual problems related to these two approaches (Al Otaiba and Fuchs, 2002). For example, although a child's performance level may be very low, they may be making important growth. Using a final status approach without considering growth could mask the student's responsiveness to instruction. Likewise, using growth alone ignores information about a child's performance relative to meaningful educational benchmarks. A child may be making steady progress, but may still be performing at such a low level that they will not likely reach an adequate performance level in a timely manner.

An alternative to final status and growth-rate-only methods is the dual discrepancy approach (Fuchs, 2003; Fuchs and Fuchs, 1998), whereby students who are discrepant from their peers in both performance level *and* growth rate would be considered in need of more intensive instruction. Researchers have provided some evidence that this approach discriminates well between readers who do and do not respond to instruction (e.g., Burns and Senesac, 2005; McMaster et al, 2005; Speece and Case, 2001). Others are testing its utility by comparing it with alternative procedures, like median split, normalized, and benchmark scores (see Fuchs, 2003). Continued research is needed to determine the best approach to gauging responsiveness to instruction.

Criteria for adequate performance levels and/or growth rates should be set a priori. Currently, there is not a consensus on grade-level performance and growth standards (Deno et al., 2001). School districts can begin by establishing criteria that are correlated with end-of-year high-stakes test results. Expected levels and rates, when calculated by individual districts, will vary. As further research is conducted and published in this area, national norms may be established.

16.4 Case Example

To illustrate the application of steps in the RTI process described above within a school context, we included a case example to show how: (1) screening data were used to identify students at risk; (2) Tier 1 instruction was implemented and student progress was monitored; and (3) progress monitoring data were used to identify a need for Tier 2 instruction.

Recently, McMaster et al. (2005) reported a study of students' response to first-grade PALS (Fuchs and Fuchs, 2005b), an evidence-based classwide peer-tutoring program focusing on critical beginning reading skills. Some of the students identified as unresponsive to PALS received Tier 2 intervention in the form of a standard tutoring protocol (other students either continued in PALS or participated in a modified version of PALS; see McMaster et al. (2005) for specific details). Figure 16.1 illustrates the progress of four at-risk students who participated in this study.

16.4.1 Screening

At the beginning of the study, students were screened using a rapid letter naming (RLN) test,

a good predictor of future reading achievement (Torgesen, Wagner, and Rashotte, 1997). Students' RLN scores were rank-ordered, and the rankings were confirmed by the students' teachers. The eight lowest performing readers in each class were identified as at risk and four average-performers were identified in each class to serve as a comparison.

16.4.2 Tier 1 Instruction and Progress Monitoring

Tier 1 instruction (PALS) was implemented three times per week for 35 min per session. PALS activities include letter-sound recognition, decoding, sight word recognition, and fluency building. Teachers pair higher performing readers with lower performing readers. The higher reader is always the tutor or "Coach" first, and the lower reader is the "Reader" first. For each activity, the Coach provides prompts, praise, and corrective feedback to the Reader. After completing each activity, the students switch roles.

For the first 2 months of PALS, the at-risk and average-performing students' progress was monitored weekly using CBM word identification probes. These probes were equivalent forms of 100 sight words selected randomly from Dolch word lists. The number of words read correctly in 1 min was recorded for each student. Performance levels and slopes on the CBM probes were calculated for each of the at-risk and average readers.

16.4.3 Identification of Students in Need of Tier 2 Intervention

After 2 months of PALS, students were identified as needing Tier 2 intervention if they were dually discrepant from their average-performing peers. In this case example, dual discrepancy was defined as a CBM performance level and slope that were both approximately one standard deviation (SD) below average. Figure 16.1 displays the growth rates of two at-risk students during the first 2 months of PALS. Student B was eventually *not* identified for Tier 2 intervention. Although her CBM performance level was well below average, her growth rate was similar to that of her peers. In contrast, Student C's performance level and slope were 1.25 SD and 1.17 SD

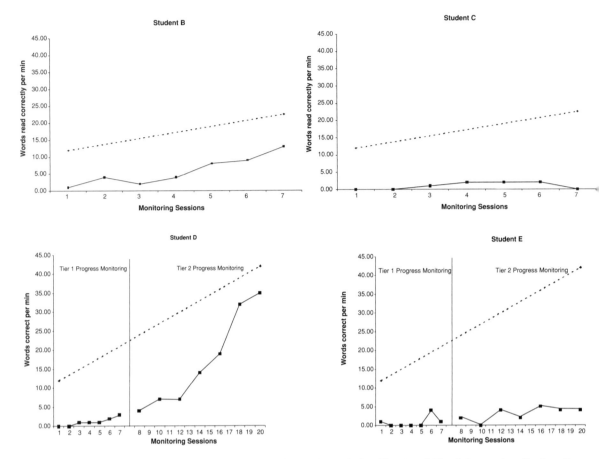

FIGURE 16.1. Case example: CBM performance of at-risk students during Tier 1 and Tier 2 instruction. Student B was identified as responsive to Tier 1, and Student C was identified as unresponsive. Student D was identified as responsive to Tier 2, and Student E was identified as unresponsive.

below average, respectively. Thus, Student C qualified for Tier 2 intervention.

The Tier 2 intervention consisted of tutoring three times each week for 35 min per session, but adult instead of peer tutors were used. The tutors were trained to teach students to mastery. The student determined how many sounds and words they needed to master and then charted this goal at the end of each lesson.

As shown in Figure 16.1, following 13 weeks of tutoring, Student D was performing at a level of 0.58 SD below average, but his growth rate was 0.24 SD *above* that of his average-performing peers. Because he no longer demonstrated a dual discrepancy, it appeared that he was responding to Tier 2 intervention. In contrast, following Tier 2, Student E's performance level and slope remained well below

those of his average peers (1.36 SD and 1.05 SD below average on level and slope, respectively). His low performance and growth indicated that he continued to be unresponsive to Tier 2. In an RTI model, this student would continue to receive Tier 2 intervention, and eventually be referred to special education if Tier 2 continued to fail to improve his performance.

16.5 Summary of Recommendations

In this chapter, we have described a process whereby general educators work in collaboration with school-based colleagues to monitor student response to general education instruction within an

RTI framework. We hope that, from our description of this process, two things are clear. First, many of the components we have outlined require further investigation. Second, monitoring response to general education instruction within an RTI framework will require a significant shift in the role of general educators. This new role will include:

1. *Identifying students at risk using technically sound screening measures that are predictive of relevant academic outcomes.* In selecting screening measures, practitioners should consider the efficiency with which measures can be administered and scored. Ideally, measures that can be given several times during the school year should be used, to catch students who may emerge as at risk later in the year. Current recommendations for identifying students at risk are either the bottom 25th percentile (Fletcher et al., 2005; Fuchs and Fuchs, 2005a) or students performing below a grade-level benchmark (Good et al., 2001; Hintze and Silberglitt, 2005).

2. *Implementing Tier 1 instruction using evidence-based core curricula and supplemental instructional programs.* This instruction should be implemented with fidelity and supported by strong professional development and support.

3. *Monitoring progress to Tier 1 instruction using tools that are sensitive to growth in brief time intervals.* Ideally, progress monitoring would occur weekly for 8 to 10 weeks during Tier 1 instruction (Fuchs and Fuchs, 2005a; Vaughn et al., 2003). Whereas CBM is currently recommended as a promising progress-monitoring tool, caution should be exercised in selecting this or any other approach, as further research is needed to establish the utility of such measures for RTI purposes. Likewise, the most appropriate criteria for judging response to instruction are still under empirical scrutiny.

4. *Selecting, implementing, and monitoring progress within Tier 2 intervention.* Students for whom Tier 1 instruction is not sufficient receive more intensive, individualized intervention. Tier 2 is distinct from Tier 1 in that it is provided in small groups, is conducted more frequently or for longer periods, includes explicit instruction targeting specific skill areas, and/or is delivered by a specialist (Fuchs and Fuchs, 2005a). Again, student progress is monitored regularly. Students for whom Tier 2 is not beneficial receive increasingly intensive intervention and are eventually referred to special education.

16.6 Conclusion

At the heart of RTI is the assumption that a student should have sufficient opportunity to learn, and that this opportunity to learn should be systematically evaluated, before the student is identified as learning disabled (Fletcher et al., 2005; Fuchs and Fuchs, 1998). Opportunity to learn should begin in the general education classroom, where, if the teacher implements evidence-based instruction with integrity, most students will progress toward important academic standards.

To implement an RTI model rooted in general education, general educators will play a critical role. They must be prepared to make data-based decisions and to differentiate instruction using evidence-based practices. School psychologists, special educators, and administrators should play a key role in working with general educators to establish appropriate screening measures, progress-monitoring tools, criteria for determining risk status and responsiveness to instruction, and appropriate Tier 1 and Tier 2 instruction. Practitioners in these roles must have solid problem-solving and communication skills, depth and breadth of knowledge about the strengths and limitations of RTI, and a commitment to staying abreast of current research and implementing best practices in special education referral and identification processes.

References

Al Otaiba, S. & Fuchs, D. (2002). Characteristics of children who are unresponsive to early literacy intervention: a review of the literature. *Remedial and Special Education, 23*, 300–315.

Berninger, V. W., Abbott, R. D., Zook, D., Ogier, S., Lemos-Britton, Z., & Brooksher, R. (1999). Early intervention for reading disabilities: teaching the alphabet principle in a connectionist framework. *Journal of Learning Disabilities, 27*, 491–503.

Burns, M. K. & Senesac, B. V. (2005). Comparison of dual discrepancy criteria to assess response to intervention. *Journal of School Psychology, 43,* 393–406.

Carnine, D., Silbert, J., & Kame'enui, E. J. (1990). *Direct Instruction Reading.* Columbus, OH: Merrill.

Cooper, H., Nye, B., Charlton, K., Lindsay, J., & Greathouse, S. (1996). The effects of summer vacation on achievement test scores: a narrative and meta-analytic review. *Review of Educational Research, 66*, 227–268.

Crawford, L., Tindal, G., & Stieber, S. (2001). Using oral reading rate to predict student performance on statewide assessment tests. *Educational Assessment, 7*, 303–323.

Delquadri, J., Greenwood, C. R., Whorton, D., Carta, J. J., & Hall, R. V. (1986). Classwide peer tutoring. *Exceptional Children, 52*, 535–542.

Deno, S. L. (1985). Curriculum-based measurement: the emerging alternative. *Exceptional Children, 52*, 219–232.

Deno, S. L. (1992). The nature and development of curriculum-based measurement. *Preventing School Failure, 36*, 507–510.

Deno, S. L., Fuchs, L. S., Marston, D., & Shin, J. (2001). Using curriculum based measurement to establish growth standards for students with learning disabilities. *School Psychology Review, 30*, 507–524.

Fletcher, J. M., Francis, D. J., Morris, R. D., & Lyon, G. R. (2005). Evidence-based assessment of learning disabilities in children and adolescents. *Journal of Clinical Child and Adolescent Psychology, 34*, 506–522.

Francis, D. J., Shaywitz, S. E., Stuebing, K. K., Shaywitz, B. A., & Fletcher, J. M. (1996). Developmental lag versus deficit model of reading disability: a longitudinal, individual growth curve analysis. *Journal of Educational Psychology, 88*, 3–17.

Fuchs, D. & Fuchs, L. S. (2005a). Responsiveness-to-intervention: a blueprint for practitioners, policymakers, and parents. *Teaching Exceptional Children, 38*, 57–61.

Fuchs, D. & Fuchs, L. S. (2005b). Peer-assisted learning strategies: promoting word recognition, fluency, and reading comprehension in young children. *Journal of Special Education, 39*, 34–44.

Fuchs, D. & Fuchs, L. S. (2006). Introduction to response to intervention: what, why, and how valid is it? *Reading Research Quarterly, 41*, 92–99.

Fuchs, D., Fuchs, L. S., Mathes, P. G., & Simmons, D. C. (1997). Peer-assisted learning strategies: making classrooms more responsive to diversity. *American Educational Research Journal, 34*, 174–206.

Fuchs, L. S. (2003). Assessing intervention responsiveness: conceptual and technical issues. *Learning Disabilities Research & Practice, 18*, 172–186.

Fuchs, L. S. & Deno, S. L. (1991). Paradigmatic distinctions between instructionally relevant measurement models. *Exceptional Children, 57*, 488–499.

Fuchs, L. S. & Fuchs, D. (1998). Treatment validity: a unifying concept for reconceptualizing the identification of learning disabilities. *Learning Disabilities Research & Practice, 13*, 204–219.

Fuchs, L. S., Fuchs, D., Hamlett, C. L., & Stecker, P. M. (1991). Effects of curriculum-based measurement and consultation on teacher planning and student achievement in mathematics operations. *American Educational Research Journal, 28*, 617–641.

Fuchs, L. S., Fuchs, D., Hamlett, C., Walz, L., & Germann, G. (1993). Formative evaluation of academic progress: How much growth can we expect? *School Psychology Review, 22*, 27–48.

Gersten, R., Chard, D., & Baker, S. (2000). Factors enhancing sustained use of research-based instructional practices. *Journal of Learning Disabilities, 33*, 443–457.

Gersten, R., Fuchs, L. S., Compton, D., Coyne, M., Greenwood, C., & Innocenti, M. S. (2005). Quality indicators for group experimental and quasi-experimental research in special education. *Exceptional Children, 71*, 149–165.

Good III, R. H., Simmons, D. C., & Kame'enui, E. J. (2001). The importance and decision-making utility of a continuum of fluency-based indicators of foundational reading skills for third-grade high-stakes outcomes. *Scientific Studies of Reading, 5*, 257–288.

Heller, K. A., Holtzman, W. H., & Messick, S. (1982). *Placing Children in Special Education: A Strategy for Equity*. Washington, DC: National Academy Press.

Hintze, J. M. & Christ, T. J. (2004). An examination of variability as a function of passage variance in CBM progress monitoring. *School Psychology Review, 33*, 204–217.

Hintze, J. M., Shapiro, E. S., & Daly III, E. J. (1998). An investigation of the effects of passage difficulty level on outcomes of oral reading fluency progress monitoring. *School Psychology Review, 27*, 433–445.

Hintze, J. M. & Silberglitt, B. (2005). A longitudinal examination of the diagnostic accuracy and predictive validity of R-CBM and high-stakes testing. *School Psychology Review, 34*, 372–386.

Hosp, M. K. & Fuchs, L. S. (2005). Using CBM as an indicator of decoding, word reading and comprehension: do the relations change with grade? *School Psychology Review, 34*, 9–26.

IDEIA (2004). *Individuals with Disabilities Education Improvement Act*, P. L. 108-446 U.S.C.

Jenkins, J. R., Zumeta, R., Dupree, O., & Johnson, K. (2005). Measuring gains in reading ability with passage reading fluency. *Learning Disabilities Research & Practice, 20*, 245–253.

Johnson, K. & Street, E. M. (2004). *The Morning-side Model of Generative Instruction.* Concord, MA: Cambridge Center for Behavioral Studies.

Juel, C. (1988). Learning to read and write: a longitudinal study of 54 children from first through fourth grades. *Journal of Educational Psychology, 80,* 437–447.

Klingner, J. K. & Edwards, P. A. (2006). Cultural considerations with response to intervention models. *Reading Research Quarterly, 41,* 108–117.

Marston, D. B. (1989). A curriculum-based measurement approach to assessing academic performance: what is it and why to do it. In M. R. Shinn (Ed.), *Curriculum-Based Measurement: Assessing Special Children* (pp. 18–78). New York: Guilford.

McMaster, K. L., Fuchs, D., Fuchs, L. S., & Compton, D. L. (2005). Responding to nonresponders: an experimental field trial of identification and intervention methods. *Exceptional Children, 71,* 445–464.

Minnesota Department of Education (2003). *Minnesota Comprehensive Assessments: Grade 3 Reading and Math Specifications.* Roseville, Minnesota: Minnesota Department of Education.

National Reading Panel (2000). Teaching children to read: an evidence-based assessment of the scientific research literature on reading and its implications for reading instruction. Retrieved March 3, 2006 from http://www.nichd.nih.gov/publications/pubskey.cfm?from=nrp.

NCLB (2002). *No Child Left Behind Act,* Public Law No. 107–110, 115 Stat. 1425, 2002 U.S.C.

O'Shaughnessy, T. E., Lane, K. L., Gresham, F. M., & Beebe-Frankenberger, M. E. (2003). Children placed at risk for learning and behavioral difficulties: implementing a school-wide system of early identification and intervention. *Remedial and Special Education, 24,* 27–35.

Psychological Corporation (2001). *Wechsler Individual Achievement Test–II.* San Antonio: Psychological Corporation.

Speece, D. L. & Case, L. P. (2001). Classification in context: an alternative approach to identifying early reading disability. *Journal of Educational Psychology, 93,* 735–749.

Speece, D. L., Case, L. P., & Molloy, D. E. (2003). Responsiveness to general education instruction as the first gate to learning disabilities identification. *Learning Disabilities Research and Practice, 18,* 147–156.

Stage, S. & Jacobsen, M. D. (2001). Predicting student success on a state-mandated performance-based assessment using oral reading fluency. *School Psychology Review, 30,* 407–419.

Stanovich, P. J. & Stanovich, K. E. (1997). Research into practice in special education. *Journal of Learning Disabilities, 30,* 477–481.

Stein, M., Silbert, J., & Carnine, D. (1997). *Designing effective Mathematics Instruction: A Direct Instruction Approach* (3rd ed.). Englewood Cliffs, MN: Prentice-Hall.

Torgesen, J. K. (2000). Individual differences in response to early interventions in reading: the lingering problem of treatment resisters. *Learning Disabilities Research & Practice, 15,* 55–64.

Torgesen, J. K., Alexander, A. W., Wagner R. K., Rashotte, C. A., Voeller, K. S., & Conway, T. (2001). Intensive remedial instruction for children with severe reading disabilities: immediate and long-term outcomes from two instructional approaches. *Journal of Learning Disabilities, 34,* 33–53, 78.

Torgesen, J. K., Wagner, R. K., & Rashotte, C. A. (1997). Prevention and remediation of severe reading disabilities: keeping the end in mind. *Scientific Studies of Reading,* 217–234.

US Department of Education (2002). *What Works Clearinghouse.* Retrieved March 3, 2006 from http://www.whatworks.ed.gov/.

Vaughn, S. & Fuchs, L. S. (2003). Redefining learning disabilities as inadequate response to instruction: the promise and potential problems. *Learning Disabilities: Research & Practice, 18,* 137–146.

Vaughn, S., Linan-Thompson, S., & Hickman, P. (2003). Response to instruction as a means of identifying students with reading/learning disabilities. *Exceptional Children, 69,* 391–409.

Vellutino, F. R., Scanlon, D. M., Sipay, E. R., Small, S., Chen, R., Pratt, P. A., et al. (1996). Cognitive profiles of difficult-to-remediate and readily remediated poor readers: early intervention as a vehicle for distinguishing between cognitive and experiential deficits as basic causes of specific reading disability. *Journal of Educational Psychology, 88,* 601–638.

Woodcock, R. W. (1987). *Woodcock Reading Mastery Test–Revised.* Circle Pines, MN: American Guidance Service.

Woodcock, R. W. & Johnson, M. B. (1989). *Woodcock–Johnson Psychoeducational Battery, Revised.* Allen, TX: DLM.

17
Monitoring Response to Supplemental Services for Students at Risk for Reading Difficulties: High and Low Responders

Sharon Vaughn, Jeanne Wanzek, Sylvia Linan-Thompson, and Christy S. Murray

Sharon Vaughn, PhD, is the H. E. Hartfelder/Southland Corp Regent Chair at The University of Texas at Austin. srvaughnum@aol.com

Jeanne Wanzek, PhD, is a Research Associate with the Vaughn Gross Center for Reading and Language Arts at The University of Texas at Austin. jwanzek@aol.com

Sylvia Linan-Thompson is an Associate Professor of Special Education at The University of Texas at Austin. sylvialt@mail.utexas.edu

Christy S. Murray, MA, is a Senior Research Coordinator with the Vaughn Gross Center for Reading and Language Arts at The University of Texas at Austin. christymurry@austin.utexas.edu

Vellutino et al. (1996) reported on first-grade students who had varying responses to a tutoring intervention in reading: many responded well (readily remediated poor readers) and some responded poorly (difficult to remediate). Vellutino et al. reported on differentiated findings for these subgroups of students providing guidance for examining students' response to intervention in future intervention studies. Subsequently, Torgesen et al. (2001) conducted an intensive intervention with students with reading disabilities who were markedly behind their peers in reading and making no progress in closing the gap between their performance and their classmates. Providing them with 2 h daily of intensive reading intervention, students made significant gains on standard scores in word attack, word identification, and comprehension (normalizing their performance in these areas), illustrating the benefits of intensive interventions for students with significant reading disabilities. These two landmark studies helped shape how future researchers considered interventions and their effectiveness demonstrating that students who were difficult to remediate might require more sustained and intensive interventions and/or better differentiated interventions than those who were more readily remediated.

One approach for intervening with students who are not readily remediated involves layering interventions to identify how students respond to increasingly more intensive treatments (Dickson and Bursuck, 1999; McMaster, Fuchs, Fuchs, and Compton, 2005; O'Connor, 2000; O'Connor, Fulmer, Harty, and Bell, 2005; O'Connor, Harty, and Fulmer, 2005; Vaughn, Linan-Thompson, and Hickman, 2003). These layering approaches (O'Connor, 2000), also referred to as multi-tiered approaches to instruction, combine prevention and intervention through ongoing assessment and implementation of successive treatments that provide increasingly more intensive and specific interventions.

Initially, with Tier I instruction, the focus is on providing effective and empirically based instruction to the class as a whole. Effective instructional practices are implemented and monitored classwide in general education as a primary level of intervention. All students are screened for the presence of risk characteristics that predict a reading problem (e.g., inadequate knowledge of letter sounds, word reading, text reading) as early as kindergarten and consistently (two or more times a year) at each grade. Students identified as at risk or who do not respond adequately to the Tier I instruction are provided successive levels of intervention as needed. These levels of intervention provide increasingly more intensive interventions (e.g. smaller groups, longer time for intervention) and even more specific focus to meet students' individual needs. For example, students who respond inadequately to the

Tier I intervention may be provided small-group instruction by the teacher in addition to the Tier I instruction for approximately 20 to 30 min each day (referred to as a Tier II intervention). For many students, a relatively brief dose of Tier II intervention (50–100 sessions) is sufficient for maintaining successful outcomes and additional intervention is not required. For fewer students, Tier II intervention is not sufficient and even more intensive interventions (Tier III) that may involve smaller group sizes or one-on-one tutoring, additional time, and/or specialization on the part of the teachers are needed to improve student outcomes.

The use and implementation of multi-tiered approaches to instruction have been recommended as a means of implementing a response to intervention model for the identification of students with learning disabilities (National Association for State Directors of Special Education, 2005). This chapter will report preliminary data on a 2-year study of two groups of first- to second-grade students identified as at risk for reading failure. The two groups consisted of students who were high responders to intervention (met criteria for exit from intervention after 10 or 20 weeks) and low responders (students who did not meet criteria for exit after 20 weeks and were provided 20 additional weeks of intervention). It is reasonable to conceptualize these students as at-risk students who received Tier II intervention and responded adequately (high responders) and students who received the same Tier II intervention and did not respond adequately (low responders).

17.1 Participants and Study Background

All teachers in this study participated in the same Tier I intervention provided by the research team that included ongoing professional development in the critical elements of reading instruction for all classroom teachers, use of progress monitoring measures to facilitate monitoring students' progress in reading and altering instruction, and occasional in-class coaching (described in more detail in Vaughn and Linan-Thompson (2003) and Vaughn, Wanzek, Woodruff, and Linan-Thompson (2007)). This Tier I program was provided to all classroom teachers in first and second grade for both years of this study.

TABLE 17.1. Criteria for identifying students for secondary and tertiary intervention.

	Risk criteria and continued risk criteria
Secondary intervention screening period	
Fall first grade	NWF < 13 or PSF < 10 and NWF < 24
Winter first grade	NWF < 30 and ORF < 20 or
	ORF < 8
Tertiary intervention screening period	
Fall second grade	ORF < 27
Winter second grade	ORF < 70

Note. NWF: nonsense word fluency; PSF: phonemic segmentation fluency; ORF: oral reading fluency.

17.1.1 Participants

The participants in the study are participating in a 5-year longitudinal study investigating the effectiveness of a three-tier intervention model on students' response to intervention and placement practices in special education (Vaughn, Linan-Thompson, and Elbaum, 2002).

The study is being conducted in a near-urban school district that is primarily minority (more than 75%; mostly Hispanic) with the majority of students receiving free and reduced lunch. There were six elementary schools (all Title I schools) in the district when the 1st treatment cohort was provided (data reported here); however, a seventh school was added to the district and included in subsequent reports. All first-grade students were screened ($n = 532$) and 152 (29%) met criteria for being at risk for reading problems in the fall of first grade (see Table 17.1 for criteria for being at risk for reading problems). Students were randomly assigned to treatment and comparison groups, with the treatment groups receiving intervention from the research team and the students in the comparison group receiving typical school services. All students who remained in the district throughout the 2-year period (first through second grade) and met the criteria for either high responders (10–20 weeks of intervention were sufficient to meet exit criteria) or low responders (40 weeks of intervention were provided) are included in the report of the findings.

17.1.1.1 High Responders (Tier II Only)

The students in this intervention group received either 10 or 20 weeks of intervention during first grade, depending upon their response to intervention, and then continued in the study through second grade, receiving only Tier I instruction from their classroom teachers (no Tier II intervention in second grade). There were 20 students (11 female, 9 males) in the treatment group and 23 students (8 females, 15 males) in the comparison group who met these criteria. All of the treatment students received the same intervention daily in first grade for 30 min provided in group sizes of four to six students with one tutor who was hired and trained by the research team. Because of their adequate or above performance, these students did not receive intervention after first grade but were tested through second grade. The intervention provided to them in first grade is described in the subsequent section.

17.1.1.2 Low Responders (Tier II Plus Tier III)

The students in this intervention group received the same 20 weeks of Tier II intervention provided to the high responders (Tier II only) in first grade. At the end of 20 weeks of intervention (end of first grade) these students still did not meet a priori established exit criteria and were provided another 100 sessions of intervention (approximately 20 weeks), Tier III, in second grade. There were seven students (two females, five males) in the treatment group and 15 students (five females, ten males) in the comparison group who were considered low responders and required the additional second-grade intervention. The Tier III intervention was conducted during second grade and occurred in small groups of two to four students, was provided by a tutor who was trained and supervised by the research team, and occurred for longer time (approximately 50 min daily). The intervention for Tier III provided in second grade is described in the subsequent section.

17.2 Description of Specific Interventions

17.2.1 Tier II: First-Grade Intervention

The Tier II research intervention provided in first grade consisted of daily 30-min sessions scheduled in addition to the Tier I reading program provided in the general education classroom. Trained graduate students and university staff provided instruction to small groups of four to six students per group.

17.2.1.1 Phonics and Word Recognition (15 min)

Phonics and word recognition instruction was provided each day. Instruction included the introduction and practice of letter names and letter sounds, including letter combinations. On average, new letter sounds were introduced once every 2 days; however, new letter sounds were introduced at a rate commensurate with student mastery. Mastered sounds were then used to provide instruction in reading and spelling regular words. Students first learned to blend sounds to read regular words. Once students had mastered blending of consonant–vowel–consonant words, daily instruction also included word family patterns (e.g., fin, tin, bin), and word building (e.g., work, works, worked, working). Irregular words were taught through reading and spelling as well. Approximately one new irregular word was introduced each day with additional practice and review of previously introduced words.

17.2.1.2 Fluency (5 min)

Daily fluency exercises addressed improving speed and automaticity in reading words (early in first grade) and then connected text (later in first grade). Each activity addressed one of three skill areas: (a) letter names and sounds, (b) word reading, or (c) passage reading. Letter name/sound and word reading fluency activities typically consisted of speed games with tutor feedback. As students progressed in their ability, fluency of passage reading was emphasized. Passage reading activities included rereading of text with the goal of improving fluency, tutor modeling of fluent reading followed by student practice, and timed readings. Tutor feedback on fluency was provided for all activities.

17.2.1.3 Passage Reading and Comprehension (10 min)

In the beginning of first grade, students read words and sentences. As their reading progressed, students read novel text daily consisting of short passages incorporating sounds and words previously taught through phonics and word recognition activities. The passages built from three or four words to over

40 words, according to student skill level. Students often read multiple passages during the session. Tutors built appropriate background knowledge on topics as needed, including relevant vocabulary instruction. Typically, students read the text twice during the session. Appropriate comprehension questions integrating literal and inferential thinking followed the reading of the passage. Students were taught strategies for locating answers or clues to answers for the comprehension questions.

17.2.2 Tier III: Second-Grade Intervention

Students receiving tertiary intervention were provided daily 50-min sessions in addition to their Tier I core reading instruction. Instruction was provided by trained graduate students and university staff to small groups of two to four students. Each session included sound review, phonics and word recognition, vocabulary, fluency, passage reading, and comprehension.

17.2.2.1 Sound Review (1–2 min)

Each day the lesson began with a review of previously taught letter sounds, letter combinations, and other phonic elements, such as affixes. The review included students saying sounds, as well as practice writing the appropriate letters to match sounds provided orally by the tutor.

17.2.2.2 Phonics and Word Recognition and Vocabulary (17–25 min)

Sound review was followed by introduction of the new decoding skills or strategies. Students learned new letter sounds, letter combinations, prefixes and suffixes, and strategies for decoding multi-syllabic words during this time. Introduction of the new material was followed by practice reading and spelling words, with emphasis on the use of the new skill or strategy to read new words. Student learning of new decoding skills and strategies was carefully scaffolded with the tutor modeling the word reading and decoding, followed by tutor guidance during initial student practice with word reading, and finally student reading of new words independently with tutor feedback. Words containing previously learned concepts were also included in word read-

ing practice for review. In addition to regular word reading, approximately two to three irregular words were introduced each day, depending on student mastery levels. Ten to twelve previously introduced irregular words were also practiced and reviewed each day. Decoding and encoding of words was emphasized in the instruction of regular and irregular words. Students blended letter sounds and word parts, read word cards, built words with letter tiles and word parts, and wrote words. In addition to the word recognition activities, three to five vocabulary words were introduced or reviewed each day. Words frequently used in reading text and with meanings unfamiliar to students were selected for vocabulary instruction.

17.2.2.3 Fluency (5 min)

Daily fluency activities were aimed at improving accuracy and speed of text reading. Activities included rereading of text with the goal of increasing fluency, tutor modeling of fluent reading followed by student practice, and timed readings. Tutor feedback on fluency was provided for all activities.

17.2.2.4 Passage Reading and Comprehension (12–20 min)

Students applied newly learned word recognition and vocabulary skills to sentences and passages daily. Sentence reading was used as a scaffold to passage reading, allowing students to apply newly learned skills to connected text. Reading passages built in length and difficulty throughout the intervention. Before reading each passage, tutors highlighted relevant vocabulary words, taught "story words"—i.e. difficult-to-decode words specific only to the current story—and implemented activities designed to build necessary background knowledge for the reading. Students read each passage two or more times. During the first reading, tutors provided corrective feedback on word recognition and phrasing when needed. During the second reading, tutors checked for understanding as appropriate while also trying not to interrupt the flow of reading the passage. After reading, instruction focused on comprehension skills and strategies. Specifically, self-questioning, story retell, main idea, and summarizing were explicitly taught. Self-questioning was addressed at least three times per week throughout the intervention. Passage reading and comprehension instruction included both narrative and expository structures.

17.3 Findings and Evidence of Effectiveness

17.3.1 High Responders (Tier II Only)

The most important question about high responders (Tier II only) is the extent to which their early difficulties and then relatively positive response to intervention would prevent further difficulties and whether their reading performance would be equal to or below grade-level expectations at the end of second grade. For both groups of students (those who participated in the treatment intervention and comparison students who met at-risk criteria but did not participate in the treatment intervention) the performance at the end of second grade was well within normative expectations on all critical elements of reading. The end of second-grade standard score means and standard deviations (SDs) on the *Woodcock Reading Mastery Test–Revised* (WRMT-R; Woodcock, 1987) were for treatment and comparison groups respectively: word identification $M = 106.05$ (SD $= 7.42$) and $M = 102.45$ (SD $= 8.76$); word attack, $M = 105.70$ (SD $= 14.20$) and $M = 103.09$ (SD $= 12.25$); passage comprehension, $M = 102.00$ (SD $= 6.55$) and $M = 99.18$ (SD $= 6.93$).

Additionally, the mean oral reading fluency scores for 1-min cold reads on end of second-grade passages was 82.65 (SD $= 25.93$) for treatment students and 76.61 (SD $= 18.48$) for comparison students. These data suggest that overall these students were performing within the average range on all critical indicators of reading success at the end of second grade.

17.3.2 Low Responders (Tier II Plus Tier III)

The most important question about the low responders is the extent to which this substantive amount of intervention would assist them in compensating for their significant at-risk status and in closing the gap towards grade-level performance. The end of second-grade standard score means and SDs on the WRMT-R for the low responders in the

treatment and comparison groups respectively were: word identification, $M = 99.86$ (SD $= 9.63$) and $M = 91.60$ (SD $= 7.14$); word attack, $M = 106.57$ (SD $= 14.75$) and $M = 91.60$ (SD $= 7.14$); passage comprehension, $M = 97.71$ (SD $= 5.22$) and $M = 86.93$ (SD $= 9.59$).

The mean oral reading fluency scores for 1-min cold reads on end of second-grade passages was 46.57 (SD $= 15.77$) for treatment students and 29.47 (SD $= 19.22$) for comparison students. These findings reveal that the end of second-grade scores for the treatment students are quite promising on all measures except oral reading fluency. Scores for the comparison students are not nearly so promising, with students falling on average more than one SD behind expected second-grade performance on reading comprehension, and two-thirds of an SD behind on word attack and word identification. Perhaps of greatest concern is students' performance on oral reading fluency measures. Treatment students' oral reading fluency on 1-min passages (end of second-grade level) were on average 47 words per minute correct for treatment students and 29 words correct per minute for comparison students. Though the oral reading fluency average for treatment students is well below expected reading fluency scores at that grade (89 words per minute correct for students in the 50th percentile; Behavioral Research and Teaching, 2005), these students' speed of reading does not appear to be interfering significantly with their understanding of text, which is well within the average range. This is not true for the comparison students whose slow and inaccurate reading ($M = 29$ words per minute) and very low comprehension scores (on average almost one SD below the norm) provides cause for concern about these students' ability to read for understanding.

Line graphs (Figures 17.1–17.4) illustrate the relative performance over time (from fall of first grade through spring of second grade) of low responders (treatment and comparison students). Students' responses on the WRMT-R are graphed using standard scores on the word attack, word identification, and passage comprehension subtests. A consistent pattern for all subtests and for both the treatment and comparison condition is that students have relative losses from spring of first grade to fall of second grade. We are not the first to notice this relative loss during the summer, suggesting that students at risk for reading and learning problems would benefit from academically oriented summer programs

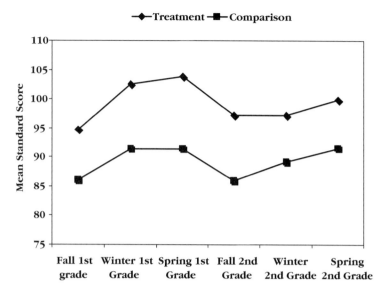

FIGURE 17.1. WRMT-R word identification mean standard score for low responders.

(Borman and Boulay, 2004). A second pattern is that students participating in the intervention progress relatively well, closing the gap with normal achieving students, whereas comparison students do not.

17.3.3 Gains per Hour of Intervention

Another way to compare the overall effectiveness of an intervention is to consider the progress made as the difference in standard score points between students' scores at the beginning of the intervention (pretest) and students' scores at the end of

the intervention (posttest) divided by the number of hours of intervention provided. This calculation can provide some insight into the standard score gains per hour of intervention (McGuiness, McGuiness, and McGuiness, 1996; Torgesen et al., 2001). In a previous review (Vaughn and Linan-Thompson, 2003), we summarized the standard score gains per hour of intervention for studies that provided early intervention in reading to students with significant reading problems for whom one or more subtest score on the WRMT-R was available. There were 12 interventions provided for more than 10 h

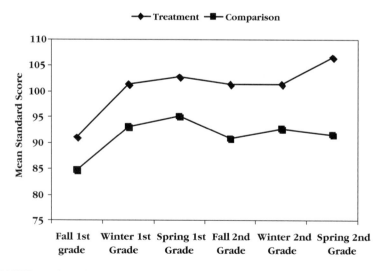

FIGURE 17.2. WRMT-R word attack mean standard score for low responders.

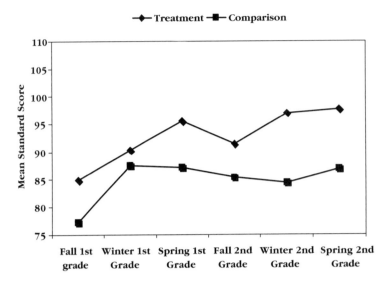

FIGURE 17.3. WRMT-R passage comprehension mean standard scores for low responders.

(fewer studies, since some studies had more than one intervention) for which word attack scores were available and the gains in standard scores per hour of intervention ranged from 0.23 to 0.47. There were 17 interventions, with gains per hour in word identification scores ranging from 0.07 to 0.34. For passage comprehension, there were 11 interventions, with gains per hour ranging from 0.05 to 0.35. To illustrate gains per hour of intervention, Table 17.2 reflects scores from the beginning to the end of intervention for the high and low responders. For the high responders, 19 of the 20 students received about

50 sessions of intervention (30-min sessions) before exiting. Therefore, the average amount of intervention for high responders was about 25 h. The low responders required approximately 100 sessions of Tier II intervention (50 h) plus approximately 100 50-min sessions of Tier III. Therefore, the average amount of intervention for the low responders was about 130 h.

As can be seen in Table 17.2, the gains per hour of intervention for high responders were within the range of previous studies. However, the gains for the high responders in this study reflect their scores

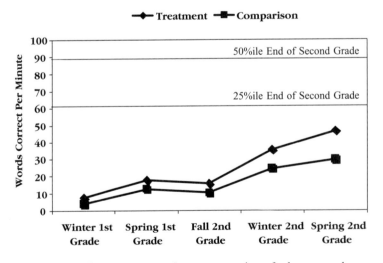

FIGURE 17.4. DIBELS oral reading fluency mean words correct per minute for low responders.

TABLE 17.2. Gains in standard scores per hour of intervention.

	WI	WA	PC
High responders (~25 h of intervention)	0.23	0.16	0.29
Low responders (~130 h of intervention)	0.04	0.12	0.10

Note. WA: word attack; WI: word identification; PC: passage comprehension.

at the "end" of second grade. This is important, because the intervention was provided in first grade; thus, the gains reflect maintenance of effects of more than 1 year following intervention for the high responders. The gains for the low responders are considerably lower for word identification, but less distinct for word attack and passage comprehension.

17.4 Implications for Using Data from Response to Intervention Treatment Protocols for Identifying Students with Learning Disabilities

The data in this chapter are organized to provide some insight into the implementation of a multi-tier model in six high-poverty, high-minority schools. Though the sample sizes in this report are relatively small (larger sample sizes are expected as we add another cohort), they provide data about response to intervention in school samples and guidance about students' responses to Tier II and Tier III interventions. Although a complete analysis of responders and nonresponders to Tier II and Tier III interventions is beyond the scope of this chapter, there are students in the Tier II intervention who maintained successful intervention responses over time and few whose responses were not maintained and are likely to require additional intervention, even if for a relatively brief period.

Similarly, with Tier III participants, there are students who demonstrated relatively successful responses to intervention after a fairly intensive course and others whose response was minimal even after the 2-year intervention. For example, Mario is an example of a relatively successful intervention student whose progress indicates that he is closing the gap in reading achievement. Mario's oral reading fluency score was 7 words per minute in the winter of first grade and 21 words per minute by the end

of first grade. During the second year of intervention, Mario had an oral reading fluency score of 19 in the fall, 47 in the winter, and by the end of second grade year was reading 60 words per minute. Nathan's progress began similarly to Mario, but his progress was considerably lower. In the winter of first grade, Nathan presented the same oral reading fluency as Mario (7); however, his progress was much slower, with a score of 12 by the end of first grade, 15 in the fall of second grade, 24 in the winter, and by the end of second grade Nathan was reading 32 words per minute. Neither student was identified as having a disability. Both students were reported to be highly motivated and interested in learning to read. Mario's tutors reported he enjoyed working in the small group and receiving attention from the teacher. In the first year of intervention, Mario demonstrated success during the lesson even before his independent assessments indicated significant progress. This success was also demonstrated in the second year of intervention, when Mario was consistently the first student in his group to master new concepts. Nathan also demonstrated quick skill learning in the Tier II intervention; however, his tutors reported significant difficulties with attention. These attention problems continued in the second year of intervention. During the second year of intervention, the tutors reported Nathan's difficulty with mastering new concepts. His daily work was often behind others in his group. He seemed to have difficulty putting the rules for decoding together to read rapidly and automatically.

17.4.1 Cost for Intervention

A prevailing issue related to effectively and consistently implementing interventions for Tiers II and III such as those described in this chapter is related to the cost of implementing the intervention. Though the exact cost of an intervention is difficult to determine, there are factors that can be considered when estimating costs, including the qualifications of the tutor and the group size. Because all of the tutors had undergraduate degrees and were highly trained, we assumed a higher cost per hour of intervention than may actually be incurred by a district. Estimating that tutors would be paid approximately $50 per hour of intervention (this high amount also allows for time for planning and training), it is readily apparent that high responders cost a great deal less than low responders. First estimating the cost for high responders, we multiply $50 per hour by 25 h and by 50 h (the two intervention amounts provided to high responders) then divided by the number of students in a group ($n = 5$) to obtain the cost per child, in this case $250 to $500 per child depending upon whether the high responder required one or two treatment cycles.

For low responders, the cost would be $50 per hour by 50 h divided by 5 (the first year of intervention). Thus, the first year cost about $500 per child. Since these students were low responders and required additional intervention we must also calculate the cost of the Tier III intervention multiplying $50 per hour by 83 h divided by 3 (the second year of intervention) for a total of $1400 per child the second year. Adding the two years together, the low responders (also known as difficult-to-remediate students) cost approximately $1900 per child for intervention. Considering that these difficult-to-treat students were within the average range on all critical indices of reading, the cost could be considered relatively low. This cost should be considered in terms of what it would cost a school district to provide special education or other specialized services for extensive periods of time. Of course, this does not also consider the cost of continued failure in reading on the child's self-concept and motivation to learn. Invernizzi, Juel and Rosemary (1997) reported an average cost per child of $595 for a tutoring program that they implemented with trained volunteers. Hiebert's analysis of the cost of reading recovery, for example, ranged from $3000 to $3488 per student at Grade 1 (Hiebert, 1994).

These preliminary findings from our multi-year study confirms findings from Vellutino, Scanlon, and Jaccard (2003), who, having examined followup data on first-grade students identified as at risk and provided tutoring, reported "that there are small but significant numbers of children who will require intensive and individualized remedial assistance for a period of time beyond that provided by the intervention project in order for them to become functionally independent readers." Learning to read for most students is a relatively easy process that occurs so readily that, as adults, they often cannot even remember how they learned to read. For other students the process is significantly more intensive, requiring ongoing interventions that may be in place well past the third grade. We believe that the data presented in this chapter suggest that the needs of these students cannot be met solely by general education and that they will require a special education.

References

Behavioral Research and Teaching (2005, January). Oral reading fluency: 90 years of assessment (BRT Technical Report No. 33). Eugene, OR: Behavioral Research and Teaching.

Borman, G. D. & Boulay, M. (2004). *Summer Learning: Research, Policies, and Programs.* Mahwah, NJ: Erlbaum.

Dickson, S. V. & Bursuck, W. D. (1999). Implementing a model for preventing reading failure: a report from the field. *Learning Disabilities Research & Practice, 14,* 191–195.

Hiebert, E. (1994). Reading recovery in the United States: what difference does it make to an age cohort? *Educational Researcher, 23,* 15–25.

Invernizzi, M., Juel, C., & Rosemary, C. A. (1997). A community volunteer tutorial that works. *The Reading Teacher, 50,* 304–311.

McGuiness, C., McGuiness, D., & McGuiness, G. (1996). Phono-Graphix: a new method for remediating reading difficulties. *Annals of Dyslexia, 46,* 73–96.

McMaster, K. L., Fuchs, D., Fuchs, L. S., & Compton, D. L. (2005). Responding to nonresponders: an experimental field trial of identification and intervention methods. *Exceptional Children, 71,* 445–463.

National Association of State Directors of Special Education (2005). *Response to Intervention: Policy Considerations and Implementation.* Alexandria, VA: National Association of State Directors of Special Education.

O'Connor, R. (2000). Increasing the intensity of intervention in kindergarten and first grade. *Learning Disabilities Research & Practice, 15,* 43–54.

O'Connor, R. E., Fulmer, D., Harty, K. R., & Bell, K. M. (2005). Layers of reading intervention in kindergarten through third grade: changes in teaching and student outcomes. *Journal of Learning Disabilities, 38,* 440–445.

O'Connor, R. E., Harty, K. R., & Fulmer, D. (2005). Tiers of intervention in kindergarten through third grade. *Journal of Learning Disabilities, 38,* 532–538.

Torgesen, J. K., Alexander, A. W., Wagner, R. K., Rashotte, C. A., Voeller, K. K. S., & Conway, T. (2001). Intensive remedial instruction for children with severe reading disabilities: immediate and long-term outcomes from two instructional approaches. *Journal of Learning Disabilities, 34,* 33–58, 78.

Vaughn, S. & Linan-Thompson, S. (2003). What is special about special education for students with learning disabilities? *Journal of Special Education, 69*, 391–409.

Vaughn, S., Linan-Thompson, S., & Elbaum, B. (2002). Centers for implementing K-3 behavior and reading intervention models preventing reading difficulties: A three-tiered intervention model. US Department of Education Grant Contract #H324XD100013.

Vaughn, S., Linan-Thompson, S., & Hickman, P. (2003). Response to instruction as a means of identifying students with reading/learning disabilities. *Exceptional Children, 69*, 391–409.

Vaughn, S., Wanzek, J., Woodruff, A. L., & Linan-Thompson, S. (2007). A three-tier model for preventing reading difficulties and early identification of students with reading disabilities. In D. H. Haager, S. Vaughn, & J. K. Klingner (Eds.), *Validated Reading Practices for Three Tiers of Intervention* (pp. 11–28). Baltimore, MD: Brookes.

Vellutino, F. R., Scanlon, D. M., & Jaccard, J. (2003). Toward distinguishing between cognitive and experiential deficits as primary sources of difficulty in learning to read: a two year follow-up of difficult to remediate and readily remediated poor readers. In B. F. Foorman (Ed.), *Preventing and Remediating Reading Difficulties: Bringing Science to Scale* (pp. 73–120). Baltimore: York Press.

Vellutino, F. R., Scanlon, D. M., Sipay, E. R., Small, S. G., Pratt, A., Chen, R., et al. (1996). Cognitive profiles of difficult-to-remediate and readily remediated poor readers: early intervention as a vehicle for distinguishing between cognitive and experiential deficits as basic causes of specific reading disability. *Journal of Educational Psychology, 88*, 601–638.

Woodcock, R. W. (1987). *Woodcock Reading Mastery Test–Revised.* Circle Pines, MN: American Guidance Service.

18

The Fundamental Role of Intervention Implementation in Assessing Response to Intervention

Kristin A. Gansle and George H. Noell

Kristin A. Gansle, PhD, is an Associate Professor in Special Education at Louisiana State University.
kgansle@lsu.edu
George H. Noell, PhD, is a Professor of Psychology with the School Psychology Program at Louisiana State
University. gnoell@lsu.edu

Although the assessment of response to intervention (RTI) as a service delivery model has undergone considerable development over the last decade, all of the critical elements that must be in place for RTI to be successful have not received similar attention. One of the fundamental elements of RTI is the implementation of interventions. However, implementation of interventions appears to be commonly assumed within discussions of RTI rather than considered a major issue to be resolved. Emerging research suggests that assuring treatment or intervention implementation is, in fact, a substantial requirement for problem-solving services to students in schools (Noell, in press). This chapter describes some of the critical conceptual issues related to intervention implementation, and provides a selected review of the research regarding the assessment and assurance of intervention implementation.

18.1 Importance and Conceptual Basis

Treatment integrity is commonly described as the extent to which independent variables or treatment plans are implemented as intended (Gresham, 1989; Moncher and Prinz, 1991; Yeaton and Sechrest, 1981). It has also been described as procedural fidelity, procedural reliability, procedural integrity, and treatment fidelity. Clear differentiation among the meanings of these terms is not evident. Fur-

thermore, treatment integrity can refer to adherence to procedures within experimental studies for the purposes of research, and within treatment plans for clinical and school cases, as well as the extent to which practitioners adhere to protocols for conducting school consultation sessions, independent of treatment plans designed in consultation (Noell, in press). For the purposes of clarifying this discussion of RTI, the convention established by Noell is followed within this chapter. *Treatment integrity* will be defined narrowly as the accuracy of the implementation of the independent variable within an experiment. Measurement and assurance of treatment integrity, then, allow the investigator to more accurately answer the question, "To what extent are changes in the dependent variable due to implementation of the independent variable?" *Treatment plan implementation* (TPI) refers to the degree to which a treatment plan developed for remediation of referral concerns is implemented as designed, and is a consideration that is critical to RTI. TPI is a result of the process of intervention development and implementation, and is not, nor is it expected to be, under experimental control.

It is important to consider that TPI, or accurate implementation of the treatment plan developed for a student, is not the only variable that may affect student behavior. A lock-and-key metaphor may be used to illustrate the point. A lock is akin to a referral concern, and a key is needed to open the lock, or to "fix" the problem. Three characteristics of the lock and key relationship are critical to opening the lock:

its fit, its strength, and whether it is put in the lock at all.

18.1.1 Treatment Fit

There are several keys that may fit into any given lock: the master key, the dedicated key, and other keys that are similar to the one designed for the lock, but which may or may not open it. When we start with the lock as the only piece of data, it is impossible to know what will open it without investigating further. Assessment data suggest pieces of the key that may be cut to open the lock, or to remediate the referral concern. A key that is cut to the specifications of the lock is likely to open it. It is possible that a variety of keys may open any given lock, as long as they have some combination of critical cuts on them (i.e., a master key and a dedicated lock key will open the same lock). In other words, interventions that are suited to the characteristics of the referral concern are most likely to have positive effects. It is important that we choose empirically validated treatments (Gresham, 2002) that are based on accurate assessment data so that we have the best chance to determine a response to intervention that will be meaningful to programming for that student.

18.1.2 Treatment Strength

Having the correct cuts on a key, however, does not assure that a lock will open. A key must be of material sufficiently strong to turn the tumblers within the locking mechanism. A key cut of gelatin will not open a lock; similarly, a treatment designed specifically for a referral concern will not have demonstrable effects if it is not of strength sufficient to change behavior. Treatment strength is a construct that is analogous to dosage (Yeaton and Sechrest, 1981). More of an intervention (e.g., time implemented) is generally presumed to be more effective, but the potential benefits must be weighed against the costs of increasing the amount of the intervention (Noell and Gresham, 1993). For the purposes of RTI, it is important to determine what strength of intervention is sufficient to evaluate student response without making the intervention so laborious that it becomes impractical for school personnel to implement.

18.1.3 Treatment Plan Implementation

In the same way that keys of gelatin will not open locks, keys that are *not inserted*, or inserted only part way into locks, are highly unlikely to open them. TPI in applied contexts is receiving increasing attention in the literature (e.g., Lentz and Daly, 1996; Mueller, Edwards, and Trahant, 2003; Rhymer, Evans-Hampton, McCurdy, and Watson, 2002; Riley-Tillman and Chafouleas, 2003). Strongly empirically supported treatments for childhood concerns usually involve the implementation of treatment by parents, teachers, and other care providers as primary treatment agents (DuPaul and Eckert, 1997; Swanson and Hoskyn, 1998; Weiss and Weisz, 1995; Weisz, Weiss, Alicke, and Klotz, 1987). However, requiring that parents and teachers take substantial responsibility for the implementation of interventions creates substantial challenges to assuring treatment is provided. A variety of factors may intervene to degrade TPI. For teachers and other service providers in schools, time demands are legion, and resources are limited. Thus, TPI is not assured from simply developing a treatment/intervention plan and providing training (Happe, 1982; Noell, Witt, Gilbertson, Ranier, and Freeland, 1997; Taylor and Miller, 1992), nor from using interventions with high acceptability (Noell et al., 2005). In fact, despite a body of literature that suggests a conceptual link between treatment acceptability and treatment implementation (Eckert and Hintze, 2000; Nastasi and Truscott, 2000), low acceptability might not prevent implementation of an intervention if environmental contingencies are sufficient to support that behavior by the treatment agent (e.g., Noell et al., 2000). At a practical level, the types of intervention commonly employed in schools (e.g., peer tutoring, school–home notes, self-monitoring) may be so consistently highly acceptable that a relationship between treatment acceptability and TPI will not be evident (Noell, in press).

Although it seems intuitive that TPI is directly linked to student outcomes, an emerging line of research suggests that the relationship may be more complicated (e.g., Greenwood, Terry, Arreaga-Mayer, and Finney, 1992; Rhymer et al., 2002). With wide varieties of treatment components, strengths, and protocols, combined with a limited number of studies conducted by several investigators, there is not yet a comprehensive body of literature that clearly defines the relationship. Some studies have suggested that low TPI leads to poorer outcomes (Greenwood et al., 1992; Henggeler, Melton, Brondino, Scherer, and Hanley, 1997; Taylor and Miller, 1992); however, some suggest that degradations in TPI may not be related to poorer outcomes for students (Gansle and McMahon, 1997; Rhymer et al., 2002).

One issue may contribute directly to the difficulties in drawing general principles from the literature that does exist: weighting of treatment steps. Often, treatment integrity and TPI are recorded using a list of the steps of treatment, having the investigator or the treatment agent mark those steps completed, and the measure of TPI or treatment integrity is the percentage of steps of treatment completed by the treatment agent. In the absence of a system for determining weights for treatment steps, each step on the list is assigned equal weight. It is unlikely that all steps of *any* treatment contribute equally to the outcome; clearly, error is introduced into the calculation without proper weighting of those steps. For example, whether a self-monitoring card is picked up by the teacher at the end of the day is less likely to influence child behavior than whether the child had recorded instances of hand raising during the school day. Furthermore, variations in outcome may be the result of *how* the steps are implemented, rather than *whether* they are implemented. Praise is an excellent example of this. A teacher who says "Good job! Yes! $6 + 5$ *is* 11!" with enthusiasm is more likely to have a positive effect on that student's achievement than a teacher who says "good" with no animation in his voice. These are not, however, the only factors that may affect outcomes, and the literature regarding the number and scope of these is still developing. Individual differences in students and their tolerance for degradations in TPI are likely to affect outcomes. In addition, high TPI may be more important during the establishment of new behavior than later in the intervention, when fluency is the concern. Finally, individual differences in intervention will affect the relationship between TPI and outcomes, as some interventions are likely robust to incomplete TPI, whereas some are more brittle in the face of incomplete implementation and small degradations in TPI will lead to large degradations in outcome (Noell, in press).

The limited literature on TPI suggests that TPI can be problematic in school-based intervention (e.g., Jones, Wickstrom, and Friman, 1997; Telzrow, McNamara, and Hollinger, 2000; Wickstrom, Jones, LaFleur, and Witt, 1998). However, documenting and assuring TPI is a critical enabling technology to permit substantive implementation of an RTI model. Even if RTI is implemented with the highest quality assessment, intervention design, progress monitoring, and data evaluation, if TPI does not occur, then the process would not be a substantive assessment of or service to the referred student.

18.2 Research

Current research suggests that for treatment providers in schools, in the absence of systematic follow up, TPI is likely to be poor (DiGennaro, Martens, and McIntyre, 2005; Noell et al., 2005; Wickstrom et al., 1998). Acknowledging that TPI is not assured and is critical to RTI raises three questions. *How much treatment is enough treatment? What is the best assessment of TPI? What is the best way to assure TPI?* See Table 18.1 for a snapshot of what is known about TPI and its implications for practice.

18.2.1 How Much Treatment is Enough Treatment?

This seemingly simple question has not yet been answered by the available research; we do not know

TABLE 18.1. Treatment plan implementation: implications for practice.

1. Intervention implementation in schools is likely to be poor and deteriorate over time without systematic data-based follow up.
2. Intervention implementation is a fundamental due process protection within RTI models for assessing entitlement.
3. Assessing RTI without *documenting* intervention implementation does not provide adequate due-process protections for referred students.
4. Current evidence suggests that self-report data regarding intervention implementation are upwardly biased and are unrelated to more direct measures of implementation. More direct measures, such as observations and permanent products, appear to be needed.
5. It is possible to dramatically improve intervention implementation using very brief weekly performance feedback meetings.

how much TPI is necessary for a given intervention/treatment to be successful. The level of implementation may also depend in part on how treatment is defined and assessed. That being said, the current literature does suggest that, as TPI decreases, the risk that treatment will become either less effective or that it will no longer be effective at all increases (Noell, in press). Studies that have empirically evaluated the effect of TPI have either systematically varied TPI or have studied uncontrolled variations in TPI in naturalistic settings for anxiety disorders (Vermilyea, Barlow, and O'Brien, 1984), classwide peer tutoring (Greenwood et al., 1992), constant time-delay instruction (Holcombe, Wolery, and Snyder, 1994), differential reinforcement (Vollmer, Roane, Ringdahl, and Marcus, 1999), disruptive behavior (Gansle and McMahon, 1997), social skills training (McEvoy, Shores, Wehby, Johnson, and Fox, 1990), strategy instruction (Noell, Gresham, and Gansle, 2002b), and multisystemic therapy for juvenile offenders (Henggeler et al., 1997). Generally, low TPI was associated with poorer treatment outcomes for some participants on at least some of the measures used, an increase in the number of participants for whom treatment was ineffective, and/or a decreased effect size for treatment. However, this is not to say that this was the outcome for *all* of the participants or studies; decreased TPI had no significant effect on some outcome measures for some participants (Gansle and McMahon, 1997; Vollmer et al., 1999).

The research literature that documents the relationship between TPI and intervention outcomes is neither sufficiently systematic nor programmatic to allow for a synthesis of research that provides a positive link between them. The heterogeneity of the treatments, populations, methods of TPI assessment, outcome measures, and types of error in TPI provide a hurdle that has not yet been cleared. It appears that as TPI begins to break down, the risk that treatment will deteriorate increases, and that the degradation of different components may affect outcomes differently for specific students.

18.2.2 What is the Best Assessment of Treatment Plan Implementation?

How, then, is a decision to be made about how to assess and set standards for TPI within RTI? Any

given treatment can be task analyzed to the point that measuring implementation of all of its steps is more costly than implementing the intervention itself. Where possible it would be prudent to identify those treatment components that have been empirically identified as critical for the intervention to be effective and assess those. However, extensive component analyses are not available for most interventions used in schools. As a practical matter, researchers will infrequently have sufficient data regarding the critical steps of treatment plans or the weighting of those steps. A reasonable strategy for coping with this weight uncertainty would be to assess those steps that are believed to be critical for successful treatment or are practically necessary to complete the intervention and then weight them equally in assessing TPI (Noell and Gansle, 2006). This strategy derives from the success of an improper linear model in dealing with cases of weight uncertainty (Dawes, 1979).

This kind of assessment of TPI leads to some interesting challenges, in that the behavior of the *treatment agent* rather than the *student* is the focus of the assessment (Noell, in press). Generally, when students are not experiencing success in the general curriculum, the student is the target for the assessment. In the implementation of intervention plans for student difficulties, it has often been assumed that treatment agents will do what they have agreed to do without consideration for other demands that compete for their time (Lentz and Daly, 1996). Educators tend to be far more comfortable measuring student behavior than their own (Noell and Gansle, 2006), and this may lead to additional issues that must be addressed before adequate TPI can be assured.

One unobtrusive method of TPI assessment that has been investigated is to have treatment agents provide self-reported data regarding their intervention implementation. Unfortunately, this method for evaluating teacher behavior has been shown to provide data that appear to be upwardly biased and are unrelated to more objective measurements of TPI (Noell et al., 2005; Wickstrom et al., 1998). These studies argue against the exclusive use of teacher report to adequately measure TPI.

Direct observation is a natural choice for collection of objectively verifiable data regarding the implementation of the intervention. However, interventions may occur at any and all times of the school day, which makes direct observation of implementation behaviors difficult to manage (Jones et al., 1997; Witt, Noell, LaFleur, and Mortenson, 1997). Direct observations that do occur, then, are likely to be small samples, which may not be representative of all treatment agent behavior due to reactivity to observation (Hintze and Matthews, 2004). To strengthen evaluations of TPI, a mixed assessment method consisting of direct observation data plus the collection and evaluation of permanent products of the intervention is a practical strategy. This strategy allows for the sampling of all occasions by using permanent products, and is unobtrusive, which decreases the effects of reactivity to observation on the entire TPI assessment (Foster and Cone, 1986). The literature in this area is limited, and future research may provide models for accurate assessments of TPI that provide a maximum of objectivity in the data, and a minimum of cost to the participants.

18.2.3 What is the Best Way to Assure Treatment Plan Implementation?

There are many factors that could influence whether a treatment plan will be implemented. Much has been written about factors that are thought to influence TPI; relatively few of these factors have been *demonstrated to* influence TPI. This literature is still in its infancy; a variety of moderating variables that may be related to TPI have not yet systematically been investigated (Noell, in press). These include, but are not limited to, teacher stress, competing time demands, the perceived importance of the referral concern, the salience of the referral concern, school climate, and parental and/or administrator interest in the referral concern. Two factors that have been investigated are training and performance feedback.

18.2.3.1 Training

Deficits in plan implementation have been hypothesized to occur as a result of inadequate training provided to treatment agents. The reasoning was that teachers did not implement interventions because they did not know how. Furthermore, it has been suggested that if teachers understood what they were asked to do they would implement intervention plans (Watson and Robinson, 1996). Taylor and Miller (1997) found that implementation of time-out was poor following didactic training alone. Di-

dactic training was followed by intensive in-vivo training, which led to better implementation. Direct instruction in intervention implementation has also been found to lead to better TPI than didactic instruction alone (Sterling-Turner, Watson, Wildmon, Watkins, and Little, 2001). Although these studies support the argument that more training leads to better TPI, substantive issues with each study suggest that this conclusion is premature. The Taylor and Miller (1997) study used an amount of training that greatly exceeded what would be considered possible in common school practice and may have sensitized teachers to the observers in their classrooms. The Sterling-Turner et al. (2001) study used undergraduate volunteers in a simulation, which decreased the external validity of its conclusions.

18.2.3.2 Performance Feedback

Most of the studies that have demonstrated a positive effect on TPI have focused on performance feedback. Performance feedback for TPI consists of reviewing implementation data with the treatment agent. Several studies have verified that performance feedback procedures can improve and maintain TPI for a variety of academic and behavioral interventions (DiGennaro et al., 2005; Jones et al., 1997; Martens, Hiralall, and Bradley, 1997; Mortenson and Witt, 1998; Noell, Duhon, Gatti, and Connell, 2002a; Noell et al., 1997, 2000, 2005; Witt et al., 1997). Furthermore, Noell et al. (1997) demonstrated that extensive training is unnecessary for performance feedback to be effective for teachers who are implementing an academic intervention.

Additional pieces of the performance feedback picture have been investigated. The teacher contact aspect of performance feedback does not appear to be responsible for improvements in TPI. Performance feedback has been shown more effective than brief follow-up meetings with teachers in which they were asked about student outcomes; in fact, these meetings increased TPI in less than half of the cases studied (Noell et al., 2000). This is especially important given the common practice in schools for psychologists to "check in" with teachers without collecting any data regarding actual implementation of the intervention. Graphs of teacher implementation behavior drawn from permanent products of the intervention have also been shown to lead to much more consistent positive effects for performance feedback than feedback with no graphs provided (Noell et al., 2002a).

Performance feedback has also been investigated in tandem with a social influence strategy designed to improve TPI. Noell et al. (2005) used a social influence strategy that included a discussion with the teacher of the commitment made to implement the intervention, common barriers to TPI, and risks and effects of poor TPI. In addition, consultants discussed strategies for maintaining good TPI with teachers. The control condition used a brief weekly meeting with teachers that is similar to a problem evaluation interview (Bergan and Kratochwill, 1990). Over the course of 3 weeks of intervention, the performance feedback condition was associated with improved intervention implementation and with child outcome. Teacher contact was faded to one contact per week, and TPI was maintained. In addition, a moderate and statistically significant relationship ($r = 0.44$) between TPI and child behavioral outcome was found (Noell et al., 2005).

Taken together, these studies suggest that, without systematic follow up, poor and deteriorating implementation of interventions in schools is likely. High acceptability and intensive training were not sufficient to insure TPI. Performance feedback leads to improved TPI, and graphing appears to lead to a more consistent effect for performance feedback.

18.3 Limitations, Future Directions, and Conclusion

Intervention plan implementation is fundamental to the successful application of RTI models of eligibility determination and service delivery for students who are experiencing failure in the general curriculum. However, it is important to acknowledge that what is not known about the relationship between TPI and outcomes, as well as how to increase TPI, may far outweigh what is known. Additional research in this area is critical to establishing general principles of assuring the TPI that will lead to possible RTI determination.

For individual students, evidence of TPI will provide a fundamental due-process protection by demonstrating that the intervention aspect of the RTI special education eligibility determination was implemented. Although it has not been shown to oc-

cur as a matter of course as a result of consultation (Wickstrom et al., 1998), TPI is often assumed. If this naïve assumption were adopted it would likely lead to systematic and substantive violation of due-process protections whose entitlement for special education services was being evaluated through an RTI model.

One of the most significant benefits from RTI would be an increase in student access to services *before* problems become sufficiently severe to warrant traditional special education evaluation and placement. Some services should begin at the point of referral within RTI (Fuchs, Fuchs, and Speece, 2002). If TPI is assured, then those services will be made available at a point that precedes where they would in a traditional model, and carries lower risks for inappropriate placement. However, if TPI is not assured, then we have merely exchanged one administrative procedure for data collection and decision based upon somewhat arbitrary standards with another.

One substantial challenge confronting professionals developing RTI systems is determining what level of TPI is necessary to constitute a valid assessment (Noell and Gansle, 2006; Noell et al., 2002b). Successful models for standards are likely to include measurable steps of treatment, determination of potent steps of treatment, and some form of direct assessment of TPI. The current state of the literature indicates that performance feedback has a positive effect on TPI; additional research into methods to enhance TPI is critical.

References

Bergan, J. R. & Kratochwill, T. R. (1990). *Behavioral Consultation and Therapy.* New York: Plenum Press.

Dawes, R. M. (1979). The robust beauty of improper linear models in decision making. *American Psychologist, 34,* 571–582.

DiGennaro, F. D., Martens, B. K., & McIntyre, L. L. (2005). Increasing treatment integrity through negative reinforcement: effects on teacher and student behavior. *School Psychology Review, 34,* 220–231.

DuPaul, G. J. & Eckert, T. L. (1997). The effects of school-based interventions for attention deficit hyperactivity disorder: a meta-analysis. *School Psychology Review, 26,* 5–27.

Eckert, T. L. & Hintze, J. M. (2000). Behavioral conceptions and applications of acceptability: issues related to service delivery and research methodology. *School Psychology Quarterly, 15*, 123–148.

Foster, S. L. & Cone, J. D. (1986). Design and use of direct observation procedures. In A. R. Ciminero, K. S. Calhoun, & H. E. Adams (Eds.), *Handbook of Behavioral Assessment* (2nded., pp. 253–324). New York: Wiley.

Fuchs, L. S., Fuchs, D., & Speece, D. L. (2002). Treatment validity as a unifying construct for identifying learning disabilities. *Learning Disability Quarterly, 25*, 33–45.

Gansle, K. A. & McMahon, C. M. (1997). Component integrity of teacher intervention management behavior using a student self-monitoring treatment: an experimental analysis. *Journal of Behavioral Education, 7*, 405–419.

Greenwood, C. R., Terry, B., Arreaga-Mayer, C., & Finney, R. (1992). The classwide peer tutoring program: implementation factors moderating students' achievement. *Journal of Applied Behavior Analysis, 25*, 101–116.

Gresham, F. M. (1989). Assessment of treatment integrity in school consultation and prereferral intervention. *School Psychology Review, 18*, 37–50.

Gresham, F. M. (2002). Responsiveness to intervention: an alternative approach to the identification of learning disabilities. In R. Bradley, L. Danielson, & D. P. Hallahan (Eds.), *Identification of Learning Disabilities: Research to Practice* (pp. 467–519). Mahway, NJ: Lawrence Erlbaum Associates.

Happe, D. (1982). Behavioral intervention: it doesn't do any good in your briefcase. In J. Grimes (Ed.), *Psychological Approaches to Problems of Children and Adolescents* (pp. 15–41). Des Moines, IA: Iowa Department of Public Instruction.

Henggeler, S. W., Melton, G. B., Brondino, M. J., Scherer, D. G., & Hanley, J. H. (1997). Multisystemic therapy with violent and chronic juvenile offenders and their families: the role of treatment fidelity in successful dissemination. *Journal of Consulting and Clinical Psychology, 65*, 821–833.

Hintze, J. M. & Matthews, W. J. (2004). The generalizability of systematic direct observations across time and setting: a preliminary investigation of the psychometrics of behavioral observation. *School Psychology Review, 33*, 258–270.

Holcombe, A., Wolery, M., & Snyder, E. (1994). Effects of two levels of procedural fidelity with constant time delay on children's learning. *Journal of Behavioral Education, 4*, 49–73.

Jones, K. M., Wickstrom, K. F., & Friman, P. C. (1997). The effects of observational feedback on treatment integrity in school-based behavioral consultation. *School Psychology Quarterly, 12*, 316–326.

Lentz, F. E. & Daly III, E. J. (1996). Is the behavior of academic change agents controlled metaphysically? An analysis of the behavior of those who change behavior. *School Psychology Quarterly, 11*, 337–352.

Martens, B. K., Hiralall, A. S., & Bradley, T. A. (1997). A note to teacher: improving student behavior through goal setting and feedback. *School Psychology Quarterly, 12*, 33–41.

McEvoy, M. A., Shores, R. E., Wehby, J. H., Johnson, S. M., & Fox, J. J. (1990). Special education teachers' implementation of procedures to promote social interaction among children in integrated settings. *Education and Training in Mental Retardation, 25*, 267–276.

Moncher, F. J. & Prinz, R. J. (1991). Treatment fidelity in outcome studies. *Clinical Psychology Review, 11*, 247–266.

Mortenson, B. P. & Witt, J. C. (1998). The use of weekly performance feedback to increase teacher implementation of a prereferral academic intervention. *School Psychology Review, 27*, 613–627.

Mueller, M. M., Edwards, R. P., & Trahant, D. (2003). Translating multiple assessment techniques into an intervention selection model for classrooms. *Journal of Applied Behavior Analysis, 36*, 563–573.

Nastasi, B. K. & Truscott, S. D. (2000). Acceptability research in school psychology: current trends and future directions. *School Psychology Quarterly, 15*, 117–122.

Noell, G. H. (in press). Research examining the relationships among consultation process, treatment integrity, and outcomes. In W. P. Erchul & S. M. Sheridan (Eds.), *Handbook of Research in School Consultation: Empirical Foundations for the Field*. Mahwah, NJ: Lawrence Erlbaum Associates.

Noell, G. H., Duhon, G. J., Gatti, S. L., & Connell, J. E. (2002a). Consultation, follow-up, and behavior management intervention implementation in general education. *School Psychology Review, 31*, 217–234.

Noell, G. H. & Gansle, K. A. (2006). Assuring the form has substance: treatment plan implementation as the foundation of assessing response to intervention. *Assessment for Effective Intervention, 32*, 32–39.

Noell, G. H. & Gresham, F. M. (1993). Functional outcome analysis: do the benefits of consultation and prereferral intervention justify the costs? *School Psychology Quarterly, 8*, 200–226.

Noell, G. H., Gresham, F. M., & Gansle, K. A. (2002b). Does treatment integrity matter? A preliminary investigation of instructional implementation and mathematics performance. *Journal of Behavioral Education, 11*, 51–67.

Noell, G. H., Witt, J. C., Gilbertson, D. N., Ranier, D. D., & Freeland, J. T. (1997). Increasing teacher intervention implementation in general education settings through consultation and performance feedback. *School Psychology Quarterly, 12*, 77–88.

Noell, G. H., Witt, J. C., LaFleur, L. H., Mortenson, B. P., Ranier, D. D., & LeVelle, J. (2000). A comparison of two follow-up strategies to increase teacher intervention implementation in general education following consultation. *Journal of Applied Behavior Analysis, 33*, 271–284.

Noell, G. H., Witt, J. C., Slider, N. J., Connell, J. E., Gatti, S. L., Williams, K. L., et al. (2005). Treatment implementation following behavioral consultation in schools: a comparison of three follow-up strategies. *School Psychology Review, 34*, 87–106.

Rhymer, K. N., Evans-Hampton, T. N., McCurdy, M., & Watson, T. S. (2002). Effects of varying levels of treatment integrity on toddler aggressive behavior. *Special Services in the Schools, 18*, 75–82.

Riley-Tillman, T. C. & Chafouleas, S. M. (2003). Using interventions that exist in the natural environment to increase treatment integrity and social influence in consultation. *Journal of Educational & Psychological Consultation, 14*, 139–156.

Sterling-Turner, H. E., Watson, T. S., Wildmon, M., Watkins, C., & Little, E. (2001). Investigating the relationship between training type and treatment integrity. *School Psychology Quarterly, 16*, 56–67.

Swanson, H. L. & Hoskyn, M. (1998). Experimental intervention research on students with learning disabilities: a meta-analysis of treatment outcomes. *Review of Educational Research, 68*, 277–321.

Taylor, J. & Miller, M. (1997). When timeout works some of the time: the importance of treatment integrity and functional assessment. *School Psychology Quarterly, 12*, 4–22.

Telzrow, C. F., McNamara, K., & Hollinger, C. L. (2000). Fidelity of problem-solving implementation and relationship to student performance. *School Psychology Review, 29*, 443–461.

Vermilyea, B. B., Barlow, D. H., & O'Brien, G. T. (1984). The importance of assessing treatment integrity: an example in the anxiety disorders. *Journal of Behavioral Assessment, 6*, 1–11.

Vollmer, T. R., Roane, H. S., Ringdahl, J. E., & Marcus, B. A. (1999). Evaluating treatment challenges with differential reinforcement of alternative behavior. *Journal of Applied Behavior Analysis, 32*, 9–23.

Watson, T. S. & Robinson, S. L. (1996). Direct behavioral consultation: an alternative to traditional behavioral consultation. *School Psychology Quarterly, 11*, 267–278.

Weiss, B. & Weisz, J. R. (1995). Relative effectiveness of behavioral versus nonbehavioral child psychotherapy. *Journal of Consulting and Clinical Psychology, 63*, 317–320.

Weisz, J. R., Weiss, B. Alicke, M. D., & Koltz, M. L. (1987). Effectiveness of psychotherapy with children and adolescents: a meta-analysis for clinicians. *Journal of Consulting and Clinical Psychology, 55*, 542–549.

Wickstrom, K. F., Jones, K. M., LaFleur, L. H., & Witt, J. C. (1998). An analysis of treatment integrity in school-based behavioural consultation. *School Psychology Quarterly, 13*, 141–154.

Witt, J. C., Noell, G. H., LaFleur, L. H., & Mortenson, B. P. (1997). Teacher usage of interventions in general education: measurement and analysis of the independent variable. *Journal of Applied Behavior Analysis, 30*, 693–696.

Yeaton, W. H. & Sechrest, L. (1981). Critical dimensions in the choice and maintenance of successful treatments: strength, integrity, and effectiveness. *Journal of Consulting and Clinical Psychology, 49*, 156–167.

IV
Lessons Learned in Implementing Problem-Solving and Response-to-Intervention Strategies

19

The Heartland Area Education Agency 11 Problem-Solving Approach: An Overview and Lessons Learned

Martin J. Ikeda, Alecia Rahn-Blakeslee, Bradley C. Niebling, Jeri K. Gustafson, Randy Allison, and James Stumme

Martin J. Ikeda, PhD, is Coordinator of Special Projects at Heartland AEA 11, and an Assessment Consultant in Special Education for the Bureau of Children, Family, and Community Services of the Iowa Department of Education. marty.ikeda@iowa.gov

Alecia Rahn-Blakeslee, PhD, is a Research & Evaluation Practitioner/School Psychologist at Heartland AEA 11, Johnston, IA. arahn@aea11.k12.ia.us

Bradley C. Niebling, PhD, is a School Psychologist/Curriculum Alignment Specialist at Heartland AEA 11, Johnston, IA. bniebling@aea11.k12.ia.us

Jeri K. Gustafson, MSEd, is a special education research practitioner on the Special Education Research Team at Heartland AEA 11 in Johnston, IA.

Randy Allison, EdS, NCSP, is Coordinator of System Supports for Educational Results, Heartland AEA 11, Johnston, IA. rallison@aea11.k12.ia.us

James Stumme, EdD, is an Associate Administrator at Heartland AEA 11, Johnston, IA. jstumme@aea11.k12.ia.us

For many educators, "response to intervention" (RTI) is a new term, part of the nomenclature only after the 2004 reauthorization of the Individuals with Disabilities Education Act (IDEIA, 2004). For other educators, RTI represents the latest evolution of alternative educational service delivery that began in the 1980s (Deno, 1985; Graden, Zins, and Curtis, 1988; Shinn, 1989, 1995). RTI involves the provision of high-quality instruction and interventions matched to student need, with frequent monitoring of student progress (i.e., responsiveness to the intervention) for data-based decision-making (Batsche et al., 2005). In general, two forms of RTI are described in the professional literature: (a) *RTI-problem solving* and (b) *RTI-standard treatment protocol*.

RTI-problem solving involves applying a problem-solving perspective to individual students whose performance differs from expectations (Upah and Tilly, 2002). Individual student problems are defined in observable and measurable terms, and the gap between what is expected (e.g., a district's benchmark, or accepted performance levels) and what is observed is used to determine the severity of the problem. Problem analysis of individual problems identifies relevant, low inference factors that are impacting student performance (Lentz and Shapiro, 1986) and determines what instructional or curricular changes might be implemented to address the problem.

A second iteration of RTI in the professional literature is called the *standard treatment protocol* (Fuchs, Mock, Morgan, and Young, 2003). After screening, rather than individually analyzing the problems of every student who does not perform at the desired level, empirically validated interventions are implemented for all students with similar instructional needs, and progress is monitored frequently. If student performance continues to be discrepant from peers, then entitlement for special education is considered.

This chapter describes a statewide effort for implementing an alternate system for special education identification and service delivery, beginning in 1985, and part of an RTI-problem solving system since 1993 (Ikeda, Tilly, Stumme, Volmer, and Allison, 1996). While there have been publications describing how Iowa and, in particular, Heartland

Area Education Agency 11 (henceforth referred to as *Heartland*) has worked to create and support a more integrated special education and general education service delivery system with a foundation in RTI (Grimes and Tilly, 1996; Ikeda et al., 1996; Ikeda, Grimes, Tilly, Kurns, Allison, and Stumme, 2002; Ikeda and Gustafson, 2002; Reschly and Ysseldyke, 2002), a descriptive chronology of the "whys" and "hows" of large-scale implementation has not appeared in the professional literature. The purpose of this chapter is to detail the steps that Iowa, and in particular Heartland, took to integrate problem-solving practices into the daily routines of staff. In addition, lessons learned and next iterations based on lessons learned, are presented. Where relevant, the steps taken at the state level are described. Similarly, where relevant, how Heartland operationalized reform occurring at the state level is described.

19.1 Background

Iowa has 12 intermediate education agencies, called area education agencies (AEAs). The purpose of AEAs is to provide leadership and service to local school districts in the areas of instructional media, special education, and other educational services (e.g., school improvement). AEAs have boundary lines that were developed by following the county-wide service delivery system from which AEAs evolved in 1975. AEAs support 365 accredited public school districts serving about 451,000 students in grades Kindergarten through 12th grade, as well as about 35,000 students in accredited nonpublic schools.

Currently, Heartland supports 54 public school districts and over 30 accredited nonpublic schools, with public school enrollment of about 119,000 students. School districts within Heartland range in total K-12 student populations of between 340 and 33,000, with a median K-12 student population of about 1000. The geographic coverage of Heartland is over 10,000 square miles in central Iowa. Heartland's boundaries contain the largest number of students, and Heartland is the second largest in the state of Iowa in physical size.

In the 1980s, in the area of special education supports and services, AEA policies and practices reflected the zeitgeist of that time: teacher referral for special education testing. Testing included a battery of measures, including aptitude, achievement, adaptive functioning, social history, medical history, and others. Regardless of the presenting problem, the test battery was administered. This "refer–test–place" system was efficient for placing children into categories that were consistent with the *Education of All Handicapped Children Act* (EHA) (now titled the *Individuals with Disabilities Education Improvement Act*).

The primary rationale for moving from a refer–test–place system to a problem-solving system was recognition by leaders in Iowa that practices for serving students with disabilities could be improved. In the 1980s, there was growing interest by leaders in Iowa with alternative practices and an emerging research base (Batsche and Ulman, 1986; Deno and Mirkin, 1977; Graden et al., 1988). With a widespread desire to improve services for students with disabilities, combined with a growing base of evidence of alternative methodology for supporting students with disabilities, Iowa began the process of the development and wide-scale implementation of alternative special education supports and service delivery. The reform effort was led by the Iowa Department of Education, with AEAs and local education agencies (LEAs) viewed as critical partners in the reform effort. The Department of Education provided technical assistance, but AEAs were given the latitude to determine the pace and magnitude of the reform effort. The Iowa Administrative Rules of Special Education (Iowa Department of Education, 2000) place child find responsibilities on AEAs, with districts (LEAs) responsible for implementation of programming.

19.1.1 Alternative Practices Emerging in the 1980s

Several influential reform efforts and practices in the professional literature drove the state to move from a refer–test–place system to a "needs-based" system. For example, the *Regular Education Initiative* (Will, 1986) described bridging the gap between segregated special education and general education services. Developing programs to better impact quality of life (Meyer and Evans, 1989) and including families in discussions about significant life outcomes for persons with even the most severe disabilities (Browder, 1991) were important for learning how to better consult with families and assess student needs.

The research on IQ also influenced development of alternative practices. For example, research examined the reliability and utility of common assessment practices like profile analysis and found that such practices did not reliably differentiate students (Barnett and Macmann, 1992; McDermott, Fantuzzo, and Glutting, 1990; McDermott, Fantuzzo, Glutting, Watkins, and Baggaley, 1992). Other studies demonstrated that IQ does not limit a child's ability to benefit from instruction (Gersten, Becker, Heiry, and White, 1984).

Finally, concepts such as (a) linking assessment and intervention (Fuchs and Fuchs, 1986), (b) focusing on measurable behaviors with lower levels of inference (Lentz and Shapiro, 1986), and (c) investing in consultation (Kratochwill and Bergan, 1990) made sense to many in leadership positions throughout the state. The attitude within the state, at the time of change, was not that the "system" was broken. The system in place was very effective in identifying that some students had disabilities. The system was not efficient, however, in identifying instructional needs and supporting teachers in improving student performance. Leadership at the Iowa Department of Education and the AEAs worked together to develop (a) a belief system that would endure as practices changed and (b) an ambitious training agenda that would better link assessment practices during entitlement decision-making with individual education plan (IEP) development and implementation.

19.1.2 Belief Systems for Supporting New Practices

In the 1980s, leaders within the Department of Education and the AEAs recognized that principles drove practices. Critical roles were filled by administrators and consultants at the Iowa Department of Education, professors of school psychology, and practitioners in leadership roles within their respective AEAs (from a variety of professional disciplines, but predominately from the School Psychology Leadership group). The philosophy adhered to during system reform was that, while technology and knowledge change over time, linking practices to core foundational beliefs would help sustain change. In addition, while the problem-solving model continues to evolve as described in this chapter, the core belief systems provide a constant against which new ideas can be anchored prior to large-scale adoption of practices.

While the reform effort was initiated at the state level, critical conversations occurred throughout Iowa's educational system, to facilitate change of practices. Initially, as part of the effort to reform both services and the belief systems about services, the Iowa Department of Education sought widespread input from constituents, including administrators, general education teachers, special education teachers, support service providers, and parents. By asking a series of questions about what was working, what could be better, and what were the barriers to change, leaders within the state developed foundational principles for organizing their change process.

The foundational principles first described in 1985 have endured to date and include: (a) integration of resources from general, compensatory, and special education; (b) increased role flexibility and function; (c) increased availability of intervention options for students; (d) increased options for local schools to provide a continuum of services to all students; and (e) the promotion of meaningful parental involvement. In addition, in the 1980s, the Iowa State made a commitment to high-quality professional development for school psychologists and educational consultants, as well as general education teachers, as pivotal for improving student performance.

19.1.3 Emerging Practices for Identifying Instructional Needs

The Iowa Department of Education organized the professional development effort, and also established priorities for what services in schools should address. Hence, professional development was provided throughout the state to: (a) increase the use of direct and functional assessment method; (b) develop appropriate teacher support strategies; (c) monitor student performance using direct and frequent measures; and (d) establish an outcomes-based perspective of student performance rather than a perspective based on a process for identifying students as having disabilities.

Given this perceptual climate in the state of Iowa, Jeff Grimes at the Iowa Department of Education, Dan Reschly at Iowa State University, and the School Psychology Leadership Group accessed an emerging professional literature that described alternatives to IQ testing and refer–test–placement of children (Deno, 1985; Marston and Magnusson, 1988; Shinn, 1989; Shinn and Marston, 1985). The research base demonstrated that more direct measures of academic competence (e.g., curriculum-based measures) could be used to establish performance gaps for students with low achievement, and those direct measures were sensitive in differentiating between low achievers and students with disabilities (Shinn and Marston, 1985; Ysseldyke, Algozzine, Shinn, and McGue, 1982). Other relevant and influential literature focused on practices like consultation in academics and behavior as a vital role for school psychologists beyond merely testing students (Curtis and Zins, 1981; Kratochwill and Bergan, 1990).

Based on the emerging research described above, Iowa engaged in statewide, systems-level reform in 1985 (Ikeda et al., 1996). A 3-year project was implemented collaboratively between the Iowa Department of Education, Iowa State University, and Iowa's AEAs. University-based experts, primarily from outside of Iowa, were hired to train curriculum-based assessment, behavior consultation, and referral/question consultation statewide. National experts traveled the state and directly worked on new assessment practices with school psychologists in the field.

Having developed a core belief system, and having received some initial training on skills relevant for reform, AEAs began aligning procedures manuals with emerging practice, to sustain change. In Heartland, the manual had breadth of content of: (a) roles and functions of all staff; (b) forms and procedures for interventions; (c) forms and procedures for entitlement; (d) forms and procedures for IEPs; and (e) other regulatory information. The manual was developed to assist staff in incorporating problem solving and data-based decision-making into their existing repertoires (Heartland AEA 11, 1989). Other AEAs developed similar procedures manuals.

This initial step in large-scale change in practice led to another statewide, 3-year project for further integrating newly learned practices. The *Renewed Service Delivery System* (RSDS) brought in additional national expertise on curriculum-based measurement (CBM; Deno, 1985, Fuchs and

Fuchs, 1986, Shinn, 1989) and functional assessment (Derby and Wacker, 1992).

Heartland leaders made the decision to build capacity of agency staff to sustain skills in the absence of the university trainers. An internal training cadre of six full-time equivalents was established to develop trainings for Heartland and district staff, in the areas of CBM norms, building assistance teaming, and progress monitoring. These trainers consisted of master's level educational consultants, school psychologists, and early childhood consultants.

School districts applied for grants that allowed training and support for teachers to work in building assistance teams. Teachers were taught to (a) identify students at risk for failure in general education, (b) brainstorm solutions to problems, and (c) refer for special education evaluation those students whose problems were not solved in general education.

It was from this second 3-year project that problem-solving practices at Heartland were developed. The procedures manual was revised (and continues to be revised annually) to reflect these new policies and procedures (e.g., collaboration, CBM and its use in a problem-solving model, building assistance teams). Because there are figures and descriptions of the problem-solving model elsewhere (e.g., Ikeda et al., 2002; Reschly and Ysseldyke, 2002), the following is a brief overview of Heartland's *problem-solving approach*. The problem-solving approach initially was piloted in the early 1990s with 10 of Heartland's then 56 public school districts.

19.1.4 A Four-Tiered Problem-Solving Approach

Heartland's problem-solving approach was designed to match resources based on the severity of the problem. For low-level problems, fewer resources are needed. As problems become more severe or in need of more instruction or other support, more expertise is used in consultation and problem solving. As operationalized in 1993, there were four levels of problem solving. First, general education teachers attempt to solve problems through accommodations in the classroom. Second, teachers work with other teachers using the building assistance team to develop and implement strategies that could resolve the problem. Third, Heartland staff work with teachers to solve the problem. Fourth, entitlement for special education is considered.

19.1.5 Use of the Problem-Solving Process in Decision-Making

Embedded within each level of the problem-solving approach is the problem-solving process. The problem-solving process entails four decisions: defining the problem, understanding why the problem is occurring, designing and implementing an intervention, and evaluating intervention effects. For a detailed description of the problem-solving process, see Tilly (2002).

Table 19.1 describes the conceptual underpinnings of problem solving first used by Heartland in 1993. Table 19.1 was developed from the master

file first written in 1993 and adapted from Hartmann, Roper, and Bradford (1979). The information in the table illustrates the strong link that Iowa and Heartland made to the professional literature, when selecting both belief systems and practices.

Distinctions made to Heartland staff in 1993 centered around assumptions of assessment, implications of assessment, use of data, and other key characteristics of linking functional assessments to appropriate instructional strategies. Staff were taught that assessment was the process of using information to make a variety of educationally relevant decisions. Tests were but one method used in decision-making, and all methods should lead to understanding of the interactions between instruction, curriculum, setting, and the learner that enable children to learn, rather than using assessment as a search for pathology within the child. Personality

TABLE 19.1. Comparison of problem solving and traditional models of practice.

	Behavioral	Traditional
I. Assumption		
1. Conception of personality	Personality constructs mainly employed to summarize specific behavior patterns, if at all	Personality as a reflection of enduring underlying states or traits
2. Causes of behavior	Maintaining conditions ought in current environment	Intrapsychic or within the individual
II. Implications		
1. Role of behavior	Important as a sample of person's repertoire in specific situation	Behavior assumes importance only insofar as it indexes underlying causes
2. Role of history	Relatively unimportant, except, for example, to provide a retrospective baseline	Crucial, in that present conditions seen as a product of the past
3. Consistency of behavior	Behavior thought to be specific to the situation	Behavior expected to be consistent across time and settings
III. Use of data	To describe target behaviors and maintaining conditions	To describe personality functioning and etiology
	To select the appropriate treatment	To diagnose or classify
	To evaluate and revise treatment	To make prognosis; to predict
IV. Other characteristics		
1. Level of inferences	Low	Medium to high
2. Comparisons	More emphasis on intra-individual or idiographic	More emphasis on inter-individual or nomothetic
3. Methods of assessment	More emphasis on direct methods (e.g., observations of behavior in natural environment)	More emphasis on indirect methods (e.g., interviews and self-report)
4. Timing of assessment	More ongoing; prior, during, and after treatment	Pre- and perhaps post-treatment or strictly to diagnose
5. Scope of assessment	Specific measures and of more variables (e.g., of target behaviors in various situations of side effects, context, strengths as well as deficiencies)	More global measures (e.g., of cure, or improvement) but only of the individual
6. Basic philosophical approach	Disconfirmatory	Confirmatory

constructs were recognized as descriptive of behavioral patterns for further functional assessment, rather than as causal or explanatory factors for poor student performance. Information that staff had historically relied upon as important, like in-depth family history, became important only to the extent that such information helped the team understand the problems *and* led the team to instructional strategies that could be taught to the child or to the family.

Hence, it became unacceptable for teams to explain behaviors through statements like, "he is behaving in such ways because he has attention-deficit hyperactivity disorder (ADHD)." Instead, the teams needed to focus assessment on the behavioral manifestations of ADHD, and the instructional, curricular, and environmental factors that preceded or followed the behavioral manifestation of "ADHD-ness." With these new assumptions, beliefs, and requirements came a new set of practices that education professionals were to engage in when collecting assessment data.

19.1.6 Changes in Linking Assessment to Interventions

Assessment practices were much different after adopting the problem-solving approach than prior. Heartland professionals worked more with teachers prior to referral to understand problems and conducted more direct observation of behavior in classrooms, rather than pulling students out for testing. When direct measures of student performance were obtained, the emphases were ongoing data collection in relevant academic skill areas rather than on one-time use of published, standardized, norm-referenced tests of aptitude or achievement. Simply obtaining and implementing new assessment practices was not sufficient to fully implement problem solving.

Skill sets needed to effectively implement problem solving, and ultimately link assessment data to instructional recommendations, included knowledge of: (a) effective instructional principles (Ysseldyke, Thurlow, Mecklenburg, and Graden, 1984), (b) effective behavioral principles (Sulzer-Azaroff and Mayer, 1994), (c) CBM (Shinn, 1989), (d) functional behavioral assessment (O'Neill et al., 1997), (e) behavioral consultation (Kratochwill and Bergan, 1990), (f) using CBM for progress monitoring (Fuchs, Fuchs, and Hamlett, 1989), and (g)

single-case research design for monitoring intervention effects (Deno, 1986).

In 1993, it was recognized that, while there were tools for establishing that students had problems in both academic and behavioral domains, practitioners working within the academic domain recognized the need for more expertise in problem analysis and research-linked instructional practice. AEA staff piloted use of curriculum-based evaluation (CBE; Howell and Nolet, 2000), a decision-making framework for considering the assumed causes of the problem, validating the hypotheses, and linking results to teaching recommendations.

19.2 Fine-Tuning Implementation of Problem Solving

Implementation of problem solving has been largely unchanged since 1993, with changes primarily in paperwork to help staff better follow the problem-solving process and to promote high levels of rigor when analyzing problems. For example, in 1995 it was recognized that there were little data on how well implementation of problem solving was occurring throughout the school districts supported by Heartland. An internal review was conducted to evaluate paperwork turned in by Heartland staff on components of problem identification, problem analysis, intervention implementation, and intervention evaluation. In a strategic and purposeful way, the results of the review led Heartland leaders to emphasize problem analysis for improving practice. Paperwork requirements were changed to provide staff with very descriptive prompts, in logical order of understanding the problem. Professional development was provided in individual and group settings, and staff were evaluated on how well problems were analyzed. As a result of the changes, an additional program review found that problem definition and problem analysis improved.

Another finding of the review projects was that Heartland had little information about intervention practices prior to special education entitlement. Consequently, Heartland supervisors changed evaluation and supervision practices to include case reviews descriptive of the problem-solving steps utilized in work with teachers and families. From these case reviews, supervisors had a built-in opportunity to engage staff in conversations around effective practices and to problem-solve barriers to practice. As Heartland leaders worked with staff, several lessons were learned in the form of positive outcomes and areas of concern.

19.2.1 Lessons Learned: Things to Celebrate

The positives in implementing problem solving include use of local data to define problems, use of more direct measures of problems, engaging general educators in supporting students experiencing difficulty, promoting access to the research base for developing interventions, and using graphed data to make decisions about instructional progress. Each concept is a positive because each concept is linked to the core foundational principles that resulted in systems reform, and merely having each concept is at some level a degree of qualitative evidence for adoption of practices endorsed in reform.

Extending the work embedded in the initial piloting of problem solving in the early 1990s, the Iowa *Administrative Rules of Special Education* codified the legitimacy for AEAs to use problem solving as part of the child-find procedures. Components of interventions were clearly described in the Iowa Rules. Any AEA that opted to engage in problem solving was required to demonstrate procedures manuals in alignment with the Iowa Rules. For AEAs who did not choose to operationalize problem-solving practices, the Iowa Rules required data from a general education intervention for all cases of students suspected of having disabilities. While there are no hard data to confirm the extent to which problem solving and general education interventions have been implemented within Heartland and across the state, all Heartland practitioners were (and still are) required to engage in problem-solving practices within all school districts that Heartland staff served directly.

Procedures were written to reflect the need for behavioral definition/operationalization of the problem; problem analysis; intervention materials and other responsibilities; duration, location, and time for the intervention; and the data decision rule for continuing or modifying the intervention. These interventions became part of the student record and were required when consent for full and individual evaluation was submitted. Additionally, the full and individual evaluation did not mean "test." Instead,

the full and individual evaluation, as defined in the Iowa Rules (Iowa Department of Education, 2000), means:

an initial evaluation of the individual's educational needs shall be completed before any action is taken with respect to the initial provision of special education services. Written parental consent as required in these rules shall be obtained prior to conducting the evaluation. The purpose of the evaluation is to determine the educational interventions that are required to resolve the presenting problem, behaviors of concern, or suspected disability, including whether the educational interventions are special education (page 18, Iowa Rules of Special Education).

The Iowa Rules then specify that the evaluation consists of: (a) an objective definition of the problem; (b) analysis of existing information about the individual; (c) identification of areas of strength or competence relevant to the presenting problem; and (d) collection of additional information needed to design interventions intended to resolve the problem. Similar language is used for describing re-evaluations. Hence, since 1995, *every student* for whom entitlement for special education was explored within Heartland has results from a general education intervention in their cumulative folder. *Every student* means, quite literally, every student supported with an IEP: speech, academic problems, motor difficulty, elementary-aged, high-school-aged, and significantly cognitively impaired.

In addition, since 1995, while over 15,000 initial special education evaluations, re-evaluations, and 3-year evaluations have been conducted by Heartland staff, it is estimated that fewer than 20 published, standardized, norm-referenced tests of aptitude have been administered by Heartland staff. Thus, measurement methods other than IQ tests or published achievement tests have been used for analyzing achievement problems and developing interventions. This is important because, in over 10 years of practice, students have been identified as having disabilities, have had IEPs written, and have been afforded other protections of IDEA without use of published tests and without use of IQ–achievement discrepancy formulas. Child-find and IEPs can be completed without the use of published, standardized, norm-referenced tests.

Other effects documented for problem solving were summarized by Ikeda and Gustafson (2002), who reported that about 25% of problems were solved at the building assistance team level (which may or may not include support from Heartland staff) without exploring eligibility and need for specialized instruction under IDEA. Building assistance teams are part of Levels 2 and 3 of the Heartland problem-solving approach. Teachers collaborate with other teachers, and in some cases with AEA staff, to resolve problems using resources other than special education. Internal surveys of school psychologists indicated similar resolution rates: about 25% of cases at Level 3 resolved, with the remaining cases moving to determination of eligibility for an IEP.

19.2.2 Lessons Learned: Addressing Unintended Impacts of Changes in Practice

Despite the positives summarized above, there have also been several unintended effects of problem solving that we view as problematic. First, some schools integrated practices but not belief systems, and other schools viewed problem-solving practices as hoops for excluding children from the general curriculum. This led to frustration on teachers' behalf and in problem solving merely serving to supplant testing practices. The intention of many general education teachers was still to "get the child into special education," rather than on understanding the child's needs and the resources needed to meet those needs.

The second unintended effect observed was that the standard of rigor for instructional interventions was higher for general education interventions than for interventions implemented through IEPs in special education. One of the purported advantages of problem solving over refer–test–place is that assessment practices in the entitlement process are more instructionally relevant. There are better data defining student present level of performance, and there are better descriptions of the curricular material and instructional sequences children need to succeed. Nevertheless, case reviews demonstrated that students sometimes made more progress on general education interventions than they made when on an IEP. Heartland staff reported that some students received more support during the intervention process than when children received specialized instructional resources, and special education teachers

reported not using the information generated during problem solving to determine how best to teach students.

The level of rigor of interventions during problem solving prior to entitlement and problem solving after entitlement is directly attributable to differences in the paperwork. As described in the Iowa Rules, components of general education interventions are very prescriptive, and specific strategies and tasks are written into the intervention. With IEPs, the general rule of thumb since 1975 is that IEPs are not instructional documents, in that IEPs describe global goals and services rather than specific instructional sequences. Hence, it is not surprising that general education interventions had more rigor than programs found in IEPs.

Another unintended effect of problem solving was that general education teachers did not view the intervention phase as "helpful." Even in circumstances in which progress in the general education intervention (a) exceeded projected progress based on the intervention goal or (b) resulted in a reduced performance gap but still below the goal, many general education teachers instead viewed only "placement into special education" as "help." Teachers complained that "it" took too long ("it" meaning the process to remove the child from the general class setting). In the traditional model, from the time of referral to the time of placement, the child received nothing. In the problem-solving model, the child receives a variety of supports, and the information gathered throughout the process is used to help generate IEP goals and, in best cases, inform instruction. However, the culture and belief system in most schools was still that many students who required "extra help" would not "get what they need" until placed into special education services.

19.3 Next Iteration of Problem Solving

Dissatisfied with how problem solving in the late 1990s was focused on lack of response to intervention, was considered "hoop jumping" by many in general education, and with statewide consensus on what constituted defensible decision-making (Iowa Department of Education, 2006), state leaders and Heartland administrators discussed strategies to get schools more engaged in using data in decision-making.

Schools were required by Iowa State law to report on multiple measures of student performance to answer four basic questions about student achievement: (a) What do data tell us about student learning needs? (b) What can be done to impact student learning? (c) What can be done to assess student performance both summatively and formatively? (d) Did the efforts work in impacting student achievement?

While Iowa schools had large-scale test results available for review (the Iowa Test of Basic Skills), teachers and administrators found that the data from these tests were available neither quickly nor frequently enough to assess short-term changes in achievement as a result of school improvement. Having moved past defending the appropriateness of using CBM data as part of special education decision-making, Heartland and school leaders were ready to explore CBM for making schoolwide, data-based decisions in the basic academic skills areas (Simmons, Kuykendall, King, Cornachione, and Kame'enui, 2000), and positive behavior supports in the realm of behavior (Sugai, Horner, and Gresham, 2002).

The culmination of local data collection, ongoing developments in the research literature, new federal and state policies, and the constant examination of practices in Heartland and the schools has all contributed to the evolution of the problem-solving model. Improved practices at Heartland and in the schools has required more than simply changing the Heartland problem-solving model and improved data collection on student learning and behavior. Hiring practices, professional development, and evaluation of staff all needed to be changed in order to promote practices aligned with systems—and individual-level problem solving.

19.4 Hiring and Training Staff to Implement Problem Solving

As early as 1993, Heartland's leadership recognized that RTI-problem-solving systems require different skill sets of staff. This recognition led to changes in hiring and evaluation practices, as well as in professional development practices.

19.4.1 Hiring and Evaluating Staff

As problem solving was implemented and evolving, job descriptions were changed to reflect changing practice. School psychologists on staff in 1995 provided input into job descriptions to redefine what "working as a school psychologist" meant. Teaming, data-based decision-making, consultation, functional assessment (i.e., academic and behavioral), intervention design, and formative evaluation were selected as critical skill sets worthy of evaluation for new and continued employment.

In addition, as job descriptions were revised, criteria for selection for employment were revisited. Several critical skill sets were identified from the literature to discriminate staff likely to be able to adapt to problem-solving practices from staff that would not be successful at applying problem solving in schools. These skill sets helped screen applicants for new school psychologists and educational consultant positions, and included (a) familiarity with nontraditional measures (e.g., CBM; Deno, 1985; Shinn, 1989), (b) instructional and behavioral consultation (Kratochwill and Bergan, 1990; Rosenfield, 1987), (c) problem analysis (Howell and Nolet, 2000), (d) effective teaching practices (Ysseldyke et al., 1984), and (e) single-case research (Deno, 1985).

Evaluation of staff also changed over time. Prior to problem solving, staff were evaluated on the numbers of tests administered, the compliance to timelines, and general people skills. Now, staff are evaluated on how well they implemented problem solving. Previously, staff and their supervisor engaged in basic reviews of performance. Now, staff have peer reviews in which interventions are critiqued, in addition to basic reviews of general performance and job management. Staff who do not demonstrate competence are provided with external supports from expert practitioners and supervisors.

19.4.2 Training Staff

Beyond hiring staff with the beginning skill sets needed to effectively practice in a problem-solving system, substantial investment has been made in training all staff to work at the systems and individual level.

19.4.2.1 Systems-Level Training

All Heartland staff are taught the connections between the initiatives that occur in agencies and schools. This includes van drivers and clerical staff, as well as consultant staff (like school psychologists) and direct service staff (like occupational therapists). Staff working at the systems level (school improvement consultants, school psychologists, educational consultants, and school social workers) receive additional training in analyzing both individual student and systems-level data using Microsoft Excel, needs assessment tools, and tools to assist in planning, implementation, and evaluation of individual student and systems-level interventions. There are sequences of training for staff for their first 2 years of employment.

19.4.2.2 Individual Problem-Solving Training

Special education staff new to Heartland (school psychologists, educational consultants, physical and occupational therapists, school social workers, speech and language pathologists, early childhood teachers, and a few others) are trained on a variety of topics on problem solving. Training was developed internally through the relationships and content expertise developed in partnership with the university faculty since 1993.

Staff are trained in the philosophies inherent in problem solving, as well as in the steps needed to write an intervention (Upah and Tilly, 2002). Staff also learn CBE (Howell and Nolet, 2000) in reading, math, writing, social–emotional behavior, and task-related behavior. Progress monitoring, building assistance teaming, and functional behavioral assessment are optional trainings. In addition, each discipline group within Heartland (e.g., school psychology, speech and language pathology, occupational therapy) has a staff development specialist. The staff development specialist spends half of their assignment as a practitioner assigned to schools, engaged in problem-solving. The other half of the assignment is assisting supervisors with support to staff, in particular new staff or veteran staff having difficulty with implementing problem solving. Hence, professional development at Heartland is more than simply "taking classes." Case reviews with peers, specialists,

and managers also help refine decision-making skills.

19.5 Next Lessons for Learning: Bridging the Research-to-Practice Gap

This chapter has described principles and practices that were used to effect changes in assessment and intervention practices starting in 1993 and continuing today. The importance of collectively establishing foundational principles cannot be overstated. The foundational principles and priorities remain today and have been at the heart of all subsequent changes or efforts that Heartland has made over the last 15 years. When better ideas, knowledge, or tools have become available, these new ideas are examined against the foundational principle structure prior to adopting or endorsing practices large scale.

Systems-level consultation, as well as full and individualized evaluations, takes time. Skills needed to engage in systems-level consultation take training time. Support to staff to engage in school improvement (including special education) takes time. Skills needed to engage in individual problem analysis and instructional consultation require ongoing support. Like most systems, schools in Iowa are still in session for 186 days. Heartland staff access teachers in a work day that is about 10 hours long. Finding time to do it all, and to do it well, is an issue. After the initial pilot (1991 or 1992), Heartland chose to scale up to all schools rather than to slowly bring schools into alignment with problem solving. By 1994, all schools within Heartland's boundaries were engaged with problem solving.

Grimes and Kurns (2003) and Tilly (2003) provide summaries of outcomes data in Heartland. Grimes and Kurns (2003) describe implementation at one elementary building in which data-based decision-making is systematized. Data indicate near 100% attainment of benchmarks on dynamic indicators of basic early literacy skills (DIBELS; Good, Gruba, and Kaminski, 2002), and increases in oral reading fluency (from a first-grade median of 32 words per minute (wpm) in 1994 to a 2003 median of 60 wpm, second-grade median of 78 wpm in 1994 to a 2003 median of 92 wpm). In addition, proficiency rates of fourth-graders as a whole, on the district-wide assessment, is improving, going from 55% of fourth-graders proficient in the triennium 1999–2001 to 70% of fourth-graders proficient in the triennium 2001–2003.

Grimes and Kurns (2003) summarize results of surveys done with between 5% and 8% of building assistance teams within Heartland's boundaries. For these teams, most referrals were at either first or second grade, and roughly half of meetings had parents in attendance. Most interventions (69%) were in the academic areas, with another 29% targeting behavior. Some 25% of students had interventions through assistance teams prior to the intervention summarized, 16% of interventions were reported as resolving the problem, and another 39% continued with intervention. About one-third of the students received specialized instruction within an IEP.

Special education placement rates within Heartland have been increasing since 1986. The trend is consistent, about 0.5% increase per year. At present, about 13% of students within Heartland are entitled to special education.

Grimes and Kurns (2003) also summarize consumer satisfaction data. Teachers and administrators are surveyed as part of the accreditation process that occurs once every 5 years. For 2003, general education teachers (90% of 416), administrators (97% of 46), and special education teachers (87% of 126) reported that the problem-solving process supports teachers in improving performance of students. Similar responses were obtained when constituents were asked about the relevancy of applying problem-solving practices to students receiving support through general education, as well as students receiving support through specialized instruction. Ikeda and Gustafson (2002) were the source of some of the data in Grimes and Kurns (2003).

Tilly (2003) described the evolution of practices at Heartland from being individual based (teacher referred) to being data based. The set of practices now emerging relies on student achievement data on systems-wide screening measures, to help school staff align instructional resources. In evaluating an early literacy project in which DIBELS were used to group students by instructional need and to help school systems enhance core and supplemental instructional practices, Tilly (2003) reported gains over time on all DIBELS measures, moderate to large effect sizes for the majority of the 36 partic-

ipating elementary schools, and reductions in new special education placement rates. Missing, however, were comparison data from nonimplementing schools.

Rahn-Blakeslee, Ikeda, and Gustafson (2005) evaluated 32 reading intervention cases generated from problem solving. Rahn-Blakeslee et al. rated interventions for quality, examined goal ambitiousness, and calculated student growth over time. Results suggested strong ratings overall for the presence of quality indices and ambitious goal setting. Most interventions were not sufficiently rigorous to impact reading performance. Most students made progress toward goals, but intervention slopes typically did not meet or exceed established growth standards or instructional placement standards. In addition, intervention data typically did not transfer to the student's initial IEP upon entitlement.

The results of the aforementioned studies provide several areas in which research can better inform RTI practice. First, simple indicators of "successful" RTI implementation need to be defined. If sites across the country used similar protocols, and if non-participating sites provided comparison data, then much could be learned.

Second, the data underscore the importance of (a) staff development, (b) implementation monitoring, and (c) integrating research-to-practice *with rigor*. Concepts embedded in RTI are not intuitive, and in many cases are counter to how people have been trained. There needs to be a wealth of teaching and support for helping staff implement RTI. Treatment integrity is critical to examine. It is important to understand if instructional practices are implemented as needed to effect change. Relatedly, research must inform practice. There are practices that effect performance. These practices, and only these practices, can be endorsed.

There are several areas in which additional evaluation data are needed. Where individual problem-solving practices are applied, relevant questions include: (a) Does problem-analysis result in interventions that effect student performance? (b) What factors predict better outcome for students? (c) How many students have problems solved without needing support through special education? (d) How many IEP goals have been developed directly from results of interventions? Note that, from our perspective, the questions around "are the right students being found?" are not as compelling, because the intent is to promote a system in which resources are aligned and student performance is effected, not a system in which child-find is the end result of the process.

From a standard treatment protocol perspective, questions include: (a) How many students receive supplemental support? For how long? With what effect? (b) How many students receive intensive support? (c) What supports do students need after their performance is "normalized"? (d) What is the cost associated with implementation?

The clock is running. By 2014, all students must be proficient on their state-approved indicator. At some point, loopholes for masking deficiencies will be eliminated. At that time, schools and supporters of schools will need to demonstrate that, through differentiated instruction, achievement happens. Problem solving and the standard treatment protocol both have potential for helping schools better align resources, and to focus intervention efforts on variables under the control of schools: (a) materials presented, (b) frequency and quality of opportunities to respond, (c) reinforcement schedules, (d) alignment between standards, instruction, and assessment, and (e) frequency and quality of formative assessment data.

19.6 Summary

Heartland began the transition from refer–test–place to an RTI-problem-solving system in the early 1990s. Heartland's educational reform efforts began 20 years ago without external funding or ongoing support from universities. Research-based practices continue to guide the Heartland reform efforts. Small-scale quantitative projects and larger scale qualitative projects support decision-making about enhancements to problem solving that are needed. Decisions about special education entitlement have been made without use of published tests of intelligence and achievement, for over 10 years, across all disability categories. The challenge now is to effect performance of the educational system, so that specialized resources are applied only to students truly in need of specialized instruction, and not to students whose academic performance is the result of a misalignment between curriculum, instruction, and assessment. The data in 2014 will differentiate sites able to implement effective whole-scale

RTI practices from those systems not able to differentiate resources. The challenge to schools is to identify formative, systems-level data to allow for change prior to the point in time at which schools are judged on leaving no child behind. At present, RTI is the best option for aligning curriculum, instruction, assessment, and resources. The effectiveness of RTI on student achievement is promising. As sites engage in RTI, more evaluation data, and more systematic evaluation data, should help judge the effect of RTI practices. Both RTI and non-RTI sites are challenged to gather student achievement data to understand the effects of practices. Only through such collaborative efforts will scientists and practitioners understand practices that impact students in meaningful ways.

References

Barnett, D. W. & Macmann, G. M. (1992). Aptitude-achievement discrepancy scores: Accuracy in analysis misdirected. *School Psychology Review, 21*, 494–508.

Batsche, G., Elliott, J., Graden, J. L., Grimes, J., Kovaleski, J. F., Prasse, D., et al. (2005). *Response to Intervention: Policy Considerations and Implementation*. Alexandria, VA: National Association of State Directors of Special Education.

Batsche, G. M. & Ulman, J. (1986). *Referral Question Consultative Decision Making*. Des Moines, IA: Department of Education, Bureau of Special Education.

Browder, D. M. (1991). *Assessment of Individuals with Severe Disabilities: An Applied Behavior Approach to Life Skills Assessment* (2nd ed.). Baltimore: Paul H. Brookes.

Curtis, M. J. & Zins, J. E. (Eds.) (1981). *The Theory and Practice of School Consultation*. Springfield, IL: Charles C. Thomas.

Deno, S. L. (1985). Curriculum-based measurement: the emerging alternative. *Exceptional Children, 52*, 219–232.

Deno, S. L. (1986). Formative evaluation of individual student programs: a new role for school psychologists. *School Psychology Review, 15*, 358–374.

Deno, S. L. & Mirkin, P. K. (1977). *Data-Based Program Modification: A Manual*. Reston, VA: Council for Exceptional Children.

Derby, K. M. & Wacker, D. P. (1992). Brief functional assessment techniques to evaluate aberrant behavior in an outpatient setting. *Journal of Applied Behavior Analysis, 25*, 713–723.

Fuchs, D., Mock, D., Morgan, P. L., & Young, C. L. (2003). Responsiveness-to-intervention: definitions, evidence, and implications for the learning disabilities construct. *Learning Disabilities Research & Practice, 18*, 157–171.

Fuchs, L. S. & Fuchs, D. S. (1986). Linking assessment to instructional intervention: an overview. *School Psychology Review, 15*, 318–323.

Fuchs, L.S., Fuchs, D., & Hamlett, C. L. (1989). Effects of instrumental use of curriculum-based measurement to enhance instructional programs. *Remedial and Special Education, 10*, 43–52.

Gersten, R. M., Becker, W. C., Heiry, T. J., & White, W. A. T. (1984). Entry IQ and yearly academic growth of children in direct instruction programs: a longitudinal study of low SES children. *Educational Evaluation and Policy Analysis, 6*, 109–121.

Good III, R. H., Gruba, J., & Kaminski, R. A. (2002). Best practices in using dynamic indicators of basic early literacy skills (DIBELS) in an outcomes-driven model. In A. Thomas & J. Grimes (Eds.), *Best Practices in School Psychology–IV* (pp. 699–720). Washington, DC: National Association of School Psychologists.

Graden, J. L., Zins, J. E., & Curtis, M. J. (Eds.) (1988). *Alternative Educational Delivery Systems: Enhancing Instructional Options for all Students.* Washington, DC: National Association of School Psychologists.

Grimes, J. & Kurns, S. (2003, December). An intervention-based system for addressing NCLB and IDEA expectations: a multiple tiered model to ensure every child learns. Paper presented at the *National Research Center on Learning Disabilities Response-to-Intervention Symposium.* Kansas City, MO. Available for download at http://www.nrcld.org/symposium2003/index.html.

Grimes, J. & Tilly, D. (1996). Policy and process: means to lasting educational change. *School Psychology Review, 25*, 465–476.

Hartmann, D. P., Roper, B. L, & Bradford, D. C. (1979). Some relationships between behavioral and traditional assessment. *Journal of Behavioral Assessment, 1*, 3–19.

Heartland AEA 11 (1989). *Program Manual for Special Education (1989–1990).* Johnston, IA: Heartland AEA 11.

Howell, K. W. & Nolet, V. (2000). *Curriculum-Based Evaluation* (3rd ed.). Belmont, CA: Wadsworth/Thomson Learning.

Ikeda, M. J., Grimes, J., Tilly III, W. D., Allison, R., Kurns, S., & Stumme, J. (2002). Implementing an intervention-based approach to service delivery: a case example. In M. R. Shinn, H. M. Walker, & G. Stoner (Eds.), *Interventions for Academic and Behavior Problems II: Preventive and Remedial Approaches* (pp. 53–69). Bethesda, MD: National Association of School Psychologists.

Ikeda, M. J. & Gustafson, J. K. (2002). Heartland AEA 11's problem solving process: impact on issues related to special education (Research Report No. 2002-01). Johnston, IA: Heartland Area Education Agency 11.

Ikeda, M. J., Tilly III, W. D., Stumme, J., Volmer, L., & Allison, R. (1996). Agency-wide implementation of problem solving consultation: foundations, current implementation, and future directions. *School Psychology Quarterly, 11*, 228–243.

IDEIA (2004). *Individuals with Disabilities Education Act Amendments.* 20 U.S.C. Sect. 1400 et seq.

Iowa Department of Education (2000). *Iowa Administrative Rules of Special Education.* Des Moines, IA Iowa Department of Education.

Iowa Department of Education (2006). *Special Education Eligibility Standards.* Des Moines, IA: Iowa Department of Education.

Kratochwill, T. R. & Bergan, J. R. (1990). *Behavioral Consultation in Applied Settings: An Individual Guide.* New York: Plenum Press.

Lentz, F. & Shapiro, E. (1986). Functional assessment of the academic environment. *School Psychology Review, 15*, 346–357.

McDermott, P. A., Fantuzzo, J. W., & Glutting, J. J. (1990). Just say no to subtest analysis: a critique on Wechsler's theory and practice. *Journal of Psychoeducational Assessment, 8*, 290–302.

McDermott, P. A., Fantuzzo, J. W., Glutting, J. J., Watkins, M. W., & Baggaley, A. R. (1992). Illusions of meaning in the ipsative assessment of children's ability. *Journal of Special Education, 25*, 504–526.

Marston, D. & Magnusson, D. (1988). Curriculum-based measurement: district level implementation. In J. L. Graden, J. E. Zins, & M. J. Curtis (Eds.), *Alternative Educational Delivery Systems: Enhancing Instructional Options for all Students* (pp. 137–173). Washington, DC: National Association of School Psychologists.

Meyer, L. H. & Evans, I. M. (1989). *Nonaversive Intervention for Behavior Problems: A Manual for Home and Community.* Baltimore: Paul H. Brookes.

O'Neill, R. E., Horner, R. H., Albin, R. W., Sprague, R., Storey, K., & Newton, J. (1997). *Functional Assessment of Problem Behavior: A Practical Guide* (2nd ed.). Pacific Grove, CA: Brooks/Cole.

Rahn-Blakeslee, A. R., Ikeda, M. J., & Gustafson, J. (2005). Evaluating the quality and responsiveness of reading interventions developed through problem-solving. *Journal of Psychoeducational Assessment, 23*, 395–412.

Reschly, D.J. & Ysseldyke, J. (2002). Paradigm shift: the past is not the future. In A. Thomas & J. Grimes (Eds.), *Best Practices in School Psychology–IV* (pp. 3–20).

Bethesda, MD: National Association of School Psychologists.

Rosenfield, S. A. (1987). *Instructional Consultation*. Hillsdale, NJ: Erlbaum.

Shinn, M. R. (Ed.) (1989). *Curriculum-Based Measurement: Assessing Special Children*. New York: Guilford.

Shinn, M. R. (1995). Curriculum-based measurement and its use in a problem-solving model. In A. Thomas & J. Grimes (Eds.), *Best Practices in School Psychology–III* (pp. 547–568). Washington, DC: National Association of School Psychologists.

Shinn, M. R. & Marston, D. (1985). Using curriculum-based measures to identify mildly handicapped students. *Remedial and Special Education, 6*, 31–45.

Simmons, D. C., Kuykendall, K., King, K., Cornachione, C., & Kame'enui, E. J. (2000). Implementation of a schoolwide reading improvement model: "no one ever told us it would be this hard!" *Learning Disabilities Research & Practice, 15*, 92–100.

Sugai, G., Horner, R. H., & Gresham, F. M. (2002). Behaviorally effective school environments. In M. R. Shinn, H. M. Walker, & G. Stoner (Eds.), *Interventions for Academic and Behavior Problems II: Preventive and Remedial Approaches* (pp. 315–350). Washington, DC: National Association of School Psychologists.

Sulzer-Azaroff, B. & Mayer, G. R. (1994). *Achieving Educational Excellence: Behavior Analysis for School Personnel*. San Marcos, CA: Western Image.

Tilly, W. D. (2002). Best practices in school psychology as a problem-solving enterprise. In A. Thomas & J. Grimes (Eds.), *Best Practices in School Psychology–IV* (pp. 21–36). Washington, DC: National Association of School Psychologists.

Tilly, W. D. (2003, December). How many tiers are needed for successful prevention and early intervention?: Heartland Area Education Agency's evolution from four to three tiers. Paper presented at the *National Research Center on Learning Disabilities Responsiveness-to-Intervention Symposium*, Kansas City, MO. Available for download at http://www.nrcld.org/symposium2003/index.html.

Upah, K. R. F. & Tilly III, W. D. (2002). Best practices in designing, implementing, and evaluating quality interventions. In A. Thomas & J. Grimes, (Eds.), *Best Practices in School Psychology–IV* (pp. 483–502). Washington, DC: National Association of School Psychologists.

Will, M. C. (1986). *Educating Students with Learning Problems—A Shared Responsibility*. Washington, DC: United States Department of Education, Office of Special Education and Rehabilitation Services.

Ysseldyke, J. E., Algozzine, B., Shinn, M., & McGue, M. (1982). Similarities and differences between low achievers and students classified learning disabled. *The Journal of Special Education, 16*, 73–85.

Ysseldyke, J. E., Thurlow, M. L., Mecklenburg, C., & Graden, J. (1984). Opportunity to learn for regular and special education students during reading instruction. *Remedial and Special Education, 5*, 29–37.

20

One Student at a Time; One Teacher at a Time: Reflections on the Use of Instructional Support

James A. Tucker and Robert O. Sornson

James A. Tucker, PhD, is Professor and McKee Chair of Excellence in Dyslexia and Related Learning
Exceptionalities, University of Tennessee at Chattanooga. jatuck@mac.com
Robert O. Sornson, PhD, is the founder and President of The Early Learning Foundation, Brighton, Michigan.
bobsornson@aol.com

The importance of intervening early and effectively to help more students achieve learning success cannot be overstated, because early learning success lays the foundation for a child's learning future. Children who come to be successful at reading, writing, mathematical thinking and learning in general tend to be more successful throughout their entire school career (Alexander and Entwisle, 1988; Snow, Burns, and Griffin, 1998; Torgesen, 1998; Tuscano, 1999; Vellutino, Scanlon, and Tanzman, 1998). Moreover, early learning success is related to the absence of adolescent and teenage risky behaviors, including violence, dropping out of school, early sexual behavior, pregnancy, substance abuse and delinquency (Barnett, 1996; Beuhring, Blum, and Rinehart, 2000; Currie and Duncan, 1995; Juel, 1996; Pfannenstiel, 1989). Conversely, poor performance in the early years almost invariable continues (Torgesen, 1998; Snow et al., 1998; Stevenson and Newman, 1986). The social costs of frustrated, unsuccessful learners who become adults in the information age is hard to overestimate.

Early learning success initiatives suggest that offering supports to students and classroom teachers in the early grades (or before) will offer better results for children, while saving school districts the greater costs associated with special-education placements for children who might have found success (Hartman and Fay, 1996). Sadly, this notion is at variance with the systems design that requires that students experience failure over a number of years before a significant discrepancy between potential and achievement can be measured, which then al-

lows a child to receive intensive support (President's Commission on Excellence in Special Education, 2002).

Months and years of frustration are of little benefit to any young learner, and quality preschool or parent training programs improve learning outcomes (Barnett, 1996; Pfannenstiel, 1989; Schweinhart, 2001; Winter, 2001). Well-trained teachers can help 85% to 95% of poor readers in kindergarten and first grade and raise their reading skills to average levels (Lyon, 1997, 1998). By helping children to establish patterns of success in the early years, programs such as Success for All and Reading Recovery have demonstrated a new awareness that young children can learn more effectively (Pinnell, DeFord, and Lyons, 1988; Slavin, 1996, 2001).

The use of instructional-support teams (ISTs) is one way to improve our response to the needs of young learners who are struggling in the early grades. Instructional support is a concept, not a program or a model, that is based on a set of principles that can be applied in various ways to "search for what works," and whatever it takes to help a student to succeed in school. Pawlowski (2001) lists the beliefs that underlie the use of instructional support: We believe: (a) in reducing the amount of time a student struggles before appropriate intervention is provided; (b) that the most effective learning occurs in the regular classroom; (c) that effective intervention must include the identification of individual learning strengths; (d) that the most powerful interventions are developed collaboratively; and (e) that teachers will accept responsibility and ownership for student learning when appropriate support is provided.

From these aforementioned beliefs, the concept of instructional support was developed to be family focused, community centered, collaborative, and data based. More specifically, instructional support identifies effective instruction is the most important force in education, instruction by parents in the home and instruction by teachers in the classroom, and that leads to a special education for all children that fosters lifelong learning. Finally, the purpose of education is to develop the capacity of every student for success as an adult. Because it is collaborative, instructional support is best provided by a team of individuals rather than by a single professional. The IST is a flexible collection of professionals and parents who can lead the search for answers in meeting the needs of individual students.

Inevitably, the question will be asked how instructional support relates to the more recent concept called response to intervention (RTI; Gresham, 2001). Although the two concepts are obviously interlinked and have similar origins, the focus of each could be different. Some have used RTI to focus on the response to a planned intervention and the use of that response as a measure of the student's learning capacity. In instructional support, the focus is on the support that a student needs to succeed. The degree to which the support is successful will be the measure of the efficacy of that support, but the assessment of success is primarily for the purpose of determining whether or not to continue the support, to alter it, or to terminate it. Furthermore, it is a mistake to assume that instructional support is a method for diagnosing a learning disability. Instructional support is simply support for instruction.

20.1 Instructional Support Concept

The term *instructional support* is one relatively recent iteration in the litany of terms used to describe the concept that we are discussing. Initially the term arose as a result of the implementation of the concept in Pennsylvania (Kovaleski, Gickling, Morrow, and Swank, 1999; Kovaleski, Tucker, and Duffy, 1995; Kovaleski, Tucker, and Stevens, 1996; Tucker, 2001), but the idea actually has its roots in Connecticut, where it was implemented under the name

"Early Intervention Project" in 1985 (Connecticut State Department of Education, 1994).

By introducing a simple collection of proven educational practices under the rubric of instructional support, schools in at least four states systematically and significantly reduced the number of referrals to special education while at the same time seeing an increase in academic achievement and a decrease in grade retention while not increasing costs over a 5- to 10-year period (Hartman and Fay, 1996).

In the early 1980s, the state of Connecticut was faced with a challenge. There was a significant disproportion of minority students in special-education classes. The state decided that something should be done about it, but what? Fortunately, Heller, Holtzman, and Messick (1982) set forth the new finding that such discrimination was not due, as had been thought, to biased testing, but rather to inefficient referral systems based on ineffective instruction. This conclusion was supported soon thereafter by Samuels (1984), who addressed specifically what should be done to provide all students with a foundation of basic skills (reading, writing, mathematics, speaking, and listening).

In 1984, the National School Psychology Inservice Training Network published *School Psychology: The State of the Art*, in which a different paradigm began to emerge to meet the needs of students who were not being successful in school (Ysseldyke, 1984). In that publication, a model for instructional intervention was provided by Samuels (1984). It is a simple statement, but it had profound results that have now extended to thousands of schools in many states:

In many ways, good athletic coaching and good classroom teaching have much in common, and principles of coaching applied to the classroom can help students master the basic skills. In essence, to master the basic skills either in sports or the classroom, three elements are necessary:

1. Motivate the student
2. Bring the student to the level of accuracy in the skill, and
3. Provide the practice necessary for the skill to become automatic (p. 27).

While there have subsequently appeared a number of useful and perhaps more comprehensive frameworks to describe the instructional process, it was this conceptual framework of instructional success, provided by Samuels, that has guided the development and implementation of instructional support from the mid-1980s to the present.

In Pennsylvania, the instructional-support concept was implemented as a statewide reform of the interaction between special education and regular education. Instructional support became the initial form of intervention to be applied when a student was experiencing academic difficulty. Subsequent referral or more intensive programming was provided if needed, but with the added benefit of the data derived from the instructional support.

In the application of instructional support that was implemented in Pennsylvania, the frame of reference begins with a student's identified need, not with an identified or suspected exceptionality. Once a student's need is determined, the services and/or programs needed to meet that need are based on the nature of the need, not on what services or programs are available or can be conveniently provided. Finally, the delivery of all services is managed at the school building level, under the direction of the building administrator or the administrator's designee, not at the district or regional level. Perhaps the most significant change in the regulations was to focus on instructional needs of students, rather than on perceived internal deficiencies of students. "The new regulations require that referral for special-education evaluation be *preceded* by interventions of an instructional support team (IST)" (Feir, 1992, p. 8).

The requirement that a referral to special education be preceded by interventions subsequently evolved into decision-making assessment models such as RTI. In the process, however, the focus has shifted from the effectiveness of the intervention to the nature of the response—a subtle and seductive distinction that can be more easily translated into special-education eligibility data.

20.2 How Does the Instructional Support Team Work on a Day-to-Day Basis?

Because instructional support is a concept, it is implemented in many ways. What follows is a general description of how instructional support is carried out at a school building level using the design developed in the Pennsylvania project. The reader should keep in mind that this is simply one representation of how the concept is put into place. Instructional support involves two primary forms of action: the action of the IST and the action of the teacher who is assigned to provide the instructional support.

20.2.1 The Instructional Support Team

The IST is the basic support-group for all of the educators in the building. There are many versions of the IST. An excellent resource for developing functional ISTs is the book by Rosenfield and Gravois (1996). They call this team an "instructional consultation team" and describe its function as follows:

...an [instructional consultation team] is created to serve as a centralized problem-solving unit, to model interactive professionalism (Fullen and Hargreaves, 1991), and to operate as a consultant panel for each other and for teachers in the building (p. 40).

The IST may meet on a regular schedule, or on an "as needed" basis, but it is a functional group of colleagues who will both model collaboration and provide expertise as needed. The membership of the IST also varies from place to place. Membership may represent various programs, or it may be an appointed group, with permanent membership supplemented by individuals with specific expertise as needed. It is often as simple as three or four individuals consisting of the building administrator, an instructional support consultant, and the teacher who is making a request.

When putting such a team structure into place, it is important not to forget the vital role of parents in the process of collaboration and problem solving that is facilitated by such a team. Each team should be built around the culture of the school building and made as formal or as informal as will facilitate the needed function of such a team in that setting.

20.2.2 The Instructional Support Consultant

In this discussion, the teacher who provides instructional support will be referred to as the instructional support consultant (ISC). This consultant is a teacher who has been trained in instructional support strategies, which are conducted for one student, a small group of students, or an entire class in the regular classroom. The assigned task on any given day may come from the IST, a request log, or by verbal request.

Typically, there is some kind of a log book or recording sheet in the building administrator's office on which teachers throughout the building are invited to place their name along with a brief description of the issue they would like to have addressed in their classroom. The issue may be a concern for an individual student, but it may also be a request for a demonstration of an instructional strategy that will be used on a class-wide basis. For some ISCs, the referrals come even more informally by a teacher or the building administrator simply asking for assistance, but it is always better to have a record of the action that is requested. This is especially true at the point that the IST comes into play. But it is important to keep the necessary recording involved to a minimum at this stage. There should be no complicated formal procedure in order to obtain the help of the ISC. A simple request log maintained in the building administrator's office is usually sufficient.

The ISC, in consultation with the building administrator, establishes the priority of issues to be addressed. And the ISC proceeds to spend the day accordingly, dealing with specific cases in regular classrooms. This is not a pull-out service, though that should not be read as disallowing one-on-one support wherever it is most advantageous. The principle here is that the location of the instructional support should be determined by the nature of the support, not by some eligibility factor.

What the ISC does in the classroom is dictated by the needs of the individual student or teacher. The action may be an instructional assessment of a student's reading fluency or comprehension, leading then to specific interventions based on that student's prior knowledge in order to maximize their achievement. It may also be a class-wide intervention to model or demonstrate a given strategy that will benefit not only one or two students, but the entire class as well. Learning these skills and becoming skilled in them is a major portion of the training that is provided in the implementation of instructional support.

20.2.3 Implementation in Northville, Michigan

Northville Public Schools (NPS) is a school district with six elementary schools, two middle schools, and one high school located in southeast Michigan. Total student enrollment is over 7000 and the district employs over 400 teachers. The IST began in NPS at Silver Springs Elementary in 1995–1996 with recognition by the staff that classroom support was needed for struggling students. The process of information gathering in collaboration with the Executive Director of Special Services, establishment of a framework by the special-education staff and analysis of feedback took place during this initial year. In 1996–97, the first year of implementation, an IST position was established, a role defined and a plan for referral became part of the school improvement plan. Since that time, a process of refinement has continued through teacher training, a modification of paperwork, fine-tuning the record-keeping system, tracking student progress, and implementation of the support partners concept. Over time, all members of the IST were trained to serve as ISCs, and to work with a teacher on a particular IST referral.

The NPS model differed somewhat from the Pennsylvania model in that a team of people was trained, as opposed to one instructional support teacher, and then one person from that team partnered with the referring general education teacher. In addition, support was not limited to 50 days, as was the case in Pennsylvania, but instead regular reviews were conducted on a shorter time-frame.

The IST became a catalyst in each elementary school to support a comprehensive early intervention model based on the premise that nearly all students can achieve academic success if provided quality education that offers classroom-based support for teachers and students, as well as pull-out support as needed. This model is designed to (a) provide early and systematic assistance to students in their regular classroom environment, (b) reduce or eliminate inappropriate referrals for special-education testing, (c) reduce unnecessary placements into special education, (d) increase the regular classroom teacher's capacity to deal with more difficult-to-teach children, (e) provide a comprehensive plan of support for students, teachers, and parents, and (f) improve the academic performance of children who are at-risk of early learning failure.

20.3 Results from Instructional-Support Teams: Lessons Learned about Outcomes

As with any innovation, the proof of the program is in the results, not in the eloquence and persuasive nature of the concepts involved. The reader is encouraged to review all of the references provided and to contact persons in the states of Connecticut, Pennsylvania, New York, and Michigan where the instructional-support concept has been operational for long enough to show the kinds of results shared below

20.3.1 Reduction in Special-Education Referrals

During the 1990–91 academic year, ISTs were implemented in 186 schools in 104 school districts throughout the state of Pennsylvania. During that year, there was an average reduction of 45% in special-education placement in those buildings. Concomitantly, there was a reduction of 15% in regular education-grade retentions. The measure of retention was used as one way of determining whether the issues requiring intervention were being ignored and, therefore, contributing to student retention as opposed to placement in special education. For a comprehensive report on this connection, see Kovaleski et al. (1996).

Beginning with the 1985–86 academic year, the instructional-support concept was implemented in individual school buildings in eight school districts in Connecticut. As an example of the results, displayed in Table 20.1 is the special-education placement rate at one of the school-building sites before and after the introduction of instructional support. The most remarkable fact illustrated by these data is the consistency over time that has resulted from the initial years of training. What is shown is a systems change at the building level. It is worth noting that the school site illustrated by the Table 20.1 data is an inner-city school where 70% of the students are Hispanic and African American.

As stated earlier in the chapter, there was concern in Connecticut as to the overrepresentation of minority students in special education. During the first 4 years of implementation, data were collected relative to the special-education placement of mi-

nority students. Table 20.2 shows that the disproportion of minority placements into special education was substantially reduced after the introduction of instructional support, and continued to remain

TABLE 20.1. The special-education placement history of one inner-city elementary school building after the introduction of instructional support.

Academic year	Total enrollment	Placements into special education
1984–85	675	53 (8%)
Introduction of instructional support		
1985–86	682	14 (2%)
1986–87	705	14 (2%)
1987–88	716	13 (2%)
1988–89	727	18 (2%)
1989–90	809	7 (1%)
1990–91	819	10 (1%)
1991–92	792	13 (1%)
1982–93	689	13 (2%)
1993–94	678	16 (2%)
1994–95	711	13 (2%)
1995–96	678	16 (2%)
1996–97	580	9 (2%)
1997–98	591	6 (1%)

TABLE 20.2. A comparison of the ethnic/racial proportion of special-education placement rates in an inner-city elementary school building before and after the introduction of instructional support.

School year	Referred	Placed	Percent
Hispanic			
1984–85 (pre IST)	40	38	95%
Introduction of instructional support			
1985–86	33	8	24%
1986–87	96	7	7%
1987–88	87	7	8%
1988–89	96	7	7%
African American			
1984–85 (pre IST)	11	4	36%
Introduction of instructional support			
1985–86	6	2	33%
1986–87	15	1	7%
1987–88	15	0	0%
1988–89	29	1	3%
Caucasian			
1984–85 (pre IST)	21	10	48%
Introduction of instructional support			
1985–86	23	3	13%
1986–87	43	9	21%
1987–88	34	6	18%
1988–89	30	1	3%

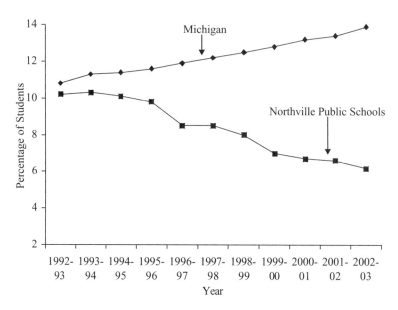

FIGURE 20.1. Percentage of students identified with a special-education disability in NPS and the state of Michigan.

at more equalized levels over the subsequent years for which data were collected. Prior to the introduction of instructional support, the percentages of referred students who were placed into special education were 95% for Hispanic students, 36% for African American students, and 48% for Caucasian students. After 3 years of instructional support, these percentages were 7% for Hispanic students, 3% for African-American students, and 3% for Caucasian students. Those who, in the past would have been referred, evaluated, and placed, were now getting instructional support in their regular classrooms and were no longer in need of special-education services.

The instructional support initiative in Michigan led to similar results at Pennsylvania. Figure 20.1 shows that, although rates of special-education eligibility have increased steadily in Michigan and across the nation as a whole since that time, the need for special-education placement decreased in the NPS (Sornson, Frost, and Burns, 2005).

20.3.2 Increase in Academic Achievement

Perhaps the most impressive outcome of instructional support is the fact that student achievement is improved. Previously struggling students are now

experiencing success; students who were not reading, are now; and students whose misbehavior was the result of boredom or frustration are declared by their teachers to be behaving.

The data exist in two forms: instructional assessment data (Kovaleski et. al., 1999) and standardized test scores. Both forms of data show consistent and positive increases when instructional support is used. The accumulation of this data will be reported elsewhere, but one example will provide the kind of results that is most often reported. Table 20.3 shows the 1-year increase in reading achievement, as measured on a standardized norm-referenced measure of reading, for 17 sixth-grade students from a special-education resource room. This classroom was in a medium-sized town in an otherwise rural part of an eastern state, which suffered serious economic slowdown with the collapse of the steel industry in the United States. To achieve these results, this resource room class of 17 students was taught as a regular class, using cooperative learning groups and the curriculum of general education, adapted to fit the prior knowledge of each student in the class; this is a strategy that is critical to the implementation of instructional support. Given these results, it is possible to suggest that the concept called instructional support, when it is applied as an instructional intervention in the regular classroom, is no more or less than "good teaching" or effective instruction.

TABLE 20.3. The change in reading comprehension for the 17 individuals of a sixth-grade resource room after the introduction of instructional support.

Student	Reading vocabulary		Reading comprehension	
	Fall	Spring	Fall	Spring
1	2.4	5.1	2.6	4.7
2	3.7	8.5	3.6	5.5
3	4.4	5.6	3.0	4.5
4	5.1	10.1	6.8	7.9
5	6.0	11.2	5.5	12.4
6	4.7	9.1	2.8	5.8
7	3.0	5.1	3.0	3.6
8	3.0	5.4	2.7	2.9
9	3.5	7.1	3.1	4.7
10	3.5	6.0	3.8	6.8
11	4.4	9.1	4.1	5.1
12	2.1	3.5	3.5	4.1
13	3.3	5.6	4.1	5.4
14	3.0	7.1	4.1	4.9
15	2.9	5.1	4.1	3.8
16	3.3	7.1	3.6	4.9
Average	3.6	6.8	3.8	5.4
		+3.2/student		+1.5/student

Note: Reading comprehension is measured by the Stanford achievement test.

20.3.3 Reduction in Grade Retention

Kovaleski et al. (1995) report the effect of the introduction of instructional support in Pennsylvania on grade retention. They report data to show that, during the initial 3-year period of providing instructional support, 99 individual school buildings involved demonstrated a 67% reduction in grade retention. It is important to note that this was accomplished with a simultaneous 33–46% reduction in special-education placement.

20.3.4 Cost Effectiveness

A comprehensive evaluation of the cost effectiveness of ISTs in Pennsylvania was performed by the Center for Special Educational Finance (Hartman and Fay, 1996). Their concluding statement by Hartman and Fay (1996, p. 32) is definitive relative to cost:

In summary, the effectiveness of the IST program was much greater than the traditional program; it was able to reduce the number of students placed in special education, while at the same time providing extensive and successful instructional services to many more children in regular education. It did this at a cost that was no greater than the traditional program over a 5 to 10-year period.

20.3.5 Pennsylvania Implementation Summary

A comprehensive review of the literature relative to the implementation of IST in Pennsylvania, specifically as the concept relates to the proposal that a multi-tiered screening and intervention system is better than the traditional test-and-place model, was provided by Kovaleski and Glew (2006, p. 24), who conclude that:

The newly revised IDEA (2004) has promoted the concept of early intervening and has given local education agencies the prerogative of using an RTI process in lieu of an ability–achievement discrepancy approach to determining LD [learning disability]. School districts that endeavor to use a multi-tiered process to implement the RTI provisions will need to put in place an extensive infrastructure of instructional supports to operationalize RTI in a defendable manner. It is suggested that the results of the Pennsylvania experience, combined with other recent advances, should be considered by local education agencies as changes to traditional practices are evaluated and implemented.

20.4 Lessons Learned for Implementation

The success of these applications of the instructional-support concept offer support for the hope that far more students can find success in the early years of school, which predicts successful learning throughout school and life. While there are other innovative concepts and models that have been proposed to support early learning success, instructional support stands out when considered by the evaluation model proposed by Ellis (2001). He proposes that any innovation being considered for adoption should pass three levels of research validation: a sound theoretical base, valid classroom application, and consistent evidence of large-scale implementation. We believe that the first two of Ellis's standards have clearly been met, and that some promising evidence exists from several large-scale implementation studies.

A recent review of the literature applied Ellis's criteria to pre-referral intervention teams and reported that the Pennsylvania implementation of the instructional-support team was "quite effective," but only "when implemented with a high degree of fidelity" (Burns, Vanderwood, and Ruby, 2005, p. 100). We suggest that before any large-scale evaluations are attempted there should be a clear understanding of what is required in implementing the model or concept in question. In Pennsylvania, for example, where several studies (Bickel, Zigmond, and McCall, 1998; Bickel, Zigmond, McCall, and McNelis, 1999) found only moderate to inconclusive results from the implementation of IST, Kovaleski et al. (1999) found significant positive effects. The clear difference between the findings of these studies was the presence in the Kovaleski et al. study of implementation criteria. Just because a school system claims that it has implemented a given model does not mean that it has done so with an acceptable degree of fidelity. Thus, it is possible for a school system to claim that it has implemented a given model, especially if mandated to do so, and show few, if any, of the desired outcomes.

Most schools continue to cling to a failure model before significant support can be given to struggling students. Requirements for significant learning discrepancies and other gross measures of disability, before help is given to struggling children, create the likelihood that help will come too late for many. The failure model also supports the mistaken notion that some students are "special," once identified as eligible for special education, and, therefore, no longer the responsibility of "general" classroom teachers. This concept reinforces low expectations and reduces the likelihood of collaboration designed to help a child succeed in the regular classroom.

The collaborative culture needed for effective instructional support takes careful and ongoing work. For a classroom teacher to ask another professional within the building for support assumes a measure of trust. Before committing to a process of ongoing collaboration and problem solving, teachers must believe that the experience will be positive and not judgmental.

A careful analysis of the learning needs of struggling students will often cause teachers to become aware of their own learning needs. Teachers involved in instructional support frequently identify professional development needs that are important to the skill development which will allow them

to be more successful with practically every child (Sornson, 2005).

The assessment strategies used in most states for their high-stakes achievement testing programs create pressure on teachers to help students prepare for the test. High test scores become the goal. Many states have increased the number of content expectations, and often moved content expectations from upper to lower grades. Unfortunately, many teachers get the message that covering the curriculum as fast as possible is a necessary response to these testing programs. Group instruction, even at the cost of teaching many children outside the appropriate zone of instructional development (instructional match), is a frequent response. When all children in the early grades are receiving the same instruction, on the same day, in the same way, we can be sure some children are being left behind.

Funding systems within districts tend to give greater priority, and more dollars per student, to secondary students than to students in the early grades. In light of the ability to predict long-term learning outcomes based on early learning success, this is hard to justify. Funding systems at the state and federal level continue to give additional dollars to districts for more identified special-education students (President's Commission on Excellence in Special Education, 2002). The more effective use of some of these funds in the early years, before significant learning failure has become a pattern, might reduce the need for special-education expenditures.

Home–school collaboration continues to be problematic in most schools (Esler, Godber, and Christenson, 2002). Creating mechanisms for ongoing trust building and collaboration between home and school could help some children get the learning and behavioral experiences at home that can improve learning success in the schools.

20.5 Conclusions

More children are coming to school at risk of early learning failure, and more children are being identified for special education. The importance of establishing patterns of early learning success has never been greater. The instructional support concept, in its varied successful applications, provides hope that we can do a significantly better job helping young children establish the patterns of early learning success, which lays the foundation for successful learning throughout life.

References

Alexander, K. L. & Entwisle, D. R. (1988). Achievement in the first two years of school: patterns and processes. *Monographs of the Society for Research in Child Development, 53*, 157.

Barnett, W. S. (1996). *Lives in the Balance: The Age-27 Benefit–Cost Analysis of the High/Scope Perry Preschool Program.* Ypsilanti, MI: High/Scope Press.

Beuhring, T., Blum, R., & Rinehart, P. M. (2000). *Protecting Teens: Beyond Race, Income and Family Structure.* Minneapolis, MN: University of Minnesota.

Bickel, W., Zigmond, N., & McCall, R. (1998). Documentation and impact of Pennsylvania's instructional support team process: final report. Pittsburgh, PA: Pennsylvania Bureau of Special Education and the University of Pittsburgh.

Bickel, W., Zigmond, N., McCall, R., & McNelis, R. (1999). Instructional support team best practices in Pennsylvania: final report. Pittsburgh, PA: Pennsylvania Bureau of Special Education and the University of Pittsburgh.

Burns, M. K., Vanderwood, M. L., & Ruby, S. (2005). Evaluating the readiness of pre-referral intervention teams for use in a problem solving model. *School Psychology Quarterly, 20*, 89–105.

Connecticut State Department of Education (1994). The *Early Intervention Project.* Middletown, CT: Special Education Resource Center, Connecticut State Department of Education.

Currie, J. & Duncan, T. (1995). Does head start make a difference? *American Economic Review, 85*, 341–364.

Ellis, A. (2001). *Research on Educational Innovations* (3rd ed.). Princeton Junction, NJ: Eye on Education Publishers.

Esler, A. N., Godber, Y., & Christenson, S. L. (2002). Best practices in supporting home–school collaboration. In A. Thomas & J. Grimes (Eds.), *Best Practices in School Psychology IV* (pp. 389–411). Bethesda, MD: National Association of School Psychologists.

Feir, R. E. (1992). Refining Pennsylvania's funding mechanism and program rules for special education. Paper presented at the *Annual Meeting of the American Education Finance Association*, New Orleans.

Fullen, M. & Hargreaves. A. (1991). *What's Worth Fighting For? Working Together for Your School.* Andover, MA: Regional Laboratory for Educational Improvement of the Northeast and Islands.

Gresham, F. (2001, August). Responsiveness to intervention: an alternative approach to the identification of learning disabilities. Paper presented at the *Learning Disabilities Summit: Building a Foundation for the Future*, Washington, DC.

Hartman, W. T. & Fay, T. A. (1996). Cost-effectiveness of instructional support teams in Pennsylvania. Policy Paper Number 9 of the Center for Special Education Finance. Palo Alto, CA: American Institutes for Research.

Heller, K. A., Holtzman, W. H., & Messick, S. (Eds.) (1982). *Placing Children in Special Education: A Strategy for Equity.* Washington, DC: National Academy Press.

Juel, C. (1996). What makes literacy tutoring effective? *Reading Research Quarterly, 31*, 268–289.

Kovaleski, J. F. & Glew, M. C. (2006). Bringing instructional support teams to scale: implications of the Pennsylvania experience. *Remedial and Special Education, 27*, 16–25.

Kovaleski, J. F., Gickling, E. E., Morrow, H., & Swank, P. R. (1999). High versus low implementation of instructional support teams: a case for maintaining program fidelity. *Remedial and Special Education, 20*, 170–183.

Kovaleski, J. F., Tucker, J. A., & Duffy Jr., D. J. (1995). School reform through instructional support: the Pennsylvania initiative, Part I. *Communiqué, 23*(8), insert.

Kovaleski, J. F., Tucker, J. A., & Stevens, L. J. (1996). Bridging special and regular education: the Pennsylvania initiative. *Educational Leadership, 53*, 44–47.

Lyon, G. R. (1997, July). Report on learning disabilities research. Testimony given before the Committee on Education and the Workforce in the US.House of Representatives, Washington, DC.

Lyon, G. R. (1998, April). Report on learning disabilities research supported by the national institute of child health and human development. Address to the Committee of Labor and Human Resources of the US Senate, Washington, DC. Available at: www.rlac.com/edarticles.htm.

Pawlowski, K. F. (2001). The instructional support team concept in action. In R. Sornson (Ed.), *Preventing Early Learning Failure.* Alexandria, VA: Association for Supervision and Curriculum Development.

Pfannenstiel, J. (1989). *New Parents as Teachers Project: A Follow-Up Investigation.* Overland Park, KS: Research & Training Associates.

Pinnell, G. S., DeFord, D. E., & Lyons, C. A. (1988). *Reading Recovery: Early Intervention for At-Risk First Graders.* Arlington, VA: Educational Research Service.

President's Commission on Excellence in Special Education (2002). *A New Era: Revitalizing Special Education for Children and their Families.* Washington DC: US Government Printing Office.

Rosenfield, S. A. & Gravois, T. (1996). *Instructional Consultation Teams.* New York: The Guilford Press.

Samuels, J. (1984). Basic academic skills. In J. E. Ysseldyke (Ed.), *School Psychology: The State of the Art.* Minneapolis, MN: National School Psychology Inservice Training Network, University of Minnesota.

Schweinhart, L. J. (2001). Getting ready for school in preschool. In R. Sornson (Ed.), *Preventing Early Learning Failure.* Alexandria, VA: Association for Supervision and Curriculum Development.

Slavin, R. E. (1996). Neverstreaming: preventing learning disabilities. *Educational Leadership, 53,* 4–7.

Slavin, R. E. (2001). Success for all: failure prevention and early intervention. In R. Sornson (Ed.), *Preventing Early Learning Failure.* Alexandria, VA, Association for Supervision and Curriculum Development.

Snow, C. E., Burns, S., & Griffin, P. (Eds.) (1998). *Preventing Reading Difficulties in Young Children. Report of the Committee on the Prevention of Reading Difficulties in Young Children.* Washington, DC: National Academy Press.

Sornson, R., Frost, F., & Burns, M. K. (2005). Instructional support teams in Michigan: data from Northville Public Schools. *Communiqué, 33*(5), 28–30.

Sornson, R. O. (2005, May). Report to Northville Public Schools Board of Education. Northville, MI: Northville Public Schools.

Stevenson, H. W. & Newman, R. S. (1986). Long-term prediction of achievement and attitudes in mathematics and reading. *Child Development, 56,* 646–659.

Torgesen, J. K. (1998). Catch them before they fall. *American Educator, 22,* 32–39.

Tucker, J. A. (2001). Instructional support teams: it's a group thing. In R. Sornson (Ed.), *Preventing Early Learning Failure.* Alexandria, VA: Association for Supervision and Curriculum Development.

Tuscano, A. (1999). When schools fail children. *Our Children, The National PTA Magazine*, (August/September), 36–37.

Vellutino, F. R., Scanlon, D. M., & Tanzman, M. S. (1998). The case for early intervention in diagnosing specific reading disability. *Journal of School Psychology, 36,* 367–397.

Winter, M. M. (2001). Parents as teachers: improving the odds with early intervention. In R. Sornson (Ed.), *Preventing Early Learning Failure.* Alexandria, VA: Association for Supervision and Curriculum Development.

Ysseldyke, J. E. (1984). *School Psychology: The State of the Art.* Minneapolis, MN: National School Psychology Inservice Training Network, University of Minnesota.

21
Implementation of the Problem-Solving Model in the Minneapolis Public Schools

Douglas Marston, Matthew Lau, and Paul Muyskens

Douglas Marston, PhD, is a special education administrator for research and evaluation in the Minneapolis Public Schools. doug.marston@mpls.k12.mn.us
Matthew Lau, PhD, is a school psychologist and program facilitator with Minneapolis Public Schools and Field Experience Coordinator with the University of Minnesota. lauxx008@tc.umn.edu
Paul Muyskens, PhD, is a school psychologist and program facilitator with Minneapolis Public Schools. paul.muyskens@mpls.k12.mn.us

In 1994 the Minneapolis Public Schools (MPS) formally adopted the problem-solving model (PSM) as an alternative approach to determining the eligibility of high-incidence disabilities. However, the groundwork for successful implementation of this approach was laid by three important initiatives which were undertaken in the years prior to adoption of the PSM: data-based decision-making, curriculum-based measurement (CBM), and collaborative teaching. In addition, the concurrent implementation of a district-wide data warehouse and screening system further facilitated implementation of the PSM.

In MPS, the initial commitment to data-based decision-making can be traced to the special-education department's adoption of the tenets outlined in Deno and Mirkin's (1977) *Data-Based Program Modification* (DBPM). In their book, Deno and Mirkin argue that the use of objective student data contributes to better educational decisions for students with learning problems when contextualized within a five-step model. The five steps outlined by Deno and Mirkin are problem identification, problem definition, designing intervention plans, implementing the intervention, and problem solution. Each step is designed to address an important question about the student, which, if answered with valid data, leads to effective programming for the student. For example, the problem identification step asks "Does a problem exist?" At the next step, problem definition, asks if the problem is important, which reflects on the impact of the student's difficulty inside and outside the classroom and pro-

vides information on the extent to which the student is discrepant from expectations. Once the student's problem has been defined and its significance determined, the educator must address "What is the best solution hypothesis?" at the designing intervention plan stage. At the next stage, which focuses on implementation of the solution, the educator must determine "Is the solution attempt progressing as planned?" Finally, at the problem solution stage, the question "Is the original problem solved?" is answered by examining student data and the response to the intervention.

The common element found across all of the steps of DBPM is student data. None of the questions posed can provide credible answers unless an objective data set is used for evaluation. Within the special education department these tenets became the framework for instructional decision-making, including the measurement of progress towards goals, instructional modifications, and program changes. For example, if a school wanted to move a student to a more restricted setting, part of the process involved an examination of data that show a student's response to different intervention strategies. These presentations were required to be data based and to show a student's responses to different instructional or intervention strategies. The steps outlined by Deno and Mirkin (1977) also provided the framework for the PSM adopted by MPS, which will be discussed later.

A second major initiative promoted within the MPS Special Education Department which impacted subsequent adoption of the PSM was the implementation of CBM (Deno, 1985). CBM was originally designed to measure the progress of students with disabilities and to examine the effectiveness of their special-education interventions. Although there are many forms of CBM, the most widely used is oral reading fluency, where students are timed while reading out loud. Research over the past 20 years has suggested that CBM data are reliable for various populations and result in valid conclusions for many types of decisions, including screening, eligibility, program planning, progress monitoring and program evaluation (Deno, 1985; Marston, 1989; Marston and Magnusson, 1985). As such, CBM provides data-based decision-makers with the student information necessary to make many of the decisions outlined by Deno and Mirkin (1977) and in the PSM process. With these purposes in mind, district administrators promoted the use of CBM for ongoing progress monitoring with special-education students throughout the district.

A third initiative influencing our district's adoption of the PSM was the Six Week Assessment Plan (SWAP; Marston and Magnusson, 1988) and the Collaborative Teaching Project (Self, Benning, Marston, and Magnusson, 1991). The SWAP was used to encourage regular education staff to implement an intervention before a referral to special education to determine whether the intervention led to adequate progress in the general curriculum. During this 6-week period, teachers were encouraged to use CBM procedures to measure student growth as a function of the pre-referral strategy that was used with the student. These ideas were adapted as part of a federally funded model demonstration project at Hiawatha Elementary School. Here, the staff implemented a data-based decision-making model where the regular education, Title I, and special-education teachers teamed to frequently review the progress of students on CBM procedures and then designed and provided the appropriate instruction.

With these three initiatives in place, the real impetus for the change to the PSM came in the early 1990s, when the state of Minnesota moved to a special-education eligibility determination process requiring the administration of a formal measure of intellectual functioning for students with academic needs. At that time, district personnel in the special-education department became concerned with the use of intelligence tests as part of the criteria in determining students as learning disabled or mild

mentally impaired, because the majority of students in MPS were, and continue to be, students of color. Moreover, there was and remain a large number of students who are English language learners. This concern led staff to begin working on the development of the PSM as an alternative means for identifying students with learning problems. The resulting alternative model was influenced by the problem-solving process being used in Iowa (Tilly, Reschly, and Grimes, 1999). As designed by staff from the Iowa Bureau of Education and educators in Heartland Area Education Agency, this process involved the use of a functional assessment approach to selecting interventions for students with learning problems, monitoring student progress, and identifying students with disabilities (Tilly et al., 1999).

21.1 Minneapolis Public Schools' Problem-Solving Model

Using the tools put in place by the special-education department, and drawing on the experience of those working in Iowa, MPS staff developed an alternative eligibility approach. Our district then sought and attained a waiver from the State Board of Education that gave us permission to use this process. That alternative was a response-to-intervention approach, which was called the PSM.

In this model, we asked staff to follow a variation of the five steps outlined by Deno and Mirkin (1977). Subsequently, a four-step PSM was created that included (1) a definition of the problem, (2) the selection and implementation of an intervention, (3) monitoring student progress and the response to intervention, and (4) recycling through this sequence if the student is not making adequate growth. This sequence is implemented within the three stages of the PSM that are described below.

21.1.1 Stages of Minneapolis Public Schools' Problem-Solving Model

Stage 1 is labeled "classroom interventions." At this stage of the model, classroom teachers are asked to define the student's difficulties, provide baseline data, specify an intervention, and document the results. The Classroom Intervention Worksheet, also known as Worksheet 1, is used to document the process. The actual prompts for the teacher on this worksheet are:

- Review cumulative file/relevant school history
- Talk with staff
- Interview student
- Interview parent
- Concerns (be specific)
- Current levels of performance (and or baseline data)
- Student strengths
- Relevant health information
- Start date, follow-up date. Were any of the interventions successful?

Those students who remain discrepant from teacher expectations move on to Stage 2 of the PSM. This stage is known as the team intervention stage, where the student difficulties are addressed through the building problem-solving team. These teams are typically composed of the regular education teacher, such as a classroom or Title I teacher, building social worker, school psychologist, special-education teacher, other specialists as indicated, and a building administrator. Again, the four stages are followed. The major elements of this stage are similar to Stage 1, with a movement towards more intensive interventions, goal setting and more frequent data collection. Staff complete the Team Intervention Worksheet (Worksheet 2), which includes the following prompts:

- Primary source of the referral
- Health/additional health related information, health review, vision/hearing screening
- Parent input, date of contact
- Define/redefine specific behavior concerns
- Current level of performance/baseline data
- Specific goal for intervention
- Intervention plan including outcome goals, results, start date, staff responsible, and follow-up date
- What is the goal for this student and expected outcome
- Intervention date/results

The responsibility of the PSM team is to ensure that high-quality interventions are implemented with the student and that the data be reviewed approximately 6–8 weeks after the intervention has been initiated.

While Stages 1 and 2 involve cycling through a series of regular education interventions and evaluating response to instruction through examination of progress monitoring data, Stage 3 marks the beginning of the formal due process and special-education evaluation. While response-to-intervention data continue to be collected at this stage, district personnel also initiate the processes of completing a Notice of Evaluation/Reevaluation, evaluation plan, evaluation report, and determination of eligibility. Most of these steps are included in our Special Education Evaluation worksheet, or Worksheet 3.

Although Stage 3 involves a formal and comprehensive special-education eligibility evaluation, it may not involve traditional eligibility diagnoses. After a child is not successful in the first two stages, the problem-solving team will continue to seek out interventions that will facilitate student success. However, these interventions may be so intensive that special-education services are needed to implement them. In this case the child is identified as a student needing alternative programming (SNAP), rather than traditional classifications of learning disabled or mildly mentally retarded, and special education is provided (Marston, Muyskens, Lau and Canter, 2003).

21.1.2 Changes to Implementation

With the strong background provided by the special-education department, and permission from the state department to begin our alternate assessment system, implementation of the PSM was initiated at a small number of elementary schools in the district. However, plans to gradually phase in the process while implementing ongoing program evaluation were altered by other events. Beginning in the 1998–1999 school year, MPS came under the direction of a voluntary compliance agreement with the United States Department of Education's Office for Civil Rights (OCR). In this agreement, OCR requested that MPS follow a plan that included: improving screening in academics and behavior, providing a wide range of interventions for students performing poorly in these areas, using a multidisciplinary team at the school to identify interventions, and monitoring the progress of these students. Implementation of this agreement resulted in several activities which bolstered the PSM.

One of the provisions included in the OCR agreement is the universal screening in grades K through 8 for difficulties in reading, math and behavior. All students are screened in the fall, with follow up data collected for identified students. Students who are below the district established cut-off scores are considered to be at risk. These students enter the first stage of the PSM. While screening is now commonly accepted as part of any response-to-intervention protocol (Burns and Ysseldyke, 2005) and is an important part of the PSM, at the time it was a new addition to our academic intervention process. The inclusion of all students, teachers, and principals in the process helped facilitate the integration of the PSM into the sphere of general education.

The second aspect of the OCR agreement that impacted our implementation of the PSM was a recommendation to implement the PSM at all schools. The original plan was to gradually introduce the PSM beginning in the elementary schools, which would allow for refinement of training and implementation protocols while evaluating the effectiveness of the model as we moved towards implementation at the secondary schools. OCR recommended a scaled-up district-wide initiative, which required us to make improvements as we went, and forced us to move to a train-the-trainers model.

The third factor was not a requirement or recommendation of the OCR agreement, but rather a decision about how to best implement the activities related to the agreement on a district-wide scale. Because of limited resources, the decision was made to create an internet-based data warehouse. This initiative has become such a major part of how our district operates that it merits further discussion. The rationale behind the creation of a district-wide data warehouse was that, in order to encourage staff to use data to make instructional decisions for students, the students' data should be easily and readily accessible. This was a major problem, because our district was using multiple platforms for the purpose of gathering and storing data (i.e., Mac and PC, Filemaker Pro and Excel), data were largely communicated through the use of printed reports, and the student population was highly mobile. In order to address these issues we needed a platform that was accessible to everyone, was fluid, and followed students instantaneously. Whereas in 2006 the decision to address these issues using a web-based application

seems simple, in 1998 the idea was relatively new, and there were few commercially available products to accomplish this.

What we eventually developed, with the help of a local web programmer, is a secure, web-based data warehouse. Staff members can now access the students in the classrooms or school(s) where they work, and the system allows different levels of access through the assignment of individual passwords. For instance, a principal has schoolwide access, whereas a general education teacher only has access to the students in their classroom. Moreover, the web-based program with security protocol allows convenient access both at school and home.

Types of data available for staff include: general demographic information and school history; academic information, such as CBM scores, district assessment results, and state assessment results; and behavioral information, such as behavioral screener scores, attendance, and suspension data. These data follow the student from school to school, and historically goes back to the time the student initially enrolled in the district. An example of how the website integrates assessment data with instructional decisions and the PSM is the application of a cut-off score or criterion (e.g., below the 25th percentile) for use in screening. In reading, math and the social/behavioral areas the score is used as an indicator that the student may be at risk academically and/or behaviorally. A three-color coding system (red, yellow, and green) is used to help staff members identify these at-risk students visually so that further interventions can be implemented. Figure 21.1 is an example of the *Summary Organizer* of a classroom in which the academic and social/behavioral data are displayed for each student.

As shown in Figure 21.2, a variety of reports are available that summarize and present the group data in graphs or tables. Many additional reports are available for principals and district administrators as well. In addition to data access, it is important for teachers to be able to input formative assessment data and intervention results onto the website. The PSM worksheets, basic graphing programs allowing individual progress monitoring (see Figure 21.3), and various program-specific data-collection forms can be completed online. For example, within 1 day of enrollment a teacher can now view the

Name	Home Room	Read NALT Scale	Read NALT %tile	Math NALT Scale	Math NALT %tile	Fall Behavior Total	Winter Behavior Total	% Attend	Abs. Exc*	Abs. UnExc*	Tardy*	# Susp.*	CBM FALL	CBM WIN
	204						15.0	100.0	0	0	0			26
	205							87.9	6	6	0			
	205							94.9	0	5	0			
	204						17.0	90.6	1	4	0			117
	204	155	1	178	11	12.0	23.0	99.0	0	1	0		21	34
	205	155	1	169	4	37.0	37.0	83.7	8	8	0		15	28
	205	161	3	185	25	12.0	12.0	96.9	0	3	0		13	21
	204	159	4	184	27		33.0	86.1	7	3	0			53
	205	161	4	173	6		12.0	100.0	0	0	0		21	59
	204	163	5	191	42	28.0	14.0	77.3	2	20	0		48	60
	205	175	15	185	25	14.0	14.0	89.8	4	6	0		38	75
	204	176	17	181	16	12.0	12.0	100.0	0	0	0		70	87
	204	179	21	179	13	24.0	23.0	93.9	4	2	0		57	85
	205	180	23	192	45	15.0	23.0	98.0	0	2	0		81	87
	205	180	23	191	42	15.0	14.0	99.0	0	1	0		75	89
	205	182	26	181	16	12.0	12.0	90.8	2	7	0		39	87
	205	183	28	187	30	21.0	24.0	100.0	0	0	0		35	52
	205	183	28	194	52	29.0	14.0	99.0	0	1	0		64	96
	205	190	44	199	69	12.0	12.0	99.0	0	1	0		55	82
	204	191	46	192	45	12.0	12.0	93.9	3	3	0		103	130
	205	192	49	197	62	12.0	14.0	95.9	0	4	0		107	112
	205	192	49	200	72	12.0	12.0	94.9	3	2	0		101	147

FIGURE 21.1. A summary organizer that displays academic and social/behavioral data for students in a classroom.

newly enrolled students' school and attendance history, test data since their arrival in the district, review interventions initiated this year and in previous years, and document the intervention(s) they will try and their results within their current classroom. In sum, the web-based data warehouse is an invaluable tool for staff to gather data for a data-driven decision-making model such as the PSM.

21.2 Lessons Learned from Implementing the Problem-Solving Model

Having implemented the PSM over the past 12 years we have a deeper understanding of how the theoretical model of response to intervention translates into everyday practices in the schools. In the remainder of this chapter we will address the topics of student outcomes, roles and responsibilities, integration with general education, and the use of data.

21.2.1 Student Outcomes

A frequent question that we are asked is the extent to which child count for students with disabilities (commonly referred to special-education placement rates) is impacted by using the PSM. Using the PSM has not had a significant effect on the prevalence of students with high-incidence disabilities in MPS. Our initial waiver from the Minnesota Department of Education allowed us to use the PSM for the special-education categories of learning disabilities and mild mental impairment. The rate of these two groups was about 7% of the student population

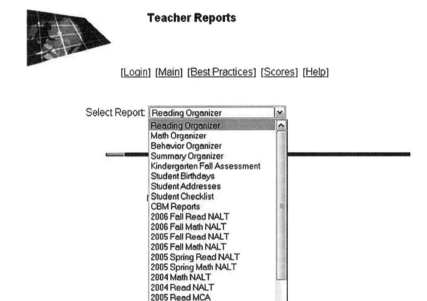

FIGURE 21.2. Examples of reports available to classroom teachers.

when we began the PSM and our follow-up analyses show that implementation of PSM did not affect this percentage (Marston et al., 2003) However, as noted earlier, the disability terms are replaced with the noncategorical SNAP classification.

Another question that is often asked about PSM is whether different types of students are identified with the response-to-intervention approach versus the traditional discrepancy model. Similarities in achievement levels of students found eligible with

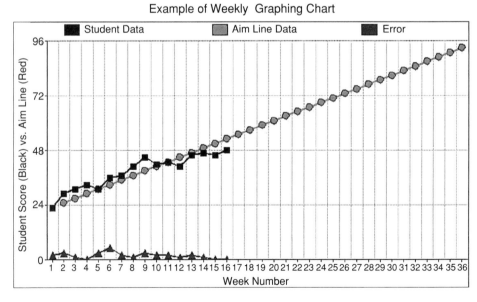

FIGURE 21.3. Example of a web-based individual student progress-monitoring graph.

PSM and those labeled using the IQ–achievement difference score were found (Marston et al., 2003). However, the interventions used by teachers during the PSM were of higher quality than those provided under the traditional approach, and students in the PSM were provided service in special education at an earlier age than students served in the traditional approach (Reschly and Starkweather, 1997).

The implementation of a new PSM initiative will undoubtedly elicit many questions and concerns from those who work in existing systems or advocate for disability groups. Knowledge about the long-term impact of a PSM on placement rates and intervention quality can be very helpful in communicating with these stakeholder groups about how implementation may impact students.

21.2.2 Roles and Responsibilities of Staff

Our experience implementing the PSM has also allowed us to discern what areas of staff development we need to address in order to move to a higher level of implementation, quality and academic progress. Of course, these needs are generalizations and many of these needs are already being addressed by the excellent work of individual teachers and schools. For teachers, the emphasis on effective instruction and academic outcomes for students in the PSM highlighted the need to further expand their skills in the area of evidence-based instruction, assessment, and progress monitoring for diverse students. Teachers are already being asked to do an incredible amount of work, but ongoing professional development is a vital part of all of our careers.

For special-education evaluations there needs to be an emphasis upon diagnostic teaching, testing of limits, differential instructional materials, and curriculum-based assessment. School psychologists need time to expand their role as a problem solver, as a building leader, and as a system change facilitator. Their training in areas such as statistics and measurement, evidence-based interventions, and effective instructional strategies behavioral consultation, and home–school collaboration will help them take a role as an effective facilitator in PSM implementation. Finally, district administrators and school principals are key players in quality implementation of the PSM. They provide vital support by establishing a common vision, incorporating data-based decision-making into the current school sys-

tem, providing tangible (e.g., budget allocation for materials, intervention programs, staff time, etc.) support for the process, and by performing essential administrative functions to ensure staff members remain on course. They also provide important leadership in system-wide change within a school district. Further discussion of the roles of various staff members within the implementation of the PSM can be found in Lau et al. (2006).

21.2.3 Integration with General Education

Another area that needs to be an ongoing and high priority for the successful implementation of the PSM is the ownership of academic difficulties and instructional interventions by general education. In MPS, the PSM originally arose from within special education. This resulted in the widely held perspective that the PSM was part of the referral process to get a student placed in special education. While the OCR aggrement made clear to us that the origin of special-education placements is the referral from general education, this perspective remains within our district.

21.2.4 The Use of Data

The final area which we have learned is vital to the implementation of the PSM is the importance of collecting progress-monitoring and formative-assessment data, and the dissemination of this data to those who need it. As noted earlier, essential to the adoption of PSM is the use of a progress monitoring system. MPS has utilized CBM for this purpose since 1982. To support the logistics of frequent measurement, district staff have developed a manual entitled, *Performance Assessment of Academic Skills in the Problem Solving Model* (Minneapolis Public Schools, n.d.). This manual includes an introduction to the use of CBM, directions for administration and scoring of measures, and passages and probes to be used for oral reading, reading expression, comprehension questions, and story retells. District norms and data relating these measures to state assessments are also included in this manual.

Over the years, district staff have implemented graphing systems (see Figure 21.4) and published research on the validity of these measures (Marston,

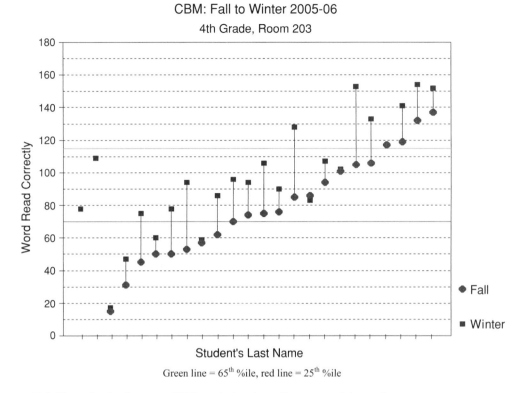

FIGURE 21.4. Example of a classroom CBM graph showing mid-year growth by student.

Muyskens, Betts, and Heistad, 2004; Muyskens and Marston, 2002; Tindal and Marston, 1996). In addition, the use of progress-monitoring measures has led district staff to expand their scope through their inclusion in district-wide assessments and the development of early literacy measures that assess letter sound fluency, onset phoneme identification, and phoneme segmentation (Marston et al., in press). These progress-monitoring systems have become a part of our district's culture. Significant advances in recent years have made valid and reliable progress-monitoring measures readily available, the adoption of which is crucial to a quality PSM program. However, it must be noted that a data-based decision-making model cannot be successful unless the data are in the hands of those who need it. All too often students must wait to fail before interventions are implemented, even though extensive test scores, background information, and prior intervention data are sitting in a drawer or a file somewhere. While our web-based data warehouse and collection system has helped greatly in this area, more work re-

mains. New tests, graphing features, and connecting data to interventions continue to be ongoing needs.

Acknowledgments. The authors would like to acknowledge Tom Hegranes, Executive Director of Special Education; Dr. Ann Casey, Assistant Director of Special Education; Dr. David Heistad, Director of Research, Evaluation and Assessment, and Elizabeth Dolan, Systems Analyst, for their support of the work described in this chapter.

References

Burns, M. K. & Ysseldyke, J. E. (2005). Comparison of existing responsiveness-to-intervention models to identify and answer implementation questions. *The California School Psychologist, 10,* 9–20.

Deno, S. L. (1985). Curriculum-based measurement: the emerging alternative. *Exceptional Children, 52,* 219–232.

Deno, S. L. & Mirkin, P. K. (1977). *Data-based program modification.* Reston, VA: Council for Exceptional Children.

Lau, M. Y., Sieler, J. D., Muyskens, P., Canter, A., VanKeuren, B., & Marston, D. (2006). Perspectives on the use of the problem-solving model from the viewpoint of a school psychologist, administrator, and teacher from a large Midwest urban school district. *Psychology in the Schools, 43,* 117–127.

Marston, D. (1989) A curriculum-based approach to assessing academic performance: what it is and why do it. In M. R. Shinn (Ed.), *Curriculum-Based Measurement: Assessing Special Children,* (pp. 19–78). New York: Guilford Press.

Marston, D. & Magnusson, D. (1985). Implementing curriculum-based measurement in special and regular education settings. *Exceptional Children, 52,* 266–276.

Marston, D., Muyskens, P., Lau, M., & Canter, A. (2003). Problem-solving model for decision-making with high-incidence disabilities: the Minneapolis experience. *Learning Disabilities Research and Practice, 18,* 187–200.

Marston, D., Pickart, M., Reschly, A., Muyskens, P., Heistad, D., & Tindal, G. (in press). Early literacy measures for improving student reading achievement: translating research into practice. *Exceptionality.*

Muyskens, P. & Marston, D. (2002). Predicting success on the Minnesota Basic Skills Test in reading using CBM. Unpublished manuscript, Minneapolis Public Schools.

Minneapolis Public Schools (n.d.). *Performance assessment of academic skills in the problem solving model.* Retrieved September 22, 2006, from http://pic.mpls.k12.mn.us/Performance_Assessment_Manual.html.

Reschly, D. & Starkweather, A. (1997). *Evaluation of an alternative Special Education Assessment and Classification Program in the Minneapolis Public Schools.* Ames, IA: Iowa State University.

Self, H., Benning, A., Marston, D., & Magnusson, D. (1991). Cooperative teaching project: a model for students at risk. *Exceptional Children, 58,* 26–34.

Tindal, G. & Marston, D. (1996). Technical adequacy of alternative reading measures as performance assessments. *Exceptionality, 6,* 201–230.

Tilly, W. D., Reschly, D., & Grimes, J. (1999). Disability determination in problem solving systems: conceptual foundations and critical components. In D. Reschly, W. Tilly, & J. Grimes (Eds.), *Special Education in Transition* (pp. 1–18). Longmont, CO: Sopris West.

22
The Ohio Integrated Systems Model: Overview and Lessons Learned

Janet L. Graden, Stephanie A. Stollar, and Rita L. Poth

Janet L. Graden, PhD, is Professor of School Psychology and Division Head at the University of Cincinnati, Cincinnati, OH. janet.graden@uc.edu

Stephanie A. Stollar, PhD, is an Educational Consultant at the Southwestern Ohio Special Education Regional Resource Center, Cincinnati, OH. stollar_s@swoserrc.org

Rita L. Poth, PhD, is Associate Director of the Southwestern Ohio Special Education Regional Resource Center, Cincinnati, OH. poth_r@swoserrc.org

Since the early 1990s Ohio has implemented state-wide or regional school-based projects focused on use of problem solving as a key method and student improvement as a primary goal. These initiatives have evolved through implementation experience, partnering with other states through the Innovations in Education Conference, and learning and improvement from emerging research. This chapter describes the evolution of Ohio's model/approach into a comprehensive, integrated model for school improvement. Ohio uses a three-tiered approach for universal, supplemental, and individualized instruction/intervention called the Ohio Integrated Systems Model (OISM). OISM involves problem solving both academic and behavior concerns at all three tiers. This model is consistent with the response to intervention (RTI) model as described by the National Association of State Directors of Special Education (NASDSE, 2005) and other authors (e.g., Tilly, 2003). In discussing the evolution of the OISM, we emphasize key components, the evaluation model and emerging data, and lessons learned. Ohio's experiences and the collective experiences described in other chapters should help inform the efforts of both practitioners and scholars as they implement and evaluate RTI practices in a systemic way to improve student outcomes.

22.1 Background and Context

For more than a decade the Ohio Department of Education (ODE), Office for Exceptional Children (OEC) has supported educational reform initiatives to remove barriers to success for students with disabilities. Areas of focus have included ensuring that students be educated in the least restrictive environment, preventing misclassification and overrepresentation of ethnic and racial minority students, and addressing suspension and expulsion rates of students in special education categories. Individual state-wide initiatives related to these goals have included intervention-based assessment/multi-factored evaluation (Telzrow, McNamara, and Hollinger, 2000), classroom management, and inclusive practices. These initiatives were all supported through Ohio's 16 Special Education Regional Resource Centers (SERRCs), state-supported agencies for professional development, technical assistance, and consultation (and, in some cases, direct services delivery to schools). Implementation for all initiatives was voluntary, based at the building level, and required training and participation of a school team that included an administrator, general and special educators, and parent representation.

The 16 Ohio SERRCs, as agencies of the ODE/OEC, regionally serve Ohio's 692 school districts. Ohio's State Standards and Procedures, including Academic Content Standards, provide a context for implementation of these initiatives. The state-wide assessment system provides another important context, as school and district performance is rated on the Ohio Report Card (in categories ranging from Excellent to the lowest ratings of Academic Watch and Academic Emergency).

Over the past two decades, Ohio's approach to these special education sponsored initiatives has evolved and improved. Three major influences have shaped Ohio's current work as it is now framed in the OISM. An important initial influence was federal support through a State Improvement Grant (SIG) from the US Department of Education to ODE/OEC of approximately $6 million over the 3-year grant. Additional compelling support was provided by federal requirements in No Child Left Behind (NCLB) and the reauthorization of the Individuals with Disabilities Education Improvement Act (IDEA 2004). These legislative mandates supported key features of the initiative (e.g., early intervention to students, using data for decisions, a school improvement focus), which in turn led to support from general and special education. Finally, research developments in specific components of the model, particularly in system-wide approaches (e.g., a comprehensive three-tiered model) for academics (e.g., Simmons et al., 2002) and behavior (e.g., Horner, Sugai, Todd, and Lewis-Palmer, 2005), provided critical empirical support and foundations for the current comprehensive OISM.

In 2005–2006, approximately 300 school buildings participated in the OISM, supported through the SIG, and 29 additional districted were supported in 2006–2007 through targeted grants from ODE to build district-level capacity for the OISM beyond the SIG, which ends in 2007. In a prior related initiative implemented from 1993–2000, over 100 schools participated in the problem-solving project called Intervention-Based Assessment. The southwest Ohio region has been particularly active in supporting school practice consistent with problem solving, with over 150 schools collaborating with the Southwestern Ohio SERRC (SWO SERRC) across both initiatives to implement systemic models as now represented in the OISM (15 of these schools are included specifically in the OISM through the SIG and the remainder have been supported in system-level school change in related practices).

22.2 Rationale and Underlying Principles for Ohio's Approach

There is research-based support and compelling rationale for all components of Ohio's model. Key rationales for both the need for an improved model

and for the overall approach (a tiered model emphasizing instruction and intervention across tiers) were detailed by the President's Commission on Excellence in Special Education (2002). A significant feature of Ohio's model is a focus on both academics and behavior in an integrated model. Support for this dual focus is provided by research demonstrating the additive effects and significantly improved outcomes of targeting academics and behavior simultaneously (e.g., Ialongo, Paduska, Werthamer, and Kellam, 2001; Kellam, Mayer, Regok, and Hawkins, 1998). Another key principle is the overall school improvement and student outcome focus in Ohio's model. The OISM is focused on improving student outcomes at all levels (district, school, classroom, and individual student) using research-based approaches and relying on data-based decision making at all tiers. Using data for school and student improvement decisions is a hallmark of effective schools (Schlecty, 2005). With this orientation, Ohio's approach is similar to models with a school improvement and student outcome orientation, such as those implemented in Iowa (e.g., Ikeda et al., 2002) and Michigan (Ervin, Schaughnency, Goodman, McGlinchey, and Matthews, 2006). This outcome orientation can be differentiated from other RTI models that focus more on alternate methods for eligibility determination (e.g., Brown-Chidsey and Steege, 2005; National Research Center on Learning Disabilities, 2006; Speece, Case, and Molloy, 2003).

Finally, other key research-based and conceptual foundations for components of the model include: collaborative strategic planning, based on systematic problem solving/data-based decision making as described in Deno (2002), Bergan and Kratochwill, (1990), and Allen and Graden, (2002); scientifically-based curriculum/instruction and research-based practices, founded in NCLB and increased emphases on research-based practice (Kratochwill and Shernoff, 2004); and culturally responsive practices, such as those described in the National Research Council's report (Donovan and Cross, 2002).

22.3 Goals and Description of the Model

22.3.1 Goals of the Model

Ohio's approach, the OISM for academic and behavior supports (Stollar, Poth, Curtis, and Cohen, 2006), has the primary goal of school improvement (with a specific focus on closing achievement gaps for all NCLB subgroups) by increasing the capacity of systems to use problem solving/data-based decision making and research-based practices to sustain high achievement over time. Secondary goals include the application of a problem-solving model to system-level issues (as well as individual student concerns) and improvement of universal literacy and behavior instruction for all students. Ohio's model has no stated goal regarding using RTI for eligibility, although RTI practices naturally occur throughout implementation of OISM components (e.g., using student performance data for decisions, using research-based instruction and intervention of increasing intensity (Barnett, Daly, Jones, and Lentz, 2004). The goals of OISM are about improving achievement for all students, not about an alternative process for determining eligibility for special education. This shift in emphasis away from improvement of special education eligibility practices to a focus on student and school improvement was one of the most difficult yet critically important lessons learned that hopefully will inform others' ef-

forts related to RTI implementation. The real benefit of this approach is improved outcomes for schools and students. Focusing primarily on RTI as an alternative set of eligibility procedures misses this important opportunity and, in our view, is limiting in scope.

22.3.2 Description of Ohio's Model

The three-tiered model used in OISM is conceptualized as a cone, with the tiers of instructional support for all students resting on a well-functioning school system that focuses on and supports academics and behavior (see Figure 22.1). As a cone, the OISM is a three-dimensional model, with six key components providing the base and also cutting across all tiers. These core components are: (a) collaborative strategic planning (using problem solving), (b) data-based decision making, (c) continuum (tiers) of academic and behavior supports, (d) scientifically-based practices, (e) administrative leadership, and (f) culturally responsive practices. These components are seen as interrelated (e.g., data-based decision making occurs within

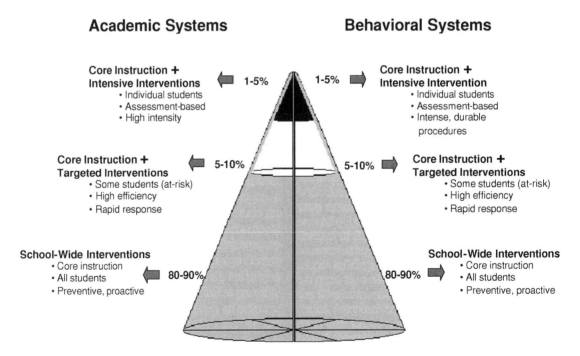

FIGURE 22.1. The OISM for academic and behavior supports.

collaborative strategic planning; all practices—assessment, culturally responsive practices, and instructional practices—must be scientifically-based).

Tier 1 represents the universal core of research-based curriculum and instructional practices provided to all students, as all children benefit from school-wide positive behavior support practices and core academic instruction. Ohio's model is specific in the components but has not been prescriptive in judging the scientifically-based curriculum. The OISM training modules contain content on criteria for determining whether approaches are scientifically-based and research-based, using definitions from NCLB and criteria from the US Department of Education. School-based teams then apply this knowledge to decisions about core curricula. Similar to other three-tiered models (e.g., Horner et al., 2005; Simmons et al., 2002), this universal instruction tier is represented as the foundation of the cone. In the OISM, Tier 1 is the foundation and also surrounds the higher tiers, reflecting that students continue to receive Tier 1 instruction even as supplemental and individualized supports are added (i.e., Tier 1 is not replaced, but remains the core).

Tier 2, the second tier in the cone, represents research-based, supplemental instruction (still within general education) directed at improving skill deficits and usually delivered in small groups. Because supports are needs based, deriving from collaborative strategic planning/data-based decision making, there typically is a need to rethink past practices regarding use of remedial and supplemental resources. In many schools, these supports had been provided without needs-based, data-based decision making and without sufficient attention to the use of scientifically-based supplemental programs. Ohio's model uses universal screening data from research-based, computer-based data systems, which allows for using the same data across various school decisions (such as Dynamic Indicators for Basic Early Literacy Skills (DIBELS; Good, Gruba, and Kaminski, 2002) or Office Disciplinary Referrals in a system such as the School-Wide Information System (SWIS; May et al., 2002)). For example, if DIBELS data indicate that the core reading curriculum and instruction are not meeting student needs in the area of phonemic awareness, then collaborative strategic planning will be used to design, implement and eval-uate Tier 2 supplemental instructional supports to meet that need. When students' DIBELS and other reading performance data indicate that they are not on track to master phonemic awareness skills, they receive Tier 2 supports already designed for that purpose. In other words, the problem solving is done at the systems/group level, not at an individual student level using a referral-based method. Frequent progress monitoring allows for data-based decisions about discontinuing Tier 2 supports (if data indicate performance has sufficiently improved) or planning Tier 3 supports (if data indicate more individualized, intensive problem solving and supports are needed).

Tier 3 instruction, in the OISM cone (still surrounded by Tier 1 to represent continuation of universal supports), is designed by applying the same data-based problem-solving process used in system-level collaborative strategic planning to individual student concerns. Data collected while students received Tier 1 and Tier 2 supports are used to plan Tier 3 interventions that are more individualized, frequent, intensive, and explicit. The goal of Tier 3 is to enable learning by finding instructional environments, materials, and strategies that close the gap for each student. In the OISM, Tier 3 is individualized and more intensive, but it is still considered general education (not equated with special education as in some other models). If the supports necessary for a student to make sufficient progress are unique, intensive, and specialized, then a disability may be suspected and procedures to determine eligibility for special education services may be instituted. Information about the interventions used and resulting data form the basis for determining eligibility and need for special education, as well as for developing the individualized educational plan (IEP). There is a seamless transition from Tier 3 to formalizing the supports in an IEP. RTI data emerge naturally from progress monitoring across instruction and intervention across tiers, so RTI is not a separate phase, set of procedures, or a "test;" and at no point is there a movement or return to "test and place." Importantly, as has been described in Iowa's model (Grimes, Kurns, and Tilly, 2006; Ikeda et al., 2002; Tilly, 2003), data continue to be collected for students on IEPs to continue data-based decision making toward improvement with a student outcome orientation.

22.4 Developing Capacity for Model Implementation: Strategies and Activities

Taking a comprehensive model to scale is a complex process requiring extensive preparation, organization, and involvement of key stakeholders (e.g., Glennan, Bodilly, Galeger, and Kerr, 2004). In Ohio's efforts, the OISM and precursor models have been supported through training and on-site technical assistance to schools through the existing network of Ohio's 16 SERRCs. Key components of the training and support are summarized in Table 22.1 and include (a) the use of a standard set of training modules and tools to support implementation accuracy, (b) training of all SERRC consultants on the model, (c) on-site coaching support to OISM districts and schools (by trained SERRC consultants at the district level and by internal district coaches at the building level) to model some practices (e.g.,

collaborative strategic planning) and provide technical assistance and coaching to support implementation of core components (e.g., use of DIBELS data for decision making).

A key feature of the state support structure is reliance on the already existing SERRC network to build capacity of districts and schools. A training-of-trainers model, using standardized materials and activities, is used. The project has evolved from a focus on supporting change at the building level to an expanded focus on district-level change and support. SERRC consultants support district-leadership teams and internal district coaches. SERRC consultants' roles in this district-capacity building structure have evolved away from direct building-level support to district-level support, training, consultation, and change facilitation. Although the primary OISM implementation activities still are focused at the building level, district-level coordination and planning are essential for sustainable systemic change and

TABLE 22.1. OISM support structure: key leadership bodies, roles, purposes, and activities.

Leadership role (members)	Purpose	Key activities
OISM state-level core group (representatives from ODE, SERRC directors, OISM leads, SIG evaluators, parent group)	Advisory function—provides overall direction and state-level decision making	Monthly core meetings Review and input on materials Input on all key decisions Guidance on directions
OISM leads (three regional leads)	Responsible for coordination and support for SERRC consultant networks (each has one-third of SERRC regions) and district leadership teams/coaches within regions	Monthly regional networking meetings Training, technical assistance, support to SERRC consultants Coordination and communication
SERRC consultants (in 16 SERRCs)	Responsible for supporting district leadership teams/coaches in SERRC region	Meet approximately monthly with district teams/coaches to support district-level efforts (training, technical assistance) Trained in all OISM components
District leadership team (representatives of central and administrators, building and special services personnel, parent representation)	Guides planning and decision making for district-level implementation of OISM	Plans for delivery of training for OISM components Collaborative strategic planning for implementation and district-level decision making
District coach (internal district person)	Responsible for on-site support of OISM—training and technical assistance	On-site training, using state OISM modules On-site technical assistance and coaching support
Building leadership team (representatives of administration, teachers, special services personnel, parent representation)	Responsible for implementation of OISM at school level	Plans for implementation of OISM components in building Collaborative strategic planning for implementation, building-level decision making regarding resources

broad and deep implementation of research-based practices.

22.5 Resources for Implementation

As has been the case in states with similar models (e.g., North Carolina, Florida), the Ohio model has been supported for the past few years through a SIG. Shapiro (2006) highlighted the importance of supporting implementation at the local level without additional external resources to (a) promote local adoption and ownership and (b) avoid the perception (or reality) that change in practices can occur only through external resource support. A key to sustaining practices has been encouraging use of local resources at the district level. Collaborative strategic planning has been used with district and building teams to plan for implementation using existing resources. In schools that have been long-term adopters of OISM practices, additional resources typically have not been added, nor have there been reductions in resources or staff (as is sometimes noted as a concern). Rather, there has been a change in how services are delivered (e.g., more resources directed to early/supplemental intervention; more collaboration among general education, remedial, and special education personnel; reorganization of schedules to allow for more targeted intervention time for more students).

22.6 Evaluation of the Program and Impact Evidence

The OISM is evaluated on multiple levels: state, regional, district/school, and student. The ODE has a contract with a consultant for state-level SIG evaluation. Components of the overall evaluation include levels of implementation (through interviews, observations, and review of permanent products, such as action plans and team self-assessment tools) and, ultimately, student outcomes (as measured by DIBELS, curriculum-based measurement, and Office Discipline Referral data). Early data reports are very promising in showing high levels of implementation and positive student outcomes.

In the southwestern region of the state, the SWO SERRC has used a scientist practitioner model to develop and measure the OISM and school/district change in prior iterations of the model. In addition to using the available research base, the evaluation model has been informed by experience and feedback during implementation. SWO SERRC uses a framework that assesses implementation of the model and impact on student outcomes (Guskey, 2000). Methods have been adapted from existing tools and/or designed for the dual purposes of aiding implementation (e.g., use by district and building-leadership teams for self assessment and strategic planning) and evaluating outcomes (e.g., use by SERRC personnel to summarize implementation data across districts and relate implementation levels to outcomes). For example, the action plan prompts use of collaborative strategic planning (implementation aid), and examination of written records on the action plan allows for measuring the extent to which leadership teams use collaborative strategic planning (evaluation purpose). OISM implementation and evaluation methods have included direct use or adaptation of existing tools such as the Planning and Evaluation Tool (Kame'enui and Simmons, 2003) and the School-wide Evaluation Tool (SET; Sugai, Lewis-Palmer, Todd, & Horner, 2001). A team survey, described in Stollar et al. (2006), is used in yearly evaluation by building-leadership teams and provides self-report data on implementation activities. An OISM Implementation Evaluation Tool, based on the SET, is used to measure the extent of implementation. DIBELS and SWIS data reports provide formative and summative evidence of the impact on student learning at a school, district, or regional level. Finally, putting the implementation data together with student outcome data allows for analysis of level of implementation as related to student outcomes. As implementation of the model is still in progress, summary data at the district and regional level are not yet available. Data from individual schools implementing the model are very encouraging, showing positive growth in areas targeted for school change; see Stollar et al. (2006) for an example.

22.7 Lessons Learned

As with any complex and large-scale change project, there are inevitable challenges to be overcome, lessons to be learned from experience, and improvements to be made resulting from these expe- riences and from emerging research. Improvements have been made based on collaboration and shar- ing with other states implementing similar projects, supported by the Innovations in Education Con- ference and follow-up communication and partner- ships (with Iowa, Michigan, Illinois, and others who have chapters in this volume). Reflecting on these challenges and improvements over time, some clear lessons and principles emerge, along with implica- tions for practice. These lessons and implications are summarized in Table 22.2.

22.8 Need for a Systems Focus and Broad Ownership

Many authors (e.g., Fullan, 2005; Fullan, Bartaini, and Quinn, 2004; Hall and Hord, 2001) have dis- cussed the importance of a system-level focus as

necessary to sustain change over time through broad ownership. Ohio's experience with a previous and related initiative, intervention-based assessment, highlighted the importance of broad ownership. This prior initiative was well intentioned (in aim- ing to remedy documented problems in a refer– test–place model) and resulted in some positive outcomes (e.g., positive parent perceptions of the practices; Telzrow et al., 2000). However, it was not sufficiently integrated across general education and special education, resulting in a lack of broad school-based ownership. Another important differ- ence between the prior initiative and the current OISM is the focus of efforts. Previously, the fo- cus was more on improving practices for individ- ual children than on overall school improvement. Thus, even though many of the core components and practices were the same (such as data-based decision making, collaborative problem solving, ef- fective intervention), the OISM has a broader focus that better connects with the needs and priorities

TABLE 22.2. Lessons learned and implications for implementation.

Lessons learned	Implications for implementation
Need for system-level focus and broad ownership	• focus on the big picture—school improvement • use universal screening/data systems • avoid focus of RTI for eligibility only
Viewing practices within a comprehensive, integrated model	• adopt a comprehensive, integrated model • explain model, components, research support, and benefits to gain understanding • avoid piecemeal approach
Attention to scaling up	• build layers of support and provide networking opportunities • build on existing structures and groups to build capacity • include representation by key constituencies on core decision making group • provide opportunities to share resources, highlight results
Maintaining accuracy in implementation	• use a well-developed, comprehensive model • use/adapt existing tools to monitor implementation • use standard materials/modules for consistency • support implementation with on-site coaching
Importance of parent participation	• include parents at all levels of decision making—advisory, district and school-level planning • provide guidance on parent participation in decisions for their children • develop materials and resources for parents
Importance of language and perceptions	• be aware of how language is perceived by various groups • communicate clearly rationale and research for core components • be open to discussion and allow for flexibility in terms where possible
Collaboration for pre-service training	• establish communication and collaboration between schools, IHE, and faculty • provide information on the model to faculty at IHEs

of general educators. A key lesson for those considering adoption of RTI models is the importance of a school-wide focus, including universal screening and the use of computerized data systems, such as DIBELS (available at http://dibels.uoregon.edu), AIMSWEB (available at www.aimsweb.com), and SWIS (available at www.swis.org), that allow for easy application of data-based decision making.

This system-wide approach is the real benefit of the OISM and similar models, and it is vastly different from a referral-based, "wait-to-fail" model that relies on a teacher or parent referral process. Significant changes to special education practices are not possible without changes to general education practices. Likewise, framing RTI as a special education, eligibility-driven initiative will work against broad adoption and focus on the most important outcome: student and school improvement.

22.9 Viewing Practices within a Comprehensive Integrated System, Not as an "Add On"

From experience in the prior project focused on improving eligibility practices, a related lesson learned was that innovative practices such as RTI will not be effectively implemented or sustained if they are conceptualized as an "add on" to an existing system, particularly if the existing system is not effective for a majority of students. An important feature of the OISM is using collaborative strategic planning to identify, analyze, and address system-level barriers to improve student academic and behavior outcomes. Universal screening data are used in collaborative strategic planning to design and evaluate all three tiers of instructional support, not only supplemental tiers (e.g., Stollar et al., 2006).

All features of the school system must be organized to facilitate implementing the comprehensive model. For example, one of the key features of RTI is determining instructional supports that enable student learning. However, to effectively do this for *one* student, a continuum of instructional services must be available to *any* student, based on data regarding student needs. This means that schools must find a way to use their general, remedial, and special education funded resources and staff flexibly—in

small groups, in co-teaching, and across traditional special education categories. Research-validated instruction that is well matched to the data-based needs of students is the foundation of RTI. Past experience with trying to implement intervention-based practices in Ohio without a focus on school-wide data-based decision making about supports led to the following unintended negative outcomes: (a) continued overreliance on teacher referral that perpetuated "wait to fail" concerns; (b) continued high numbers of students who did not meet grade expectations, straining resources for supplemental services (e.g., referral to intervention assistance teams, overuse of interventions delivered in collaboration with special services personnel); (c) perpetuation of thinking of general and special education as separate systems; (d) continued practice of passing students from grade to grade without necessary skills; (e) maintenance of belief that poor academic or social skills are the result of child characteristics rather than consideration of instructional variables; and (f) discontinuation of intervention-based practices due to teacher burn out and an overwhelmed system. Others early in implementation of RTI models can learn from our experiences to focus efforts on a model with a school-wide, instructional emphasis rather than implementing minor adjustments to special education practices.

22.9.1 Careful Attention to Scaling Up Implementation of the Model

There are many important considerations and activities that require extensive effort and planning in scaling up a model or innovation (Glennan et al., 2004). In Ohio, significant implications follow from evolution of OISM as solely a voluntary project, to being conceptualized as a state-wide model for all students, aligned with federal regulations and state policies. Rather than just working with highly motivated, volunteer partners, some districts may be involved in the OISM because of their school improvement status or their outcomes for student subgroups (e.g., disproportionate number of minority students in special education or in suspension or expulsion rates). Taking this model to a larger scale in districts with varying points of entry and levels of motivation is presenting new challenges and has implications in creating collaborative partnerships, local ownership, and addressing concerns. Systems-change literature (e.g., Fullan, 2005; Hall and Hord, 2001) has emphasized the importance of readiness for change (i.e., starting with districts/schools that have some core components in place). However, to take change to scale, particularly in the context of mandates, will require changes in thinking and practices. All involved will need to encourage school change through incremental "baby steps," set clear goals and targets for change that provide tangible benefits to implementers, promote positive movement in the right direction, and carefully support and build upon ongoing change efforts.

Given the larger-scale focus of the OISM, Ohio is applying change principles and effective practices from research-based sources on sustaining change (e.g., Adelman and Taylor, 1997; Curtis and Stollar, 2002; Denton, Vaughn, and Fletcher, 2003; Slavin, 2004). Ohio has developed layers of decision making and support (summarized in Table 22.1), including: a core state-wide team with representation across key constituencies; regional networks for collaboration, support, and training; a district-level structure for training and on-site support; and communities of practice to support continued planning, discussion, and partnership for key groups (e.g., administrators, teachers, parents, school psychologists). Training consistent with the OISM is occurring within several existing groups (e.g., elementary and secondary principal academies, school psychology interns). Also importantly, there has been attention to networking, sharing, and celebration of successes. Both at the state and regional levels, there are networking meetings of school and district teams implementing the change (e.g., DIBELS and Positive Behavior Support summits, "Partnering for Progress" celebrations to share and celebrate outcome data and experiences).

22.9.2 Maintaining Implementation Accuracy in Scaling-Up Efforts

A common challenge faced in large-scale adoption of a comprehensive model is retaining accuracy of implementation of core model components and practices while allowing flexibility and local adaptation in other features. Grimes et al. (2006) discussed the importance of relying on a strong

model with clear components. Consistent with this practice, Ohio has a clear visual model as a guide with required components that are carefully defined and delineated (e.g., data-based decision making, scientifically-based practices as components of the model that are specifically trained in module content). Instruments have been developed to support implementation accuracy. The implementation checklist is used for self-assessment, goal setting, and planning for fidelity of implementation of OISM components, as well as for evaluation. Also vitally important to promoting implementation accuracy is use of a comprehensive professional development model and practices consistent with NCLB's emphasis on high-quality professional development and the recommendations for effective professional development to sustain change (e.g., National Staff Development Council, 2001). Ohio's model for supporting the OISM through the SER-RCs has incorporated these principles and practices, and thus includes district and school planning to incorporate and support the change, the use of a coaching model to support implementation, and standardized training modules and materials to assure consistency.

22.9.3 Importance of Parent Participation in Planning and Implementation

One important commitment Ohio has had throughout initiatives is encouraging active, meaningful parent involvement in all aspects of planning and implementation of the model. As has been well documented, encouraging and maintaining parent involvement at a systems level is challenging and requires sustained efforts and a commitment to the importance of partnerships (e.g., Esler, Godber, and Christenson, 2002). Although there is continued need for improvement, particularly at the systems level, Ohio has made important strides in encouraging parent participation. This includes participation on the state-level OISM core planning group by representatives of the Ohio Coalition for the Education of Children with Disabilities, a state-wide advocacy and training group for parents. In addition, all district and building planning teams are required to have parent representation, and parent participation in all decisions is described in training materials across tiers and activities (in naturally occurring ways consistent with emphases of decisions at tiers—from general education to special education decision making). Many schools have developed brochures and web-based descriptions of OISM practices for parents, and the OISM website (www.iesystems.org) will includes information, links, and resources specifically for parents. The importance of strong parent participation has been a firm commitment across initiatives. However, there is ongoing learning about ways to enhance this participation and improvements to make.

22.9.4 Importance of Addressing Language and Different Perceptions

An issue related to enhancing broad ownership state wide is the challenge involved in language used in describing components and differing perceptions about these components. As the OISM is being implemented on a broad scale across districts and different state agencies, there has been heightened awareness of how language and model concepts can sometimes be barriers to understanding and ownership. Some concepts and language used in OISM may be more familiar to special educators (e.g., positive behavior support), and other key concepts (e.g., use of DIBELS, scientifically-based instruction) can raise discussion and different understandings among educators with different perspectives. In working toward a state-wide OISM model, efforts continue to be made to use language that is understandable to various constituencies across general and special education, including parents. Where language is a barrier, some districts have relabeled core components in more understandable language for their local contexts. This issue will be a continuing one to address as the model is discussed across various agencies, including mental health agencies and partners. The core principles of OISM, including collaborative strategic planning and reliance on scientifically-based approaches, will help provide a framework for working through these issues.

22.9.5 Collaboration for Change in Pre-Service Training

A consistent need expressed from administrators across the state is a lack of congruence between what is being taught at the pre-service level and the skills needed by educators in OISM schools. National reports also have addressed this training gap specifically as related to reading instruction (National Council on Teacher Quality, 2006). Some areas cited in Ohio as needing to be addressed include core components of data-based decision making (including assessment methods for decision making and use of data systems), scientifically-based instruction, and collaborative strategic planning. To support increased collaboration and alignment, in 2005–06, the ODE provided grants to Institutions of Higher Education (IHEs). Projects were funded with specific goals of (a) developing a framework for self-study to address alignment of personnel preparation with OISM components and (b) bringing together IHE faculties, across disciplines and in partnership with the SERRCs and OISM school personnel, to collaborate and align training efforts. These projects are in initial phases, but have the potential to begin examination of pre-service preparation and increasing collaboration across IHEs and practitioners. As one positive example of changes in pre-service preparation for a core constituency group, the nine Ohio school psychology training programs have committed to align training consistent with the OISM, promote internships in OISM schools, and work collaboratively with the Ohio School Psychologists Association on professional development for the OISM.

22.10 Concluding Comments

With advances in educational research and support from legislative initiatives, foundations are set for implementation of models that enhance school practices for all students (NASDSE, 2005). Ohio's approach reflects use of these research-based advances and links to these key legislative foundations. There is great potential for broad-based change to incorporate effective practices at a school-system level to improve outcomes for all students. As has been described in this chapter and related chapters in this volume, there are key similarities among these approaches, including use of a school-wide, tiered model, focus on school and student improvement, using data-based decision making, and relying on scientifically-based approaches. These components represent significant advances and opportunities to address many of the challenges schools have faced over the past decades in meeting the needs of increasing numbers of students experiencing significant academic and behavioral difficulties. Adoption of a model with features similar to the OISM is an important step in making strides toward this school improvement.

References

Adelman, H. S. & Taylor, L. (1997). Toward a scale-up model for replicating new approaches to schooling. *Journal of Educational and Psychological Consultation, 8,* 197–230.

Allen, S. J. & Graden, J. L. (2002). Best practices in collaborative problem solving for intervention design. In A. Thomas & J. Grimes, (Eds.), *Best Practices in School Psychology IV* (pp. 565–582). Bethesda, MD: National Association of School Psychologists.

Barnett, D. W., Daly III, E. J., Jones, K. M., & Lentz, F. E. (2004). Response to intervention: empirically-based special services decisions from single-case designs of increasing and decreasing intensity. *Journal of Special Education, 38,* 66–79.

Bergan, J. R. & Kratochwill, T. R. (1990). *Behavioral Consultation and Therapy.* New York: Plenum Press.

Brown-Chidsey, R. & Steege, M. (2005). *Response to Intervention: Principles and Strategies for Effective Practice.* New York: Guilford.

Curtis, M. J. & Stollar, S. (2002). Best practices in systems-level change. In A. Thomas & J. Grimes (Eds.), *Best Practices in School Psychology IV* (pp. 223–234). Bethesda, MD: National Association of School Psychologists.

Deno, S. L. (2002). Problem solving as "best practices." In A. Thomas and J. Grimes (Eds.), *Best Practices in School Psychology IV* (pp. 37–55). Bethesda, MD: National Association of School Psychologists.

Denton, C. A., Vaughn, S., & Fletcher, J. M. (2003). Bringing research-based practice in reading to scale. *Learning Disabilities Research and Practice, 18,* 201–211.

Donovan, M. S. & Cross, C. T. (Eds.) (2002). Minority students in special education and gifted education. Washington DC: National Academy Press. Available at http://www.nap.edu/catalog/10128.html.

Ervin, R. A., Schaughnency, E., Goodman, S. D., McGlinchey, M. T., & Matthews. A. (2006). Merging research and practice agendas to address reading and behavior school-wide. *School Psychology Review, 35,* 198–223.

Esler, A. N., Godber, Y., & Christenson, S. (2002). Best practices in supporting home-school collaboration. In A. Thomas & J. Grimes (Eds.), *Best Practices in School Psychology IV* (pp. 389–411). Bethesda, MD: National Association of School Psychologists.

Fullan, M. (2005). Resiliency and sustainability. *Educational Leadership, 59,* 16–20.

Fullan, M., Bartaini, A., & Quinn, J. (2004). New lessons for district reform. *Educational Leadership, 6,* 42–46.

Glennan, T. K., Bodilly, S. J., Galegher, J. R., & Kerr, K. A. (2004). Summary: toward a more systematic approach to expanding the reach of educational interventions. In T. K. Glennan, S. J. Bodilly, J. R. Galegher, & A. Kerr (Eds.), *Expanding the Reach of Educational Reforms: Perspectives from Leaders on the Scale-Up of Educational Interventions.* Rand Corporation. Available at http:;://www.rand.org.

Good III, R. H., Gruba, J., & Kaminski, R. A. (2002). Best practices in using dynamic indicators of basic early literacy skills in an outcomes-driven model. In A. Thomas & J. Grimes (Eds.), *Best Practices in School Psychology IV* (pp. 699–720). Bethesda, MD: National Association of School Psychologists.

Grimes, J., Kurns, S., & Tilly III, D. (2006). Sustainability: an enduring commitment to success. *School Psychology Review, 35,* 224–244.

Guskey, T. R. (2000). *Evaluating Professional Development.* Thousand Oaks, CA: Corwin Press.

Hall, G. E. & Hord, S. M. (2001). *Implementing Change: Patterns, Principles, and Potholes.* Boston: Allyn & Bacon.

Horner, R. H., Sugai, G., Todd, A. W., & Lewis-Palmer, T. (2005). School-wide positive behavior support: an alternative approach to discipline in schools. In L. Bambara & L. Kern (Eds.), *Individualized Supports for Students with Problem Behaviors: Designing Positive Behavior Plans* (pp. 359–390). New York: Guilford.

Ialongo, N., Poduska, J., Werthamer, L., & Kellam, S. (2001). The distal impact of two first-grade preventive interventions on conduct problems and disorders in early adolescence. *Journal of Emotional and Behavioral Disorders, 9,* 146–160.

Ikeda, M. Grimes, J., Tilly III, W. D., Allison, R., Kurns, S., & Stumme, J. (2002). Implementing an intervention-based approach to services delivery: a case example. In M. R. Shinn, G. Stoner, & H. M. Walker (Eds), *Interventions for Academic and Behavior Problems II* (pp. 53–69). Bethesda, MD: National Association of School Psychologists.

Kame'enui, E. J. & Simmons, D. C. (2003). *Planning and Evaluation Tool for effective School-Wide Reading Programs–Revised.* Eugene, OR: Institute for the Development of Educational Achievement. Available at http://oregonreadingfirst.uoregon.edu/downloads/PET-R.doc.

Kellam, S. G., Mayer, L. S.., Regok, G. W., & Hawkins, W. E. (1998). Effects of improving achievement on aggressive behavior and of improving aggressive behavior on achievement through two preventive interventions: an investigation of causal paths. In B. Bohrenwend (Ed.), *Adversity, Stress, and Psychopathology* (pp. 486–550). London: Oxford University Press.

Kratochwill, T. R. & Shernoff, E. S. (2004). Evidence-based practice: promoting evidence-based interventions. *School Psychology Review, 33*, 34–48.

May, S., Ard, W. I., Todd, A. W., Horner, R. H., Glasgow, A., & Sugai, G. (2002). *School-Wide Information System*. Education and Community Supports, University of Oregon. Available at www.swis.org.

NASDSE (2005). *Response to Intervention: Policy Considerations and Implementation*. Washington, DC: National Association of State Directors of Special Education.

National Council on Teacher Quality (2006). What education schools aren't teaching about reading and what elementary teachers aren't learning. Available at www.nctq.org/actq/images/nctq_reading_study_app.pdf.

National Research Center on Learning Disabilities (2006). Responsiveness-to-intervention. Available at http://nrcld.org.publications/papers/mellard/html).

National Staff Development Council (2001). *Standards for Staff Development (Revised)*. Oxford, OH: National Staff Development Council.

President's Commission on Excellence in Special Education (2002). *A New Era: Revitalizing Special Education for Children and Their Families*. Washington, DC: US Department of Education. Available at www.ed.gov/inits/commissionsborads/whspecialeducation.

Schlecty, P. S. (2005). *Creating Great Schools: Six Principles*. San Francisco: Jossey-Bass.

Shapiro, E. S. (2006). Are we solving the big problems? *School Psychology Review, 35*, 260–265.

Simmons, D. C., Kame'enui, E. J., Good, R. H., Harn, B. A., Cole, C., & Braun, D. (2002). Building, implementing, and sustaining a beginning reading model: lessons learned school by school. In M. R. Shinn, H. M. Walker, & G. S. Stoner (Eds.), *Interventions for Academic and Behavior Problems II: Preventive and Remedial Approaches* (pp. 537–570). Bethesda: MD: National Association of School Psychologists.

Slavin, R. E. (2004). Built to last: long term maintenance of "Success for All." *Remedial and Special Education, 25*, 61–66.

Speece, D. L., Case, L. P., & Molloy, D. E. (2003). Response to general education instruction as a first gate to learning disabilities identification. *Learning Disabilities Research and Practice, 18*, 147–156.

Stollar, S. A., Poth, R. L., Curtis, M. J., & Cohen, R. M. (2006). Collaborative strategic planning as illustration of the principles of systems change. *School Psychology Review, 35*, 181–197.

Sugai, G., Lewis-Palmer, T., Todd, A. W., & Horner, R. H. (2001). School-wide evaluation tool—version 2.0. Education and Community Supports, University of Oregon. Available at www.pbis.org/files/SET_v2.1.pdf.

Telzrow, C. F., McNamara, K., & Hollinger, C. L. (2000). Fidelity of problem-solving implementation and relationship to student performance. *School Psychology Review, 29*, 443–461.

Tilly III, W. D. (2003, December). How many tiers are needed for successful prevention and early intervention? Heartland Area Education Agency's evolution from four to three tiers. Paper presented at the *National Research Center on Learning Disabilities Responsiveness-to-Intervention Symposium*, Kansas City, MO. Available at http://www.nrcld.org/ symposium2003/tilly.pdf.

23
The Illinois Flexible Service Delivery Model: A Problem-Solving Model Initiative

David W. Peterson, David P. Prasse, Mark R. Shinn, and Mark E. Swerdlik

David W. Peterson, MS, is Co-Director of FED ED, an organization that represents the interests of suburban schools in Washington. peterson@nssed.org
David P. Prasse, PhD, Professor and Dean of School of Education, Loyola University of Chicago. dprasse@luc.edu
Mark R. Shinn, PhD, is a Professor of School Psychology at National Louis University, Skokie, IL. markshinn@mac.com
Mark E. Swerdlik, PhD, is a Professor of Psychology and Coordinator of Graduate Programs in School Psychology at Illinois State University, Normal. meswerd@ilstu.edu

The Illinois Flexible Service Delivery System (FSDS) model is a problem-solving and response-to-intervention (RTI) service delivery model that has evolved since its conception in 1994. It began as the result of a systems change effort to develop a more flexible and responsive delivery system for all students (NSSED, 2005). The first portion of this chapter outlines some of the basic principles that underlie the model, discusses some of the historical influences that supported its development, and provides a brief history of the growth of the model in Illinois schools. A description of sustaining structures for this initiative and a more complete discussion of the unique features and basic principles of the FSDS will follow this section. The statewide evaluation of the program, including evidence of its impact, is also addressed. This chapter concludes with a discussion of the lessons learned from the authors' work as consultants/trainers in implementing FSDS in a number of Illinois school districts.

The Illinois FSDS model was founded upon broad premises that have evolved over time and have historically shaped educational thinking about children with special learning needs (Peterson and Casey, 1991). Most basic among these premises is the underlying assumption that the academic and social/emotional difficulties experienced by students in school are at least partially the result of the interactions between the child and the classroom or instructional environment, and that the causes of those difficulties do not solely lie "within" the child. Consequently, such models also assume that school difficulties can be ameliorated through interventions aimed at modifying the instructional environment. Originally labeled as "alternative" service delivery models, these conceptions of service delivery also are based on the premise that categorical "test-and-place" models of special education service delivery have not been as effective as desired.

23.1 Basic Principles of the Illinois Model

The Illinois FSDS encompasses basic principles and components similar to those found in the Iowa problem-solving service delivery model (Heartland Area Education Agency 11, 2005), as well as in others that have developed concurrently in other states (e.g., Pennsylvania). These models include, but are not limited to: (a) merging all of the compensatory resources in a school to support the learning of all students; (b) implementing a multi-tiered model of service delivery for all students experiencing difficulty; (c) preventing and intervening early in academic and social/emotional difficulties; (d) involving parents in a meaningful way in the implementation of interventions; (e) using a systematic problem-solving model to guide decision-making; (f) using research-based, scientifically validated interventions; (g) developing increased levels of collaboration between school psychologists, general classroom teachers, and other special education staff; (h) frequently monitoring student progress using performance-based measures (e.g., curriculum-based measurement) and using data from those measures to evaluate intervention effectiveness; and (i) determining student eligibility for ongoing special education services based upon the student's RTI.

23.2 Historical Foundations

The roots of the Illinois FSDS (as well as those in other states) can be traced to the late 1980s when the then Assistant Secretary for Education, Madeline Will, published her White Paper, *Educating Children With Learning Problems: A Shared Responsibility* (Will, 1986), on special education services. In that paper, she called for greater cooperation between regular (now referred to as general) and special educators, and issued a call for all educators to create a more integrated and interdependent system for educating students with disabilities. Will's paper began a national discussion on the efficacy of traditional special education services and helped to create the inclusion movement that significantly changed the assumptions about how special education services should be delivered. In a more recent call for education reform, the report from the *President's Commission on Excellence in Special Education* cited the need for significant change, and stressed the need to implement research-based prevention and intervention approaches to assess and intervene with academic and behavioral problems in young children (President's Commission, 2002). The President's Commission report criticized the psychometric model of assessment of children suspected of having learning disabilities, and called for models based upon RTI. Similarly, *School Psychology: A Blueprint for Training and Practice II* (Ysseldyke et al., 1997, p. 3) stated, "it has been clear for some time that children and schools could do well with less of categorical delivery systems." They also stated (p. 3), "school psychologists' expertise in . . . problem-solving can be used to move toward more diverse assessment of stu-

dent learning and increased accountability in the schools."

Concurrent with the need for change being discussed nationally in the publications referenced above, the documented origins of FSDS in Illinois can be traced to work begun at the Northern Suburban Special Education District (NSSED). NSSED is a special education consortium of 19 school districts. In 1994, educators at NSSED developed a proposal to address problems in the existing special education service delivery system. This proposal was based upon the perspective that the existing special education service delivery system was flawed, because it was based upon a student assessment framework driven by deficit labels that were not logically related to the development of effective interventions and rigid procedural requirements that make it difficult to offer preventive interventions or that result in unacceptable time delays before service is initiated (NSSED, 2005).

Because of existing state rules and regulations regarding the provision of special education services, NSSED sought permission from the Illinois State Board of Education (ISBE) to implement an alternative service delivery model. After a series of meetings and correspondence, ISBE approved the model in the fall of 1995 (Broncato, 1995). The approval by ISBE was very bold and innovative. Although pockets of reform were emerging in other states as well, it was still 2 years before the federal reforms of the Individuals with Disabilities Education Act (IDEA) of 1997. After receiving ISBE approval, NSSED began an evolving series of planning and professional development activities to implement the new model and developed an evaluation design to begin to evaluate the effects of the initiative within their special education cooperative.

What happened next in Illinois solidified three important components necessary for successful reform. The components were (and still are) local district initiative (i.e., the choice/desire to implement a different way of doing business), meaningful state support, and independent evaluation of the programs. Following the NSSED approval, other districts in the state began to develop and submit proposals to ISBE that would allow them to provide services to special education students via an FSDS approach. By 1998, ISBE had developed a mini-grant program for FSDS sites directed to support training for school-based personnel. At the same time, the ISBE also initiated a statewide evaluation of FSDS programs such that independent evaluators would handle evaluation of the programs.

The number of school districts and cooperatives choosing to participate consistently grew after NSSED initially received approval. At the end of 1995, six districts were approved as FSDS sites. Ten years later there were close to 90 school districts, 81 of which were within 12 special education districts, including 30 grant sites. The state of Illinois has approximately 883 school districts. Each participating district developed and implemented professional development activities to ensure successful implementation.

23.2.1 Sustaining Structures

To the extent the Illinois initiatives have enjoyed success, one reason is the attention to sustaining structures developed at a state, regional, and district level. The four essential structural elements include building-based commitment and involvement, communication and learning networks, professional development, and an evaluation plan. Implementation throughout the state has been based on these four elements, and the support structures built around them. Building-based commitment in Illinois means initial professional development and training requires building-level (i.e., school) commitment, including active participation of the school principal. Training occurs via building teams and is ongoing over a planned training cycle. Although differences exist across sites, most districts follow a common training template. Training materials, curriculum, and resources are commonly shared among sites.

Communication and learning networks take the form of a statewide FSDS consortium made up of several regions. By 2000, the statewide and regional consortium was developed to promote collaboration between schools and districts across state FSDS sites. District-level professionals within regions regularly meet to focus on developing training cycles within regions, and sharing material and problem-solving implementation challenges. Each summer a statewide planning session is held with representatives from each region participating. Via committees, year-long plans are made that include evaluation of progress, professional development, and political action. Along with the support of ISBE, a statewide conference is held annually. Sessions are structured for those districts just beginning and for those districts who are years into their effort.

Early in the process (mid 1990s), it was understood that systemic change resulting from FSDS would not occur without the necessary support for changing professional behavior and the accompanying structures in the schools. Attention to training sequences that addressed the need to acquire both a different knowledge base and a new skill set were given priority. There was also acknowledgement that even the best inservice seldom, if ever, resulted in changes in professional behavior, especially at the scale necessary for successful implementation. Therefore, professional development activities were structured to address these challenges. As mentioned previously, participation began at a building level and required the commitment of the building principal along with a building team. Training of this team (principal led) would continue over an extended period of time (4 years in some places). Many districts worked at the regional level, sharing training sessions, personnel resources for training, and materials. The scope of the curriculum was developed to apply concepts and skills from the beginning for individual students, targeted groups, and system-level cases. Participation in professional development brought an obligation to complete homework assignments and follow a sequence that provided opportunities for practice, with feedback, and on-site applications of learned skills. In many training sites, coaches/facilitators were provided to the school teams implementing the FSDS to assist in both learning and implementation.

The importance of a statewide evaluation initiative (described in the following sections) was recognized at the onset of the program. Two key elements guided the evaluation approach. The first was a focus on implementation. Knowing that student outcome data would lack validity without evidence of implementation, early evaluation systems focused on the degree of implementation. By 2000, evaluation efforts expanded to begin looking closely at student outcome data. Systems were being developed to collect, aggregate, and analyze performance data, such as that obtained from progress monitoring.

Structural support continues through the consortium and through a recent grant program from ISBE. Beginning in 2006, an Illinois State Personnel Development Grant, I-ASPIRE (Alliance for School-Based Problem-Solving and Intervention Resources in Education), supported by Office of Special Education personnel preparation funds, was established to implement a coordinated, regionalized system of personnel development that would increase the capacity of school systems to provide early intervening services, aligned with the general education curriculum, to at-risk students and students with disabilities, as measured by improved student progress and performance. Similar to the statewide Positive Behavioral Intervention Support (PBIS) project, there will be a statewide, centralized evaluation system that will permit a focus on both the training/professional development component and student outcome data.

The following section provides a more extensive discussion of the features and basic concepts of the FSDS. Many of these concepts are common to problem-solving models.

23.3 Flexible Service Delivery as a Form of Problem Solving

Flexible service delivery is a variation of a problem-solving model that has its roots in Deno's conceptual model (Deno, 1989, 2002, 2005; Deno and Mirkin, 1971) and the cornerstones of a practice first implemented in Pine County, Minnesota, in 1978 (Germann and Tindal, 1985; Tindal, Wesson, Deno, Germann, and Mirkin, 1985). At its most fundamental level, all variations of a problem-solving model are based on the presumption that *all* students (i.e., with and without disabilities) receive programs of sufficient quality with the intensity and duration necessary for all students to *benefit*. In other words, problem solving is not just about special education or identifying students as eligible for special education.

For most students, this benefit can be obtained through general education. However, some students will not learn what is expected of them unless modifications to the standard instructional or behavioral interventions are made (Deno, 1989, 2005). One

of the options for students with severe educational needs, who need intensive or specialized instruction in order for them to learn what is expected, is special education. Four other cornerstones define problem-solving models like FSDS:

1. problems are defined ecologically;
2. problem solving starts with prevention;
3. special education eligibility is defined by both need and services required to benefit;
4. scientifically based assessment tools that fit problem solving are used.

23.4 Problems are Situationally Defined: An Ecological Approach

Since 1977, states have been required to specify the diagnostic criterion for each of the 13 federal disability categories because of a lack of national consensus. Criteria vary from state to state and, significantly, across districts within states. To be identified as learning disabled in Illinois, a student must have severe ability–achievement discrepancy and significant processing problems. With respect to ability–achievement discrepancies, the state does not specify what constitutes "severe." With respect to significant processing problems, the state does not specify what processing is, how to measure it, or what constitutes "significant."

In a problem-solving approach, a problem is defined as a *discrepancy between what is expected and what is occurring in a given situation* (Deno, 1989). The *situation*, or context, is a prominent part of the definition of a problem. What *occurs* is the achievement level of the student. What is *expected* is the level of typical achievement of other students. The *situation* is the classroom, school, or school district context. This is an ecological model that posits the *interaction* between a student and the instructional contextual expectations that defines an academic problem. In practice, there must be a discrepancy, but in this instance the discrepancy is *inter-individual* (i.e., between students) rather than *intra-individual* (i.e., within the student).

An illustration of who is identified as eligible for special education when an ecological perspective is operationalized is shown in Figure 23.1 (Peterson and Shinn, 2002). Students who are the

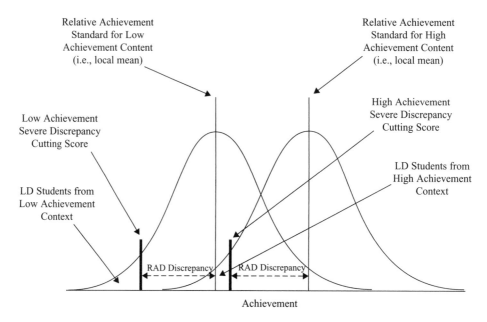

FIGURE 23.1. The problem-solving ecological performance discrepancy.

most severely discrepant academically in one situation (e.g., a higher performing school district) may differ from those who are the most severely discrepant academically in another situation (e.g., a lower performing school district).

Students identified with severe achievement problems and eligible for special education are the lowest achievers in a specific situation or context. Interestingly, the available research evidence suggests that, despite special education eligibility practices that emphasize within-the person disabilities, this relative achievement discrepancy (see Peterson and Shinn (2002) and Shinn, Good, and Parker (1999) for more details) has greater explanatory power in determining who schools identify as learning disabled.

23.5 Problem Solving Starts with Prevention

Prevention of academic problems is fundamental to a problem-solving model. Without this emphasis, problem solving becomes a wait-to-fail model. So, rather than sustaining separate "systems" for intervention (e.g., special education, remedial programs, English language learning programs) with unique

identification/eligibility, assessment, funding, and instructional practices, in problem-solving models the schools are creating a single heuristic system based on a three-tiered intervention model, such as the one shown in Figure 23.2 (Batsche et al., 2005).

The first level of problem solving, Tier 1 or core instructional interventions, is designed to bring science-based, validated interventions to *all* students. If these interventions are effective (e.g., a science-based reading program), then the needs of perhaps 80% of students can be met. However, even with effective Tier 1 interventions, some students will need more intensive or individualized programs to be successful (Deno, 1989). Tier 2 or targeted group interventions; provide *selected interventions* (e.g., Title I reading programs) to meet the needs of at-risk students.

If a student benefits from intervention in Tier 1 or Tier 2, then they may not be need special education. However, even with effective secondary prevention programs, a small proportion of students will need more intensive, and likely more expensive, Tier 3 or targeted individual interventions. These interventions are typically delivered through special education. In a problem-solving model, professional efforts are directed toward identifying, implementing, and strengthening interventions across all

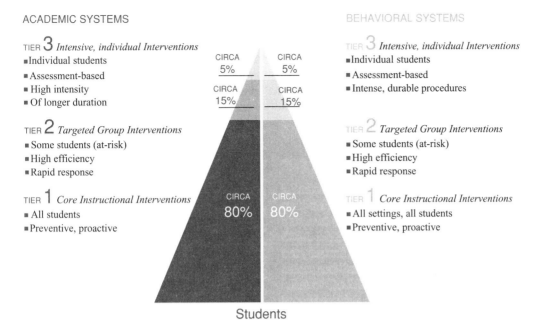

FIGURE 23.2. A three-tiered intervention model. From the National Association of Directors of Special Education, NADSE, Batsche et al. 2005.

three tiers rather than focusing efforts on identifying disabilities and presuming that the student "needs" special education to benefit from their educational program.

23.6 The Importance of Educational Need and Benefit

The third fundamental principle of identification within a problem-solving model is that the entitlement decision (i.e., the student needs special education) is based on the interaction of *severe educational need* and *educational benefit* (Shinn, 2005a, 2005b). It is not the disability status, a within-person characteristic that "confers" special education eligibility, but instead it is a severe educational need that requires intensive or specialized intervention services beyond what can be provided in general education (i.e., supplemental aids and services) in order for the student to benefit from the instruction. The combination of severe educational need and insufficient benefit (e.g., rate of improvement) results in what is called a *dual discrepancy* (Fuchs, Fuchs, and Speece, 2002; Pericola-Case, Speece, and Eddy-Molloy, 2003).

23.7 Scientifically Based Assessment Tools That Fit Problem Solving

To be able to implement a problem-solving model, it is critical that *assessment tools must fit the other design principles of problem solving*. That is, the assessment data must be able to: (a) reflect the "situation" or school and community context (i.e., provide a "local norm"); (b) provide an intervention focus (i.e., help identify effective interventions); (c) support a three-tiered model; and (d) allow educators to make statements about educational need and benefit. The assessment system(s) also must be consistent *across the three tiers* of the prevention model, so that a continuous database can be collected across levels of interventions and over time.

Implementation of a problem-solving model has been successful, in part, because of the use of curriculum-based measurement (CBM), a set of standardized and validated short-duration tests in the basic skills (Deno, 1985, 1986; Fuchs and Deno, 1991). CBM, and other members of the CBM family (e.g., dynamic indicators of basic early literacy skills, or DIBELS), is a set of short tests of

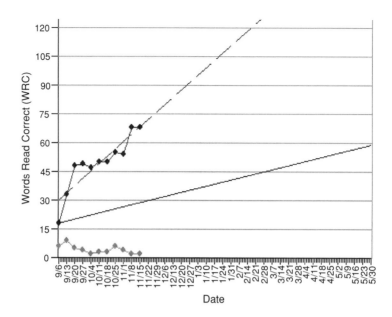

FIGURE 23.3. A student's benefit from special education as monitored toward the IEP goal using CBM.

reading, early literacy, mathematics computation, and problem solving, including early numeracy, spelling, and written expression (Shinn, 1989, 1998). A thorough explanation of CBM is not possible in this chapter; the reader is referred, for example, to the works of Deno (1985, 2002), Fuchs and Deno (1992), and Shinn (1989, 1998), among numerous others. For purposes of illustration, this chapter will use reading CBM (R-CBM), in which students read aloud from standard, high-quality passages for 1 min. The number of words read correctly is counted.

CBM was developed more than 25 years ago by Deno as an accurate and time-efficient way to monitor student progress and determine a student's *benefit* from intervention. CBM is reliable, valid, and, importantly, sensitive to improvement during short-term intervention for students wherever they receive their instruction (i.e., general, remedial, or special education). Therefore, CBM is ideal for use in a three-tier model.

Figure 23.3 provides an illustration of frequent progress monitoring for a grade 2 student in Tier 3 problem solving (special education). In R-CBM, students are tested one to two times per week using a single but different standard assessment passage from their expected grade-level curriculum. Figure 23.3 shows the student's benefit in Tier 3 problem solving.

This student's rate of progress (the dashed line) exceeded the expected rate progress (the solid line) toward the individualized education program (IEP) goal. With a high degree of certainty, educators can feel confident that this student is benefiting from the intervention.

When students are not benefiting from the intervention, in a problem-solving model, educators revise the intervention so that increased benefit can be obtained. An illustration is provided in Figure 23.4, where the student's progress monitoring data were used to modify the intervention as necessary to increase benefit (Shinn, 2005a, 2005b).

In the first intervention, the student's progress was below the expected rate of progress and the intervention was revised. The effects of Program Change 1 were then evaluated. Although the student was benefiting more from the modified intervention, it was still not a sufficient rate of improvement. Therefore, more changes to the intervention were made that were to be evaluated in Program Change 2.

In problem solving, CBM is used in a three-tier model to assess *all* students' educational needs in addition to their benefit. The process begins in Tier 1 (general education) using a benchmark assessment approach where students are tested three times per year on their grade placement level. For example, grade 4 students read grade 4 reading passages. For more detail, see Shinn, Shinn, Hamilton, and Clarke

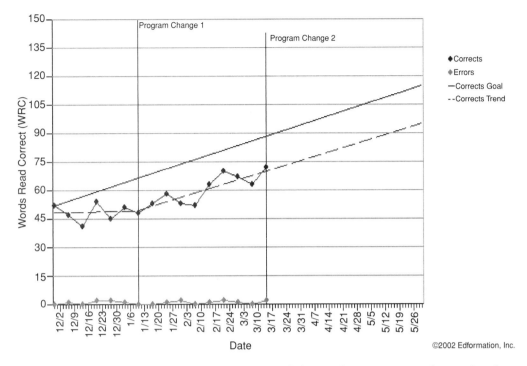

FIGURE 23.4. Student's progress monitoring data used to modify intervention as necessary to increase benefit.

(2002) or Shinn (2003). This benchmark process takes approximately 5 min; then, an individual student's scores are compared with the scores from other students in the school or community. Benchmarking allows schools the ability to conduct universal screening to identify students with potentially severe needs.

Benchmark scores plot the individual student's score against a box-and-whisker chart corresponding to how other students read. In this grade 4 fall benchmark, scores in the "box" show the average range (25th–75th percentiles). Scores below the lower whisker (10th percentile) are used to identify students with potentially severe educational needs. Typically, in this example, teams would begin problem solving to identify interventions that may improve achievement.

A theme in problem solving is the presence of *both* educational need and lack of benefit as a basis for decision-making. Not all students who are identified with severe educational needs, using CBM and benchmarks, require special education. Special-education eligibility decisions would be made only when there is a validated severe (e.g., below the

5th or 7th percentile) educational need *and* the student is not benefiting significantly from intensive, high-quality, scientifically based interventions *without* special education resources.

An example of a student with severe needs that does *not* need special education in order to benefit follows. A grade 2 student was identified for problem solving based on the fall benchmark data and placed in the school's Tier 2 intensive remedial *general education* program. By the grade 2 winter benchmark, it is evident that this student is improving at a faster rate than typically developing students. Placement in a more restrictive environment would not be warranted.

In sharp contrast, consider the lack of benefit from the Tier 2 intervention for the grade 4 student described in the following example. A student who does not demonstrate progress as a result of an intervention would move to a more intensive stage of problem solving where the RTI would be assessed more intensively and frequently (e.g., one to two times per week) in a process that would be structured and include due process, documentation of attention to state and federal regulations,

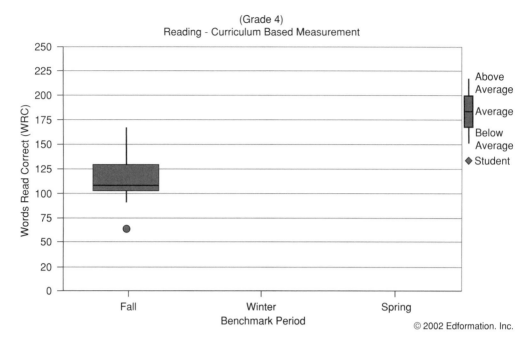

FIGURE 23.5. A student with potentially severe educational need.

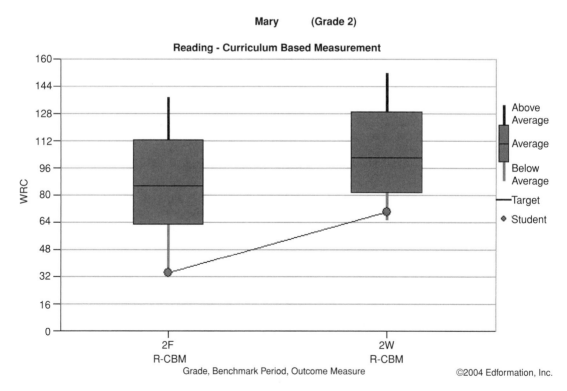

FIGURE 23.6. A student with potentially severe educational need who is benefiting from intervention.

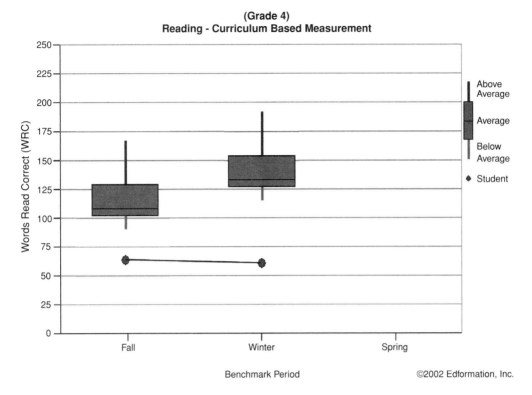

FIGURE 23.7. A student with potentially severe educational need who is not benefiting from the intervention.

and team decision-making leading to the decision about special education eligibility. For more information about using CBM for the RTI intervention process, see Shinn (2005a, 2005b).

Having discussed the history of the FSDS in Illinois and describing its basic features, we now focus on a summary of the evaluation of the initiative. The evaluation was part of the original approval process from the ISBE and the results provided further impetus for flexible service delivery to expand.

23.8 Evaluation of Program and Evidence of Impact

As noted earlier, one of the key components of the Illinois FSDS initiative from the beginning was the development and implementation of an evaluation plan. As more districts and special education co-operatives became involved in this "experiment," a statewide evaluation plan was implemented for each of the four years 1999–2003 (Aloia and Swerdlik,

1999; Swerdlik, 2003; Swerdlik et al., 2000, 2001, 2002; Swerdlik, Aloia, Peterson, Morrison, and Thor, 1999; Swerdlik and Hoff, 2003; Swerdlik, Hoff, Morrison, Swastek, and Sibley, 2003; Swerdlik, Hoff, Prasse, Swastek, and Sibley, 2004). The evaluation was focused on student outcomes, but another goal was to generate data that could be used to guide implementation.

Over the course of the 4 years of the statewide evaluation, data collection was focused on answering the following four questions, generated by participating districts and approved by the ISBE. The questions were: (1) Is the FSDS an effective method of meeting the needs of students? (2) What effect, if any, does FSDS have on resources and services for students eligible for special education services? (3) What effect, if any, does FSDS have on the timeliness of referral, evaluation, and subsequent entitlement for special education services for those students suspected of having a disability? (4) Are parents and educational staff satisfied with the use of FSDS? The evaluation plan included criteria to insure that participating districts had

TABLE 23.1. Samples for four statewide evaluations.

Evaluation year	Population of districts*	Sample districts	School buildings**	School personnel	Parents	Student cases
I (99–00)	15	6	16	258	41	269
II (00–01)	undetermined	9	23	414	64	316
III (01–02)	19	16	32	NA	108	557
IV (02–03)	22	7	26	NA	82	556

*Number of districts that were implementing the FSDS and met inclusion criteria at the time of the statewide evaluation. There are approximately 883 school districts in Illinois.
**There are approximately 4200 schools in Illinois.

been implementing flexible service delivery with fidelity.

The criteria for inclusion in the sample used for each year of the statewide evaluation included: (a) the sites had been implementing the FSDS for a minimum of 2 years; (b) the staff at the selected sites had been trained in the skills essential to the implementation of FSDS; and (c) the implementation of FSDS was proceeding in a satisfactory manner based on the Flexible Service Delivery: Rubric of Quality Indicators (see http://www.fsds.org). A primary limitation of this sampling procedure was a nonrandom sample and the fact that no comparison groups were used. More recent evaluation efforts, as part of the previously mentioned ISBE-funded project Illinois ASPIRE, are employing a stronger evaluation design including random sampling and comparison groups. The samples for each of the evaluation years are described in Table 23.1. The total number of districts implementing FSDS in a given evaluation year is also provided.

23.9 Data Sources

A survey of school personnel, including administrators, general and special education teachers, paraprofessionals, and related service personnel, such as school psychologists, school social workers, speech pathologists, and counselors, was conducted during each of the first 2 years of the statewide evaluation. Parents of children participating in FSDS were also surveyed for each of the four years of the evaluation. Student case data, all from elementary students enrolled in grades K-8, were drawn from the files of students participating in FSDS during each of the four evaluation years. Historical data relating

to numbers of referrals and percentage of children found eligible for special education were collected for the last 2 years of the study.

23.10 Key Findings

The following presents information regarding each of the questions delineated above.

23.10.1 Are Parents and Educational Staff Satisfied with the Use of the Flexible Service Delivery System?

23.10.1.1 High Level of Satisfaction with the Flexible Service Delivery System among School Personnel

School personnel completing surveys during the first 2 years of the statewide evaluation indicated that they were satisfied with the implementation of the FSDS in their buildings. Although all groups of school personnel surveyed were satisfied, using a five-point scale, with 5 corresponding to "strongly agree" and 1 to "strongly disagree" with the statement "I am satisfied with the implementation of the FSDS in my school", there was a clear and consistent pattern in the average scores of principals (4.4), school psychologists and social workers (4.1) being the most satisfied with the implementation of the FSDS, followed by special education (3.7) and general education (3.3) teachers. In reviewing the data on the level of knowledge about the FSDS, there was a relationship with those respondents being most (administrators) and least familiar (general education teachers) as having the highest and relatively lower levels of satisfaction with the implementation of FSDS.

23.10.1.2 Parents High Level of Satisfaction with the Flexible Service Delivery System

Over the four years of the statewide evaluation, parents were particularly satisfied with their experience with the FSDS. Over 75% of parent respondents indicated that their child received help in a timely fashion and that the assistance provided as part of the FSDS contributed to their child being successful in school.

23.10.1.3 Parent's High Level of Involvement in the Flexible Service Delivery System

A median of 91% of the FSDS problem-solving meetings convened had a parent in attendance. Of the parent respondents, a median of 77% indicated that they had a better understanding of their child's strengths, weaknesses, and educational needs as a result of participating in the FSDS. Over 90% of parent respondents perceived they were a partner in the FSDS problem-solving process.

23.10.2 Is the Flexible Service Delivery System an Effective Method of Meeting the Needs of Students?

23.10.2.1 Positive Student Outcomes

School personnel surveyed during the first 2 years of the statewide evaluation agreed that their students improved both academically (mean rating of 3.6, with 5 "strongly agree" and 1 "strongly disagree" with the statement "the FSDS resulted in improved academic performance for my students") and behaviorally (mean rating of 3.4 with the statement "the FSDS resulted in improved behavioral performance for my students") from interventions developed as part of the FSDS. School personnel viewed their students as being more successful in school due to the FSDS.

Based on the review of student case files over the 4 years of the statewide evaluation, more than 75% of the goals identified for students involved with the FSDS were met, exceeded, or not met, but performance improved. Only a median of 18% of the goals identified for students were not met and performance did not improve over the 4 years of the study. A median of 68% of parents surveyed indicated that their child's performance improved significantly or improved due to the FSDS.

Related to the dispositions of cases of students who were a part of the FSDS, over the 4 years of the evaluation that these data were colleted, a median of 3% transferred out of the district, 15% of the students were discontinued from the FSDS, 44% were continued to the next school year, 20% were referred for consideration for special education (entitlement), and 18% of all students participating in the FSDS were found eligible for special education. Of the students participating in the FSDS who were referred for entitlement, the median percentage of those found eligible was 96%.

CBM data in reading were collected only during the last 2 years of the statewide evaluation. Data indicated a small average increase (13) in correct words per minute from reading probe 1 to 2 and probe 2 to 3, controlling for grade and minutes of engaged time per week, with a large standard deviation across the different grade levels. Systematic collection and analyses of CBM data are included as part of the evaluation component of the ISBE-funded grant, I-ASPIRE.

The relationship between goal attainment and year-end outcomes/case dispositions was investigated and students who had goals that were rated "met or exceeded" were more likely to have the year-end outcomes of the FSDS discontinued. Students who had goals that were rated as "not met but performance improved" were more likely to have the year-end outcome of continuing in the FSDS. Students that had goals that were rated as "not met and performance did not improve" were more likely to be referred for consideration of special education and found eligible for entitlement.

23.10.2.2 Flexible Service Delivery System Leads to More Timely Interventions

School personnel respondents indicated that the FSDS leads to more timely services. A review of case files indicated the mean number of days between referral for problem solving and implementation of an intervention was 24 days compared with 60 or more days between referral for special education and convening of an IEP meeting to determine eligibility for special education. It might be even longer before a placement is implemented. Further, 75% of parent respondents agreed that their child was receiving the help they needed quickly as a result of the FSDS.

23.10.2.3 More Reading Goals Developed as Part of the Flexible Service Delivery System

Related to the types of goal developed as part of the problem-solving process, over 99% of the students had multiple goals developed for them. FSDS problem solving was being used to address a wide variety of concerns, including academic, behavioral, and social–emotional problems. Most of the goals were developed in reading (median: 37%) followed by social–emotional/behavioral (24%), written language (14%), math (11%), and other areas (11%).

23.10.3 What Effect, If Any, Does the Flexible Service Delivery System Have on Resources and Services for Students Eligible for Special Education Services?

23.10.3.1 Little Impact of the Flexible Service Delivery System on Other Entitled Students

One of the concerns noted above by parents of children with identified special education needs was that the FSDS would negatively impact the provision of services to their children. This concern was addressed by collecting data during the first year of the statewide evaluation. Findings indicated that the presence of the FSDS was not adversely impacting the delivery of special education services. Only 4% of the school staff respondents indicated that services specified on a student's IEP were not being provided, whereas 72% indicated they were provided. The remaining 24% of the staff respondents were not in a position to make a determination. When asked if appropriate services were being provided to students in special education, less than 2% of the staff respondents said no and 98% said either yes or stated they did not know (72% and 26%, respectively).

23.10.3.2 A Variety of Individuals Are Implementing Interventions as Part of the Flexible Service Delivery System

Prior to the implementation of the statewide evaluation, parent groups expressed some concerns that the interventions developed as part of the FSDS would place a heavy burden on the special education teacher, in that it would fall to the special educa-tion teacher to implement the majority of interventions. However, data collected over the 4 years of the statewide evaluation consistently indicated that the bulk of the interventions implemented as part of the FSDS fell to the general education teacher with a median of 48% of the interventions being implemented by the classroom teacher and a median of only 12% with a range of 7–16% of the interventions being implemented by the special education teacher. Others who were involved in implementing interventions included reading improvement/chapter teachers (12%), teacher assistants (6%), related service personnel, including school psychologists, social workers, counselors, and speech pathologists (17%), and administrators, tutors, and volunteers implemented less than 2% of interventions.

Over the course of the 4 years of the statewide evaluation, 99% of the interventions developed for students as part of the FSDS had multiple implementers with a mean of two and a range of one to six individuals implementing interventions per goal. A median of 68% of parents responded that they also served as an implementer of an intervention developed as part of the FSDS for their child. There was also a significant relationship ($r = 0.40$) between parents who reported they implemented an intervention and perceived that their child was performing better as a result of the FSDS.

23.10.4 What Effect, If Any, Does the Flexible Service Delivery System Have on the Timeliness of Referral, Evaluation, and Subsequent Entitlement for Special Education Services for those Students Suspected of Having a Disability?

23.10.4.1 Preliminary System-Level Outcomes

During the last year of the statewide evaluation, more system-wide outcomes were investigated. The numbers of problem-solving requests tended to remain relatively consistent after the initial year that the FSDS was implemented in a particular building. This suggests that buildings that are implementing the problem-solving model, as part of the FSDS, continue to use the model over the years.

Historical data reported by buildings (and some districts) indicate that requests for initial evaluations (i.e., referrals for special education) remain relatively stable over the years of implementing the FSDS, with an average absolute change of a decrease of 1% for all of the participating schools or districts. In terms of referrals increasing or decreasing while the FSDS is being implemented in a building or district, 10 buildings and districts reported declines, two reported increases, and one remained the same from the year of implementation to data reported to the most recent year (FY03). These data suggest that, although the absolute change in small, there is a trend towards decreasing numbers of initial evaluations for special education.

Special education enrollment data, based on the size of the building or district, remained relatively stable since implementation of the FSDS with an average absolute change of 1.4% over the years of the FSDS implementation. Seven buildings and districts reported an increased special education enrollment percentage, two remained the same, and three decreased from the first year of implementation of the FSDS to the most current year (FY03). Although the trend was towards increased special education enrollment, the absolute magnitude of the increase is quite small, averaging just above 1% with a range of 0–5% and a modal increase of 1%. Owing to small sample sizes for different lengths of time (i.e., years) after implementation, the impact of the FSDS on systems-level outcomes, such as number of referrals for special education and placement rates, will need to be monitored to determine whether these trends continue. This monitoring is part of the evaluation plan for the ISBE I-ASPIRE grant referenced earlier.

Further analysis of data from year 4 of the statewide evaluation indicated that the number of the FSDS problem-solving requests, the number of initial referrals for special education, nor the percentage of students in special education per year were impacted if the FSDS was implemented in an entire building (i.e., at all grade levels) or only in selected grades. Schools that have implemented the FSDS longer or have more experience with the FSDS do have different outcomes for students than those with less experience in terms of the number of closed cases, referred to as problem-solving discontinued. There was a moderate correlation ($r = 0.26$) between years implementing the FSDS and problem-solving discontinued. Problem-solving discontin-

ued refers to students who were making adequate progress in their general education program to the degree that they no longer required interventions provided as part of the FSDS.

23.10.4.2 Role Change Was Significant for Some Personnel under the Flexible Service Delivery System

Perception of role change was assessed during the first year of the statewide evaluation. Thirty-one percent of school personnel felt that their role had not changed as a result of the implementation of the FSDS, whereas 44% of the respondents felt that their role had changed to a moderate or large degree. The role and function of the school psychologist and social worker were perceived to have changed the most and expanded to provide more interventions to students. Open-ended responses further suggested that school psychologists and social workers were conducting fewer full and individual evaluations to determine special education eligibility and spending more time participating in problem solving meetings/consulting with teachers, implementing academic and behavioral interventions, and using more direct measures (e.g., CBM/DIBELS) of assessments for progress monitoring purposes.

23.11 Lessons Learned

This section provides an opportunity to share the lessons learned from the implementation of the FSDS. These lessons were formulated based on the evaluation data collected, but also on the experience of the authors in consulting with a number of school districts across Illinois, and providing training on implementation of the FSDS.

Creating lasting change and reform is incredibly complex in multiple layered systems like school districts. Illinois began planning for the FSDS in 1995 and it has taken more than a decade to finally start to take hold in the school districts that began implementation of the FSDS more than a decade ago. However, the changes in federal law, including No Child Left Behind Act (2002) and IDEA 2004, have accelerated the rate of implementation.

Reform initiated at the local level can take hold and become widespread. In Illinois, local districts

TABLE 23.2. Summary of implications for practice.

1. Change is a process and not an event and can take up to a decade.
2. Successful change can be initiated from the "bottom up" (individual school districts).
3. Maintain dialogue with your state board of education.
4. Significant professional development resources are required for implementation.
5. Training must be sequential, ongoing, and provided to all staff.
6. Training must include coaching providing opportunities for practice and feedback.
7. Include general educators on problem solving/RTI and district-wide planning teams.
8. A strong evaluation component, focused on student outcomes, is critical from the start.
9. The evaluation plan should be both formative (to guide implementation efforts) and summative.
10. Parents should be included as part of the evaluation plan.
11. Implementation integrity is a major challenge and should be addressed in the formative evaluation plan.
12. The principal is the most important catalyst for change to problem solving/RTI.
13. Problem solving/RTI requires a paradigm shift to thinking about student problems from an ecological perspective.
14. Problem solving/RTI must be "institutionalized" in school improvement plans, school board policies, building handbooks, and new staff orientation programs.
15. Communication systems such as a website, listserv, and convening statewide and/or regional conferences facilitate the change process by providing ongoing support and technical assistance.
16. Develop collaborative/networking mechanisms, such as regional and statewide consortia, that include learning networks that address challenges/barriers to implementation and provide social support.
17. Disseminate information to all "stake-holders" through presentations at conferences and in newsletters for allied groups (e.g., principals, superintendents).

initiated flexible service delivery, and the ISBE's initial reaction was less than enthusiastic. Only through persistent dialog with the ISBE bureaucracy was the state's consent able to be secured. Once that consent was obtained, other districts began to study similar service delivery reforms and the use of the problem-solving model began to expand. Now, the ISBE is a strong advocate for the FSDS and has recently secured a large professional development grant (I-ASPIRE) to integrate the FSDS with other state initiatives (Reading First and Standards Aligned Classrooms) throughout the state. ISBE is now one of the strongest supporters for problem solving/RTI in Illinois and in the nation.

Reform is a long, slow, and evolutionary process. Implementing the FSDS has taken a long time (over 10 years now) and there still is a long way to go. The lesson learned is that significant professional development resources need to be devoted to this reform and accountability mechanisms need to be put in place to assure that outcomes are measured.

School personnel need the district to provide continuing professional development. School staff (general and special education classroom teachers, related service personnel, administrators) need continuing professional development, so that the staff can learn the skills related to effective implementation of the FSDS. Most of the staff were not exposed to the FSDS in their preparation programs. District administrators need to stress that "no staff member will be left behind" related to implementation of the FSDS and staff members need to "retool" their skill sets.

University programs have a major impact on effective implementation and positive outcomes. Recently trained school psychologists and other related service personnel and changes in teacher/administrator preparation programs have made a major contribution to effective implementation of the FSDS in Illinois. Recent graduates of university programs are skilled in more instructionally relevant assessment approaches, interventions, and problem-solving techniques. As always, people and their skills make the difference.

The complexity of the FSDS reform contributes to implementation integrity and poses a major challenge. Making sure that the FSDS is implemented with integrity is the single most difficult issue. In the absence of rules and regulations, which are currently being developed but are as yet not approved, but with consistent monitoring and training, systematic program evaluation is constantly needed. When a district/building indicates they are implementing the FSDS, one must observe changes in the school culture (e.g., problem-solving team meets on a regular basis, progress monitoring occurs as part of the part of the problem-solving process at all tiers) consistent with this service delivery approach. It must become the philosophy and cornerstone of service delivery when implemented with integrity.

Progress monitoring is a significant challenge to effective implementation. It has been our experience that many school personnel see progress monitoring as outside their job description and as a significant burden. This component is critical, because successful implementation of a tier system of problem solving/RTI requires consistent progress monitoring.

The support of the school principal is paramount to FSDS success. If the school principal did not support the FSDS and provide resources (e.g., time for the problem-solving team members to meet) for implementation, the change effort was always unsuccessful. Principals must be trained on skills related to effectively implementing the FSDS. We found that many principals had developed creative solutions to common problems/barriers to implementation of the FSDS, but typically there existed no mechanism to share these creative solutions with other principals within the school districts.

The FSDS implementation requires a "paradigm shift" when thinking about student problems. School personnel need to recognize that the student's problem(s) are not solely attributable to "within the child" factors, but one must also assess environmental factors and focus on the instructional environment. This heavy reliance on "within the child" factors led some school personnel to refer to a new disability group—"flex kids." However, it is these "external to the child factors/variables" that school personnel have the most control over and can intervene successfully.

Evaluation is a major key to successful implementation. Implementation should include a detailed evaluation plan. Both individual student outcomes (e.g., student performance on high-stakes tests) and broader "systems level" impact (e.g., number of referrals, placement rate, etc.) should be monitored. State boards of education and individual school boards are particularly interested in parent perceptions/satisfaction, which should be assessed as well as student outcomes. As part of the evaluation plan, an assessment of treatment integrity should be included to be sure that data collected are from buildings that are actually implementing this reform initiative.

School staff benefit from observing how other schools have implemented the FSDS. Because the FSDS is a systems-wide and building-wide approach, having staff visit other schools has proved helpful. In particular, providing an opportunity for principals to talk to other principals and classroom teacher's talk to other general education teachers was found to be quite valuable. Efforts to keep school staff trained in the skills associated with the FSDS were found to be important and a challenge. "Booster sessions" for already-trained staff together with new training for unskilled staff should be part of an implementation plan.

Training and mentoring of all staff insures implementation success. Efforts to include annual training and a mentoring system to help new staff are critical for long-term success. Further, trainings in scientifically supported interventions for targeted groups, and more intensive intervention for individuals, must be provided for all school personnel, including classroom teachers. These training sessions need to go beyond information sharing and move to skill building. Coaching is necessary to bring staff up to skill levels in the different areas. For example, more intensive training should occur linking assessment to intervention. In particular, classroom teachers, who are often expected to implement interventions developed as part of the FSDS process, require more training in interventions. When interventions are suggested as part of problem solving they need to be modeled and then teachers given opportunities for guided practice. Further, if teachers are to implement particular interventions developed as part of the FSDS, then principals must support this action and communicate this expectation to their staff.

Continual communication with and between school staff enhances the FSDS value. Communication mechanisms, such as a periodic newsletter, e-mail listserv, and website, should be available to all school personnel to provide support, share successes, communicate ideas to overcome barriers, and announce other successful efforts to implement a large-scale change effort such as the FSDS.

The FSDS resources require scheduling time for preparation. Preparation time is needed to engage in problem solving, including the assessment and intervention component of the FSDS. Buildings that have successfully implemented the FSDS have made problem solving a priority and have modified scheduling and reallocated resources to make this a reality.

The FSDS works best in conjunction with other school initiatives. Although the FSDS is perceived by some school administrators to be a separate freestanding program, it is actually a process that is most effective when it is organizationally/systemically combined or integrated with other initiatives. The FSDS provides a mechanism (i.e., systematic data-driven collaborative problem solving) to deliver

other interventions such as those developed as part
of PBIS and other mental health and educational
initiatives. To move towards sustainability, it is important to integrate the FSDS with these other initiatives.

*The FSDS must be realized beyond the students
and the classroom.* Efforts also must occur to "insti-
tutionalize" reform efforts such as the FSDS at the
school board and building levels. This effort would
mean including the FSDS in school improvement
plans, school handbooks, and as part of the fall orientation program for all new staff at the district and
building levels.

*The FSDS teams should be inclusive and di-
verse.* When selecting participants for building-
based problem solving the FSDS teams, efforts
should be made to include a cross-section of staff,
including general education classroom teachers representing various grade levels, the school principal, and related service staff. It is very important
not to include just special education staff on the
building-based problem-solving team, because the
FSDS may then be considered a special education
initiative and result in less buy-in from general education staff, hence hindering implementation efforts.

*Students benefit from individual and direct inter-
vention.* There is a need for staff to be dedicated
to providing individual direct interventions to the
at-risk students who are part of the FSDS process.
However, those schools that appear most successful utilize *all* available staff (e.g., including classroom aides, custodians, community volunteers, and
librarians) to implement the targeted group and individualized interventions developed as part of the
FSDS.

*School districts need to communicate success-
ful FSDS implementations.* When communicating
about a reform initiative such as the FSDS, it is important to disseminate information, including evaluation data, to allied groups such as principals, school
superintendents and directors of special education
through presentations at their professional conferences and articles in their newsletters.

Develop collaborative/networking efforts. In Illinois, a website (www.fsds.org) was created and a
statewide consortium was begun that also met regionally. These consortia included developing and
implementing learning networks on such topics as
CBM and early literacy. During the statewide con-

ference, it is important to have topics geared to
districts just beginning implementation, as well as
those at more advanced levels.

Implementation of the FSDS is expanding in
Illinois. As noted earlier, the ISBE has recently
funded four regional professional development centers with monies from the US Department of Education, Office of Special Education Programs. In
partnership with school districts, special education
cooperatives, regional offices of education, parent
groups, statewide educational initiatives, and institutes of higher education, these four centers will
provide research-based professional development
and technical assistance based on integrating established training frameworks developed by the FSDS,
PBIS, and Standards-Aligned Classroom initiatives,
all of which represent statewide initiatives in Illinois. Other I-ASPIRE goals include increasing the
participation of parents in the decision-making process and incorporating this professional development content into the general and special education
preservice curricula of Institutes of Higher Education in the state of Illinois.

References

Aloia, G. F. & Swerdlik, M. E. (1999, September). Eval-
    uation of the Illinois flexible service delivery system.
    Paper presented at *National Conference on Reform in
    Special Education*, Seattle, WA.
Batsche, G. M., Elliott, J., Graden, J., Grimes, J., Ko-
    valeski, J. F., & Prasse, D. (2005). *Response to In-
    tervention: Policy Considerations and Implementation.*
    Alexandria, VA: National Association of State Direc-
    tors of Special Education.
Broncato, M. J. (1995). A letter dated November 22, 1995
    from the Illinois State Board of Education to David
    W. Peterson, Superintendent of the Northern Suburban
    Special Education District in Highland Park, IL.
Deno, S. L. (1985). Curriculum-based measurement: the
    emerging alternative. *Exceptional Children, 52,* 219–
    232.
Deno, S. L. (1986). Formative evaluation of individual
    student programs: a new role for school psychologists.
    School Psychology Review, 15, 358–374.
Deno, S. L. (1989). Curriculum-based measurement and
    alternative special education services: a fundamen-
    tal and direct relationship. In M. R. Shinn (Ed.),
    *Curriculum-Based Measurement: Assessing Special
    Children* (pp. 1–17). New York: Guilford.
Deno, S. L. (2002). Problem-solving as best practice. In A.
    Thomas & J. Grimes (Eds.), *Best Practices in School*

Psychology IV (pp. 37–55). Bethesda, MD: National Association of School Psychologists.

Deno, S. L. (2005). Problem-solving assessment. In R. Brown-Chidsey (Ed.), *Assessment for Intervention: A Problem-Solving Approach* (pp. 10–40). New York: Guilford.

Deno, S. L. & Mirkin, P. (1977). *Data-Based Program Modification: A Manual.* Reston, VA: Council for Exceptional Children.

Fuchs, L. S. & Deno, S. L. (1991). Paradigmatic distinctions between instructionally relevant measurement models. *Exceptional Children, 57*, 488–500.

Fuchs, L. S., Fuchs, D., & Speece, D. L. (2002). Treatment validity as a unifying construct for identifying learning disabilities. *Learning Disability Quarterly, 25*, 33–45.

Germann, G. & Tindal, G. (1985). An application of curriculum based assessment: the use of direct and repeated measurement. *Exceptional Children, 52*, 244–265.

Heartland Area Education Agency 11 (2005). *Program Manual for Special Education: Heartland Area Education Agency 11.* (Intra-agency manual) Johnston, IA.

Northern Suburban Special Education District (2005). Flexible service delivery executive summary. Retrieved October 1, 2005, from http://www.nssed.org/Pages/flex/execsummary.htm

Pericola-Case, L., Speece, D. L., & Eddy-Molloy, D. (2003). The validity of response-to-instruction paradigm to identify reading disabilities: a longitudinal analysis of individual differences and context factors. *School Psychology Review, 32*, 557–582.

Peterson, D. W. & Casey, A. (1991). The contribution of school psychological services to the regular education initiative. In G. Stoner, M. Shinn, & H. Walker (Eds.), *Interventions for Achievement and Behavior Problems* (pp. 37–48). Washington, DC: National Association of School Psychologists.

Peterson, K. M. & Shinn, M. R. (2002). Severe discrepancy models: which best explains school identification practices for learning disabilities? *School Psychology Review, 31*, 459–476.

President's Commission on Excellence in Special Education (2002). *A New Era: Revitalizing Special Education for Children and their Families.* Washington, DC: US Office of Education.

Shinn, M. R. (Ed.) (1989). *Curriculum-Based Measurement: Assessing Special Children.* New York: Guilford.

Shinn, M. R. (Ed.) (1998). *Advanced Applications of Curriculum-Based Measurement.* New York: Guilford.

Shinn, M. R. (2003). *Aimsweb™ Training Workbook: Organizing and Implementing a Benchmark Assessment Program.* Eden Prairie, MN: Edformation.

Shinn, M. R. (2005a). *Aimsweb Response to Intervention (RTI): A Standard Protocol-Based System for Managing and Reporting Problem-Solving Outcomes.* Eden Prairie, MN: Edformation.

Shinn, M. R. (2005b). Identifying and validating academic problems. In R. Brown-Chidsey (Ed.), *Assessment for Intervention: A Problem-Solving Approach* (pp. 219–246). New York: Guilford.

Shinn, M. R., Good, R. H. I., & Parker, C. (1999). Noncategorical special education services with students with severe achievement deficits. In D. J. Reschly, W. D. I. Tilly, & J. P. Grimes (Eds.), *Special Education in Transition: Functional Assessment and Noncategorical Programming* (pp. 81–106). Longmont, CO: Sopris West.

Shinn, M. R., Shinn, M. M., Hamilton, C., & Clarke, B. (2002). Using curriculum-based measurement to promote achievement in general education classrooms. In M. R. Shinn, G. Stoner, & H. M. Walker (Eds.), *Interventions for Academic and Behavior Problems: Preventive and Remedial Approaches* (pp. 113–142). Bethesda, MD: National Association of School Psychologists.

Swerdlik, M. E. (2003, September). Flexible service delivery system in Illinois: statewide evaluation results. Paper presented as part of the *National Innovations in Special Education Conference*, Charleston, SC.

Swerdlik, M. E. (Chair), Aloia, G. F., Brown, R., Morrison, D., Nolten, P., Peterson, D., et al. (2001, April). The Illinois initiative in alternative service delivery: The flexible service delivery system (FSDS). Symposia presented at the *33rd Annual Convention of the National Association of School Psychologists*, Washington, DC.

Swerdlik, M. E. (Chair), Aloia, G., Morrison, D., Strain, L., Swastek, R., Surber, J., et al. (2002, March). The Illinois initiative in alternative service delivery: Implementation of system reform. Symposium presented at the *Annual Conference of the Illinois School Psychologists Association*, Springfield, IL.

Swerdlik, M. E., Aloia, G. F., Peterson, D., Morrison, D., & Thor, K. (1999, April). Flexible service delivery system: evaluation results. Paper presented at the *Annual Conference of the National Association of School Psychologists*, Las Vegas, NV.

Swerdlik, M. E. (Chair), Brown, R., Schuck, L., Morrison, D., Sibley, D., Nolten, P., et al. (2000, March). The Illinois initiative in alternative service delivery: The flexible service delivery system. Symposium presented at the *Annual Conference of the National Association of School Psychologists*, New Orleans, LA.

Swerdlik, M. E. & Hoff, K. (2003). Flex in Illinois: what are the outcomes? *School Psychology in Illinois, 24*(3), 6–8.

Swerdlik, M. E. (Chair), Hoff, K. E., Morrison, D., Swastek, R., & Sibley, D. (2003, April). The Illinois initiative in alternative service delivery: parent satisfaction, student outcomes, and guidelines for successful implementation. Symposium presented at the *Annual Meeting of the National Association of School Psychologists*, Toronto Ontario, Canada.

Swerdlik, M. E. (Chair), Hoff, K. E., Prasse, D., Swastek, R., & Sibley, D. (2004, April). The alternative service delivery system in Illinois-flexible service delivery system. Symposium presented at the presented at the *Annual Meeting of the National Association of School Psychologists*, Dallas, TX.

Tindal, G., Wesson, C., Deno, S. L., Germann, G., & Mirkin, P. (1985). The Pine County model for special education delivery: a data-based system. In T. Kratochwill (Ed.), *Advances in School Psychology* (vol. IV, pp. 223–250). Hillsdale, NJ: Lawrence Erlbaum.

Will, M. C. (1986). Educating children with learning problems: a shared responsibility. *Exceptional Children, 52*, 411–415.

Ysseldyke, J., Dawson, P., Lehr, C., Reschly, D., Reynolds, M., & Telzrow, C. (1997). *School Psychology: A Blueprint for Training and Practice II*. Bethesda, MD: National Association of School Psychologists.

24

The St. Croix River Education District Model: Incorporating Systems-Level Organization and a Multi-Tiered Problem-Solving Process for Intervention Delivery

Kerry A. Bollman, Benjamin Silberglitt, and Kimberly A. Gibbons

Kerry A. Bollman, SSP, is the Academic Collaborative Planner and Reading Center Director with the St. Croix River Education District in Rush City, MN. kbollman@scred.k12.mn.us

Benjamin Silberglitt, PhD, is a Senior Consultant, Assessment and Implementation with Technology and Information Educational Services in St. Paul, MN. benjamin.silberglitt@ties.k12.mn.us

Kimberly A. Gibbons, PhD, is the Director of the St. Croix River Education District in Rush City, MN. kgibbons@scred.k12.mn.us

The provision of the 2004 reauthorization of the Individuals with Disabilities Education Improvement Act (IDEIA) that allows school districts to identify learning disabilities (LDs) by measuring student response to scientifically based instruction/intervention (RTI) will undoubtedly make the LD classification process more instructionally relevant. Another goal of RTI in the larger context is to prevent large numbers of students from ever becoming labeled LD in the first place (Fletcher, Coulter, Reschly and Vaughn, 2004). With new legislation mandating scientifically based reading instruction and an accountability scheme for ensuring that all children learn to read effectively (No Child Left Behind Act; No Child Left Behind, 2001), it seems that the pendulum is swinging towards requiring effective reading instruction as a way to prevent LD identification (President's Commission on Excellence in Special Education, 2002).

The St. Croix River Education District (SCRED) has been involved in promoting these RTI "preventative" practices for the past two decades. SCRED serves five school districts in east central Minnesota with a total population of approximately 9000 students. SCRED manages special education services for all of its member districts and provides leadership and guidance to regular education in a variety of areas, including basic academic skills instruction. There is a long history of data-based decision making through problem-solving processes within the district. In fact, SCRED was one of the initial pilot sites for examining the efficacy of curriculum-based measurement (CBM) in the early 1980s (Tindal et al., 1984). For the past 10 years, SCRED has worked with its member districts to implement a model that coordinates three critical elements: (a) frequent and continuous measurement using general outcome measures (CBM), (b) evidence-based instruction, and (c) schoolwide organization to ensure the most effective instruction possible for each student.

24.1 Importance of the Issue: Key Elements to Improving Reading Achievement

Recent research has identified the three basic elements of the SCRED model as important for improving reading achievement in particular (Kameenui and Simmons, 1998). Each of these elements are critical to student success, but none affects student achievement adequately on its own. Within the

319

Saint Croix River Education District model, measurement, instruction, and problem-solving organization are visualized as three sides of a triangle. Additional information regarding each component is provided in the following sections.

24.1.1 Measurement

The first requirement in the triangle of critical elements is measurement. The federal government mandates that all students must be assessed by at least grade 3 (No Child Left Behind, 2001). While the goal to have students reading proficiently by grade 3 is admirable, schools cannot afford to wait that long to assess student reading. Educators must know from the earliest possible moment who is and who is not succeeding and intervene accordingly.

SCRED uses data-based measurement practices, including CBM, that allow for evaluation of instruction for each student during learning. CBM is a general outcome measure that allows teachers to formatively evaluate their instruction for individual students on an ongoing basis (Deno, 1985; Deno, Marston, Shinn, and Tindal, 1983; Deno, Mirkin, and Chiang, 1982). Such frequent measurement prompts teachers to adjust instruction as needed to affect more progress for each student (Deno and Fuchs, 1987). Further, schools can use the same measure to evaluate their overall instructional programs regularly (Deno, 2003).

SCRED schools follow a protocol in which students are measured on three schedules: *benchmark* for all students grades K-8 (three times a year), *strategic* for students of some concern (once a month), and *intensive* for students of great concern (once a week). All districts use general outcome measures of reading (i.e., oral reading fluency), early literacy measures (letter naming fluency, letter sound fluency, nonsense word fluency, and phonemic segmenting and blending tasks), and mathematics (math fact fluency, and math concepts and applications).

24.1.2 Scientifically Based Reading Instructional Practices

The second side of the triangle of critical elements is instruction. In the area of reading, three syntheses of reading research are available to guide us. *Beginning to Read: Thinking and Learning About Print* (Adams, 1990) and *Preventing Reading Difficulties* (Snow, Burns, and Griffin, 1998), both commissioned by the US Department of Education, give the field a common and trustworthy path for reading instruction. The final and most recent synthesis of beginning reading research is the report of the National Reading Panel's review of the last 30 years of research in reading (National Institute of Child Health and Human Development, 2000).

In addition to the research on *what* should be taught to beginning readers, a synthesis on effective teaching principles gives us information on *how* to teach. Students learn best when, among other things, they are actively engaged, have high to moderate success rates, have multiple opportunities to cover content, spend most of their time being directly taught by the teacher, have instruction that is scaffolded, have strategic instruction, and have explicit instruction (Swanson, Haskyn, and Lee, 1999). SCRED has incorporated the three syntheses of reading research in assisting member districts with curriculum adoption and the incorporation of research-based instructional practices.

24.1.3 Schoolwide Organization

The third critical element in the triangle is schoolwide organization. Although the National Reading Panel has research-based suggestions for assessment and instruction in beginning reading, it is silent on the topic of school organization. Without a school-level system of implementation, it is nearly impossible for assessment and instruction best practices to be put into place effectively. The school as the "host environment" must be organized to ensure that research-based practices can thrive and be sustained (Coyne, Kameenui, and Simmons, 2001). At SCRED, five elements of school organization are promoted to ensure that effective instruction can be provided to every student: continuous measurement, grade-level team meetings, flexible grouping, grade-level scheduling, and concentrated resources. These elements will be described in further detail later in the chapter.

The purpose of this chapter is to describe a multi-tiered problem-solving process for intervention delivery. First, we discuss the necessary conditions in which the problem-solving process can thrive. Second, we describe a specific approach to the problem-solving process. Third, we provide data demonstrating the effectiveness of the SCRED model. Fourth, we discuss elements that must be in place prior to using RTI in a special education decision-making framework. Finally, we provide directions for future research.

24.2 Conceptual Basis: Schoolwide Organization to Allow for Effective Problem Solving

In order for the problem-solving process to work effectively, schools must be organized such that problem solving does not exist in a vacuum, but is instead integrated into the overall system of communication and decision-making in the school (Kameenui and Simmons, 1998). As mentioned earlier, SCRED schools employ a process of school organization that provides this necessary context in which effective problem solving can take place. Below is a description of these school organization strategies; see Howe, Scierka, Gibbons, and Silberglitt (2003) for a more complete discussion of this model.

24.2.1 Continuous Measurement

A prerequisite to RTI implementation is schoolwide continuous measurement. As mentioned earlier, all children in grades K through 8 in SCRED are assessed three times each year. Some children are assessed more frequently as needed. Since measurement was already described earlier, we will not discuss it again here. It is included at this point only to emphasize its critical nature, as a necessary component to effective implementation of the model.

24.2.2 Grade-Level Team Meetings

Once schools are organized to measure student progress on a regular basis, the system needs to be organized to use the data to make instructional decisions. SCRED has worked with building principals to ensure that teams of grade-level teachers meet regularly to review student achievement data. The frequency of meetings may vary from three times per year to weekly but is most often one time per month. The goal is to have grade-level staff members collectively consider all students as one group to be supported together rather than considering students in each particular classroom to be the primary responsibility of the teacher of that class.

Several activities are completed during grade-level team meetings. First, shortly after each benchmark assessment, teams review data and evaluate the percentage of students that are at or above target (tier 1), somewhat below target (tier 2), or significantly below target (tier 3). Target scores are developed via methods that will be described later in this paper. Second, after reviewing the benchmark data, grade-level teams set goals for the percentage of students they would like to have performing at or above target by the end of the year. For example, if in the fall a second-grade class had 72% of students performing at or above target, then the team might establish a goal to have 80% of students performing at or above target by spring. Third, grade-level teams discuss the programming they plan to provide to students in each tier group. For example, the team may discuss the organization of a 90-min core reading block for all students, the specific contents of an additional 30 min of supplemental small-group instruction for all students below target, and possibly another more intensive plan for students in tier 3. Finally, grade-level teams typically meet monthly to review the progress of all students in tiers 2 and 3, and to discuss program changes that would increase success for all students. Program effectiveness is evaluated in large part based on the extent to which students on grade level stay on grade level, and the students below grade level are able to catch up.

24.2.3 Grade-Level Scheduling

Another aspect of schoolwide organization is the common scheduling of basic skill instruction within grade levels. For example, all grade 1 teachers may agree to teach reading from 9:30–11:00 each morning and math from 12:30–1:30 each afternoon. Setting up a schedule such as this for all grades requires some planning and coordination with regard to lunch/recess and special class schedules, but is entirely feasible within the context of a typical school schedule. In addition, SCRED has encouraged principals to schedule basic skill instruction at different times *across* grade levels. There are two primary benefits to this type of grade-level scheduling. First, it is possible that teachers may opt to create flexible instructional groups that are different from initial classroom assignments. Second, it allows building-level resources to be concentrated at each grade level during the most opportune times each day.

24.2.4 Flexible Grouping

For the past 10 years, SCRED schools have been implementing flexible grouping procedures. Students are grouped according to their achievement groups, but, unlike traditional grouping procedures, students move in and out of groups regularly as determined by their progress. Because all teachers of a particular grade level teach the same instructional content at the same time each day, the possibility of flexibly regrouping across classrooms becomes available. For example, the few students in each classroom who are performing well above grade level in reading might be pulled together for a specific enrichment unit for a period of time. Alternatively, a group of students who are determined to need additional phonics instruction might be grouped to receive instruction at their current level of need. One role of the grade level teams is to make decision about student grouping each month.

24.2.5 Concentrated Resources

Another important facet of schoolwide organization is the notion of concentrating resources in an efficient and effective manner. A benefit of grade-level scheduling is the availability of concentrated resources (e.g., reading specialists, special education teachers, etc.) to each grade-level team. When each grade level has some unique period of the school day in which reading is taught, then all additional nonclassroom-based staff members can be assigned to support reading at that grade level during that time. This often includes special education, title 1, or paraprofessional staff members. If a school has five sections of third grade, they may have access to additional three or four staff members to assist with reading instruction during that instructional block. Building principals have given grade-level teams the authority to decide as a group the best use for these additional resources.

24.3 Description of the Specific Approach: The Problem-Solving Process

After all of the schoolwide organizational procedures have been implemented, schools need to have a problem-solving system in place to address the needs of unique learners. While grade-level teams are able to solve many problems, they need a mechanism for obtaining additional assistance when they have exhausted their collective resources. Most school buildings across the nation have a team that meets regularly to discuss the needs of students experiencing difficulty and to consider possible supports for these students (Buck, Polloway, Smith-Thomas, and Cook, 2003). These teams have a wide variety of names (teacher assistance teams, student assistance teams, student support teams, student success teams, etc.), as well as a wide variety of behavioral norms and activities completed (Burns, Vanderwood, and Ruby, 2005). SCRED has worked with buildings to establish a problem-solving team in each building. At the grade-level team level, teachers work to meet the needs of all children by utilizing grade-level resources. In instances where their efforts do not result in student success, a referral to the problem-solving team is made. Each building-based problem-solving team follows a specific process for responding to identified student concerns. There are several specific attributes of these problem-solving teams that appear to differentiate them from many other types of school-based teams in other districts.

24.3.1 St. Croix River Education District Problem-Solving Teams

Each problem-solving team consists of 5–10 building staff members. The membership of this group is specifically arranged to be representative of the staff at large. That is, the majority of problem-solving team members are general education teachers. The principal is always a member of this team for several significant reasons. First, as instructional leader of the building, the principal communicates values and expectations with regard to student service through their actions. Full participation on the problem-solving team establishes a data-based problem-solving orientation as the behavioral norm for all building staff. Second, the authority of the principal is needed to make decisions regarding allocation of resources. Problem-solving teams need this authority to design intervention plans that may utilize resources in new or different ways to meet student needs. Third, principals benefit from and appreciate active and ongoing knowledge of specific efforts supporting at-risk students in the building. Often a "specials" teacher (gym, music, art) acts as a team member, and brings the unique perspective of knowing referred students in a less traditional academic setting, and often across multiple years. One or two special education staff members and the building school psychologist act as consistent members of these teams, but it is critical that the majority of the problem-solving team membership comes from the general education staff. Some buildings elect to train a large number of staff on the problem-solving process and use different subsets of these members depending on the individual student of concern.

Teams meet one time per week for approximately 45 min each meeting. For buildings that elect to have "part-time" members, all members agree to keep the pre-established weekly meeting time open in their schedules with the understanding that they may not participate in every meeting. Following this schedule, elementary buildings with as many as 600 students and secondary buildings with as many as 1000 students operate successfully with a single team. Buildings with larger student enrollment may find that multiple teams are needed to meet building needs. Teams often meet in a building-level conference room, although classrooms are also used in some buildings that lack dedicated meeting space.

24.3.2 Decision-Making Process used by Problem-Solving Teams

Problem-solving teams within SCRED buildings follow a specific five-step problem-solving process (Batsche and Knoff, 1995; Knoff, 2002), answering explicit questions at each step. The steps and questions are as follows:

1. *Problem identification.* What is the discrepancy between what is expected and what is occurring?
2. *Problem analysis.* Why is the problem occurring?
3. *Plan development.* What is the goal? What is the intervention plan to meet this goal? How will progress be monitored?
4. *Plan implementation.* How will intervention integrity be ensured?
5. *Plan evaluation.* Was the intervention plan successful?

Using a systematic problem-solving process differentiates SCRED problem-solving teams from many traditional student support teams. Teams need a decision-making framework as they work towards developing interventions and evaluation of the ef-

fects of these interventions. The problem identification step helps teams consider a variety of data to prioritize areas of concern for referred students. Of equal importance, the second outcome of problem identification is to define the prioritized problem in specific quantifiable terms using data that have technical adequacy for this purpose. For example, rather than identifying a "problem in reading", a team might identify that the second-grade student is currently reading grade-level passages at a rate of 18 correct words per minute while the expectation for second-grade students at that time of the year is a rate of 43 correct words per minute. Inherent in this practice is the necessity for ongoing schoolwide data collection so that behavioral expectations are known.

Once the team has identified the problem, the next step for the team is to develop an alterable hypothesis about why the problem is occurring. Student difficulty is regarded as the result of a mismatch between student need and the resources that have been provided. Rather than considering a problem to be the result of inalterable student characteristics, teams are compelled to focus on changes that can be made to the instruction, curriculum, or environment that would result in positive a student outcome (Deno, 1989). For example, rather than considering a student's failure to master basic math facts to be the result of low IQ or lack of home support, a team may consider whether increasing student motivation, providing additional practice opportunities, or increasing levels of explicit instruction with immediate feedback would effectively ameliorate this problem. This is, of course, not to say that factors including low IQ or lack of home support do not exist, only to say that it is inefficient for teams to spend time discussing factors over which they have little to no control when there are other avenues for intervention in which they can effect timely and meaningful change.

After a hypothesis has been developed about the cause of the problem, the next step is for the teams to develop a plan. When teams arrive at the plan development stage of the problem solving and before any discussion regarding possible intervention plans can take place, the team must agree upon a specific goal, including a timeline for reaching this goal, and develop an individualized graph. Goals are derived from existing local or broader normative data, criterion referenced targets, or local professional expectation for acceptable performance (Fuchs and Shinn, 1989). SCRED schools have established criterion-referenced targets for CBM that predict future successful performance on the Minnesota statewide assessments. These targets are used as goals for students in problem solving, as they represent performance in reading that is equivalent to meeting grade-level standards as set by the state. The line on the graph that connects baseline data to the goal data point defines the desired rate of progress for the student. Subsequent evaluation of interventions is based in large part on the extent to which student progress follows this aim-line.

Once the goal has been defined, the team moves on within the plan development step to create the specific intervention plan for the student. The team works to decide what the intervention will be, who will implement it, where, when, and how often. Within SCRED buildings, a combination of standard treatment protocol and individually designed interventions is used. Often, the first intervention plan attempted with a student will be selected from a series of standardized options. Standard treatment protocol interventions have a variety of benefits to teams and students (see Chapter 17 for more information). Empirical documentation exists to support the likely effectiveness of many standard intervention programs (Kovaleski, 2003). Often, the materials needed are already developed, requiring little to no prep time on the part of the interventionist. Districts can provide standard training on these interventions so that multiple staff members are prepared to implement them with students. If students do not make the expected rate of progress using standard treatment protocols, then the problem-solving team may create a more individualized intervention using the problem-solving approach. In all instances, intervention plans are clearly defined in written form, including explicit instructions on the duration, frequency, location, materials, participants, and individual steps of the interaction. This information is recorded in "script" format, such that any person could pick up the intervention plan and follow the steps, and such that an observer could view the intervention, read along on the script, and mark "yes" or "no" to the presence of each step of implementation.

The third part of the plan development step is the determination of a progress-monitoring plan. Teams utilize the same data-collection mechanism that was used to set the goal, and agree upon a frequency for assessment, as well as who will collect the data and

when it will be collected (Fuchs, 1989). Students involved in problem solving are most often monitored weekly toward their goals. This rate of data collection allows a sufficient number of data points to be collected in a timely manner for decision-making.

After teams have developed an intervention plan, the next step is to implement the plan and determine whether the intervention is being implemented with integrity. This fourth step of the problem-solving process, plan implementation, is often an overlooked phase of many traditional intervention teams (Upah and Tilly, 2002), yet difficulty with implementation integrity is a common cause for low rates of student success (Noell, Gresham, and Gansle, 2002). For example, an intervention designed for 30 min per day may only actually occur for 20 min 3–4 days out of each week due to scheduling difficulty or student absence. Moreover, the interventionist may inadvertently omit a step in the intervention that affects student performance. At the very least, if a team has defined a specific intervention to be delivered to a student, and the intervention that was actually delivered was in some way different from the plan, then success, or lack thereof, cannot be attributed to the original plan. During the plan implementation step within SCRED schools, an observation of the intervention in action is conducted for all interventions. Observers are other members from the problem-solving team, who utilize a copy of the intervention script to document implementation integrity. This is admittedly a time-intensive process, and one that takes some advanced planning and scheduling. However, the effort is strongly warranted given the significance of potential decisions being made for students as a result of their reaction to the intervention. In the extreme, teams may use these data to identify a student as meeting criteria for entitlement to special education services. Ethical practice standards should insist that teams make concerted efforts to ensure that lack of student progress is in no way caused by a lack of intervention integrity.

During the final step, plan evaluation, teams review the student graph, complete with progress monitoring data collected as planned, and make a determination regarding the success of the plan. Specifically, in reviewing the data, teams determine whether the current discrepancy between what is expected and what is occurring for a student is smaller, the same as, or greater than the original discrepancy that was identified at the start of the process. The team then determines the next steps to take. Teams may consider how to fade an intervention for a student who has experienced success or how to continue an intervention for a student who is making excellent progress but who has not yet met grade-level expectations. Alternately, for plans that have not been effective, teams may review data to determine whether the original hypothesis concerning the cause of the problem was not accurate, and whether a different hypothesis better accounts for the problem. Or, teams may feel that the hypothesis is correct, but the specific intervention plan would be more successful if alterations were made for that student. Teams cycle back through this five-step process as many times as necessary to meet student needs. Importantly, the problem-solving process is used for students receiving both general and special education services, and entitlement decisions do not change the theoretical model or practical activities of teams working toward student success.

24.4 Evidence of Effectiveness

While several elements of the model described above have been in place for longer, the districts in SCRED began collecting systematic CBM data for reading performance in 1996. Since that time, SCRED has seen a steady increase in performance on this measure, as well as on other general outcome measures of early literacy and mathematics, implemented more recently. Districtwide math data exist and are promising, but due to both space considerations and emphasis of this chapter on reading, only reading data will be presented.

First, the percentage of students reaching benchmark target scores on CBM-reading (CBM-R) has increased significantly over the past decade. Figure 24.1 presents the percentage of students reaching target on benchmark reading and literacy measures in spring, across all of SCRED, in grades K-8, over the past decade. While the targets themselves have increased with changes in state standards, the current set of targets have been applied to all data in

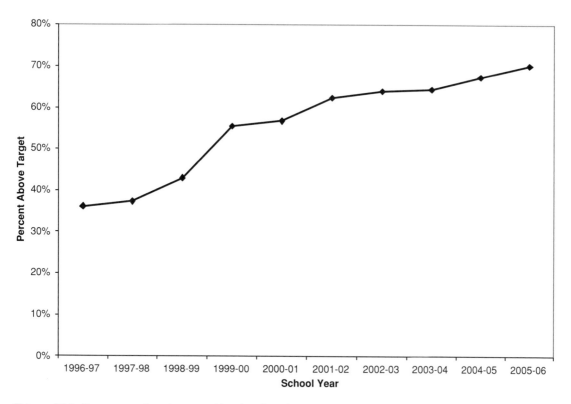

FIGURE 24.1. Percentage of students reaching benchmark targets on literacy measures, SCRED-wide, grades K through 8.

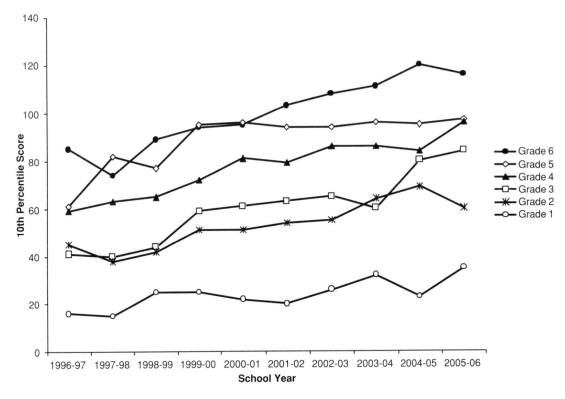

FIGURE 24.2. Historical 10th percentile scores on CBM-R at SCRED, by grade level.

this graph to ensure consistency. One especially notable aspect of this increase in performance lends support to the notion that the improvement is due in large part to effective prevention techniques. The score representing the 10th percentile at SCRED has risen dramatically over the same time period. Figure 24.2 presents the increase in the 10th percentile scores on CBM-R in grades 1 through 6.

Districtwide CBM data support the effectiveness of SCRED innovations, but No Child Left Behind requires assessment of student learning on group achievement tests. The percentage of students reaching grade-level standard on the statewide assessment has increased from 51% at its inception in 1998 to 80% in 2005. This is a slightly faster increase than that of the state overall. Again, there is strong evidence that this increase is a result of a prevention model. The statewide assessment in Minnesota is divided into five levels, with level 1 representing the lowest level of performance, and levels 3 and above representing success in reaching grade-level standards. Where SCRED has seen its greatest gains has been in reducing the number of students falling

in that lowest level on the statewide assessment, as shown in Figure 24.3. This percentage has declined from over 20% in 1998 to 6% in 2005, which is also faster than the state's rate of improvement in this area.

Finally, there is some concern in the education community that the use of RTI models will cause a rapid increase in the rate of special education referrals (Hale, Naglieri, Kaufman, and Kavale, 2004). The data from SCRED run counter to this notion. Figure 24.4 displays the LD rate at SCRED, compared with the state of Minnesota, and, more specifically, SCRED's geographic region (region 7) within the state. SCRED data were not removed from region 7 or state totals. As can be seen, the LD rate at SCRED has dropped dramatically over the past decade, by more than 40%. We feel this is primarily because special education referrals are not the only means for getting effective interventions in place for students with reading difficulties. In addition, we believe that, because of the increase in student achievement over the years, many "LDs" have been prevented.

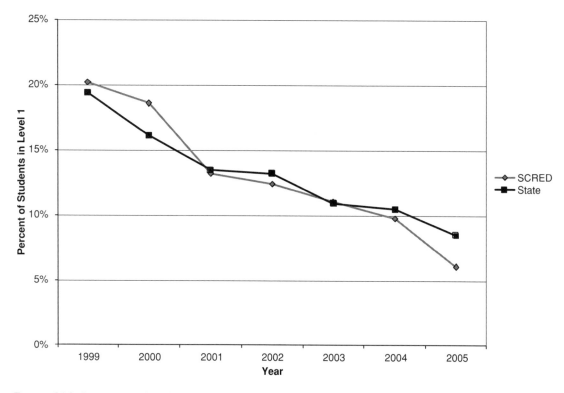

FIGURE 24.3. Percentage of students scoring in the lowest achievement level on the Minnesota comprehensive assessment–reading (MCA-R), SCRED vs. State of Minnesota.

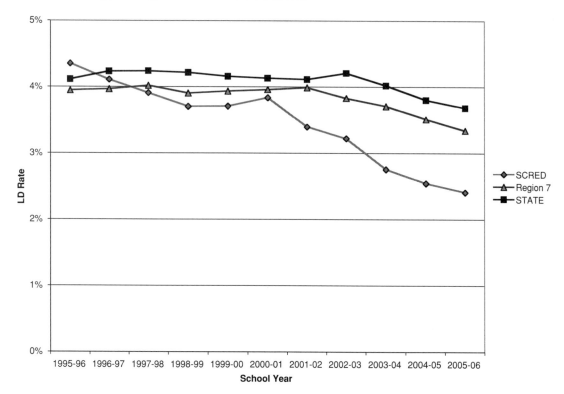

FIGURE 24.4. Incidence of specific learning disabilities, SCRED vs. Region 7 vs. State of Minnesota.

24.5 Limitations: Necessary Conditions for Response to Intervention as an Eligibility Tool

In order to effectively establish an RTI model within a school building, a number of elements need to be in place. For one, although the notion of RTI has commonly been considered as a special education framework, buildings are strongly encouraged to consider this systems change as one that first occurs within general education. A consideration of the tasks to be completed prior to a special education entitlement decision on behalf of an individual student makes this classification clear. First, all students must be provided with scientifically based core instruction in academic skill areas. Next, students participate in universal screening to identify those at risk for academic failure. Once students are identified as at risk, they must be then provided with scientifically based interventions. Notably, suggestions for time estimates for these interventions range from 90 to 150 additional minutes per week, include weekly progress monitoring, and implementation integrity checks. In most models, those students who continue to demonstrate below-target performance and insufficient rates of growth on the first intervention attempt are provided a second intervention with greater intensity or specificity for each student, and with the continuation of weekly data collection and integrity checks. All of these tasks are completed through the utilization of general education resources, with special education entitlement considerations being initiated once these tasks have been completed, for students who continue to demonstrate low levels of response to intervention attempts. Given the extensive work that needs to be completed within general education prior to special education decision-making, it would be inaccurate to describe this systems change as a special education initiative.

A second consideration for buildings considering a move to an RTI framework is the knowledge and application of a range of scientifically based core instructional programs and interventions provided through general education that address common reasons for school failure. Conceptualization of instructional delivery within a three-tier model is particularly helpful in this way, as is the organization of general education resources so that students not meeting grade-level standards can access powerful supplemental support. Ongoing professional development and support to ensure that core and supplemental instruction are delivered with high levels of integrity becomes a significant goal of students pursuing an RTI framework.

Third, buildings need the ability to use valid and reliable methods of assessment for the purposes of screening, diagnostics, progress monitoring, and outcomes evaluation. To do this, district or school buildings need to establish a system-wide measurement net that defines what data is collected at what time for which students. It is helpful to align this measurement net to the established instructional three-tier model. For example, identify data that are collected for all students and those that are collected only for specific subsets of students. As with instructional implementation, ongoing professional development and support must be provided to ensure that staff are appropriately trained to administer and score all assessments in standardized format. In addition, frameworks for organizing and communicating these assessment data for efficient use by grade-level and problem-solving teams must be established.

Fourth, a structured format for problem solving must be in place in order to effectively respond to student concerns as they arise. Establish teams for completing these activities, define the team membership, the process to be followed, the meeting schedule, and the paperwork to be utilized. Communication to all building staff members and parents regarding the procedures for proactive identification of students in need of assistance, as well as implementation of additional support to students at risk, must be an ongoing activity of buildings engaged in an RTI model.

24.6 Future Directions

The RTI process at SCRED has evolved considerably over the past two decades, and will continue to grow in ways that allow for greater integrity and consistency of the process across districts, schools, and teams. One strategy that has recently been adopted is the development of formal decision-making guidelines. These guidelines are benchmarks of both level and slope of performance, to aid in making decisions about the need for and effectiveness of interventions.

While it is emphasized to staff that these benchmarks are guidelines, rather than lines in the sand, they provide a means for ensuring more consistent decision-making. The guidelines, developed by Silberglitt and Gibbons (2005), use a norm-based score for establishing that a student is discrepant on level of performance, while simultaneously using a criterion-based score for establishing that a student is discrepant on slope.

Specifically, the criterion for slope is based on the rate of increase of the fall, winter, and spring benchmark target scores on curriculum-based measures. These target scores were developed using methods described by Silberglitt and Hintze (2005), which link performance at each benchmark period to the desired outcome, in this case reaching grade-level standard on the statewide assessment. This linking process provides a consistent method for establishing the target scores, and gives us a reasonable estimation of the growth necessary to maintain "on-track" status, or "a year's growth in a year's time." Students who fall below this rate of growth are not making adequate progress in their current curriculum, and some change or supplementation needs to be made.

One significant advantage of this approach is that the slope goal is known at the beginning of the year and is relevant to the student. Slope goals based on normative information do not possess these characteristics. If the slope goal is to be based on the growth rates of the student's current cohort, then the goals cannot be established until that cohort has completed at least two benchmark assessments (fall and winter), and preferably all three. An alternative is to base the slope goals on the norms of previous cohorts or on national or state norms, but this reduces the relevance of the goal. Previous cohorts or other districts may have meaningfully different instructional experiences, such as not having all-day every-day kindergarten or using less current versions of curricula, which would make their norms less applicable to the current local cohort. Burns, Silberglitt, Christ, and Gibbons (2007) explored the efficacy of various guidelines for LD incidence, and found that the Silberglitt and Gibbons (2005) model yielded the greatest consistency across grades, with higher LD rates in the early grades than with other models. This seems to support the usefulness of this model for early intervention and prevention of later reading difficulties.

24.7 Conclusion

This chapter summarizes the experiences of one group of school districts from a single region of the country. However, this education district has watched the model it began implementing over a decade ago evolve into a systematic and highly effective process for preventing LDs and academic failure. Now, the law has caught up to science, allowing school districts greater flexibility in their application of similar models. Based on our experiences, we feel confident that implementing a best-practices RTI framework is a step forward for prevention, a step forward for better academic outcomes, and a step forward for schools and the children they serve.

References

Adams, M. J. (1990). *Beginning to Read: Thinking and Learning About Print*. Cambridge, MA: MIT Press.

Batsche, G. M. & Knoff, H. M. (1995). Best practices in linking assessment to intervention. In A. Thomas & J. Grimes (Eds.), *Best Practices in School Psychology* (3rd ed., pp. 569–586). Bethesda, MD: National Association of School Psychologists.

Buck, G. H., Polloway, E. A., Smith-Thomas, A., & Cook, K. W. (2003). Prereferral intervention processes: A survey of state practices. *Exceptional Children, 69*, 349–361.

Burns, M. K., Silberglitt, B., Christ, T. J., & Gibbons, K. A. (2007). comparing norm- and criterion-referenced criteria for non-response (manuscript in submission).

Burns, M. K., Vanderwood, M., & Ruby, S. (2005). Evaluating the readiness of prereferral intervention teams for use in a problem-solving model: review of three levels of research. *School Psychology Quarterly, 20*, 89–105.

Coyne, M. D., Kameenui, E. J., & Simmons, D. C. (2001). Prevention and intervention in beginning reading: two complex systems. *Learning Disabilities Research & Practice, 16*, 62–73.

Deno, S. L. (1985). Curriculum-based measurement: the emerging alternative. *Exceptional Children, 52*, 219–232.

Deno, S. L. (1989). Curriculum-based measurement and alternative special education services: a fundamental and direct relationship. In M. R. Shinn (Ed.), *Curriculum-Based Measurement: Assessing Special Children* (pp. 1–17). New York: Guilford Press.

Deno, S. L. (2003). Developments in curriculum-based measurement. *The Journal of Special Education, 37*, 184–192.

Deno, S. L. & Fuchs, L. S. (1987). Developing curriculum-based measurement systems for data-based special education problem solving. *Focus on Exceptional Children, 19*(8), 1–16.

Deno, S. L., Marston, D., Shinn, M., & Tindal, G. (1983). Oral reading fluency: a simple datum for scaling reading disability. *Topics in Learning and Learning Disabilities, 2*(4), 53–59.

Deno, S. L., Mirkin, P., & Chiang, B. (1982). Identifying valid measures of reading. *Exceptional Children, 49*, 36–45.

Fletcher, J. M., Coulter, W. A., Reschly, D. J., & Vaughn, S. (2004). Alternative approaches to the definition and identification of learning disabilities: some questions and answers. *Annals of Dyslexia, 54*, 304–331.

Fuchs, L. S. (1989). Evaluating solutions, monitoring progress and revising intervention plans. In M. R. Shinn (Ed.), *Curriculum-Based Measurement: Assessing Special Children*. New York, NY: Guilford Press.

Fuchs, L. S. & Shinn, M. R. (1989). Writing CBM IEP objectives. In M. R. Shinn (Ed.), *Curriculum-Based Measurement: Assessing Special Children* (pp. 130–152). New York, NY: The Guilford Press.

Hale, J. B., Naglieri, J. A., Kaufman, A. S., & Kavale, K. A. (2004, Winter). Specific learning disability classification in the new Individuals with Disabilities Education Act: the danger of good ideas. *The School Psychologist, 6–13, 29.*

Howe, K. B., Scierka, B. J., Gibbons, K. A., & Silberglitt, B. (2003). A school-wide organization system for raising reading achievement using general outcome measures and evidence-based instruction: one education district's experience. *Assessment for Effective Intervention, 28*, 59–72.

Kameenui, E. J. & Simmons, D. C. (1998). Beyond effective practice to schools as host environments: building and sustaining a schoolwide intervention model in beginning reading. *Oregon School Study Council, 41*(3), 3–16.

Knoff, H. M. (2002) Best practices in facilitating school reform, organizational change, and strategic planning. In A. Thomas & J. Grimes (Eds.), *Best Practices in School Psychology* (4th ed., pp. 235–253). Bethesda, MD: National Association of School Psychologists.

Kovaleski, J. F. (2003, December). The three tier model of identifying learning disabilities: critical program features and system issues. Paper presented at the *National Research Center on Learning Disabilities Responsiveness-to-Intervention Symposium*, Kansas City, MO.

National Institute of Child Health and Human Development (2000). Report of the National Reading Panel, teaching children to read; an evidence-based assessment of the scientific research literature on reading and its implications for reading instruction-reports of the subgroups. D. N. Langenberg, Chair, National Reading Panel.

No Child Left Behind (2001). *No Child Left Behind Act.* Pub. L. No. 107–110.

Noell, G. H., Gresham, F. M., & Gansle, K. A. (2002). Does treatment integrity matter? A preliminary investigation of instructional implementation and mathematics performance. *Journal of Behavioral Education, 11*, 51–67.

President's Commission on Excellence in Special Education (2002). *A New Era: Revitalizing Special Education for Children and their Families*. Washington, DC: US Department of Education.

Silberglitt, B. & Gibbons, K. A. (2005). *Establishing Slope Targets for Use in a Response to Intervention Model (Technical Manual)*. Rush City, MN: St. Croix River Education District.

Silberglitt, B. & Hintze, J. M. (2005). Formative assessment using CBM-R cut scores to track progress toward success on state-mandated achievement tests: a comparison of methods. *Journal of Psychoeducational Assessment, 23*, 304–325.

Snow, C. E., Burns, S. M., & Griffin, P. (Eds.) (1998). *Preventing Reading Difficulties in Young Children*. Washington, DC: National Academy Press.

Swanson, H. L., Haskyn, M. & Lee, C. (1999). *Interventions for LD Students: A Meta-Analysis Of Treatment Outcomes*. New York: Guilford Publications.

Tindal, G., Germann, G., Deno, S., Marston, D., Shinn, M., & Fuchs, L. S. (1984). A measurement system for integrating assessment, intervention, and evaluation. Paper presented at the *Annual Meeting of the National Association of School Psychologists*, Philadelphia, PA.

Upah, K. R. & Tilly, W. D (2002). Best practices in designing, implementing, and evaluating quality interventions. In A. Thomas & J. Grimes (Eds.), *Best Practices in School Psychology* (4th ed., pp. 483–502). Bethesda, MD: National Association of School Psychologists.

25

The Idaho Results-Based Model: Implementing Response to Intervention Statewide

Wayne A. Callender

Wayne A. Callender, EdS, is a Regional Coordinator and RTI Trainer/Consultant at the University of Oregon.
waynec@uoregon.edu

Quality is never an accident; it is always the result of high intention, sincere effort, intelligent direction, and skillful execution; it represents the wise choice of many alternatives.

Willa A. Foster

Response to intervention (RTI) is receiving significant national attention. For many schools and districts, and even a few states, RTI has been "in the works" for several years. While empirical evidence regarding RTI continues to be collected and reviewed, its popularity with parents and educators can be viewed as a function of dissatisfaction with the traditional approach (i.e., achievement—ability discrepancy) and a desire for more immediate and meaningful solutions for struggling students.

Questions surrounding RTI implementation at the building level are practical in nature. What are the time and resource requirements to carry out effective interventions? What constitutes research-based interventions and practices? What is the relevant definition of "response"? How does RTI impact regular education? And how does RTI impact special education resources within a building? At the district and state levels, RTI raises additional issues, including how it will impact the percentage of students who qualify for special education, how to provide large-scale trainings and support, and how to ensure proper and uniform practice within schools.

This chapter provides insights to the questions posed regarding implementation and ongoing practice of RTI, both at the state and local levels. It provides a description of Idaho's statewide implementation of RTI, also known in Idaho as the Results-Based Model (RBM). This chapter emphasizes the major lessons learned at the local and state levels as a result of experience, program evaluation, and school feedback. Cautionary recommendations along with implications for practice are offered.

25.1 Response to Intervention in Idaho: The Results-Based Model

In 1997, the Idaho State Department of Education, Bureau of Special Education, applied for and was awarded a state improvement grant to begin implementation of a "proactive, dynamic, problem-solving process that is responsive to individual student needs." Included in the grant were provisions for training school-based problem-solving teams, hiring a state-level project coordinator, and conducting ongoing project evaluation. School recruitment followed several introductory meetings that were held across the state. During the first year, three elementary schools were identified and school personnel were trained to implement the model. Over the years, as interest in the project increased, additional schools were added. As of 2005, approximately 150 elementary and secondary schools were trained across the state of Idaho. Approximately 40% of all districts within the state have one or more buildings participating in the program, several are district-wide.

25.1.1 Idaho's Approach to Response to Intervention

RTI in Idaho combines both a standard-protocol and problem-solving approach. Early in the project, it was recognized that problem solving alone did not adequately meet the needs of most schools. It was neither practical nor efficient for schools with a disproportionate number of students below academic proficiency to engage in individual student problem solving. Often, the school's system itself was identified as contributing to a lack of student proficiency. For instance, a student below grade level in reading often came from a class that included other poor readers. Closer examination typically revealed systemic concerns (e.g., use of a non-research-based reading program, lack of effective interventions for struggling readers, no method for monitoring student progress, or an overall system limited in its design to respond to struggling readers). When a systemic approach was established, far fewer students needed individualized problem solving. Changes to core trainings were subsequently made in an effort to emphasize effective overall systems. Within this framework, individual student problem-solving became one component of a systemic approach, as outlined below in the four levels:

1. *Level I.* Basic/general education: all students.
2. *Level II.* Standard protocol treatments: small-group instruction for intensive and strategie students in general education/Title I/special education.
3. *Level III.* Problem-solving: targeted individual interventions in general education/Title I/special education. Available to all students as needed.
4. *Level IV.* Special education/individual education plan: intensive, long-term services.

25.1.2 Guiding Principles of Idaho's Results-Based Model

The Results-Based Model seeks to improve results for all students and to provide support for parents and teachers. Its guiding principles are (Idaho State Department of Education, 2006):

1. Improving results for all students, including students with disabilities; requires a strength-based, rather than a deficit-based or categorical, model.
2. It is necessary to integrate the resources and shared expertise of general education, compensatory education, and special education in addressing the needs of students with learning and behavior difficulties.
3. Parents are key players in improving educational results for their children and should be empowered to participate fully in making and implementing educational decisions.
4. Collaboration between general and special educators and parents improves access to and participation in general education curricula, as well as success in meeting the standards and benchmarks set for all students.
5. Idaho's educational system for serving all students is proactive and responsive; it provides for early identification and intervention of academic or behavioral difficulties.
6. Ongoing training and technical assistance for all staff are critical to system change and improvement.
7. Professionals have flexible roles, based on expertise and student needs, as well as assignment.
8. Functional assessment is used to gather data to design, implement, and monitor the effectiveness of interventions.
9. Improving results for students with disabilities incorporates Individuals with Disabilities Education Act requirements and best-practices to assessment and interventions.
10. Idaho's system includes frequent progress monitoring and data-based decision-making.

25.1.3 Key Practices of the Results-Based Model

Idaho's approach to RTI is comprised of several key practices, or "big ideas." They form a comprehensive, integrated process that stretch far beyond an alternative method for identifying students with disabilities and includes (1) addressing the system, (2) problem-solving teams, (3) parental involvement, (4) functional assessment, (5) outcome-oriented intervention, (6) ongoing progress monitoring, (7) systemic data-based decision-making, and (8) dual discrepancy eligibility. The following section provides a brief description of each of these facets.

25.1.3.1 Addressing the System

The RBM most effectively impacts schools through evaluation of the effectiveness of the overall system. The fundamental goal is to be proactive and preventative. Key strategies include:

Regular evaluation of the system. System change relies on the ongoing assessment of all students in an effort to: (a) evaluate the effectiveness or "health" of the system, including the levels of benchmark, strategic and intensive; (b) pinpoint areas of concern, including analysis of instruction, curriculum and environment; and (c) determine the extent to which adjustments to the system are effective as measured by student performance.

A context-based view of problems. Student achievement (or lack of it) is a product of the student in the school context, not simply a problem within the student. School context includes instruction, curriculum, and environment.

Early identification of problems. Universal assessments in the fall, winter, and spring evaluate whether students are meeting expectations in the basic skill areas of reading, writing, and math.

Providing standard, but differentiated intervention according to students need, including:

A. Strategic interventions. These include standard, small-group interventions available for students in need within regular education. Strategic interventions are provided in addition to the effective core program.

B. Intensive interventions. These include explicit instructional methods a replacement to the core program, such interventions may either already be available for students as part of a differentiated and flexible system or require development by a collaborative problem-solving team.

25.1.4 Problem-Solving Teams

When system-wide interventions prove unsuccessful, a student or a group of students may be referred to the problem-solving team. At the individual student level, a student intervention plan (I-Plan) is created. A modified version of Branford and Stein's (1984) IDEAL problem solver is utilized by the team as a structured approach to break down a problem. It includes the steps illustrated in Table 25.1.

TABLE 25.1. Steps in the IDEAL problem-solving model.

IDEAL steps		What questions are explored?
I	Identify the problem	What is the specific concern?
D	Define the problem	What is causing the problem?
E	Explore intervention options	What is the goal and how can it be addressed?
A	Act on the intervention plan	How will the plan be implemented? How will progress be monitored?
L	Look at results	What were the results? What is the next course of action?

Problem-solving teams generally consist of four to eight people. Participants include grade level teachers, the student's teacher, special education representatives, a school psychologist, the building principal, specialists (e.g., speech pathologist, occupational therapist, or others professionals), parents, and in most circumstances, the student. Using the problem-solving steps outlined above, teams typically meet weekly for 45 to 60 min. Two students can be discussed at each meeting—a first student for whom the goal is to complete preplanning and a second student for whom preplanning was previously completed. Preplanning involves determining what information will be collected to gain in-depth information about the student in question (such as present level of performance and functional academic assessments, etc.) as well as the system context (e.g., effectiveness of curriculum, instruction, and environment).

At the problem-solving level, interventions are provided along with progress monitoring for a period spanning 9 to 27 weeks. During the "Look at Results" step, teams consider the student's overall progress and determine if and what further action may be necessary. Options include: (a) continue the plan as is; (b) change the current plan; (c) discontinue the plan; or (d) refer to extended problem solving (i.e., determining eligibility and need for special education).

25.1.5 Parental Involvement

Parents are vital members of the problem-solving team. They provide critical information regarding their child, which helps to more accurately define the problem. They also participate with the team

TABLE 25.2. Sources used to identify research-based practices and programs.

Northwest Regional Education Laboratory*	Educational Resources Information Center*
National Reading Panel*	National Research Council*
National Council of Teachers of Mathematics*	Center of Research on Standards and Student Testing (CRESST)*
Eisenhower National Clearinghouse*	An Educator's Guide to School-wide Reform*
Achieving Student Success Handbook*	Positive Behavior Supports Literature
Peer refereed scientific journals (e.g., *Exceptional Children*)	The What Works Clearinghouse
Oregon Reading First	Florida Center for Reading Research

Source: US Department of Education, Institute of Education Sciences (2003).

TABLE 25.3. Example of a school's K–3 intervention list for reading.*

Supplemental program (used in addition to a core reading program)	Intervention program (supplants the core program)
Early reading intervention (K–1) PA, P	Early reading intervention plus language for learning (K) PA, P, V
Road to the code (K–1) PA	Horizons (1–3) PA, P, F, V, C
Phonics for reading (1–3) PA, P	Reading mastery (K–3) PA, P, F, V, C
Language for learning (K–1) V	Corrective reading (3) PA, P, F, V, C
Language for thinking (1–3) V, C	
Read naturally (1–3) F	

*PA: phonemic awareness; P: phonics; F: fluency; V: vocabulary; C: comprehension.

in brainstorming possible solutions and provide a home-based intervention component identified by the problem solving team, designed to reinforce critical skills being taught at school. Necessary materials and training for carrying out the home-based intervention are provided to the parent by the school.

25.1.6 Functional Assessment

Informal, functional academic assessments are used for problem analysis in the RBM approach. Functional assessment is used to identify specific skill deficits for instructional purposes/identifying appropriate programming. For instance, knowing that a student's poor reading performance is primarily related to difficulty in decoding multi-syllabic words enables the problem-solving team to identify advanced decoding instruction as the appropriate intervention. With this information, the team then identifies the most appropriate research-based approach/program to address the identified skill deficits.

25.1.7 Outcome-Oriented Intervention

Identifying the most effective interventions is dependent on problem analysis. Only interventions based in research are typically considered. Various sources are used to identify research-based practices and programs such as those identified in Table 25.2.

Having access to research-based interventions is critical for schools to reliably identify effective interventions and achieve positive outcomes using an RTI approach. To minimize time and effort, teams are assisted in establishing a list of intervention programs available at the various grade levels within the building. The list further divides interventions according to area or domain, specific skills addressed, and specifies if used to supplants the core program. Schools are encouraged to identify fewer, yet powerful interventions. To increase intervention fidelity, schools are encouraged to arrange for appropriate training and on-going follow-up from program specific experts/consultants.

By utilizing an intervention list, problem solving teams match student skill deficits to the most powerful, direct interventions available. For instance, at the k-3 elementary level in reading, a school's intervention list might include the programs outlined in Table 25.3.

25.1.8 Progress Monitoring

Monitoring student progress is central throughout all levels of the RBM. Student progress is evaluated in reference to benchmark, strategic, and intensive levels. At the benchmark level, all students are assessed in the fall, winter, and spring using curriculum-based measurements (e.g., DI-BELS, CBM Math or CBM Writing). The resulting data help to evaluate overall progress towards grade-level expectations and assess student risk levels. An additional benefit of benchmark assessment is evaluation of overall program efficacy.

At the strategic level, all students receive small-group, supplemental instruction and are progress-monitored every three to four weeks to ensure ample growth and learning. Programs at the strategic level are generally specialized and designed to accelerate specific skill areas, such as social skills or reading fluency. Intensive students, in contrast, have marked difficulties and require sustained, intense programming. Progress monitoring for these students occurs twice monthly to ensure that expected growth in skill acquisition is occurring at the necessary rate.

25.1.9 Systematic Data-Based Decision-Making

The key to RTI is the capacity for making informed instructional decisions. That is, schools must have precise methods for determining when an intervention is working and when it is not. In the Idaho experience, collecting and accurately using progress monitoring data can be difficult for schools to perfect. Often student data are collected and graphed, but decision rules are not consistently engaged for any number of reasons. Most notably, schools report time and resources as the most common barrier to changing interventions. As a result, unsuccessful interventions (i.e., those that don't promote growth as identified by the I-Plan's goal or aimline), may be continued for extensive periods. Even successful interventions typically require periodic adjustments to maximize student response.

25.1.10 Dual-Discrepancy Eligibility

Idaho requires schools to complete five days of core training and to demonstrate proficiency in key skill areas (e.g., progress monitoring, decision rules, research-based interventions) prior to receiving a state-issued waiver. The waiver allows schools to use a dual-discrepancy criterion for making special-education eligibility decisions. A definition of dual discrepancy is when a student: (a) exhibits large differences from typical peer levels of performance in achievement, social behavior, or emotional regulation, *and* (b) shows insufficient response to high-quality interventions in academic and/or behavioral domains.

According to the President's Commission on Excellence in Special Education (2002), the use of the classification of disabilities and their relation to instruction is not established and remains a questionable practice. In Idaho, the dual discrepancy criterion does not require assignment of a disability category. Rather, students may be placed noncategorically. Idaho's noncateogorical eligibility is defined as:

Without regard to category of disability, a student may be determined eligible for special education when (1) data from progress monitoring demonstrate the student's academic or behavioral performance is significantly discrepant from peers, (2) the student has not significantly progressed despite the application of research-based interventions and (3) special education interventions are necessary to provide an appropriate education (Idaho Special Education Manual, 2001).

Idaho Noncateogorical Eligibility Requirements:

Discrepancy from Peers	The student exhibits large differences from typical levels of peer performance in academic achievement, social behavior or emotion/regulation. In Idaho the discrepancy may be demonstrated through various means (i.e., at or below the 7th percentile compared to peers, two grade levels below current grade placement, a standard score of 74 or lower and a discrepancy ratio of 2.0 or greater)
Multiple Indicators Required:	
Response to Intervention	Evidence and data from progress summaries show insufficient response to research-based interventions applied with fidelity in academic or behavioral areas of concern. Adequate progress is evaluated by comparing a student's growth pattern relative to expected progress established during the development of the I-Plan. Comparisons of expected growth to actual growth require that the goal is

both realistic, yet ambitious enough to significantly close the achievement or performance gap within a specified period of time. A student's response or progress trajectory is a primary consideration.

Need for Specially Designed Instruction — The student's needs cannot be adequately met within regular education; the student requires accommodation and ongoing intense intervention that is most appropriately provided long-term through special education.

In practice, the above eligibility requirements are established through completion of an eligibility report consisting of four components as outlined in Table 25.4. If done well, the completed I-Plan and progress-monitoring graphs provide the essential documentation necessary for establishing eligibility. Noteworthy is that, over the course of the project, special education placements in RBM schools fell a medium of 3%, whereas placements in non-RBM schools across the state increased a medium of 1% during the same time period.

In summarizing key practices of the RBM, major emphasis and effort is placed on prevention and intervention. When long-term, intensive intervention and support are necessary, a student may qualify for special education using the dual-discrepancy criteria. This method requires that information collected as part of the intervention process (which is also most relevant to special-education program planning) be used for determining eligibility. The need for additional evaluation beyond that completed during the intervention period is left to the discretion of the intervention team. More often, additional evaluation measures (i.e., IQ, diagnostic testing) are not deemed necessary.

25.1.11 Statewide Implementation of Response to Intervention

Applying RTI methodology was a radical departure from how schools in Idaho were used to conducting prereferral and special-education evaluations. The degree of change presented considerable challenges to the staff of participating schools, as

TABLE 25.4. Eligibility report form.

1. The response of the presenting problem or behaviors of concern to general education interventions indicates the need for intense and sustained resources for an indefinite time period. • Attempt to resolve problems at the least restrictive, least intrusive level • Evaluate improvement relative to level of risk • Rate of learning and progress toward the goal or aimline is the indicator of most interest • Directly addresses the educational needs of the student	2. The resources necessary to support the child to participate and progress in the general education curriculum are beyond those available in the general education curriculum, or require intense intervention and support for sustained periods of time. • Specific questions about the student's learning are addressed (e.g., what level in the curriculum can the student be instructed; what environmental conditions are related to improved student success?) • Determine amount of resources necessary to support the student • Is a direct statement of the student's need for special education
3. Evidence of a severe discrepancy from peer's performance in the area(s) of concern. (Must use multiple sources of data): • Performance on CBM tests e.g., 16%ile at one grade level below and/or 7%ile at grade level on local curriculum measure • Standard deviations below peers on norm referenced tests (1.75 SD below mean on nationally standardized assessments) • Two grade levels below peers in areas of concern • Discrepancy ratio of 2.0 • Direct observations of student behavior in the performance domain • Interviews with the child's teacher and parent about the student's performance compared to peers	4. Convergent evidence logically and empirically supporting the teams' decisions • The presence of exceptionality is substantiated by convergent data from multiple sources including general education interventions, record reviews, interviews, observations and tests • A preponderance of the data must support the eligibility of a child as a child with an exceptionality. • Must collect broad based information related to the problem • Must collect targeted information to satisfy initial three criteria

well as to the state's ability to provide adequate training and support. Efforts to help schools implement RTI include introducing a web-based training clearinghouse and the creation of learning communities. Both have increased the access to information, materials, and resources and improved communication between the participating schools and the Department of Education.

The importance of training school personnel to use problem solving and related practices was realized after the first year, as sites initially demonstrated low or unacceptable levels of implementation. As a result, at the beginning of year two, and with greater levels each year thereafter, trainings were emphasized placing greater focus on (a) establishing effective overall systems (tier 1 and tier 2) within schools, (b) providing more direct, explicit training regarding the key components of problem identification, problem analysis, research-based interventions, and progress monitoring; and (c) raising expectations for implementation of key RBM practices.

Regional trainings have maximized limited resources for statewide implementation of RTI. Building-level teams attend 5 days of core training, approximately 1 day per month, September through January. This allows teams the opportunity to initiate each segment of the training, in succession, within their schools. A state consultant trained in RBM provides monthly on-site support to each school, answering questions, demonstrating problem-solving procedures, and providing technical assistance.

The difficulty of executing complex systems change requires regular, on-site professional support and strong instructional leadership. School feedback and program evaluations confirm its value. Schools not adequately supported demonstrated considerable difficulty with system reform, implementing key problem-solving components, and successfully carrying out RTI.

25.1.12 Lessons Learned

Although there is still much to discover about RTI, valuable lessons have been learned through the implementation of the Idaho RBM. Based on these, several considerations for implementing and practicing RTI are offered.

25.1.13 Problem Solving or Standard Protocol?

Neither problem solving (as described in the previous section) nor standard protocol (i.e., level I and II programming) alone adequately address the needs of all students. Each approach presents advantages and limitations. For instance, concerns at the student level are often due, in part, to the system itself, such as the student whose limited reading skills are actually the product of a poor reading program or inadequate instruction. Problem solving will often address the individual student's concerns, but not necessarily impact the source of the problem. Conversely, standard protocol will not be sufficient in all situations. Students who do not respond to predetermined interventions will require additional analysis and extended planning. The problem-solving process is well suited to addressing their needs. Standard protocol requires that multiple intervention "packages" be available to meet a variety of student needs and that student skill deficits be sufficiently identified so as to match specific learning needs to available packages.

Owing to the limitations inherent in both the standard-protocol and problem-solving approaches, a combined effort offers significant advantages, namely allowing the strength of problem solving to address the weaknesses of standard protocol and vice versa. This framework more adequately addresses all students and improves alignment between programs and interventions throughout all levels of the overall system.

25.1.14 What Constitutes Adequate Response?

Although no single definition of what constitutes adequate response to intervention has been widely established, a statewide standard provides important guidance to schools as they begin to implement RTI. Establishing a statewide definition is necessary and helps ensure the use of a uniform standard across schools and districts. Such a standard also guards against the inappropriate placement of a nondisabled student into special education.

While "response" may be viewed from different perspectives (see Table 25.5), a combined approach (idiographic and criterion) has evolved over time within the state of Idaho. The RBM defines

TABLE 25.5. Ways to view "response" to intervention.

"Response" may be viewed in different ways:
1. Normative—an increase in relation to national norms (i.e., move from the 7th percentile to the 15th percentile, etc.)
2. Local norms—measured in relation to the class or grade-level norm (i.e., move from 10th percentile to 13th percentile of peers)
3. Idiographic—measured against the student's prior performance (i.e., increase slope)
4. Criterion—meeting a predesignated goal or level (grade-level expectations or benchmarks)

"response" according to levels of student growth or slope (idiographic) in relation to student risk status (criterion). That is, a student's response to intervention is a measure of student progress toward pre-established goals (i.e., skill proficiency) and decreased risk. For instance, "nonresponding" means that a student's slope of progress is not moving in the direction of the goal. In such instances, the student's rate of progress need not, over time, substantially reduce risk or enable them to be an independent learner anytime in the foreseeable future. This is evident when the student's medium rate of progress, based on previous progress, is projected into the future. Conversely, a student making adequate response will, given the right interventions and adequate time, progress towards a level where treatments available for all students can appropriately support the student.

Consider the following example. Kaylee participates in a reading intervention for 18 weeks. During this period, the intervention is altered four times as indicated by progress-monitoring decision rules. Despite the school's best efforts, Kaylee's reading level remains well below her original goal, although her score has improved slightly. Examination of Kaylee's performance over the course of the intervention period reveals that she is still firmly within the intensive level of risk, where, according to progress-monitoring projections, she is likely to remain despite continued intervention into the foreseeable future. As a result, Kaylee will continue to require extensive intervention and accommodations. At this point, Kaylee is considered for long-term support, perhaps through special education services. It should be noted that special education interventions and interventions provided through the RBM do not significantly differ in quality or intensity. Indeed, the most powerful interventions available

are applied in both instances regardless of the student's placement. Interventions provided through special education differ primarily in terms of duration. Whereas problem-solving interventions are often short-term (carried out for 9 to 27 weeks—sometimes longer; there is no maximum time limit for implementing interventions within RBM), special education is typically reserved for those students in need of long-term support, accommodations, and sustained direct intervention.

25.1.15 Length and Intensity of Intervention

Most concerns referred to problem solving are not easily or quickly resolved and often require resources or a level of intervention beyond those available within level 2. They typically represent severe skill deficits that have occurred over time and, thus, will require substantial time and effort to remedy. Beyond research-based and scientifically proven programs, intervention periods exceeding 18–27 weeks may be necessary. Even then, students often require continued support through supplemental support programs. When sufficient student progress is not being realized, schools must know how and be willing to intensify interventions. This often requires regular interventions firmly unavailable through regular education alone. This often entails altering certain variables rather than replacing entire programs. Alterable variables include: (a) modifying opportunities to learn; (b) examining program efficacy; (c) adjusting program implementation and grouping for instruction; (d) improving the coordination of instruction.

25.1.16 System is Key

What educators and parents want is straightforward: timely, effective help for struggling students. Although individual problem solving is effective in achieving this goal, it is not always efficient. More efficient is an overall school design that meets the needs of all students. Within the state of Idaho, it was clearly revealed that schools trained to incorporate well-defined levels of student support (basic, targeted, and intensive) were also more successful at meeting the needs of individual students. The key is providing differentiated levels of support to meet student needs without delay. In most cases, only students not responding at anticipated rates within tier 2 interventions are referred for problem solving.

25.1.17 Sharing Responsibility

A successful RTI approach requires the efforts of parents and regular and special education professionals. Regular education must be arranged to take on a more direct and active role in providing support and interventions for all students, including those in special education. Likewise, special education must be available to provide expertise and resources to support the overall system, especially for nondisabled students at the tertiary levels. In Idaho, the schools most successful in implementing RTI were those most conscientious at involving parents and sharing resources across programs. Sharing across programs (e.g., Title I, special education, etc.) was not only allowed, but also encouraged by the State Department of Education.

25.1.18 Discontinue Prereferral Teams

Schools should consider replacing prereferral teams with problem solving teams/processes so as to reduce duplicated effort and discourage meetings for the sole purpose of determining whether a student should be referred for special education evaluation. Once trained, a problem-solving team, which may be composed of members from the prereferral team, serves several purposes: developing intervention plans, arranging for specific interventions and support, reviewing student progress, and making recommendations for additional action based on the student's RTI.

25.1.19 Team Training and On-Site Support

Perhaps the most important lesson learned throughout the implementation of RTI in Idaho is that schools need extensive training and support implementing the essential components of RTI. Successful execution requires extensive knowledge of how to implement and apply research-based programs with fidelity, problem analysis, progress monitoring, use of decision rules, and strategic goal setting. Explicit training is required in determining special education eligibility based on an RTI approach. From

the Idaho experience, it is recommended that states ensure well-designed, comprehensive trainings for schools to complete prior to using an RTI approach. On-site support for implementing RTI during and after training is also recommended. Finally, ongoing evaluation of the school's implementation of RTI components and subsequent feedback are important and necessary.

25.1.20 Establishing Accurate Expectations for Student Growth

RTI requires that educators be able to establish accurate expectations for student academic growth and improvement. Establishing goals that are not adequately ambitious typically results in less academic growth. Likewise, establishing expectations that are unrealistically high or do not allow enough time (e.g., expecting a student to improve as a result of 3 weeks of intervention) will result in erroneous decision-making regarding effectiveness of interventions. In both instances, expecting too little growth or setting unrealistically high goals will negatively impact the team's ability to assess a student's response to intervention. Without realistic goals and judicious decision-making, RTI will ultimately be flawed, offering little advantage to the traditional discrepancy method for determining eligibility.

25.2 Program Evaluation

As part of a state improvement grant, Idaho commissioned ongoing evaluation of RBM. Results from five years of program evaluation were summarized in a report available from the Idaho State Department of Education (Nunn, 2005), including data on RBM and special-education placement and reading performances for students in participating schools. Also presented are findings regarding knowledge, skills, and perceptions of problem-solving practices. Some of these findings are summarized below.

25.2.1 Special Education Placements

Between fall of 2002–2003 and fall of 2004–2005 the overall enrollment of public schools in Idaho increased by 3%. During the same period, enrollment statewide in special education increased 1%. Districts with at least one participating RBM school (most districts have multiple schools) demonstrated a 3% decrease in special-education placements. In such districts, RBM schools accounted for the majority of the decrease.

25.2.2 Reading Performances

A comprehensive study compared the reading improvement of 1400 K–3 students. Students were divided into two groups, those at RBM schools on intervention plans (for reading) versus students from non-RBM schools with like reading performances but not placed on intervention plans. Students with intervention plans progressed significantly more than those without intervention plans (effect size: 1.10).

25.2.3 Knowledge, Skills and Perceptions of Problem-Solving Practices

The growth of participant knowledge and skills regarding essential problem-solving practices (e.g., problem analysis, progress monitoring, decision rules) were evaluated using a pre- and post-assessment before and after completion of 5 days of core training. The percentage of pre- and post-assessment items answered correctly were 26% and 90%, respectively.

Observations of problem-solving team activities early in the project lead to the need for increased training and on-site support. Initial observations revealed relatively low levels of important problem-solving activities actually occurring (see Table 25.6). These findings reveal the imperative for well-designed training and on-site follow-up.

TABLE 25.6. Problem-solving activities initially observed during team meetings.

Activity	Observed (%)
Parent participation	22
Problem analysis	9
Obtaining present level of performance	5
Writing goals	2
Graphing student performance	0
Following decision rules	0

25.2.4 Information Obtained from End-of-Year Reports Submitted by Participating Schools

Fidelity and overall success of RBM is strongly tied to administrative and instructional leadership within the school. Extensive trainings/support is highly related to quality of RTI practices. First-year schools report spending significant time and effort implementing RBM-related components. However, first-year schools also report a high degree of satisfaction with RBM components, attributable to a significant decrease in the number of students "falling between the cracks."

25.2.5 Results-Based Model Policy Committee Recommendations

In the spring of 2005, a policy group consisting of State Department of Education representatives and educators from veteran schools implementing the RBM met to identify key recommendations for the future development of the RBM. The recommendations are as follows:

- Encourage districts to consider the number of students being served on intervention plans as part of the overall need for resources within a building. Consider use of 15% of special education funding for carrying out interventions in such buildings.
- Schools participating in the RBM should use only RTI (dual discrepancy) for qualifying students. Discontinue use of the discrepancy formula.
- Do not decrease the number of core training days (five) required for beginning schools.
- Explore ways to expand RBM to early childhood education.
- Communicate changes regarding eligibility and classification of students to related agencies involved in providing services to special education students, including colleges and vocation rehabilitation centers.
- Decreased the use of categorical labels within special education.

25.2.6 Implications for Practice

In Idaho's experience, one of the keys to successfully implementing RTI is providing quality and explicit training for schools. Site-based support is also

TABLE 25.7. Implications for practice.

Key idea/practice	Recommendation
RTI approach: combine problem solving and standard protocol	A combination of both the problem-solving and standard-protocol approaches will more effectively meet the challenges facing schools. Together, they present an array of safety nets for students and greatly increase resources available to educators.
Address the system	It is important to devote extensive attention to developing an overall effective system of supports for all students. Areas addressed are curriculum, instruction, and environment.
Problem-solving teams in place of prereferral teams	Referral-based teams should be discontinued and replaced by intervention- and solution-oriented problem-solving teams whose primary function is to create individualized intervention plans for students not addressed through tier 1 and 2 interventions. Referrals for evaluation should be the responsibility of a team primarily concerned with brainstorming solutions and ensuring interventions are carried out.
Dual discrepancy eligibility criteria	Eligibility requires both (a) response to research-based interventions and (b) a severe discrepancy from peers in area of concern.
Research-based interventions	Use only interventions aligned to specific skill deficits that are research based or scientifically based and applied with fidelity. Guidelines for quality, duration and intensity of interventions should be established.
Duration of interventions	Interventions should be carried out for an adequate period of time (18–27 weeks).
Training and support	Schools receive training prior to initiating RTI. Training focuses on development of key skills and knowledge required for implementation of key components of RTI.
Precision goals	Required for accurate decision-making during progress monitoring and in determining a student's response to instruction.
Progress monitoring	Progress monitoring is used throughout the system to evaluate effectiveness of programs and interventions; documents RTI.
Noncategorical eligibility	Schools should consider using a noncategorical approach to special education eligibility. Classification of disabilities, especially "soft" categories, is not instructionally relevant or supported in science. Noncategorical increases focus on student's individual instructional needs rather than conditions of disorder or label category.
Defining "Response" to Intervention	A standard and uniform definition of "response" is recommended across schools within a given state.

critical. However, effective training and support is not easily accomplished. The potential for RTI to improve upon Idaho's existing system, as well as to improve outcomes for students, is directly related to how well and how thoughtfully it is implemented. Ensuring correct practice of RTI components is key, as is establishing effective standard-protocol and problem-solving systems. Table 25.7 summarizes the implications for practice gleaned from the Idaho experience.

25.3 Conclusion

Effective RTI depends on thoughtful planning and implementation. Beyond the training of personnel, RTI requires a significant philosophical shift in how we view problems and the school's responsibility in addressing the needs of all students. Educating parents regarding the philosophy of this new approach, is an important step towards securing their support.

Finally, RTI, as in Idaho's experience, can be implemented with great success. It can provide educators with real solutions to increasingly complex problems and offer the assurance that assistance will not be delayed and that students will not "fall through the cracks." Perhaps the greatest concern is that RTI, as it becomes implemented across the nation, will inadvertently become just a new way to identify students for special education without adequate attention to its most appealing and powerful quality: improving the results for students while supporting teachers and parents. For this to be accomplished, considerable thought and effort will be required.

References

Bransford, J. D. & Stein, B. S. (1984). *The IDEAL Problem Solver: Improving Critical Thinking, Improving Learning and Memory Skills, Solve Problems Creatively*. New York: W. H. Freeman.

Idaho State Department of Education. (2006). An overview of the results-based model in Idaho. Website available, from http://www.idahotc.com/rbm/rbmoverview.htm.

Nunn, G. D. (2005). Evaluation summary report: results-based model SI final summary of evaluation findings 1999–2004. Boise, ID: Idaho State Department of Education.

Nunn, G. D. & Callender, W. A. (2005). Results-based model overview presentation and summary of evaluation report. Presented at the *National Association of School Psychologist Annual Conference*, Atlanta, GA.

US Department of Education, Institute of Education Sciences (2003). *Identifying and Implementing Educational Practices Supported by Rigorous Evidence: A User Friendly Guide*. Washington, DC: US Department of Education, Institute of Education Sciences, National Center for Education Evaluation and Regional Assistance.

US Department of Education Office of Special Education and Rehabilitative Services. (2002). *A New Era: Revitalizing Special Education for Children and their Families*. Washington, DC: US Department of Education Office of Special Education and Rehabilitative Services.

26

The System to Enhance Educational Performance (STEEP): Using Science to Improve Achievement

Joseph C. Witt and Amanda M. VanDerHeyden

Joseph C. Witt, PhD, is the Director of Research and Development iSTEEP Learning. joe@JoeWitt.org
Amanda VanDerHeyden, PhD, is a Private Researcher and Consultant living in Fairhope, Alabama.
amanda@education.ucsb.edu

The System to Enhance Educational Performance (STEEP) is a program that provides a blueprint for implementation of response to intervention (RTI). RTI has been defined as the practice of "(a) providing high quality instruction/intervention matched to student needs and (2) using learning rate over time and level of performance to (3) make important educational decisions" (NASDSE, 2006, p. 5). In other words, RTI is a process for gathering data, applying decision rules, and making decisions. As a generic process, RTI may include various types of screening procedure, decision-making processes, and, interventions. Implementation and decision-making with RTI by professionals using a problem-solving model may differ from case to case and school to school. STEEP represents a specific set of decision rules and procedures that, together, help to operationalize the RTI process. The purpose of this chapter is to describe the empirical and epistemological foundation for STEEP.

STEEP is a research-based RTI model. STEEP consists of a series of assessment and intervention procedures with specific decision rules to detect and remediate students with academic deficits in reading, mathematics, or writing in kindergarten through eighth grade. STEEP begins with screening, which utilizes curriculum-based measurement (CBM). Decision rules are applied to screening data to determine whether or not there is a Tier 1 or core curriculum problem. If so, then classwide problems are addressed with classwide intervention. If a Tier 1 problem is not present or has been successfully resolved with intervention, then a subset of students are identified to participate in a brief assessment of

the effect of incentives on child performance. Decision rules are then applied to the results of the performance/skill deficit assessment and students are matched to either a skill or performance intervention. For skill deficit students, a standard protocol is used to select and implement an appropriate intervention. Progress monitoring data are used to determine whether or not the intervention response was adequate or inadequate. Hence, STEEP is a set of procedures that functions to detect and assist students who might benefit from academic intervention. Interventions are quickly delivered and monitored for effectiveness.

26.1 Background and Original Problem

The purpose of schooling is to assist students to acquire academic proficiency. It follows, then, that a major problem for schools occurs when students do not achieve the academic skills that schools have been entrusted to impart. Such students have always been present in schools, and educators have struggled with the question of how best to respond to their needs. In the 1980s there was increased use of special education as a solution for the problem of low achievement. It was assumed that students who were intellectually capable and yet had significant achievement deficits must have a specific learning disability (SLD), and SLD classification became a widely used tool for the problem of low achievement. The classification of students as having an SLD was viewed as positive for all: good for students, in that they were provided with "small class size and specially trained teachers," and good for schools because there was no need to make extraordinary accommodations in instruction for low-achieving students.

In hindsight it appears this approach was wrong for students and wrong as a method for improving overall achievement. The dramatic rise in special education placements in the United States occurred in the face of increasing evidence that special education outcomes were poor. Once placed, students stayed in special education for their entire school career. Students enrolled in special education disproportionately failed to graduate from high school and employment options were more limited. Many professionals were not surprised by the inadequacy of SLD diagnosis to improve achievement, because common sense dictates that fundamental problems cannot be solved using solutions that do not address the causes of those problems. Diagnosis as SLD and subsequent eligibility for special education services under the category of SLD did not address the root cause of low achievement. Students could show low achievement for reasons other than SLD. Special education was not the answer for many of the students placed there.

In 1975 with the passage of PL 94-142, which has since evolved into the Individuals with Disabilities Act and practitioners and educators began viewing special education as a solution for students who could fit into one of the diagnostic categories within PL 94-142 (e.g., SLD, mental disability). Decision-makers in schools, when considering the problem of a specific low-achieving student, have the option of examining student-focused solutions or system-focused solutions. System-focused solutions examine the interaction between instruction and student response to instruction. The most common student-focused question is, "Why is this student not learning?" The most common answer in the 1980s and 1990s was, "Because he has SLD." System-focused questions move beyond the individual student and include:

1. Why are referrals so much higher in school A relative to school B when they have similar populations?
2. Why are so many Hispanic students not meeting district standards?
3. With five first-grade teachers, why are students from one teacher's class far less prepared for second grade relative to students in the other four classrooms?
4. Why are African American students overrepresented in special education?
5. Why are pre-referral interventions unsuccessful 90% of the time?

Student-focused solutions were preferred by school systems because system problems are difficult to "diagnose" and system solutions can require great effort to implement. For example, placing 10 low-achieving English language learners in special education is easier for a school than analyzing curriculum deficits and implementing a comprehensive language and vocabulary program in the early grades. This statement is not intended to offend the hard-working and well-meaning individuals who work in the schools to help children learn; rather, it is our contention that many schools are overwhelmed with multiple problems and, by default, focus on quick and reactive solutions because they have not had the time, resources, or leadership to proactively identify and attempt to address problems before they become crises.

26.2 The Science of Education

The overuse of special education was one symptom of the much larger question faced by schools: How can schools most effectively assist low-achieving students? Schools should provide students with solid research-based instruction every day and initiate and faithfully implement research-based interventions for those students who do not initially succeed. Frequent progress monitoring should be used to evaluate progress. Basically, these common-sense notions summarize what has come to be referred to as a three-tiered model or RTI.

Curiously, parts of this model have been around for at least 30 years. Not only were components of this model not used, they were an anathema in education in the 1980s and 1990s. The idea of evidence-based core instruction that is effective for *all* students was well known. Project Follow-Through, which remains the single largest educational research project of all time, clearly established the superiority of direct instruction over other models examined (Carnine, 2002). Beyond a failure to embrace something that was shown to work, educators and administrators seemed to dislike it so intensely that it was generally discounted despite the efficacy data demonstrating that it was a powerfully effective program (Carnine, 2000). However, students who were given direct instruction succeeded, especially those who were characterized as "difficult to teach" or low achieving. The success of direct instruction with students from poverty who lacked an academic background created an alternative to special education for poor students (Carnine, 2002).

If low achievement is the primary symptom used to trigger the process that results in a diagnosis of SLD *and* it is demonstrated that low achievement may be caused by factors other than SLD and that powerful instruction can change achievement profiles and even IQ estimates (Carnine, 2002), then diagnosis of SLD becomes an error-prone process indeed. Core instruction is obviously a key component for the problem of low achievement, and at least one strong option has existed for schools in the form of direct instruction. Beyond that, there was a research base on instructional principles that were fundamental for any type of instruction to be effective (e.g., opportunities to respond, feedback, practice).

Similarly, procedures such as universal screening in reading and mathematics were available before CBM was "invented." For example, the work of Ogden Lindsley and his precision teaching called for the direct measurement of reading using oral reading fluency probes. Lindsley was a student of B. F. Skinner, and reading and math were behaviors for Skinner. Teaching those behaviors required drafting a task analysis of the skill and then designing instruction to facilitate initial acquisition and fluency of the required tasks. Dynamic indicators of basic early literacy skills, for example, was foreshadowed by at least 10 years by precision teaching proponents. Starlin (1971) developed a comprehensive task analysis of reading, including assessment, intervention, and progress monitoring procedures that included an analysis of letter sounds, letter blends, and words read correctly. Ray Beck and others, with the fabled Sacagawea project (Beck, 1979) in Montana, were using 1-min timed reading and math probes for universal screening and showed 20–40 percentile increases in achievement scores across schools using the universal screening and progress monitoring versus control schools.

Lentz and Shapiro (1986) summarized much of the existing assessment foundation for education and school psychology:

1. Assessment must reflect an evaluation of the behavior in the natural environment.
2. Assessment should be idiographic rather than nomothetic.
3. What is taught and expected to be learned should be what is tested.
4. The results of the assessment should be strongly related to planning interventions.
5. Assessment methods should be appropriate for continuous monitoring of student progress, so that intervention strategies can be altered as indicated.
6. Measures used need to be based upon empirical research and have adequate validity.
7. Measures should be useful in making many types of educational decision.

This article connected the fundamental practices of applied behavior analysis, precision teaching, and other fields to education and what was then the evolving field of CBM.

Another crucial component of the early RTI tool box that was also readily available in the 1970s and 1980s was intervention for struggling students. The literature was replete with research on effective strategies for struggling learners (cf., Shinn, Walker, and Stoner, 2002). Under 94-142, schools were directed to use pre-referral interventions. Many such interventions were available but do not appear to have been utilized or implemented in schools.

In addition to screening and intervention, progress monitoring has also been available. Again, the precision teaching group (Starlin, 1971) was generating aimlines and trendlines in the 1970s and had a rigorous system for evaluating intervention effectiveness and analyzing the conditions of learning. The work of Stan Deno in the area of progress monitoring was also becoming widely known. Deno adapted and improved some of the work of precision teaching (Deno and Mirkin, 1977).

Beyond the tools that were available, the development of those tools was guided by an epistemology that has also guided the development of STEEP. The epistemological differences are nowhere more evident than in the question of "Why are low students low?" This starts with the measurement process and especially the interpretations of the measurement. It is important to say that a student is low because there is a *discrepancy* between where the student is and where the student needs to be. Commonly, however, low scores on a test are presumed to mean a *deficiency*. This distinction remains present but more subtle, even among those who utilize CBM. In the field of CBM, two groups have emerged. One group's thinking is heavily grounded in "normal curve" logic. First, some property of the student is defined and measured. Intelligence is such a construct. Then intelligence test scores are collected from a large number of students. Following that, a line is drawn on the normal curve at two standard deviations below the mean. These students who score below the line are labeled as "deficient" (i.e., students with a mental disability). The reason they are deficient is that they are low on this construct. With CBM, one group generally views academic performance measures as a construct. This group collects data from a large number of students and those who are in the bottom $x\%$ are said to be "at risk" or deficient. In other words they apply classical measurement theory to CBM. The other group views academic performance such as oral reading fluency as a behavior. Behavior is considered to vary as a function of the student interacting with the learning environment. Importantly, the interpretation of CBM scores is relative to a meaningful functional standard rather than relative to a norm. Students are considered to need instruction if they fall below this meaningful standard, regardless of their normative position. By analogy, if there were a test of surgical ability for doctors, then the view of the first group is that those who score in the bottom 16% of the class fail. The view of the second group is that there is an absolute standard that surgeons must meet pertaining to the use of proper technique. It does not matter if one is in the top 5% on the test; if one cannot perform these specific behaviors, then that individual "needs instruction." Similarly, an individual may be in the bottom 1% and not require instruction because that person meets the appropriate standard. STEEP is a process that is grounded in a criterion-referenced approach where performance problems are defined as a discrepancy from a standard. The causes of the discrepancy are presumed to be a result of the student interacting with the environment (e.g., instruc-

tion, feedback, early literacy experiences) and not purely the result of student-centered problems.

26.3 The Origins of STEEP

Collectively, the tools noted above represented an answer to the question of "what" to do about the problem of low achievement. A central goal in developing STEEP was to bring the rigor of applied behavior analysis (ABA) to education. For any problem, the ABA approach called for an analysis of the problem involving rigorous data collection methods and then an analysis of instruction and other environmental conditions that could correct the problem.

In developing STEEP, the emphasis was not so much what needed to be done, but how. That is, there was less of a need to create *new* tools for the problem of low achievement than to identify methods that would assist schools to use the right tools (e.g., to strengthen general education rather than to overuse special education) and to use those tools correctly. It appeared that there was an abundance of good tools available and the problem was that those tools were not being utilized.

In considering whether the more rigorous procedures from ABA could be evaluated to determine whether they had value and applicability, two key problems were identified. The first problem was the ubiquitous use of self-report in all phases of the solution design and plan implementation process. Perhaps the primary determinant of referral was a series of meetings of the school-based team. At these meetings, decisions were made almost exclusively based on teacher self-report. The student was presumed to have a problem because *someone said so*. Based upon teacher self-report, a pre-referral intervention was implemented. The intervention was presumed to have been implemented with fidelity *because someone said so*. Based upon teacher self-report, intervention data were considered reliable and were used for decision-making. And invariably the intervention was found to be ineffective *because someone said so*. In developing STEEP, the interest was in evaluating the utility of the more direct assessment methods deriving out of ABA instead of, or in addition to, self-report. This work benefited immensely not only from those who were using direct measurement procedures, but also from those who were were using very sophisticated functional analysis processes to analyzing academic behaviors (Daly, Martens, Hamler, Dool, and Eckert, 1999). The second problem addressed in a series of studies was implementation fidelity (Noell et al., 2000; Witt, Noell, LaFleur, and Mortenson, 1997) . Research and anecdotal observations revealed that there was a surprising but pervasive and consistent lack of fidelity in the implementation of procedures and processes surrounding the assistance provided to low-achieving students.

Both of the above problems led to referral; and, once referral was made, placement was inevitable. STEEP initially evolved out of the interest in the first problem, and some of the procedures that eventually found their way into STEEP were called problem validation screening (PVS). The purpose of this process was to validate that a referred student was truly exhibiting a problem that merited intervention. Some of the research reviewed below pertains to PVS. The issue of implementation fidelity and the research on that topic has also found its way into STEEP because STEEP training procedures, the intervention implementation protocol, and the management of the process in schools are built around what is known about implementation fidelity and the use of performance management, including training, antecedent control, monitoring, and feedback.

An overriding principle guiding the development of STEEP is that it is not enough to find something that "works"; instead, what is developed must function well in all types of school. Many methods will be effective in a well-funded suburban district with the full support of university research assistants. However, what is most needed are tools that can be utilized by low-capacity schools with the greatest need.

This research approach led to a variety of collaborative projects with all types of schools. For instance, one project included taking responsibility for second-grade math instruction across an entire grade within a school where 99% of the students were African American and 100% received free and reduced lunch. The purpose of this particular project was to provide evidence that the presence of low achievement is not pathognomonic for learning disability. Whereas the project produced significant improvement in state test scores for the students, the school did not continue the program the next year. This experience influenced future work related to developing procedures that build local capacity and are sustainable by systems over time.

Other collaborative projects with school districts did take hold and became independently successful. For instance, a collaborative endeavor with St. Charles Parish in Louisiana became known as the PAM project, which incorporated the direct measurement of student performance as a means of problem validation. The process in that district has continued to evolve. Another success was a collaboration with a group headed by Louisiana Region 7 Service Center that included the efforts of Louisiana State University Health Sciences Center Shreveport, Louisiana State University Shreveport, Region 7 Services Center, Caddo Parish schools, and DeSoto Parish schools. The approach used incorporated problem validation, but was much broader. This effort also evolved into an independent effort which was eventually called PRISM (Pyramid of Research-based Instructional Supports Model). Similarly, Plaquemine's Parish school district in Louisiana began using STEEP problem validation procedures, then subsequently modified the process and included other elements and have called their effort the Plaquemine Screening System. Initially, spin-off-type efforts were fostered and encouraged as part of a series of efforts to disseminate research-based practices in the state of Louisiana. Through these collaborative projects, much was learned about the performance management of district conversion from the "old" way to the "new" way. It became clear that hard work was required when the initial change was introduced. This understanding subsequently led to the development of materials and procedures that simplify system response requirements and encourage fidelity to the process.

26.4 Review of Research

STEEP is a program that includes several components (e.g., screening, intervention, progress monitoring). In creating or selecting components for the process, there were two fundamental criteria related to efficacy and fidelity. First, there was a need to have a research basis for every component. Second, each component and the components as a whole needed to be simple. A basic test of the research basis for anything is to have a data-based answer for the question, "How do you *know*?" For example, when asked, "How do you know that a 1-min oral reading sample is valid for the purpose of identifying students who may need intervention?" an evidence-based response was provided. Ongoing evaluation of the "fidelity factor" was more subjective. It is important that professionals implement procedures (i.e., assessments, decisions, and interventions) with fidelity. Research on intervention fidelity and acceptability indicated that fidelity could be enhanced by minimizing the effort and complexity of procedures. There has been a constant and necessary tension between the guiding principles inherent in the "research factor" and "fidelity factor." It is easier to have allegiance to one of these factors or the other, *but not to both*. Simply put, the objective is to establish components that are both simple and supported by research.

Furthermore, it is recognized that merely because each part has its own research base does not mean the system as a whole would produce meaningful outcomes for students. Also, if the system was comprised of too many components, then the fidelity of the system likely would be reduced. Therefore, in any multicomponent system (e.g., any comprehensive RTI system), it was important that not only each "part" of the system be effective, but, in addition, that the system as a whole should be effective. Hence, the process as a whole has also been evaluated with respect to outcomes that might be expected from RTI systems (e.g., improved achievement and reduced referrals). The latter is important. Merely because one component is research based does not mean that the complete system can also be considered research based. In describing the research base for STEEP, the information will be divided into (a) the research support for the program as a "whole" integrated process and (b) the research support for the individual components.

Over the last several years the term "research based" has lost its meaning because commercial publishers have overused the term. When we use the term we will refer to procedures that have been directly tested in the literature. Also reported here are studies that directly evaluated STEEP or STEEP components and were published in peer-reviewed journals. For example, CBM is a tool which is research based because it has been extensively evaluated within the literature. Hence, CBM within STEEP is "research based." In reading, STEEP utilizes one CBM probe, not the three that are commonly done within CBM. This component has been directly evaluated in peer-reviewed research. The latter type of research is a stronger form of research support.

26.5 Research on the Model as a Whole

Researchers have investigated and evaluated the STEEP model as a whole. This type of research is needed because it is possible to select the very best screening procedures, the very best progress monitoring procedures, and the best research-based intervention and still not produce good outcomes because the various components do not work well together to produce good academic outcomes for students.

26.5.1 Improving Referral Accuracy

As noted above, STEEP initially began as a method for problem validation. New methodological ground was broken in studying referral accuracy (VanDerHeyden, Witt, and Naquin, 2003). A major problem in the study of referral accuracy is knowing whether a referral is truly accurate or not. For example, if a teacher makes a referral of a student, how does one know if the referred child truly has a problem or if the teacher made an inaccurate judgment or false positive error (i.e., teacher indicated the student had a problem when in actuality the student did not have a problem)? Whereas it is tempting to use the actual referral as the standard, placement is often affected not only by test scores, but also by team deliberations. The deliberations would include input from the teacher. Hence, placement may not be a clean and unbiased indicator of "true" need. VanDerHeyden et al. (2003) studied students in the southeastern USA and used a comprehensive assessment and intervention process to establish a criterion against which to determine whether a child truly did or did not have an academic problem in reading or mathematics. Importantly, to be labeled a true positive, students were required to meet a definition of low achievement; in addition, students did not respond to a research-based intervention. The findings indicated that teacher referral was accurate 19% of the time in 406 cases, whereas the

STEEP process was accurate in 52% of the cases. Given that teacher referral is so important in a traditional problem-solving model, the researchers concluded that data-based decision-making involving universal screening and basic functional assessment techniques should play an important role in determining who needs assistance. In particular, given the finding that teacher referral was accurate less than 20% of the time and given the importance assigned to teacher judgment, it seemed important to take a closer look at a broader range of variables. In a related study, VanDerHeyden and Witt (2005) found that classroom context significantly and negatively affected the accuracy of teacher referral. That is, teachers were less accurate at identifying students who did and did not have a problem in both low-achieving and high-achieving classrooms (compared with "normally" achieving classrooms), whereas the STEEP process maintained or achieved even greater accuracy across those contexts.

More recently, VanDerHeyden et al. (in press) studied students in the southwestern USA and showed reductions in referrals and improvements in achievement as STEEP was sequentially introduced across five schools (one by one) within one district. They also found that the quality of the referral increased. That is, students who did not respond to the STEEP program were more likely to qualify for special education, but fewer students were referred. The program had a generally positive effect with respect to disproportionality in terms of sex and language proficiency. The goal of RTI is to improve achievement. However, as a result of screening and improved achievement, the need for special education is reduced. With respect to reducing referrals, STEEP increases the accuracy of referrals and it improves achievement (VanDerHeyden and Witt, 2005).

26.5.2 Overidentification and Disproportionality

VanDerHeyden and Witt (2005) examined the effect of STEEP in situations where there were either many high-achieving students or many low-achieving students. The findings indicated that teacher referral was markedly affected by the situation. For example, the "low" student in a high-achieving classroom tended to be referred even though the "low" student was still in the normal range. However, these students "stood out" to the teacher because they were low relative to high-performing peers. STEEP places an objective lens on the situation and is much more accurate regardless of context. A very interesting finding in this study was that minority children (who were primarily African American) were disproportionately represented as "low achievers" and fell into the bottom 16% of classes. However, the minority students were more likely to have rapid acceleration of learning when given a strong intervention. Specifically, with universal screening, more than half of the minority students in the school performed in the bottom 16% of their classes; however, following intervention, only 7% of the minority group failed to respond adequately to individual intervention. The researchers hypothesized that the quality of the intervention used may have been more in line with the needs of minority students than was their core curriculum.

26.5.3 Improving Achievement in General Education

VanDerHeyden and Burns (2005) found that STEEP intervention procedures produced statistically significant gains in mathematics performance for at-risk students. This study, along with VanDerHeyden et al. (2006), will be of interest to principals and teachers, because these studies show the importance and relevance of RTI to general education. VanDerHeyden and Burns found that CBM assessment and intervention produced significant achievement gains in mathematics and produced statistically significant improvements in state testing scores on the Stanford achievement test (SAT-9). RTI is best viewed as an instructional model, and these studies showed that RTI can produce gains for all students. A "side effect" of improved achievement is reduced need for special education and reduction of problems such as disproportionality. Disproportionality and overreferral are problems that are reduced when achievement is improved.

26.6 Research on the Components of STEEP

In addition to being evaluated as an integrated process, the various components of STEEP (screening, intervention, and progress monitoring) within the program have undergone separate testing. Each of the components will be discussed separately.

26.6.1 Universal Screening and Progress Monitoring

Universal screening and progress-monitoring procedures have undergone extensive testing by a large number of researchers. These procedures rely on CBM, a measurement approach that has been around for many years and for which hundreds of studies have supported its use in decision-making.

26.6.2 Readability

Each of the STEEP reading benchmark passages is written around words that are common for each grade level. The passages also contain no words that are uncommon for the grade level of the student. This step is taken to improve the match between the assessment and the words that students encounter daily at school. To determine high- and low-frequency words, the *Word Frequency Guide* (Zeno, 1995) was used. This database of words is based upon an analysis of 17 000 000 words from 60 500 samples that include textbooks, works of literature, and nonfiction. The database can be analyzed by grade to give common and uncommon words. For the lower grades, words with frequencies below 100 in 100 000 words were not used in the passages. For the upper grades, frequencies below 50 words in 100 000 words were not included in the passages. After the passages were written, they were evaluated using an appropriate readability formula.

Early on in the development of STEEP, passages were written based upon readability alone. At one point there was concern that readability may not be the best method to level a passage, and so the interest became the study of readability formulas. Thus, a study was initiated in which the accuracy of many different methods for estimating passage readability was evaluated (Ardoin, Suldo, Witt, Aldrich, and McDonald, 2005). The research indicated that many readability methods are not very accurate. STEEP continues to use readability in constructing passages; however, readability has been bolstered using the methods described above. Scholars continue to

look for improved methods for leveling a reading passage. The use of a readability formula is unlikely ever to yield an accurate estimate for any *one* student. This is because readability is more or less a norm-referenced concept. In general, most fourth-grade students can read the word "horse." However, a particular student may have difficulty with that word. Therefore, passages leveled with a readability formula will be appropriate "in general," but there will be some individual differences between students.

26.6.3 Three versus One Benchmark Probe

With universal screening, the most common CBM method is to administer three benchmark probes to each student and calculate a median score. With STEEP, only one benchmark probe is used. This, combined with more efficient administration procedures, means that STEEP requires less than one-third the time of the typical CBM procedure. However, the question is, do you still get valid results using only one probe? VanDerHeyden et al. (2003) investigated the stability of scores across two trials of CBM for reading and math and found that student rank-order remained remarkably stable across trials but that there was a significant improvement on average for all students on the second trial. These authors then examined the correspondence between scores on the first trial and a median score obtained using the three trials and a median score for students. They found that screening decisions based on a single trial corresponded with decisions based on median scores. A follow-up study by Ardoin, Suldo, Witt, and McDonald (2004) indicated that one probe yielded equivalent results to three probes.

STEEP, contrary to other CBM-based systems, uses three probes for progress monitoring. The use of three probes derives from studies (e.g., Poncy, Skinner, and Axtell, 2005) indicating that the standard error of measurement for CBM reading probes can range from 4 to 18 words correct per minute. If the standard error markedly exceeds the expected rate of progress during progress monitoring, then, by inference, one probe is not sufficient for progress monitoring. One probe results in too much "bounce" in the data, and this is very problematic when intervening and making important decisions about progress in the context of RTI. STEEP, therefore, incorporates three probes for progress monitoring. This is an area where research is needed to specifically address the number of trials needed to make decisions about student progress.

26.6.4 Can't Do/Won't Do Assessment

The can't do/won't do assessment has also undergone research and evaluation. Peer-reviewed published research has appeared in scholarly journals to support its use (sometimes under the term skill/performance deficit assessment). Duhon et al. (2004) used functional academic assessment procedures to directly test the effects of incentives on performance and subsequently validated the assessment by providing intervention based on the assessment data. In each case, Duhon et al. found that brief functional analysis procedures correctly identified the most effective intervention to use in all cases. An earlier study by Noell et al. (1998) yielded similar results. It should be mentioned that the can't do/won't do procedure cannot rule out unequivocally a "won't do" problem. Therefore, implementers may assume that the student has a skill problem when, in fact, the student has a performance problem and simply was not interested in the incentive offered. The logic and limits of the scientific method preclude knowing with certainty that something, such as a performance deficit, does not exist. However, use of the procedure has been shown to be valuable as part of a package of assessment activities to identify children for whom adjustments to the general education environment will improve instructional outcomes.

26.6.5 Intervention Selection

Within RTI research through the 1990s, two basic approaches were identified (Fuchs, Mock, Morgan, and Young, 2003): the problem-solving approach and the standard-protocol model. As described by Fuchs et al., the problem-solving model calls on the team, through discussion and brainstorming, to identify student needs and to determine an appropriate intervention. With the standard-protocol model, each step (e.g., identifying students in need of intervention, determining which intervention they need and whether the intervention is effective) is guided by research-based decision rules. Using research to guide decisions means that consultants can connect an academic problem with an intervention that *has been shown* to be effective for that problem. This increases the likelihood that the correct intervention is matched with each problem. STEEP (and many models that have reported data since 2000) uses a hybridized approach that combines the merits of problem-solving assessment and standard-protocol procedures. STEEP is a hybridized model that uses a standard-protocol method at all stages with associated integrity checks (i.e., components attributed to standard-protocol approaches) *and* collects individual child data up-front to select the "right" intervention, uses frequent progress monitoring to troubleshoot the intervention, and links the resulting data to team decision-making to inform referral and eligibility decisions (i.e., components attributed to problem-solving approaches). STEEP's standard-protocol method uses data to recommend a specific intervention to match the student's unique needs.

To implement a standard protocol for intervention selection, one needs an instructional model, an assessment that determines student status within the instructional model, and research showing that students with a specific status in the instructional model improve more with specific interventions and improve less or not at all with other interventions. STEEP's intervention selection is based upon an instructional model called the Instructional Hierarchy (Haring, Lovitt, Eaton, and Hanson, 1978). The research in support of the STEEP standard protocol is based upon work conducted by Jones and Wickstrom (2002) and by Daly et al. (1999) showing that the outcomes are better when interventions are matched to a student level within the instructional hierarchy than when interventions are not matched. Similarly, Duhon (2006) found that use of the intervention indicated by the standard protocol was markedly superior to using an intervention that was not matched or was contraindicated by the protocol. The practical utility of using standard approaches to intervention is that it simplifies the decision-making process that must occur at school to get an effective intervention in place, and simplifies the logistics of implementing interventions (i.e., teams do not have to creatively assemble new interventions and intervention materials each time an intervention is needed). These simplifications reduce errors in implementation.

26.7 Future Directions

Whereas the research for major components of the STEEP model has come along considerably, there is work to be done. Below is a list of topics that require investigation.

1. *Instructional placement standards.* STEEP has utilized the instructional placement standards advanced by Deno and Mirkin (1977) as a basis for identifying students who need intervention. Recently, Burns and VanDerHeyden and Jiban (2006) have used a methodology that is promising for the purpose of setting standards for students needing intervention in mathematics. This method, as well as others, may be explored in the future.

2. *Standard protocol and problem solving.* There are some logical combinations of the standard protocol and what is known as the problem-solving model. Good problem-solving is analogous to rule-governed behavior. That is, professionals follow rules derived from science. The standard-protocol approach is simply making those rules more explicit. Research is needed to explore discrete outcomes, such as intervention selection, conducted via a standard protocol or a problem-solving model.

3. *The efficiency of screening.* Currently, all students are screened three times per year. In average- to high-achieving schools, most students perform adequately. Arguably, it is not necessary to screen a student more than once per year if they are not at risk, especially after third grade. However, research is needed to more definitively determine error rates if only one screening per year is used or if only students who perform poorly on the state test should be screened.

4. *Decision rules.* RTI requires many decisions. There is a need for more research to provide a foundation for more definitive decision rules regarding issues such as expected rates of progress, duration of interventions of various types, frequency of intervention, and intensity of intervention (and how to measure and increase intensity). Very preliminary data were reported by VanDerHeyden, Witt, and Barnett (2005), who detailed a plan of research questions requiring investigation related to RTI.

5. *Middle- and high-school screening and progress monitoring.* There is a growing demand for RTI services at the middle and high school levels. However, the research pertaining to all phases of RTI is less advanced than for elementary school students. Additional research is needed.

6. *Preschool screening and progress monitoring.* Similarly, there is perhaps an even stronger need for research with preschool students.

It is an exciting time for researchers who are eager to see their findings inform actual practices in real schools. Never before has there been such impetus and opportunity to bring data to bear upon everyday instructional practices in classrooms. RTI is a science of decision-making whose meaning is evaluated by its use and effect on child and system outcomes. In this regard, researchers have an opportunity to operationalize and examine procedures that may make a difference in schools. STEEP is an example of an operationalized RTI model that has been extensively researched and widely field-tested. It has been an honor to work among educators in schools to develop and build the procedures associated with STEEP. It has been incredibly fulfilling to be part of a process that has resulted in better learning and more equitable identification in schools. Future studies are on the horizon, and nearly all are geared to improving the efficiency and effectiveness in using RTI in schools.

References

Ardoin, S. P., Suldo, S., Witt, J. C., & McDonald, E. (2004). Accuracy of readability estimates' predictions of CBM performance. *School Psychology Review, 33,* 218–233.

Beck, R. (1979). Report for the Office of Education joint dissemination review panel. Great Falls, Montana: Precision Teaching Project.

Burns, M. K., VanDerHeyden, A. M. & Jiban C. (2006). Assessing the instructional level for mathematics: a comparison of methods. *School Psychology Review, 135,* 401–418.

Carnine, D. (2000). Why education experts resist effective practices (and what it would take to make education more like medicine). Retrieved March 16, 2004, from http://www.edexcellence.net/foundation/publication/publication.cfm?id=46.

Daly III, E. J., Martens, B. K., Hamler, K. R., Dool, E. J., & Eckert, T. L. (1999). A brief experimental analysis for identifying instructional components needed to improve oral reading fluency. *Journal of Applied Behavior Analysis, 32,* 83–94.

Deno, S. L. & Mirkin, P. K. (1977). *Data-Based Program Modification: A Manual.* Reston, VA: Council for Exceptional Children.

Duhon, G. J. (2006). A standard protocol for selecting an appropriate intervention: evaluating the generalizability component of construct validity for the instructional hierarchy by examining the interchangeability of intervention components. *School Psychology Review* Submitted for publication.

Duhon. G. J., Noell. G. H., Witt J. C., Freeland. J. T., Dufrene. B. A., & Gilbertson, D. N. (2004). Identifying academic skills and performance deficits: the experimental analysis of brief assessments of academic skills. *School Psychology Review, 33,* 429–443.

Fuchs, D., Mock, D., Morgan, P. L., & Young, C. L. (2003). Responsiveness-to-intervention: definitions, evidence, and implications for the learning disabilities construct. *Learning Disabilities Research & Practice, 18,* 157–171.

Haring, N. G., Lovitt, T. C., Eaton, M. D., & Hansen, C. L. (1978). *The Fourth R: Research in the Classroom.* Columbus, OH: Merrill.

Jones, K. M. & Wickstrom, K. F. (2002). Done in sixty seconds: further analysis of the brief assessment model for academic problems. *School Psychology Review, 31,* 554–568.

Lentz, F. E. & Shapiro, E. S. (1986). Functional assessment of the academic environment. *School Psychology Review, 15,* 346–357.

NASDSE (2005). *Response to Intervention: Policy Considerations and Implementation.* Washington, DC: National Association of State Directors of Special Education.

Noell, G. H., Gansle, K. A., Witt, J. C., Whitmarsh, E. L., Freeland, J. T., LeFleur, L. H., et al. (1998). Effects of contingent reward and instruction on oral reading performance at differing levels of passage difficulty. *Journal of Applied Behavior Analysis, 31,* 659–664.

Noell, G. H., Witt, J. C., LaFleur, L. H., Mortenson, B. P., Ranier, D. D., & LeVelle, J. (2000). Increasing intervention implementation in general education following consultation: a comparison of two follow-up strategies. *Journal of Applied Behavior Analysis, 33,* 271–284.

Poncy, B., Skinner, C., & Axtell. P. (2005). An investigation of the reliability and standard error of measurement of words read correctly per minute using curriculum-based measurement. *Journal of Psychoeducational Assessment, 23,* 326–338.

Shinn, M. R., Walker, H. M., & Stoner, G. (Eds.) (2002). *Interventions for Academic and Behavior Problems II: Preventive and Remedial Approaches.* Bethesda, MD: National Association of School Psychologists.

Starlin, C. (1971). Evaluating progress towards reading proficiency. In B. Bateman (Ed.), *Learning Disorders,* vol. IV. Seattle: Special Child Publications.

VanDerHeyden, A. M. & Burns, M. K. (2005). Using curriculum-based assessment and curriculum-based measurement to guide elementary mathematics instruction: effect on individual and group accountability scores. *Assessment for Effective Intervention, 30,* 15–31.

VanDerHeyden, A. M. & Witt, J. C. (2005). Quantifying the context of assessment: Capturing the effect of base rates on teacher referral and a problem-solving model of identification. *School Psychology Review, 34,* 161–183.

VanDerHeyden, A. M., Witt, J. C., & Barnett, D. A. (2005). The emergence and possible futures of response to intervention. *Journal of Psychoeducational Assessment, 23,* 339–361.

VanDerHeyden, A. M., Witt, J. C., & Naquin, G. (2003). Development and validation of a process for screening referrals to special education. *School Psychology Review, 32,* 204–227.

VanDerHeyden, A. M., Witt, J. C., Naquin, G., & Noell, G. (2001). The reliability and validity of curriculum-based measurement readiness probes for kindergarten students. *School Psychology Review, 30,* 363–382.

Witt, J. C., Noell, G. H., LaFleur, L. H., & Mortenson, B. P. (1997). Teacher use of interventions in general education settings: measurement and analysis of the independent variable. *Journal of Applied Behavior Analysis, 30,* 693–696.

Zeno, S. (Ed.) (1995). *The Educator's Word Frequency Guide.* Brewster, NJ: Touchstone Applied Science Associates.

27
Moving from a Model Demonstration Project to a Statewide Initiative in Michigan: Lessons Learned from Merging Research-Practice Agendas to Address Reading and Behavior

Ruth A. Ervin, Elizabeth Schaughency, Steven D. Goodman, Margaret T. McGlinchey, and Amy Matthews

Ruth A. Ervin, PhD, is an Associate Professor of School Psychology and Special Education at University of British Columbia, Vancouver, Canada. ruth.ervin@ubc.ca
Elizabeth Schaughency, PhD, is a Senior Lecturer in the Department of Psychology at University of Otago, Dunedin, New Zealand. schaughe@psy.otago.ac.nz
Steven D. Goodman is a Teacher Consultant at the Ottawa Area Intermediate School District, Holland, Michigan. sgoodman@oaisd.org
Margaret T. McGlinchey is an Educational Consultant at Kalamazoo Regional Educational Service Agency, Kalamazoo Michigan. mmcglinc@kresanet.org
Amy Matthews, PhD, is an Associate Professor of Psychology at Grand Valley State University, Allandale, Michigan. matthewa@gvsu.edu

This chapter describes how lessons learned from attempting to facilitate adoption of separate empirically derived practices, namely functional assessment and curriculum-based measurement (CBM), evolved into more promising and systematic capacity building at the school, district, county, and state level. More specifically, the chapter describes the evolution of a model demonstration project into a statewide dissemination/replication project in Michigan. The initial federally funded model demonstration project involved four elementary schools across four school districts, representing different communities with differing demographic characteristics (Ervin, Schaughency, Goodman, McGlinchey, and Matthews, 2006). Recognizing that many school reform efforts fail, the preliminary project incorporated features found to be successful in developing school-wide behavioral and academic support programs to implement (and sustain) evidenced-based practice and decisions. Promotion of visibility of the model demonstration project conveyed its compatibility with global policies and initiatives at the federal (e.g., passage of No Child Left Behind, Reading First) and state level (e.g., Michigan Positive Behavioral Support Initiative), enhanced political support, and created momentum for expanding the project to other schools across the state. The initial model demonstration project focused on the development and refinement of a prototype for addressing reading and behavior school-wide, and the logical extension of this work at the state level involved widespread "scaling up" (Adelman and Taylor, 1997) or replication of this prototype.

The sections that follow describe how the initial project evolved and how efforts are currently underway to replicate effects in many schools across the state. The model demonstration project is described herein in the past tense; however, it should be noted that, subsequent to the termination of grant support and funding in December of 2005, the schools in the project sustained adopted project activities into the 2005–2006 school year in which this chapter was written. Further, the state replication project is ongoing and expanding and, therefore, is described in the present tense. The following begins with background information regarding local needs and conditions that served as catalysts for both projects. Next, a rationale for the school-wide reading/behavior approaches adopted in these systems-change projects is provided, followed by a description of the underlying principles and goals of the approach, empirically derived methods for capacity building and sustainability embedded within these projects, their course, and preliminary evaluation data. The chapter concludes with discussions of preliminary student outcomes, indicators of increased capacity and sustainability, lessons learned, and implications for practitioners and practitioner–researcher partnerships.

27.1 Background Regarding Local Needs

Carnine (1999) called for a campaign to move research into practice, highlighting the urgency to align research and practice agendas to target important, visible problems of interest to a broad number of stakeholders and which affect the larger community (e.g., literacy, school violence). The initiation of efforts in Michigan to merge research and practice agendas to build capacity for addressing reading and behavior school wide coincided with this call. More specifically, in 1999, a core team (i.e., the authors of this chapter) comprised of school-based practitioners and university trainers was formed in the southwest region of Michigan. This core team, frustrated with failed attempts to promote the sustained use of various evidence-based practices (e.g., functional assessment, data-based decision-making, CBM) in schools, embarked on a mission to work collaboratively to develop and implement a replicable model for promoting the sustained use of a data-informed problem-solving approach to build schools' capacity to promote academic and behavioral competence. *Successful collaboration and merging of research-practice agendas* focused on *targeting important issues of literacy and school violence* formed the foundation for systemic reform efforts in Michigan. Further, it appears that a combination of global and local conditions and infrastructures that aligned with project

aims created conditions of readiness for successful systemic change (Fullan, 2000). Thus, these factors are highlighted as important background issues or contextual factors hypothesized to set the stage for sustainable and portable adoption of school-wide approaches to addressing reading and behavior in Michigan.

27.1.1 Successful Collaboration and Targeting Important Problems

According to Adelman and Taylor (2006, p. 297), "the aim [of collaboration] is to build potent, synergistic, *working* relationships, not simply to establish positive connections." There were five members of the initial core team, including two school practitioners and three university faculty members. Three team members (i.e., Team Member 1, 2, 3) were located in close proximity to one county regional school area from which three schools (School A, B, C) were selected for participation and two team members (i.e., Team Member 4 and 5) were located in close proximity to a second county regional school area from which a fourth school (School D) was selected for participation.

Team Member 1 was a PhD-level Special Education Consultant who was working for a county regional service agency that served three of the participating schools in the project. He had worked in the district for 17 years in a variety of capacities (e.g., teacher, teacher consultant, behavioral consultant) and had been working for some time to train school personnel to use functional assessment and data-based decision-making in the school settings. In addition to conducting trainings in positive behavioral support (PBS), his efforts had focused on his individual caseload and working with special education teachers on using formative data collection to guide instructional decision-making.

Team Member 2 was a clinical psychologist and university faculty member at a comprehensive regional university located in close proximity to the county regional service agency that served Schools A, B, and C. She began her research career studying disruptive behavior disorders from a clinical perspective, leading to the recognition of the importance of early school experience for the developmental outcomes of this population. Over her career, she became increasingly involved in in-service and pre-service professional development with a variety of child-serving professionals (e.g., general and special educators, school psychologists, early childhood educators). Prior to participation in this project, her experience with successful implementation of grant-supported practice innovations across settings with differential sustained adoption led to an appreciation of the role that systemic and organizational factors may play in professionals' capacity for integrating new empirically based practices in their work and a professional interest in supporting this process.

Team Member 3 was a PhD-level clinical psychologist who, when the project began, was teaching classes in childhood disorders and applied behavior analysis at the same local university as Team Member 2. She also offered practicum experiences in the area of developmental disabilities and was coordinating a 4-year statewide autism training and resource grant. The autism project involved a significant level of systems change and professional development in school systems across the state. As part of the autism project, this team member had developed professional training activities in the areas of teaming and collaboration, coaching and problem solving, positive behavior support, effective educational supports for students with autism, and early intervention, among others.

Team Member 4 was a PhD-level school psychologist who worked within the county regional service agency that served School D. She had worked in this capacity at an urban school district for 17 years. Team Member 4 had been collecting CBM data and attempting to gain support in using this information to inform instructional decision-making for a period of 7 years prior to the start of this project. Her efforts included preliminary norming of oral reading fluency data at a district level and analyses of the relationship between these data and performance on statewide fourth-grade assessments. These efforts resulted in county and state funding to support training of teachers and school psychologists in CBM, but had not yet resulted in sustained use of these measures at the school and classroom level. In addition to her work at the district level, this team member contributed to preparation of school psychologists and continued education of teachers and special educators at a local university.

Team Member 5 was a university faculty member and researcher in school psychology who had

focused her efforts on the use of a data-driven problem-solving approach (including functional assessment and CBM) to address the needs of students with severe behavior problems in general education settings. Efforts to address these issues from a tertiary prevention approach led this team member to shift her attention to the need to address issues in a more proactive fashion via primary and secondary prevention efforts, team building, and systems change.

Together, core team members (i.e., school personnel and university researchers) developed the goals and objectives of the reading and behavior model demonstration project. In doing so, they sought input from their colleagues at the university level (e.g., conversations with scholars in the field of systems change and school-wide approaches to reading and behavior, literature reviews in the areas of reading, behavior, and systems change) and at the school practitioner level (e.g., general and special education teachers, school psychologists, administrators, parents).

In recognition of her efforts to promote systematic use of CBM data to identify need for reading support, during the 2002–2003 school year Team Member 4 was invited to attend the annual Innovations in Education Conference. The aim of this annual invited conference is to provide an opportunity for states working to develop a school-level service delivery system to address needs of all students to share progress, challenges, and solutions. Team Member 4 formed a group to represent the state of Michigan at the conference. To promote visibility of project efforts, Team Members 4, 5 (university-based partner), and 1 (other practitioner) attended the conference with seven additional education stakeholders. Among these individuals were the Director and Deputy Director of Michigan Office of Special Education and Early Intervention Services, an Administrator for Monitoring, Compliance and Data Collection, two school psychologists, a curriculum director, and supervisor of Title I and special education programs.

This shared experience served to increase political support for extension of model demonstration project activities and contributed to a request for proposals to scale up project activities to schools across the state (Ervin et al., 2006). Team Members 1 and 4 subsequently extended their collaboration to become members of the core team for the state project.

They joined with another school practitioner who was actively involved with PBS activities being implemented through another county service agency elsewhere in the state. This team was augmented by administrators and specialists from regional service areas with input from an advisory team that consisted of parents of children with disabilities, as well as national experts in school-wide PBS, developing literacy, and successful systems change toward noncategorical service delivery. Together, they developed a successful proposal for expanding school-wide approaches across the state.

27.1.2 Alignment with Global and Local Infrastructures in Michigan

Global infrastructure provides the policy, legal, and financial framework necessary to facilitate systemic reform, and local infrastructure provides a useful translation of the global principles and establishes networks of support for local agency personnel who are responsible for implementing the innovative practices (Grimes, Kurns, and Tilly, 2006). The project focus was on building schools' capacity to address reading and behavior aligned with state leadership vision and policies in Michigan. In 2000, the Director of the Office of Special Education and Early Intervention Services in Michigan described the 1997 reauthorization of the *Individuals with Disabilities Education Act* (IDEA) as marking a revolution in the theory and practice of behavior intervention by mandating the inclusion of functionally based PBS for students with disabilities (Thompson, 2000). She also commented, however, that IDEA did not prescribe how this support was to be provided (Thompson, 2000). In response, the state of Michigan set out to develop an umbrella framework for understanding the concept of PBS and guiding its implementation in Michigan schools as part of its State Improvement Plan/State Improvement Grant (SIP/SIG; Michigan Department of Education, 2000—hereafter referred to as *Executive Summary*).

Michigan's SIP/SIG aimed to build capacity for schools to provide safe and productive learning environments via information development, awareness and dissemination activities, and opportunities for further learning for Michigan educators. Although identifying IDEA as the setting event for their development, the documents developed by the SIP/SIG moved beyond a special education umbrella by stating that the PBS principles presented were not limited to students who had been determined to be eligible for special education services (Michigan Department of Education, 2000b—hereafter referred to as *Overview Document*). Instead, Michigan's *Executive Summary* described pre-referral PBS as a discretionary "promising practice" for *all* students, with or without disabilities. In other words, the state's leadership was arguing for a prevention focus to proactively address the needs of all students, not just those students with identified disabilities.

To accommodate a multi-leveled public health orientation that focuses on all students from a prevention standpoint, however, service delivery models developed with an individual student focus, such as special education, need re-engineering (Grimes et al., 2006). Adoption of pre-referral interventions and school-wide approaches to prevention implies that capacity exists to provide pre-referral supports to students who have not been determined eligible for special education. Unfortunately, existing systems may not readily allow for such changes to take place without altering infrastructure. Within Michigan, for example, some special services personnel members (e.g., resource teachers, school psychologists), who were equipped with potential expertise to assist in the delivery of these pre-referral and prevention-oriented services, perceived that their mandate was to only serve students eligible for special education. In some districts, in fact, this perception was also held by the district leadership and included in policy statements. Thus, in Michigan, as in other states considering the use of a preventative problem-solving approach to addressing learning and behavior, the need existed to either redefine professional roles to break down traditional general education–special education organizational boundaries (Grimes et al., 2006) and/or to develop other resources to build capacity for provision of services outside of special education (Atkins, Graczyk, Frazier, and Abdul-Abil, 2003). State and local leadership within model demonstration project schools and districts supported redefining roles and linking services across special and general education to varying degrees. The alignment of this project's goals with perceptions of district leaders at participating schools and with state leadership, when present, helped facilitate sustained adoption and replication of project activities within and across schools.

Moreover, although "pre-referral" interventions are often described as "alternative delivery systems," they retain focus on individual students who are experiencing difficulties (Strein, Hoagwood, and Cohn, 2003). Achieving a multi-leveled public health approach to service delivery involves broadening focus from reactive, individually oriented problem-solving to proactive, population-level (e.g., school) service delivery (Strein et al., 2003), with pre-referral interventions along a continuum of instructional and intervention strategies (e.g., Coyne, Kame'enui, and Simmons, 2004; Horner, Sugai, Todd, and Lewis-Palmer, 2005). Facilitating systematic, rather than ad hoc, implementation of pre-referral interventions entails consideration of local infrastructure, or systems, to support practice (Grimes et al., 2006; Horner et al., 2005).

In Michigan, as elsewhere, schools vary in community characteristics, resources, and challenges (Harris, 2006; Kozol, 2005; US Department of Education, 2000–2001, 2005). Therefore, an adaptive approach, in which strategies are tailored to meet local needs, is indicated (Schaughency and Ervin, 2006). The projects focus on building capacity to address reading and behavior issues via development of a preventative, data-informed, problem-solving approach. By carefully attending to efficient allocation and utilization of school resources and focus on the establishment of systems and networks to support projects locally, the aim is to aid in the development of *local infrastructures* to sustain adoption of new practices in targeted Michigan schools.

27.2 Rationale and Underlying Principles of the Approach

It was desirable to develop an approach that was comprehensive, provided a spectrum of services to meet the needs of *all* students, and allowed for adaptations to meet local circumstances (Graczyk, Domitrovich, and Zins, 2003). The rationale for integrating school-wide reading and behavior targets stemmed from a synthesis of research on the development of antisocial behavior, reading difficulties, their intervention, and the potentially more powerful preventive effects of combined approaches (Ervin

et al., 2006). The following overarching principles provide the framework for this work:

1. The research literature provides clues as to the developmental course of learning and behavioral difficulties, windows of opportunities for intervention, and evidenced-based practices (Hunter, 2003; National Reading Panel, 2000; Power, 2003; Walker, Ramsey, and Gresham, 2004).
2. A public health prevention orientation provides a useful, and efficient approach for developing a systematic continuum of academic and behavioral supports and interventions (Coyne et al., 2004; Hunter, 2003).
3. Site-specific development and capacity building are important for socially valid and efficient allocation of resources and sustainability (Adelman and Taylor, 2003; Graczyk et al., 2003; Schaughency and Ervin, 2006).
4. Recognizing that "more" is not necessarily "better" and that fragmented, piecemeal programs are less likely to be effective and maintained (Adelman and Taylor, 2006; Grimes et al., 2006), coordination of project activities with ongoing local, state, and national initiatives and priorities is important.
5. Evidenced-based problem solving, linking assessment to intervention and using systematic formative evaluation to subsequently refine intervention, improves efficiency and effectiveness of intervention efforts (cf., Campbell, 1988; Elliott and Fuchs, 1997; Fuchs and Fuchs, 1986; Grimes et al., 2006).

The content and process used in this approach to systems change was consistent with school-wide approaches to behavior described extensively by Horner et al. (2005) and school-wide reading described by Simmons and colleages (e.g., Coyne et al., 2004). Conceptually, the main ideas driving methodology and procedures used to facilitate this process were as follows: (a) the impact of effective strategies is constrained by the support for implementation provided by host environment; (b) data-based information must be used to make effective support decisions; (c) a proactive (i.e., positive and preventative) instructional approach is required to realize meaningful and sustainable change in school climate; (d) the intensity of interventions must be matched to intensity of the problem; and (e) supporting and educating students with severe difficulties is possible if effective and efficient systems are in place.

27.3 Goals

The overall building-level and student-level outcome goals for the model demonstration and state projects were the same and derived from the school-wide approach (e.g., Coyne et al., 2004; Horner et al., 2005). The primary goals of the model demonstration and state projects included: (a) increasing reading performance at the school-wide level; (b) reducing behavior problems at the school-wide level; (c) increasing socially appropriate behavior at the school-wide level; (d) building capacity for localized service delivery and continuous improvement to serve purposes of school improvement planning, goal setting, resource allocation, and student intervention planning via establishing mechanisms for ongoing gathering and review of accurate information about behavior and reading performance; (e) institutionalizing school-wide academic and behavior support systems for long-term sustainability and capacity to evolve and adapt as needed.

To extend the model demonstration project to the state level, goals were expanded to also include several areas necessary for a broader delivery system. Expanded goals included: (a) establishing a foundation for statewide implementation via replication of the model in 100–200 schools across Michigan; (b) building capacity for state-level coordination and oversight via creation of a project leadership team, including the state department, state school board, school personnel, and parents; (c) building training and technical assistance capacity via cultivation of a cadre of state trainers in behavior and reading and development of a web-based system to access information, technical assistance and support; (d) building capacity for formative evaluation for continuous quality improvement via gathering and reviewing accurate information about behavior and reading performance from participating school sites across the state to target training and technical assistance.

27.4 Levels of Intervention/Implementation

In the model demonstration project, the aim was to facilitate development of school-wide approaches to improving reading and behavior that provided multiple levels of intervention (for all students in a school, for selected settings or groups of students displaying some difficulties, and individualized interventions for students experiencing significant difficulties). Emphasis was placed on developing levels of prevention and intervention across four targeted schools (Ervin et al., 2006). In total, the four schools served over 1300 students, with two schools serving grades K–5, one K–6, and one serving grades 2–3. To build capacity with sustainable implementation of school-wide approaches across larger numbers of schools, the state project targets a multilayered infrastructure that includes the following: building teams, coaching supports, local content expertise, state trainer/technical assistance, leadership, and national support through technical assistance. To do so, existing school structures (e.g., school improvement teams) are utilized, when available, to build capacity to provide these levels of support.

Building teams are the foundations for implementation at the building level. The team includes the building administrator and representation of the school staff. When possible, existing school improvement teams serve as site-based steering teams for implementation and provided leadership for development of school-wide activities. Some schools, however, decide to create a team outside of the school improvement team to implement the school-wide support activities. In such cases, communication and collaboration is encouraged with the school improvement team. Site-based steering teams focus on developing whole-school strategies to promote literacy and social competence and prevent behavior and/or reading difficulties. Grade-level teams adapt school-wide strategies to a particular grade level or classroom needs. Grade-level teams periodically review student performance data to make adjustments to the core reading or social program specific to their grade level and provide problems-solving support for classroom teachers looking for additional ideas to help their students. Existing school-based student assistance teams are key participants in problem-solving processes for students in need of indicated interventions. Thus, personnel involved in development of intervention activities for selected settings, groups of students, or individual students varies, often involving individuals with relevant content knowledge (e.g., reading specialist, school counselor) in collaboration with teachers and members of the school improvement team.

Coaching support is provided primarily through external coaches (individuals who may be employed in the local or regional school district and provide service to the school). A number of schools also use additional internal coaches (staff who are employed within the school). External and internal coaches support building teams by providing information to guide the implementation process, problem-solving assistance when difficulties arise, and celebration of the team's successes. External coaches may support multiple school teams directly or, through the internal coaches, indirectly. External and internal coaches attend training events with teams to facilitate understanding of content and implementation of innovative practices.

Local content experts in reading or behavior are utilized to develop or enhance student-specific supports. Typically, the local experts are employed at the local or regional district level. These individuals may be called upon to help develop a student intervention plan or to provided additional training in a specific content area. *State trainer/technical assistance* personnel provide regional training to building teams in the school-wide model of prevention and intervention for reading and behavior difficulties. The state trainers also provide building teams and coaches with additional information or help in problem solving, as needed.

A *state leadership team* provides administrative oversight and addresses broader issues of developing capacity and sustainability. The team was strategically established to include those with decision-making roles and responsibilities to support expansion to the state level (Grimes et al., 2006) and serves to promote visibility and political support (Sugai and Horner, 2006). It includes high-ranking administrators within the state department of education, state school board members, directors of Reading First, parent advocate, and project directors. Thus, it includes those who are skilled in policy development and knowledgeable about the educational and political landscape and potential funding mechanisms.

The state project is also connected to several national initiatives and support networks. As the state project continues with scaling-up efforts, new situations are encountered that benefit from the expertise and experience of those individuals involved in the national networks. The Center on Positive Behavioral Intervention and Support, for example, has been instrumental in expansion planning and execution, in collaboration with the state leadership team.

27.5 Resources Necessary for Developing Capacity

Efforts to create readiness and build capacity for implementation for the model demonstration project are described more fully elsewhere (Ervin et al., 2006). Funding to support model demonstration project activities was sought through the State of Michigan's PBS Initiative and in response to a US Department of Education request for proposals for school-wide reading and behavior model demonstration projects. State funding from Michigan Department of Education provided the seed money to begin awareness-level training and school-specific needs assessment with personnel from participating schools prior to initiation of federal funding. State seed money totaled $6000 from 2000 to 2003 (i.e., $2000 in 2000–2001, $3000 in 2001–2002, and $1000 in 2002–2003). Federal funds, totaling $720 000, were used to support training and technical assistance, provide resources for information systems, and provide mechanisms for planning and problem-solving meetings within participating schools (e.g., by funding substitute teachers to allow team members to meet during the school day). Federal funding began in January of 2001 and funding was extended through December of 2005.

In addition to supporting training in, implementation, and evaluation of school-wide approaches at the local level, state funding (i.e., $500 000 in the initial 2002–2003 year and over $1 000 000 per year from 2003 to 2006) for the statewide Michigan's Integrated Behavior and Learning Support Initiative (MiBLSi) provides for resource development (team training, materials, website development) to build training and technical assistance capacity at the local area and regional support levels. These activities support the efforts of state trainer/technical assistance personnel by designing resources for professional development, including curricula for regional training trainers, an annual conference, and participation in national networks. With each year of project implementation, the number of schools involved in MiBLSi has increased, as has state funding support (e.g., 22 schools were involved in 2003–2004, with $1 013 837 in support, and 102 schools were involved in 2005–2006, with $1 704 699).

27.6 Overview of Specific Approach

Implementing innovative practices involves consideration of the content (or what) of change and the process (or how) of change (Schaughency and Ervin, 2006). The content of the approach taken in Michigan schools was derived from school-wide models to improve behavior (Horner et al., 2005) and reading (Coyne et al., 2004). For the model demonstration project, frameworks for replicating promising prototypes at the school level (Adelman and Taylor, 1997) and for supporting expanded implementation (Sugai and Horner, 2006) helped to conceptualize and guide the implementation process.

27.6.1 The "What" of the Approach: School-Wide Approaches to Behavior and Reading

School-wide approaches to reading and behavior employ a public health framework to provide a continuum of prevention and promotion activities. They represent a paradigm shift from a reactive, "illness care" paradigm, in which services are provided only to those already afflicted (Weist, 2003). Preventive interventions aim to curtail negative outcomes, such as antisocial behavior and illiteracy. Promotion efforts extend beyond preventive efforts and aim to build wellness (e.g., academic and behavioral/social competence) and establish conditions that maintain and enhance it (e.g., learning climate of schools) (Graczyk et al., 2003). As applied in school-wide approaches, levels of prevention and promotion activities are provided to: (a) all students, independent of risk for academic and/or social/behavioral difficulties (*universal* intervention activities); (b) students/settings determined to be at risk for academic

and/or social behavioral difficulties (*selective* interventions); (c) individualized supports for students who are experiencing significant learning or behavioral difficulties (*indicated* interventions); for discussion, see Graczyk et al. (2003).

Four interrelated common elements guide school-wide models: (a) explicit focus on student outcomes; (b) selection and implementation of evidence-based practices; (c) ongoing collection and use of local performance data to guide decision-making; (d) focus on development of systems, or infrastructure, to support and sustain practice (Horner et al., 2005). Defining desired student outcomes provides criteria by which local needs are determined and progress is gauged (Stollar, Poth, Curtis, and Cohen, 2006). To maintain focus on enhancing student outcomes, practices selected are those that have been previously demonstrated to have positive results in the empirical literature. Controversy surrounding what constitutes an "evidence-based" practice or intervention has resulted in distinctions between intervention *efficacy* (i.e., interventions with promising outcomes in the scientific literature) and intervention *effectiveness*, "demonstration(s) of socially valid outcomes under normal conditions of usage in the target settings(s) for which the intervention was developed" (Walker, 2004, p. 399). In keeping with the notion that sustained systems change is facilitated by focus on principles rather than specific practices (Grimes and Tilly, 1996), a focus on the principle of evidence-based interventions, rather than specific practices, provides for localized choice in intervention selection (Schaughency and Ervin, 2006) and change as new techniques are developed (Grimes et al., 2006). In other words, schools were asked not only to consider the scientific evidence (efficacy) support of specific practices or interventions, but also the effectiveness of the intervention within the target context. From this perspective, ongoing collection and review of local performance data via data-informed problem solving provides a mechanism for identifying local needs and determining whether practices should be modified via systematic formative evaluation (Schaughency and Ervin, 2006).

Various factors are related to the likelihood that innovative practices will be implemented (Graczyk et al., 2003; Gresham, 2004). Therefore, the fourth element of the model involves cultivating the infrastructure to support successful implementation.

Developing mechanisms for training and technical assistance around evidence-based practices (EBPs)/ evidence-based interventions (EBIs) to address knowledge gaps are a necessary, although not necessarily sufficient, component of this infrastructure. In addition to mechanisms that promote professional knowledge and skill development, infrastructure should also likely consider professional time in at least two ways (Gresham, 2004). First, time to implement a practice has been found to be related to the likelihood that it will be implemented, arguing for selection of effective and efficient practices or intervention strategies and discontinuation of those practices or activities that are redundant, ineffective, or inefficient. Second, time is needed to effectively engage in program planning and formative evaluation activities. Therefore, infrastructure is needed that provides both a mechanism and time for program planning, review of local performance data, and problem solving, as needed. Further, these infrastructures should allow for flexibility and responsiveness to the natural ebb and flow of events and to changing demands on the system.

Within school-wide approaches, a similar problem-solving process occurs at multiple levels, but the unit of analysis and the target for intervention varies (i.e., school, setting/group, individual) (Ervin, Schaughency, Matthews, Goodman, and McGlinchey, 2007). Guiding questions include who are the stakeholder groups to be involved in efforts (e.g., which students, school personnel, community members), what will be the content and structure of activities (i.e., promotion and prevention practices, intervention activities), and how and when activities will be implemented.

Assessment, prevention, and intervention increase in intensity with increased risk or student needs. All students receive *universal* prevention and promotion activities. According to school-wide approaches, at the universal level, the goal is to create environments that promote student learning and engagement and decrease students' risk for learning and/or social/behavior problems. Evidence-based effective instruction is emphasized to promote academic competence and to prevent behavioral difficulties, and requisite and prerequisite social skills for succeeding within the school community are identified, taught, and supported (Coyne et al., 2004; Ervin et al., 2007). Assessments and reviews of student performance take place several times throughout the year to screen for potential difficulties and

to evaluative the effectiveness of the universal program. *Selected* and *indicated* levels of prevention examine local performance information in context to guide localized problem solving, matching resources with problem intensity (e.g., Grimes et al., 2006). Examples of selected prevention activities might include adjustments such as instructional grouping (e.g., Coyne et al., 2004) or setting level interventions (e.g., Ervin et al., 2006, 2007), with progress monitoring occurring somewhat more frequently than at the universal level (e.g., monthly) to determine whether modifications or additional supports are indicated. Indicated prevention activities are individualized instructional support plans based on individualized assessment of skill deficits (Coyne et al., 2004) and functional behavioral assessment (Ervin et al., 2007), with frequent progress monitoring (e.g., weekly) to evaluate whether intervention efforts are meeting student needs.

As illustrated in the preceding paragraph, information is important for identifying local needs and determining when these needs are not being met by universal supports and adapting practice (Schaughency and Ervin, 2006), with depth of assessment and frequency of review of student performance increasing with the intensity of the difficulties experienced by the student. At least two levels of measurement may be included in school-wide approaches to reading and behavior support: *Student performance indicators* in target areas of reading and behavior, and measures assessing reading and behavior support *systems*. Examples of measures included in these projects are described in Section 27.8.

27.6.2 Considering the "How": Replicating Promising Prototypes of School Reform

School-wide approaches are viewed as promising prototypes for school reform because they consider EBPs, EBIs, *and* contextual fit to promote and sustain effective practice (Ervin et al., 2006). Adelman and Taylor (1997) describe the process of replicating promising prototypes of school reform as consisting of four, overlapping, phases: (a) creating readiness; (b) initial implementation; (c) institutionalization; (d) ongoing evolution. In this collaborative model, a core team of skilled personnel facilitates replication activities, with meaningful involvement of stakeholders across all phases of the systems-change process.

27.6.2.1 Creating Readiness

Tasks at this stage include promoting awareness, interest, and consensus around the decision to adopt the proposed change.

27.6.2.2 Initial Implementation

To promote the transition from the decision to adopt to actual implementation, infrastructure is re-engineered to foster stakeholder leadership of the reform, with support from the core team. This is often in the form of a site-based steering team that works with the core team, administration, and other stakeholders in developing and implementing the innovation plan.

27.6.2.3 Institutionalization

At this stage, the primary tasks are promoting effective integration of the innovation into the organization and the infrastructure to sustain the innovation across time and changing conditions (Adelman and Taylor, 1997; Grimes et al., 2006).

27.6.2.4 Ongoing Evolution

Mechanisms fostering continued refinement of procedures to meet local needs are supported, emphasizing principle-based innovation, guided by formative evaluation (Adelman and Taylor, 1997; Grimes et al., 2006).

Although the logic model guiding replication of school-wide approaches followed the sequence described by Adelman and Taylor (1997), the process of systems change is not linear. Thus, in Michigan, there was differential progression across schools (Ervin et al., 2006), domains (behavior versus reading), and levels of intervention (universal, selected, indicated) (Ervin et al., 2007). This required recursive planning and supported implementation within each school.

27.6.3 Considering the "How": Supporting Expanded Implementation of School-Wide Approaches

There were 4008 schools in Michigan 2003–2004 (US Department of Education, 2003–2004), with approximately 12% of Michigan's schools identified as not making adequate yearly progress and 13% in need of improvement for 2005–2006

(Education Research Center, 2006). These numbers indicate that a school-by-school approach to reform, as used in this model demonstration project, is likely inadequate to meet the demand for taking the school-wide prototype to scale across the state. Building on the idea that adoption and sustainability of EBPs and EBIs are linked to coordinated infrastructure and leadership, larger organizational units (e.g., districts, educational services districts) will likely need to establish infrastructure to develop and sustain local capacity (Sugai and Horner, 2006).

Michigan's schools are located within 553 districts, supported by 57 instructional school districts/regional educational service areas. However, failure to coordinate initiatives at school, district, or intermediate school district/regional educational service agency levels sometimes impedes efficient and effective service delivery (Michigan Department of Education, 2002). To address this, the MiBLSi establishes leadership teams comprised of individuals with policy and programmatic decision-making responsibilities across relevant content areas and administrative units (e.g., reading, discipline, special education) to coordinate reform efforts (Sugai and Horner, 2006).

Amount and quality of training and technical support also correlate with successful implementation (Graczyk et al., 2003). Therefore, developing and sustaining local capacity includes building-level *training* (providing relevant information and concepts) and *coaching* (modeling, opportunities to practice, and performance feedback) capacity (Graczyk et al., 2003; Sugai and Horner, 2006). Thus, the MiBLSi is developing both state- level trainers and local "coaches" to link training experiences and implementation efforts.

27.7 Description of Activities

Table 27.1 provides a summary of goals, relevant project activities, and measurement tools. Project activities for the model demonstration project are described in more detail elsewhere (Ervin et al., 2006, 2007). Briefly, participating schools met recommended guidelines for engaging in school reform activities (Horner et al., 2005), were proximate to the core team for frequent interaction, and comprised of diverse school communities to field test an adaptive, flexible model in varying school contexts. Guidelines for inclusion were: (a) minimum

TABLE 27.1. Model demonstration and state projects goals, activities, and measures.

Goals	Activities	Measures
Increase reading performance	Data-based decision-making. Including: • school-wide reading assessment three times per year to identify needs at school-wide, grade, classroom and individual student levels; • progress monitoring; • pre-referral problem solving. Evidence-based practice curriculum and interventions across levels of support	DIBELS,[a] high-stakes assessment (MEAP[b])
Decrease behavior problems	Data-based decision-making. Including: • ODRs tracked using SWIS and analyzed for intervention planning and resource allocation; • pre-referral problem-solving and FBA-based intervention planning. Strategies and processes for responding to inappropriate behavior included in school discipline policies	ODR/SWIS[c]
Increase socially appropriate behavior	Behavior expectations and requisite social skills identified, taught, and supported across contexts	Archival implementation data (e.g., "caught being good" ticket counts)
Build capacity for localized service delivery and continuous improvement	Data-based decision-making for localized service delivery and continuous improvement. Including: • DIBELS and ODR/SWIS data reviewed for school improvement planning, goal setting, resource allocation, and intervention planning. Activities to build local service delivery capacity: • school leadership team training; • professional development in evidence-based practices. Coaching support and technical assistance	SET,[d] PET,[e] EBS-TIC,[f] EBS Self-Assessment Survey,[g] ERS-TIC,[h] School Improvement Plan Goals
Institutionalize school-wide academic and behavior support systems for long-term sustainability	Project support thinned and ownership transferred to local teams via: • school developed action plans; • regular funding mechanisms.	SET, PET, EBS-TIC, EBS Self-Assessment Survey, ERS-TIC, School Improvement Plan Goals

[a] DIBELS: dynamic indicators of basic early literacy skills (Good et al., 2002a).
[b] MEAP: Michigan Education Assessment Program (Michigan Department of Education, 2004).
[c] ODR/SWIS: Office Discipline Referrals/School-Wide Information System (Irvin et al., 2006).
[d] SET: School-wide Evaluation Tool (Horner et al., 2004).
[e] PET: Planning and Evaluation Tool for Effective Reading Programs (Simmons et al., 2002).
[f] EBS-TIC: Effective Behavior Support Team Implementation Checklist (Sugai et al., 2002).
[g] EBS Self-Assessment Survey: Effective Behavior Support Self-Assessment Survey (Sugai et al., 2003).
[h] ERS-TIC: Effective Reading Support Team Implementation Checklist (McGlinchey, 2006).

staff vote of 80% to participate; (b) principal commitment, including attendance at monthly meetings with other participating principals; (c) agreement to designate a school leadership team for project activities; (d) prioritization of improved reading and behavior among school improvement goals; (e) agreement to ongoing data collection for formative and summative evaluation.

In contrast to the recruitment efforts involved in the model demonstration project, schools are selected for participation in the state project via an application process. Inclusion criteria include those used in the model demonstration project (e.g., administrative support, staff buy-in, and school priorities of improved reading and behavior), plus district-level administrative support, and agreement to share data collected through project activities with MiBLSi staff. Preference for participation is given to schools identified as low performing by *Michigan Yes!*, the Michigan Department of Education accreditation system for schools.

At the school level, activities in both projects were consistent with those described for schoolwide approaches of behavior (Horner et al., 2005) and reading (Coyne et al., 2004). Early activities supported implementation of information systems for use in needs assessment and formative evaluation, and project personnel facilitated schools attainment of prerequisites for their use (e.g., Good, Gruba, and Kaminski, 2002a; Irvin et al., 2006). Information obtained through systems-level assessments and student performance data, which are described in Section 27.8, were reviewed by members of the school improvement team to establish school-based action plans. These action plans guided capacity building, professional development, and technical assistance activities and functioned as a mechanism for schools to take ownership of, and self-direct, project activities (Ervin et al., 2006).

As described elsewhere (Ervin et al., 2006), schools in the model demonstration project generally elected to begin implementation with schoolwide approaches for behavioral support. All projects began with development of universal levels of support. Development of selected and indicated levels of behavioral support took longer to develop. At times, development of selected levels of support seemed to evolve in response to data-guided problem solving, whereas in other instances explicit teaching, modeling, and coaching appeared necessary to promote implementation of a new activity (e.g., pre-referral intervention, functional assessment-based behavior support planning). Development of reading supports followed a similar course. With demonstration of the instructional utility of performance data over time, school personnel were more likely to engage in data-guided, problem solving and consider adoption of instructional interventions to meet student needs.

In both projects, a scaffolded approach to support was taken, with the intent to promote implementation in the early phases and support institutionalization over time. That is, in early stages, project personnel interacted with building-level personnel more frequently, thinning to less frequent interactions as project activities were up and running (e.g., monthly). In addition, in the model demonstration project, schools seemed most likely to successfully sustain project activities when they considered ongoing funding support mechanisms to continue project activities, received external validation for these practices (e.g., being granted permission to substitute dynamic indicators of basic early literacy skills (DIBELS) measures for other district-used early literacy assessment practices), and became part of a larger network of like-minded innovators (Ervin et al., 2006).

27.8 Evaluation of Program: Preliminary Evidence of Impact

Multiple methods and sources of data were collected to provide ongoing monitoring of systems-level practices related to behavior and reading and to assess each school's progress in development and implementation of multi-tiered problem solving to address reading and behavior. In addition to systems variables (e.g., changes in organizational goals, structures, processes, and procedures), ongoing measures of student reading performance and behavior were obtained. These data were collated to guide problem-solving efforts at whole-school, grade, class, small-group, and individual student levels. In the following section, systems-level assessment tools and student outcome measures, as well as preliminary findings from the model demonstration and statewide project, are described.

27.8.1 Systems-Level Assessment Tools

27.8.1.1 School-Wide Evaluation Tool

The SET assesses features of school-wide PBS using multiple sources of information (Horner et al., 2004).

27.8.1.2 Effective Behavior Support Self-Assessment Survey

This survey is completed annually by school staff to evaluate the status of positive behavior support within the school and to provide information for planning. Questions from this survey assess school-wide, nonclassroom, classroom, and individual student systems of support (Sugai, Horner, and Todd, 2003).

27.8.1.3 Effective Behavior Support Team Implementation Checklist

The checklist is completed quarterly by the building team to track progress in implementing PBS activities. Information obtained from this checklist is used in creating and revising teams' action plans to improve behavior support (Sugai, Horner, and Lewis-Palmer, 2002).

27.8.1.4 Planning and Evaluation Tool for Effective Reading Programs

The PET was developed to assist with development of school-wide reading programs by determining a school's current policies and practices in beginning reading and identify areas for improvement (Simmons et al., 2002).

27.8.1.5 Effective Reading Support Team Implementation Checklist

This checklist was developed by McGlinchey (2006). Its format parallels that of the EBS-TIC. The checklist is completed quarterly by the building team to track progress in implementing reading support activities. Information obtained from this checklist is used in creating and revising teams' action plans to improve reading support.

27.8.2 Student Performance Outcome Measures

27.8.2.1 School-Wide Information System

The SWIS provides a systematic and standardized approach to use of ODR data (Irvin et al., 2006). These data are commonly available in schools and may be used for monitoring performance at the individual, setting, or school-wide level (Ervin et al., 2007; Irvin et al., 2006). Normative data regarding ODR converge with the three-tiered public health model of behavioral support needs (Horner et al., 2005). Based on normative data, the target percentage of students at each risk category are: (1) 85%

or more of students would have zero or one ODRs per year (universal level); (2) fewer than 10% would have two to five ODRs (selective prevention level); (3) fewer than 5% would have greater than six ODRs per year (indicated prevention level).

27.8.2.2 Dynamic Indicators of Basic Early Literacy Skills

DIBELS provides research-based, norm-referenced measures of reading and pre-reading skills (Good et al., 2002a). DIBELS scores may be used to place students in risk categories derived using a rational–empirical approach (Good, Simmons, Kame'enui, Kaminski, and Wallin, 2002b). Students reading at recommended benchmark cut-points are likely to reach literacy goals; students performing below benchmark are at risk for not reaching literacy goals and in need of strategic (selective) or intensive (indicated) supports (Good et al., 2002b).

27.8.3 Preliminary Findings: Model Demonstration Project Schools

Data collected across the four schools involved in the model demonstration project were promising, with changes occurring in desired directions across most targeted areas (e.g., Ervin et al., 2006, 2007). Figure 27.1 illustrates the number of ODRs per day per 100 students and Figure 27.2 displays the percentage of students at the universal, selected or indicated level of prevention based on the number of ODRs per student per year of the project. Both figures include reprinted data, from Ervin et al. (2006), indicating effects during years in which the model demonstration project schools were supported by federal funds and follow-up data for the 2005–2006 year. Further, follow-up data collected during the 2005–2006 school year suggest that improvements in behavior and reading outcomes were sustained when grant support and funding was discontinued. Data during 2005–2006 reflect sustainability of project outcomes despite termination of grant funding. In addition, evidence of continued improvements of behavioral outcomes at School D, a school faced with the unique challenge of serving a significantly impoverished community, are particularly promising.

Figure 27.3 displays the percentage of students performing at benchmark or within a risk category

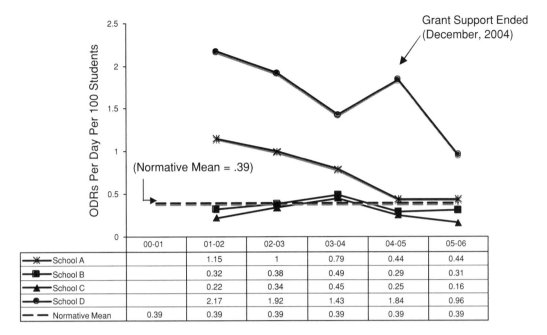

FIGURE 27.1. ODRs per day per 100 students across years for schools participating in model demonstration project. From Ervin et al. (2006). Merging research and practice agendas to address reading and behaviour school-wide. *School Psychology Review*, 35, 198–223. Copyright 2006 by the National Association of School Psychologists, Bethesda, MD. Reprinted/adapted by permission of the publisher. www.nasponline.org

on the DIBELS at the whole-school level for schools within the model demonstration project. Follow-up data in 2005–2006 demonstrate promising maintenance of effects for School A and B, and continued difficulties at School D, with less than 50% of the whole school population reaching benchmark goals. Maintenance of efforts to implement early reading interventions targeting grades K and 1 at School D (for a description of these interventions, see Ervin et al. (2006)), however, reflect sustained commitment to improving reading performance, despite the complexity of doing so when faced with such large numbers of struggling readers (see Figure 27.4).

27.8.4 Preliminary Findings: Statewide Project Schools

When evaluating widespread replication of prototypes for systemic change, such as Michigan's statewide MiBLSi project, premature emphasis on impact (e.g., effects on achievement test performance data) has been argued to be "one of the surest ways to undercut efforts to sustain promising innovations" (Adelman and Taylor, 2003, p. 23). Instead, initial evaluation of systems-level replication

projects should emphasize the collection of formative evaluation data (i.e., data that inform decision-making problem-solving efforts). Thus, this section presents preliminary formative evaluation data pertaining to MiBLSi.

In February of the 2003–2004 school year, the first cohort of schools began participation in MiBLSi. Of the initial 22 schools in Cohort 1, 21 schools sustained participation through the 2004–2005 and 2005–2006 school years. Cohort 2, 31 schools, commenced participation during February of the 2004–2005 school year and all schools have maintained participation throughout the 2005–2006 school year. In January of the 2005–2006 school year, 50 additional schools joined MiBLSi, creating an overall total of 102 schools (100 elementary and 2 middle schools) involved in widespread replication of school-wide approaches to addressing reading and behavior. Figure 27.5 illustrates the general locations of project schools across the state.

To provide preliminary data reflecting statewide efforts, formative evaluation data from Cohort 1 are presented in Tables 27.2 and 27.3. Table 27.2 displays demographic data for each school in Cohort 1, as well as student behavior (ODRs per day

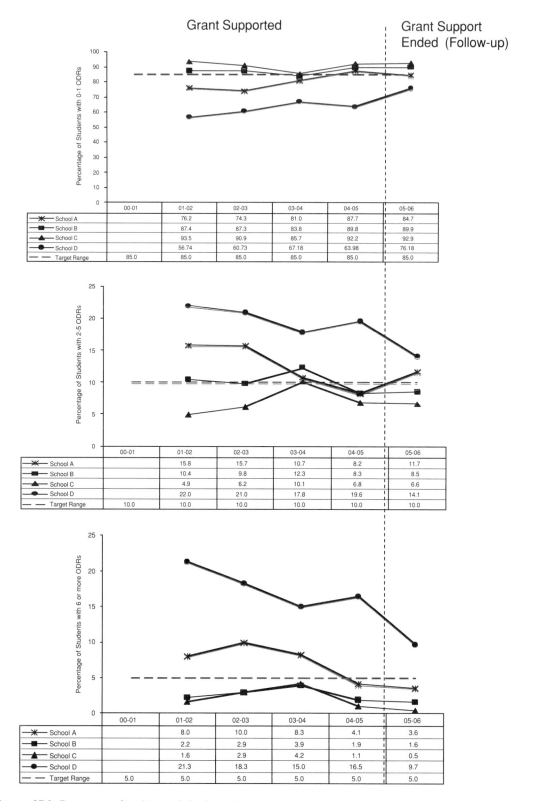

Top chart — Percentage of Students with 0-1 ODRs

	00-01	01-02	02-03	03-04	04-05	05-06
School A		76.2	74.3	81.0	87.7	84.7
School B		87.4	87.3	83.8	89.8	89.9
School C		93.5	90.9	85.7	92.2	92.9
School D		56.74	60.73	67.18	63.98	76.18
Target Range	85.0	85.0	85.0	85.0	85.0	85.0

Middle chart — Percentage of Students with 2-5 ODRs

	00-01	01-02	02-03	03-04	04-05	05-06
School A		15.8	15.7	10.7	8.2	11.7
School B		10.4	9.8	12.3	8.3	8.5
School C		4.9	6.2	10.1	6.8	6.6
School D		22.0	21.0	17.8	19.6	14.1
Target Range	10.0	10.0	10.0	10.0	10.0	10.0

Bottom chart — Percentage of Students with 6 or more ODRs

	00-01	01-02	02-03	03-04	04-05	05-06
School A		8.0	10.0	8.3	4.1	3.6
School B		2.2	2.9	3.9	1.9	1.6
School C		1.6	2.9	4.2	1.1	0.5
School D		21.3	18.3	15.0	16.5	9.7
Target Range	5.0	5.0	5.0	5.0	5.0	5.0

FIGURE 27.2. Percentage of students at behavioral risk categories, according to ODRs, across years for schools participating in model demonstration project. From Ervin et al. (2006). Merging research and practice agendas to address reading and behaviour school-wide. *School Psychology Review, 35*, 198–223. Copyright 2006 by the National Association of School Psychologists, Bethesda, MD. Reprinted/adapted by permission of the publisher. www.nasponline.org

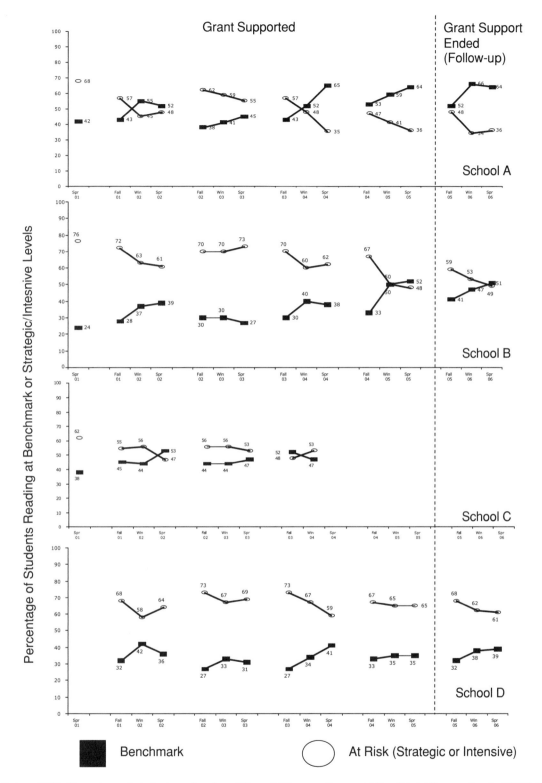

FIGURE 27.3. Percentage of students performing at "low risk" versus "some risk" or "at risk", according to DIBELS benchmarks, within and across years for schools participating in the model demonstration project. From Ervin et al. (2006). Merging research and practice agendas to address reading and behaviour school-wide. *School Psychology Review, 35*, 198–223. Copyright 2006 by the National Association of School Psychologists, Bethesda, MD. Reprinted/adapted by permission of the publisher. www.nasponline.org

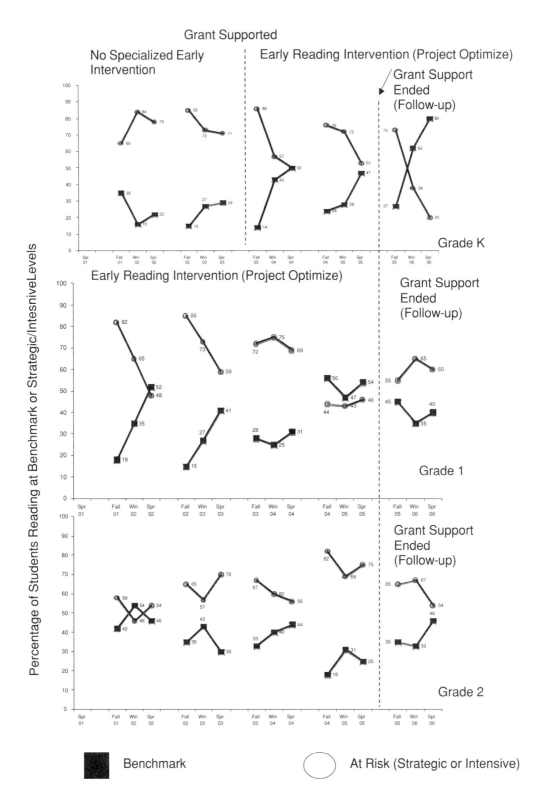

FIGURE 27.4. Percentage of students in kindergarten and Grade 1 performing at "low risk" versus "some risk" or "at risk", according to DIBELS benchmarks, within and across years before and during Project Optimize Early Reading Intervention curriculum. From Ervin et al. (2006). Merging research and practice agendas to address reading and behaviour school-wide. *School Psychology Review, 35*, 198–223. Copyright 2006 by the National Association of School Psychologists, Bethesda, MD. Reprinted/adapted by permission of the publisher. www.nasponline.org

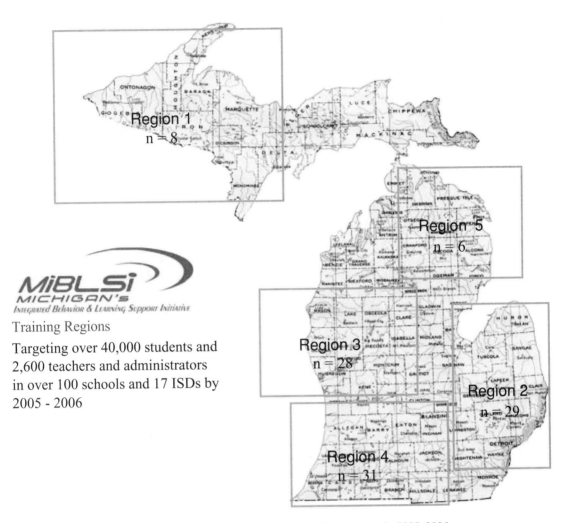

FIGURE 27.5. Distribution of schools participating in statewide scale-up project in 2005–2006.

per 100 students), and PBS systems indicators (staff perceptions on the EBS self-assessment survey and EBS-TIC). Table 27.3 displays the percentage of students at each school who were assessed with DI-BELS, the percentage of students assessed who were reading at benchmark goal levels (i.e., low risk for later reading problems), and measures of systems-level implementation of effective reading supports (i.e., PET, ERS-TIC). Schools are currently involved in building their capacity to collect formative measures of student outcomes and systems-level implementation of reading and behavior supports. Thus, data are presented to reflect preliminary establishment and use of formative evaluation tools rather than evidence of project impact on intended goals.

In general, data collected across schools in Cohort 1 suggest that, with each project year, use of measures increased across schools. Further, preliminary student reading and behavior data suggest that, as with the model demonstration project, schools varied with respect to demographic characteristics and student reading and behavior needs. Some schools (e.g., School #21), for example, were faced with high rates of discipline problems (see Table 27.2) and low numbers of students meeting reading benchmark goals (see Table 27.3), whereas other schools (e.g., School #20) presented with relatively low rates of discipline problems (see Table 27.2) and a majority of students reaching reading benchmark goals.

TABLE 27.2. Student population and behavioral performance and systems indicators for Cohort 1 of Michigan's Behavior and Learning Support Initiative, by region.[a]

| | | Behavioral performance and systems indicators across project years | | | | | | | | |
| | | 03–04 | | 04–05 | | | 05–06 | | |
School #	Student population	ODR[b]/day/100 students	EBS survey[c] (%)	ODR/day/100 students	EBS survey (%)	EBS-TIC[d] (%)	ODR/day/100 students	EBS survey (%)	EBS-TIC (%)
Region 1 schools									
1	42		29	2.28	83	94	0.38	89	65
6	110		23	0.64	46		0.18	56	88
13	143		48	0.86	49	59	0.92	49	88
Region 2 schools									
2	145		22		43	41	0.70	62	94
9	294		32	0.21	54	88	0.11	79	94
10	348	0.20	23	0.05		100	0.01		
14	564	0.10	45	0.14	42	71	0.08		76
16	244		48	0.61	57	65	0.46	75	100
17	396		28	0.87	33	65	0.49		94
20	459		30		57	82	0.23		76
Region 3 schools									
3	365	0.71	27	2.35	40	65	0.72	55	82
4	334	0.45	63	0.36			0.13		100
5	507		21	0.18		100	0.26	67	88
8	232	0.41	49	0.11	77	88	0.12	75	100
12	538		22	0.09	61	71	0.06		71
19	105		25		96	100	0.16	99	100
Region 4 schools									
7	355		28	0.34		94	0.25	94	100
11	475		36		39	47	0.11		59
15	304	0.43	25	0.55	62	69	0.30	73	100
18	501	0.32	67	0.11	72	65	0.18	71	100
21	344	2.63	40	3.33	71	88	4.67	94	100
Descriptive statistics for Cohort 1									
M	324.0	0.66	34.8	0.77	57.8	76.4	0.50	74.1	88.8
SD	153.7	0.82	13.6	0.96	17.4	17.9	0.99	15.7	13.0

[a] Region refers to geographical location of school (1: northwest; 2: southeast; 3: central west; 4: southwest; see Figure 27.5).
[b] ODR: office discipline referrals.
[c] EBS Self-Assessment Survey: Effective Behavior Support Self-Assessment Survey (Sugai et al., 2003).
[d] EBS-TIC: Effective Behavior Support Team Implementation Checklist (Sugai et al., 2002).

27.9 Lessons Learned

In Michigan, many lessons have been learned from efforts to merge research and practice agendas to address the continuum of students' reading and behavior needs at a school-wide level. In keeping with a data-informed problem-solving approach to decision-making, efforts in Michigan have been informed by, and have evolved based on, the empirical literature and formative information collected from participating schools along the way. Michigan's systems-change story is ongoing, and the impact of attempts to build schools' capacity to implement school-wide approaches to reading and behavior are yet to be determined. Thus, in this section, preliminary lessons, or working hypotheses, are articulated in the hope of contributing to general practice and future research in this area.

Scholars have argued that federally funded projects can serve as important catalysts for large-scale replication of promising prototypes for systemic school reform (Adelman and Taylor, 2003). In Michigan, for example, it is likely that promising preliminary data taken across four model

TABLE 27.3. Student reading performance and instructional systems indicators for Cohort 1 of Michigan's Behavior and Learning Support Initiative, by region and time of assessment.

School #	03–04		04–05					05–06					
	In assess[a]	At BM[b]	In assess	At benchmark			PET[c]	In assess	At benchmark			PET	ERS-TIC[d]
		S[e]		F[f]	W[g]	S	F		F	W	S	F	S
Region 1 schools													
1	59	32	97	46	46	54	92	71	40	55	56	89	50
6	88	44	88	65	59	63	51	65	42	59	67	70	62
13	55	53	83	63	62	74	51	76	57	72	72	70	
Region 2 schools													
2	73	42	73	28	41	47	49	83	40	37	49	83	96
9	100	50	96	66	68	71	60	99	66	72	71	94	73
10		29	93	55	63	56	91	98			56		
14	30	12	100	27	39	38	45	100	35	45	50		18
16	50	42	96	46	49	42	57	97	43	57	56	44	55
17		11	53	16	26	21	74	44	36	32	39		50
20	77	57	100	60	64	60	68	100	59	63	67	53	55
Region 3 schools													
3	0		93	31	28	30	80	77	25	38	45	80	68
4	34	28	91	36	36	33	60	89	31	35	35	56	27
5	49	45	100	34	49	49	83	100	42	53	55	81	64
8	23	43	98	54	50	48	65	100	47	50	48	66	50
12	12	52	96	59	65	71	50	96	63	72	72	84	64
19	76	39	45	37	58	56	89	82	41	62	63	93	95
Region 4 schools													
7		39	100	40	47	48	62	90	41	48	61	67	77
11	57	60	92	53	56	60	55	94	61	63	65	57	59
15	60	37	100	37	48	50	75	97	45	51	68	60	50
18	71	29	94	32	36	53	47	79	48	50	53	78	
21	100	32	100	33	33	37	66	100	35	37	39	76	
Descriptive statistics for Cohort 1													
M	53.4	38.8	89.9	43.7	48.7	50.5	65.2	87.5	44.9	52.6	56.5	72.3	58.5
S	30.5	13.1	15.2	14.4	12.6	13.9	15.0	14.8	11.1	12.6	11.3	14.4	20.1

Note. All values are percentages. Blank values represent missing data.

[a] In assess: % of student population assessed.

[b] BM: benchmark, % of students who achieved benchmark on the DIBELS (Good et al., 2002a).

[c] PET: Planning and Evaluation Tool for Effective Reading Programs (Simmons et al., 2002).

[d] ERS-TIC: Effective Reading Support Team Implementation Checklist (McGlinchey, 2006).

[f] S: spring data collection.

[g] F: fall data collection.

[h] W: winter data collection.

demonstration project schools (Ervin et al., 2006) set the stage for a statewide initiative focused on widespread replication. The model demonstration project, which was conducted over a period of 5 years, indicated that change occurred in desired directions across schools during implementation of the project (Ervin et al., 2006, 2007). Further, follow-up data from model demonstration schools illustrated maintenance of effects and continued improvement despite termination of federal funds to support project efforts.

Within the initial years of implementation of the model demonstration project, efforts to replicate project activities spread to other schools and other school districts across the state. For example, in the district serving School D, eight additional schools are currently participating in MiBLSi (one school in Cohort 1, four schools in Cohort 2, and three schools in Cohort 3), with a district-wide plan for all schools to participate. School D now serves as a model school in its district, with other schools visiting to learn from its experience.

One key working hypothesis reinforced from observing replication efforts across schools is that implementation and systems change should be viewed as iterative processes, requiring continued attention and responsiveness. Innovation efforts should not be conceptualized as a commitment to implement a specific program; instead, they are a commitment to be responsive and to continuously monitor, modify, and adjust. Moreover, schools, and their respective school districts, are unique, dynamic systems (Curtis and Stollar, 2002) and move through the implementation and change process differentially. Thus, frameworks for promoting change must be flexible and in keeping with an *experimenting society* approach to science and practice (Campbell, 1988). Schools new to the innovation process can learn about the nature and course of successful efforts undertaken at other schools, yet should take an idiographic approach to organizational change and development (Shapiro and Elliott, 1999). Ongoing collection and efficient use of systems monitoring and student performance data provides a formative feedback mechanism that is integral to the systems-change process and appears to be a powerful motivator (Horner et al., 2005). However, skills to interpret data and, particularly, infer instructional implications cannot be assumed. School personnel need training and technical support for these skills to be embedded in daily practice (Stecker, Fuchs, and Fuchs, 2005).

A second working hypothesis was that the time needed and intensity of support needed to achieve change varies across schools. Replication may focus on dispersal of a prototype (breadth of scale up) and/or quality of implementation (depth) (Grimes et al., 2006). Supports and depth of implementation needed to impact change appeared to vary along with the nature and course of implementation. For example, model demonstration School D, a school faced with significant challenges, showed continued declines in ODRs (approaching normative levels) following termination of grant funding. In other words, school-wide improvement at School D was associated with sustained implementation supported by continued emphasis on implementation *depth* to address the continuum of students' behavioral and academic needs (Grimes et al., 2006). We consider these findings to be encouraging and to highlight the need for "realistic optimism" for schools faced with significant behavior and academic challenges

(Elias, Zins, Graczyk, and Weissberg, 2003). The finding that school-wide evidence of impact may be delayed relative to impact evidence from schools faced with less severe challenges and occur following longer periods (e.g., 5–6 years) is in keeping with recommendations for emphasis on formative rather than summative evaluation of impact during initial years of implementation (Adelman and Taylor, 2003). Moreover, the finding that improvement at challenged schools was associated with more sustained and intensive focus on implementation depth is consistent with scale-up models providing for differentiated levels of technical assistance and support (e.g., Stollar et al., 2006).

The model demonstration project illustrates emphasis on depth of implementation, whereas, the statewide project focuses on breadth of implementation (see Grimes et al., 2006). External supports and resources involved in supporting the development of each of the four model demonstration school sites in Michigan far exceeded current funding for each school involved in the statewide project, MiBLSi. Whether or not schools facing significant challenges (e.g., School #21) involved in the statewide project are able to establish the depth of implementation necessary to impact the continuum of student needs without the extensive external support and funding that was provided to the model demonstration schools has yet to be determined. Although the state project targets breadth of replication across large numbers of schools, it is important to balance this focus on replication with sufficient emphasis on the integrity in which activities are implemented (Graczyk et al., 2003).

As described above, school-wide approaches consist of four interrelated elements (focus on student outcomes, selection of evidence-based practices, collection and use of local performance data, and development of systems), with each element a potential focus for considerations of treatment integrity. Data presented in Tables 27.2 and 27.3, for example, suggest that, statewide, there is increasing demonstration of establishment of data systems to monitor student outcomes (SWIS, DIBELS) in reading and behavior and to monitor systems development (i.e., EBS survey, PET). Improvements are also noted on performance indicators in some schools over time, but should be interpreted with caution for two reasons. First, initial evaluation should focus on formative, rather than summative evaluation, as previously noted (Adelman and Taylor, 2003). Second, the primary focus at this stage should be on levels directly targeted for change (e.g., school level), with evaluation moving to more distal levels (e.g., student) as intermediary levels are shown to demonstrate change (e.g., teaching practices) (Schaugheny and Ervin, 2006).

27.9.1 Directions for Future Research

Future research should help to determine key factors that enhance implementation integrity. Potential areas for consideration include factors related to both local and global alignment (Fullan, 2000). For example, the model demonstration project and the statewide project in Michigan identify the unit of change to be the building level. At the local, or within-school level, all schools involved in the Michigan projects established commitment from at least 80% of the staff prior to initiating project activities. In addition to staff commitment, schools were required to demonstrate administrative commitment and support to project activities. Anecdotal information collected from school personnel involved in project activities suggests that it may be important to periodically review staff commitment.

School buildings operate in broader contexts (e.g., districts), and experience suggests that global alignment is also likely important to reduce risk of detrimental effects of competing initiatives and to provide validation for change efforts. Finally, involvement in learning communities (Adelman and Taylor, 2006) and larger networks of like-minded innovators at all levels of participation in these projects (from school practitioner through project director) seemed to be positively associated with positive outcomes, such as successful implementation and sustainability (Ervin et al., 2006) and involvement with further efforts to take innovation to scale.

Acknowledgments. Preparation of this manuscript was supported in part by grants from the Office of Special Education Programs, US Department of Education (CFDA Award# H324T000024) and the Michigan Department of Education (Award#060470-1D50). Opinions expressed herein do not necessarily reflect the position of the US Department of Education nor the Michigan Department of Education and such endorsements should not be inferred. The authors would like to acknowledge and express our gratitude to the schools that participated in this project as well as the advisory team of experts who provided assistance and support as needed. Special thanks to Jacuelyn Thompson, David Tilly, Rob Horner, and Roland Good.

References

Adelman, H. S. & Taylor, L. (1997). Toward a scale-up model for replicating new approaches to schooling. *Journal of Educational and Psychological Consultation, 8*, 197–230.

Adelman, H. S. & Taylor, L. (2003). Commentary: advancing mental health science and practice through authentic collaboration. *School Psychology Review, 32*, 53–56.

Adelman, H. S. & Taylor, L. (2006). Mental health in schools and public health. *School Report on Child Mental Health, 121*, 294–298.

Atkins, M. S., Graczyk, P. A., Frazier, S. L., & Abdul-Adil, J. (2003). Toward a new model for promoting children's mental health: accessible, effective, and sustainable school-based mental health services. *School Psychology Review, 32*, 503–514.

Campbell, D. T. (1988). The experimenting society. In S. Overman (Ed.), *Methodology and Epistemology for Social Science* (pp. 290–314). Chicago: University of Chicago Press.

Carnine, D. (1999). Campaigns for moving research into practice. *Remedial and Special Education, 35*, 2–6.

Coyne, M. D., Kame-enui, E. J., & Simmons, D. C. (2004). Improving beginning reading instruction and intervention for students with LD: reconciling "all" with "each". *Journal of Learning Disabilities, 37*, 231–239.

Curtis, M. J. & Stollar, S. A. (2002). Best practices in system-level change. In A. Thomas & J. Grimes (Eds.), *Best Practices in School Psychology IV* (Vol. 1, pp. 223–234). Bethesda, MD: National Association of School Psychologists.

Education Research Center (2006). *Quality Counts at 10: A Decade Of Standards-Based Education.* Washington, DC: Education Week.

Elias, M. J., Zins, J. E., Graczyk, P. A., & Weissberg, R. P. (2003). Implementation, sustainability, and scaling up of social-emotional and academic innovations in public schools. *School Psychology Review, 32*, 303–319.

Elliott, S. N. & Fuchs, L. S. (1997). The utility of curriculum-based measurement and performance assessment as alternatives to intelligence tests. *School Psychology Review, 26*, 224–233.

Ervin, R. A., Schaughency, E., Goodman, S. D., McGlinchey, M. T., & Matthews, A. (2006). Merging research and practice agendas to address reading and behavior school-wide. *School Psychology Review, 35*, 198–223.

Ervin, R. A., Schaughency, E., Matthews, A., Goodman, S. D., & McGlinchey, M. T. (2007). Primary and secondary prevention of behavior difficulties: developing a data-informed problem-solving model to guide decision-making at a school-wide level. *Psychology in the Schools, 44*, 7–18.

Fuchs, L. S. & Fuchs, D. (Eds.). (1986). Linking assessment to instructional intervention: An overview. *School Psychology Review, 15*, 318–323.

Fullan, M. (2000). The three stories of education reform. *Phi Delta Kappan, 81*, 1–11.

Good, R. H., Gruba, J. & Kaminski, R. A. (2002a). Best practices in using dynamic indicators of basic early literacy skills (DIBELS) in an outcomes driven model. In A. Thomas & J. Grimes (Eds.), *Best Practices in School Psychology IV* (Vol. 1, pp. 699–720). Bethesda, MD: National Association of School Psychologists.

Good, R. H., Simmons, D. C., Kame'enui, E. J., Kaminski, R. A., & Wallin, J. (2002b). Summary of decision rules for intensive, strategic, and benchmark instructional recommendations in kindergarten through third grade. Technical Report No. 11. Eugene, OR: University of Oregon.

Graczyk, P. A., Domitrovich, C. E., & Zins, J. E. (2003). Facilitating the implementation of evidence-based prevention and mental health promotion efforts in schools. In M. D. Weist, S. W. Evans, & N. A. Lever (Eds.), *Handbook of School Mental Health: Advancing Practice and Research* (pp. 301–318). New York: Kluwer Academic/Plenum.

Gresham, F. M. (2004). Current status and future directions of school-based behavioral interventions. *School Psychology Review, 33*, 326–343.

Grimes, J., Kurns, S., & Tilly, W. D. III (2006). Sustainability: An enduring commitment to success, *School Psychology Review, 35*, 224–244.

Grimes, J. & Tilly, D.W. (1996). Policy and process: means to lasting educational change. *School Psychology Review, 25*, 465–476.

Harris, P. (2006). Detroit blacks taking the rap in one of America's poorest cities. *World Focus*, (May), 1–7, 12–13.

Horner, R. H., Sugai, G., Todd, A. W., & Lewis-Palmer, T. (2005). Schoolwide positive behavior support. In L. M. Bambara & L. Kern (Eds.), *Individualized Supports for Students with Problem Behaviors* (pp. 359–390). New York: Guilford.

Horner, R. H., Todd, A. W., Lewis-Palmer, T., Irvin, L. K., Sugai, G., & Boland, J. B. (2004). The school-wide evaluation tool (SET): a research instrument for assessing school-wide positive behavior support. *Journal of Positive Behavior Interventions, 6*, 3–12.

Hunter, L. (2003). School psychology: a public health framework III. Managing disruptive behavior in schools: the value of a public health and evidence-based perspective. *Journal of School Psychology, 41*, 39–59.

Irvin, L. K., Horner, R. H., Ingram, K., Todd, A. W., Sampson, N. K., & Boland, J. B. (2006). Using office discipline referral data for decision making about student behavior in elementary and middle schools: an empirical evaluation of validity. *Journal of Positive Behavior Interventions, 8*, 10–23.

Kozol, J. (2005). *The Shame of the Nation: The Restoration of Apartheid Schooling in America*. New York: Crown.

McGlinchey, M. (2006). *Effective Reading Support Team Implement Checklist*. Kalamazoo, MI: Kalamazoo Area Regional Service Agency, Instructional Center.

Michigan Department of Education (2000a). *Positive Behavior Support for ALL Michigan Students: Creating Environments that Assure Learning. Executive Summary*. Lansing, Michigan: Michigan Department of Education, Office of Special Education and Early Intervention Services.

Michigan Department of Education (2000b). *Positive Behavior Support for ALL Michigan Students: Creating Environments that Assure Learning. Overview Document*. Lansing, Michigan: Michigan Department of Education, Office of Special Education and Early Intervention Services.

Michigan Department of Education (2002). Making reading first in Michigan. Proposed Reading First Plan submitted to the US Department of Education. Lansing, MI: Michigan Department of Education.

Michigan Department of Education (2004). Michigan Educational Assessment Program (MEAP) frequently asked question. Retrieved August 2, 2005, from www.michigan.gov.

National Reading Panel (2000). *Teaching Children to Read: An Evidence-Based Assessment of the Scientific Research Literature on Reading and its Implications for Reading Instruction*. Washington, DC: National Institute of Child Health and Human Development/National Institutes of Health.

Power, T. J. (2003). Promoting children's mental health: reform through interdisciplinary and community partnerships. *School Psychology Review, 32*, 3–16.

Schaughency, E. & Ervin, R. (2006). Building capacity to implement and sustain effect practices to better serve children. *School Psychology Review, 35*, 155–166.

Shapiro, E. E. & Elliott, S. N. (1999). Curriculum-based assessment and other performance-based assessment strategies. In C. R. Reynolds & T. B. Gutkin (Eds.), *The Handbook of School Psychology* (3rd ed., pp. 383–408). New York: Wiley.

Simmons, D. C., Kame'enui, E. J., Good, R. H., Harn, B. A., Cole, C., & Braun, D. (2002). Building, implementing, and sustaining a beginning reading improvement model: lessons learned school by school. In M. R. Shinn, H. M. Walker, & G. Stoner (Eds.), *Interventions for Academic and Behavior Problems II: Preventive and Remedial Approaches* (pp. 537–570). Bethesda, MD: National Association of School Psychologists.

Stecker, P. M., Fuchs, L. S., & Fuchs, D. (2005). Using curriculum-based measurement to improve student achievement: review of research. *Psychology in the Schools, 42*, 798–819.

Stollar, S., Poth, R. L., Curtis, M. J., & Cohen, R. M. (2006). Collaborative strategic planning as an illustration of the principles of systems change. *School Psychology Review, 35*, 181–197.

Strein, W., Hoagwood, K., & Cohn, A. (2003). School psychology: a public health perspective I. Prevention, populations, and systems change. *Journal of School Psychology, 41*, 23–38.

Sugai, G. & Horner, R. H. (2006). A promising approach for expanding and sustaining school-wide positive behavior support. *School Psychology Review, 35*, 245–259.

Sugai, G., Horner, R., & Lewis-Palmer, T. (2002). *Effective Behavior Support Team Implementation Checklist (Version 2.2)*. Eugene, OR: University of Oregon, Educational & Community Supports. Retrieved from http://www.pbis.org/tools.htm.

Sugai, G., Horner, R., & Todd, A. (2003). *Effective Behavior Support Self-Assessment Survey (Version 2.0)*. Eugene, OR: University of Oregon, Educational & Community Supports. Retrieved from http://www.pbis.org/tools.htm.

Thompson, J. J. (2000). Letter of support. In *Positive Behavior Support for ALL Michigan Students: Creating Environments that Assure Learning. Executive Summary*. Lansing, MI: Michigan Department of Education, Office of Special Education and Early Intervention Services.

US Department of Education (2000–2001). *Public Elementary/Secondary School Universe Survey*. Common Core of Data, National Center for Education Statistics. Washington, DC: US Department of Education.

US Department of Education (2003–2004). *State Education Data Profiles*. Common Core of Data, National Center for Education Statistics. Washington, DC: US Department of Education. Retrieved July 23, 2006, from http://nces.ed.gov/programs/profiles/.

US Department of Education (2005). *1992–2005 Reading Assessments*. National Assessment of Educational Progress (NAEP), Institute of Education Sciences, National Center for Education Statistics. Washington, DC: US Department of Education.

Walker, H. M. (2004). Commentary: use of evidence-based interventions in schools: where we've been, where we are, and where we need to go. *School Psychology Review, 33*, 398–407.

Walker, H. M., Ramsey, E., & Gresham, F. M. (2004). *Antisocial Behavior in Schools: Evidence-Based Practices* (2nd ed.). Independence, KY: Thomson Wadsworth.

Weist, M. D. (2003). Challenges and opportunities in moving toward a public health approach in school mental health. *Journal of School Psychology, 41*, 77–82.

28

The Florida Problem-Solving/Response to Intervention Model: Implementing a Statewide Initiative

George M. Batsche, Michael J. Curtis, Clark Dorman, José M. Castillo, and Larry J. Porter

George M. Batsche, EdD, is Professor and Co-Director of the Institute for School Reform in the School Psychology Program at the University of South Florida in Tampa, Florida and serves as the Co-Director of the Florida PSM/RTI Project. batsche@tempeset.coedu.usf.edu

Michael J. Curtis, PhD, is Professor and Co-Director of the Institute for School Reform in the School Psychology Program at the University of South Florida and serves as the Co-Director of the Florida PSM/RTI Project. curtis@tempest.coedu.usf.edu

Clark Dorman, EdS, is the Project Leader for the Florida PSM/RTI Project and a former school psychologist in the Orange County (Orlando) School District. dorman@coedu.usf.edu

José M. Castillo, MA, is a doctoral student and Presidential Fellow in the School Psychology Program at the University of South Florida. jcastillo@tampabay.rr.com

Larry J. Porter is a doctoral intern in the Pasco County School District in Land O' Lakes, Florida and a student in the School Psychology Program at the University of South Florida. ljporter@mail.usf.edu

The Florida Department of Education (FLDOE) approved and funded ($1.2 million/year) a 5-year project in spring, 2006, to implement the problem-solving/response-to-intervention (PSM/RTI) model throughout the state. The project was awarded to the School Psychology Program at the University of South Florida. However, building the infrastructure necessary to implement the PSM/RTI model actually began in 1991, and the state systematically built capacity to support the implementation of this model. This chapter describes how the state built capacity to implement the PSM/RTI model, the three-stage implementation process, the training model, the implementation plan and the evaluation protocol.

The Florida PSM/RTI Project incorporated two simultaneous initiatives: statewide training available to all school districts and district-specific training delivered to a small number of districts each year (based on a competitive grant process). There are two reasons that this two-pronged method was chosen to implement the project. First, a clear need exists to provide training to all districts to support their implementation of the requirements of the In-dividuals with Disabilities Education Improvement Act (IDEIA, 2004). Second, funding levels and the need to conduct a valid evaluation of the impact of this innovation model on students and educators required that a limited number of sites be selected for controlled implementation. The activities associated with each of these initiatives are explained more fully later in this chapter.

28.1 Principles of Systems Change that Support Implementation

What is known about factors essential for successful systems change efforts has increased significantly in recent years (Fixsen, Naoom, Blasé, Friedman, and Wallace, 2005). It has become apparent that the most successful large-scale implementation projects are those that use well-established strategies supported by research. Accordingly, systems theory and principles identified in the systems-change literature as critical for success were used to guide the design and implementation of the statewide project in Florida.

28.2 Education as a Social System

First, it must be recognized that the P-12 educational system in Florida is a social system, as defined in the literature, that includes a wide array of interconnected parts, ranging all the way from the Governor, Legislature, and FLDOE through each of the 67 county school districts to each school and each classroom. It is also important to recognize that there is an ongoing reciprocal influence among all of those parts and that the influences are dynamic and transactional. Whether intended or not, change in one part of the system causes change in other parts of the system.

28.3 The Capacity to Solve Problems

An effectively functioning system has the capacity to assess and understand internal as well as external forces that are or will impact it and to address those forces in ways that facilitate the system's ability to attain its goals (Curtis and Stollar, 2002). Of course, systems differ markedly in their capacity to solve problems effectively. One goal of any system-change initiative is to improve the general capacity of the system to solve any problem confronting it. Although part of the larger educational system, in this project, each building represents a specific system in which change is desired and the problem-solving capacity of the building is one of the project goals.

28.4 Critical Issues in Systems-Change Initiatives

The active involvement of as many organizational members as possible through collaborative planning and problem-solving efforts is essential for meaningful and sustainable system-level change. Change cannot be dictated. Initiatives that are mandated from above, even through legislation, and even when supported, can fail if those who must implement the change lack an understanding of the justification and lack a commitment to the innovation (Fullan, 1997). The desired change must be seen as integral to and interrelated to other key elements of the school (Senge, Kleiner, Roberts, Ross, and Smith, 1994). Therefore, all primary stakeholders (e.g., classroom teachers, parents, student support services personnel, building principals) must be involved in every stage of the change process, from initial discussions through evaluation of outcomes and modification of the change process, as needed (Curtis and Stollar, 2002). At the same time, change is unlikely in the absence of support from persons in key leadership positions and policy makers (Hall and Hord, 2001) or when there is no visionary leadership present (Fullan, 2003).

The success of a change effort will be determined primarily by those who are members of the system, rather than by an outside expert (Fuchs, Fuchs, Harris, and Roberts, 1996). Therefore, continuous on-site understanding of commitment to and support for the initiative must be present. Initiatives must be followed by regular and reliable communication, ongoing staff development, on-site coaching, and adequate time for implementation (Hall and Hord, 2001).

The Florida PSM/RTI project has used a three-stage process for implementation: development of *consensus*, *infrastructure* support, and finally *implementation* of the complete model.

28.5 Development of Consensus

The primary purpose of the activities designed to promote consensus was to ensure that a wide range of key stakeholders were provided with the information and knowledge necessary to understand the rationale and design of the PSM/RTI model and to support its implementation. Developing the consensus at a statewide level occurred as a result of several strategic activities: (1) disseminating knowledge about PSM/RTI at a statewide level; (2) establishing partnerships with related and relevant initiatives; (3) conducting a statewide assessment of beliefs, practices, and identified needs necessary for successful implementation; (Porter, Batsche, Curtis, Castillo, Witte, 2006) (4) developing statewide interactive webcasts directed to all relevant stakeholders; (5) conducting research on the impact of statewide initiatives related to PSM/RTI and disseminating those findings to stakeholders.

28.5.1 Disseminating Knowledge

Information about No Child Left Behind Act (NCLB, 2002), the reauthorization of the Individuals with Disabilities Education Act (IDEA) and knowledge about PSM/RTI was disseminated systematically over a 3-year period of time beginning in 2003. Five primary groups of individuals were the target of the dissemination process: general and special education administrators, general and special education teachers and curriculum supervisors, student services professional associations, university training programs, and parent groups.

Workshops and informational meetings for general and special education administrators were conducted each year at an annual conference (The Administrators Management Meeting (AMM)) convened by the FLDOE. This conference is designed to bring general and special education administrators together to discuss new initiatives, laws and rules, and other state-level administrative issues. The primary focus of these presentations was the role of the central office and building administrators in the implementation of NCLB and IDEA 2004. Presentations at this statewide meeting were followed up with regional meetings, such as those conducted by the Institute for Small and Rural Districts. Similar presentations were made over that 3-year period of time at the statewide Curriculum, Instruction and Assessment Conference attended by general education curriculum supervisors, master teachers and classroom teachers. The State Network of Association Presidents, a group comprised of the leadership (president, past-president, president-elect) of the student services organizations (school psychology, social work, counseling, nursing), was convened twice each year by the FLDOE. The topics discussed during this period of time focused primarily on issues related to PSM/RTI and accountability within the student services professions. This venue served to strengthen the role of the professional associations in providing professional development in PSM/RTI. The Florida State Improvement Grant funding was used to support activities (e.g., developing a web-based interactive training module on PSM/RTI) to involve the university training programs in school psychology, social work, counseling, and speech/language therapy. In addition, presentations were made to parent groups (e.g., state advisory council), and parent and advocacy

groups were active partners in state-level meetings convened to address regulatory changes necessary to comply with IDEA 2004.

28.5.2 Establishing Partnerships

The FLDOE has funded and facilitated three primary initiatives that are related directly to the PSM/RTI model: Just Read, Florida! (includes Reading First), Statewide Positive Behavior Support, and early intervention (Voluntary Pre-Kindergarten). The Florida Center for Reading Research (FCRR; www.fcrr.org) has been instrumental in implementing evidence-based reading curricula, progress monitoring assessment (e.g., dynamic indicators of basic early literacy skills (DIBELS), curriculum-based measurement (CBM)), and a statewide data management system for reading. The statewide Positive Behavior Support Project has implemented similar systems to address behavior issues in schools. The early intervention program includes a statewide support for preschool education, the use of evidence-based curricula and assessment protocols that link with entry assessment to kindergarten statewide. The statewide PSM/RTI Project has partnered with these initiatives to ensure that each of these projects is integrated in school districts throughout Florida.

28.5.3 Statewide Surveys

Prior to the implementation of the statewide model, it was important to understand the attitudes and beliefs, perceived skill levels, and professional development needs of professionals who would be called upon to provide skill support, coaching, data management, and training in the model. In the state of Florida, school psychologists were identified as professionals likely to posses these skills.

A survey was developed to gauge Florida's readiness to implement the PSM/RTI model and to identify the specific training needs of school psychologists in the state. The survey consisted of three sections: (1) the current practices of school psychologists, specifically activities related to problem solving; (2) the beliefs of school psychologists about problem solving and RTI; (3) the perceived professional development needs for the implementation of problem-solving and RTI. Demographic information (e.g., highest level of training and number of students served) was also collected. The survey was mailed on two separate occasions to 823 members of the Florida Association of School Psychologists. There were a total of 308 responses, resulting in a 42% response rate.

28.5.4 Attitudes and Beliefs

Among the school psychologists surveyed, 80% were currently satisfied with their job role and 82% indicated that they would be happy with their job role if PSM/RTI were implemented in their district. A majority of school psychologists believed that they could use PSM/RTI with training (84%), that PSM/RTI could accurately identify at-risk students (75%), and that PSM/RTI would accurately identify students for special education eligibility/determination (64%). Approximately two-thirds of the school psychologists surveyed supported the use of RTI for special education determination (64%).

28.5.5 Practices

School psychologists responding to the survey indicated that they did not consistently graph progress monitoring or baseline data (81% sometimes or never), establish peer-group level of functioning (69% sometimes or never), monitor progress of students (66% sometimes or never) or implement interventions based upon verified hypotheses (57% sometimes or never). Problem identification occurred consistently approximately half of the time (49% often or always). School psychologists were most likely to use grades (82% often or always) and teacher report (70% often or always) for progress monitoring data and were least likely to use norm-referenced achievement and cognitive assessments (80% sometimes or never). School psychologists were likely to be involved in developing individual behavior management interventions (67% often or always). School psychologists were less likely to be involved in building-level curricular decisions (92% sometimes or never), individual academic interventions, and group therapy/social skills training. School psychologists were most likely to use clinical training (64% often or always) and programs available at the school district (60%) for intervention development rather than information from research/professional journals (less than 20%).

28.5.6 Training Needs

Responses of school psychologists surveyed also identified that skills related to PSM/RTI were a high priority for training (e.g., problem-solving steps, academic intervention development, behavior intervention development, RTI, consultation and tiered model of service delivery). Skills relating to ability/achievement testing were identified as low priority (e.g., norm referenced cognitive assessment and achievement assessment). Approximately 25% of school psychologists indicated that they had no training in tiered service delivery models or program evaluation. Approximately 10–15% of school psychologists indicated that they had no training in goal setting, progress monitoring, or response to intervention.

The results of this survey suggested that a significant amount of training would be required if school psychologists were to play a significant role in the implementation of PSM/RTI. The results also suggested that school psychologists would embrace the opportunity to be involved in this effort and that they did not believe the shift to this model presented a significant threat to their job security. The Florida Association of School Psychologists established a PSM/RTI committee and appointed a committee chairperson. The PSM/RTI committee was charged with ensuring that school psychologists had the skills and opportunity to provide leadership to the statewide implementation.

28.5.7 Webcasts

One method of disseminating information across a large state is through the use of technology. The FLDOE developed five webcasts for broadcast in fall, 2006. The webcast content is targeted toward the following stakeholders: administrators and supervisors, school-based problem-solving/intervention teams, general education and support teachers, special education and support staff, and parents, guardians, and advocacy groups. The purpose of the webcasts was to increase awareness and knowledge, not to promote specific skill development. Many sources of information exist regarding PSM/RTI, and the FLDOE wanted to present consistent information to all stakeholders. The intent was to support an activity that resulted in all stakeholders "being on the same page" regarding basic information about PSM/RTI at the beginning of the statewide implementation. The following content was presented to each of the stakeholder groups, with differential emphasis on the information depending on the stakeholder group: overview and purpose of the state project; statutory and regulatory authority for PSM/RTI; research supporting positive outcomes for students using PSM/RTI; three-tiered model of service delivery; components of and steps in the PSM/RTI model; data-based decision-making; decision rules for modifying interventions and special education eligibility; evidence-based academic and behavior interventions; and integrating PSM/RTI with existing state initiatives.

28.5.8 Disseminating Research on the Impact of Early Intervention Programs: Reading First

Evaluating the impact of early intervention programs in the state was important to the project for several reasons. First, data on the impact of implementing early intervention programs could be disseminated to key stakeholders across the state to help build consensus. These data also informed the project in terms of programs that would be useful for schools implementing the problem-solving model. Finally, data from early intervention programs served as a baseline when evaluating the impact of implementing the problem-solving model.

One such early intervention program that the project evaluated (Castillo, Batsche, Curtis, Porter, and Smith, 2006) was the state's *Reading First* initiative. The Reading First (FCRR, 2006) initiative is funded to individual states through Title I of NCLB and is designed as an early intervention (K–3) program that provides intensive, scientifically proven reading instruction to students in low socioeconomic status (SES) schools. Beginning with the 2003–2004 school year, Reading First funds (approximately $275 million) were provided to districts containing schools with significant proportions of low-SES students. The purpose of the additional funding was to help schools improve the quality of reading assessment, instruction, and intervention in kindergarten through third grade. The FCRR (www.fcrr.org) was established to implement the Reading First initiative. The center provides

technical assistance, research support, intervention support and Reading First coaches for all Reading First schools. The research, intervention, and technical assistance support is available through the website to all schools in Florida. It was important to assess the impact of implementing the early reading intervention program on referrals for special education evaluations. Referrals were believed to be a sensitive indicator of the immediate impact of early intervention on the proportion of students not responding to general education instruction. Examining referrals was a way to assess the impact of Reading First on disproportional representation among the students referred.

To assess the impact of Reading First on referral rates and disproportionality, a random sample of schools, stratified by condition (i.e., Reading First versus comparison schools) and district size (i.e., the number of students in a school's district) was selected. The sample consisted of 100 schools that received Reading First funding since the program's inception and 92 comparison schools. Because the state of Florida requires schools to submit information on each of their students, including demographic data and special education status, information was obtained from the state's management information system. Each student's race/ethnicity, gender, and free–reduced lunch status was obtained for each of the schools in the study sample. In terms of referrals, two data elements were used by the state of Florida that proved useful as indicators of referral trends. One element provided an index of the rate at which students were referred and had an evaluation pending at the conclusion of the school year. The other element indicated the rate at which students had been evaluated for special education and found ineligible. No other data elements adequately provided an index of referral rates. Both the demographic and referral data were obtained for the 2002–2003, 2003–2004, and 2004–2005 school years.

The primary method used to analyze the referral data involved calculating proportional changes in the risk of being referred across years. Risk indices were calculated for all of the students in the sample to obtain an index of overall referral rates. Risk indices were calculated by racial/ethnic group, gender, and free–reduced lunch status to examine disproportionality. All risk indices were derived by dividing the number of students referred in a given group by the total enrollment for that group (Donovan and Cross, 2002). The risk indices were compared across years to determine the proportional changes in the risk of being referred for all students and disaggregated subgroups.

Based on the two referral indicators, results indicated that Reading First had a positive impact on referral rates and reduced disproportionality. In Florida, 50% of all placements in special education occur in programs for students with learning disabilities (LDs). Approximately 95% of the LD placements occurred because of low performance in reading and language arts. Therefore, about 47% of all special education placements are related directly to reading and language arts. Noteworthy findings included: a 49% decrease in the proportion of students referred and pending in Reading First schools, compared with a 70% increase in comparison schools; a 4% decrease in the proportion of students evaluated and ineligible in Reading First schools, compared with a 76% increase in comparison schools. The risk of being referred and pending referrals in Reading First schools decreased for traditionally overrepresented groups. For males, African American students, Hispanic students, and students on free–reduced lunch, reductions of over 50% occurred. The opposite trend occurred for the same groups in the comparison schools, with 13–63% increases in risk found. The risk of being evaluated and ineligible decreased in Reading First schools for the majority of disaggregated groups. Decreases in risk of 19–69% occurred for males, African American students, and students on free–reduced lunch. The opposite trend occurred for comparison schools, with 32–78% increases in risk observed for the same groups. Inexplicably, the risk of being evaluated and ineligible for Hispanic students increased by 67% in the Reading First schools, but decreased by 31% in the comparison schools.

In order to assess the impact of the PSM/RTI model on outcomes such as referrals for special education and student academic performance, it is important to separate the effects of the PSM/RTI model from the effects of other programs (e.g., Reading First) with parallel outcomes implemented during similar timeframes. It is clear that programs such as Reading First have a significant impact on the number of students referred for special education, particularly in elementary grades. IDEIA (2004) provides local educational agencies with the option to use PSM/RTI to determine eligibility for LD programs. The PSM/RTI model will provide school districts with the tools and data necessary to assess the impact of early intervention programs (Tier 1 and 2) on student performance, individually or in groups. These data can then be used to determine whether student performance might be attributed to the effectiveness of core curriculum and supplemental instruction (Reading First immediate instruction and intensive instruction) or to variables associated with a disability.

28.6 Development of the Infrastructure

A statewide project such as PSM/RTI must incorporate and build on the skills and infrastructure that exist in the public schools across the state. Any attempt to implement a problem-solving/RTI model without consensus and the necessary infrastructure *already in place* will fail. Sarason (1982) stressed that it was necessary both to understand and to use the behavioral regularity of the existing system in order to build additional skill and capacity. Therefore, it was important to understand both the historical contributions and present artifacts of the infrastructure in Florida prior to organizing the salient components of the model. The existing infrastructure for the current statewide project was comprised of: (1) practices that resulted from early statewide projects addressing curriculum-based assessment, school-wide problem solving and student support teams; (2) contemporary statewide projects, including Just Read, Florida!, Reading First, Positive Behavior Support, and Universal Pre-K; (3) state regulations that support problem-solving/RTI; (4) use of technology; (5) existing pilot projects; (6) annual conferences to communicate effective practices and outcomes.

28.6.1 Historical Perspective

In 1991, the FLDOE funded three major projects in the state: curriculum-based assessment (Orange County School District), school-wide problem solving (University of South Florida), and student support teams (Broward County School District). Although rudimentary in their beginning stages, these three programs served as incubators for the development of many practices in the ensuing 16 years. These programs contributed directly to the current assessment and intervention practices in Florida. For instance: (1) all kindergarten students in Florida are screened with DIBELS within the first 21 days of school; (2) CBM and DIBELS are used as the progress-monitoring tool in all Reading First schools in Florida and in a significant number of non-Reading First schools; (3) a statewide project (Project Central) provides training and technical assistance to any district in the state that wishes to use DIBELS/CBM as a method of early identification and progress monitoring; materials and statewide norms exist for these assessment practices; (4) State regulations require interventions in the general education setting and the use of response to intervention prior to consideration of any referral for special education; (5) virtually all schools in the state use problem-solving teams to facilitate decision-making for at-risk students; (6) a strong foundation exists for the use of a tiered system of service delivery at the universal (e.g., early screening/intervention, school-wide positive behavior support, K-3 academic support plan). Furthermore, the historical presence of authentic assessment, school-wide perspectives on intervention and problem-solving teams makes the transition to practices consistent with the basic principles involved in PSM/RTI less formidable.

Currently, a number of statewide initiatives exist that will provide additional infrastructure to support statewide implementation of the PSM/RTI model. Each is described briefly.

28.6.2 Just Read, Florida!

The FLDOE invested significant resources in the Just Read, Florida! (FLDOE, 2005a) (www.justreadflorida.com) initiative that focuses on practices ranging from early literacy skills through post-secondary programs. This emphasis on reading skills has resulted in significant improvements in the reading skills of students in Florida. In Florida, approximately 95% of students in LD programs were referred for problems in the reading/language arts areas. Therefore, any program that significantly improves reading/language arts skills should result in a positive impact on referrals resulting in LD eligibility. In fact, recent trend data indicate that LD placements in Florida

have stabilized or indicate a downward trend. Once again, this is important baseline information to know when interpreting evaluation data on the PSM/RTI initiative. More importantly, the Just Read, Florida! initiative provides schools with a rich resource of interventions in the area of reading.

28.6.3 Reading First

Florida was the second state in the United States to receive funding under Title I of NCLB for Reading First. The Reading First initiative is the responsibility of the FCRR under the directorship of Joseph Torgeson. The FCRR has implemented a number of programs that support the PSM/RTI project. These include:

1. Resources for evidence-based interventions in reading, K–12.
2. A statewide reading assessment system comprised of both DIBELS and CBM.
3. The statewide Progress Monitoring Reporting Network (PMRN). The PMRN is a web-based system of data storage and management through which DIBELS/CBM data are archived and available for progress monitoring and reporting at the individual student, classroom, building and district levels. The PMRN is available to every public school in the state of Florida.
4. Blueprints for a three-tiered intervention support system for reading instruction, K–3.
5. Technical assistance and support to improve the quality of reading instruction and student outcome.
6. Statewide evaluation of the effects of Reading First on student performance.

Thus, the infrastructure provided by the FCRR provides support to the PSM/RTI project in the areas of assessment, data management, and intervention support and implementation in the area of reading/language arts.

28.6.4 Statewide Positive Behavior Support

The FLDOE (2002) has supported the implementation of a statewide positive behavior support (PBS; www.flpbs.fmhi.usf.edu) initiative for a number of years. The project, housed at the Florida Mental

Health Institute at the University of South Florida, provides training, technical assistance, and support to implement school-wide PBS (SW-PBS). The components of the PBS project that support the implementation of the PSM/RTI project include; (1) evidence-based interventions that improve behavior at the building, classroom, and individual student levels; (2) evidence-based assessment procedures to evaluate the degree to which the key features of the PBS system are present at the school (SET) and classroom (TACL) levels; (3) training and technical assistance to implement the School-Wide Information System (SWIS) to organize and interpret data assessing student behavior; (4) evaluation data that assess the effects of PBS on both student social behavior and the effects of improved behavior on academic performance.

28.6.5 Early Intervention Programs

In 2003, the citizens of the state of Florida passed a constitutional amendment requiring the availability of "universal pre-kindergarten" programs throughout the state. This program has been modified to a "voluntary pre-kindergarten" (VPK) (FLDOE, 2005a) program for all 4-year-old children in the state. The components of the VPK initiative that impact the PSM/RTI project directly include: (1) the development of state standards of performance for children ages 3–5 that guide basic curriculum and interventions for pre-kindergarten programs; (2) a requirement that all students beginning kindergarten be assessed using both the DIBELS and the Early Screening Inventory for Kindergarten during the first 21 days of kindergarten, which provides a baseline data point on all beginning kindergarten students; (3) a requirement that the progress of all kindergarten students be monitored using the DIBELS three times during the year.

28.6.6 State Education Regulations

The successful implementation of any statewide PSM/RTI initiative required state regulations that support the practices, procedures, and funding sources necessary to implement the initiative. The FLDOE promoted the PSM/RTI as a general education initiative that will impact special education. The FLDOE promulgated a series of regulations that support the PSM/RTI model with requirements that

strengthen the general education programs for at-risk students. In addition, the FLDOE changed the regulations regarding eligibility for programs serving students with emotional/behavioral disorders. When preparing this chapter, the regulations regarding eligibility for programs serving students with LDs were also being revised. The most important regulations, however, are those that impact general education. Selected excerpts from those regulations that have direct relevance to the PSM/RTI initiative appear in Table 28.1.

28.6.7 Use of Technology

The geography of the state of Florida requires that technical assistance and training be supported through the use of distance learning and interactive CD-ROM technology. In addition, data from the needs assessment survey indicated clearly that practitioners would require technology to organize, manage, and display data to implement the PSM/RTI model with integrity. Of the practitioners responding to the survey, 69% indicated that the lack of technology to support the model represented a "somewhat or large threat" to successful implementation.

The first phase of the PSM/RTI project included the use of statewide webcasts and an interactive CD-ROM to support implementation of the PSM/RTI model. The interactive CD-ROM guides practitioners and school-based teams through the steps of the problem-solving/response to intervention process and provides them with feedback regarding accuracy in decision-making. The primary purpose of the CD-ROM is to control the amount of drift that naturally occurs when a process is implemented without widespread coaching support or other methods of providing implementation fidelity feedback to participants.

The PSM/RTI project provided two types of technology support for data management and display. First, additional information regarding the use of the PMRN was provided during the statewide training. The goal was to increase the use of this data management system for reading interventions. Second, the project compiled and disseminated information regarding software programs that facilitate and support data management and display. The project's technology staff will obtain, review, and evaluate all available computer programs that can accomplish this task. The information was provided to school

TABLE 28.1. Excerpts from regulations that support PSM/RTI (Florida Department of Education, 2006b, 2006c)

Rule 6A-6.0331 Identification and Determination of Eligibility of Exceptional Students for Specially Designed Instruction	Rule 6A-6.03016. Exceptional Student Education for Students with Emotional or Behavioral Disabilities.
• It is the local school board's responsibility to address through appropriate interventions and, to the extent possible, resolve a student's learning or behavioral areas of concern *in the general education environment*....	(1) Definition. Students with an emotional/behavioral disability (E/BD). A student with an emotional/behavioral disability has persistent (is not sufficiently responsive to well-implemented evidenced-based interventions) and consistent emotional or behavioral responses that adversely effect performance in the educational environment that cannot be attributed to age, culture, gender or ethnicity.
• The initial conference with the parents must include discussion of the student's learning or behavioral areas of concerns, the *general education interventions planned, and the anticipated effects of the interventions.*	(6) Characteristics not indicative of a student with an emotional/behavioral disability:
• Other conferences must include discussion of the student's *responses to interventions*....	(a) normal temporary (less than 6 months) reactions to life event(s) or crisis, or
• For students with academic learning problems, the *general education interventions must include an AIP.**	(b) emotional/behavioral difficulties that improve significantly in the presence of well-implemented evidenced-based interventions, or
• Pre- and post-intervention measures of the academic and/or behavioral areas of concern must be conducted to assist in identifying appropriate interventions and *measuring their effects.*	(c) social maladjustment unless also found to have an emotional/behavioral disability.

*Academic Improvement Plan.

districts throughout the state. In addition, a number of the large school districts (e.g., Broward County School District, Ft. Lauderdale) in Florida developed district-specific information management systems designed to monitor student progress and manage/display data. These districts served as resources to other districts that decided to develop their own district-specific system.

28.6.8 Pilot Projects

In the 5 years prior to the initiation of the statewide project, a number of school districts supported small pilot projects to implement and evaluate the PSM/RTI model. A few of these districts developed policies and procedures that support implementation of the problem-solving model. Orange County School District (Orlando, FL) began a pilot project with six elementary schools. The district provided a summary of the pilot project, 2 years of outcome data, and a compilation of "lessons learned" for this chapter:

In September of the 2003–04 school year, a three-person team comprised of two school psychologists and a read-

ing specialist was assembled. The sole responsibility of that team was to develop and implement a problem solving/RTI initiative in 6 pilot schools. At that time we had a better than fair knowledge base regarding PS/RTI but had no experience at all with implementation. The schools were chosen for us and covered a broad range of socioeconomic, achievement, and geographical categories. We gave a brief PS/RTI presentation to the administrative teams at each of the schools and made subsequent presentations to the school faculty. Our initiative was focused initially on reading, so we became DIBELS trainers and trained all the teachers in our buildings in DIBELS administration. Upon examining our schoolwide data, it became apparent to our team that there were systemic problems in each building that needed correcting prior to beginning problem solving with individual students. We were not especially successful in communicating that message to the leadership in our school buildings. Throughout the 2003–04 school year we spent time observing the instruction during the entire 90-minute reading block in each of our K–3 classrooms. After each administration of DIBELS, we would meet with teachers, one grade level at a time, to discuss the results and implications. We used those sessions as 'on the job' training opportunities to teach both problem solving and DIBELS interpretation (very bad idea!).

Noting our struggles at informal training with a 'learn by doing' model, over the summer following the 2003–04 academic school year, we set up a three-day summer institute and brought in Dave Tilly and Randy Allison (Heartland Area Education Agency, Des Moines, IA). Randy did a full day of system-wide problem solving, Dave did a full day of individual student problem solving, and our team wrapped with a third day of problem solving in Orange County. We invited teams from all our schools, set them up at their own table, provided them with a packet of data from their school from the previous year, and walked them through digesting their data and action planning for the next year. We also provided each school with a tub of resources which included a variety of books (Ken Howell's CBE book, Special Ed in Transition, Direct Instruction Reading, Bringing Words to Life, and others).

With the beginning of the 2004–05 school year, our reading specialist became ill and was out the entire year. Thus, our three-person team was now two. We met with principals to impress upon them the need for the development of teams at their schools who would function independently of us, but met with moderate success. We continued to provide scattered presentations on problem solving ideas and practice. We spent our second year with a bit more success than the first, but still floundering much more than was acceptable. By the end of 2004–05 we had a much better skill set in PS/RTI in general, but more importantly now had a well developed sense of what does not work in implementation. We took an objective and critical look at our success and failures and decided to dedicate a significant amount of time and effort toward creating a deliberate, systematic, and comprehensive set of training modules and materials.

We spent the summer following the 2004–05 academic year and the beginning of the 2005–06 academic year in the development and refinement of that professional development package. Our goal was to implement a train the trainers model, with those trained trainers responsible for delivering training to identified teams at the schools. We trained 40 trainers—12 of those were identified as "core" personnel who would have training responsibilities and the others as "ancillary" personnel who desired the information, but were unable to commit to training at schools. At this point (May, 2006), we have completed the training of trainers and those trainers have completed training in 8 of 10 additional pilot schools. The benefits to a structured, thoughtful process of professional development cannot be overstated. We now have school teams who have ownership of the change process at their schools, who cannot wait for the new school year to begin so they can use their newly developed skills.

The positive results in Orange County have been both qualitative and quantitative. The RTI team has developed into an Information/Professional Development/Best Practices resource for the district. Dialogue between district committees, departments, and projects has increased. Needs in instructional integrity and curricular consistency have been identified and addressed. At successful sites, teachers have moved from a mindset of making decisions about special education eligibility to making decisions of what to teach and how to teach it.

Quantitatively, we have documented (Figure 1) the positive impact on student performance when data are used to make systemic programming decisions. At one particular site at the kindergarten level, the percentage students with the most intense academic needs making a defined amount of progress increased from 50% in year one to 89% in year two. In first grade, the percentage of students with the same instructional need making progress increased from 0% during year one to 60% in year two. In second and third grades, the results were somewhat different. In second grade, the percentage of students who maintained the top level benchmark status increased from 58% to 83%. Likewise, in third grade the students maintaining benchmark status increased from 57% to 89%. However, in both second and third grades, the percentage of students with the highest instructional needs making progress was negligible. Some contextual information helps to explain the differences noted between the increased progress made by students with intense need in kindergarten and first and the limited progress made by those students in second and third. Upon analyzing the first year data, the school made decisions to alter the content and structure of instructional delivery to the most struggling students in kindergarten and first grade, but elected to maintain the same instructional and intervention strategies in second and third grade. The data accurately reflect the outcomes of these decisions.

The training package consists of 6 half-day instructional modules: 1) Overview of PS/RTI; 2) Problem Identification; 3) Problem Analysis (part one); 4) Problem Analysis (part two); 5) Intervention Design; and 6) Intervention Evaluation.

The Orange County School District provided a summary of what they learned from this three-year experience (See Appendix A).

28.6.9 Statewide Meetings

The FLDOE and the associations representing administrators, teachers, and student services personnel provide multiple opportunities each year for districts with pilot projects to convene and share their experiences, outcomes, and policy/procedures information. The PSM/RTI statewide project will convene a state-level "innovations conference" each

Progress in reading is defined using DIBELS data with three conditions resulting in "progress": 1) a student who begins the year at an instructional recommendation level of Intensive and reaches either Emerging or Established end of year goal status ; 2) a student who begins the year at an instructional recommendation level of Strategic and reaches Established end of year goal status; 3) a student who begins the year at an instructional recommendation level of Benchmark and maintains Established end of year goal status.

FIGURE 28.1. Pinewood elementary outcome data: years 1 and 2.

year to ensure that information regarding implementation strategies, professional development, and evaluation data are shared throughout the state. In addition, this annual conference provides a venue to identify and develop solutions for systemic problems that threaten successful implementation statewide.

28.6.10 Technical Assistance Papers

Technical assistance papers (TAPs) is a method used primarily by the FLDOE to provide technical assistance to practitioners regarding the implementation of a wide range of practices and initiatives. The TAPs provide a background, literature review, specific practice guidelines, and a frequently asked question section for each of the areas addressed by the TAP. In September 2005, the FLDOE released a TAP titled, "The Response to Intervention (RTI) Model" (FLDOE, 2006a) (available at http://sss.usf.edu). The purpose of this TAP was to communicate general information about the PSM/RTI model and to clarify the position of the FLDOE regarding the implementation of the model and to communicate the expectations of this model for general and special education administrators and teachers, student services personnel and parents and advocates. The TAP was a critical component in the development of the statewide infrastructure.

The successful implementation of a statewide PSM/RTI model requires the presence of critical infrastructure components. These include funding and personnel support, regulations, intervention support, technology, and technical assistance. During the 2004–2005 school year, an evaluation of the existing infrastructure in the state of Florida resulted in the decision that sufficient components were in place to justify implementation of the statewide project.

28.7 Statewide Implementation

28.7.1 Overview of the Method of Implementation

Implementation of the PSM/RTI model is slated to occur through two separate, but linked, initiatives. First, statewide training is made available to all school districts in the state of Florida and implemented over a 5-year period of time. This training

is facilitated by regional coordinators/trainers and supported by project staff. Second, demonstration districts and pilot schools within those districts were selected through a competitive, Request for Proposal (RFP) process. Each of the districts selected received funds to support building-level coaches, as well as training and support from the project staff. The demonstration districts and pilot schools were required to meet pre-established criteria, to agree to support the activities of the project, agree to participate in project evaluation research and to support the coaches who they chose to employ. Project staff monitored the training regimen, implementation integrity, and evaluation process closely. Three districts and six pilot schools (elementary) in each district (total of 18 schools) were selected for the first year of implementation. Approximately 10 000 students were enrolled in the 18 schools. Project funding for districts and schools selected is maintained for 3 years, after which districts will be strongly encouraged to assume responsibility for continued support and expansion of the implementation process. Districts and pilot schools will be added to the project in each of the subsequent years of funding. Table 28.2 illustrates the differences between the two separate, but linked, initiatives.

TABLE 28.2. Differences between statewide training and demonstration site activities.

	Statewide training	Demonstration districts
Training model	Large group	Pilot schools only
Follow-up support	Limited to time and resources of regional coordinators/trainers	One coach, full-time, for three pilot schools
Funding	None to districts specifically	Support to hire coaches, purchase computers, materials/supplies, conduct training, collect data
Data collection	Discretion of district	Requirement for project participation. One specific job responsibility of coaches
Evaluation	Discretion of district	Evaluation plan developed and implemented by project staff

The two-pronged implementation model (statewide training and demonstration districts) was selected to ensure that all districts had access to training in order to implement the requirements of both NCLB and IDEIA (2004) *and* to ensure that implementation in controlled settings occurred in order to conduct a rigorous evaluation protocol. The project goals and activities are delineated in Table 28.3.

The PSM/RTI project staff facilitate the implementation of both the statewide training and the demonstration site initiatives. The project is funded for approximately $1.2 million a year for 5 years by the FLDOE using IDEA discretionary project funding sources. The central project staff are identified in Goal 1 in Table 28.3.

28.7.2 Training Protocol and Agenda

The training protocol for both the statewide training and the training of school-based teams in the demonstration sites is the same. The basic training occurs over a three-year period of time with the option of advanced training in areas to be determined by the site(s). The basic training cycle and agenda includes:

Cycle 1/Year 1 Training
  Day 1: Introduction to grant: special ed law and systems change
  Day 2: problem solving overview with case examples
  Day 3: problem identification and data sources and types
  Day 4: problem analysis and plan development/implementation/fidelity
  Day 5: managing/displaying data and intervention/eligibility decision-making
Cycle 2/Year 2 Trainings
  Day 1: facilitator's training
  Day 2: strengthening building-level tier systems
  Day 3: program evaluation
Cycle 3/Year 3 Trainings
  Day 1: implementation in other settings (transferring training)
  Day 2: strengthening and enhancing intervention options
  Day 3: technical assistance on system problems

28.7.3 Statewide Training Initiative

The state of Florida was divided into three geographic regions. Each region was assigned one re-

gional coordinator/trainer (RCT). Each RCT is responsible for the following activities:

1. To serve as a member of the statewide planning and implementation team.
2. To communicate project goals and activities to all school districts in the region.
3. To conduct needs/readiness assessments regarding the PSM/RTI model with districts in the region.
4. To deliver/facilitate Cycle 1–3 training at multiple sites within the region.
5. To provide technical assistance, based on time available, to districts implementing the model within the region. This is delivered through large group meetings with district designated "point persons" for this initiative.
6. To provide feedback to the FLDOE and the project staff regarding implementation successes and challenges.
7. To meet quarterly with the evaluation consultant regarding data for the evaluation protocol.
8. To meet monthly with coaches from demonstration districts in their respective regions.

The RCTs spend the majority of their time in the first 2 years ensuring that the training cycles are delivered successfully in their region. Owing to the size of each region, the Cycle 1 content must be delivered multiple times within the region. The RCTs schedule meetings quarterly to communicate with district designated "point persons" and to provide technical assistance for problems identified during these meetings. Owing to the size of the state, the number of RCTs and the geography to be covered in each region, technical assistance at this level of the project is limited to these quarterly meetings.

28.7.4 Demonstration Districts/Sites

The selection of demonstration districts/pilot schools is accomplished through the use of a statewide RFP. Selection of demonstration districts is a competitive process with a limited number of districts selected each year. During the first year of the project, three districts were selected. Additional districts will be added each subsequent year of the project. Each district will implement the project in six schools for a total of 18 school sites during the first year. Each district selected received funding to support the following activities for three years: 1) Hire one full-time PSM/RTI

TABLE 28.3. Florida statewide PSM/RTI project goals and activities.

Goal 1: Establish an infrastructure through which the statewide problem-solving initiative will be implemented statewide and in select school districts as pilot/demonstration sites over a period of 5 years

Activities:

1.1 Employ and evaluate staff who possess the knowledge and skills necessary to achieve implementation of the problem-solving project. Project personnel will include:

- project leader
- technology consultant(s)
- training module consultant(s)
- accountability consultant
- support staff
- technical assistance staff
- 3 regional coordinators/trainers.

1.2 Create and maintain a systematic process and structures for communication and dissemination of information and products relative to the project. Products of this activity will include:

- website
- newsletter.

1.3 Establish an advisory/articulation panel to provide guidance relative to activities and the accomplishment of project objectives, and to facilitate communication between the project and other major school-based initiatives (e.g., Reading First, PBS, voluntary pre-kindergarten), current and prospective implementation sites and other relevant constituencies (e.g., school districts, professional associations).

1.4 Create and/or identify print and web-based training modules to support the training of school district personnel relative to the successful implementation of a problem-solving model for improving student performance. This will be an ongoing activity throughout the life of the project. Priority will be assigned to resources that are based on interactive computer or other technological methodologies. The resources must reflect methods shown through research to be critical for effective problem solving.

- Initiation of identification and evaluation of resources that already exist across the United States.
- Initiation of collection of effective training resources.
- Identified training needs for which existing resources cannot be identified will be addressed through the development of training modules in subsequent years of the project.

1.5 Create (or use existing) a clearinghouse for technologically based resources (1) directly supportive of the problem-solving process or (2) effective in facilitating improved student performance for dissemination to and use by schools.

- Initiation of identification and evaluation of resources that already exist across the United States.
- Initiation of directory of available resources.
- Identified needs for which existing resources cannot be identified will be addressed through the development of resources in subsequent years of the project.

1.6 Develop a comprehensive evaluation plan of the project. This plan will include evaluation of: project goals and outcomes, training processes and outcomes, effectiveness of the RFA process and impact data for both students and personnel. The evaluation plan will be developed prior to the implementation of any project activities.

Goal 2: Create an RFP process through which schools and school districts will be selected to serve as pilot/demonstration sites

Activities:

2.1 Identify criteria for the selection of pilot/demonstration schools and school districts. Some factors for consideration have been generated through discussions with and input from school and school district personnel in conjunction with presentations relating to the implementation of a problem-solving model at various statewide conferences (e.g., professional association conferences, Curriculum, Instruction and Assessment, AMM, Attendance Symposium) over the last 4 years. Establish the timeline, procedures, and associated documents relating to the dissemination of an RFP and the selection of pilot/demonstration schools and school districts.

2.2 Initiate the RFP process and select three districts with six schools in each district for implementation during the 2006–2007 school year.

2.3 Provide infrastructure grants to each of the selected districts to fund the following activities:

- Hire one full-time PSM/RTI coach to serve three buildings. During the first year each district selected received funding for two coaches to serve the six buildings.
- Purchase computers/software and other technology necessary to manage student/building data.

(Continued)

TABLE 28.3. (*Continued*)

- Purchase materials and supplies to support the training and implementation of the model in the sites.
- Hire substitute teachers, as necessary, to ensure access to training.
- Travel and telephone/internet access.

Goal 3: Develop a training agenda for both the statewide training initiative and the training of school-based teams in the demonstration sites

Activities:

Develop training content to be implemented in yearly cycles over a three-year time period. Content will focus on the following topics:

- overview of problem-solving/RTI and legal bases
- problem identification
- data sources and types
- problem analysis
- management and implementation of interventions
- managing and displaying data
- intervention and eligibilty decision-making.

Deliver content in cycles in the following manner:

- Cycle 1/Year 1: five training days
- Cycle 2/Year 2: three training days
- Cycle 3/Year 3: three training days.

Deliver optional content each year depending on the results the needs assessment data. Optional content might include:

- advanced training in data management and display
- advanced training in academic and behavioral assessment methods
- additional training in intervention development and support
- program evaluation methods for use by districts.

Goal 4: Conduct a statewide conference for the purpose of familiarizing school and school district personnel, as well as personnel from other major school-based initiatives with the PSM/RTI model, the statewide PSM/RTI initiative, and the RFP process for the selection of pilot/demonstration sites

---

coach to serve three buildings. During the first year each district selected received funding for two coaches to serve the six buildings; 2) Purchase computers/software and other technology necessary to manage student/building data; 3) Purchase materials and supplies to support the training and implementation of the model in the sites; 4) Hire substitute teachers, as necessary, to ensure access to training; and 5) Travel and telephone/internet access.

Clearly, the most important component of the demonstration site initiative is the presence of a coach to support the implementation of the model. The roles assumed by the coaches include:

1. To participate in training school-based teams.
2. To facilitate the implementation of the training at the school level.
3. To provide on-site technical assistance to implement each step of the process at the site level.
4. To collect school-based data on implementation integrity and student outcome data.

5. To conduct a group meeting monthly with coaches, principals, and identified central office staff to communicate issues related to project implementation.
6. To meet quarterly with the state project staff to evaluate project implementation, to receive "social support" from other coaches and project staff, and to obtain technical assistance from the project staff.
7. To meet quarterly with the evaluation consultant and RCTs to ensure integrity of data collection for the evaluation protocol.
8. To meet monthly with the RCT for their respective region.

28.7.5 Training

The focus of training for the demonstration sites is the school-based team and follows the protocol in Table 28.3. Each site identifies a school-based team to facilitate the implementation of the model. Each team is made up of a building administrator, general and special education teachers, student services personnel, and other instructional support staff (e.g., Title I reading). In addition, the district is invited to include district-level supervisors (e.g., reading) and administrators on school-based teams during training sessions. Unlike the statewide training that is conducted through large-group regional training activities, the demonstration site training is conducted at the district level for the school-based teams from the six schools in the district. The school-based coaches participate as trainers during these sessions and provide training follow-up at the building level following training sessions.

28.7.6 Support for Site-Based Coaches

Coaches are supported by the project staff through training and social support activities. Project staff meet monthly with the demonstration site coaches to ensure that they have the support needed to address issues related to personnel, conflict resolution, communication with district staff, and to share successes and challenges. In addition, project staff provide direct training to the coaches in any areas of the problem-solving/RTI process that are needed. In addition, coaches are provided training regarding data collection, management, and organization of data needed both for the project evaluation and program evaluation at the district level. The building-based coaches are the individuals responsible for collecting all of the site-based data for the statewide evaluation protocol.

28.7.7 Evaluation Model

The evaluation model was developed to assess the impact of the PSM/RTI model on district/building-level variables, student outcomes, and satisfaction/beliefs of educators and parents. Evaluation data are collected only from the demonstration school sites. A "comparison" school will be selected for each of the demonstration-site schools and data will be collected from both the demonstration-site school and its comparison school. Districts must agree to collect data from both types of school in order to be eligible for one of the demonstration-site grants. Data are analyzed at different points in time and both within and across demonstration and comparison schools. Table 28.4 provides an outline of the components and data sources for the evaluation protocol.

TABLE 28.4. Florida PSM/RTI project evaluation model.

Evaluation component	Data source
1. Staff beliefs/attitudes about PSM/RTI and perceptions of skills and professional development needs	1. RTI assessment survey PSM/RTI building readiness survey
2. Impact on district/building variables	1. Percentage of students referred and placed in special education by program 2. Risk indices and odds ratios for referral and placement by race, gender, SES 3. Percentage of students referred to the office for discipline referrals 4. Percentage of students suspended, expelled or placed in alternative education programs 5. Percent of students retained
3. Student outcome data	1. Reading progress (DIBELS/CBM) from the PMRN 2. Florida comprehensive achievement test 3. Behavioral office discipline referrals
4. Satisfaction indices	1. Teacher, administrator and parent satisfaction with intervention services survey

28.7.8 Current Status

The educational system in the state of Florida is comprised of 67 county-based school districts, approximately 2700 public schools and 2.7 million students. At the end of the 2006–2007 school year, the following activities were completed:

1. Senior administrators from all 67 districts had received training on the basic components of PSM/RTI, statutes and regulations, and orientation to the statewide project.
2. Cycle 1 training was initiated in all three regions of the state. School-based teams from each of the 67 districts had the opportunity to participate in the training and to become part of a communication/technical assistance support group. The number of teams varied by region, but all 67 districts sent representative teams.

3. The year 1 demonstration-site districts were selected (3 districts, 18 school buildings, consisting of approximately 10 000 students) following a statewide conference for districts interested in completing an RFP.

4. Year 2 demonstration site RFPs were announced for additional districts and sites.

5. Year 1 of the evaluation model was completed. Baseline data on student outcomes, staff attitudes and beliefs, and district level and demographic data were collected.

28.7.9 Summary

Most states have chosen to implement the PSM/RTI model through pilot projects rather than attempting statewide implementation. At the time that this chapter was written, few states were attempting statewide implementation (e.g., Florida, Idaho, Illinois, Michigan, and Pennsylvania) through the state department of education. Presently, no models exist that provide evidence-based practices for such an undertaking. Therefore, this process can best be described as a grand experiment at this point. However, each of the states currently implementing PSM/RTI state wide have strong evaluation models, using continuous progress-monitoring strategies, to identify problem areas early in the process and to attempt problem solving to ensure continued implementation. Only time and data will tell whether the strategies enhance the educational outcomes of students.

Appendix A: Orange County School District Pilot Site Summary

A.1 "Lessons Learned"

What we thought	What we learned
Schools would have a consistent core curriculum in reading, implemented with integrity, successfully teaching 80% of the students.	Far fewer than 80% of students were successful with core curriculum.
Learning *rates* of 80% of students would be satisfactory to *maintain* benchmark or strategic status.	The percentage of students was far lower.
Specific LDs placement would result in learning gains.	Data reflecting growth of SLD students indicated limited gains.
Presentations and ongoing inservice provided by OCPS PSM Team would be limited to pilot schools.	There has been much larger demand for presentation and in-service from district literacy team, literacy coaches, learning communities, and school psychologists.
A "learn by doing" approach would be sufficient to give school team members the necessary skills.	A deliberate, structured, sequenced program of professional development is necessary.
Training was an event, which once completed, was done.	Professional development is, indeed, *development*. Learning occurs over time.

References

Castillo, J. M., Batsche, G., Curtis, M. J., Porter, L. J., & Smith, J. C. (2006, March). Early reading intervention: a preliminary analysis of a state initiative's impact on special education outcomes. Paper presented at the *National Association of School Psychologists Annual Convention*, Anaheim, CA.

Curtis, M. J. & Stollar, S. A. (2002). Best practices in system-level change. In A. Thomas & J. Grimes (Eds.), *Best Practices in School Psychology IV* (Vol. 1, pp. 223–234). Bethesda, MD: National Association of School Psychologists Publications.

Donovan, M. S. & Cross, C. T. (2002). *Minority Students in Special and Gifted Education*. Washington, DC: National Academy Press.

Fixsen, D. L., Naoom, S. F., Blasé, K. A., Friedman, R. M., & Wallace, F. (2005). *Implementation Research: A Synthesis of the Literature*. Tampa, FL: University of South Florida, Louis de la Parte Florida Mental Health Institute, The National Implementation Research Network (FMHI Publication #231).

Florida Center for Reading Research (2006). *Reading First*. Retrieved July 6, 2006, from http://www.fcrr.org/technicalassistanceReadingFirst.htm.

Florida Department of Education (2005a). *About Just Read Florida!* Retrieved July 6, 2006, from http://www.justreadflorida.com/about.asp.

Florida Department of Education (2005b). *VPK program overview*. Retrieved July 6, 2006, from http://myfloridaeducation.com/earlylearning/.

Florida Department of Education (2006a). *Technical assistance paper: the Response to intervention (RTI) model*. Retrieved July 6, 2006, from the University of South Florida, Student Support Services website: http://sss.usf.edu/pdf/y2006-8.pdf.

Florida Department of Education (2006b). Proposed Regulations for Identification and Determination of Eligibility of Exceptional Students for Specially Designed Instruction, Rule 6A-6.0331.

Florida Department of Education (2006c). Proposed Regulations for Exceptional Student Education for Students with Emotional or Behavioral Disorders, Rule 6A-6.03016.

Florida's Positive Behavior Support Projects (2002). *About us*. Retrieved July 6, 2006, from http://flpbs.fmhi.usf.edu/aboutus_projectmission.asp.

Fuchs, D., Fuchs, L., Harris, A. H., & Roberts, P. H. (1996). Bridging the research-to-practice gap with mainstream assistance teams: a cautionary tale. *School Psychology Quarterly, 11*, 244–266.

Fullan, M. (1997). *The Challenge of School Change*. Arlington Heights, IL: IRI/SkyLight Training and Publishing.

Fullan, M. (2003). *The Moral Imperative of School Leadership*. Thousand Oaks, CA: Corwin Press.

Hall, G. E. & Hord, S. M. (2006). *Implementing Change: Patterns, Principles, and Potholes*. Boston: Allyn and Bacon.

IDEIA (2004). *Individuals with Disabilities Education Improvement Act*, U.S.C. H.R. 1350.

NCLB (2002). *No Child left Behind Act*, U.S.C. 115 STAT. 1426.

Porter, L. J., Batsche, G., Curtis, M. J., Castillo, J. M., & Witte, R. (2006, March). Problem-solving and response-to-intervention: school psychologists' beliefs, practices, and training needs. Paper presented at the *National Association of School Psychologists Annual Convention*, Anaheim, CA.

Sarason, S. (1982). *The Culture of the School and the Problem of Change* (rev. ed.). Boston: Allyn & Bacon.

Senge, P. M., Kleiner, A., Roberts, C. Ross, R. B., & Smith, B. J. (1994). *The Fifth Discipline Fieldbook*. New York: Doubleday.

29

Using Technology Tools to Monitor Response to Intervention

James E. Ysseldyke and Scott McLeod

James Ysseldyke, PhD, is a Birkmaier Professor with the School Psychology Program at the University of Minnesota. jim@umn.edu
Scott McLeod, JD, PhD, is an Assistant Professor in Educational Policy and Administration with the University of Minnesota. mcleod@umn.edu

School psychologists and other educational professionals are faced with increasingly demanding data collection needs. There is increasing pressure to engage in data-driven decision-making for the purpose of making eligibility, instructional planning, program evaluation, and accountability decisions. For example, school psychologists are expected to engage in all of the data-driven decision-making activities specified in the *Blueprint for Training and Practice in School Psychology III* (Ysseldyke et al., 2006), and to help teachers identify evidence-based instructional practices while monitoring the effectiveness of those practices. Thus, school psychologists need to be knowledgeable about and capable of implementing continuous and periodic monitoring systems designed for use at universal, targeted, and intensive levels of intervention.

Along with increasing demands to gather data on student performance, educational professionals are faced with enhancing the competence of an increasingly diverse student population. Of considerable importance for instruction is the significant diversity of academic skills of students enrolled in today's schools. For example, our experiences in working with students in classrooms in the Minneapolis Public Schools have shown us that, when we assess skill development in mathematics of students enrolled in sixth grade, there typically is at least a 6-year range in performance. Some students, those recently immigrated, demonstrate very low-level math skills (or at least perform at a very low level on math tests). Other students in the same class are solving algebra problems. We even found two students who had mothers who were software engineers for local computer firms and, together,

those mothers and students solved quadratic equations "for fun"! Therein lays the dilemma for teachers. The logistics of implementing what is known about effective instruction is incredibly difficult.

The big need for teachers, principals, and school psychologists is for objective information that enables teachers to differentiate instruction, allows principals to lead and manage school improvement, and helps superintendents ensure success for entire districts. Thus, psychometrically sound data are needed to guide these decisions, but often there is a significant shortage of reliable, instructionally sensitive assessment information.

One method of enhancing data collection and increasing the frequency of data-based decision-making could be the use of technology to facilitate the process. School psychologists and related services personnel need to be aware of, and know how to use, the many technology tools that now are available for use in monitoring student progress. These tools have been shown to be essential components of schools' data-driven educational strategies and intervention efforts; indeed, it often is quite difficult to collect, manage, and analyze data meaningfully without the use of such tools (McIntire, 2002; McLeod, 2005b; Pierce, 2005; Wayman, 2005). Technology tools could help school psychologists use continuous data on pupil performance to collaborate with teachers in adjusting or adapting instruction, to demonstrate accountability for performance and progress of all students, and to gather data within a variety of problem-solving models, some of which require monitoring response to intervention (RTI).

In this chapter we make a case for the need to use technology to enhance progress monitoring in school settings. We argue that progress monitoring is a labor-intensive process and one that is nearly impossible without the assistance of technology. We refer the reader to many of the technology tools now available to enhance the assessment and accountability practices of educational professionals. We provide empirical evidence on the extent to which the use of technology tools enhances assessment and accountability practices (and ultimately student outcomes).

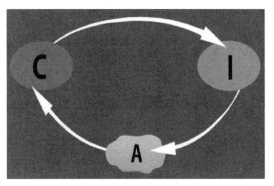

A lack of adequate assessment (A) information severely limits the effectiveness of curriculum (C) and instruction (I).

FIGURE 29.2. How most continuous improvement loops look.

29.1 The Problem(s)

Educational professionals who address continuous improvement of teaching and learning often describe a continuous improvement loop (Paul, 2003). The loop is presumed to look like the one pictured in Figure 29.1. It is presumed that instruction is reciprocally linked to curriculum and to assessment. It is presumed that assessments are instructionally sensitive and sufficiently frequent to drive data-based decisions about what to teach, how to teach, and what curriculum to use. Unfortunately, most curriculum, instruction, and assessment (CIA) loops look like the one pictured in Figure 29.2: a lack of adequate assessment information (A) severely limits the effectiveness of curriculum (C) and instruction (I).

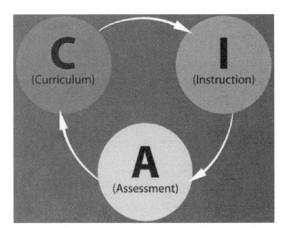

Each of the three elements is equally important to teaching and learning.

FIGURE 29.1. The continuous improvement loop.

There are a number of problems or challenges we confront in current practice:

- The large-scale tests (both norm referenced and standards referenced) used for accountability purposes are too little and too late. They typically lack instructional sensitivity and in most instances are administered once a year (Shepard, 2000; Shepard and Dougherty, 1991). Turnaround for scoring and interpretation takes time (often 3 or 4 months), and students have moved from the teacher they tested with to another teacher by the time the results are available.
- The prediction paradigm in which we try to use the results of norm-referenced tests to plan instruction has not worked. There is an absence of evidence of aptitude by treatment interactions for the tests and treatments that have been used (Reschly and Ysseldyke, 2002).
- The quantity of hourly, daily, and monthly formative assessment information necessary to effectively manage a classroom could be overwhelming, and gathering it can be expensive.
- Nearly the entire burden for collecting formative assessment information falls on the teacher, which creates a time, paperwork, and record-keeping burden (Paul, 2003).

29.2 Current Important Activity

In 2005, the United States Department of Education issued the third national education technology plan.

As part of the development efforts for the plan, and in conjunction with other activities related to the *No Child Left Behind Act* (NCLB), the department sponsored two technology leadership summits. Both the national plan and the summits emphasized the importance of using technology for making assessment and accountability decisions. Corporations are moving quickly to create continuous and periodic assessment tools for use by educational professionals in their assessment and accountability practices. The federal government also has funded both a National Center on Student Progress Monitoring and a Research Institute on Progress Monitoring.

29.2.1 National Education Technology Plan

The third national education technology plan was officially released at a launch event on January 7, 2005. To help states and districts prepare students for the opportunities and challenges of tomorrow, a set of seven action steps and accompanying recommendations were included in the plan. These steps were to:

1. Strengthen technology leadership
2. Consider innovative budgeting for technology
3. Improve teacher training in the use of technology-enhanced assessment and accountability systems
4. Support e-learning and virtual schools
5. Encourage broadband access
6. Move toward digital content
7. Integrate data systems.

29.2.2 National Summit on Empowering Assessment and Accountability Using Technology

In March 2004, the first national summit on assessment and accountability focused on the provision of technical assistance to state and local education leaders by:

1. Identifying technology tools and resources that are available to support the accountability, student information, and data management requirements of the NCLB.
2. Demonstrating how to use data and decision-making to achieve the requirements and intent of the NCLB.

3. Demonstrating how online assessments can improve and strengthen state assessments.
4. Providing guidance on how a state can implement an online assessment statewide.
5. Exploring opportunities for multi-site consortiums to foster collaboration on the development of policies to move toward a system for computer-based assessment, illustrating how online assessments can inform instruction at the classroom level (diagnostic tests, real-time reporting, performance-based assessment, etc.).

Two important papers were released at the first summit: "How states can use information technology to support school improvement under NCLB" (Dougherty, 2004) and "Empowering accountability and assessment: the road ahead" (Patrick, 2004). Both addressed the intricate role of technology in enhancing educational assessment and accountability activities.

29.2.3 The Push by Test Publishers to Develop Technology-Enhanced Assessment and Accountability Tools

Since development of computers for public use, test publishers have been developing and improving online testing systems. Over the past 10 years there has been a significant increase in the number of test publishers who are developing technology-enhanced progress monitoring systems. Early entrants into this arena were PLATO Learning (http://www.plato.com/products.aspeduTest), Renaissance Learning (Accelerated Reader, Math, and Writer; Assessment Master; http://www.renlearn.com), McGraw-Hill Digital Learning (Yearly Progress Pro; http://mhdigitallearning.com/prod_tour.jsp), Scantron (Achievement Series, Performance Series; http:// www.edperformance.com), Pearson NCS (PASeries, Prosper; http://www. pearsonassessments.com), AIMSweb (http://edformation.com), and others.

29.2.4 National Center on Student Progress Monitoring

To meet the challenges of implementing effective progress monitoring, the United States Department of Education Office of Special Education Programs (OSEP) funded the National Center on Student Progress Monitoring. Housed at the American

Institutes for Research, and working in conjunction with researchers from Vanderbilt University, the center is a national technical assistance and dissemination center dedicated to the implementation of scientifically based student progress monitoring. The center's mission is to provide technical assistance to states and districts and disseminate information about progress-monitoring practices proven to work in different elementary-level academic content areas. The Student Progress Monitoring Center's integrated program of services is intended to:

- Raise knowledge and awareness by forming partnerships and communicating with states, districts, associations, technical assistance providers, institutions of higher education, and other interested groups.
- Provide implementation support for using and sustaining proven progress monitoring practices to states and districts.
- Provide for national dissemination by developing resources and supporting ongoing information sharing through advanced web services, regional meetings, and a national conference.

The center provides a wealth of resources on progress monitoring, including publications and presentations specifically geared toward RTI, as well as corporate vendor comparison charts.

29.2.5 Research Institute on Progress Monitoring

The OSEP funded the Research Institute on Progress Monitoring to develop a system of progress monitoring that can be used to evaluate the effects of individualized instruction on access to and progress within the general education curriculum. The institute is housed at the Institute on Community Integration and the Department of Educational Psychology in the College of Education and Human Development at the University of Minnesota. The center is developing measures that can be used to enhance the assessment and accountability activities in which school personnel are engaged.

29.2.6 Technology Tools

As noted above, a number of technology solutions exist to assist educators with student progress monitoring. These technology tools typically are designed to facilitate assessment at one or more of the following levels: continuous, periodic, or annual. These levels should not be confused with the three levels of intervention (universal, targeted, and intensive) often described in the literature on RTI and problem solving (e.g., Ysseldyke et al., 2006). Rather, these levels indicate how frequent assessment occurs within the school organization.

More direct and continuous measurement systems typically are more relevant and useful to instructional planning (Burns and Ysseldyke, 2005). Direct, frequent measures of student performance and progress administered as an integral part of classroom instruction (continuous assessment) provide teachers with information that is more instructionally relevant than high-stakes state and national assessments. Paul (2003) estimated that continuous assessment systems generate 50 times more information than periodic and large scale systems combined.

29.2.7 Continuous Progress Monitoring Systems

Continuous progress-monitoring (CPM) systems are designed to assess student performance and to increase time on task. They provide daily, even hourly, formative assessment with direct feedback to students on their performance. They act as instructional management systems because they give educators daily feedback, which is useful in targeting students who are experiencing difficulty, matching level of instruction to level of individual skill development, and grouping students for instruction. These technology-enhanced systems (Table 29.1) reduce paperwork for the teacher, increase student motivation, and are said to reduce discipline problems. In Table 29.2 we list several of the multiple vendor solutions available for CPM. Some of these CPM systems are also described below. All of these tools are intended to facilitate educators' easy collection and analysis of student progress-monitoring data.

29.2.7.1 AIMSweb

AIMSweb is a formative assessment system which uses curriculum-based measures in oral reading fluency, reading comprehension, phonics and phonological awareness, early numeracy, math computation, spelling, and writing. The product is

TABLE 29.1. Technology-enhanced CPM systems.

Provider	Product	URL
AIMSweb	Basic, Pro, RTI	www.aimsweb.com
Essential Solutions	Kid Compass	www.kid-compass.com
Hosts Learning	LearnerLink	www.hosts.com
LeapFrog SchoolHouse	LeapTrack	www.leaptrack.com
Princeton Review	Homeroom	www.k12.princetonreview.com
Pro-Ed	Monitoring Basic Skills Progress	www.proedinc.com
Renaissance Learning	Accelerated Math, Accelerated Reader, Accelerated Writer	www.renlearn.com
Riverdeep	Destination Success, Skill Detective, Skill Navigator	www.riverdeep.net
Scantron	Skills Connection, Classroom Wizard	www.scantron.com
Wireless Generation (and Harcourt Achieve)	e*assessment	www.wirelessgeneration.com

a web-based data management and reporting system that uses standardized probes and protocol consisting of 1- to 5-min probes. The developers of AIMSweb initially took its measures from curricula. Now they are configured as standardized protocol measures in order to account for frequent changes in curricula.

AIMSweb offers three products: Basic, Pro, and RTI. The Basic product is designed to be used with dynamic indicators of basic early literacy skills (DIBELS; see below). Once educators input data into Basic, it creates graphs and charts showing progress of individuals and groups. AIMSweb Pro is available at three levels: a benchmark level, in which probes are given three times per year; a strategic level, in which probes are given monthly; and a progress monitoring level, in which probes are given CPM measures. The RTI product is designed to help manage the problem-solving aspects of the RTI process. Users proceed through a series of steps, much like those in the Heartland Problem Solving Model (see Chapter 19). Assessors document educational

need, monitor individual student progress, and evaluate the effectiveness of interventions. Task lists, forms, and program evaluation tools are included in the product. AIMSweb users can input data using online web forms, on Palm OS handheld computers, or with a digital pen system that uses a digital pen and special paper to upload handwritten scores into the database.

29.2.7.2 Accelerated Math

Accelerated Math (Renaissance Learning, 1998) is an integrated, computerized continuous monitoring system. Users perform a computer-adaptive initial assessment of student skills and competence using a math test called STAR Math. Teachers then use the data they obtain from STAR Math to make judgments about the appropriate match of instructional level to student skill level. Students are assigned to graded sets of math objectives called math libraries, which enhance a teacher's ability to provide individualized instruction and practice to students. The

TABLE 29.2. Some example software packages for CPM.

Provider	Product	URL
AIMSweb	Basic, Pro, RTI	www.aimsweb.com
Essential Solutions	Kid Compass	www.kid-compass.com
Hosts Learning	LearnerLink	www.hosts.com
LeapFrog SchoolHouse	LeapTrack	www.leaptrack.com
Princeton Review	Homeroom	www.k12.princetonreview.com
Pro-Ed	Monitoring Basic Skills Progress	www.proedinc.com
Renaissance Learning	Accelerated Math, Accelerated Reader, Accelerated Writer	www.renlearn.com
Riverdeep	Destination Success, Skill Detective, Skill Navigator	www.riverdeep.net
Scantron	Skills Connection, Classroom Wizard	www.scantron.com
Wireless Generation (and Harcourt Achieve)	e*assessment	www.wirelessgeneration.com

teacher has complete control over the assignment and organization of math objectives for the classroom and for individual students.

Once assigned to libraries, students are given pages of problems to work on, which are selected by the system from a database of millions of problems. Students work individually or in groups to solve the problems. Answers are then scanned into a computer, via scantron sheets, and students receive immediate feedback in the form of what is called The Opportunity to Praise a Student (TOPS) report. Accelerated Math uses a mastery learning paradigm in which students must achieve mastery on their work in order to take a test. Once students demonstrate sufficient mastery on daily work, teachers are signaled via computer reports that the student is ready to take a test on the specific objective. Mastered objectives are spiraled back for skill maintenance and nonmastered objectives are paired with new objectives for additional practice and instruction. The computer uses algorithms to generate problems sets, and these differ for individual students working on the same objective, which could also this facilitate the use of peer-assisted learning.

Accelerated Math includes a number of preformatted reports, including the aforementioned TOPS report, as well as diagnostic, goal history, and other reports. These reports provide immediate feedback to students and teachers and allow instructors to easily monitor student progress and assess student mastery.

Like AIMSweb, Accelerated Math affords school personnel the opportunity to create a cycle of continuous improvement at the student, teacher, and classroom level. In addition to being a technology-enhanced CPM system, the program provides students with many of the components of effective instruction, including increased practice time at the appropriate level with information feedback, personalized goal setting, and universal success (Ysseldyke and Christenson, 2002)

29.2.7.3 Monitoring Basic Skills Progress

Monitoring Basic Skills Progress (MBSP; Fuchs and Fuchs, 2004) is another curriculum-based measurement product intended to assist educators with CPM. MBSP offers a multitude of different products, including Basic Reading, Basic Math Computation, and Basic Math Concepts and Applications. Most of the MBSP assessment lines are computer based in which students complete tests that are instantaneously scored and feedback provided. Teachers have access to graphs of student progress over time, as well as class-wide reports with instructional recommendations.

29.2.8 Periodic Progress Monitoring Systems

Periodic progress monitoring (PPM) systems (Table 29.3) include assessments that are given less frequently than those in continuous progress-monitoring systems, but more frequently than annually. Periodicity can range from once every 2 or 3 weeks to only two or three times per year.

TABLE 29.3. Technology-enhanced PPM systems.

Provider	Product	URL
Compass Learning	Explorer	www.compasslearning.com
CTB McGraw-Hill	i-know	www.ctb.com
McGraw-Hill Digital Learning	Yearly Progress Pro	www.mhdigitallearning.com
Northwest Evaluation Association	Measure of Academic Progress	www.nwea.org
Pearson Education	Pearson Prosper	www.pearsonncs.com
Pearson School Systems	Pearson Benchmark	www.personschoolsystems.com
PLATO Learning	eduTest	www.edutest.com
Renaissance Learning	AssessmentMaster, STAR Math, STAR Reading, STAR Early Literacy	www.renlearn.com
Riverside Publishing	Assess2Know	www.riverpub.com
Scantron	Achievement Series	www.scantron.com
ThinkLink Learning	Predictive Assessment Series	www.thinklinklearning.com
Tungsten Learning	Benchmark Assessment System	www.tungstenlearning.com
Vantage Learning	Learning Access!	www.vantagelearning.com
Wireless Generation	mCLASS DIBELS	www.wirelessgeneration.com

These systems are used to monitor learning growth throughout the year, often in the form of progress toward specific state standards, and to predict performance on state tests. The purpose of the test is to identify students who are experiencing difficulty so that educators can intervene and quickly adjust level or pace of instruction, change materials being used, or change instructional strategies.

Typically, PPM systems are more prevalent than CPM systems. Data from PPM systems are more easily integrated into districts' data warehouses and most school systems are just now recognizing the power of PPM to improve student learning outcomes. As the NCLB forces schools to better incorporate the use of student performance data into daily practice, school districts typically follow a natural progression from using data warehouses for annual summative data to PPM systems to CPM systems. As educators realize the value and limitations of the data at each level, they become increasingly interested in student information that is more fine-grained and thus more useful.

29.2.8.1 mCLASS DIBELS

Most school psychologists have at least passing familiarity with DIBELS (Good and Kaminsky, 2003). A set of standardized measures of early literacy development, DIBELS assessments are taken individually by students periodically throughout the year. DIBELS probes are short (1 min) and address a variety of student capacities in areas such as phonemic awareness, nonsense word fluency, and oral reading fluency. DIBELS is used widely across the country: at least 45 state Reading First plans include DIBELS as an assessment measure. The University of Oregon DIBELS Data System website allows educators to upload student data and generate automated reports. Similarly, AIMSweb also has licensed DIBELS as part of its Basic product.

Another version of DIBELS is available from Wireless Generation for Palm OS-based handhelds. The mCLASS version of DIBELS (http://www.wirelessgeneration.com/web/DIBELS.html) includes internet-based reporting mechanisms, automatic scoring, and data management and progress monitoring tools. To administer DIBELS in mCLASS, teachers simply use the handheld stylus to tap on a name from the preloaded student roster. The system selects the appropriate set of

probes and helps classroom instructors with the administration of the DIBELS probes by including teacher prompts, a built-in timer, and other help resources. Upon completion of the probe, mCLASS DIBELS immediately displays the student's score and assigns the student to relevant risk categories. Teachers have the ability to include notes and observations along with the score results. mCLASS DIBELS includes some unique features designed to help teachers identify specific student reading strategies and includes graphical charts for progress monitoring that are instantly available on the handheld. Synchronization of the handheld with an Internet-connected computer uploads all student data into a central database, which allows for more sophisticated reporting and printing of student-, class-, school-, and district-level data.

29.2.8.2 AssessmentMaster

AssessmentMaster, formerly known as Standards-Master (Renaissance Learning, 2005), is a progress-monitoring system designed to help educators monitor student progress toward state standards. The assessments are matched to each state's particular standards so the assessments differ from state to state. Assessments are administered up to nine times per year, typically to all students in a class. Most educators give the assessments to their students three or four times a year in preparation for the state's yearly test. Educational personnel receive comprehensive reports that are customizable for all levels: district, school, class, and student. Data can be disaggregated by any student characteristic (e.g., special education status, gender, and ethnicity). Like for Accelerated Math, a bevy of reports are available to school personnel to assist with individualized student feedback, teacher diagnosis and classroom monitoring, and building- or district-level trend analysis. Educators can then use these reports to guide instructional interventions, as well as whole-school reform initiatives and staff training programs.

29.2.8.3 Yearly Progress Pro

Yearly Progress Pro (McGraw-Hill Digital Learning, 2004), is representative of many PPM systems that offer item banks of questions that can be used to create customized assessments. Other vendors that offer similar products include Pearson (Prosper),

Renaissance Learning (STAR Math, STAR Reading, and STAR Early Literacy), and others. Yearly Progress Pro also includes a number of curriculum-based assessments that can be administered as often as weekly, as well as a sophisticated data management and reporting system. Yearly Progress Pro also exemplifies a growing trend, which is to also include instructional resources that can be used after receipt of assessment results to boost student proficiency in the skills just assessed. Assessment companies increasingly are partnering with or acquiring curriculum providers to build up the post-assessment resources that they can offer to school districts.

29.2.8.4 STAR Early Literacy

STAR Early Literacy (Renaissance Learning, 2004) is a computer-adaptive assessment that students can complete in less than 10 min. Teachers receive immediate results that help them intervene faster and provide effective instruction during the most critical years of literacy development. The assessment includes measures of general readiness, phonemic awareness, graphophonemic knowledge, phonics, structural analysis, vocabulary, and comprehension, all of which can be given three to nine times per year.

As Table 29.4 indicates, there are a number of other PPM systems from other educational publishing companies.

29.2.9 Teacher-Created Assessments

Like data warehouse solutions, CPM and PPM systems typically are fairly expensive. Such systems often are beyond the financial capacities of most small and/or rural school districts. As a result, many districts have teacher teams create their own assessments instead,, both because of cost considerations and because of the powerful, shared understandings about what students need to know that occur when teachers collaboratively create high-quality assessments rather than merely using off-the-shelf tests from an outside company (Stiggins, 2000, 2001; Stiggins, Conklin, and Bridgeford, 1986). These schools also need technology tools that allow them to easily collect and analyze formative data. Otherwise, the process becomes too cumbersome and teachers will abstain due to other pressing duties and time demands. Unfortunately, schools proceeding in this direction quickly find that, to date, vendors have paid little attention to the technological needs of educators that wish to create, store, and analyze their own assessments (McLeod, 2005a).

29.2.9.1 Mastery Manager

Mastery Manager, from GoldStar Learning, is a tool that allows teachers to input the results of their self-made assessments. Once student data are entered, Mastery Manager allows teachers to conduct item analysis, link to state standards, and export results to an electronic gradebook. Mastery Manager has a variety of reporting capabilities and includes the

TABLE 29.4. Some example software packages for PPM.

Provider	Product	URL
Compass Learning	Explorer	www.compasslearning.com
CTB McGraw-Hill	i-know	www.ctb.com
McGraw-Hill Digital Learning	Yearly Progress Pro	www.mhdigitallearning.com
Northwest Evaluation Association	Measure of Academic Progress	www.nwea.org
Pearson Education	Pearson Prosper	www.pearsonncs.com
Pearson School Systems	Pearson Benchmark	www.personschoolsystems.com
PLATO Learning	eduTest	www.edutest.com
Renaissance Learning	AssessmentMaster, STAR Math, STAR Reading, STAR Early Literacy	www.renlearn.com
Riverside Publishing	Assess2Know	www.riverpub.com
Scantron	Achievement Series	www.scantron.com
ThinkLink Learning	Predictive Assessment Series	www.thinklinklearning.com
Tungsten Learning	Benchmark Assessment System	www.tungstenlearning.com
Vantage Learning	Learning Access!	www.vantagelearning.com
Wireless Generation	mCLASS DIBELS	www.wirelessgeneration.com

ability to export data to Microsoft Excel and other spreadsheet software programs.

29.2.9.2 Osseo Data Templates Project

Finally, in an attempt to create progress monitoring tools that are free or low cost, the University Council for Educational Administration Center for the Advanced Study of Technology Leadership in Education (CASTLE) at the University of Minnesota is working with the Osseo (MN) Area Schools to create formative data collection and analysis templates using the pivot charting capabilities inherent in Microsoft Excel (McLeod, 2005b). After entering student assessment results, teachers can use the template to easily track student progress and disaggregate by the NCLB demographic categories. The district assessment and evaluation staff pre-load the Excel worksheets with student data to minimize teachers' initial data entry burden. Teachers and administrators are using the templates to track and analyze student reading and math fluency, discipline referrals, attendance, library book usage, and other data of interest.

Tools such as Mastery Manager or CASTLE's Excel data templates that incorporate teacher-created data can be designed or developed to include multiple assessment periods as desired. As such, these tools cross over between both the CPM and PPM paradigms. A few companies, such as Scantron and Pearson, have recently begun modifying their CPM and/or PPM systems to try and incorporate data from teacher-made assessments. We anticipate that assessment companies in the near future will explore partnerships that marry their software's item analysis, diagnostic reporting, and other analytical strengths with the ease of use and reporting capabilities of electronic gradebook software.

29.3 Research on Technology-Enhanced Assessment Systems

Over the past 25 years, research has shown that curriculum-based measurement and other research-based formative assessment practices can have powerful effects on student learning outcomes and on closure of student subgroup achievement gaps. Un-

til recently, benchmarking assessments were completed on paper and scored by hand. As the power and potential of personal computing technologies literally transform our entire society, educators and corporations are taking advantage of the computational power, mobility, networking, and graphical display features of new hardware and software systems to create powerful tools for student progress monitoring. It has never been easier for educators to regularly and continuously collect and analyze student performance data. We still have much to learn about these assessment technologies, however. In particular, helping educators understand how to implement these tools and interpret the data to benefit students is of primary importance.

In this section of the chapter we describe and report the results of several studies of using Accelerated Math as a progress monitoring and instructional management system. The studies were not evaluations of the efficacy of Accelerated Math, though the results obviously can be interpreted as supporting or negating the use of this tool. Rather, we studied the effects of monitoring student performance and implementing a technology-enhanced monitoring system that met the components of effective instruction as outlined by Carroll (1963), Walberg (1984) and Ysseldyke and Christenson (2002). Specifically, Accelerated Math was selected because it provided instruction matched to student skill level, immediate corrective feedback, realistic, yet high expectations, effective strategies for heightening student motivation and interest, large amounts of relevant practice, and direct, frequent measurement of student progress while continuously checking for student understanding.

We view these studies as support for those components of RTI that involve continuous monitoring of student performance, data-driven decision-making, and problem solving. They provide evidence of what happens when continuous monitoring and data-driven decision-making are added to existing curricula in math. Accelerated Math is not a curriculum; rather, it is a continuous monitoring system that works with any existing math curriculum.

The initial progress monitoring study conducted was a 3-year classroom-based math intervention in the Minneapolis Schools. The project actually consisted of a set of multiple studies over a 3-year period. Specific methods and results are reported in a separate set of papers in refereed journals (Spicuzza et al., 2001, 2003; Ysseldyke, Spicuzza, Kosciolek, and Boys, 2003). Results of these investigations are summarized in the following list.

- Students who had failed state and district tests and attended an intensive summer school program gained more in 6 weeks than they had in the previous entire academic work.
- Across all studies, students with whom progress monitoring and instructional management were used gained significantly more than those who did not participate in progress monitoring, and the gains were evidenced on multiple math measures.
- Low-, middle-, and high-performing students who participated in instruction enhanced by progress monitoring and data-driven decision-making outperform those who do not.
- Application of progress monitoring and data-driven decision-making results in significant positive changes in the instructional ecology used in classrooms (more individual instruction, more cognitive emphasis, increased adaptive instruction, etc.).
- When a technology-enhanced progress monitoring system is used, students engage in more active academic responding and less task management time as measured by Ecobehavioral assessment instruments (Ecobehavioral Assessment System Software).
- Intervention integrity is critical. When teachers implement the program as intended, gains are far greater than when this is not the case.

Ysseldyke and Tardrew (2002) also conducted a 5-month study of the implementation of a technology-enhanced monitoring system (Accelerated Math) with 2202 students enrolled in 125 classrooms (67 experimental and 58 controls) in 47 schools in 24 states. The study was quasi-experimental rather than experimental, because the students were not randomly assigned to classrooms and there was no reason to believe that assignment of classrooms to conditions was random. There were 1072 students in the experimental group and 1130 in the control group.

At grades 3, 4, 5 and 6, students in classrooms in which teachers used the progress monitoring system (AM) gained significantly more in math than in control classrooms. At grades 7–10, students in the experimental group outperformed those in the control group, though the difference in performance was not significant. At every grade there were large differences in grade equivalent score and percentile point gains between students in the experimental and control groups. Gains were consistent across low-, average-, and high-performing groups. There was considerable variability in student performance, and level of teacher implementation had a definite, significant effect on gain in math performance across the entire sample.

Over the course of running several experiments on progress monitoring, intervention integrity was found to be a critical factor. When teachers actually enhance their instructional efforts with technology-assisted monitoring systems, and when they do so consistent with the intent of developers of the monitoring systems, students profit more than when the progress monitoring systems are not used.

29.3.1 Subgroup Analyses

We were interested in the extent to which technology-enhanced progress monitoring worked consistently for students in different subgroups (e.g. Title I, gifted and talented). We learned that gifted and talented students whose teachers use a technology-enhanced progress monitoring system outperform gifted and talented students whose teachers do not use such a system (Ysseldyke, Tardrew, Betts, Thill and Hannigan, 2004). Title I students who participate in technology-enhanced progress monitoring systems also outperform those Title I students who do not (Ysseldyke, Thill, Hannigan and Betts, 2004).

29.3.2 Additional Studies

Ysseldyke and Bolt (in press) conducted a 2-year randomized controlled experiment in 136 school districts in 11 states. Data from the first year of the study suggested that intervention integrity is absolutely critical. Teachers in the experimental group did not implement the intervention with large numbers of students, and without the use of technology-enhanced systems this information likely would have been lost (Ysseldyke and Bolt, in press). Knowledge of the information enabled the investigators to exclude from the experimental group students who had not actually participated in the program. Whereas nonparticipation masked differences between groups, use of the technology-enhanced system showed that the groups differed.

29.4 Summary

After highlighting the importance of progress monitoring and RTI techniques for school psychologists and the students they serve, this chapter described a number of technology tools currently available to assist educators with academic benchmarking tasks. Several of these tools were described in some detail and some recent research on the effectiveness of these tools was reported. It is thought that, for most school psychologists, the technology domain is relatively new. This chapter was intended to give a broad an overview of some of the existing technologies currently being marketed to schools.

It is our hope that school psychologists will attempt to stay abreast of the technological trends related to student progress monitoring, The power and breadth of these technologies is literally astounding compared with a mere 5 years ago. Recent purchasing and partnership trends, such as the acquisition of Alpha Smart (Palm OS-based handhelds) and incorporation of a student response system into Renaissance Learning's software systems, the development of digital pen input by AIMSweb, and the synergistic partnership between Scantron and Techna Data (a major data warehouse vendor), indicate that assessment companies are continuously looking for ways to enhance product value and marketability. Over the next few decades it is anticipated that the dual trends toward ubiquitous, wireless, mobile computing and more powerful data management and reporting technologies, together, including voice recognition, will result in a convergence of assessment solutions that today are barely imaginable. Moreover, they will enable us to engage in a seamless system of continuous and periodic assessment linked directly to district and statewide accountability systems that will make the traditional administration of the norm-referenced test superfluous, if not obsolete.

References

Burns, M. K. & Ysseldyke, J. E. (2005). Comparison of existing responsiveness to intervention models to identify and answer implementation questions. *California School Psychologists, 10*, 9–20.

Carroll, J. (1963). A model of school learning. Teachers College Record, *64*, 723–733.

Good, R. & Kaminsky, R. (2003). *Dynamic Indicators of Basic Early Literacy Skills (DIBELS)*. Longmont, CO: Sopris West.

Dougherty, C. (2004, March). How states can use information technology to support school improvement under NCLB. Paper presented at the *National Summit on Empowering Assessment and Accountability Using Technology*, St. Louis, MO.

Fuchs, D. & Fuchs, L. (2004). *Basic Skills Monitoring System*. Austin, TX: Pro Ed.

McGraw-Hill Digital Learning (2004). *Yearly Progress Pro*. Columbus, OH: McGraw-Hill Digital Learning.

McIntire, T. (2002). The administrator's guide to data-driven decision making. *Technology & Learning, 22*(11), 18–28, 32–33.

McLeod, S. (2005a). *Data-driven teachers*. Retrieved October 1, 2005, from Microsoft Innovative Teachers Thought Leaders at http://www.microsoft.com/ education/ThoughtLeadersDDDM.mspx.

McLeod, S. (2005b). *Technology tools for data-driven teachers*. Retrieved October 1, 2005, from Microsoft Innovative Teachers Thought Leaders at http://www.microsoft.com/education/ThoughtLeadersDDDM.mspx.

Patrick, S. (2004, March). Empowering accountability and assessment: the road ahead. Paper presented at the *National Summit on Empowering Assessment and Accountability Using Technology*, St. Louis, MO

Paul, T. D. (2003). *Guided Independent Reading: An Examination of the Reading Practice Database and the Scientific Research Supporting Guided Independent Reading as Implemented in Reading Renaissance*. Madison, WI: Renaissance Learning.

Pierce, D. (2005). *Formative assessment rates high at FETC*. Retrieved February 15, 2005, from eSchoolNews Online at www.eschoolnews.com.

Renaissance Learning (2004). *STAR Early Literacy*. Wisconsin Rapids: Renaissance Learning.

Renaissance Learning (2005). *Assessment Master*. Wisconsin Rapids: Renaissance Learning.

Renaissance Learning (1998). *Accelerated Math*. Wisconsin Rapids, WI: author.

Reschly, D. J. & Ysseldyke, J. E. (2002). Paradigm shift: the past is not the future. In A. Thomas & J. Grimes (Eds.), *Best practices in School Psychology IV*. Bethesda, MD: National Association of School Psychologists.

Salvia, J. A. & Ysseldyke, J. E. (in press). Assessment in special and inclusive education (10th edition). Boston: Houghton-Mifflin.

Shepard, L. (2000). The role of assessment in a learning culture. *Educational Researcher, 27*(7), 4–14.

Shepard, L. & Dougherty, K. (1991, April). Effects of high stakes testing on instruction. Paper presented at the *Annual Meeting of the American Educational Research Association*, Chicago, IL.

Spicuzza, R. Ysseldyke, J., Lemkuil, A. Koscioleck, S., Boys, C., & Teelucksingh, E. (2001). Effects of using a curriculum-based monitoring system on the classroom instructional environment and math achievement. *Journal of School Psychology, 39*, 521–542.

Spicuzza, R., Ysseldyke, J., Kosciolek, S., Teelucksingh, E., Boys, C., & Lemkuil, A. (2003). Using a curriculum-based instructional management system to enhance math achievement in urban schools. *Journal for the Education of Students Placed at Risk, 8*, 247–265.

Stiggins, R. (2000). *Student-Involved Classroom Assessment* (3rd ed.). Englewood Cliffs, NJ: Prentice Hall.

Stiggins, R. J. (2001). The unfulfilled promise of classroom assessment. *Educational Measurement: Issues and Practice, 20*(3), 5–15.

Stiggins, R. J., Conklin, N. F., & Bridgeford, N. (1986). Classroom assessment: a key to effective education. *Educational Measurement: Issues and Practice, 5*(2), 5–17.

Walberg, H. (1984). Families as partners in educational productivity. *Phi Delta Kappan, 65*, 397–400.

Wayman, J. C. (2005). Involving teachers in data-driven decision-making: using computer data systems to support teacher inquiry and reflection. *Journal of Education for Students Placed At Risk, 10*, 295–308.

Ysseldyke, J., & Bolt, D. (in press). Effect of technology-enhanced continuous progress monitoring on math achievement. *School Psychology Review.*

Ysseldyke, J. E., Burns, M. K., Dawson, M., Kelly, B., Morrison, D., Ortiz, S., et al. (2006). *School Psychology: A Blueprint for the Future of Training and Practice III.* Bethesda, MD: National Association of School Psychologists.

Ysseldyke, J. E. & Christenson, S. L. (2002). *Functional Assessment of Academic Behavior: Creating Successful Learning Environments.* Longmont, CO: Sopris West.

Ysseldyke, J. E., Spicuzza, R., Kosciolek, S., & Boys, C. (2003). Effects of a learning information system on mathematics achievement and classroom structure. *Journal of Educational Research, 96*, 163–174.

Ysseldyke, J. E. & Tardrew, S. (2002). *Differentiating Math Instruction.* Wisconsin Rapids: Renaissance Learning.

Ysseldyke, J. E. & Tardrew, S. (in press). Use of a progress monitoring system to enable teachers to differentiate mathematics instruction. *Journal of Applied School Psychology, 24* (1).

Ysseldyke, J. E., Tardrew, S., Betts, J., Thill, T., & Hannigan, E. (2004). Use of an instructional management system to enhance math instruction of gifted and talented students. *Journal for Education of the Gifted, 27*, 293–310.

Ysseldyke, J. E., Thill, T., Hannigan, E., & Betts, J. (2004). Use of an instructional management system to improve mathematics skills for students in Title 1 programs. *Preventing School Failure, 48*(4), 10–15.

30
Response to Intervention for English Language Learners: Current Development and Future Directions

Michael L. Vanderwood and Jeanie E. Nam

Mike L. Vanderwood, PhD, is an Assistant Professor of School Psychology in the Graduate School of Education at the University of California–Riverside. mike.vanderwood@ucr.edu
Jeanie Nam is a School Psychology Graduate Student in the Graduate School of Education at the University of California–Riverside. jeanie.nam@email.ucr.edu

The concept of providing scientifically based instruction, progress monitoring, and data-based decision-making within a tiered model seems like an appropriate and promising approach for English language (EL) learners (Klinger and Edwards, 2006). Unfortunately, making an assumption that what works with native English speakers will work with students from diverse language backgrounds may be inaccurate (McLaughlin, 1992). Although substantial empirical support exists for the use of a response-to-intervention (RTI) approach to address literacy problems with native English speakers (e.g., Burns, Appleton, and Stehouwer, 2005; Mathes et al., 2005; Vellutino, Scanlon, and Tanzman, 1998), very little data exist about the effectiveness of this approach with EL learners (Vaughn et al., 2006).

This chapter will define the challenges associated with serving students from diverse language backgrounds and will review what is currently known about using an RTI approach with EL learners. The review will focus on evidence related to literacy assessment and instruction due to the relationship between literacy and other academic pursuits and the paucity of research in other academic domains. The chapter will end with an example and a presentation of the issues related to using an RTI approach for making critical education decisions for EL learners.

30.1 Importance of the Issue: The Growing Concern

In recent years, the number of EL learners in US schools has increased dramatically. In 1989–1990, 2.1 million students in grades K–12 were classified as limited English proficient (LEP) and a decade later the number increased to 4.4 million (National Clearinghouse for English Language Acquisition, 1999, 2002). In at least one state (i.e., California), the EL learner population has grown to almost 25% of the total public school enrollment (National Clearinghouse for English Language Acquisition, 2004). Hopstock and Stephenson (2003) found that the EL learner population represented more than 350 native languages in 2001–2002. Of these languages, Spanish was the native language for approximately 77% of EL learners. Whereas the growth of total K–12 enrollment was about 11% between 1991–2000, the EL learner population expanded by 89% during the same decade (National Clearinghouse for English Language Acquisition, 2002). The growing number of EL learners has dramatically increased the demand on classroom teachers to diversify their instruction; however, in a national survey of teachers, only 20% reported that they were trained to teach students from diverse language and cultural backgrounds (National Center for Education Statistics, 1999).

EL learners come from diverse cultures, languages, and educational backgrounds. Differing levels of conversational and academic language proficiency may also exist among students of the same ethnic background. Some students may know how to read and write in their native language, whereas others may not. Owing to their language disparities, EL learners have exhibited considerable achievement gaps on state and national assessments compared with native English-speaking students (Snow and Biancarosa, 2003). As with native English-speaking students, a key factor for academic success for EL learners is a solid foundation in literacy in the early grades (Garcia, 1991; Gonzalez and Garcia, 1995). Whereas research for effective literacy interventions for English speakers is prevalent, literacy interventions for EL learners has been much less well-researched (Vaughn et al., 2006).

30.1.1 Language of Instruction and Transfer Across Languages

There has been much debate about the appropriate language of instruction for EL learners. Studies on this topic have generally found that reading instruction that uses a student's native language or paired bilingual strategies is more effective than English-only instruction (Garcia, 1991). Like native English speakers, many EL learners go to school with many well-developed skills in their first language. Evidence has shown that these native language literacy skills can be transferred into the second language (Cummins, 1984). A review by Garcia (1998) cited extensive evidence that EL learners use knowledge of their native language to learn to read in English. Once a firm foundation has been established in a child's native language, the student is able to apply their background knowledge of the first language to make sense of the second language. Freeman and Freeman (1992) found that even when the written forms of the native language and English are distinctly different, such as the Chinese characters and the English alphabet, children are still able to apply the skills and strategies used in their native language to read and write in English.

Although students that speak another language develop social proficiency, or basic interpersonal conversation skills (BICS), within the context of everyday living and without formal instruction, cog-

nitive academic language proficiency (CALP) requires formal schooling and takes about 5 to 7 years to develop (Cummins, 1984). CALP development has been found to be essential for school success (Cummins, 1984); therefore, it may take significantly longer for EL learners to develop the academic language proficiency needed for school success.

30.2 The Assessment Challenge: Current Practices

Owing to the complexity of assessing students from diverse linguistic backgrounds, the authors of the *Test Standards* (AERA, APA, and NCME, 1999) devoted an entire chapter to aspects that need to be considered when selecting and using assessment tools with EL learners. One of the biggest issues related to assessment for EL learners is the lack of inclusion of the group in the development, validation, and norming of the most popular tools, and deciding how many separate groups are needed to capture the unique aspects of language and culture (Salvia and Ysseldyke, 2004). The issues of adequacy of group representation in the norms and the degree to which culture is addressed is especially critical when the measure is used for critical education decisions like special education eligibility (AERA et al., 1999).

The limitations of current assessment tools and the discrepancy approach for determining special education eligibility with native English-speaking students also apply to EL learners. As previously mentioned, it is clear that parallel skills are involved in reading both English and Spanish, and there are certain processes basic to reading across languages that can be applied to almost any language (Goodman and Goodman, 1978). Whereas there are a variety of approaches to assessing EL learners' intellectual and academic functioning, some have suggested that the most optimal approach is to have a bilingual school psychologist administer a test in the native language and in English (Kamphaus, 2000; Lopez, 1997). The challenge with this approach is finding a test with appropriate psychometric characteristics and a bilingual school psychologist who speaks the student's native language. Alternate approaches include using nonverbal tests, interpreters, and translations of English tests, yet all of these approaches have significant limitations and some are considered inappropriate (Bainter and Tollefson, 2003). Finally, traditional single-point-in-time measures administered in a student's native language or in English are insufficient to estimate capacity to learn given high-quality instruction. Hence, RTI-based decision-making is a promising alternative to the discrepancy model for EL learners (Klingner and Edwards, 2006).

Another assessment challenge related to EL learners is determining how to appropriately evaluate a student's language proficiency in their native language and English. At this point there is no consensus among researchers regarding the nature of language proficiency and how best to measure the proficiency of EL learners. The nature of language proficiency has been understood by some researchers as consisting of 64 separate language components (Del Vecchio and Guerrero, 1995), whereas Oller (1979) has suggested that one underlying factor, termed the global language proficiency factor, accounts for the majority of the variance in language proficiency test scores. According to Cummins (1984), not all aspects of language proficiency can be incorporated into one dimension. Instead, language proficiency can be separated into two categories: BICS and CALPS. As a result of the contrasting theories on the nature of language proficiency, language proficiency tests may differ from each other in many fundamental ways (Del Vecchio and Guerrero, 1995).

Some commonly used language proficiency tests have been found to differ in their classification of students as non-English speaking, LEP, or fluent English proficient (FEP) (Ulibarri, Spencer and Rivas, 1981). Three commonly used tests of language proficiency are the idea proficiency test (IPT), the language assessment scales (LASs), and the Woodcock language proficiency battery–revised (WLPB-R). According to Del Vecchio and Guerrero (1995), the IPT is used to assess four areas of English oral language proficiency: comprehension, syntax, vocabulary, and verbal expression.

The IPT oral language proficiency test used in conjunction with the reading and writing tests assesses overall language proficiency for individuals from the age of 3 years to adulthood. The oral measure must be individually administered, but the reading and writing tests can be administered in small groups. The LASs consist of an oral, reading, and written language proficiency test that can be used to assess language ability and proficiency for individuals from age 4 years to adulthood. As with the IPT, the oral measure must be individually administered, but the reading and writing tests can be administered in small groups.

The WLPB-R (Woodcock, 1991) is used to diagnose English and Spanish language proficiency skills, providing cluster scores for the following categories: broad ability, oral language ability, reading ability, and written language ability. The test can be used for individuals from age 2 years to adulthood. All parts of this test must be individually administered.

Schrank, Fletcher, and Alvarado (1996) examined the validity of three tests of English oral language proficiency tests in terms of Cummin's BICS/CALP distinction. The IPT, the LASs, and the WLPB-R were found to measure similar and dissimilar aspects of oral language proficiency, supporting the BICS/CALP distinction. Test correlations provided evidence of concurrent validity among the three tests.

The oral language scores for the IPT, LASs, and WLPB-R were highly correlated with one another at the kindergarten and second-grade levels; however, when subtests from one test were compared with those of another, differences in correlational patterns were detected. Differences were found at both grade levels, indicating that the subtests measured different components of language proficiency. For example, at the second-grade level, the WLPB-R verbal analogies subtest appeared to measure different aspects of language proficiency than did the LASs oral pronunciation subtest, resulting in a low correlation between the two subtests. Whereas the WLPB-R verbal analogies subtest measured the ability to comprehend and complete word relationships, a component of CALPS, the LASs oral pronunciation subtest measured the ability to listen to and repeat specific phonemes, a component of communicative language, or BICS.

These data suggest that language proficiency measures should be carefully examined to determine what components of language proficiency are being assessed prior to their use. Tests that measure BICS may mistakenly lead educators to assume that a student possesses CALP. Language proficiency tests are often used to make high-stakes decisions about the program of instruction in which a child is best suited to learn. For example, results may be used to determine whether a student is able to meet the academic demands of English-only instruction or whether the student would be better served in a bilingual or English-as-a-second-language instructional program (Schrank et al., 1996). Incorrect placement decisions or denial of services may result from misinterpretations of test scores. As a result, the scores obtained must exhibit technical adequacy, providing evidence of reliability and validity for assessing the type of language proficiency relevant to the questions at hand (i.e., CALP or BICS).

30.3 What We Know About English Language Learner Literacy Assessment, Instruction, and Intervention

The challenge for those working with EL learners is deciding how to apply literacy research to the education of students who come from a significantly different educational background than those who participated in almost all recent literacy research (Klingner and Edwards, 2006). For example, if phonological awareness is established in a student's native language, is it necessary to teach phonological awareness in English if a student has a low score on an English phonological awareness measure? If an intervention is determined to be effective for native English speakers, to what extent does English proficiency affect an EL learner's response to intervention? How should a student's background and culture be integrated into decision-making about needed services?

30.3.1 Early Literacy Assessment and English Language Learners

It is fairly clear that phonological knowledge can transfer across languages. Lindsey, Manis, and Bailey (2003) investigated the cross-linguistic transfer of early reading skills. The study examined the reading ability of 249 Spanish-speaking EL learners during three times from kindergarten through first grade. They found that phonological awareness transferred from Spanish to English and was predictive of word identification skills. The cor-

relation between Spanish measures of phonological awareness and English measures of phonological awareness during two time periods was in the range of $r = 0.21$–0.36. Spanish measures of phonological awareness were also correlated with developing English reading and word decoding skills ($r = 0.19$–0.37). These results indicate that phonological awareness is a general, not a language-specific, process involved in early reading; therefore, once phonological processing is acquired in one language, it may be more readily applied to a second language (Lindsey et al., 2003).

Durgunoglu, Nagy, and Hancin-Bhatt (1993) examined factors influencing English word identification performance of Spanish-speaking EL learners. First-grade native Spanish speakers with strong phonological awareness and word decoding ability in their native language were better at decoding words and pseudowords in English than were those with poor native-language abilities in these areas. Performance on English word and pseudoword recognition tests was predicted by the levels of both Spanish phonological awareness and Spanish word recognition, indicating cross-language transfer. The results of this study indicate that it is possible to build on the strengths that a child already has in their first language to aid in the beginning stages of reading in a second language. Therefore, developing phonological awareness and word recognition skills in the first language is likely to help in second-language recognition.

The results of a recent study suggest that pseudowords can predict future reading performance for Spanish-speaking EL learners. Edelston, Vanderwood and Healy (in press) conducted a longitudinal study examining the relationship between nonsense word fluency (NWF) scores from dynamic indicators of basic early literacy skills (DIBELS; Kaminski and Good, 1996) and performance on a statewide accountability measure of reading comprehension (i.e., CAT6). Across the sample of 134 EL learners, the correlation between first-grade NWF scores and their scores in third grade on the California Achievement Test 6th Edition (CAT6) was $r = 0.34$. This correlation was significantly higher than the relationship between a first-grade reading accountability measure (i.e., SAT9) and their third grade CAT6 score ($r = 0.17$). The correlation between the first-grade NWF score and the third-grade CAT6 score was consistent across all levels of English fluency as determined by a statewide measure of English proficiency. These data suggest that, based on the results from this study, NWF (the ability to rapidly decode nonsense words in English) could be an effective literacy screener for first-grade EL learners. Future research is needed to identify the most efficient way to promote phonological awareness in EL learners (i.e., establish in native language first, then train in English or begin with English-only phonological awareness training).

Given the strong correlation of phonological awareness across languages, as well as the prevalence of studies that have shown phonological awareness to be predictive of reading ability for non-English-speaking children, there is significant reason to believe that phonological awareness interventions would assist EL learners in developing early reading skills. Whereas phonological awareness and phonics are intertwined, they are different. Whereas phonological awareness focuses on the auditory and oral manipulation of sounds, the main focus of phonics instruction is to help beginning readers understand how letters are linked to sounds to form letter–sound correspondences and spelling patterns. The National Reading Panel (2000) identified and evaluated a number of studies relevant to phonics instruction. An analysis of the literature indicated that phonics instruction improved success in reading.

30.3.2 Comprehension and Fluency Assessment and Intervention

Although research has shown that instruction in phonological awareness is a significant predictor of word recognition skills (Durgunoglu et al., 1993), there is significantly less evidence that instruction in phonological awareness has any significant effects on the development of reading comprehension for EL learners. Hence, phonological awareness may be thought of as a necessary but insufficient skill for comprehension with EL learners. Garcia (1991) found that reading test performance of fifth- and sixth-grade Spanish speaking children greatly underestimated their reading comprehension potential. The author hypothesized that test performance was adversely affected by unfamiliar English vocabulary.

There is also evidence that time engaged in reading and access to printed reading materials are strong predictors of reading comprehension development as students advance through school (Elley and Mangubhai, 1983; Taylor, Frye, and Maruyama, 1988). Elley and Mangubhai (1983) found that fourth- and fifth-grade students in Fiji exposed to a daily English reading program showed significant language growth. Prior to the study, the schools had a very limited collection of books for their students to read. During the study, students were provided access to a variety of high-interest, illustrated books and were required to read 30 min per day. After 8 months, the students in the "Book Flood" schools were found to perform significantly better than control group schools on tests of English reading, writing, listening, comprehension, and speaking. The control group schools continued to use the ongoing English language program that put less emphasis on reading.

Exposure to a daily reading program, in which children were given the opportunity to read a variety of appealing books, led to considerable improvements in literacy skills (Elley and Mangubhai, 1983). Cummins (2003) also suggested that the development of reading comprehension is best supported by a program that combines some phonological awareness and phonics instruction with strategies for decoding and comprehending text, including exposure to meaningful and wide-ranging texts.

Reading instruction that incorporated phonics was found to be more effective than instruction that taught little or no phonics for students in kindergarten through sixth grade, as well as for children having difficulty learning to read (National Reading Panel, 2000). Students in kindergarten who received beginning phonics instruction were found to have enhanced abilities to read and spell. First-graders who were taught phonics showed considerable improvements in their ability to comprehend text, as well as progress in decoding and spelling skills. Older students who received phonics instruction also exhibited significant progress in decoding and spelling skills.

According to the National Reading Panel (2000), the goal of phonics instruction is to provide children with knowledge and skills that can be applied to their daily reading and writing activities. The panel, however, also noted the importance of a comprehensive approach to reading instruction. The National

Reading Panel (2000, p. 11) reported "Teachers must understand that systematic phonics instruction is only one component, albeit a necessary component, of a total reading program; systematic phonics instruction should be integrated with other reading instruction in phonemic awareness, fluency, and comprehension strategies to create a complete reading program." The current literacy research suggests that instruction for EL learners must take a comprehensive approach. Effective literacy programs must include systematic phonics instruction, as well as additional instruction to develop phonological awareness, reading comprehension skills, and fluency.

30.4 Response-to-Intervention Research with English Language Learners

The review of what we know about applying early literacy research with an EL learner population suggests that members of this group likely should respond to the same types of intervention used for native English speakers struggling with literacy development. Yet, to this point, very few systematic applications of an RTI approach have been conducted in school settings. Two studies that combined screening with high-quality measures, targeted interventions, and progress monitoring are presented as examples of how the RTI model can be applied to an EL learner population. Interestingly, significant differences exist across the approaches in the measures selected for screening, language of the targeted instruction, and length of the intervention.

Healy, Vanderwood, and Edelston (2005) applied a three-tier prevention model with first-graders at a school that was comprised of over 90% EL learners in a large urban district in southern California. All of the first-grade students were screened with English measures of phonological awareness and phonics from DIBELS (Good and Kaminski, 2002). English was selected as the language of assessment and instruction to be consistent with the district's and school's practice of English-only instruction. The 15 lowest performing students across the two measures received a small-group structured intervention in English for 30 min twice per week for 16 weeks. The groups consisted of five students taught

by two school psychology graduate students who used *Sounds and Letters for Readers and Spellers* (Greene, 1997), a structured intervention program that consisted of phonological awareness, phonics, and vocabulary instruction. Observations were conducted to assess treatment integrity during the intervention, which indicated the program was delivered as intended.

At several different points during the 16-week intervention period, students who had reached the recommended cutoff scores on DIBELS were exited from the intervention. By exiting students, the interventionists were able to provide more individual attention to the students who were still struggling to improve to the desired level. At the end of the intervention period, only two students were still classified in the deficit category in phonological awareness and phonics. One student achieved the cutoff for NWF but was still at a deficit level on the phoneme segmentation task. Figure 30.1 is an example of the decision-making approach used by the team to determine whether a student was improving at the expected rate.

Vaughn et al. (2006) designed and implemented an oral language and literacy intervention to be provided in Spanish that was pedagogically similar to literacy intervention programs conducted in English. The team used the letter-word identification (LWID) subtest from the Woodcock language proficiency battery–Spanish version (Woodcock, 1991) and an experimental Spanish five-word reading ability test to screen 361 students attending seven different schools who reported speaking Spanish at home. Sixty-nine students, who performed below the 25th percentile on the LWID subtest and were not able to read one or more of the words on the Spanish word-reading test, were randomly assigned to either a treatment or comparison group.

The intervention program was provided in Spanish to match the core literacy program and was designed to improve Spanish oral language and literacy skills. The treatment was provided in groups of three to five students for 50 min a day from October to May. The interventionists were six bilingual certified teachers who received 12 h of instruction and regular feedback throughout the year about the intervention's implementation from the program's authors. Analysis of pre- and post-intervention test scores on several measures of English and Spanish oral language and literacy indicated the treatment

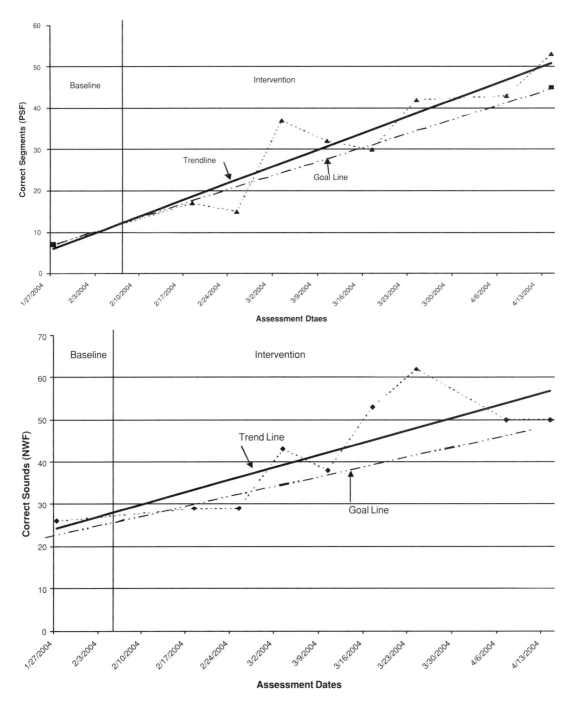

FIGURE 30.1. Phoneme segmentation fluency (PSF) and nonsense word fluency (NWF) scores of a student who exited the intervention.

group improved significantly more than did the comparison group on most of the Spanish measures, but did not perform better than the comparison group on the English assessments (Vaughn et al., 2006).

The study's results support the idea that intensive reading intervention for EL learners designed to match the language of core instruction can significantly improve student outcomes in the language

TABLE 30.1. Questions to address when using RTI with EL learners.

Instruction/Intervention
1. To what extent does the universal academic curriculum address language diversity?
2. Is a continuum of English language acquisition options offered?
3. What is the appropriate language of instruction?
4. To what extent do the supplemental (Tier 2) interventions address issues related to language and cultural diversity?
5. To what extent does empirical evidence support the use of the intervention with EL learners?

Assessment
1. What measures are used to determine English language proficiency and are there psychometric data to support their use?
2. What evidence exists to supports the use of the academic screening measures used to determine who receives Tier 2 services?
3. Is the expected rate of growth for EL learners, as measured by the progress monitoring measures, the same as for native speakers?
4. Should progress monitoring be conducted in the student's native language or English?

of instruction whether the philosophy is to provide core instruction in English or Spanish.

30.5 Conclusion

The purpose of this chapter was to review what is currently known about using an RTI process with EL learners (Table 30.1). There is clearly a need to determine how to best serve this growing population of students who are overrepresented in the group of students who struggle academically (Snow and Biancarosa, 2003). Yet, using assessment tools and interventions based on the results from studies with native English speakers is not consistent with recommended practices (e.g., Test Standards; APA et al., 1999) or experience (McLaughlin, 1992).

Although research about the application of an RTI approach with an EL learner population is very limited, the data that do exist suggest that using this model with EL learners will produce results that are similar to those achieved when RTI is used with native English speakers. It appears that some of the same assessment and intervention tools that are used to screen and intervene with native English speakers can be used to improve the outcomes for EL learners who receive core literacy instruction in English (Healy et al., 2005; Edelston, Vanderwood, and Healy, in press). Similarly, EL learners who receive core instruction in Spanish can benefit from targeted small-group intervention in Spanish significantly more than those students who continue to receive classroom-based literacy instruction (Vaughn et al., 2006).

Despite these promising findings, it is premature to conclude that RTI should be used with all low-achieving EL learners. There are still questions about how to best assess non-native English speakers to determine which students are most in need of intensive intervention and to determine how to account for the effect of cultural and language variations on student performance. Most research with EL learners and RTI has been conducted with primarily Spanish speakers, yet in many parts of the country Spanish is only one of many languages represented in the EL learner population. Finally, additional intervention research is needed to determine the most optimal intensity and length of treatment and to further address the relative effectiveness of English versus native-language instruction or intervention.

References

AERA, APA, & NCME (1999). Testing individuals of diverse linguistic backgrounds. In AERA, APA, & NCME (Eds.), *Standards for Educational and Psychological Testing* (pp. 91–97). Washington, DC: American Educational Research Association.

Bainter, T. R. & Tollefson, N. (2003). Intellectual assessment of language minority students: what do school psychologists believe are acceptable practices? *Psychology in the Schools, 40*, 599–603.

Burns, M. K., Appleton, J. J., & Stehouwer, J. D. (2005). Meta-analytic review of responsiveness-to-intervention research: examining field-based and research-implemented models. *Journal of Psychoeducational Assessment, 23*, 381–394.

Cummins, J. C. (1984). *Bilingual and Special Education: Issues in Assessment and Pedagogy.* Austin, TX: Pro-Ed.

Cummins, J. (2003). Reading and the bilingual student: fact and fiction. In G. G. Garcia (Ed.), *English Learners: Reaching the Highest Level of English Literacy* (pp. 2–33). Newark, Delaware: International Reading Association.

Del Vecchio, A. & Guerrero, M. (1995) *Handbook of English Language Proficiency Tests*. Albuquerque, NM: Evaluation Assistance Center-West, New Mexico Highlands University. Retrieved February 13, 2006, from http://www.ncela.gwu.edu/pubs/eacwest/elptests.htm#IPT.

Durgunoglu, A. Y., Nagy, W. E., & Hancin-Bhatt, B. J. (1993). Cross-language transfer of phonological awareness. *Journal of Educational Psychology, 85*, 453–465.

Edelston, D., Vanderwood, M. L., & Healy, K. (in press). Early predictors of future reading performance: an English language learner population. *School Psychology Review*.

Elley, W. B. & Mangubhai, F. (1983). The impact of reading on second language learning. *Reading Research Quarterly, 19*, 53–67.

Freeman, D. & Freeman, Y. (2003). Teaching English learners to read: learning or acquisition. In G. G. Garcia (Ed.), *English learners: reaching the highest level of English literacy* (pp. 34–54). Newark, Delaware: International Reading Association.

Garcia, G. E. (1991). Factors influencing the English reading test performance of Spanish speaking Hispanic children. *Reading Research Quarterly, 26*, 371–392.

Garcia, G. E. (1998). Billingual children's reading. In M. Kamil, P. Mosenthal, P. D. Pearson, & R. Barr (Eds.), *Handbook of Reading Research, Vol. 3*. Mahway, NJ: Lawrence Erlbaum and Associates.

Goodman, K. & Goodman, Y. (1978). *Reading of American Children Whose Language is a Stable Rural Dialect of English or a Language other than English* (NIE-C-00-3-0087). Washington D.C.: U.S. Department of HEW, National Institute of Education.

Good, R. H. & Kaminski M. A. (Eds.) (2002). *Dynamic Indicators of Basic Early Literacy Skills* (6th ed.). Eugene, OR: Institute for the Development of Education Achievement.

Gonzalez, J. E. J. & Garcia, C. R. H. (1995). Effects of word linguistic properties on phonological awareness in Spanish children. *Journal of Educational Psychology, 87*, 193–201.

Greene, J. F. (1997). *Sounds and Letters for Readers and Spellers*. Longmont, CO: Sopris West.

Healy, K., Vanderwood, M., & Edelston, D. (2005). Early literary interventions for English language learners: support for an RTI model. *The California School Psychologist, 10*, 55–63.

Hopstock, P. J. & Stephenson, T. G. (2003). *Special Topic Report #1: Native Languages of LEP Students*. Report submitted to US Department of Education, Office of English Language Acquisition. Arlington, VA: Development Associates, Inc.

Kaminski, R. & Good, R. (1996). Toward a technology for assessing basic early literacy skills. *School Psychology Review, 25*, 215–227.

Kamphaus, R. W. (2000). Current trends in psychological testing of children. *Professional Psychology: Research and Practice, 31*, 155–164.

Klingner, J. K. & Edwards, P. A. (2006). Cultural considerations with response to intervention models. *Reading Research Quarterly, 41*, 108–117.

Lindsey, K. A., Manis, F. R., & Bailey, C. E. (2003). Prediction of first-grade reading in Spanish-speaking English-language learners. *Journal of Educational Psychology, 95*, 482–494.

Lopez, E. C. (1997). The cognitive assessment of limited English proficient and billingual children, In D. P. Flanagan, J. L. Genshaft, & P. L. Harrison (Eds.), *Contemporary intellectual assessment* (pp. 503–516). New York: Guilford.

Mathes, P. G., Denton, C. A., Fletcher, J. M., Anthony, J. L., Francis, D. J., & Schatschneider, C. (2005). An evaluation of two reading interventions derived from diverse models. *Reading Research Quarterly, 40*, 148–182.

McLaughlin, B. (1992). *Myths and Misconceptions about Second Language Learning: What Every Teacher Needs to Unlearn*. Santa Cruz, CA and Washington, DC: National Center for Research on Cultural Diversity and Second Language Learning.

National Center for Education Statistics (1999). *Teacher quality: A report on the preparation and qualification of public school teachers*. Washington, DC: US Department of Education.

National Clearinghouse for English Language Acquisition (1999). *State K-12 LEP enrollment and top languages 1989–90 to 1997–98*. Retrieved November 30, 2005, from http://www.ncela.gwu.edu/pubs/reports/state-data/1998/index.htm.

National Clearinghouse for English Language Acquisition (2002). *The growing number of LEP students 1991/91–2001/02*. Retrieved November 30, 2005, from http://www.ncela.gwu.edu/policy/states/stateposter.pdf.

National Clearinghouse for English Language Acquisition (2004). *California rate of LEP growth 1993/1994–2003/2004*. Retrieved November 30, 2005, from http://www.ncela.gwu.edu/policy/states/reports/statedata/2003LEP/California-G.pdf.

National Reading Panel. (2000). *Teaching children to read: an evidence-based assessment of the scientific research literature on reading and its implications for reading instruction*. Retrieved November 17,

2005, from http://www.nationalreadingpanel.org/ Publications/summary.htm.

Oller, J. (1979). *Language Tests at School: A Pragmatic Approach*. London: Longman.

Salvia, J. & Ysseldyke, J. E. (2004). *Assessment in Special and Inclusive Education* (9th ed.). Boston, MA: Houghton Mifflin.

Schrank, F. A., Fletcher, T. V., & Alvarado, C. G. (1996). Comparative validity of three English oral language proficiency tests. *The Bilingual Research Journal, 20,* 55–68.

Snow, C. E. & Biancarosa, G. (2003). *Adolescent Literacy and the Achievement Gap: What Do We Know and Where Do We Go From Here?* Washington, DC: Carnegie Corporation of New York.

Taylor, B. M., Frye, B. J., & Maruyama, G. M. (1990). Time spent reading and reading growth. *American Educational Research Journal, 27,* 351–362.

Ulibarri, D. M., Spencer, M. L., & Rivas, G. A. (1981). Language proficiency and academic achievement: a study of language proficiency tests and their relationship to school ratings as predictors of academic achievement. *NABE Journal, 5,* 47–80.

Vaughn, S., Linan-Thompson, S., Mathes, P. G., Cirino, P. T., Carlson, C. D., Pollard-Durodola, S. D., et al. (2006). Effectiveness of Spanish intervention for first grade English language learners at risk for reading difficulties. *Journal of Learning Disabilities, 39,* 56–73.

Vellutino, F. R., Scanlon, D. M., & Tanzman, M. S. (1998). The case for early intervention in diagnosing specific reading disability. *Journal of School Psychology, 36,* 367–397.

Woodcock, R. W. (1991). *Woodcock Language Proficiency Battery–Revised, English and Spanish forms.* Itasca, IL: Riverside.

31
Using Response to Intervention to Promote Transition from Special Education Services

Kristin Powers, Kristi Hagans, and Megan Miller

Kristin Powers, PhD, NCSD, is an Associate Professor of School Psychology, and Director of the Educational Psychology Clinic, California State University, Long Beach. kpowers@csulb.edu
Kristi Hagans, PhD, Assistant Professor and School Psychology Program Coordinator, California State University, Long Beach. khagansm@csulb.edu
Megan Miller, BA, is a graduate student of school psychology, California State University, Long Beach. mmiller8@csulb.edu

A response-to-intervention (RTI) approach to determining when and how to best exit students from special education has the potential to improve current educational practices and outcomes for students with disabilities. We know that post-secondary outcomes of students with disabilities are considerably less favorable than those of students without disabilities (National Council on Disability, 2004). Compared with adults without disabilities, those with disabilities are (a) twice as likely to be unemployed, (b) three times as likely to live in poverty, (c) twice as likely to have inadequate transportation, and (d) significantly less likely to socialize, eat out, or attend religious services than their nondisabled counterparts (National Organization on Disability, 2004). In addition, a disturbing upward trend has been observed in the rates of youth with disabilities who experience some type of disciplinary action at school, work, or with law enforcement (Wagner, Newman, Cameto, and Levine, 2005). RTI strategies, such as using continuously collected progress data to guide instruction and interventions, may improve the services designed to transition students from special education to general education and adulthood.

RTI shifts the duties of school personnel from diagnosing within-child deficits toward identifying conditions that enable learning and there is no reason for this process to end once eligibility is established (Grimes, 2002). Collecting data on students' educational progress and responding with a targeted intervention when it is determined that they are not achieving the expected outcomes will likely improve students' achievement, school persistence,

and transition to adulthood. For example, students with disabilities in 27 states must pass a graduation exam to be eligible to receive a high-school diploma (Johnson, Thurlow, Cosio and Bremer, 2005). An RTI methodology could be used to evaluate the effectiveness of instruction delivered to students with disabilities prior to the exit exam in order to make mid-course instruction or curricular adjustments. This practice may promote optimal performance on the exam and other important achievement benchmarks.

31.1 Importance of Response to Intervention in Exiting Special Education Students

RTI, because is an approach to evaluating a student's response to an intervention or instruction (Christ, Burns, and Ysseldyke, 2005), can be applied to many more types of educational decision beyond determining eligibility. For example, RTI strategies can be used to determine whether a student is ready to exit special education and be reintegrated into general education. Currently, 11% of students with disabilities, 14 years of age and older, are exited from special education each year because they no longer require services (US Department of Education, Office of Special Education Programs, 2004). This number could increase with an RTI approach to reintegration. The emphasis of RTI on direct assessment of student behavior, adjusting the instructional

418

context based on assessment results, and monitoring progress toward meaningful achievement goals can assist in making informed decisions about fading and discontinuing special education services (Grimes, 2002). In an RTI reintegration model, a plan to support the student in general education is developed based on the student's skills and the demands of the classroom ecology, the plan is implemented, and the student's performance in general education is monitored to determine whether the reintegration intervention was successful (Powell-Smith and Ball, 2000). Essentially, the RTI process used to qualify students for special education in the first place is repeated to determine whether, with appropriate accommodations, the student is able to meet the behavioral and academic demands of general education. An RTI reintegration model would require special educators to become knowledgeable about general education grade-level expectations and to use curriculum-based assessments (rather than traditional nomothetic measures) in order to make data-based decisions about when and how to exit a student from special education.

RTI can also guide transition planning and services. In transition planning, the individualized education program (IEP) team assists the student with a disability in achieving his/her individualized goals for adulthood, such as attending college or trade school, living in an assisted-living apartment, or securing medical insurance and access to primary care services. Transition planning became mandatory with the passage of the 1990 Individuals with Disabilities Education Act (IDEA, 1990) in response to the dismal adult outcomes of students with disabilities. Subsequent reauthorizations of this law served to strengthen the transition planning mandate. IDEA 1997 required the IEP team to clarify transition services needed by the student and to identify adult service agencies for assistance when appropriate (Shearin, Roessler, and Schriner, 1999). Since transition planning became mandatory, students with disabilities' high school graduation rates, postsecondary enrollment and participation in organized community groups improved considerably. Yet, adults with disabilities continue to achieve and participate in adult society at rates well below the general population (Wagner et al., 2005).

IDEA 2004 increased the emphasis in transition planning on outcomes by requiring postsecondary goals to be measurable, progress toward the goals to be monitored, and summative evaluations for students with disabilities who age-out of special education to be conducted (Johnson, 2005). IDEA 2004 defined transition services as "a coordinated set of activities for a child with a disability that is designed to be within a *results-oriented process* that is focused on improving the academic and functional achievement of the child with a disability to facilitate the child's movement from school to post-school activities" (Johnson, 2005, p. 61, emphasis added). IEP teams are required to identify postsecondary goals based on the students' preferences and design an intervention, which may include direct instruction, community experiences, and related services to achieve those goals. The mandate to identify transition services based on a results-oriented process is congruent with RTI, which is simply a method of efficiently organizing interventions to accomplish a desired outcome.

Unfortunately, a legal mandate does not guarantee immediate widespread adoption. Numerous studies have documented the shortcomings of transition planning, including use of vague goals that do not easily permit direct measurement, absence of data in identifying student needs, and poorly defined and ineffective interventions (Grigal, Test, Beattie, Wood, 1997; Lawson and Everson, 1993; Powers et al., 2005; Shearin et al., 1999). For example, Powers et al. (2005) examined 399 transition plans collected from two large urban districts and found little evidence that objective data were collected or used in the transition-planning process. Only 6% of the transition plans referenced data; thus, most of the 1747 postsecondary goals listed on the transition plans were not data based. The following types of data were found in proportion to all the IEPs (not just the transition component of the IEP) that were reviewed: work sample or portfolio (47%), grades (23%), observation (23%), vision-, hearing- or other health-related indices (21%), standardized test results (17%), career preference scales (<1%) and behavior rating scales (<1%; Balandran and Powers, 2004). Powers et al. (2005) hypothesized that lack of progress-monitoring data contributed to the problem of vague or nonexistent goals in the transition plans. Developing transition plans through an RTI model may enhance the quality of transition planning by encouraging IEP teams to identify measurable goals and monitor students' progress toward those goals using ongoing data collection.

31.2 Conceptual Basis of a Response to Intervention Model for Special Education Exit Practices

Generally, there are two assumptions inherent in an RTI model that drive the selection and implementation of assessment and intervention procedures: (1) interventions represent testable hypotheses that must be evaluated for each student; (2) implemented interventions focus on alterable contextual variables that empirically relate to improved student outcomes. Conceptually, RTI's methodology is based on the applied behavior analysis and single-subject research literature that promote the use of direct ongoing methods of assessment that measure socially important behaviors to make intraindividual or idiographic comparisons to evaluate the effectiveness of interventions (Baer, Wolf, and Risley, 1987). Additionally, RTI's grounding in applied behavior analysis theory asserts that child outcomes are influenced by a reciprocal interaction between student characteristics and environmental conditions. As a result, the focus of the problem does not reside solely within the child; rather, academic and behavioral challenges require an analysis of specific environmental conditions that support or thwart the development of academic competence (DiPerna and Elliot, 2002). Conversely, the identification and implementation of special education services traditionally operates from a deficit, child-centered model, with an assessment methodology that embraces and largely expects evaluations that measure within-person, unobservable, and unalterable characteristics (e.g., aptitude-by-treatment interactions) and produce data that do not relate to the development of targeted interventions and improved academic achievement (Ysseldyke, 2002). Because RTI focuses on the collection of individual time-series data within the context of a student's unique environment (Barnett, Daly, Jones, and Lenz, 2004), RTI-driven services may increase the quantity and quality of successfully exiting youth from special education programs and increase postsecondary outcomes for students transitioning to adulthood.

An ecological systems theory, first conceived by Bronfenbrenner (1977), is based on the assertion that a child's development is influenced by the interrelation of four ecological systems: (a) the microsys-

tem, or immediate setting(s) in which the child spends a majority of their time; (b) the mesosystem, or the linkage of two or more microsystems; (c) the exosystem, or those settings not directly experienced by the child but which influence the child's microsystems; and (d) the macrosystem, the wider society and culture that encompasses the other systems (Bronfenbrenner, 1988, 1989). An ecological framework can assist transition-planning teams in determining which skills to target for intervention and can facilitate collaboration among agencies and individuals. For example, a student with the postsecondary goal of attending college may require direct instruction in college study and test-taking skills if demands for these skills differ from the expectations within the high-school microsystem. At the mesosystemic level, individuals from the local University Disabled Student Services may attend the student's IEP to help identify the requisite college study and test-taking skills and identify sources of support in the college microsystem. Furthermore, knowledge of exosystemic influences on a student's success in a microsystem (e.g., university policies regarding test accommodations) and an awareness of the larger macrosystem that dictates the skills and abilities imperative to success in a society will guide the transition-planning process.

31.3 Description of an Response to Intervention Approach to Special Education Exit Practices

Using an ecological systems framework, an RTI approach to transition planning would include collecting data from multiple microsystems to determine the skills needed to be successful in each system. Instruction would then be developed and implemented to teach those skills, and is formatively evaluated at predetermined intervals to ensure student attainment of skills. Ecological systems theory defines success as a match between the environmental demands and the developing capabilities of the individual (Conoley and Haynes, 1992). Accordingly, preparing a student for success after special education may involve altering post-special education environments (i.e., providing accommodations in general education, mentoring in the workplace, modifying public transportation to be more accessible), as well as increasing the student's capacity to interact successfully within these various social systems. As targeted skills are mastered, the focus of instruction changes to the next skill in the hierarchy deemed necessary for success. A primary assumption of this model is that interventions cannot be guaranteed in advance to be successful with a student despite the empirical evidence of their effectiveness (Bergan and Kratochwill, 1990). Thus, if progress-monitoring data indicate that skills are not increasing to a desired level or rate, then instructional strategies or interventions are altered. Some promising transition practices that an RTI approach may improve include community mapping, interagency collaboration, and self-determination training. Each of these promising approaches is described in the following sections.

are offered. By becoming more invested and knowledgeable about the community resources available to students, educators are better equipped to prepare their students with disabilities for the transition from high school to postsecondary education or the workforce (Crane and Skinner, 2003); however, there are no empirical studies to confirm this hypothesis. In an RTI-driven transition-planning process, community mapping would be essential to identifying resources that could be used in planned interventions. The RTI emphasis on objective, measurable, and meaningful goals could refine the focus of community mapping on achieving objectives most salient to adjustment in adulthood. RTI methods of measuring progress toward those goals could remove the "guesswork" in community mapping by empirically testing the efficacy of various community-based interventions.

31.3.1 Community Mapping

In community mapping, educators, family members, or students investigate resources in their communities (e.g., employment and recreational opportunities, mental health agencies, possible mentors) by searching internet resources, calling agencies, and personally visiting organizations (Tindle, Leconte, Buchanan, and Taymans, 2005). Community mapping consists of determining a goal or vision, choosing data collection approaches, and establishing a timeline to finish the process. Community mapping is a type of person-centered planning in which the needs and preferences of the individual with disabilities results in *searching* for community assets, sometimes in unlikely places, that will allow the individual to attain their goals. In contrast, most transition planning is based on program availability rather than student needs (Johnson, Stodden, Emanuel, Luecking, and Mack, 2002). Community mapping is one method for improving the match between an individual's needs and the resources that are accessed.

Once the community resources have been identified, the team discusses gaps and overlaps in available resources. Community mapping is intended to proactively address insufficiencies in needed resources, to forge partnerships between institutions that provide complimentary resources, and to overall exert stronger influence on the types of community resource available and how such resources

31.3.2 Interagency Collaboration

Interagency collaboration occurs primarily at the state and local system level and involves agencies collaborating to plan and implement services in the most efficient and comprehensive way possible (Asselin et al., 1993). Collaboration between agencies, such as vocational rehabilitation, workforce development agencies, and community health and mental health providers, is essential in creating integrated service plans that support youth into adulthood (Johnson et al., 2002). School districts typically enter into a formal collaboration with community agencies articulated in a memorandum of understanding (MOU; Johnson et al., 2002). Yet, reviews of the transition component of the IEP found that representatives from community organizations rarely participate in transition planning meetings (Defur, Getzel, and Kregel, 1994; Powers et al., 2005). Collaborations that include cross-agency staff development, resource sharing, and mechanisms for sharing information across agencies on individuals' needs and outcomes are thought to produce optimal postsecondary outcomes (Johnson et al. 2002). RTI may improve such collaborations by focusing individuals' attention on the student's progress toward established postsecondary goals and providing a standard and common way to evaluate the absolute and relative effectiveness of various services and supports provided by different agencies.

31.3.3 Self-Determination Training

Self-determination is a set of interpersonal skills that gives one the ability to make decisions and set and attain goals based on one's own preferences and desires (Field, Martin, Miller, Ward and Wehmeyer, 1998, as cited in Test, Fowler, Brewer, and Wood, 2005). This skill set is necessary to developing individual identity, controlling one's life, and to obtaining others' respect for individual decisions and goals. Self-determination skills are considered essential to the full participation of individuals with disabilities in society. Self-determination training teaches goal setting and attainment, self-regulation, self-understanding, self-confidence, autonomy, and self-advocacy to students with disabilities who are transitioning from secondary education to adulthood. Self-determination training, much like social skills training, can be delivered to a whole class or a small group. Self-determination programs include *Whose Future Is It Anyway?* (Wehmeyer and Lawrence, 1995), *Self Advocacy: A Training Manual* (Rumrill, Roessler, and Brown, 1994), and *TAKE CHARGE* (Powers et al., 2001). Adequate evidence exists to suggest that self-determination training leads to short-term gains in the self-determination skills of students with disabilities (Test et al., 2005); however, less is known about the impact of this intervention on other skills (e.g., academic achievement, social skills, and cognitive skills) and its long-term benefits.

31.4 Relevant Research and Evidence of Effectiveness

To date, there are no published empirical studies on the effectiveness of using RTI to plan transitions from special education to either a less restrictive environment, or to adulthood beyond the immediate school environment, or both. Much of the research on improving students' post-special education outcomes is grounded in ideological premises or descriptive methodology; little is founded on empiricism. Research on evidenced-based transition practices is limited because of the complexity associated with the multiple contexts and multitude of skills that youth with disabilities must master to achieve well-adjustment in adulthood (National Council on

Disability, 2004). Yet, this is exactly the type of research that is most needed, as Bronfenbrenner (1977, p. 514) wrote:

... the understanding of human development demands going beyond the direct observation of behavior on the part of one or two persons in the same place; it requires examination of multi-person systems of interaction not limited to a single setting and must take into account aspects of the environment beyond the immediate situation containing the subject.

One notable example of this type of research was conducted by Sinclair, Christenson, and Thurlow (2005), who randomly assigned 164 students with special needs to either a treatment or control group. The intervention condition included many RTI strategies, including routine progress monitoring and individualized, data-based interventions. The interventionists also developed relationships with the students and their families and emphasized school persistence. The results of this study found this intervention led to improved school persistence and transition-planning quality. By the end of 4 years, only 39% of the students who received the intervention dropped out, compared with 58% of the students in the control group (effect size ES = 0.18). The effect sizes for persistence attendance ranged from 0.22 to 0.48, depending on the year, with greater effects for later years. The effects of the intervention on IEP and transition-planning quality were reported to be: (a) more up-to-date IEP, ES = 0.26; (b) student participation in IEP meeting (ES = 0.30); (c) high-quality goals and activities (ES = 0.32 to 0.34, depending on the transition area).

Whereas the remaining research on transition planning is more descriptive than experimental, a short summary exemplifies the ecological nature of transition planning. Benz, Lindstrom, and Yovanoff (2000) reviewed the literature and identified the following phenomenological and microsystemic factors as beneficial to postsecondary schooling outcomes: paid work experience within 2 years of exiting school; functional academic, independence living, vocation, self-determination, and social skills; participation in transition planning; participation in vocational education; graduation from high school; and an absence of academic, vocational and social deficits. Wehmeyer and Schwartz (1997) found that students who received self-determination training in school achieved more positive adult outcomes, such as a higher rate of employment and greater monetary earnings, in their follow-up study of youth with mental retardation or learning disabilities. Similarly, Martin et al. (2003) found that teaching goal setting and self-monitoring to eight students with severe behavioral problems led to gains in self-regulatory and academic skills.

Mesosystemic supports for transition services include collaboration between: (a) general and special education to increase students' participation in general education curriculum and extracurricular activities (Sands, Bassett, Lehmann, and Spencer, 1998); (b) parents and teachers to establish reasonably ambitious goals for youth who are about to exit special education (Whitney-Thomas and Hanley-Maxwell, 1996); and (c) school personnel and rehabilitation counselors to increase the range of services that are available (Hagner, Cheney, and Malloy, 1999) and students' opportunities for accessing services (Johnson et al., 1994).

Exosystemic factors that appear to support favorable transitions to adulthood included written interagency agreements and dedicated personnel in school districts to provide transition services (Benz et al., 2000). Similarly, Hasazi, Furney, and DeStefano (1999) compared schools with exemplary transition services with those that were representative of current practices and found model sites to have system-wide (rather than program-specific) leadership devoted to transition, professional development activities, self-determination training, and interagency collaboration. At the model sites, special education transition initiatives were linked to the School-to-Work Opportunities Act programs, which seemed to benefit general and special education students.

Macrosystemic influences on transition include cultural expectations about disability, gender, race, and social economic status. A failure to acknowledge and respond to these biases or assumptions can have a negative impact on students' transitions to adulthood. The influence of gender stereotypes has been observed in the types of employment in which young women and men with disabilities are engaged. Men with disabilities are more often employed in "masculine" jobs, such as machinists, and are subsequently paid higher wages and work more hours than females with disabilities, who pop-

ulate lower paid "feminine" jobs, such as childcare providers and personal assistants (Cameto, Marder, Wagner, and Cardoso, 2003). Powers et al. (2005) found students with developmental disabilities to be less involved in the IEP process and more frequently engaged in disability-stereotypic work (e.g., working with food, flowers, or filth) relative to students with other disabilities, despite their non-stereotypic career aspirations. Geenen, Powers, and Lopez-Vasquez (2001) found variations among European American and African American parents of students with disabilities in their self-report levels of engagement with 10 different transition-related activities. For example, African American parents were more likely than European American parents to report frequently talking to their children about life after high school (average score of 4.22 compared with 3.72 on a five-point Likert scale), yet they were less likely to report frequent involvement in school-based transition meetings (3.12 versus 4.39). These researchers also found school personnel to underestimate culturally and linguistically diverse parents' involvement in preparing their children for unfettered transitions to adulthood. Preliminary studies of RTI models of eligibility determination suggest racial and cultural bias is reduced by the focus on observable outcomes (Marston, Muyskens, Lau, and Canter, 2003). Accordingly, improving transition planning by incorporating RTI strategies may be most important for females, minorities, and students with developmental disabilities.

31.5 Critique and Implications of Response-to-Intervention Model for Existing Special Education

Embracing RTI practices, such as those listed in Table 31.1, may result in more targeted and data-based transition planning and greater service delivery effectiveness. However, RTI is not a panacea, and assessment and intervention issues related to preparing for adulthood are quite complex. Bronfenbrenner (1977) described development, in part, as an increase in the number of contexts in which the developing individual must operate. The RTI process of identifying student's needs, meaningful goals, and learning conditions to reach those goals may be

TABLE 31.1. Summary table of RTI enhancements to special education exit practices.

Outcome	RTI enhancement
Increased reintegration	Identify progress toward general education standards to determine when special education services are no longer needed. Establish interventions in general education that were successful in special education.
Increased graduation rate	Progress toward graduation standards continuously monitored to make necessary adjustments to curriculum and instruction and/or to provide targeted interventions.
Improved transition planning	Data-based transition plans: present level of performance and preferences measured. Meaningful and measurable post-secondary goals are identified. Monitor progress toward postsecondary goals with goal attainment scaling, rating scales, etc. Results of interventions (self-determination training, community mapping, etc.) identified, failure to respond leads to additional transition services.

more easily implemented for a single skill (reading) in a specific context (classroom) than applied to multiple skills in multiple contexts, as is necessitated by transition to adulthood. Transition-related activities, such as transition planning, person-centered planning, community mapping, and interagency collaboration, reflect this ecological complexity.

The implementation of an RTI model for transitioning students with disabilities would involve collecting data to inform decision-making about achieving socially important outcomes. There are technical challenges to monitoring progress toward complex skills such as self-determination, independence in career and living, and employability; the measurement of these skills is not as well developed as oral reading fluency or phonemic awareness. Fuchs and Fuchs (1999) described adequate progress-monitoring assessments to be sensitive to small changes in behavior, independent from specific instructional techniques, capable of modeling growth toward important goals, relevant to instruction and intervention efforts, and feasible. Currently, few measures of postsecondary skills meet these criteria.

Goal attainment scaling (GAS) is one promising intervention evaluation methodology. GAS offers considerable flexibility for measuring a wide range of skills, provides an explicit structure for identifying goals, and may increase the acceptability of transition services because the goals are derived from consensus (Sladeczek, Elliott, Kratochwill, Roberston-Mjaanes, and Stoiber, 2001). GAS scales a student's performance of a target behavior from -2 to $+2$, with, "0" being their current level of performance. The IEP team defines each anchor point $(-2, -1, 1, 2)$ in terms of advancing or declining performance of the behavior. For example, the following rubric may be created for a student who has identified the long-term goal of maintaining steady employment:

- $+2 =$ arrive at work on time, complete quality work, accept constructive criticism from co-workers
- $+1 =$ arrive at work on time, complete quality work
- $0 =$ tardy to work 2 of 5 days
- $-1 =$ tardy to work more than 2 days
- $-2 =$ tardy to work and/or altercation with supervisor/co-worker.

The individual's performance at work would be rated each week, and this monitoring would allow targeted interventions to be introduced when a clear downward trend became apparent.

Informant and self-report checklists, such as self-determination scales, might also be used to monitor students' progress toward important outcomes. Checklists are often very feasible, and commercially available checklists such as the Scales of Independent Behavior-Revised (SIB-R), Responsibility and Independence Scale for Adolescents (RISA), and the Behavioral Assessment System for Children (BASC) generally have adequate reliability and validity estimates (Salvia and Ysseldyke, 2004). Further research on whether checklists provide intervention evaluation data is needed.

31.6 Conclusion

An RTI model for exiting students from special education directs the efforts of families, schools, and community partners toward achieving meaningful and measurable outcomes. While not all desired outcomes are measurable, a select group of key results, such as reintegration into general education, employment with a living wage, and self-determination can be systematically monitored. With this monitoring, greater resources can be applied in the form of multisystemic interventions when failure appears eminent. Such formative use of data is superior to the "train and hope" or "transition and hope" approach that is currently prevalent (Stokes and Baer, 1977). Current practices in reintegration and transition planning constitute the "level one" of an RTI service delivery model. Many students with disabilities do succeed in response to currently provided services; however, some students are not successful and require more support. Right now there is no mechanism for identifying and responding to the students who are faltering as they exit special education services. RTI in combination with increased commitment of resources to assisting students who are exiting special education will lead to more favorable outcomes for young adults with disabilities.

References

Asselin, S. B., & Clark, G. M. (1993). Understanding and implementing secondary education transition programs. In B. Billingsley, B. V. Cline, S. B. Cohen, L. Cook, et al. (Eds.), *Program Leadership for Serving Students with Disabilities* (pp. 299–314). Blacksburg, VA: Virginia Polytechnic Institute and State University."

Baer, D. M., Wolf, M. M., & Risley, T. R. (1987). Some still-current dimensions of applied behavior analysis. *Journal of Applied Behavior Analysis, 20*(4), 91–97.

Balandran, J. & Powers, K. (2004). Enhancing the transition planning process of students with disabilities. *National Association of School Psychologists Annual Conference*, Houston, TX and *California Association of School Psychologists Annual Convention*, Burlingame, CA.

Barnett, D. W., Daly, E. J., Jones, K. M., & Lentz, F. E. (2004). Response to intervention: Empirically based special decisions from single-case designs of increasing and decreasing intensity. *The Journal of Special Education, 38*, 66–79.

Benz, M. R., Lindstrom, L., & Yovanoff, P. (2000). Improving graduation and employment outcomes of students with disabilities: predictive factors and student perspectives. *Exceptional Children, 66*, 509–529.

Bergan, J. R. & Kratochwill, T. R. (1990). *Behavioral Consultation and Therapy.* New York: Plenum.

Bronfenbrenner, U. (1977). Toward an experimental ecology of human development. *American Psychologist, 32*, 513–530.

Bronfenbrenner, U. (1988). Interacting systems in human development. In N. Bolger, A. Caspi, G. Downey, & M. Moorehouse (Eds.), *Persons in Context* (pp. 25–49). New York: Cambridge University Press.

Bronfenbrenner, U. (1989). Ecological systems theory. In R. Vasta (Ed.), *Annals of Child Development* (Vol. 6, pp. 187–251). Greenwich, CT: JAI.

Cameto, R., Marder, C., Wagner, M., & Cardoso, D. (2003). Youth employment. *Data Brief from the National Longitudinal Transition Study, 2*(2).

Christ, T. J., Burns, M. K., & Ysseldyke, J. E. (2005). Conceptual confusion within response-to-intervention vernacular: clarifying meaningful differences. *Communiqué, 34*(3), 1, 6–7.

Conoley, J. C. & Haynes, G. (1992). An ecological approach to intervention. In R. C. D'Amato & B. A. Rothlisberg (Eds.), *Psychological Perspectives on Intervention: A Case Study Approach to Prescriptions for Change* (pp. 177–188). White Plains, NY: Longman.

Crane, K. & Skinner, B. (2003). Community resource mapping: a strategy for promoting successful transition for youth with disabilities. *Information Brief: Addressing Trends and Developments in Secondary Education and Transition, 2*(1). Retrieved January 28, 2006.

Defur, S., Getzel, E. E., & Kregel, J. (1994). Individual transition plans: a work in progress. *Journal of Vocational Rehabilitation, 4*, 139–145.

Diperna, J. C. & Elliot, S. N. (2002). Promoting academic enablers to improve student achievement: an introduction to the mini-series. *School Psychology Review, 31*, 293.

Fuchs, L. S. & Fuchs, D. (1999). Monitoring student progress toward the development of reading competence: a review of three forms of classroom-based assessments. *School Psychology Review, 28*, 659–671.

Geenen, S., Powers, L. E., & Lopez-Vasquez, A., (2001). Multicultural aspects of parent involvement in transition planning. *Exceptional Children, 67*, 265–282.

Grigal, M., Test, D. W., Beattie, J., & Wood, W. M. (1997). An evaluation of transition components of individualized education programs. *Exceptional Children, 63*, 357–372.

Grimes, J. (2002). Responsiveness to interventions: the next step in special education. In R. Bradley, L. Danielson, & Hallahan, D. P. (Eds.), *Identification of Learning Disabilities: Research to Practice* (pp. 531–547). Mahwah, NJ: Lawrence Erlbaum.

Hagner, D., Cheney, D., & Malloy, J. (1999). Career-related outcomes of a model transition demonstration for young adults with emotional disturbance. *Rehabilitation Counseling Bulletin, 42*, 228–242.

Hasazi, S. B., Furney, K. S., & DeStefano, L. (1999). Implementing the IDEA transition mandates. *Exceptional Children, 65*, 555–566.

IDEA (1990). *Individuals with Disabilities Education Act*, P.L. 101-476.

Johnson, D. R. (2005). Key provisions on transition: a comparison of IDEA 1997 and IDEA 2004. *Career Development for Exceptional Individuals, 28*(2), 60–63.

Johnson, D. R., Rydell, C., Hunt, P., Gibbons, C., Corbey, S., & Thompson, S. J. (1994). *Transition Strategies that Work. Volume II. Profiles of Community Collaboration.* Minnesota: Publications Office.

Johnson, D. R., Stodden, R. A., Emanuel, E. J., Luecking, R., & Mack, M. (2002). Current challenges facing secondary education and transition services: What research tells us. *Exceptional Children, 68*(4), 519–531.

Johnson, D. R., Thurlow, M., Cosio, A., & Bremer, C. D. (2005). High school graduation requirements and students with disabilities. *Information Brief: Developments in Secondary Education and Transition, 4*(2), 1–3. Returned November 11, 2005.

Lawson, S. & Everson, J. (1993). *A National Review of Statements of Transition Services for Students who are Deaf–Blind.* Great Neck, NY: Helen Keller National Center/Technical Assistance Center.

Marston, D., Muyskens, P., Lau, M., & Canter, A. (2003). Problem-solving model for decision making with high-incidence disabilities: the Minneapolis experience. *Learning Disabilities: Research and Practice, 18*, 187–200.

Martin, J. E., Mithaug, D. E., Cox, P., Peterson, L. Y., Van Dycke, J. L., & Cash, M. E. Increasing self-determination: teaching students to plan, work, evaluate, and adjust. *Exceptional Children, 69*, 431–447.

National Council on Disability (2004). *Improving Educational Outcomes for Students with Disabilities.* Washington, DC: National Council on Disability.

National Organization on Disability (2004). *Landmark disability survey find pervasive disadvantages.* Retrieved July 29, 2004, from http://www.nod.org/

Powell-Smith, K. A. & Ball, P. L. (2000). Best practices in reintegration and special education exit decisions. In A. Thomas & J. Grimes (Eds.), *Best Practices in School Psychology* (4th ed., pp. 255–263). Bethesda, MD: National Association of School Psychologists.

Powers, K., Gil-Kashiwabara, E., Geenen, S., Powers, L.E., Balandran, J., & Palmer, C. (2005). Mandates and effective transition planning practices reflected in IEPs. *Career Development for Exceptional Individuals, 28*, 47–59.

Powers, L. E., Turner, A., Westwood, D., Matuszewski, J., Wilson, R., & Phillips, A. (2001). Take charge for the future: a controlled field-test of a model to promote student involvement in transition planning. *Career Development for Exceptional Individuals, 24*, 89–104.

Rumrill, P. D., Roessler, R. T., & Brown, P. L. (1994). *Self-Advocacy: A Training Manual.* Hot Springs, AR: Arkansas Research and Training Center in Vocational Rehabilitation.

Salvia, J. & Ysseldyke, J. E. (2004). *Assessment in Special Education.* NY: Houghton Mifflin Co.

Sands, D. J., Bassett, D. S., Lehmann, J., & Spencer, K. C. (1998). Factors contributing to and implications for student involvement in transition-related planning, decision making, and instruction. In M. L. Wehmeyer & D. J. Sands (Eds.), *Making It Happen: Student Involvement in Education Planning, Decision Making and Instruction* (pp. 25–44). Baltimore, MD: Paul H. Brookes.

Shearin, A., Roessler, R., & Schriner, K. (1999). Evaluating the transition component in IEPs of secondary students with disabilities. *Rural Special Education Quarterly, 18*(2), 22–35.

Sinclair, M. F., Christenson, M. L., & Thurlow, M. L. (2005). Promoting school completion of urban secondary youth with emotional or behavioral disabilities. *Exceptional Children, 71*, 465–482.

Sladeczek, I. E., Elliott, S. N., Kratochwill, T. R., Robertson-Mjaanes, S., & Stoiber, K. C. (2001). Application of goal attainment scaling to a conjoint behavioral consultation case. *Journal of Educational and Psychological Consultation, 12*, 45–58.

Stokes, T. F. & Baer, D. M. (1977). An implicit technology of generalization. *Journal of Applied Behavior Analysis, 10*, 349–367.

Test, D. W., Fowler, C. H., Brewer, D. M., & Wood, W. M. (2005). A content and methodological review of self-advocacy intervention studies. *Exceptional Children, 72*, 101–125.

Tindle, K., Leconte, P., Buchanan, L., & Taymans, J. M. (2005). Transition planning: Community mapping as a tool for teachers and students. *National Center on Secondary Education and Transition (NCSET), Research to Practice Brief, 4*(1).

US Department of Education, Office of Special Education Programs (2004). *Individuals with Disabilities Education Act (IDEA) data. Number of students with disabilities exiting special education, by age year and disability, 2002–2003 all disabilities.* Retrieved April 18, 2005 from http://www.ideadata .org/tables26th/ar_ad2.htm and http://www.ideadata .org/tables27th/ar_ad2.htm

Wagner, M., Newman, L., Cameto, R., & Levine, P. (2005). *Changes over time in the early postschool outcomes of youth with disabilities. A report from the national longitudinal transition study–2 (NLTS2).* Menlo Park, CA: SRI International.

Wehmeyer, M. L. & Lawrence, M. (1995). Whose future is it anyway? Promoting student involvement in transition planning. *Career Development for Exceptional Individuals, 18*, 69–83.

Wehmeyer, M. L. & Schwartz, M. (1997). Self-determination and positive adult outcomes: a follow-up study of youth with mental retardation or learn-ing disabilities. *Exceptional Children, 63*, 245–255.

Whitney-Thomas, J. & Hanley-Maxwell, C. (1996). Packing the parachute: parents' experiences as their children prepare to leave high school. *Exceptional Children*, 63, 75–87.

Ysseldyke, J. (2002). Intended and unintended consequences of high-stakes assessment systems .*Trainers Forum: Periodical of the Trainers of School Psychologist, 22*(2), 1–3, 11.

32
Toward a Unified Response-to-Intervention Model

Matthew K. Burns, Stanley L. Deno, and Shane R. Jimerson

Matthew K. Burns, PhD, is an Associate Professor of Educational Psychology and Coordinator of the School Psychology program at the University of Minnesota. burns258@umn.edu
Stanley L. Deno, PhD, is a Professor of Educational Psychology with the Special Education program at the University of Minnesota. denox001@umn.edu
Shane R. Jimerson, PhD, is a Professor in the Department of Counseling, Clinical, and School Psychology at the University of California, Santa Barbara. jimerson@education.ucsb.edu

"Research says" is perhaps one of the most commonly used statements in education and is often used to support current practice (Cochran-Smith, 2004). However, there may very well be an insufficient research base for the practices for which the statement is invoked (Ellis, 2005). There is a long history of practices in K–12 schools that both lack research support and are resistant to change (Ysseldyke, 2001). One example relevant to this chapter is the use of a discrepancy model to identify learning disabilities (LDs).

The discrepancy model was adopted in federal special education regulations in 1977 as a result of a political compromise because there was no approach to identifying LDs for which there was widespread empirical support (Gresham et al., 2005). Moreover, a long line of research demonstrating the lack of reliability of various procedures for classifying students as learning disabled began shortly after the discrepancy model's inception (Aaron, 1997; Algozzine and Ysseldyke, 1982; Fletcher et al., 1998). Beginning with the reauthorization of the Individuals with Disabilities Education Act (IDEA, 2004), local education agencies were released from the requirement to use a discrepancy model for determining eligibility for LD services and allowed to assess response to scientifically based interventions as an alternative. This language in the federal mandate, commonly referred to as response to intervention (RTI), represented the first significant reform in the regulated procedures for identifying learning-disabled students since 1977. Federal regulations supporting the use of RTI as an alternative approach to identification is encouraging. However, for the RTI approach to avoid a similar fate as the discrepancy model, additional research is needed.

Although the inclusion of RTI in federal special education legislation is a significant innovation, the concept of identifying LDs by measuring student learning is not new (Fuchs and Fuchs, 1998; Vellutino et al., 1996). Several large-scale RTI models described in previous chapters of this book are already in place. Specifically, models implemented in the Iowa Heartland Area Education Agency (Chapter 19), Instructional Support in Pennsylvania (Chapter 20), Illinois Flexible Service (Chapter 22), St. Croix River Education District (Chapter 23), the Idaho Results-Based Model (Chapter 24), the System to Enhance Educational Performance (STEEP) model (Chapter 25), the Michigan statewide initiative (Chapter 26), and the Florida Problem-Solving/Response-to-Intervention Model (Chapter 27) were described.

Some have categorized RTI approaches as either standard protocol or problem solving (Fuchs, Mock, Morgan, and Young, 2003), or as preventative, reactive, or eligibility-oriented (Burns, Vanderwood, and Ruby, 2005). These distinctions between different types of RTI and descriptions of different school district models may prove useful in some respects, but they could also contribute to inconsistency in RTI implementation, which will be one of the major obstacles to RTI use on a national level (Noell and Gansle, 2006).

As with the discrepancy model, the success of RTI will depend, ultimately, on integrity of its implementation and effectiveness enhancing student outcomes. In the worst case, using RTI procedures to identify LD with low implementation fidelity would be equivalent to conducting a traditional LD assessment without actually administering the tests (Noell and Gansle, 2006). Inconsistent use of the discrepancy model was a common criticism of efforts to identify LD students (Dean and Burns, 2002; Haight, Patriarca, and Burns, 2001), which makes it critical that evidence be developed demonstrating that the RTI models are more consistently implemented. One step toward increasing the consistency of identification would be to move away from a collection of district-specific models to a model that can be implemented on a large scale and assessed for fidelity.

As stated in the first chapter of *The Handbook of Response to Intervention*, the value of classifying the RTI models as either the "problem-solving" or "standard-protocol" models has been questioned. It has been suggested that the subclass "problem solving" be renamed "problem analysis," because both subtypes actually are aspects of problem solving (Christ, Burns, and Ysseldyke, 2005). Perhaps the first step, then, in developing a unified RTI model is to conceptualize the RTI approach as problem solving and to identify the common elements of problem solving rather than to examine or test diverse models currently being implemented.

Framing RTI in terms of the basic steps involved in problem solving also could serve to unify efforts to operationalize RTI and to test its efficacy in identifying students for service. Several generic problem-solving models exist in the literature, but perhaps the most specific details the steps as: (a) identify the problem, (b) define the problem, (c) explore alternative solutions to the problem, (d) apply a solution, and (e) look at the effects of the application (IDEAL; Bransford and Stein, 1984). When this model is applied to solving the problems addressed through RTI, the problem to be solved is how "to eliminate the difference between 'what is' and 'what should be' with respect to student development" (Deno, 2002, p. 38), and RTI is an attempt to identify resources necessary for sufficient student learning to occur. This chapter examines current practice and research using the steps in the IDEAL model and uses this as the basis for recommending

RTI practices that would construct a unified model (Figure 32.1).

32.1 Identify the Problem

32.1.1 Current Practice

Recent legal mandates, such as *No Child Left Behind*, have fostered a school culture within the United States that emphasizes assessment and data-based decision making (Ysseldyke et al., 2006). Moreover, data are becoming more prominent in designing interventions for individual students and groups of children (Shapiro, 2000), and have moved from high-inference data regarding cognitive processes to direct assessment of the academic problem (Shapiro and Elliott, 1998). There are many depictions of RTI models in the literature that emphasize data collection as a means to identify problems for individual students (Howe, Scierka, Gibbons, and Silberglitt, 2003; Ikeda, Tilly, Stumme, and Volmer, 1996; Marston, Muyskens, Lau, and Canter, 2003; VanDerHeyden and Burns, 2005), and many states are implementing statewide assessment systems, such as the dynamic indicators of basic early literacy skills (DIBELS; Kaminski and Good, 1998). Thus, assessment appears to play a prominent role in districts in which RTI practices are engaged, and is becoming commonplace in K–12 schools.

32.1.2 Research-Based Practices

General outcomes measures, such as curriculum-based measurement (CBM), are especially useful in identifying areas of skill deficits for children. CBM could serve as an effective first step in any problem-solving effort, in that data could be compared with various standards and be used to identify individual children in need of additional intervention (Shinn, 2002). Moreover, CBM has been identified as an essential component of any effective RTI model (Burns, Dean, and Klar, 2004; Burns and Ysseldyke, 2005; Gresham, 2002).

The research regarding CBM is valuable both from a psychometric and an instructional perspective. Data obtained from CBM have consistently been shown to be sufficiently reliable for instructional decisions among various student populations (Deno, 2005), and using those data for instructional

		IDEAL Problem Solving Model				
		Identify the problem	Define the problem	Explore alternative solutions to the problem	Apply a solution	Look at the effects of the application
Three-Tier Response to Intervention Model	Tier I	Implement core curriculum and universal screening to identify problems	Collect data to rule out classwide or curricular problems	Generate potential classwide interventions if necessary	Implement classwide remedial interventions or make instructional modifications	Continue benchmark assessment to determine if the class progresses
	Tier II		Collect data that are essential to understanding and clearly defining the basis for the problem	Generate a list of evidence-based strategies to intervene class-wide or small group level	Implement explicit instructional strategies to address the problem area for a small-group of children	Outcome assessment to examine progress on at least monthly basis
	Tier III		Collect additional data that are essential to understanding and clearly defining the basis for the problem	Generate a list of evidence-based intensive individualized interventions	Implement evidence-based intensive individualized interventions to address the problem area	Frequent (twice weekly) outcome assessment to examine progress

FIGURE 32.1. Matrix representing the three-tier RTI model and the IDEAL problem-solving model (Bransford and Stein, 1984).

decision led to increased student learning (Fuchs and Fuchs, 1986). However, more important than the type of data used for problem identification is the system with which they are collected. Data obtained from brief assessments of academic skills for all students can be used to identify children with potential difficulties. Thus, the first step of the problem-solving process is to screen the academic skills of all students, called universal screening. Research is beginning to identify the effectiveness of using screening data in enhancing the learning outcomes of all children (Ardoin, Witt, Connell, and Koenig, 2005, VanDerHeyden and Burns, 2005; VanDerHeyden, Witt, and Naquin 2003).

As stated above, data need to be collected for all children on a continuous basis in order to screen for academic deficits, and CBM is an effective approach for continuous progress monitoring. However, other assessments could also serve as screening instruments, including those developed from a CBM tradition, such as DIBELS or norm-referenced measures such as the *Test of Oral Reading Efficiency* (Torgesen, Wagner, and Rashotte, 1999). Research is needed to identify which approach is superior, but likely advantages of the former over the latter are the

sensitivity to growth, ease of use, lower costs, dynamic nature, and the ability to inform other aspects of problem solving (Shinn, 2002).

32.2 Define the Problem

32.2.1 Current Practice

Clearly and explicitly defining the problem is the "key to success" of problem solving (Deno, 2002, p. 46). Although many RTI models articulated in the literature involve what is called problem solving, few convey steps to defining the problem. STEEP (VanDerHeyden et al., 2003) begins this process by first examining whether the difficulty is specific to the child or the classroom of children and then determining whether the deficit is primarily due to a lack of skill or lack of motivation (Ardoin et al., 2004; VanDerHeyden et al., 2003).

Other approaches to defining the problem usually involve comparing the child's rate of progress with a projected rate of growth necessary to obtain a level of proficiency (Burns, 2002; Shinn, 1989). After determining what rate of growth is necessary, school personnel then identify interventions that enable students to obtain that rate of learning (Tilly, 2002). The result of this analytic approach is an inference about the cause of the deficit.

32.2.2 Research-Based Practices

There is a considerable research base supporting the effectiveness of functional analysis of problem behaviors to define the problem (Iwata, Dorsey, Slifer, Baumann, and Richman, 1982; Mace, Yankanich, and West, 1988; McComas, Hoch, and Mace, 2000; McComas and Mace, 2000), but none addressed academic deficits. Thus, the model proposed by Shapiro (2004) may be optimal, in which assessment data are gathered to assess the academic environment, instructional placement, and instructional modifications to define the problem. The first step is to compare current skill level with desired skill level to clarify and define discrepancies (Deno, 2002). The term discrepancy often has a negative connotation in special education, because for 30 years the discrepancy of interest was between intelligence and academic achievement, but the discrepancy of interest here is between the child's skill level and rate of growth to acceptable levels of both. A child who scores below a given proficiency level of skills and below an acceptable rate of growth is demarked as dually discrepant (DD; Fuchs, 2003). Empirical investigations were unsuccessful in validating the discrepancy between achievement and intelligence (Aaron, 1997), but several studies support the validity of the DD approach (Burns and Senesac, 2005; Fuchs, 2003; Speece and Case, 2001; Speece, Case, and Molloy, 2003).

After examining dual discrepancy, school personnel should assess the instructional placement of children and the instructional modification (Shapiro, 2004). This essentially involves assuring a match between student skill level and task demands, and implementing interventions to align the two. Several assessment models adequately inform this decision, but few are as well researched as Gickling's model (Gickling and Havertape, 1981) of curriculum-based assessment for instructional design (CBA-ID). Several studies have supported the reliability of CBA-ID data and the validity of decisions made from them (Burns, 2001, 2004a, 2004b; Burns and Mosack, 2005; Burns, Tucker, Frame, Foley, and Hauser, 2000). Moreover, implementing

an intervention to better align student skill and task demand has consistently led to increased learning (Burns, 2002, in press; Shapiro, 1992; Shapiro and Ager, 1992). Howell and Nolet (1999) articulated an extensive instructional decision-making model called curriculum-based evaluation that emphasizes task analyses, direct observation, and systematic hypothesis testing. Although research supports the components of this approach, few studies have examined outcomes associated with the model in its entirety.

32.3 Explore Alternative Solutions to the Problem

32.3.1 Current Practice

Almost all RTI models that currently exist in K–12 schools use a multidisciplinary problem-solving team (PST) to generate alternatives solutions for student problems (Burns and Ysseldyke, 2005). Most publications describing various PST approaches specifically discuss who should be members of the team, but few discuss what specific process the team uses to generate and explore potential solutions. Those articles that do address a problem-solving process tend to use vague language, such as, after identifying the problem, "the next step is to identify why it is occurring. For problems at a low level of intensity, hypotheses about why the problem is happening may be derived informally. As problems become more intense, a more rigorous and systematic problem analysis procedure will be necessary" (Heartland Area Education Agency 11, 2006, p. 101). Moreover, there seems to be a wide range of activities in which educators engage in the name of problem solving (Burns et al., 2005).

32.3.2 Research-Based Practices

Research has consistently supported the use of PSTs to generate potential solutions (Burns and Symington, 2002; Marston et al., 2003; Reschly and Starkweather, 1997), but an empirical investigation as to whether PSTs are a critical component of RTI has yet to be completed. Moreover, little research has examined who should serve on those teams. Burns (1999) found that teams that included a special education teacher and/or school psychologist referred fewer students to special education and recommended fewer grade retentions, but no other studies addressing PST personnel were found.

There appear to be several forces that affect the role of PSTs within RTI. The research supporting the effectiveness of PSTs is balanced by a lack of research examining how critical PSTs are to RTI; and the overwhelming use of PSTs within RTI should be weighed against the aforementioned lack of research and the lack of implementation consistency among PSTs in practice. It seems reasonable to recommend the use of a PST to generate potential solutions within RTI, but additional research is clearly needed. However, the terms PST and RTI are not synonymous and, whereas it is not clear that PST is essential to RTI, it is clear that PST alone would not be an effective RTI approach.

Perhaps more importantly than who should generate solutions is *how* those solutions should be generated. Research suggests two approaches to generating interventions that are linked to the severity of the problem. The first approach is based on the work of the National Reading Panel (2000), in which phonemic awareness, phonetic decoding, reading fluency, vocabulary, and comprehension were identified as critical aspects of reading instruction. Children for whom the problem is deemed less severe could participate in small-group instruction, which has been shown to be effective for improving reading skills of children at risk for reading failure (see Chapters 14, 15; and 17). However, the specific intervention would be based on the individual child's need, which would be assessed and grouped according to the National Reading Panel's five areas. For example, a child who lacks reading fluency would participate in a small-group intervention to increase reading fluency; and those for whom phonemic awareness is a particular difficulty, small-group interventions would be based on that critical area. The National Reading Panel meta-analysis was quite extensive, which suggests confidence in their findings, but how the data fit within the RTI model would require additional research.

A second approach for intervention development, probably for children whose problems are more severe or who do not respond to small-group interventions, would involve using a brief experimental analysis (BEA) to identify interventions that are mostly likely to be successful. Daly and colleagues (Daly, Bonfiglio, Mattson, Persampieri,

and Foremann-Yates, 2005; Daly and Martens, 1994; Daly, Martens, Dool, and Hintze, 1998; Daly, Martens, Hamler, Dool, and Eckert, 1999; Daly, Witt, Martens, and Dool, 1997) proposed the BEA framework for developing reading interventions and have consistently found positive results. A BEA process consists of implementing a series of hypothesis-driven interventions over a short period of time, assessing the immediate effect on the targeted skill, and then withdrawing the interventions to return to baseline conditions (Barnett, Daly, Jones, and Lentz, 2004). Perhaps the most substantial advantage of the BEA approach is the systematic and empirical testing of interventions based on a heuristic such as the five hypotheses for student failure (Daly et al., 1997). The BEA assessment technology has been shown to be effective in improving student learning among children with significant reading difficulties (Burns and Wagner, 2006) and an effective component of RTI (Petursdottir, 2006).

32.4 Apply a Solution to the Problem

32.4.1 Current Practice

Once interventions are found to be effective for an individual student, they are implemented over an extended period, but the delivery system can vary substantially between models. Some models match delivery system with student need and may include special education services as a delivery option (Lau et al., 2006; Tilly, 2002); and others more or less restrict remedial efforts to general education but could utilize individual, small-group, or classwide interventions (Kovaleski, Tucker, and Stevens, 1996). Generally speaking, interventions implemented to solve a problem are categorized as problem solving or standard protocol, with the defining difference being the uniformity of remedial efforts (Fuchs et al., 2003). Although, as stated earlier, this dichotomy is probably artificial (Christ et al., 2005), many RTI models currently in place probably fit into one or the other category.

32.4.2 Research-Based Practices

Research has consistently supported the effectiveness of both the problem-solving approach (Heartland Area Education Agency, 2004;

Kovaleski, Gickling, and Morrow, 1999; Marston et al., 2003; Reschly and Starkweather, 1997; Tucker, 2001) and standard-protocol approach (McMaster, Fuchs, Fuchs, and Compton, 2005; Speece and Case, 2001; Torgesen et al., 1999; 2001; Vaughn, Linan-Thompson, and Hickman, 2003; Vellutino et al., 1996) to RTI. Thus, the efficiency, rather than effectiveness, should probably drive the delivery of interventions within RTI. Some children have needs that are best addressed in the small-group standardized interventions associated with the standard-protocol approach, but some require more individualized interventions.

It would require more resources to plan for an individual student rather than a group of three to four students receiving a scripted intervention, but those resources should be committed if the child benefits. The STEEP model (Chapter 26) combines both approaches by implementing a small-group intervention if the class median on the benchmark assessment falls below the desired criterion, but it uses a more individualized approach if the problem is determined to be more child specific (Van-DerHeyden and Burns, 2005). Moreover, given that small-group interventions are the more efficient approach, then that may be the first option for most students.

32.5 Look at the Effects of the Application

32.5.1 Current Practice

The culture of schools in this country has recently embraced data-based decision-making (Ysseldyke et al., 2006), but many of those decisions are based on state-mandated group achievement tests administered for accountability purposes. More instructionally relevant measures, such as DIBELS (Kaminski and Good, 1998) and CBM, have become more common. This is probably due to the readily available and easily used electronic data warehouses for PK–12 schools (Chapter 29). Moreover, some districts have developed somewhat sophisticated analyses to link CBM data to state accountability test scores and to derive benchmark criteria (Chapter 24).

32.5.2 Research-Based Practices

The recent use of CBM for data-based decision-making follows a long line of research support-

ing its effectiveness (Deno, 2005; Fuchs and Fuchs, 1986). Recent efforts have demonstrated a moderate to strong link between CBM scores and state accountability test scores (Stage and Jacobsen, 2001; McGlinchey and Hixson, 2004; Silberglitt, Burns, Madyun, and Lail, 2006), but standards for educational assessment suggest the need to directly examine the accountability and eligibility decision-making utility of CBM (American Educational Research Association, American Psychological Association, and National Council for Measurement in Education, 1999). Thus, additional research is needed. However, research has consistently supported that CBM is ideally suited to measure the effectiveness of interventions within a problem-solving model (Burns et al., 2004).

Recent developments in psychometric aspects of CBM shed some light on current practices. Perhaps most important is the effect that standard error of measure has on CBM scores. In typical assessment situations, approximately 8 weeks' worth of data are needed before the value of the standard error of measure of student growth rates is smaller than the value of the slope of growth (Christ, 2006). In other words, a slope of 1.5 words/minute/week, which indicates the child increases their reading fluency by 1.5 words/minute each week, would likely have a true score range of −0.5 to 3.5 or larger until data are collected for 8 weeks.

32.6 Unified Response-to-Intervention Model: Problem Solving

Implementation integrity remains a substantial threat to RTI implementation (Burns et al., 2005; Noell and Gansle, 2006; Ysseldyke, 2005) unless the field can articulate a common model, or at least the core components of an effective practice. As a result of a review of the research literature and current practice, a three-tiered model that infuses the principles of problem solving throughout is endorsed.

32.6.1 Tier I

The first tier of an RTI model should be defined by a quality core curriculum and universal screening of all children with instructionally sensitive and psychometrical adequate tools. Fortunately, an extensive literature exists regarding both, so we refer readers to other sources for specific information. The primary aspect of problem solving that occurs within the first tier is *identifying a problem*. Student skills should be compared with benchmark criteria to determine whether a problem exists, but identifying the problem and searching for a solution occur in later stages of problem solving and subsequent tiers in RTI. The previous statement is only true, however, if the problem is determined to be specific to the individual child. Examining whether the deficit is class wide would rule out instructional and curricular explanations for the individual child, but could suggest the need for an intervention or modification in Tier I that would affect all children in the class.

32.6.2 Tier II

32.6.2.1 Define the Problem

On average, approximately 20% of children will not respond adequately to Tier I instruction (Burns et al., 2005) and should receive a Tier II intervention. After identifying the problem, further defining of the difficulty should occur by first analyzing the magnitude of the discrepancy between what is expected and how the child is performing. Next, data for the child's classroom should be examined to determine whether the low performance is specific to the child or a residual effect of an ineffective Tier I. This is done by comparing the mean of the classroom benchmark data with a criterion to assure that it is the child and not the class that lacks proficiency. Other data should be collected, such as curriculum-based assessment (Gickling and Havertape, 1981), criterion-referenced assessment, and an ecological analysis of contextual influences (Chapter 11) to better understand and define the problem area for individual children.

32.6.2.2 Explore Alternatives

If the class median falls below the benchmark criterion, then the intervention should be delivered to the entire class. If the median score is above the benchmark criterion, then the intervention should be delivered to the child. Potential interventions should be examined within the framework of the National Reading Panel (2000) by assessing the child's skills in phonemic awareness, phonics, fluency, vocabulary, and reading comprehension. After identify-

ing which area is most likely linked to the reading deficit, a specific intervention can be attempted.

32.6.2.3 Apply a Solution

Interventions within Tier II should be delivered in a small-group format based on National Reading Panel areas. Generally speaking, these groups will have three to four members, but should be limited to six members. After grouping children according to needs, explicit instruction in the deficit area should occur for at least 30 to 60 min each day with at least supervision by a highly qualified teacher.

32.6.2.4 Look at Effectiveness

Outcome assessment within Tier II needs to occur at least monthly and should address the same general outcome measure as used in Tier I universal screenings. The reason that consistency between tiers is important is because the level of student skill and slope of growth (dual discrepancy) should both be compared with the general population, which requires that the data obtained within that general population be directly comparable to those used to monitor progress in Tier II. Those students found to respond sufficiently would either return to Tier I or continue with Tier II support. Those whose skill level falls below a criterion, such as those published by DIBELS, and whose rate of growth falls below the normative standard would next receive a Tier III intervention to continue exploring alternative interventions.

32.6.3 Tier III

32.6.3.1 Define the Problem

Shapiro's (2004) assessment-to-intervention model proposes that curriculum-based assessment data are needed to modify instruction. These data seem critical in Tier III, but other data will be needed as well and could include norm-referenced measures of word reading, reading comprehension, or phonological processing. Again, the severity of the problem can be defined normatively, but baseline and functional data are also required.

32.6.3.2 Explore Alternatives

Interventions in Tier II are designed to be efficient, in that they focus on standardized approaches for groups of children. Interventions in Tier III are more clearly focused on effectiveness rather than efficiency, because intensive individualized interventions will be explored until some individual or combination of interventions leads to student success. Perhaps the best method to explore interventions over the short term, to then implement over the long term, is BEA. Children who are not successful in Tier II should be presented to a PST, which adheres to the principles of an effective PST (Burns, Wiley, and Viglietta, in press), after a BEA has identified potential interventions. The PST would then brainstorm how to make those interventions as practical and effective as possible. This approach would match the functional analysis aspect of most problem-solving models.

32.6.3.3 Apply a Solution

Interventions within Tier III should be limited to small groups of three or less, and could even be delivered in a one-on-one format. Although the exact intervention will likely vary from child to child, it should target the deficit area, explicitly teach the skill, provide frequent opportunities to respond, use materials that provide an appropriate level of challenge, and contain sufficient feedback to inform the child of successes and errors (Burns, VanDerHeyden, and Boice, in press a). Moreover, the intervention should consist of at least 60 min of daily instruction beyond the general education core curriculum.

Special education services could be utilized in Tier III, but only if they are needed to assure success. The goal of RTI is to keep searching until the solution to the child's problem is found, and then to implement it as efficiently as possible. For some children, the level of need and/or intensity of intervention may be such that the child cannot be successful unless special education resources are allocated. At that point the child would be identified as having a special education disability and special education would be invoked.

32.6.3.4 Look at Effectiveness

CBM data are clearly needed in Tier III. Data should be collected at least twice weekly and progress toward a goal should be closely monitored. A goal can be established for an individual child based on normative criteria (e.g., average reading rate for children in their grade) and an aimline can be drawn

to monitor progress toward the goal. Data will then be plotted and compared with the aimline, with adequate response being data points that fall at or above the aimline. Data points below the aimline suggest that the intervention is not leading to success, and so a different intervention should be considered.

32.7 Implications for Behavioral Difficulties

It is important to note that the three-tier problem-solving model, described above using examples to address achievement problems, is also appropriate for addressing behavior problems (National Association of State Directors of Special Education, 2005). Scholarship addressing the use of problem-solving models has established an empirical foundation to build upon (Chapter 12), and many of the early RTI models address behavior as well. For example, many point to Deno and Mirkin (1977) as the origin of both CBM and RTI, and the data-based decision-making process outlined in that seminal document was also applied to behavioral difficulties by the authors. Furthermore, several statewide RTI models have included both achievement and behavior problems (cf., Florida: Chapter 28; Idaho: Chapter 29; Illinois: Chapter 23; Michigan: Chapter 27). This information is particularly important in the context of an increasing number of children in special education programs for children with emotional disturbance (US Department of Education, 2003). Given the interplay of social, emotional, and behavioral adjustment with academic achievement, addressing problems in these areas is also critically important to enhance student success at school. The following provides a brief description of activities at each tier.

32.7.1 Tier I

Universal screening is important to identify children at risk or developing or displaying social, emotional, or behavior problems. Annual school-wide screening provides an opportunity for school-based professionals to better understand the student population and identify both individual students and systems-level areas of need. Some schools may administer brief student surveys or rating scales addressing social, emotional, or behavior problems to all students. In addition, students' cumulative records, teachers' gradebooks, or behavioral referral databases may be available in some schools. Another screening technique that may be used is to have all teachers identify children in their classrooms they are concerned about regarding specific social behaviors (e.g., peer relationship problems, inattention, poor classroom behavior, depression) (Demaray and Elliott, 2001). In many schools, it is anticipated that such universal screening would reveal that 80–85% of students would be in the healthy range (Walker and Shinn, 2002). For those students identified at risk or currently engaging in problem behaviors (e.g., affective problems, externalizing problems, social-relationship problems, risky behaviors), it is anticipated that core-curriculum modifications would benefit many students. For instance, school-wide positive behavioral interventions and supports (e.g., Sugai, Sprague, Horner, and Walker, 2000; Crone and Horner, 2003) have been associated with promoting positive student behaviors.

32.7.2 Tier II

For those students who continue to display problem behaviors it would be essential to gather and carefully examine data for these individual students. The problem-solving process in Tier II would involve both general and special education personnel, and is within the administrative and fiscal responsibility of general education. These data would be used to facilitate problem analysis and clearly define the problem(s). For instance, it would be important to identify the conditions under which the student is displaying problems and those where the student is not. These data can then be used for developing interventions for individual students or groups of students, as well as evaluating the effectiveness of those interventions, and may also be used to determine eligibility for special education services (Gresham and Kern, 2006). Evidence-based interventions for small groups and individuals would be implemented in the classroom with appropriate evaluation to determine whether the problem behaviors were improving and whether the interventions led to success on established behavioral objectives.

32.7.3 Tier III

For those students who continue to display problem behaviors following Tier I and II prevention and in-

tervention activities, it would be important to carefully review available data and discern whether additional information was necessary to understand why the problem behaviors persist. Assessment would include a comprehensive multidisciplinary assessment of the child's educational needs. The process should focus on gathering information that will help to clearly define the problem and facilitate the development of individual intensive interventions. Through the intervention process, data should be gathered repeatedly and often to monitor student improvement. Depending upon the student's response to interventions during this third tier, the student may or may not require additional support services. If the results of this comprehensive evaluation indicate that a student's instructional needs cannot be met exclusively in the general education program, then an individualized education program team meeting would be convened to determine appropriate supports and services in special education.

32.8 Summary

The quote "dwarves standing on the shoulders of giants" (Bernard of Chartres, 1159) is especially true for contemporary RTI activities. Previous efforts of scholars and practitioners across the country provide a robust foundation of knowledge and insights to build upon to enhance the success of students through identifying and addressing their needs. Recent federal mandates and special education regulations serve as a catalyst to consider consolidating approaches rather than operating in a field of connected yet distinctly different models. The core components identified above may establish the basis from which to unify RTI efforts and assure the implementation integrity that could be the most significant threat to a national movement. Moreover, using core components would enhance the likelihood of success and continue to enhance the educational success of children.

References

Aaron, P. G. (1997). The impending demise of the discrepancy formula. *Review of Educational Research, 67,* 461–502.
Algozzine, B & Ysseldyke, J. (1982). Classification decisions in learning disabilities. *Educational and Psychological Research, 2,* 117–129.

American Educational Research Association, American Psychological Association, & National Council on Measurement in Education (1999). *Standards for Educational and Psychological Testing.* Washington, DC: American Psychological Association.

Ardoin, S. P., Witt, J. C., Connell, J. E., & Koenig, J. L. (2005). Application of a three-tiered response to intervention model for instructional planning. *Journal of Psychoeducational Assessment, 23,* 362–380.

Barnett, D. W., Daly, E. J., Jones, K. M., & Lentz, F. E. (2004). Response to intervention: empirically based special service decisions from single-case designs of increasing and decreasing intensity. *The Journal of Special Education, 38,* 66–79.

Bransford, J. & Stein, B. (1984). *The Ideal Problem Solver: A Guide for Improving Thinking, Learning and Creativity.* San Francisco: W. H. Freeman.

Burns, M. K. (1999). The effectiveness of including special education personnel on intervention assistance teams. *The Journal of Educational Research, 92,* 354–356.

Burns, M. K. (2001). Measuring acquisition and retention rates with curriculum-based assessment. *Journal of Psychoeducational Assessment, 19,* 148–157.

Burns, M. K. (2002). Utilizing a comprehensive system of assessment to intervention using curriculum-based assessments. *Intervention in School and Clinic, 38,* 8–13.

Burns, M. K. (2004a). Using curriculum-based assessment in the consultative process: a useful innovation or an educational fad. *Journal of Educational and Psychological Consultation, 15,* 63–78.

Burns M. K. (2004b). Age as a predictor of acquisition rates as measured by curriculum-based assessment: evidence of consistency with cognitive research. *Assessment for Effective Intervention, 29,* 31–38.

Burns, M. K. (in press). Reading at the instructional level with children identified as learning disabled: potential implications for RTI. *School Psychology Quarterly.*

Burns, M. K., Dean, V. J., & Klar, S. (2004). Using curriculum-based assessment in the responsiveness to intervention diagnostic model for learning disabilities. *Assessment for Effective Intervention, 29*(3), 47–56.

Burns, M. K. & Mosack, J. L. (2005). Criterion-related validity of measuring sight-word acquisition with curriculum-based assessment. *Journal of Psychoeducational Assessment, 23,* 216–224.

Burns, M. K. & Senesac, B. K. (2005). Comparison of dual discrepancy criteria to assess response to intervention. *Journal of School Psychology, 43,* 393–406.

Burns, M. K., & Symington, T. (2002). A meta-analysis of pre-referral intervention teams: student and systemic outcomes. *Journal of School Psychology, 40,* 437–447.

Burns, M. K., Tucker, J. A., Frame, J., Foley, S., & Hauser, A. (2000). Interscorer, alternate-form, internal consistency, and test–retest reliability of Gickling's model of curriculum-based assessment for reading. *Journal of Psychoeducational Assessment, 18,* 353–360.

Burns, M. K., VanDerHeyden, A. M., & Boice, C. H. (in press). Best practices in delivering intensive academic interventions for individual students. In A. Thomas & J. Grimes (Eds.), *Best Practices in School Psychology* (5th ed.). Bethesda, MD: National Association of School Psychologists.

Burns, M. K., Vanderwood, M., & Ruby, S. (2005). Evaluating the readiness of prereferral intervention teams for use in a problem-solving model: review of three levels of research. *School Psychology Quarterly, 20,* 89–105.

Burns, M. K. & Wagner, D. (2006). Determining an effective intervention within a brief experimental analysis for reading: a meta-analytic review. Manuscript submitted for publication.

Burns, M. K., Wiley, H. I., & Viglietta, E. (in press). Best practices in implementing effective problem-solving teams. In A. Thomas & J. Grimes (Eds.), *Best Practices in School Psychology* (5th ed.). Bethesda, MD: National Association of School Psychologists.

Burns, M. K. & Ysseldyke, J. E. (2005). Comparison of existing responsiveness-to-intervention models to identify and answer implementation questions. *The California School Psychologist, 10,* 9–20.

Christ, T. J. (2006). Short-term estimates of growth using curriculum-based measurement of oral reading fluency: estimating standard error of the slope to construct confidence intervals. *School Psychology Review, 35,* 128–133.

Christ, T. J., Burns, M. K., & Ysseldyke, J. E. (2005). Conceptual confusion within response-to-intervention vernacular: clarifying meaningful differences. *Communiqué, 34*(3).

Cochran-Smith, M. (2004). Promises and politics: images of research in the discourse of teaching and teacher education. In J. Worthy, B. Maloch, J. V. Hoffman, D. L. Schallert, & C. M. Fairbanks (Eds.), *53rd Yearbook of the National Reading Conference* (pp. 28–44). Oak Creek, WI: National Reading Conference.

Crone, D. A. & Horner, R. H. (2003). *Building Positive Behavior Support Systems in Schools: Functional Behavioral Assessment.* New York: Guilford.

Daly, E. J. III, Bonfiglio, C. M., Mattson, T., Persampieri, M., & Foremann-Yates, K. (2005). Refining the experimental analysis of academic skills deficits: Part I. An investigation of variables that affect generalized oral reading performance. *Journal of Applied Behavior Analysis, 38,* 485–497.

Daly, E. J., III, & Martens, B. K. (1994). A comparison of three interventions for increasing oral reading performance: application of the instructional hierarchy. *Journal of Applied Behavior Analysis, 27*, 459–469.

Daly, E. J., III, Martens, B. K., Dool, E. J., & Hintze, J. M. (1998). Using brief functional analysis to select interventions for oral reading. *Journal of Behavioral Education, 8*, 203–218.

Daly, E. J., III, Martens, B. K., Hamler, K., R., Dool, E. J., & Eckert, T. L. (1999). A brief experimental analysis for identifying instructional components needed to improve oral reading fluency. *Journal of Applied Behavior Analysis, 32*, 83–94.

Daly, E. J. III, Witt, J. C., Martens, B. K., & Dool, E. J. (1997). A model for conducting a functional analysis of academic performance problems. *School Psychology Review, 26*, 554–574.

Dean, V. J. & Burns, M. K. (2002). Inclusion of intrinsic processing difficulties in LD diagnostic models: a critical review. *Learning Disability Quarterly, 25*, 170–176.

Demaray, M. K. & Elliot, S. N. (2001). Perceived social support by children with characteristics of attention-deficit/hyperactivity disorder. *School Psychology Quarterly, 16*, 68–90.

Deno, S. L. (2002). Problem solving as best practices. In A. Thomas & J. Grimes (Eds.), *Best Practices in School Psychology* (4th ed., pp. 37–56). Bethesda, MD: National Association of School Psychologists.

Deno, S. L., & Mirkin, P. K. (1977). *Data-Based Program Modification: A Manual*. Reston, VA: Council for Exception Children.

Ellis, A. K. (2005). *Research on Educational Innovations* (4th ed.). Larchmont, NY: Eye on Education.

Fletcher, J. M., Francis, D. J., Shaywitz, S. E., Lyon, G. R., Foorman, B. R., Stuebing, K. K., et al. (1998). Intelligence testing and the discrepancy model for children with learning disabilities. *Learning Disabilities Research & Practice, 13*, 186–203.

Fuchs, D., Mock, D., Morgan, P. L., & Young, C. L. (2003). Responsiveness-to-intervention: definitions, evidence, and implications for the learning disabilities construct. *Learning Disabilities Research & Practice, 18*, 157–171.

Fuchs, L. S. (2003). Assessing intervention responsiveness: conceptual and technical issues. *Learning Disabilities: Research & Practice, 18*, 172–186.

Fuchs, L. S. & Fuchs, D. (1986). Effects of systematic formative evaluation: a meta-analysis. *Exceptional Children, 53*, 199–208.

Fuchs, L. S. & Fuchs, D. (1998). Treatment validity: a unifying concept for reconceptualizing the identification of learning disabilities. *Learning Disabilities Research and Practice, 13*, 204–219.

Gickling, E. E. & Havertape, S. (1981). *Curriculum-Based Assessment (CBA)*. Minneapolis, MN: School Psychology Inservice Training Network.

Gresham, F. & Kern, L. (2006, May). Project REACH: An overview of literature, methods, and research strategies. In L. Kern (Chair), *Project REACH: Interventions for Severe Emotional and Behavioral Challenges. Symposium Conducted at the 2006 Annual Convention of the Association for Behavior Analysis*, Atlanta, GA.

Gresham, F. M. (2002). Responsiveness to intervention: an alternative approach to the identification of learning disabilities. In R. Bradley, L. Danielson, & D. Hallahan (Eds.), *Identification of Learning Disabilities: Research to Practice* (pp. 467–519). Mahwah, NJ: Lawrence Erlbaum.

Gresham, F. M., Reschly, D. J., Tilly III, W. D., Fletcher, J., Burns, M., Crist, T., et al. (2004). Comprehensive evaluation of learning disabilities: a response-to-intervention perspective. *Communiqué, 33*(4).

Haight, S. L., Patriarca, L. A., & Burns, M. K. (2001). A statewide analysis of the eligibility criteria and procedures for determining learning disabilities. *Learning Disabilities: A Multidisciplinary Journal, 11*(2), 39–46.

Heartland Area Education Agency 11 (2006). *Program Manual for Special Education*. Johnston, IA: Heartland Area Education Agency.

Howe, K. B., Scierka, B. J., Gibbons, K. A., & Silberglitt, B. (2003). A schoolwide organization system for raising reading achievement using general outcome measures and evidence-based instruction: one district's experience. *Assessment for Effective Intervention, 28*(3–4), 59–71.

Howell, K. & Nolet, V. (1999). *Curriculum-Based Evaluation: Teaching and Decision Making*. Pacific Grove, CA: Brooks/Cole.

IDEA (2004). *Individuals with Disabilities Education Improvement Act*. Pub. L. 108-446.

Ikeda, M. J., Tilly III, W. D., Stumme, J., & Volmer, L. (1996). Agency-wide implementation of problem-solving consultation: foundations, current implementation, and future directions. *School Psychology Quarterly, 11*, 228–243.

Iwata, B. A., Dorsey, M. F., Slifer, K. J., Bauman, K. E., & Richman, G. S. (1982). Toward a functional analysis of self-injury. *Analysis and Intervention in Developmental Disabilities, 2*, 1–20.

Kaminski, R. A. & Good, R. H. (1998). Assessing early literacy skills in a problem-solving model: dynamic indicators of basic early literacy skills. In M. R. Shinn (Ed.), *Advanced Applications of Curriculum-Based Measurement* (pp. 113–142). New York: Guilford Press.

Kovaleski, J. F., Gickling, E. E., & Morrow, H. (1999). High versus low implementation of instructional support teams: a case for maintaining program fidelity. *Remedial and Special Education, 20*, 170–183.

Kovaleski, J. F., Tucker, J. A., & Stevens, L. J. (1996). Bridging special and regular education: the Pennsylvania Initiative. *Educational Leadership, 53* (5), 44–47.

Lau, M. Y., Sieler, J. D., Muyskens, P., Canter, A., Vankeuren, B. & Marston, D. (2006). Perspectives on the use of the problem-solving model from the viewpoint of a school psychologist, administrator, and teacher from a large midwest urban school district. *Psychology in the Schools, 43*, 117–127.

Mace, F. C., Yankanich, M. A., & West, B. J. (1988). Toward a methodology of experimental analysis and treatment of aberrant classroom behaviors. *Special Services in the Schools, 4*(3–4), 71–88.

Marston, D., Muyskens, P., Lau, M., & Canter, A. (2003). Problem-solving model for decision making with high-incidence disabilities: the Minneapolis experience. *Learning Disabilities Research & Practice, 18*, 187–200.

McComas, J. J., Hoch, H., & Mace, F. C. (2000). Functional analysis. In E. S. Shapiro & T. R. Kratochwill (Eds.). *Conducting school-based assessments of child and adolescent behavior* (pp. 78–120). New York: Guilford.

McComas, J. J., & Mace, F. C. (2000). Theory and practice in conducting functional analysis. In E. S. Shapiro, & T. R. Kratochwill (Eds.), *Behavioral assessment in schools: Theory, research, and clinical foundations* (2nd ed.; pp. 78–103). New York: Guilford.

McGlinchey, M. T. & Hixson, M. D. (2004). Using curriculum-based measurement to predict performance standards on state assessments in reading. *School Psychology Review, 33*, 193–203.

McMaster, K. L., Fuchs, D., Fuchs, L. S., & Compton, D. L. (2005). Responding to nonresponders: an experimental field trial of identification and intervention methods. *Exceptional Children, 71*, 445–464.

National Association of State Directors of Special Education (2005). *Response to Intervention: Policy Considerations and Implementation*. Alexandria, VA: National Association of State Directors of Special Education.

National Reading Panel (2000). *Report of the National Reading Panel: Teaching Children to Read*. Washington, DC: US Department of Health and Human Services.

Noell, G. H. & Gansle, K. A. (2006). Assuring the form has substance: treatment plan implementation as the foundation of assessing response to intervention. *Assessment for Effective Intervention, 32*(1), 32–39.

Petursdottir, A. L. (2006). Brief experimental analysis of early reading interventions. Doctoral dissertation.

Reschly, D. J. & Starkweather, A. R. (1997). *Evaluation of an alternative Special Education Assessment and Classification Program in the Minneapolis Public Schools*. Minneapolis, MN: Minneapolis Public Schools.

Shapiro, E. S. (1992). Use of Gickling's model of curriculum-based assessment to improve reading in elementary age students. *School Psychology Review, 21*, 168–176.

Shapiro, E. S. (2000). School psychology from an instructional perspective: solving big, not little problems. *School Psychology Review, 29*, 560–572.

Shapiro, E. S. (2004). *Academic Skill Problems: Direct Assessment and Intervention* (3rd ed.). New York: Guilford.

Shapiro, E. S. & Ager, C. (1992). Assessment of special education students in regular education programs: linking assessment to instruction. *Elementary School Journal, 92*, 283–296.

Shapiro, E. S. & Elliott, S. N. (1998). Curriculum-based assessment and other performance based assessment strategies. In C. Reynolds & T. R. Gutkins (Eds.), *The Handbook of School Psychology* (3rd ed., pp. 383–408). New York: Wiley.

Shinn, M. R. (2002). Best practices in using curriculum-based measurement in a problem-solving model. In A. Thomas & J. Grimes (Eds.). *Best Practices in School Psychology* (4th ed; pp. 671–698). Bethesda, MD: National Association of School Psychologists.

Shinn, M. R. (Ed.). (1989). *Curriculum-Based Measurement: Assessing Special Children*. New York: The Guilford Press.

Silberglitt, B., Burns, M. K., Madyun, N. H., & Lail, K. E. (2006). Relationship of reading fluency assessment data with state accountability test scores: a longitudinal comparison of grade levels. *Psychology in the Schools, 43*, 527–536.

Speece, D. L. & Case, L. P. (2001). Classification in context: an alternative approach to identifying early reading disability. *Journal of Educational Psychology, 93*, 735–749.

Speece, D. L., Case, L. P., & Molloy, D. E. (2003). Responsiveness to general education instruction as the first gate to learning disabilities identification. *Learning Disabilities Research & Practice, 18*, 147–156.

Stage, S. A. & Jacobsen, M. D. (2001). Predicting student success on a state-mandated performance-based assessment using oral reading fluency. *School Psychology Review, 30*, 407–419.

Sugai, G., Sprague, J. R., Horner, R. H., & Walker, H. M. (2000). Preventing school violence: the use of office discipline referrals to assess and monitor school-wise discipline interventions. *Journal of Emotional and Behavioral Disorders, 8*, 94–101.

Tilly III, W. D. (2002). Best practices in school psychology as a problem-solving enterprise. In A. Thomas & J. Grimes (Eds.), *Best Practices in School Psychology* (4th ed., pp. 21–36). Bethesda, MD: National Association of School Psychologists.

Torgesen, J. K., Alexander, A. W., Wagner, R. K., Rashotte, C. A., Voeller, K. S., & Conway, T. (2001). Intensive remedial instruction for children with severe reading disabilities: immediate and long-term outcomes from two instructional approaches. *Journal of Learning Disabilities, 34*, 33–58.

Torgesen, J. K., Wagner, R., & Rashotte, C. (1999). *Test of Word Reading Efficiency.* Austin, TX: Pro-Ed

Torgesen, J. K., Wagner, R. K., Rashotte, C. A., Rose, E., Lindamood, P., Conway, T., et al. (1999). Preventing reading failure in young children with phonological processing disabilities: group and individual responses to instruction. *Journal of Educational Psychology, 91*, 579–593.

Tucker, J. A. (2001). Instructional support teams: it's a group thing. In R. Sornson (Ed.), *Preventing Early Learning Failure.* Alexandria, VA: Association for Supervision and Curriculum Development.

U.S. Department of Education. (2003). *25th Annual Report to Congress on the Implementation of the Individuals with Disabilities Education Act.* Washington, D.C.: U.S. Department of Education, Office of Special Education and Rehabilitative Services, Office of Special Education Programs.

VanDerHeyden, A. M. & Burns, M. K. (2005). Using curriculum-based assessment and curriculum-based measurement to guide elementary mathematics instruction: effect on individual and group accountability scores. *Assessment for Effective Intervention, 30*, 15–29.

VanDerHeyden, A. M., Witt, J. C., & Naquin, G. (2003). Development and validation of a process for screening referrals to special education. *School Psychology Review, 32*, 204–227.

Vaughn, S., Linan-Thompson, S., & Hickman, P. (2003). Response to instruction as a means of identifying students with reading/learning disabilities. *Exceptional Children, 69*, 391–409.

Vellutino, F. R., Scanlon, D. M., Sipay, E. R., Small, S., Chen, R., Pratt, A., et al. (1996). Cognitive profiles of difficulty-to-remediate and readily remediated poor readers: early intervention as a vehicle for distinguishing between cognitive and experimental deficits as basic causes of specific reading disability. *Journal of Educational Psychology, 88*, 601–638.

Walker, H. M. & Shinn, M. R. (2002). Structuring school-based interventions to achieve integrated primary, secondary, and tertiary prevention goals for safe and effective schools. In M. R. Shinn, H. M. Walker, & G. Stoner (Eds.), *Interventions for Academic and Behavior Problems II: Preventive and Remedial Approaches* (pp. 1–25). Washington, DC: National Association of School Psychologists.

Ysseldyke, J. E. (2001). Reflections on a research career: generalizations from 25 years of research on assessment and instructional decision-making. *Exceptional Children, 67*, 295–310.

Ysseldyke, J. (2005). Assessment and decision making for students with learning disabilities: What if this is as good as it gets. *Learning Disability Quarterly, 28*, 125–128.

Ysseldyke, J., Burns, M., Dawson, P., Kelley, B., Morrison, D., Ortiz, S., et al. (2006). *School Psychology: A Blueprint for Training in Practice III.* Bethesda, MD: National Association of School Psychologists.

Author Index

Subject Index

Printed in the United States of America.